BOXING

©2003 Feierabend Verlag oHG
Mommsenstraße 43, D-10629 Berlin

Project management: Bettina Freeman and Alex Morkramer
Translation from German: Aingeal Flanagan, Anna L. Grant, Rebecca Holmes-Löffler
Editing: Jardi Mullinax
Picture Editing: Uta Büxel, Petra Ahke
Layout and Typesetting: Roman Bold & Black, Cologne
Lithographs: Digiprint, Erfurt
Printing and Binding: Mladinska Knijga, Ljubljana

Printed in Slovenia

ISBN 3-936761-67-1
61 01019 1

Idea and Concept: Ute Edda Hammer, Bertram Job
Art Direction: Peter Feierabend

Cover illustration
©Werner Stapelfeldt, Düsseldorf

The publishing company and the author would like to thank all organizations who contributed
to this book for their generous cooperation.
Our special thanks go to Christian Abbew, Eric Armit, Bert Blewett, Tierry Chambefort, Nigel Collins,
Glynn Evans, Steve Farhood, Fight Fax, Herbert G. Goldman, Ivan G. Goldman, John Hogg, Carlos
Irusta, Joe Koizumi, Jean-Marcel Nartz, Per-Ake Persson, Mario Rivera Martino, Olaf Schröder, Fritz
Sdunek, SPT Sportmotion, Rinze van der Meer, Ulli Wegner and Axel Zielke.

Captions for the introductory pages of each chapter, see p. 419.

IN COOPERATION WITH GETTY IMAGES

BOXING

BERTRAM JOB

Feierabend

CONTENTS

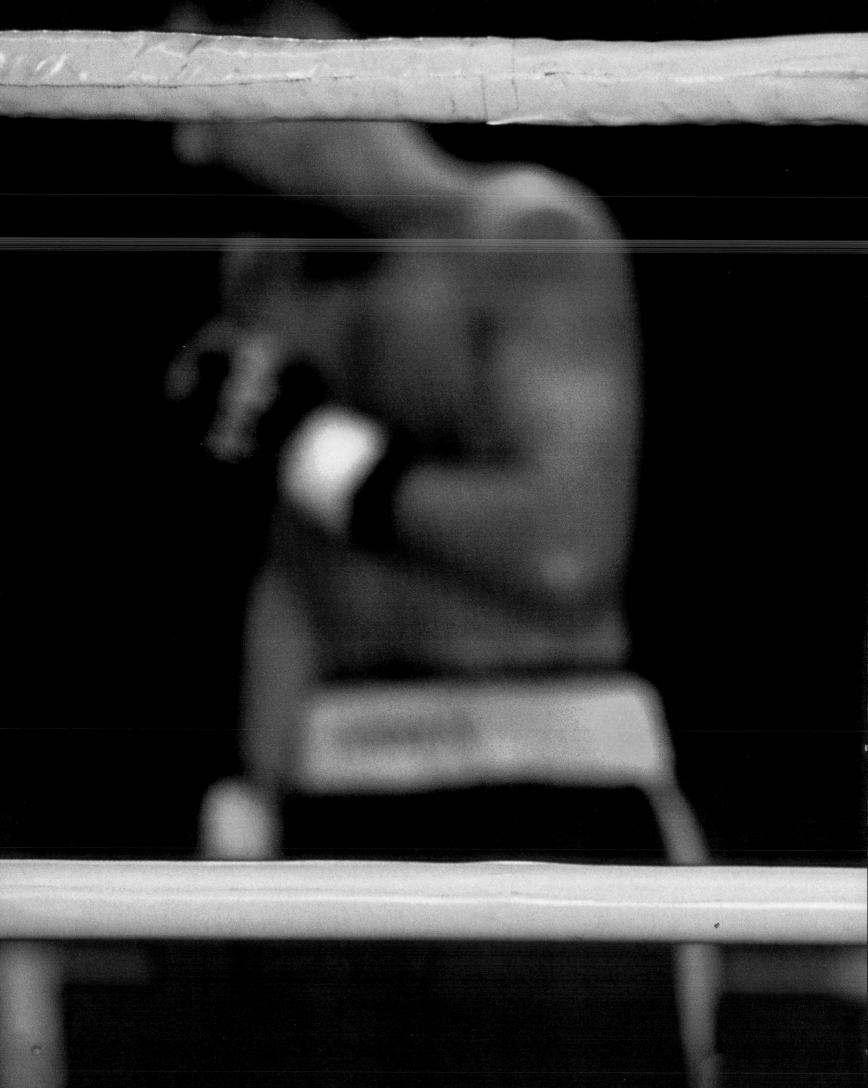

GLOBAL FASCINATION

There are not many sports that are pursued and followed with the same intensity on all five continents and across all cultural boundaries. Boxing, however, is the one form of physical exercise that has fitted into this category longer and more naturally than any other. From the ostentation of a hotel casino in Las Vegas to the spartan back-room of a small bar in the outskirts of Brisbane; from the open stadiums of Bangkok to the sophisticated atmosphere of a boxing dinner in London: whatever the backdrop, the fistic language tells the same tale of courage, self-assertion, downfall and comeback all over the world. This language is just as graphic as it is universal: everyone on the planet can understand what goes on between the two opponents in the brightly-lit ring.

Boxers win and lose more triumphantly, humiliatingly, dramatically and spectacularly than most other athletes. What's more, the outcome of their matches is often charged with fate: a single blow can make the career or even the life of one boxer while at the same time bringing the career of the other to an abrupt end. This makes every duel in the ring a crossroad fight: a battle for a better existence, which only one of the two combatants can move toward on the evening of the bout. That's what

makes prizefighting a "brutal sport," as former middleweight champion Rocky Graziano once put it. After all, "the fight for survival is the fight." But, in this sport, it is not only the stronger man but, in a more complex sense, the better and the cleverer man who generally comes out on top.

Down through the centuries, the performances of both the better men and the all-time greats—from Onomastos and James Figg to Jack Dempsey and Muhammad Ali—have attracted overwhelming public attention. Roman emperors and modern-day heads of state alike have endeavored to stage flamboyant events while Greek poets and American literary figures have been known to rub shoulders with the fans at megafights. Hardly any other sport has such a mixed following of people from all walks of life and backgrounds. From the down-at-heel to the well-to-do, who today pull up to the arenas in stretch limousines rather than horse-drawn carriages, the entire pyramid of society has always been represented in the ringside seats.

Despite everything they know about the sport, the pugilists' fascination with boxing has endured in modern times. Neither the sometimes dubious, manipulatively organized

sports deals nor the scandals and defeats of its protagonists have succeeded in causing any lasting damage to the status of the so-called "sweet science" (A. J. Liebling). Boxing may not be held in high esteem, but it is still hugely popular. And just like auto racing, the occasional fatal accident has done nothing to diminish its attraction.

Just what the source of this fascination is remains controversial to this day. Skeptics like to see the cult surrounding the mighty champions as nothing more than a backlash to primitive, handed-down, tribal behavioral patterns. Enthusiasts, on the other hand, prefer to honor boxing as a truly existential discipline: an uninterrupted, perfect metaphor for life. It is more likely that this contact sport does not fit neatly into any one non-boxing function: it is neither the last bastion of the male ego nor a modern stage for tragicomical heroes, because it continually creates its own, complete world in which its protagonists rise, triumph and fall in a different way than in real life.

This unique world, with all its transitory kings, rich history and grandiose rituals, is both the starting point and theme of this book.

Bertram Job

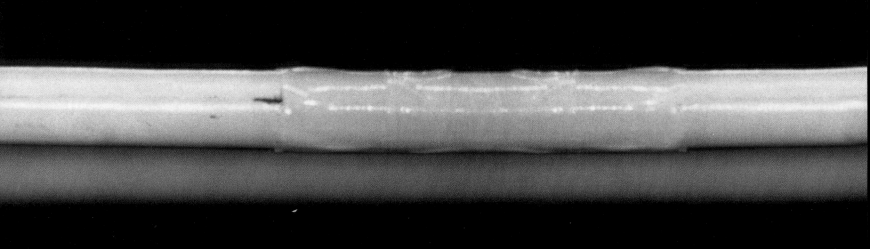

THE BOXERS

PSYCHE

EGO

IMAGE

HEART

SKILLS

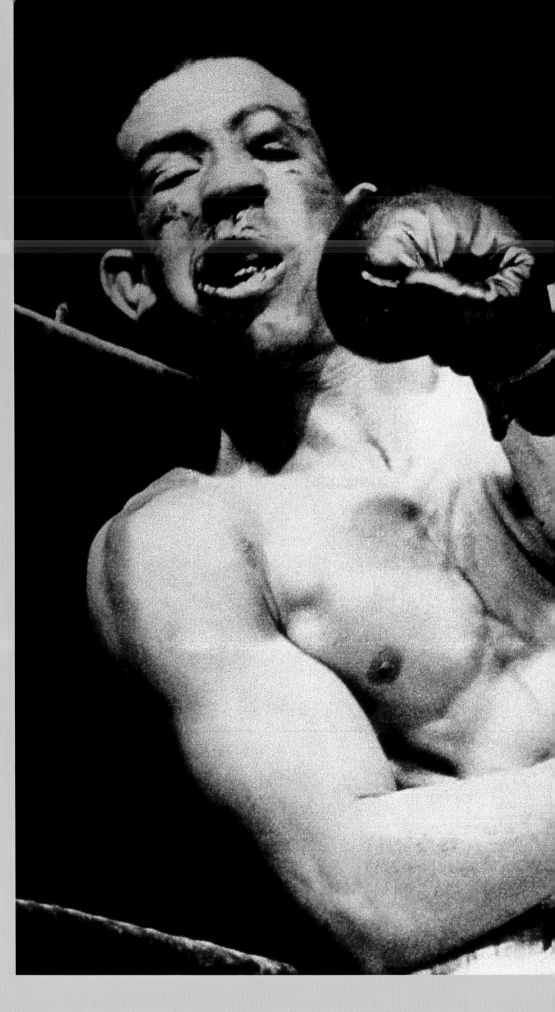

THE TRUE SPIRIT

PSYCHE

The canvas beneath their feet is not very large. There is no place to hide in a ring measuring between 16 and 20 square feet. And as soon as the gong sounds, there is no one up there to help them. Is it not understandable that athletes who willingly walk into this situation are repeatedly celebrated as heroes?

It may well be that for *aficionados* of this terribly beautiful sport, the loneliness of the boxer, who feels the impact of his mistakes on his bare body, exudes something existential. For the boxer, however, this inescapable situation in the ring is more than just a beautiful metaphor; it is the essence of what he does

and demands from him the mental attributes he needs to pull through. The best techniques and the most imposing state of mind are all just theory if frayed nerves block the realization of full athletic potential when it matters. Some people think that boxers know no doubt or fear. But what sentient person is completely free of either?

"I never wanted to go out there," Michael Spinks once freely admitted at the end of his career. But he did go out there, 32 times in all, and became both light heavyweight and heavyweight champion in that order. Instead of letting it overcome him, Spinks was able

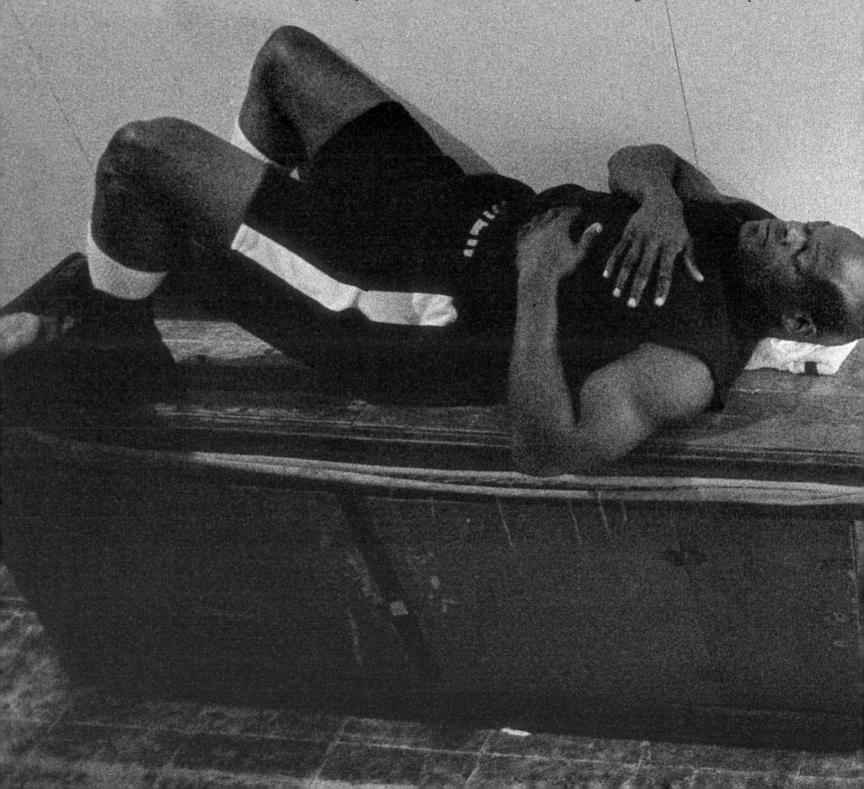

"I NEVER WANTED TO GO OUT THERE."

MICHAEL SPINKS

to control the tension inside. The same can be said for José Torres, his Puerto Rican predecessor on the light heavyweight throne, who compared his fear with fire: "If you control it, you can make good use of it. But if you lose control, it will kill you." And that is what often happens. Polish-born Andrew Golota suffered a nervous attack in his changing room ahead of his duel with Lennox Lewis in 1997. Twelve months earlier, WBA champion Bruce Seldon was visibly paralyzed on the way to defending his title against Mike Tyson. The result was the same in both bouts: a knockout in the first round.

Such incidents encourage spectators to take every opportunity to read the behavior of the combatants as if they were reading tea leaves: at press conferences, during the pre-fight weigh-in or in the final moments before the bell. They hope to see something that will reveal the boxers' state of mind. For similar reasons, many boxers try to impress their opponents up close with displays of self-assurance. They do so with good reason: psyching out an opponent is a tried and trusted weapon in fights where psyche is an indisputable factor in deciding the outcome of a fight.

Prince Naseem Hamed *(above left)* and Kevin Kelley display
self-confidence before their match in New York, 1997.
Large photo: Joe Roberts before his bout in the Blue Horizon
in Philadelphia, 1996.

EGO

When asked what his golf game was like, Muhammad Ali gave one of the most noteworthy of all his entertaining replies: "I'm the best," burst out the self-proclaimed "greatest of 'em all," "I just haven't played yet." There is probably no better introduction to the self-perception of an ambitious boxer than this.

Ali knew—and demonstrated—that when in doubt, a complete and utter lack of humility can get a talented boxer farther than modesty. While in civilian life, fitting in and taking a back seat are praised as virtually indispensable secondary virtues; in the "sweet science" they are considered a sign of unforgivable weakness. A boxer who craves success must be convinced of his superiority. This is the only way he can be assured of dominating his opponents in this sport. Ali once said: "To be a great champion you must believe you are the best. If you're not, pretend you are."

When a trainer or manager says that his protégé is a nice guy, the statement is usually accompanied by an expression of concern because, as the old saying goes, "nice guys don't win." On the other hand, a boxer's corner crew can be very ecstatic when their man is particularly difficult and irritable in the days before a fight—even if they are on the receiving end of his bad mood. Such unwavering belief in the power of the egoist might justifiably appear to outsiders as a confirmation of Darwin's theory. After all, what is a boxing match all about if not the survival of the fittest?

However, it is also true to say that the history of prizefighting is peppered with champions who don't come anywhere near the cliché of the egocentric, narcissistic victor. The permanently obliging and polite heavyweight champion of the world, Floyd Patterson, or more recently, Vuyani Bungu, the silent king who sat on the light welterweight throne from 1994 to 1999, are the living proof that modesty is no hindrance to winning great titles. However, once inside the ropes, even the most courteous boxers quickly show another side to their character. Once the first punches have been thrown, they focus more on saving their own skin than that of their opponent. Self-centeredness rules supreme in the ring.

This is why it helps boxers to develop a certain egocentricity—at least for their time in the ring—that narcissists like Ali and Pernell Whitaker had the good fortune to be born with. Of course, whether they have to take it as far as "Sweet Pea" Whitaker did is debatable. At the peak of his career, Whitaker, the welterweight star who until his demise was considered almost unbeatable, even considered the Almighty as no match for him. Whitaker announced that he wouldn't be worried about getting into the ring with God himself: "If I don't want God to hit me, then he won't hit me." These words clearly demonstrate that "Sweet Pea" didn't get his champion's belt from the Association for the Promotion of Modesty.

"IF I DON'T WANT GOD TO HIT ME, THEN HE WON'T HIT ME."

PERNELL WHITAKER

Pernell Whitaker ahead of his bout with James "Buddy" McGirt in Norfolk, 1994.

IMAGE

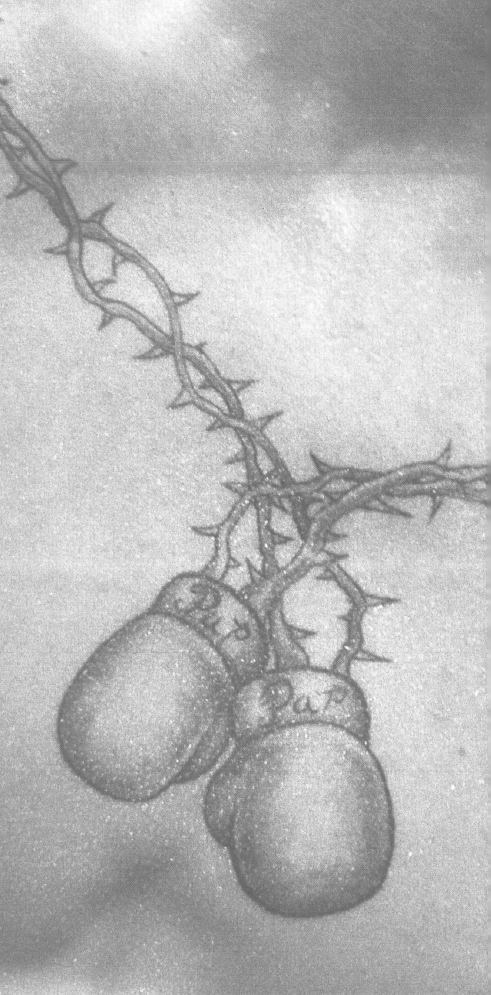

When it comes to acceptance and popularity with the punters, the style of a boxer's performance—his image in the ring—is just as important as, if not even more important than, his sporting performance. Beneath the watchful eyes of the spectators, the athlete in the glistening, illuminated ring becomes a protagonist who is supposed to embody certain stances and characteristics. As a performer in gloves, a boxer can be good or bad, brutal or cunning, fair or arrogant. Whatever he is, there is one thing he should never be: dull. After all, has anyone ever wanted to identify themselves with an actor who has no profile?

The contemporary American author Joyce Carol Oates once accurately wrote, "Each boxing match is a story—a unique and highly condensed drama without words." It could also be described as a three-dimensional comic strip because the characters in the ring are exaggerated and tend to be invariable. This makes it necessary for boxers to rethink their overall public image, if not even to map it out in advance. To avoid being pigeon-holed in the wrong category or quite simply ignored, they have to go into the offense and display easily remembered characteristics, regardless of whether they are authentic or have been invented specially for this purpose.

Gifted eccentrics such as former featherweight champion Jorge Paez, also known as the "Clown Prince of Boxing," have a talent for boosting their relatively ordinary sporting performance for the benefit of their public appeal with entertaining interludes and shrill apparel. On the other hand, clearly introverted souls like former heavyweight world champion Larry Holmes have difficulty earning respect—let alone great popularity—despite their outstanding performances. A critic once joked that Muhammad Ali could have sold anyone the Brooklyn Bridge in New York while Holmes wouldn't manage to sell a loaf of bread to a starving man. This is how this glamour-obsessed scene punishes an anti-hero who doesn't follow its flamboyant personality cult. However, positive aspects of public image are not the only key. The success of the British superstar Prince Naseem Hamed, for example, once again demonstrates that the public can also be held in trance by a purposefully arrogant persona. Even supposed bad guys like Marvin Hagler, Mike Tyson and Nigel Benn command a staunch and loyal ringside following. The aura of self-assurance and strength, which is often reflected in the boxers' nicknames ("Thunder," "Lights Out," "The Executioner"), is imperative. At an economic level, these symbols of superiority correspond to the pose of the self-satisfied, up-and-coming boxer, who proudly and openly presents his new status as if to say "look at me, I've arrived!"

Confirmed in a larger-than-life self-image of his own creation, the boxer returns to his supporters and is celebrated as a globally acknowledged winner.

The poses of the professionals are outlandish and unambiguous: Hector Camacho, Evander Holyfield, John Brown, Oliver McCall, Prince Naseem Hamed, Nigel Benn, Iran "Blade" Barkley, Hector Camacho *(clockwise from top left).*

HEART

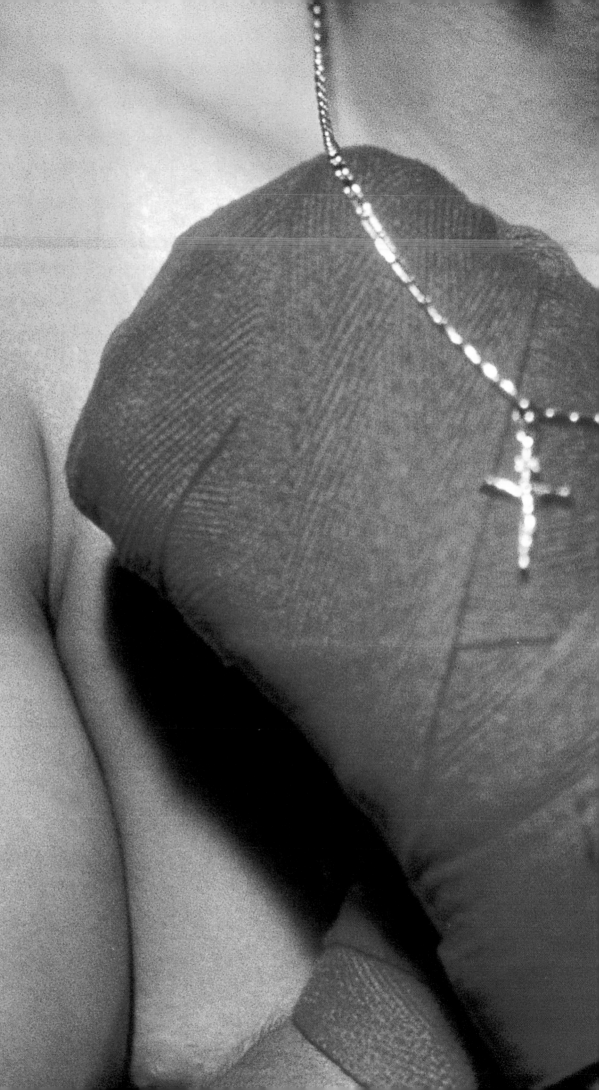

A willingness to bear extraordinary effort and even pain that borders on self-contempt; a stubborn and sometimes unreasonable refusal to concede defeat: for the fans, "heart" is the mental essence of boxing and its most essential attribute. More so than in any other discipline, the duel in the ring is a trial of strength that goes far beyond its sporting target. As middleweight champion Rocky Graziano once put it "the fight for survival is the fight."

No dyed-in-the-wool boxing fan in the United States will ever forget the bout in 1973 that saw Muhammad Ali hold on for several rounds despite a broken jaw just to see through to the bitter end his first match with Ken Norton. And almost every Australian still gets excited at the memory of Atlantic City in 1989, when Jeff Harding, who was clearly inferior to his opponent and bleeding profusely from a broken nose, knocked out the then light heavyweight champion of the world, Dennis Andries, in the final round. The last-minute triumph of the diehard, the man who overcomes every trial and handicap to finally reach his ultimate goal, is the key figure in a sport that counts more male myths than any other. According to boxing enthusiast Hemingway, "the best thing about men, is that we hold out, survive and carry on."

This admiration for a guy with heart means that even stylistically rather inadequate boxers like Jake LaMotta or George Chuvalo are stamped on the collective memory as true giants of the

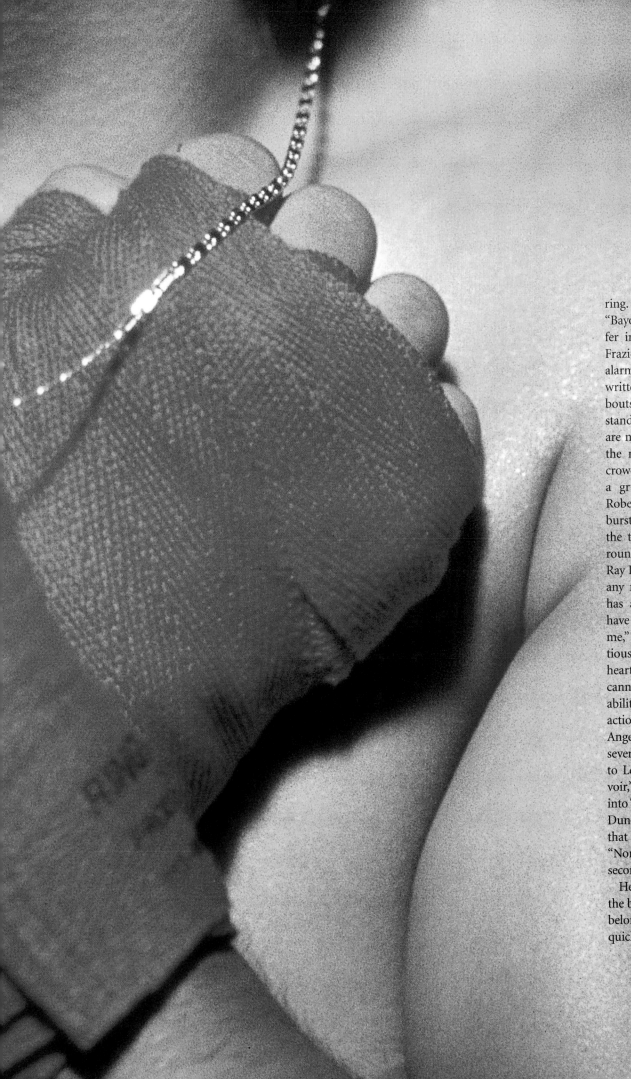

ring. In Chuvalo's case, the Canadian "Bayonne Bleeder's" willingness to suffer in his hopeless fights against Ali, Frazier, Foreman and others assumed alarming proportions, a fact that was written all over his face after the bouts. On the other hand, even outstanding champions find that they are not easily forgiven for withholding the required dose of heart from the crowd. To this day, the public still bears a grudge against multiple-champion Roberto Duran for his "No mas!" outburst (No more!), when he threw in the towel in frustration in the eighth round of his rematch against Sugar Ray Leonard on November 25, 1980. In any martial art, voluntary submission has always been a mortal sin. "He'll have to kill me if he wants to beat me," is a phrase often coined by ambitious challengers as evidence of their heart before a title fight. Even insiders cannot explain where boxers get the ability to transform this attitude into actio once they step inside the ropes. Angelo Dundee, the man who trained several dozen champions from Basilio to Leonard, called it "an innate reservoir," which allows great boxers to shift into "second gear" when the need arises. Dundee considered it highly unlikely that anyone could learn this technique: "Normal people just don't have this second gear."

Heart, also known as guts or balls, is the badge of a rank to which you either belong or you don't. It is a matter quickly settled in the ring.

SKILLS

A boxer's body is like a machine: each and every part has to be finely tuned in a training program. Nothing is left out. When the heat is on, everything between the soles of his feet and the top of his head is called into play; all the boundaries of human capability are pushed back: static and dynamic force, calculation, intuition, and reflexes. That is why it is hardly surprising that even housewives, students, and managers undergo physical training in boxing gyms in their spare time. A more comprehensive fitness-training program just doesn't exist.

For boxers and ambitious amateurs, the complexity of boxing requires particularly intense devotion and dedication. To meet the high demands of their sport, they need a large number of skills that have to be coordinated with one another. Unlike height and an ability to move, boxers are not born with these skills; they have to learn them. This is why the former American coach and subsequent TV commentator Gil Clancy once said that: "Boxing is not about power, it's about skill."

The footwork alone is a science in its own right. How and at what distance the feet must be positioned and in what direction the boxer must move to dodge his opponent's attack; this choreography must be second nature to the boxer. Add to this the bobbing and weaving of the upper body, the shift from static to dynamic force, the allocation of physical resources, the creative intelligence needed to devise and change the fight strategy and not least the development of outstanding reflexes. This has much less to do with fists than with brains, nerves and eyes, and is the reason why great boxers and trainers never tire of describing fist fighting as a "mind game."

Before his bout against Lennox Lewis, Croatian world championship hopeful Zeljko Mavrovic was asked what his best weapon in the ring was. The feared puncher with the Mohican haircut, who had previously knocked out 22 of his 27 opponents, didn't think long and pointed at his eyes. This was a throwback to the legendary Sugar Ray Robinson who distanced himself from obvious violence whenever he could. "I like sussing people out and outwitting them," said Robinson, "but I still don't enjoy beating them up."

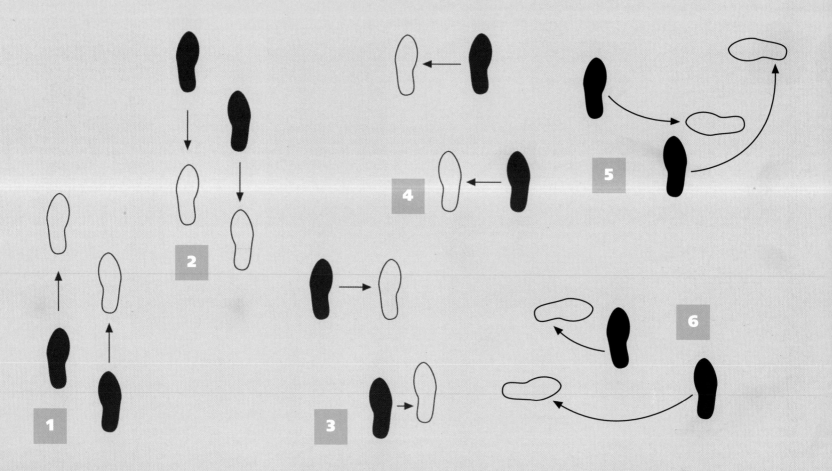

The basics of footwork have a major influence on the intricate and complex choreography of boxing. These pictures show the correct footwork sequences for advancing (1), retreating (2), shuffle (3–4) and side-stepping (5–6).

It is vital that the boxer finds his balance as quickly as possible in every situation.

Opposite page: Phantom punch in Philadelphia—Buster Mathis Jr.'s quick reactions help him duck beneath Mike Tyson's dreaded left hook during their bout in 1995. Despite his abilities, the fight ended in the third round.

WINNERS AND LOSERS

Cinderella has a brother. He calls himself "Thunder," "Sugar," "Hurricane" or "The Hammer" and looks too smashed up to be a real-life king. Nevertheless, he has made it in his own way: after many strenuous years and bouts he has fought his way to the top and is now world champion of one of the numerous boxing federations. This will bring him astronomical purses as long as he successfully defends his title. All of a sudden he is living in a whitewashed house with three bathrooms and there is gold everywhere: around his neck, on his fingers and on his over-crowned teeth. Could he be dreaming?

The transition from social underdog to the universally respected, affluent man is as omnipresent in the world of prizefighting as the tale of Cinderella is in the nurseries of the world. And just like this fairytale, the myth of the successful outsider feeds a dream. The only difference is that in the ring, real miracles happen often enough to make this impossible dream look like an achievable ambition. These miracles are as American as it gets. Just like the saga of Joe Frazier, the semi-skilled temporary worker who earned (and spent) millions as the heavyweight champion of the world, or the convicted ghetto flower from Brooklyn called Mike Tyson who became the undisputed king of purses (and has since almost gone bankrupt).

Such rags-to-riches stories stir the imagination, particularly in societies where the independent struggle for personal success has virtually achieved cult status. This is why the American social historian Jeffrey T. Sammons considers professional boxers to be the "key part of a system of faith" that believes the ultimate reward comes to those who make an effort. "The myths of success in prizefighting," believes Sammons "are caricatures of the American dream." This is in sharp contrast to the day-to-day reality of the gyms and arenas between New York and Los Angeles and elsewhere. According to a long-range study of 127 professional boxers conducted by the sociologists Weinberg and Arond between 1938 and 1951, 92.9 percent of the sportsmen examined never made it past a modest regional level of recognition; 7.1 percent at least made it into the national rankings and one actually became champion.

But the extremely slim chances of success in this dangerous sport obviously don't deter ambitious amateurs or young professionals. On the contrary, driven by the statistical improbability of his undertaking, the ambitious athlete views the merciless selection process as a personal challenge. His ambition is also fired by the realization that there are hardly any other, easier roads to affluence—a supposition that is backed up by the fact that in most countries, the underprivileged

FROM RAGS

Part-time work at a large London meat market helped former British bantamweight champion Alan Rudkin keep his head above water in the early 1970s.

Full-time professionals like Prince Naseem Hamed thoroughly enjoyed the status their hard-won success brought them in the 1990s.

то **RICHES**

and immigrant populations are breeding grounds for boxing. This also explains why Sylvester Stallone's Rocky Bilboa practiced combination punches on slabs of frozen meat in a Philadelphia slaughterhouse in the first of the five *Rocky* films. The message here is that boxing is the only thing that can save these boys from such dreary shift work in the medium term.

This is why the first large purses in an up-and-coming boxer's career are much more than a welcome means of payment. Together with the new public respect, they symbolize a huge regard for the professional boxer: suddenly he is somebody who people recognize and court. In the euphoria of this new self-esteem, the first big money is often spent quickly, as if it were "only" of symbolic value. "I just couldn't wait to go back to the old neighborhood and spread a bit of the money around

with my friends," recalled the former middleweight champion Rocky Graziano on one occasion. Just like his childhood friend, Jake LaMotta, Graziano grew up in pitiful conditions in the New York Bronx and committed his first criminal offence at an early age. Other boxers, like the Ugandan John Mugabi, the former light middleweight champion of the world, spent their money on the most pointless yet expensive products. "He has a black belt in shopping," was how English coach George Francis once described Mugabi's habits.

Later—after the first dispute with the tax authorities or the first divorce case—the elation gives way to a very sober perception of professional sport. As the wear on his physical substance increases, the experienced professional realizes that the whole thing is a straightforward barter: he gets money in exchange for pain.

While he was breaking prize money records for the lower weight divisions in the 1980s with purses of \$10 million and more, the legendary Sugar Ray Leonard was asked how long a bout hurts. He replied: "Until the check comes through."

It goes without saying that the figures on the checks for lesser-known professionals, who have to stand in the ring and endure the same pain as Leonard, are a little smaller.

OSCAR'S AWARD: THE MAKING OF A SUPERSTAR

Did someone tell him beforehand or did he come up with the idea himself? The fact is that on the evening of August 8, 1992, Oscar De La Hoya did exactly the right thing. Having just won the gold medal in the lightweight division at the Olympic Games in Barcelona, the 19-year-old descendant of Mexican immigrants from East Los Angeles did a dance while holding a flag in each of his bandaged hands. One was the Mexican flag and the other the Stars 'n' Stripes. This was to be the basic pattern used to market De La Hoya when he turned professional before the year was out: the Latino Oscar became an all-

Never before had a Hispanic succeeded in being seen as such a true American protagonist of his sport. But promoter Bob Arum immediately recognized his golden boy's potential, which would allow them to overcome all ethnic barriers together.

Outside the ring, De La Hoya was so well behaved and charming that even those who don't like boxing or knew nothing about the sport liked listening to him. What's more, with his broad smile, which he could switch on in an instant, and his perfect face, Oscar soon became a hit with the ladies. Mothers wanted the eloquent youth as a son-in-law and daughters set up

for a popularity-seeking pugilist to break out of the inner circle of the boxing scene.

So "Team De La Hoya" did everything it could to make the most of this unique opportunity. Golden Oscar, who previously had nothing against a five o'clock shadow, now always appeared in public clean-shaven. On the advice of a publicist, he was soon appearing in popular general interest magazines that presented the boxer as a fashionable gentleman. He was invited to all sorts of trendy dinner parties and golf tournaments in sophisticated country clubs. Arum was even able to exploit the disapproval that this interest in the well-to-do

Olympic champion Oscar De La Hoya was not only larger-than-life at the reopening of the Olympic Auditorium in Los Angeles in 1994. In real life too, he always plays the role of the presentable star.

Whenever De La Hoya met another Hispanic in the ring—and Arum made sure he did—the fans packed into the halls. Some came to admire the exceptional boxer while others wanted to see the upstart get a good hiding at last. Whatever their reason for coming, every one of them paid to get in.

And De La Hoya certainly didn't make it easy for his opponents. Whatever big names Arum drummed up for him to fight—some of whom were admittedly on their way out—he usually dismissed them in a few rounds. This is how De La Hoya became champion in three weight divisions in just 22 professional bouts, earning himself the respect of boxing experts as he did so. In the

October 1996 edition of the famous magazine *The Ring*, it was said that "timing is everything for the development of a superstar, and as far as that is concerned, De La Hoya is truly a blessed boxer." Any remaining sporting reservations were done away with when "probably the most marketable boxer of all time" (Dan Hirshberg) challenged the best boxers in the hotly contested welterweight division in the late 1990s and won regularly, with the exception of two bouts, which he lost on points to the Puerto Rican Felix Trinidad (1999) and Shane Mosley (2000).

But the titles in the ring were not the only triumphs recorded by product "Oscar."

Others include the spectator figures, the purses and the money he earns from the transmission of his bouts in pay TV. De La Hoya clocked up over 10,000 spectators in New York and Las Vegas (1995), 30,000 in San Antonio (1997) and 45,000 in El Paso (1998): numbers like that have not been achieved by a boxer beneath the heavyweight division since Sugar Ray Leonard. By the end of 1999, De La Hoya's career purses alone totaled over $100 million. He has earned several more million with advertising contracts for men's cosmetics, sports outfitters etc.

Oscar, the golden boy from the *barrios* has long since gone platinum.

FROM RICHES

If he had kept as tight a rein on the dollar bills as he did on the leaves he raked up in the parks of Philadelphia in later life, Bennie Briscoe would certainly have been a wealthy man. As it is, the former boxing star once respectfully referred to as "Bad Bennie" is now not much more than a fallen legend. Sometimes, people taking a walk recognize him as a man who used to feature in the world rankings and remember his unique career: 70 professional fights in 15 years, two lost middleweight championship bouts (1972 and 1974), and many grandiose performances in front of a capacity crowd in the Spectrum, the city's largest arena. Few have equaled his achievements. But those who didn't experience it, only see Bennie Briscoe for what he is today: an elderly, part-time worker who moves with measured steps between the trees and bushes.

Having said that, "Bad Bennie" hasn't actually done all that badly. As a city employee, he gets a fixed wage at the end of each month, which allows him to make ends meet in his modest life. Similarly, other former colleagues now work as janitors, museum attendants, and night porters to pay the rent. Many retired boxing professionals have a much worse time of it: the former lightweight champion of the world, Beau Jack, whose bouts regularly filled New York's Madison Square Garden in the early 1940s, later struggled to earn a living as a shoe-shine boy close the arena. Bobby Chacon, featherweight and super featherweight champion between 1974 and 1982, was seen collecting empty bottles and cans in parking lots in Los Angeles in the late 1990s. Former champions in England and elsewhere in Europe often experience similar downfalls.

The melodramatic courses taken by the lives of former pugilists are so numerous that they should be considered the rule rather than the exception. Regardless of how determined and agile they might have been in the ring, very few boxers have been able to emerge victorious from the so-called 13th round: their post-career lives. All too often, the abrupt fall that can follow a professional boxer's sudden rise to fame can lead to social impoverishment, drug addiction, and crime.

Alternatively, a lack of prospects tempts some boxers to make one comeback bid after another and so on. It may well be that the personal ambition of once again establishing themselves in the sport they know and love plays as important a role as the financial motivation. Generally, however, it is the purse that has the greater pull: a fact admitted by former light welterweight champion Billy Costello when he returned to the ring in 1999, fourteen years after losing his title. "I'm not boxing because I need boxing. I'm boxing because I need the money."

But what happens to the vast amounts of money earned by stars like Costello? It is usually swallowed up by cars and houses that end up being bigger and more expensive than planned, golden faucets, closets full of tailored suits and the boxer's 200 closest friends.

The reason for this is that successful boxers generally suffer from what sociologists refer to as the "big man, big spender" syndrome: they always want to show off to themselves and those around them their new status as "king of the castle." But experience has shown time and again that the trappings of wealth and those they attract cost more money than an unsuspecting, up-and-coming boxer usually realizes. And if he can't rely on his advisors, he will wake up one day to face an opponent he hadn't reckoned with: the man from the Internal Revenue Service (IRS). This is how even the big earners in the boxing business suddenly find themselves owing taxes. Legends of the ring like Sugar Ray Robinson and Joe Louis, whose entire bout purses were seized toward the end of his career, also number among these ranks. In the well-publicized case of Joe Louis in the mid-1950s, the debt that the former heavyweight champion was supposed to pay back to the IRS was valued at about $1.25 million. The "Brown Bomber" had to sweat it out

for ten difficult years before his third wife, a lawyer, could arrange a settlement. Payment of back taxes was also the main reason why the Mexican idol Julio Cesar Chavez was as good as bankrupt in the late 1990s despite having contested more than 30 world championship fights. In short, an opponent in the ring rarely poses as great a threat to a professional boxer as his so-called friends, business partners, and very often his own wastefulness. It is only in the last few years that world boxing associations like the International Boxing Federation (IBF) have begun keeping back a percentage of their champions' purses for a pension that will be paid out to them at the end of their careers. In this way, boxing has finally come around to the idea of social insurance to ensure that today's world champions are spared the necessity of raking leaves and the bitter irony that Joe Louis retained until the very end: "They say that money talks," he said, "but the only thing it ever said to me was good-bye."

TO RAGS

Massive demands for outstanding taxes left one-time national hero Joe Louis teetering on the brink of financial ruin: it was only the dedication of his lawyer-wife that led to an agreement with the IRS.

THE MIDDLE-OF-THE-ROAD MEN

Julius Francis *(above left)* didn't stand a chance against Mike Tyson in January 2000.

If modern-day prizefighting has seen better heavyweight boxers than Julius Francis, it has certainly seen worse title contenders than this experienced, London-based professional. And when it comes to the money that can be made in the ring, there are definitely more tragic stories to be told in this world than his. Despite his limited abilities, Francis has made his fortune as the permanent contender: today he could help some boxers out of a tight spot, even those who were once far ahead of him in the rankings.

Francis is the perfect example of a boxer who found his niche somewhere between the champions and the chronic losers. He belonged to that small class of boxers who have no place in this world of interminable ups and downs. The people usually want to

see winners and losers and maybe a few good guys who succeed in making a comeback, but no mediocre sportsmen who even go so far as to be content with their lot. Nevertheless, there are always a few who manage to make their way at a modest level in this incredibly dynamic subculture.

The career of the clever guy from Woolwich in London peaked when he made it as a respected professional in the second half of the 1990s. A few victories over fellow boxers pushed him up to sixth place in the British rankings in 1996. This was obviously as high as manager Frank Maloney's protégé could go at that time. When he challenged the reigning European champion Zeljko Mavrovic in February 1997, he hadn't a hope: the referee waved off the fight in the eighth round. After

"I COULD'VE BEEN
A CONTENDER (...)"

Terry Malloy's monologue from the film
"On the Waterfront," 1954:

"Remember that night in the Garden
and you came down to my dressing room
and you said 'Kid, this ain't your night.
We're going for the price on Wilson.'
You remember that?
This ain't your night! My night!
I could have taken Wilson apart!
So what happens?
He gets a title shot outdoors in a ballpark
and I get a one-way ticket to palookaville!
You was my brother Charley, you should've
looked out for me just a little bit so
I wouldn't have to take them dives for
the short-end money."
(...) I could have had class.
I could've been a contender!
I could've been somebody, instead of a bum,
which is what I am!"

such a defeat, lesser-known boxers would have been passed down the rankings. Not Francis. Together, he and Maloney transformed his limitations into a marketable quality: he was always just good enough but did not—thank heavens—pack the all-important, decisive punch.

Other defeats in 1998 at the hands of Axel Schulz and Vitali Klitschko earned Francis more money than most of his victories. In 1999, he outpointed Scott Welch to become British champion. But it was a year later, in late January 2000, when he landed his biggest coup as Mike Tyson's hand-picked knockout victim in Manchester. His four minutes in the ring, during which he was floored by the former world champion exactly five times, earned Francis his personal

record purse of about £150,000, not including the advertisement payment for a daily newspaper on the soles of his shoes!

But outside England too, stories like this are frequent enough to sustain the dream of the happy ending without the world championship belt. In Germany, for example, the heavyweight boxer Mario Schießer became a lucky loser around the same time by competing against—and being a worthy loser to—some of the big promoters' darlings. In the Italian city of Pesaro, the talented Andrea Magi funded his own covered beach chair empire with the money he earned in unsuccessful international title bids, while in the United States in the mid 1980s, Bobby Crabtree managed to set himself up as an internationally popular tune-up opponent

for up-and-coming stars. Crabtree considered the money he got for the bouts as a nice little nest egg.

Back home in Fort Smith, Arkansas, this late-starter and owner of a car accessory store generally considered his duels in the ring to be paid excursions to foreign parts. Crabtree lost to former and future champs like Michael Moorer, Trevor Berbick, and George Foreman, even though he actually won most of his fights. But Crabtree remained unimpressed by what he had always considered an insignificant adventure: "It keeps me in shape and out of trouble." Financial independence is surely the best insurance against major boxing triumphs. But just like every thing else in life, the trick is finding that out.

The unfortunate professional Billy Gibbs only managed to chalk up 5 wins in 400 bouts.

LOSERS AND HAS-BEENS

Sometimes it's funny. Whenever the American professional boxer Bruce "The Mouse" Strauss stepped up for one of the 145 paid fights he contended between the 1970s and the 1990s, he rarely had a chance worth speaking of. All the same, the nice guy from Neola, Iowa, usually stepped through the ropes in a cheery mood and promptly let himself be beaten up, usually very quickly too. The notorious loser, who officially lost a total of sixty contests, was just happy to be taking part for a fistful of dollars. What's more, as the years went by, he was proud to be almost as well known in the boxing scene as the champs and hopefuls who had often defeated him. "Anyone who hasn't seen me knocked out," Strauss used to like to say, "don't know nothing about boxing."

But sometimes it's just tragic. This was the case with James Pritchard who, unlike his compatriot Strauss, had once seen better days. Pritchard was a respected, ranked, cruiserweight boxer when he fought James Warring for the vacant IBF belt in the Italian town of Salemi in 1991. He was knocked out after only 24 seconds of the first round. A few fights later,

he was nothing more than "the other guy." From then on, he pocketed his purses for getting into the ring with boxers who were considered better than he was. As expected, he lost every time. Many years and pounds down the road, a bulkier Pritchard was passed back and forth across the Atlantic as a mediocre heavyweight: a sluggish shadow of his former self.

Usually everything goes according to plan. It's almost always "another day at the office." After all, the machinery that is professional boxing needs a steady stream of losers to produce its radiant victors. These losers are the tune-up opponents or, as they are known in the business, "bums" or "tomato cans." In other words, they are the boxers who, due to either a lack of great talent or ambition, willingly slip into the role of designated victim. They can only box well enough to win a bout somewhere between Pittsburgh, Cologne or Doncaster every now and then, but don't have enough ability to become the best in their division. So they are hired for an average of $1,000 to $3,000 to do just that: to compete against the best in their division and to lose more or less convincingly.

It is estimated that about 70 percent of all professional boxers are tune-up opponents who pursue a career in boxing to secure their financial survival rather than to fulfill a personal dream. But the more talented among them try almost as honestly as the stars within their weight category. Only those who put up a fight earn the respect of the punters and organizers; those who just give in probably won't be booked again. The New York booking agent Johnny Bos, who trades worldwide in tune-up opponents from the United States, once summed it up neatly: he was looking for boxers who were "capable, but beatable." In other words, the opponent should put up a decent fight before being brought to his knees. This is the only way to turn a potential walkover into a test for the favorite, and a victory into a triumph.

Mostly, in any case. It very rarely happens that a "bum" outboxes or even drops his supposedly stronger opponent. And this usually has more fatal consequences for the surprise winner than for the loser: he will probably never be booked again by that promoter.

BOUT IN ROTTERDAM

THE STORY OF A LOSER

Everett "Bigfoot" Martin posts a record weight when he steps on the scales shortly after 6:00 p.m. on the Friday evening. The officials at the small table in Rotterdam's Central Hotel enter 251 pounds after his name in their records. There are a few raised eyebrows among the observers but the procedure continues without delay. A number of professional boxers are waiting to be weighed in and, to be honest, Martin's flabby belly is nothing to worry about. Quite the opposite, actually.

After all, the heavyweight from Houston, Texas, wasn't booked to celebrate an illustrious victory on the following evening. He is a tune-up opponent who will step into the ring to fight the organizer's protégé and he knows exactly what is expected of him. "They don't bring you here so you can kill the other guy," says Martin. The plan is that

a young Pole called Albert Sosnowski—and not the 36-year-old veteran of 58 professional bouts—will come up trumps on this occasion. Sosnowski is a former kick boxer. After 17 easy victories, no one really knows what his boxing caliber is.

But Everett Martin is not happy with his paunch. When he began professional boxing back in 1983, he started out as a super middleweight. Prior to this, he won the regional Golden Gloves three times in a row. Things are different now. These days, he is slow and mostly tired. He set out from Houston two days ago. From there he flew to Las Vegas and then, six hours later, to New York. He then flew to London, where he took a bus from Heathrow to Sedgwick, from where he took a plane to Rotterdam after a four-hour delay. He has been traveling two and a half days for a purse of about $2,000. "Waiting

is a big part of my job," says "Bigfoot," with a hint of humor in his voice.

On the afternoon of the fight, the American doesn't know how to kill the time until the evening: there's nothing good on television. He and his "agent" Eric Drath spend an hour or two wandering through the shopping streets of the city before Drath convinces him to go back to the hotel. "Take it easy for a while," says Drath in the lobby, "the taxi will be here at 7:00 p.m." The young New Yorker considers his client to be "a winner" because "he refuses to feel like a loser. He doesn't let all of this get to him."

But when "Bigfoot" takes off his pants in the changing rooms of the Schiebroek sporting complex at 7:30 p.m., he discontentedly slaps his bulging midriff. Having completed the first few stretching exercises, he begins to fool around: "Man, these legs are gettin'

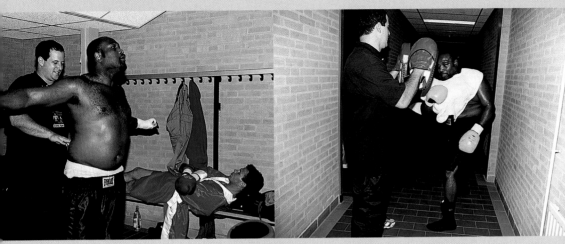

old!" Today, Drath just doesn't seem to be able to bandage his hands to his satisfaction and he halfheartedly goes through the motions on his punching bag. Even so, the American's dark skin is covered in sweat after only a few minutes of exertion. A little earlier, he briefly shook his opponent's hand on the corridor outside the changing rooms. He now knows that "the guy is even more nervous than I am."

As a sparring partner, Martin once caught Sosnowski with a right-hander that really shook the Pole. But there is no sign of this in front of the 600 spectators in the sporting complex. Like a light shower that doesn't really bother him, the Texan allows the jabs and combinations dealt out by his well-prepared opponent to rain down on him. Only one or two well-disguised counter-attacks per round remind the spectators

of what the man who once beat world championship contender Bert Cooper is capable. That's enough to make sure that Albert Sosnowski doesn't get too impetuous.

Everett Martin sometimes shakes his head and grins when he is hit. The show is on his side. But after a hit on a lower rib in the seventh of eight rounds, he throws in the towel with a pained expression on his face. Later on, once the doctor has submitted his superfluous diagnosis that no bones have been broken, "Bigfoot" makes his way to the Pole's changing room. He congratulates Sosnowski and warns him never to show his opponents too much respect. "Never show 'em respect, ya'hear?"

It's 11:30 p.m. when "Bigfoot" and Drath leave the hall for the hotel. They hope there will be another bout in two or three months; wherever and against whomever.

Ring veteran Everett Martin whiles away an afternoon in the streets of Rotterdam in fall 2000. That evening, his manager Eric Drath helps him get ready in the changing rooms. The bout against the Pole Albert Sosnowski is a dubious highlight to the day: after seven rounds of very little resistance, the former ranked boxer from Houston throws in the towel.

IN THE NEIGHBORHOOD

When they become successful professionals whose names grace the rankings, boxers can become the heroes of an entire city, region, or even nation. But before it comes to that, their world is limited to their immediate environment: the ethnic or socially encoded district, the *barrio,* or their neighborhood. Future champions usually have to assert themselves in these social "biotopes" long before they put on their first pair of boxing gloves. Because, as everybody knows, no one is handled with kid gloves in the places these guys were either born in or moved to as adolescents. Here, the streets are also battle zones and, if needs be, the kids' challengers come from the next street on the block.

This is why it is no big surprise that the biographies of countless champions begin with stories of early humiliation and brutal conflicts. Even at the end of his career, the former lightweight champion Ike Williams could still remember the name of his archenemy that bullied him almost on a daily basis during his time at school in Trenton, N.J. All of this changed when Williams, the slim newcomer with the unmistakable southern accent, began to train in a gym and learned how to defend himself effectively. The story of Williams' opponent and predecessor on the world championship throne, Beau Jack, is almost identical. As a shoeshine boy, the Georgia-born teenager learned how to use his fists to defend the tools of his trade against the competition on the streets of Miami. Decades later and long before their double Olympic victory (1978) and professional titles, brothers Leon and Michael Spinks were forced to fend off the regular attacks of a street gang in the state-subsidized welfare housing estate they called home in St. Louis. Similarly, heavyweight champions Mike Tyson and Riddick Bowe had to survive a few turbulent years in Brownsville, one of the less salubrious parts of Brooklyn, in the 1980s.

But the social misery in the suburbs and disadvantaged districts, which seems to evaporate in the anecdotes recounted by those who have left it behind them, is not an invention of American society. Middleweight champion Nigel Benn grew up in the London suburb of Ilford and was an underage member of a gang whose leader often beat him to within an inch of his life when there was no other victim to be had. In Soweto, South Africa's biggest township, Dingaan Thobela had to win countless street fights many years before being honored as the "Rose of Soweto" and holding titles in the light and super middleweight divisions. These tough conditions were also to be found in socialist countries, even though the authorities there claimed they were a typical side effect of the capitalist system. After unsuccessfully challenging Lennox Lewis for the world championship in 1998, title contender Zeljko Mavrovic told of his participation in unofficial fights among young people in the Srednjaci district of Zagreb. These sorts of contests were exactly like the ones fought by the young Sugar Ray Robinson and his adolescent friends in Harlem in the 1940s.

This means that the future boxer does not grow up surrounded by true and loyal fans. And in line with the "survival of the fittest" theory that rules supreme in these districts, it does them no harm. On the contrary: there is no better place to learn self-assertion than on the streets. This is why in hindsight, Michael Spinks was utterly convinced that all the street fights he contended in St. Louis "prepared him for Larry Holmes," the man he overmatched for the heavyweight belt in 1985. Only early successes in the ring turn a talented junior into a hopeful and gradually transform the neighborhood kids into a loyal following. The boxer then becomes "one of us" because he is defending the honor of the street in amateur cross-town fights. If he then manages to make his way in the national rankings or even become a professional international boxer, the guy next door finally becomes a local hero, even though his newly acquired wealth has, by that time, taken him to a safer, more comfortable neighborhood.

No matter where his career takes him and how long he stays at the top, it all began in the *barrio,* the neighborhood. And nothing can change that.

In the early 1960s, British middleweight champion Terry Downes knew all about the children on the streets, they were part of his social identity.

The social history of African Americans in boxing
SLAVES, HEROES & OUTSIDERS

Britain's Tom Cribb ("The Black Diamond") and America's Tom Molineaux ("The Moor") fought the first major interracial duels in 1810 and 1811.

of American strength and racial superiority"—the ruling class proved to be much less conciliatory. John L. Sullivan, who became champion in 1882, made it known that he would fight neither the hotly tipped Peter Jackson from Australia nor any other black challenger for that matter. Jack Dempsey also upheld this color bar when he relieved Jess Willard of his title in 1919. Between these two titleholders came Jack Johnson, the first black world champion, who shook American society to its foundations, the effects of which were felt for a long time afterwards.

In 1908, Johnson beat Tommy Burns to become champion and then proceeded to give every one of his challengers a decided dressing-down one after the other. He used his purses to fund an unprecedented, extravagant lifestyle that Americans found totally unacceptable. In response, a shocked America began a (futile) search for the "Great White Hope" that would

Because the history of professional pugilism closely resembles that of the underprivileged classes, the majority of professional boxers have always been African-American. At the start of the third millennium, 21 of the 51 champions in the three most respected world boxing federations were African-American. While they enjoyed the same rights as their paler-skinned counterparts both inside and outside the ring, they did not necessarily have the same opportunities. Their sporting domination would appear to be so secure that it is now almost taken for granted. However, on closer examination it becomes clear that the road to this point has been long and difficult, and paved with social prejudice, riots, and taboos.

African-Americans began to box in the United States as slaves. From time to time, their owners amused themselves by pitching their slaves against each other in no-holds-barred "Battle Royals." This involved locking five or more adversaries in a room and letting them loose on each other until only one remained standing (the practice of blindfolding the

fighters survived in the southern states until the middle of the last century). While the best fighters may have been released from bondage to make their way in the world by contesting bareknuckle fights, they gained hardly any notoriety. It was only in the early 19th century that Bill Richmond and his protégé Tom Molineaux began to arouse the interest of the American public with title fights in England. The 1810 and 1811 duels between Englishman Tom Cribb and Molineaux, who was also known as "The Virginia Slave," were the first noteworthy mixed-race championship bouts. But matches between blacks and whites remained the exception in the United States and Europe for a long time after that.

The world had to wait until 1891 to witness the first black champion in modern professional boxing: featherweight boxer George Dixon ("Little Chocolate"). "Jersey" Joe Walcott (welterweight, 1897) and Joe Gans (lightweight, 1902) soon followed in his footsteps. When it came to the holder of the heavyweight title, however—which the historian Jeffrey T. Sammons referred to as "an example

Jack Johnson married Etta Duryea in 1911: the heavyweight champion was never forgiven for his taste for white women and his extravagant lifestyle.

Joe Louis' decoration as a soldier in World War II went a long way towards cementing his general social acceptance.

without ever really getting a look-in. When Joe Louis became the second black titleholder 22 years later, his team imposed a strict code of behavior: no flashy performances and no disparaging remarks about white opponents. Louis became the modest "good" black who put himself at the service of his country in the Second World War and donated two purses to the war fund. Social equality, however, was a long time coming. Champions like Archie Moore and Muhammad Ali later told of repeatedly being refused hotel rooms or seats in restaurants until well into the 1960s.

It was not least Ali's promotion to All-American icon that carved out a new status for black boxers. After Ali, skin color was no longer a major issue and the once so widespread practice of hyping title bouts into symbolically charged interracial battles became a thing of the past.

topple the misfit from the champion's throne. Former champion James J. Jeffries fitted the bill and was accordingly induced out of retirement and back into the ring. His famous showdown with Johnson was built up to be a symbolic war of the races. So much so, that Johnson's swift knockout of his opponent on July 4, 1910 unleashed incredible resentment. Violent riots erupted around the country. The authorities responded by banning the distribution and transmission of film footage of the bout. In 1912, Johnson fell victim to dubious charges of white slavery (traffic in women). He was convicted of violating the Mann Act by taking his wife across state lines before their marriage and was sentenced to a year in prison. While out on appeal, he escaped first to Canada and later to Europe, and remained a fugitive for seven years. Jack Johnson defended his heavyweight championship three times in Paris before, intimidated and out of form, he eventually lost his title to Jess Willard in Havana in 1915.

Johnson's triumphs were to be the last celebrated by an African-American in the heavyweight division for more than twenty years. Huge talents like Sam Langford, Harry Wills, and Joe Jeannette were forced to fill in their time with series of duels against one another

Did he lose on purpose or was his opponent superior? Jack Johnson's KO at the hands of Jess Willard in Havana (1915) remains a mystery.

Boxing as a means of rehabilitation

THE SECOND CHANCE

How would people react if it became known that a respected tennis star like Pete Sampras had as a kid stolen a driver's cash box from a street car and spent 22 months in a reform school in Boonville, Miss.? And what would happen to Golf icon Tiger Woods' public standing if it was discovered that he had been sentenced to two five-year prison sentences for being involved in an armed robbery? It is pointless to speculate about either eventuality because, like almost all of their competitors, neither Sampras nor Woods have provoked courts of justice to find them guilty of any crimes.

environment, this raw sport is considered to be a good opportunity for rehabilitating underprivileged kids with criminal records through successes in the ring. The delinquent who has got a record, whether as a result of social hardship or because he fell in with a bad crowd, but manages to reverse his fortunes through the disciplinary influence of boxing training is actually one of the most popular success stories in those states that have taken up the ethical cause of reforming criminals.

"I thought to myself that it would be better to start thinking about how I wanted to live my life before I was released rather than after-

talent they had nurtured in reform school to improve their prospects for their lives outside. Others, like Sonny Liston and the notoriously conspicuous Mike Tyson, seemed to accept their sentences with a shrug of the shoulders and without any tangible signs of reformation.

To this day, the "second chance" is seen as a major social feature of a sport in which the supposedly cleansing effect of channeling aggressive energy is considered a sort of social therapy. It also produces enough reformed heroes to allow some to claim the success of this ideal. In the 1970s, for example, the story of world championship contender

Mike Tyson's court appearances (here in Indianapolis in 1992) aroused huge public interest.

Tyson supporters welcome their hero at a religious ceremony at the National Islamic Center in Plainfield, Ind., in March 1995 after his release from a three-year prison sentence.

In boxing, on the other hand, criminal records—like those of the young street car thief Archie Moore or the violent Sonny Liston—are as about as unusual as seagulls at a pier. Rocky Graziano, Jake LaMotta, Floyd Patterson, Dwight Muhammad Quawi, and Jeff Fenech are just some examples of professional champions who attended their first training sessions in penitentiaries and reform schools. And no one in their sphere would think of condemning them for their past history. More than any other

wards," said the subsequent light heavyweight world champion Archie Moore of his time in Boonville. He did just that: "I decided never to get into trouble again and to always look for something that would keep other youngsters out of trouble." Floyd Patterson reached a similar conclusion in a correctional institution in Wiltwyck, describing it as the "key experience" in his life, while Rocky Graziano discovered "that this shit ain't for me and that I'd get outta there no matter what I had done." All three used the boxing

Ron Lyle caused a stir around the world: the convicted murderer completed the majority of his professional bouts while on release from a seven and a half year sentence in Colorado before finally getting a shot at the title against Muhammad Ali in May 1975. Even though Lyle was knocked out in the 11th round, his six-digit purse drastically improved his social standing. A few years later, Matthew Saad Muhammad's star rose on the horizon. Muhammad was an abandoned orphan from Philadelphia who, after

Joe Louis' decoration as a soldier in World War II went a long way towards cementing his general social acceptance.

without ever really getting a look-in. When Joe Louis became the second black titleholder 22 years later, his team imposed a strict code of behavior: no flashy performances and no disparaging remarks about white opponents. Louis became the modest "good" black who put himself at the service of his country in the Second World War and donated two purses to the war fund. Social equality, however, was a long time coming. Champions like Archie Moore and Muhammad Ali later told of repeatedly being refused hotel rooms or seats in restaurants until well into the 1960s.

It was not least Ali's promotion to All-American icon that carved out a new status for black boxers. After Ali, skin color was no longer a major issue and the once so widespread practice of hyping title bouts into symbolically charged interracial battles became a thing of the past.

topple the misfit from the champion's throne. Former champion James J. Jeffries fitted the bill and was accordingly induced out of retirement and back into the ring. His famous showdown with Johnson was built up to be a symbolic war of the races. So much so, that Johnson's swift knockout of his opponent on July 4, 1910 unleashed incredible resentment. Violent riots erupted around the country. The authorities responded by banning the distribution and transmission of film footage of the bout. In 1912, Johnson fell victim to dubious charges of white slavery (traffic in women). He was convicted of violating the Mann Act by taking his wife across state lines before their marriage and was sentenced to a year in prison. While out on appeal, he escaped first to Canada and later to Europe, and remained a fugitive for seven years. Jack Johnson defended his heavyweight championship three times in Paris before, intimidated and out of form, he eventually lost his title to Jess Willard in Havana in 1915.

Johnson's triumphs were to be the last celebrated by an African-American in the heavyweight division for more than twenty years. Huge talents like Sam Langford, Harry Wills, and Joe Jeannette were forced to fill in their time with series of duels against one another

Did he lose on purpose or was his opponent superior? Jack Johnson's KO at the hands of Jess Willard in Havana (1915) remains a mystery.

THE ROAD TO RECOGNITION

December 18, **1810** Tom Molineaux, "The Virginia Slave," becomes the first black to take part in a championship title bout. He loses to local hero Tom Cribb over 33 rounds in London's Copthall Common.

September 25, **1886** Peter Jackson, an immigrant from the Virgin Islands, goes down in history as the first black to win the Australian heavyweight title in Sydney. Jackson outmatched his opponent Tom Leeds in the 30th round.

May 21, **1891** San Francisco is the backdrop for the first major heavyweight contest between a black and a white in the United States. The fight between future champion James J. Corbett and Peter Jackson was declared a draw after 61 rounds. Some 14 months previously, a match between Jackson and the white Gus Lambert in Troy, N.Y., was broken up by the police after four rounds. July 28, **1891** George Dixon wins a KO victory over the Englishman Abe Willis in the fifth round of their bout in San Francisco to become the first internationally recognized black champion in history; some federations had already listed Dixon as world featherweight champion after his victory over Nunc Wallace in London on June 27, **1890**. March 25, **1907** Welterweight boxer Andrew Jephta knocks out Curly Watson in the fourth round of their London match to become the first black British champion. Jephta remains the exception to the rule because soon after his victory, the National Sporting Club declares that it will only accept white contenders for the Lonsdale Belt.

December 26, **1908** Jack Johnson becomes the first black heavyweight champion by winning in Sydney against Tommy Burns on a technical knockout in the 14th round. July 4, **1910** Jack Johnson's KO victory over James J. Jeffries in the 15th round of their world championship title fight in Reno, Nev., causes racially motivated riots in numerous American cities. Several people are killed and countless others sustain serious injuries. In an immediate reaction to the rioting, 15 American states ban the transmission of all boxing films. England, South Africa, and parts of Canada follow suit. **1913** Jack Johnson is arrested and sentenced to 12 months penitentiary for alleged offences against the "White Slave Traffic Act" (Mann Act). After being released on bail, the champion flees to Canada and then to Europe. January 1, **1914** Having knocked out Arthur Pelkey in San Francisco, the New Yorker Ed "Gunboat"

Smith is declared the holder of the "White Heavyweight Title." This strange title is a defiant reaction to Johnson's ongoing reign as champion. April 5, **1915** The Johnson era comes to an end with a controversial KO defeat in the 26th round at the hands of Jess Willard in Havana. The amnesty deal that promised Johnson impunity in the United States in return for a defeat never came into effect. The "Galveston Giant" spent eight months in Leavenworth Penitentiary, Kansas, on his return in 1920. **1924** The New York boxing authorities rule that title holder Jack Dempsey must fight Harry Wills, the universally avoided "Black Panther." But the first mixed-race heavyweight title bout since 1915 never comes about because Dempsey's promoter, Tex Rickard, replaces Wills with Gene Tunney. Wills never gets the chance to compete for the title before going into retirement in 1932. June 22, **1937** Joe Louis' KO triumph over James J. Braddock in the 8th round smashes the color bar in the heavyweight division. Since then, only two whites have succeeded in becoming universally acknowledged champions: Rocky Marciano and Ingemar Johansson. **1947** The British umbrella federation overturns the ruling that only allows whites to take part in title fights. The first black boxer to benefit from this ruling is Dick Turpin, who wins a victory on decision over Vince Hawkins for the national middleweight title in London on June 28, 1947. June 5, **1952** Zack Clayton becomes the first black referee to umpire a title fight. In Philadelphia, Clayton referees the rematch between "Jersey" Joe Walcott and Ezzard Charles for the heavyweight title. Walcott wins on points. December 1, **1973** South Africa sanctions the first mixed-race title fight in the apartheid state. In a rematch in front of over 40,000 spectators in Johannesburg's Rand Stadium, white local favorite Pierre Fourie is outpointed by the African-American light heavyweight champion Bob Foster. **1977** Fights between South Africans of different races are officially permitted, thereby enriching national competition. **1983** With the establishment of the International Boxing Federation (IBF), a splinter organization that grew out of the World Boxing Association (WBA), Bob Lee Sr. becomes the first African-American president of a professional world boxing federation.

Boxing as a means of rehabilitation

THE SECOND CHANCE

How would people react if it became known that a respected tennis star like Pete Sampras had as a kid stolen a driver's cash box from a street car and spent 22 months in a reform school in Boonville, Miss.? And what would happen to Golf icon Tiger Woods' public standing if it was discovered that he had been sentenced to two five-year prison sentences for being involved in an armed robbery? It is pointless to speculate about either eventuality because, like almost all of their competitors, neither Sampras nor Woods have provoked courts of justice to find them guilty of any crimes.

environment, this raw sport is considered to be a good opportunity for rehabilitating underprivileged kids with criminal records through successes in the ring. The delinquent who has got a record, whether as a result of social hardship or because he fell in with a bad crowd, but manages to reverse his fortunes through the disciplinary influence of boxing training is actually one of the most popular success stories in those states that have taken up the ethical cause of reforming criminals.

"I thought to myself that it would be better to start thinking about how I wanted to live my life before I was released rather than after-

talent they had nurtured in reform school to improve their prospects for their lives outside. Others, like Sonny Liston and the notoriously conspicuous Mike Tyson, seemed to accept their sentences with a shrug of the shoulders and without any tangible signs of reformation.

To this day, the "second chance" is seen as a major social feature of a sport in which the supposedly cleansing effect of channeling aggressive energy is considered a sort of social therapy. It also produces enough reformed heroes to allow some to claim the success of this ideal. In the 1970s, for example, the story of world championship contender

Mike Tyson's court appearances (here in India-napolis in 1992) aroused huge public interest.

Tyson supporters welcome their hero at a religious ceremony at the National Islamic Center in Plainfield, Ind., in March 1995 after his release from a three-year prison sentence.

In boxing, on the other hand, criminal records—like those of the young street car thief Archie Moore or the violent Sonny Liston—are as about as unusual as seagulls at a pier. Rocky Graziano, Jake LaMotta, Floyd Patterson, Dwight Muhammad Quawi, and Jeff Fenech are just some examples of professional champions who attended their first training sessions in penitentiaries and reform schools. And no one in their sphere would think of condemning them for their past history. More than any other

wards," said the subsequent light heavyweight world champion Archie Moore of his time in Boonville. He did just that: "I decided never to get into trouble again and to always look for something that would keep other youngsters out of trouble." Floyd Patterson reached a similar conclusion in a correctional institution in Wiltwyck, describing it as the "key experience" in his life, while Rocky Graziano discovered "that this shit ain't for me and that I'd get outta there no matter what I had done." All three used the boxing

Ron Lyle caused a stir around the world: the convicted murderer completed the major-ity of his professional bouts while on release from a seven and a half year sentence in Colorado before finally getting a shot at the title against Muhammad Ali in May 1975. Even though Lyle was knocked out in the 11th round, his six-digit purse drastically improved his social standing. A few years later, Matthew Saad Muhammad's star rose on the horizon. Muhammad was an aban-doned orphan from Philadelphia who, after

dedicating his young life to crime, turned his life around, went pro, and fought his way to the WBC light heavyweight title (1979–81). The 1990s also had its champions with criminal records: both Johnny Tapia and William Guthrie had contacts in the drugs scene. Guthrie, IBF light heavyweight champion from 1997 to 1998, earned millions at the head of the biggest drugs cartel in St. Louis before being sentenced to three years in prison for dealing in heroin, and cocaine. He later said that it was this sentence that gave him "a second chance in life."

The unusual tolerance that is shown to boxers who break not only records but also the law, may well be a concession granted by a society trying to compensate for the fact that it is becoming increasingly incapable of dealing with its urban social problems. But there is also a more inherent, traditional reason for this reaction. In the ancient world,

Boxing practice behind bars can give prisoners a sense of discipline and self-respect: professional boxing stars like Prince Naseem Hamed *(below)* receive a rapturous reception from British delinquents.

prisoners and slaves were obliged to take part in duels that could result in death for the loser and freedom for the victor. In more recent times, British noblemen in the 17th and 18th centuries often got the more robust of their footmen to fight for their honor in bare knuckle fights. Here, too, victory meant independence.

Today, prizefighting is about much the same thing: it gives those at the bottom the chance to climb up the social ladder through outstanding performances in the ring.

JOHNNY
LIFE ON THE ROLLERCOASTER

There are plenty of amazing and even some unbelievable biographies in the recent history of boxing, but the turbulent vicissitudes of Johnny Tapia's life story certainly outdo them all. The former world champion in two weight divisions has, as he said himself in 1997, been "to hell and back" in the course of his boxing career in the American southwest. That's putting it mildly: it would be more accurate to say that he is always either in one extreme or the other.

Tapia was born in Albuquerque, the capital of New Mexico, in February 1967. But the complications of his life began a few months before his mother gave birth when his father was shot, in a case that has never been solved. His life as the son of a single parent didn't last long: when Johnny was eight years of age, his mother was kidnapped, raped, and murdered. Her murderer was never caught. The young Tapia was raised along with 14 half brothers and sisters by his grandparents. He soon channeled his energies into a variety of pursuits. As an amateur boxer, he became Junior Olympic champion, won two titles at the Golden Gloves and the American Championships. On the streets of Albuquerque, he got involved in a variety of criminal activities and came in contact with a wide range of drugs. "You name it, I did it!" was how Tapia once summed up his life.

Tapia turned pro when he failed to qualify for the American Olympic team in the winter of 1988. By the end of 1990, an almost uninterrupted series of 21 victories and a draw in 22 fights had pushed him up the rankings and put a title contention within his reach. It was at this stage that cocaine and its derivatives took the upper hand in his life. Tapia wasn't seen in a ring for three and a half years. Instead, he was regularly in an out of detention cells during this period. Looking back in 1997, Tapia explained what was going on at the time: "I was so full of rage about all the things that have happened in my life." But this wasn't meant as an excuse: "I never made anyone else responsible for what's happened and I've paid for it all myself."

It was only his girlfriend Teresa's ultimatum to either straighten up or get out that persuaded Tapia to get his wayward life back on track. Tapia renounced the white stuff, married and returned to the ring in March 1994 with a KO victory. More determined than ever before and unaffected by his long break from boxing, he won the WBO super flyweight title in the same year and soon became a real crowd-puller with his varied style and numerous entertaining performances. He concluded lucrative deals with promoter tycoons and American pay TV channels. And Tapia certainly didn't let anyone down: he defended the WBO and (since 1997) IBF belt a total of 13 times before switching to the bantamweight division, where he enjoyed success as a WBA champion until the first defeat of his professional career in June 1999, when he was outpointed by Paulie Ayala.

TAPIA

The grand finale would not have been possible if a civil court in Albuquerque had not shown some mercy in January 1996. Tapia received an 18-month suspended sentence for supposedly threatening his wife with a firearm. Teresa stuck to her version of the story, namely that her husband had threatened to kill himself during the incident in June 1995. Since then, the couple has moved away from Los Angeles to the "wild, wild East." Here, near Big Bear Lake, Johnny Tapia remains a former junkie who is constantly at risk from the influence of his own evil spirits—despite the fact that he has the image of the Virgin Mary tattooed on his chest. He still boxes, too. In the ring, he always wears shorts with his motto "Mi vida loca" (My crazy life) emblazoned on the waistband.

Again, that's putting it mildly.

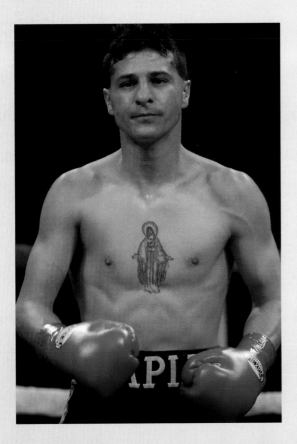

Tapia's triumphs are as spectacular as his life. He is never alone in the ring. The memory of his deceased mother and his faith in the Virgin Mary are always with him.

Women in boxing
IN A CLINCH WITH PREJUDICE

At first, it was just an exception to the rule and was mentioned more out of curiosity than out of any real interest in the sport. At least that is how it all began: in 1722, a London newspaper reported a bout between a certain Ms. Elizabeth Wilkinson and a Ms. Hannah Hyfield. Ms. Wilkinson won three guineas for her boxing prowess. From here it continued with reports on isolated ring duels between women that were published in the late 19th century in the New York *Police Gazette*, the leading American sports publication of the day. One such duel was probably the first official women's title fight held in Buffalo, N.Y., in 1888, which ended in Hattie Leslie's knock-out victory over Alice Leary in the 7th round. Not much has changed since then. Today, the most famous women boxers are those whose dubious and unconvincing qualifications are based on either their appearance or the reputations of their famous fathers.

For many people women's boxing remains a tolerated, albeit little promoted sport of peripheral importance. It is no surprise, therefore, that the generally held opinion—and not just that of the male of the species—is that women are completely out of place in this sport. Nor is it a coincidence that boxing audiences in old engravings and early photographs are made up entirely of men's caps and top hats. The reason for this is that for many years, women were denied entrance to public boxing events. It is only in recent times that members of the gentle sex have been permitted to play a supporting role in this sport and decorate this male-dominated world: initially as an attractive companion and, since the 1950s, in the form of scantily-clad round card girls. As was the case in other areas of society, the road that brought women leading roles in this sport has been long and tortuous.

Shortly after World War II, Baby Bear James from Kansas City became the first woman in America to be granted a referee's license. Thirty years later, in September 1977, Eva Shain became the first woman to sit on a world championship jury in New York for the title fight between Muhammad Ali and Earnie Shavers. In May 1993, for the first time ever, the three ringside officials that judged the world championship bout between Riddick Bowe and Jesse Ferguson in Washington, D.C. was made up entirely of women. However, just how much resentment can be shown to women in important positions in boxing became apparent after the title fight between Lennox Lewis and Evander Holyfield in 1999: ringside official Eugenia Williams had to face public ridicule that went far beyond formal criticism for her admittedly strange judgment of the fight (she pointed Holyfield ahead of Lewis).

Nevertheless, America has also given women a chance to establish themselves as active participants in the manly art of self-defense. After being denied a boxing license in Yorkshire, England, in the early 1950s, Barbara Buttrick moved across the Atlantic, where she fought any woman between Mexico and Canada who was willing to get into the ring with her. Other

In the 1990s, promoter Don King turned Christy Martin, "The Coalminer's Daughter," into the most popular woman boxer in America. This did not make her any more convincing in her match against Belinda Laracuente in March 2000.

Women professionals even succeeded in conquering the ring in New York's legendary Madison Square Garden in the late 20th Century. The big lights were all switched on when Melissa Salamone and Cora Webber let their fists fly in front of a large audience in February 1999.

Joe Frazier's daughter Jaqueline started her boxing career late in life to challenge Laila Ali in the summer of 2001 to the high-profile bout entitled "Ali vs. Frazier IV."

better-known women boxers include Cathy "Cat" Davis, who was the first woman boxer to be the subject of a title story in the cult magazine *The Ring* in 1978, and Christy Martin who—alongside Lucia Rijker, Laura Serrano, Regina Halmich, and other talented women boxers—heralded in a golden era in women's boxing. The Women's International Boxing Federation (WIBF) was established and Buttrick nominated as its president. It became the first reputable professional world boxing federation for women and organized the first all-women boxing evenings in London (1994) and Las Vegas (1995).

At the start of the new millennium, the WIBF has just under 1,000 women members in 20 affiliated states. Their average level of athletic training would not, however, convince the skeptics. However, at least the admission of women into amateur boxing, as agreed in 1993 by the AIBA, and their inclusion in tournaments such as the Golden Gloves has laid the foundation for more systematic groundwork.

Since 1994, Regina Halmich of Germany, WIBF world champion in junior flyweight and flyweight, has been one of Europe's most outstanding women athletes.

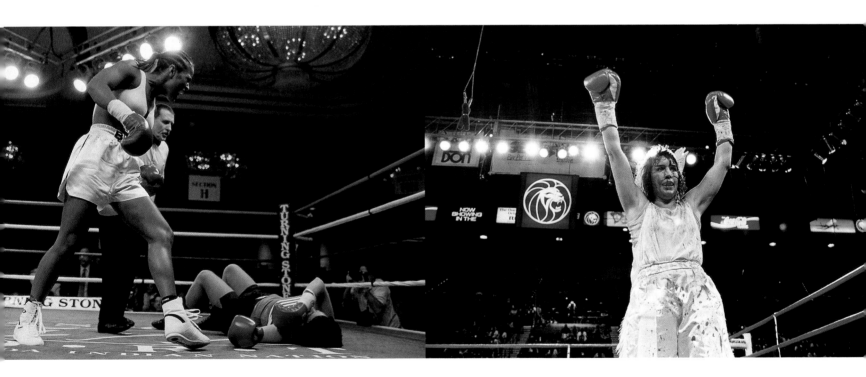

With quick technical KOs and an appealing technique, Laila Ali awakened memories of her father Muhammad around the turn of the millennium. In August 1999, she knocked out April Fowler in the first round of their bout in Verona, N.Y.

Despite being on the undercard, Christy Martin has more than once stolen the show from the men at the top of the card in front of capacity crowds in Las Vegas' casinos. In recent times, however, this feisty fighter's sporting career has stagnated in an alarming manner.

THE STAGES OF SPORTING EMANCIPATION
WOMEN AND BOXING

1722 For the first time, a boxing match contested by two women is mentioned in a publication: a London journal reports the victory of Elizabeth Wilkinson over Hannah Hyfield. **1888** The first American title fight between two women is held in Buffalo, N.Y. Hattie Leslie is declared the winner by KO over Alice Leary in the 7th round. **1904** A first at the Olympic Games in St. Louis: women stage demonstration bouts for the very first time. **1918** Bella Burge becomes the first noteworthy woman boxing promoter of modern times. After the death of her husband Dick, Mrs. Burge manages "The Ring," an arena that was located in the South London district of Blackfriars and steeped in tradition. **1942** Similarly, Aileen Eaton becomes the first important woman boxing promoter in the United States: she continues the work of her deceased husband Cal by managing the Olympic Auditorium in Los Angeles. September **1977** Eva Shain goes down in history as the first woman ringside official to judge a professional world championship fight alongside two male colleagues: Muhammad Ali's successful defense of his title against Ernie Shavers in New York. **1978** Cathy "Cat" Davis becomes the first woman boxer to grace the front page of the respected boxing magazine *The Ring,* which makes women's boxing the theme of its August issue. **1993** At its 13th World Congress in Peking, the umbrella organization for amateur boxers, the AIBA, agrees to admit women to official competitions. In the United States, a district court rules that the amateur boxer Dallas Malloy has the right to take part in amateur competitions. The American umbrella organization USA Boxing had initially denied her this right. **1994** The Women's International Boxing Federation, the first world association for women professional boxers, is established in Miami. Former boxer Barbara Buttrick is elected president. On April 20, the first all-women professional American boxing evening takes place in Las Vegas. On February 19, a similar event is held in London's York Hall for the first time in Great Britain. **1995** Women boxers take part in the regional Golden Gloves tournament in the state of New York for the first time. A total of 30 female amateurs register for the tournament. **2001** The first amateur European championships for women are held in Budapest. In June, the first six-digit purses are paid out for a women's fight when Laila Ali takes on Jaqueline Frazier in Verona, N.Y. The fight is billed as a sort of revenge of the daughters ("Ali vs. Frazier IV").

BARBARA BUTTRICK

THE LITTLE TERROR

As a pioneer of her sport, Barbara Buttrick contested a total of 26 professional fights and countless show matches between 1949 and 1959.

She might not have been able to contest bouts as a boxer all her life, but to this day, she still fights for women's boxing. Born in 1929, Barbara Buttrick has demonstrated an unusual and unprecedented dedication to the sport she loved. Since her youth, she has fought for the acceptance of women in what is, even today, in every respect a male-dominated sport. For her, there are no specific differences: "It is equally damaging or beneficial for everyone."

Buttrick was a petite teenager growing up in the English county of Yorkshire when she saw photos of boxing matches in the sports section of the newspaper. She was instantly hooked. At the age of 18 she moved to London to train in boxing and prepare herself for a professional career. But the British federation refused to grant her a license. The 5-foot bundle of energy ended up fighting in traveling boxing booths, demonstrating her talent by fighting every woman who had the courage to step into the ring with her and by taking on the more lightweight of her male colleagues in show fights. She contested up to 1,000 such fights a year in Great Britain and France.

Between 1949 and 1959, "Little Barbara" toured through the United States, Canada, and Mexico, earning herself the new nickname "Little Terror" in 26 official professional bouts. Apart from a match against the 33-pound heavier Joann Hagen, against whom she lost over eight rounds in Calgary in September 1954, Buttrick never dropped a fight in ten years. With the outstanding record of 25:1, she started a new life as a bookkeeper in Miami in 1960 at the age of 31. But her interest in a new generation of women undercard boxers—American women like Yvonne Barkley, Marian "Lady Tyger" Trimiar, Gwen Gemini or Ernestine Jones—ensured that she never lost touch with women's boxing.

This explains why the retired Buttrick didn't think twice when, riding on the crest of the most successful wave of women's boxing in history, the chance of establishing a women's boxing federation arose. The Women's International Boxing Federation (WIBF) was eventually set up in Miami in 1994 and its first president was Barbara Buttrick. She held this post into the new millennium. Since then, this tough but friendly lady has frequently been a guest of honor at major women's boxing evenings in America and Europe, where she ties the champion's belt around the waist of the winners: the insignia of recognition that she never had the chance to win. As the sport's most important female pioneer in modern times, her name is—and always will be—synonymous with women's boxing.

THE AMATEURS

Protective headgear is a definitive characteristic of amateur bouts: Gaidarbek Gaidarbekov (RUS, *opposite page*) vs. Jeff Lacy (USA) at the Olympic Games in 2000.

While boxing duels at the professional level may resemble fights in the true sense of the word, at the amateur level, they are more like sporting contests. Amateur boxing—also known as Olympic-style boxing—has always deliberately sought its own specific style. The spirit of the sport shines through in the preamble of the articles of the AIBA (Association Internationale de Boxe Amateur), which outlines the basic principles of amateur boxing. It defines the aim of the sport as follows: "to score victory by means of technical skills and not to win the contest by bringing about an early stoppage." This goal is firmly backed up by an appropriately strict set of rules and regulations.

Referees are obliged to count out a boxer who has been knocked down for the first time instead of allowing more blows to rain down on him. That being said, a knockdown does not earn a boxer extra points. Three knockdowns in a round—or a total of four in the entire match—also lead to immediate stoppage, as does the clear superiority of one boxer: if the difference between the number of scoring blows counted for each boxer reaches 15, an alarm

THE 12 WEIGHT DIVISIONS IN AMATEUR BOXING

Light flyweight:	less than 106 lbs
Flyweight:	less than 112 lbs
Bantamweight:	119 lbs
Featherweight:	125 lbs
Lightweight:	132 lbs
Light welterweight:	139 lbs

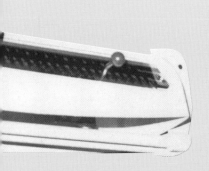

sounds and the contest is automatically stopped. The referee can also decide to wave off a bout even before this point is reached. This is not a rare occurrence, much to the annoyance of some spectators who come expecting some action-packed boxing. The rule obliging boxers to wear protective headgear was introduced in 1983 to minimize the risks to the boxers' health. Official statistics say that it has helped reduce the number of cuts and ear injuries.

All of these preventative measures have given amateur boxing the profile of a comparatively unspectacular, less risky, "light" version of boxing. And this is exactly what the sport's officials hoped to achieve. In response to the ever-changing moods of the International Olympic Committee (IOC), which in the 1990s openly discussed removing the reviled sport from the Olympic program, the AIBA is making every effort to tone down amateur boxing. In 1992, the association proudly announced that the average KO rate in amateur boxing had been cut to just under 0.8 percent. This explains why Dr. Robert Voy, president of the AIBA Medical Commission, dismissed any comparison between professional and amateur boxing as outdated: "Comparing the two is like mixing apples and oranges."

Some doctors and experts, on the other hand, doubt that amateur boxing is really all that much safer than the professional version of the sport. They think that the wearing of protective headgear can give athletes a false sense of security. Confident that they are well protected, boxers may be more willing to take a worrying amount of blows. This trend is actually reinforced by a computer-assisted judging system—the so-called scoring machine—which was introduced in the 1990s. Because only those hits that are credited in the system as a scoring blow by at least three of the five judges are actually counted as such, the matches—which were changed from three rounds of three minutes to four rounds of two minutes in 1998—are increasingly focused on clearly identifiable punches. While this amendment has made things more objective and transparent, it has done nothing to enhance the style of the contests. Stamina is often more decisive than technical skill.

Nevertheless, Olympic-style boxing upholds its tradition of spearheading the introduction of new safety standards and rules. Whether it is the introduction of standing eight counts or gloves for competition bouts, most amendments originate in amateur boxing. The dense network of boxing clubs in over 170 member states of the AIBA are the foundation for the entire sport of boxing and the competitions they organize in the various divisions are a training ground for the champions of tomorrow. Any boxer who survives the countless match series at regional level and, in later years, the international tournaments, and does well in them can justifiably be considered a winner, even if he doesn't turn professional.

Welterweight:	147 lbs
Light middleweight:	156 lbs
Middleweight:	165 lbs
Light heavyweight:	178 lbs
Heavyweight:	201 lbs
Super heavyweight:	over 201 lbs

OLYMPIC SPRINGBOARD

The Olympic boxing tournament at the Sydney Games in 2000 was held in Exhibition Hall 3 in Darling Harbor.

The description of Olympic boxing tournaments as a "springboard" to a professional boxing career has long been a standard phrase in the repertoire of sporting reporters. "First the laurels, then the checks" is the modern-day formula for a successful career in the ring. This formula has worked on occasions in the past. In the heavyweight division, for example, former American gold medallists like Floyd Patterson, Cassius Clay, Joe Frazier, George Foreman and the Spinks brothers passed the world championship belt from one to the other as if it was a family heirloom. Generally speaking, however, a successful Olympic start is no guarantee for the transition to the professional camp. Nor is it the ultimate goal of every amateur boxer.

Pugilism was an integral part of the Ancient Olympics after its introduction at the games of the 23rd Olympiad in 688 B.C. Centuries later, 28 American hopefuls became the first boxers to compete for modern-day Olympic honors in 7 weight divisions at the St. Louis Games in 1904. Back then, the athletes were permitted to try their luck in more than one weight division. This explains why Oliver Kirk is the only boxer to date to have won two Olympic gold medals

for boxing in one year (bantamweight and featherweight). Nevertheless, early Olympic champions rarely succeeded in transforming their gold medals into sizeable purses. The world had to wait until 1925 to witness two gold medallists win professional titles: Frankie Genaro and Fidel LaBarba (1920 and 1924 respectively in the flyweight division). By 1945, only two other Olympic champions followed in their footsteps: bantamweight Willie Smith (1924) and featherweight Jackie Fields (1924).

It was only after the Second World War that the Olympics became a world stage for amateurs from non-socialist countries who were considering turning pro. Regardless of the political system, however, Olympic success became increasingly important for a country's medals table. Unfortunately, this did not always have a positive effect on the quality of the judges: in 1948, for example, 66 of the 85 judges in attendance were sent home early as a result of their catastrophic decisions. Exactly 20 years later, the same thing happened again to 16 of the 32 supposedly unbiased officials. Since then, a steady stream of protests and scandals has dogged the competition. In 1976, 81 African boxers left Montreal ahead

of schedule in protest at the questionable decisions of the judges, while in 1984, half the world was infuriated when the American team shamelessly handed itself a total of nine gold medals in the previously announced "Operation Gold" at the Los Angeles Games.

Escapades such as these certainly do not help a young professional to his first million dollars. With the exception of Meldrick Taylor, Pernell Whitaker and bronze medallist Evander Holyfield, the majority of their teammates didn't get very far once they took off their protective headgear after the Los Angeles Games. Not even Mark Breland, who was named outstanding boxer of the tournament, enjoyed the glorious career many experts had predicted for him: soon after surrendering his welterweight title for the second time in 1990, the five-time Golden Gloves champion went into retirement. The stories of American Andrew Maynard, Irishman Michael Carruth or Germany's Torsten May are similar: none of them made it right to the top despite their triumphs in Seoul and Barcelona.

Lenny Mancini's famous "One day headlines, the next day bread-lines" remark can easily be applied to the "Children of the Olympics."

A LONG-LOST TREASURE

The 18-year-old boxer from Louisville, Kentucky, was the proudest victor at the Games in Rome. Wherever he went in the Olympic Village, he wore his gold medal for light heavyweight boxing around his neck. It is even reported that he wore his beloved trophy in bed. Years later, Cassius Clay's gold was gone and the men in his posse, who now called him Muhammad Ali, knew the reason why. Bitterly disappointed by racist America, Clay threw the gold medal into the Ohio river in his home town one evening after being thrown out of a restaurant and having a run-in with a motorbike gang. This, at least, is how co-author Richard Durham, dramatist and publisher of the Muslim newspaper *Muhammad Speaks,* described the incident in the biography *The Greatest,* which was published in 1975.

The Olympic champion later admitted as a professional boxer that he never met the

Cassius Clay as an Olympic champion in Rome in 1960 (top) and as Muhammad Ali in Atlanta in 1996.

supposed group of Hells Angels. And he was rarely able to recall the moment he disposed of his medal by throwing it into the river from the highest point of the Jefferson County Bridge. When it suited him, this polished performer recounted the more dramatic version of the tale. But when among friends, he admitted that the actual reason for the disappearance of his medal was much less exciting: he obviously mislaid it sometime after his return from Rome. Some 36 years later, another tournament brought closure on the matter: in 1996, the ailing champion was presented with a replica of the lost medal after he lit the Olympic flame in Atlanta. Officially, this was the end of the reconciliation between the Black Muslim convert and the America he had helped to change. With this gesture, the legend of the gold medal that was thrown into the river, disappeared into the mists of time.

GOLDEN GLOVES

It is the biggest talent-spotting amateur boxing tournament in the world and it is truly steeped in history. Any man—and, since 1994, any woman—from the United States can take part as long as he or she is considered fit enough to do so by the doctor. But the idea behind the "Golden Gloves" is more than just a gigantic knock-out competition: the tournament was also born in 1923 out of the principle of giving young people's lives some direction and supporting charities with the earnings from the tournament. It was in this year that the sports journalist Arch Ward raised the idea of organizing a regional tournament under the patronage of his newspaper, the *Chicago Tribune* as a reaction to demands for a ban on boxing in Illinois made by civil initiatives. Ward considered boxing to be a school of self-discipline and declared the event to be a success when 424 participants competed for the laurels in eight weight divisions in March of that year. Massive anti-boxing protests and a court order prevented the competition from being staged in the following years. It was the eventual legalization of the sport in Illinois in 1926 that paved the way for a return of the Golden Gloves. From 1928 onwards, the tournament joined

GOLDEN GLOVES TOURNAMENT REGIONS:

Chicago	New England
Cincinatti	New Jersey
Cleveland	New York Metro
Colorado-New Mexico	Pennsylvania
Detroit	Rocky Mountains
Great Plains	California
Hawaii	St. Louis
Indiana	Sunshine State
Iowa	New York State
Kansas City	Texas
Kansas-Oklahoma	Toledo
Knoxville	Tri-State
Michigan	Upper Midwest
Mid-South	Washington, DC
Nevada	Wisconsin

Not all of the regional divisions that offer Golden Gloves titles coincide exactly with U.S. state borders.

Top left: Boxing went on in three rings in Reno in 2001. John Santiago *(above right)* was named the most courageous boxer of the tournament.

THE SCORING MACHINE

forces with the *Tribune* and the associated newspaper, the *Daily News,* which had organized a similar tournament in New York City a year previously. The winners at this event received a miniature golden glove as a reward.

Initially, both cities selected their own champions and allowed them to compete against each other for the title "Golden Gloves Champion" every year. The earnings and gates from these competitions were, among other things, used to finance the U.S. team's trip to the 1936 Olympic Games in Berlin. Over the years, the idea spread to the rest of the Unites States. Today, competitions are held in 30 regions nationwide, including Hawaii, and are organized by the same number of franchise companies of the Golden Gloves Association of America, Inc., which was established in 1964. These competitions culminate in different locations every year and coincide with the U.S. Army Golden Gloves Championships, the reputation of which is even greater than that of the national amateur championships. It can safely be said that down through the years, anyone who became anybody in professional boxing usually first drew attention to themselves at these competitions.

HALL OF FAME: GOLDEN GLOVES CHAMPIONS

Barney Ross	1929
Joe Louis	1934
Ezzard Charles	1939
Sonny Liston	1953
Cassius Clay	1959, 1960
Sugar Ray Leonard	1974
Mike McCallum	1979
Roy Jones Jr.	1986, 1987
Oscar De La Hoya	1989
Floyd Mayweather Jr.	1993, 1994, 1996

Four buttons for two opponents: this is how the judges enter punches and warnings in the scoring machine. The scoring system remains controversial to this day.

It isn't really a machine. It's a computer-assisted registration system. Quite literally, the scoring machine, which was used for the first time at the World Amateur Boxing Championships in Moscow in 1989, provides a blow-by-blow account of the match.

The five judges no longer make their decisions based on their general impressions or by awarding each round to the stronger of the two opponents. Instead, they operate four buttons on a tiny machine. They enter the scoring blows for the blue and red corner (blue and red buttons respectively) and note warnings made by the referee (one white button each). These points are then registered by the connected computer. The scoring blows are only recorded when at least three of the five judges press the appropriate button within a reaction period of one second.

In this way, the scoring blows and point penalties that have been noted by the majority of the officials add up to a score that quickly indicates the winner.

Because electronic scoring cannot function without human intervention, subjectivity is all part of the process. It has been observed that the willingness to credit a punch as a scoring blow depends not least on the judge's personal opinion of an athlete.

Preferences for a specific style, a certain nationality, or some other factor are still part of the sporting decision. This means that the computer-assisted evaluation is not fully objective.

However, an official that points a match in a one-sided manner is easily identifiable for the organizing association: the computer registers every single point entered by all five officials along with their individual time intervals.

Cuba and its amateurs

THE LAND OF WORLD CHAMPIONS

Can you cultivate outstanding boxers as methodically as sugar? The socialist state of Cuba has done so to great effect. The excellently trained amateurs from the Caribbean island republic win gold so often at the world championships and Olympic Games that winning would appear to be a national pastime. In Barcelona (1992), Castro's most famous squadron of combatants walked away with 7 of the 12 Olympic titles, while in Atlanta (1996), 7 of the 24 finalists came from Cuba (4 gold medallists). This outstanding performance was almost repeated in Sydney in the year 2000 when the country provided gold medallists in four weight divisions and semifinalists in two other classes.

World champion three times each between 1972 and 1980. A patriot through and through, the globally admired king of the super heavyweights declined every offer made by American promoters: "What are 8 million dollars compared to the love of 8 million Cubans?" The reaction of his successor Felix Savon was similar when he returned to his hotel room in the Olympic Village in Barcelona to find a catalogue of luxury items and the telephone number of a manager waiting for him. There was just no point. Savon was just as uninterested in a lucrative bout against Evander Holyfield or Mike Tyson as Stevenson had been about turning pro to contest a prestigious duel with Muhammad Ali. "Professional boxers

"WHAT ARE 8 MILLION DOLLARS COMPARED TO THE LOVE OF 8 MILLION CUBANS?"

TEOFILO STEVENSON

There is a method behind this success. Nowhere else can so many fulltime trainers (it is said there are 600 in Cuba) encourage talent and train youngsters from such an early age. Thousands of school kids are channeled into sports promotion programs in the *areas* (regions) and filtered through countless local competitions. After all this, only a small number of the 4,000 active boxers are selected for the national training center, the Finca Orbein Quesada, on the outskirts of Havana. Here, head coach Alcides Sagarra channels his authority and conviction into training the elite of his sport to become the people on whom the nation's hopes are pinned in two ways: for almost forty years now, this member of the central committee has done all he can to "give people an integral sporting and social shape."

Sagarra's model athlete clearly was Teofilo Stevenson, who became both Olympic and

are exploited," said the heavyweight gold medallist, "exploited by people."

But cracks are starting to appear in the patriotic front. In the 1990s, highly talented top boxers like Joel Casamayor and Ramon Garbey left the economically fragile island republic for Florida. Junior world champion Juan Carlos Gomez moved to Germany, where he was built up to become a professional champion. These success stories are a continuation of the tradition started by famous exiles who made Cuba famous for professional boxing. Kid Chocolate and Kid Gavilan were already champions in the capitalist world before Castro arrived on the scene; Sugar Ramos, José Napoles, and José Legra repeated this success in the 1960s from Mexico and Spain respectively. This leaves the officials from the National Sports Institute cold: for them, a champion only becomes a hero when he stays in his home country.

Sparring partners improvising a bout is almost part of day-to-day life in Cuba: in the streets of the old town in Havana, the kids box for the love of the sport.

CUBA: OLYMPIC CHAMPIONS IN AMATEUR BOXING

1972 Munich
Orlando Martinez, bantamweight
Emilio Correa, welterweight
Teofilo Stevenson, heavyweight

1976 Montreal
Jorge Hernandez, light flyweight
Angel Herrera, featherweight
Teofilo Stevenson, super heavyweight

1980 Moscow
Juan Hernandez, bantamweight
Angel Herrera, lightweight
Andres Aldama, welterweight
Armando Martinez, light middleweight
José Gomez, middleweight
Teofilo Stevenson, heavyweight

1984 Los Angeles Olympic boycott
1988 Seoul Olympic boycott

1992 Barcelona
Rogelio Marcelo, light flyweight
Joel Casamayor, bantamweight
Hector Vincent, light welterweight
Juan Lemus, light middleweight
Ariel Hernandez, middleweight
Felix Savon, heavyweight
Roberto Balado, super heavyweight

1996 Atlanta
Maikro Romero, flyweight
Hector Vincent, light welterweight
Ariel Hernandez, middleweight
Felix Savon, heavyweight

2000 Sydney
Guillermo Rigondeaux, bantamweight
Mario Kindelan, lightweight
Jorge Gutierrez, middleweight
Felix Savon, heavyweight

Total number of medals from Olympic participation
27 gold, 13 silver and 7 bronze medals

THE PROFESSIONALS

CUBA: OLYMPIC CHAMPIONS IN AMATEUR BOXING

1972 Munich
Orlando Martinez, bantamweight
Emilio Correa, welterweight
Teofilo Stevenson, heavyweight

1976 Montreal
Jorge Hernandez, light flyweight
Angel Herrera, featherweight
Teofilo Stevenson, super heavyweight

1980 Moscow
Juan Hernandez, bantamweight
Angel Herrera, lightweight
Andres Aldama, welterweight
Armando Martinez, light middleweight
José Gomez, middleweight
Teofilo Stevenson, heavyweight

1984 Los Angeles Olympic boycott
1988 Seoul Olympic boycott

1992 Barcelona
Rogelio Marcelo, light flyweight
Joel Casamayor, bantamweight
Hector Vincent, light welterweight
Juan Lemus, light middleweight
Ariel Hernandez, middleweight
Felix Savon, heavyweight
Roberto Balado, super heavyweight

1996 Atlanta
Maikro Romero, flyweight
Hector Vincent, light welterweight
Ariel Hernandez, middleweight
Felix Savon, heavyweight

2000 Sydney
Guillermo Rigondeaux, bantamweight
Mario Kindelan, lightweight
Jorge Gutierrez, middleweight
Felix Savon, heavyweight

Total number of medals from Olympic participation
27 gold, 13 silver and 7 bronze medals

YOUNGSTERS

In the beginning they were dragged along by their big brother, a friend or someone else. Later on, they actually tried it out for themselves at the gym and began to enjoy it. This is how the boxing biography of almost all future champions begins. But it is here that the similarities in their junior days end. Just like in all other areas of life, everyone makes their own way in boxing.

According to their first trainers, some demonstrate their unique talent immediately; others are only mediocre—or even worse—at their first attempt. For their coaches, what is even more important than this is their spirit or, as it is known in the business, the flame, the special will or, quite simply, determination. According to Goody Petronelli, the man who for many years trained champion Marvin Hagler, this spirit begins to show itself after the first few sparring rounds. "I don't care whether the new boy is pulverized in the gym," says Petronelli. "If he shows me that he has guts, if he comes back again the next evening and asks 'what did I do wrong?' then I know that there is a chance he will become a boxer."

But when does that moment arrive? Here, too, the answer varies from boxer to boxer. Oscar De La Hoya was just seven years of age when he contested his first official fight in East Los Angeles. By the time he was 14, he had already over 100 bouts under his belt. Sugar Ray Robinson was 14 when he contested his first fight in a gym in Harlem, and Hagler, Petronelli's model protégé in Brockton near Boston, was 15. There are no fundamental restrictions such as a minimum age for boxing in either the United States or Latin America. This explains why French photographer Martine Barrat came face to face with mere school kids in the ring when she worked on a long-range project about day-to-day life in American gyms in the 1980s. Barrat's portraits of these children in training or competition situations later toured European galleries where they tended to appall some visitors.

While the various associations in Europe don't have a uniform regulation for young novices, their umbrella organization the EABA (European Amateur Boxing Association) has reached a sort of consensus. Between Moscow and Madrid, children who are required to

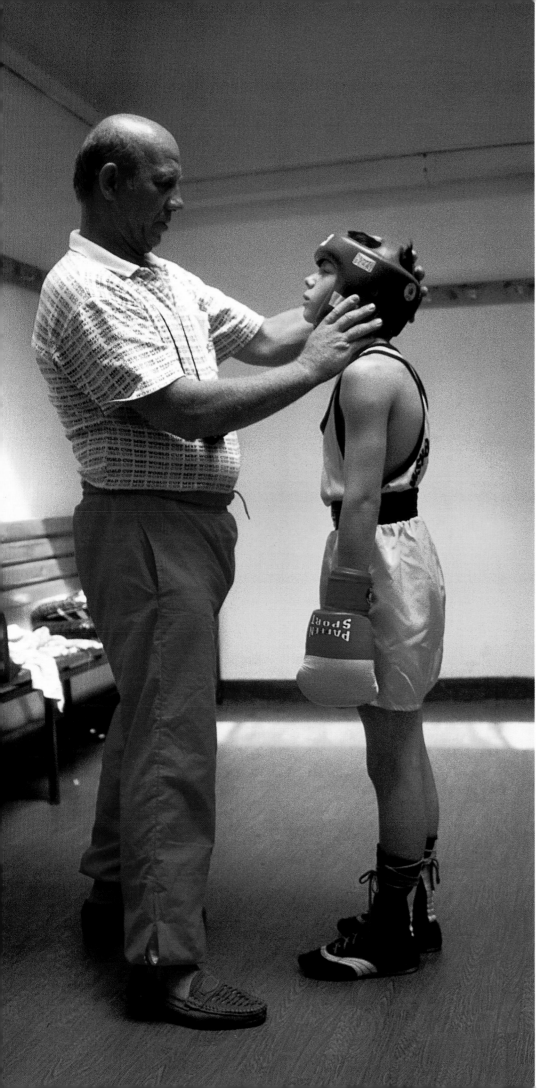

& KIDS

attend school are only allowed to attend training from the age of ten and can only take part in official matches from the age of twelve. Young boys are only allowed to participate in international junior competitions like the Balaton Tournament in Hungary, the Brandenburg Cup in Germany or the Italy Cup on Sardinia once they reach the cadet division (age 14 to 16 years). Below this age, competitions are only organized at a regional level and only once special precautions have been taken. If a youngster has to be counted out twice, he is usually taken out of the ring immediately by the referee.

Nevertheless, bloody noses, black eyes and cut lips are still unavoidable souvenirs of training and competition at junior level. But what always inspires skeptics to question whether kids should be allowed to compete in the sport in the first place, is an integral part of the toughness test for those working in boxing. This is in line with Goody Petronelli's philosophy. In his time, he saw legions of kids come and go in his Brockton gym. "The kid might have looked good on the punch bag," he once said, "but the punch bag don't punch back. No one has punched back yet. And he hasn't punched anybody either."

Despite some methodical and cultural differences, every coach in the world believes that this "flame" only bursts out when the going gets tough.

Juniors can try their hand at the sweet science while at school. A high level of responsibility is demanded of coaches and supervisors at this stage.

THE PROFESSIONALS

Formalities and health checks

THE ROAD TO A LICENSE

In the days when brave men fought without gloves, it was extremely easy to get into prizefighting. Courage and the most impressive physique possible were virtually all that was needed for fistfighting. What's more, these requirements were only tested when the going got tough during the bout, never beforehand. The establishment of national and international umbrella organizations have changed all that: pre-fight eligibility tests were introduced soon after the birth of modern boxing. Since then, only those boxers who can prove they are fit and have both the necessary reflexes and perfect vision are allowed to step into the ring. But in almost every corner of the world, even this is no longer enough for a boxer to be granted a professional license.

Boxers who are registered with any halfway reputable association are obliged to submit a long list of test results with their license applications. These include the aforementioned medical examinations, the result of a recent HIV test (the results may not be more than ten weeks old), and computer tomography (CT scan or CAT scan) pictures, which are used to check the brain for any early signs of damage (such as blood clots). The license itself must be renewed and the CAT scan repeated annually. The rules governing the submission of HIV test results, on the other hand, are starting to be tightened: boxers must prove that they are not infected with the virus before every bout.

The road to getting and renewing a professional boxing license is paved with forms and

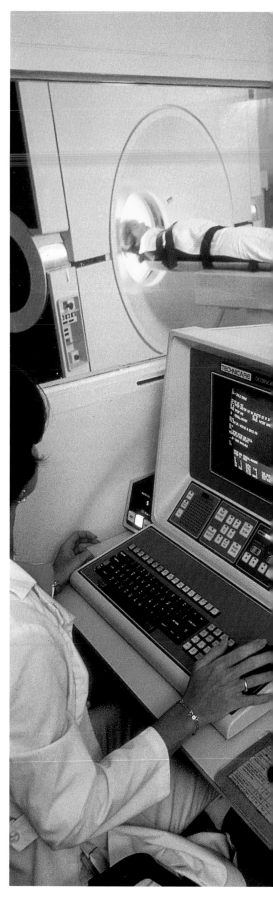

Computer tomography (CAT scan) pictures are used to determine the boxer's eligibility: a longitudinal section of the head *(left)*.

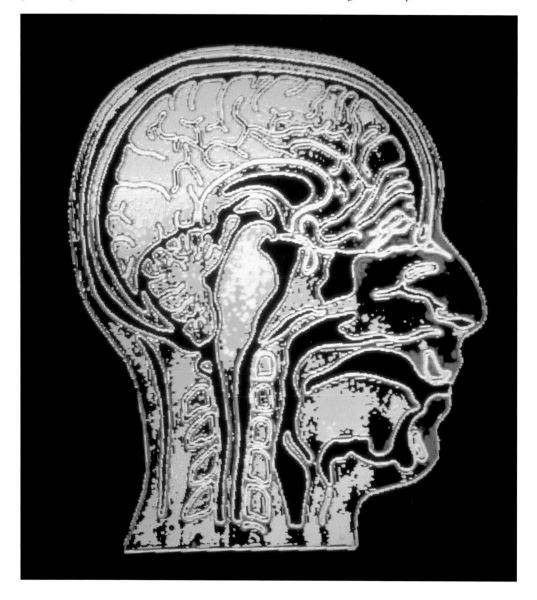

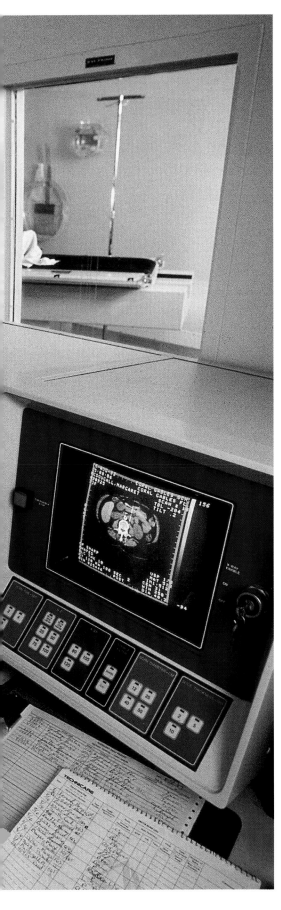

certificates. But for novices, who usually graduate to professional boxing from the amateur sport, the procedure is not really a serious hurdle. Hardly anyone who has boxed as a junior fails these tests. Once the hopeful has been given the green light by the association, there is nothing to stop him from turning pro. Before his debut fight, he has to go through the usual procedures that have been part of his routine since his amateur days: the weigh-in and the brief examination by the ringside physician. Professional boxing careers generally kick off with a four-round match. After this, it is usual for both the number of rounds and the quality of the opponents to be steadily increased.

Of course, the more daring might choose to follow the example set by Pete Rademacher: the American heavyweight gold medallist at the Melbourne Games in 1956 thought he would take a shortcut and launch his professional career in style by immediately challenging the world champion of the day, Floyd Patterson. The outcome was, quite literally, shattering: Rademacher succeeded in dropping the champion once in the second round of their bout in August 1957. But four rounds and seven knockdowns later, his dream of making history was in pieces. Not to be dissuaded by the fate of his predecessor, Rafael Lovera from Paraguay tried the same trick 18 years later in September 1975. He suffered a swift KO in round 4 of his match against the Venezuelan light flyweight WBC champion Luis Estaba.

A certain warm-up period is essential. That being said, the way boxers make their way to a title fight varies greatly. While former Thai boxer Saensak Muangsurin was crowned WBC light welterweight king in 1975 in only his second professional fight, Archie Moore first succeeded in snatching the light heavyweight crown in the 175th bout and 18th year of his professional career. The ideal route to the title lies somewhere between these two extremes.

Today, it is impossible to get a professional license without perfect CAT scan results; a scan of the brain, eyes and naval cavities *(right)*.

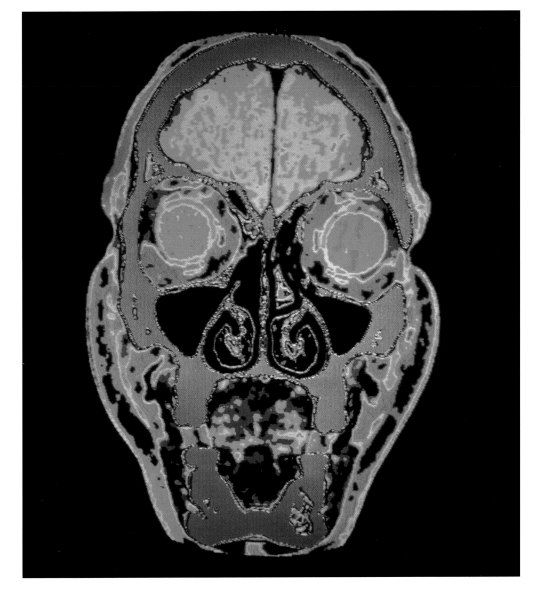

THE FINAL HOURS

"By the time you get into the changing room, half of your nerves are in bits," says Dariusz Michalczewski. "I hang up my stuff and check that nothing is missing. Then I ask for a coffee, sit down, stand up again … it's the impatience. You've got to have that."

Hamburg, December 1997. In two and a half hours time, Michalczewski, the Polish WBO light heavyweight champion who holds

German citizenship, will defend his title for the eleventh time. But until then, just like any other conscientious professional boxer, he will run through a complete program of preparations, warm-ups and official maneuvers. These are the final hours before the fight.

Cut off from the excited crowds in the hall, where the regulars are being entertained and warmed up by the undercard bouts, the

champion is surrounded by his team and is busy going through the all-important rituals of his sport. The lacing of his boots, the grinding of the lower jaw, the spitting and nose-blowing in the bathroom that is generally supposed to keep the respiratory tracts clear—it's all part of the ceremony that helps Michalczewski not least to control the rising tension inside.

The bandages applied by the trainer are checked by the opponent's trainer and the referee, who then seals them with a signature. A short time later, the champion starts stretching and shadow boxing to warm up. His inner engine starts to kick in while he is practicing a few combinations on his punching bag. "Keep cool," warns trainer Fritz Sdunek as he dries off his sweating protégé with a towel. This is followed by more advice: "Sit down again." Once again, the coach and the athlete run through the strategy for the first few rounds. The "Tiger"—as he is called—is now ready to pounce. Dressed in an embroidered robe and surrounded by his entourage, he dances lightly down the long corridor to the ring. Does he hear his theme tune, *Eye of the Tiger,* and the frantic applause of the crowds? He's not too sure himself.

"You just look straight ahead and want to get into the ring as quickly as possible. And once up there, you don't see or hear anything. In my head I am running through my tactics and trying to concentrate." Obviously the tactics worked. On the evening in question, Dariusz Michalczewski beat his Canadian challenger Daren Zenner: the fight was stopped in the sixth round. He has still not surrendered his title at the time of going to press.

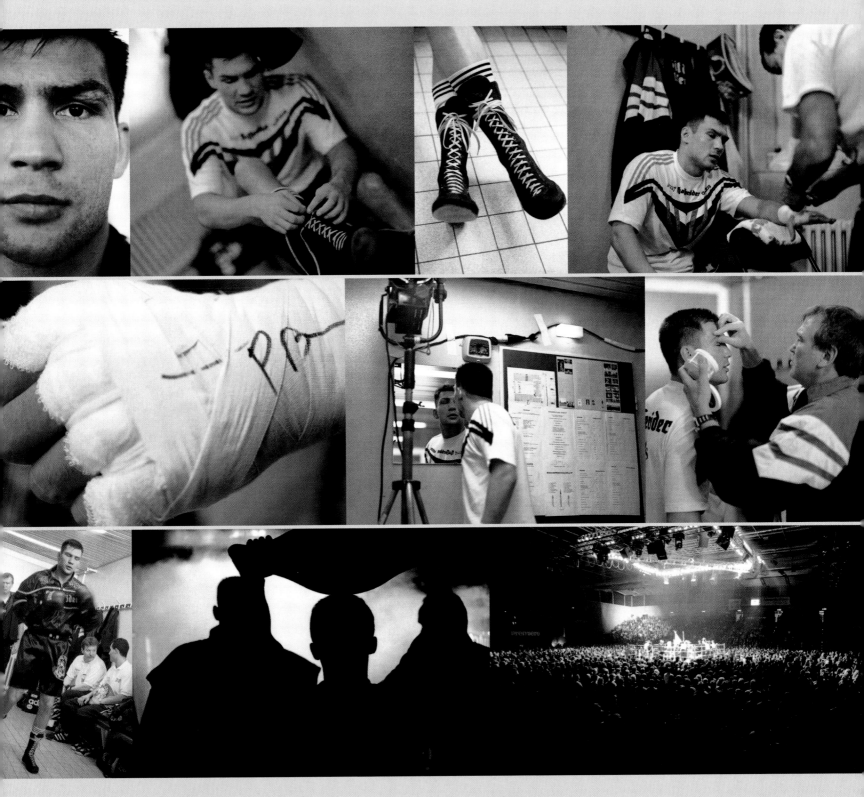

THE BANGER

The banger is a specialist. He doesn't pull any punches and hits hard and fast: bang, bang! His blows are lethal and his goals straightforward. The banger wants to hit his opponent so effectively that he is either knocked out or taken out of the fight by the referee before the final bell. This is why point decisions and technically versed opponents who avoid direct confrontation are his natural foe. This might make him appear easy to size up but caution is always advised. Given his unusual power, the banger always keeps his options open and an effective blow in reserve right until the fat lady sings. Typical bangers include Iran Barkley *(left)* and David Tua.

BOXING STYLES

One is a bit more powerful; the other much more nimble. One is tall; the other rather small. Whatever the different physical and motor characteristics boxers bring with them into the ring, they always try to emphasize their strengths and hide their weaknesses. The sum of all these strategies is the personal style of the athlete. But despite all these individual characteristics, there are stereotypes: those basic prototypes that crop up repeatedly. Some of the most common are described here. The styles outlined here should be considered prototypes. Athletes do not always adopt them one-to-one, preferring to combine them with other stylistic elements. When training and preparing for a fight, technically versed boxers—like Archie Moore, Muhammad Ali or Sugar Ray Leonard—adapt their style to suit their opponents' typical maneuvers or are able to modify their adversaries' style and strategy during the actual bout.

THE BRAWLER

The brawler is often unorthodox and tireless, and always on the attack. He pursues his goals in a permanent hail of punches: from half distance, he prefers to inundate his opponent with blows—preferably hooks. This is his way of compensating for any technical deficiencies or lack of reach. A mediocre brawler uses his sheer energy to overpower a talented technical boxer by embroiling his opponent in an almost uninterrupted shower of blows. This is the preferred style of robust, extremely fit boxers who drag their opponents down with unwavering relentlessness. Typical brawlers include Joe Frazier *(right)* and Marcelo Dominguez.

THE BOXER

Landing a blow without actually being hit, punching and immediately ducking—this is the classic art of fistfighting, which no one masters more convincingly than the boxer. He is a talented and stylish boxer who demonstrates his superiority in the ring with razor-sharp techniques and outstanding reflexes. He misleads his attacker with swift bobbing and weaving or dance-like footwork only to mount a surprise attack as soon as he spots an opening. He usually avoids the infight and prefers aiming for a clear decision to risking too much on a premature victory. Typical boxers include Muhammad Ali *(right)* and Lennox Lewis.

THE BOXER-PUNCHER

This multi-talented boxer is that rare breed of athlete that boasts both superior techniques and immense power, and can clinch a victory by forcing a stoppage or by going the distance. This combination of boxer and banger is versed in all the styles of a successful pro and is capable of choosing the right "tools" for the fight depending either on his own mood or the style of his opponent. Typical boxer-punchers include Sugar Ray Robinson and Prince Naseem Hamed *(left)*.

THE COUNTER-BOXER

The first move can reveal a boxer's weaknesses, a situation that should always be avoided in a bout. This is why the counter-boxer waits for his opponent to make the first move before he strikes. He wants to hit him just when his opponent has thrown a punch. After all, those who let down their defenses are more vulnerable. But this tactic sometimes earns the counter-boxer the reputation of a strategic parasite (or stinker) who has nothing to contribute to the duel. However, it can also be said that to counter successfully, a boxer needs some of the greatest abilities known to the sport: excellent opponent observation skills, outstanding reflexes and convincing defensive tactics. Typical counter-boxers include Gene Tunney and Henry Maske *(far right)*.

JOHN L. SULLIVAN · JAMES J. CORBETT · BOB FITZSIMMONS · JAMES J. JEFFRIES
MARVIN HART · TOMMY BURNS · JACK JOHNSON · JESS WILLARD · JACK DEMPSEY
GENE TUNNEY · MAX SCHMELING · JACK SHARKEY · PRIMO CARNERA · MAX
BAER · JAMES J. BRADDOCK · JOE LOUIS · EZZARD CHARLES · "JERSEY" JOE WALCOTT
ROCKY MARCIANO · FLOYD PATTERSON · INGEMAR JOHANSSON · SONNY LISTON
CASSIUS CLAY · ERNIE TERRELL · MUHAMMAD ALI · JOE FRAZIER · JIMMY ELLIS
GEORGE FOREMAN · LEON SPINKS · LARRY HOLMES · JOHN TATE · MIKE WEAVER

HEAVYWEIGHT

MICHAEL DOKES · GERRIE COETZEE · TIM WITHERSPOON · PINKLON THOMAS · GREG PAGE · TONY TUBBS · MICHAEL SPINKS · TREVOR BERBICK · MIKE TYSON · TONY TUCKER JAMES "BONECRUSHER" SMITH · JAMES "BUSTER" DOUGLAS · EVANDER HOLYFIELD RIDDICK BOWE · MICHAEL MOORER · LENNOX LEWIS · OLIVER MCCALL · BRUCE SELDON FRANK BRUNO · JOHN RUIZ — CRUISERWEIGHT — MARVIN CAMEL · CARLOS DELEON · DWIGHT MUHAMMAD QUAWI · EVANDER HOLYFIELD · ANACLET WAMBA BOBBY CZYZ · AL COLE · ORLIN NORRIS · FABRICE TIOZZO · JUAN CARLOS GOMEZ

THE ABSOLUTE KINGS

"The class of classes," "the champion of champions"—these popular names for the heavyweight division and its protagonists speak volumes about the special status of boxing's top weight class. This reverence for the heaviest group of pugilists reflects the dominance of their duels in the minds of the public down through the years. A world featherweight champion will always be a world featherweight champion. The world heavyweight champion, however, is considered to be something absolute. The title has something of the old-fashioned circus title, "world's strongest man," about it and is potent in its populism.

For many years, the man referred to as "boxing champion" was often none other than the "heavyweight champion" because until the middle of the 19th century, no other categories existed. The first bantamweight boxing match took place in 1856. Another 56 years were to pass by before the other six classic weight limits were to witness their own champions (the first world flyweight champion was crowned in 1912). Since then, the fight to determine the champion in this top weight division (over 195 lbs) has remained an intercontinental affair of incomparable dimensions. It is in the heavyweight division that icons are created, from Dempsey and Ali to Tyson, and it is here that myths are born, from the "white hope" to "they never come back." It is also the division that is full of the money that prizefighting is ultimately all about and this is not least why the end of the 20th century witnessed such a large migration of boxers from other classes, the like of which had only previously been seen in individual cases. Talented professionals and world champions pile on the pounds to move from the light heavyweight and cruiserweight classes into the top and supposedly most lucrative division. But just because they are the heaviest doesn't mean they have it any easier: the competition in the royal division is tougher than anywhere else. What's more, the trend is toward the colossal. Like other earlier champs, Rocky Marciano weighed just under 182 lbs and measured 5'8." Today, however, at least 220 lbs and 6'2" are the norm for the world elite.

Lennox Lewis vs. Michael Grant, New York City 2000.

LENNOX LEWIS

"Anyone. Anytime. Anywhere." This was the text of a striking advertisement for the U.S. television channel HBO in the late 1990s, in which Lennox Lewis—captured by the camera in an arrogant pose—justified his claim to the world heavyweight throne. The reigning WBC champion was ready and willing to take on anyone who dared to challenge him and to go down in the history of boxing as an all-time great. As he continues to dominate his class, there is no longer any doubt that he has reached this goal.

The son of Jamaican immigrants, Lewis was a tall twelve-year-old when he began his first training session in Kitchener, Ontario. In 1988, at the age of 23, he won Olympic gold for the Canadian team by scoring a stoppage over Riddick Bowe. After moving to Britain, the almost 6'5" colossus became one of the best and most agile professionals in the heavyweight division. Trained by Pepe Correa, Lewis notched up a spectacular KO victory over Donovan "Razor" Ruddock in October 1992, earning himself the right to challenge Bowe. He became WBC champion without having to throw a single punch when Bowe refused to fight him. It now seemed as if

he had made it to the top—and into the hearts of the British public—at lightning speed. But after a few weak title defenses, some in the United States had reservations about this eloquent and unapproachable world champion. His skeptics felt they had been proven right when in 1994, "Double L" was knocked out by the virtually unknown American Oliver McCall in front of a capacity crowd in London. With his new coach, Emanuel Steward, it would take the phlegmatic Lewis, who was now considered open to attack, two and a half years to win back his title in a rematch against McCall. But it took him much longer to win back the respect of the international boxing community because McCall and his next two opponents, Henry Akinwande and Andrew Golota, denied him a reasonable fight. So, while Lewis retained his world championship title, he remained "a guy who just can't win" *(Boxing Monthly).*

It was only his two matches against rival champion Evander Holyfield (one draw, one victory) that established Lewis as the top of his class in 1999. This was not changed by his second KO defeat, this time at the hands of the little known Hasim Rahman, on whom he

exacted his revenge in a rematch in fall 2000. Even though he weighs in at a massive 220 lbs, hardly anyone else in this division is as agile and powerful and has such as wide variety of punches in his repertoire as Lewis. No one else knows how to control a fight with the jab as well as he does. In 2001, even *The Ring* admitted that: "No one, or at least hardly anyone, disputes that he is the world's best heavyweight boxer." Lewis' predecessor George Foreman even went as far as to say that Lewis "is at present better than Muhammad Ali" and is "unbeatable in top form."

To underpin his superiority once again for publicity's sake, the world champion agreed to a contest with the rusting former champion Mike Tyson in June 2002. The one-sided duel in Memphis, Tenn., became yet another triumph for the intelligent titleholder who also considered the contest to be a match between good and evil. After all, Lewis has made it his acknowledged goal to use his own, impeccable behavior to improve the image of the discredited sport. This is another goal reached by the self-confident businessman, who is estimated to have earned over $100 million to date.

"THERE IS NO VICTORY OVER LENNOX LEWIS."

LENNOX LEWIS

SPECIAL: The first undisputed modern world champion from England
BORN: 09-02-1965 in London (GBR)
NICKNAME: Double L
HEIGHT: 6'5"
MATCH WEIGHT : 242.5 lbs
BOXING RECORD:
  43 professional bouts
  40 wins, 1 draw
  2 losses
FIRST WORLD CHAMPIONSHIP BOUT:
  1993 (win on points 12th round Tony Tucker, WBC)
LAST WORLD CHAMPIONSHIP BOUT:
  2002 (KO win 8th round Mike Tyson, WBC, IBF)
WORLD CHAMPIONSHIP TITLES:
  1992–94 (WBC), 1997–2001
  (WBC, WBC/WBA/IBF, then WBC/IBF),
  since 2001 (WBC/IBF);
  overall 15 title defenses

MIKE TYSON

If Jack Dempsey and Sonny Liston were honored for their furious style of fighting as demigods of wrath, then Mike Tyson would have to go down in the recent history of boxing as their only legitimate successor. No other pugilist in the last two decades of the 20th century presented himself in such an uncompromising and terrifying light as the self-proclaimed "baddest man on the planet"—and that covers both his performances both inside and outside the ring.

Michael Gerard Tyson was on record as having committed 38 crimes in the streets of Bedford-Stuyvesant in Brooklyn, N.Y., when at the age of 13 he made a confession to a teacher at the Tryon School for Boys near Johnstown: "I want to become a boxer." The teacher in question, a former amateur called Bobby Stewart, made Tyson promise to turn over a new leaf and taught the brawny teenager the first steps and punches there and then. Tyson learned so quickly that only a few years later, Stewart placed him in the care of the legendary trainer Cus D'Amato in the Catskill Mountains, where Tyson soon became a hot tip on the amateur scene. Blessed with huge dynamic force and short leverage, the stocky 5'8" youngster perfected an extremely

SPECIAL: The youngest heavyweight world champion to date
BORN: 06-30-1966, Brooklyn, New York (USA)
NICKNAME: Iron Mike
HEIGHT: 5'11½"
LOWEST WEIGHT: 215.7 lbs
HIGHEST WEIGHT: 223.5 lbs
BOXING RECORD: 55 professional bouts, 49 wins, 4 losses, 2 no-decision bouts, 16 title defenses (1986–2002)
FIRST WORLD CHAMPIONSHIP BOUT: 1986 (TKO win 2nd round Trevor Berbick, WBC)
LAST WORLD CHAMPIONSHIP BOUT : 2002 (KO loss 8th round Lennox Lewis, WBC/IBF)
WORLD CHAMPIONSHIP TITLES: 1986–90 (WBC, WBA, IBF), 1996 (WBC, WBA)

high-pressure, offensive style of fighting that overpowered almost every single one of his opponents in mid fight.

The dark but attractive flair of a destroyer remained when Tyson became the youngest professional world champion in the modern history of his division only 20 months after turning pro. After knocking out WBC champion Trevor Berbick in November 1986, he secured himself the belts of the rival associations WBA and IBF by defeating both James "Bonecrusher" Smith and Tony Tucker within

His defeat at the hands of Douglas reflected the languid attitude that Tyson now adopted toward his preparation for his title defenses. It is also typical of the moody complacency into which the manic depressive champion sank during his period of success. Once torn from the fatherly care of his manager Jim Jacobs and his trainer—both of whom had since passed away—there seemed no holding back for the inadequately socialized champion. There followed a series of sexual assaults and brawls and his marriage with the actress

recaptured the world title in March 1996 after administering brief but effective corporal punishment to Frank Bruno. But only eight months later, his duel with Evander Holyfield demonstrated that his earlier perfection was gone forever. Round after round, Holyfield fearlessly withstood Tyson and clearly outboxed his strategically depleted opponent until the referee waved off the fight in the eleventh round. A rematch in June 1997 began similarly and ended in a scandal when the frustrated challenger was disqualified for

»THERE'S TYSON AND THERE'S THE REST« THE RING

nine months to become the first undisputed heavyweight champion of the world since 1978. After demolishing Michael Spinks in only 91 seconds in the late 1980s, "Iron Mike" was surrounded by an aura of invincibility. The boxing magazine *The Ring* summed it up as follows: "There's Tyson and there's the rest." But all that was to change in February 1990: The 42-1 favorite was knocked out by a certain James "Buster" Douglas in the tenth round of their match in Tokyo. It took him six years to regain his title.

Robin Givens in 1988 turned into a short, turbulent farce. In March 1992, shortly before the long-awaited showdown against world champion Evander Holyfield, a civil court called a halt to the proceedings: despite the dubious evidence presented in court, Tyson was sentenced to six years in prison and got a four-year suspended sentence for rape and sexual harassment.

"Iron Mike" seemed to be almost the same horrifically effective boxer when, only twelve months after his early release from prison, he

biting a chunk out of Holyfield's ear. Hot on the heels of his suspension from the sport, Tyson was back in prison again for six months in 1999 for inflicting bodily harm. Most people didn't spare a second thought on his sentence.

After his second release, Tyson contested relatively unspectacular bouts in Europe in exchange for weighty purses. A world championship title fight against Lennox Lewis in June 2002 showed how things really stood: Tyson lost incontestably in the eighth round.

GEORGE FOREMAN

SPECIAL: Boxer and minister; managed to reclaim the world championship title at the age of 46
BORN: 01-22-1948, Marshall, Texas (USA)
NICKNAME: Big George
HEIGHT: 6'3"
LOWEST WEIGHT: 217.5 lbs
HIGHEST WEIGHT: 256 lbs
BOXING RECORD:
 81 professional bouts
 76 wins, 5 losses
 8 world championship bouts
FIRST WORLD CHAMPIONSHIP BOUT:
 1973 (TKO win 2nd round Joe Frazier)
LAST WORLD CHAMPIONSHIP BOUT:
 1995 (win on points 12th round Axel Schulz, IBF)
WORLD CHAMPIONSHIP TITLES:
 1973–74 (WBA, IBF) 1994–95 (WBA, IBF)

SPECIAL: The youngest heavyweight world
  champion to date
BORN: 06-30-1966, Brooklyn, New York
  (USA)
NICKNAME: Iron Mike
HEIGHT: 5'11½"
LOWEST WEIGHT: 215.7 lbs
HIGHEST WEIGHT: 223.5 lbs
BOXING RECORD: 55 professional bouts,
  49 wins, 4 losses, 2 no-decision bouts,
  16 title defenses (1986–2002)
FIRST WORLD CHAMPIONSHIP BOUT:
  1986 (TKO win 2nd round Trevor
  Berbick, WBC)
LAST WORLD CHAMPIONSHIP BOUT :
  2002 (KO loss 8th round Lennox Lewis,
  WBC/IBF)
WORLD CHAMPIONSHIP TITLES: 1986–90
  (WBC, WBA, IBF), 1996 (WBC, WBA)

high-pressure, offensive style of fighting that overpowered almost every single one of his opponents in mid fight.

The dark but attractive flair of a destroyer remained when Tyson became the youngest professional world champion in the modern history of his division only 20 months after turning pro. After knocking out WBC champion Trevor Berbick in November 1986, he secured himself the belts of the rival associations WBA and IBF by defeating both James "Bonecrusher" Smith and Tony Tucker within

His defeat at the hands of Douglas reflected the languid attitude that Tyson now adopted toward his preparation for his title defenses. It is also typical of the moody complacency into which the manic depressive champion sank during his period of success. Once torn from the fatherly care of his manager Jim Jacobs and his trainer—both of whom had since passed away—there seemed no holding back for the inadequately socialized champion. There followed a series of sexual assaults and brawls and his marriage with the actress

recaptured the world title in March 1996 after administering brief but effective corporal punishment to Frank Bruno. But only eight months later, his duel with Evander Holyfield demonstrated that his earlier perfection was gone forever. Round after round, Holyfield fearlessly withstood Tyson and clearly outboxed his strategically depleted opponent until the referee waved off the fight in the eleventh round. A rematch in June 1997 began similarly and ended in a scandal when the frustrated challenger was disqualified for

»THERE'S TYSON AND THERE'S THE REST« THE RING

nine months to become the first undisputed heavyweight champion of the world since 1978. After demolishing Michael Spinks in only 91 seconds in the late 1980s, "Iron Mike" was surrounded by an aura of invincibility. The boxing magazine *The Ring* summed it up as follows: "There's Tyson and there's the rest." But all that was to change in February 1990: The 42-1 favorite was knocked out by a certain James "Buster" Douglas in the tenth round of their match in Tokyo. It took him six years to regain his title.

Robin Givens in 1988 turned into a short, turbulent farce. In March 1992, shortly before the long-awaited showdown against world champion Evander Holyfield, a civil court called a halt to the proceedings: despite the dubious evidence presented in court, Tyson was sentenced to six years in prison and got a four-year suspended sentence for rape and sexual harassment.

"Iron Mike" seemed to be almost the same horrifically effective boxer when, only twelve months after his early release from prison, he

biting a chunk out of Holyfield's ear. Hot on the heels of his suspension from the sport, Tyson was back in prison again for six months in 1999 for inflicting bodily harm. Most people didn't spare a second thought on his sentence.

After his second release, Tyson contested relatively unspectacular bouts in Europe in exchange for weighty purses. A world championship title fight against Lennox Lewis in June 2002 showed how things really stood: Tyson lost incontestably in the eighth round.

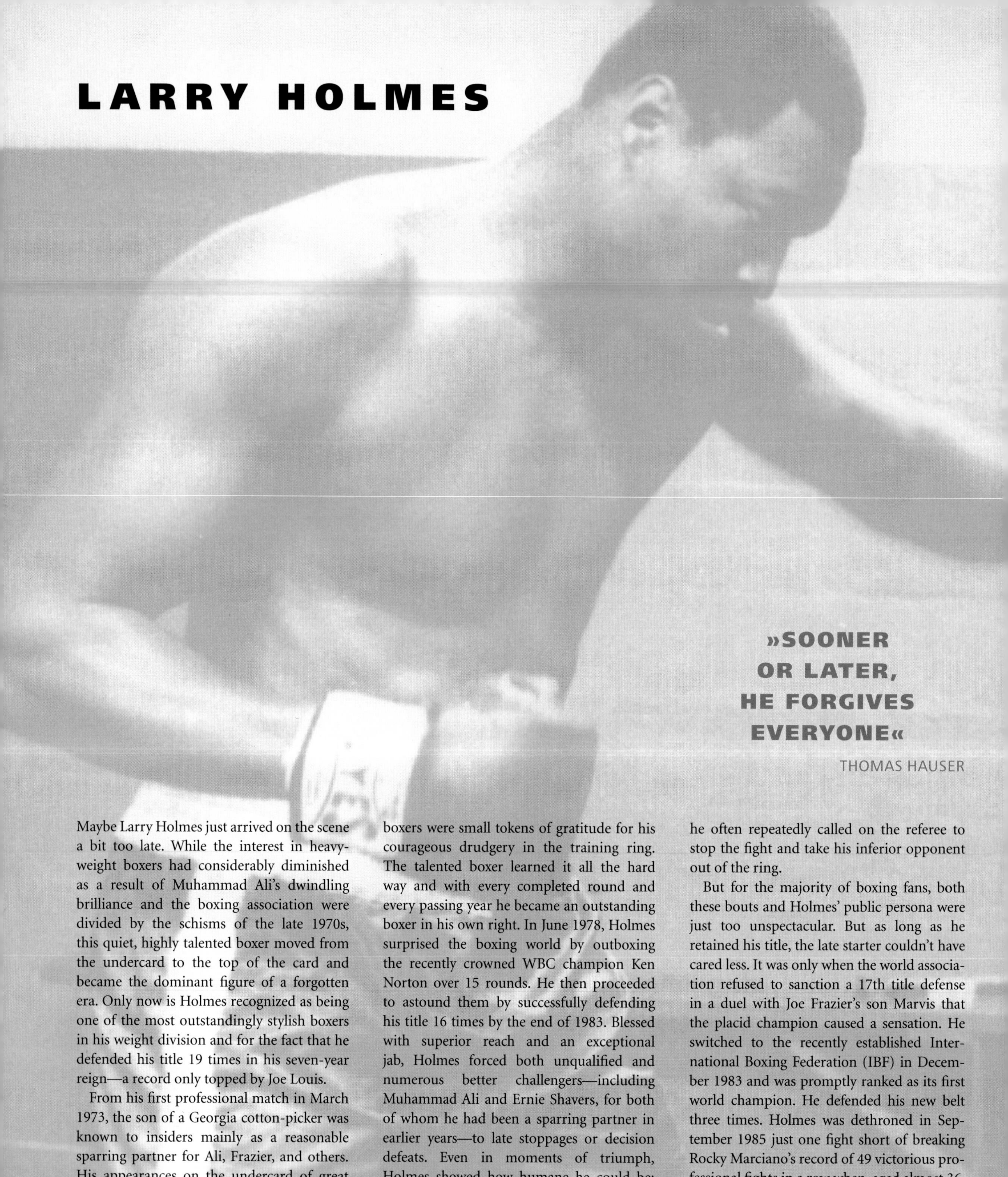

LARRY HOLMES

> »SOONER
> OR LATER,
> HE FORGIVES
> EVERYONE«
>
> THOMAS HAUSER

Maybe Larry Holmes just arrived on the scene a bit too late. While the interest in heavyweight boxers had considerably diminished as a result of Muhammad Ali's dwindling brilliance and the boxing association were divided by the schisms of the late 1970s, this quiet, highly talented boxer moved from the undercard to the top of the card and became the dominant figure of a forgotten era. Only now is Holmes recognized as being one of the most outstandingly stylish boxers in his weight division and for the fact that he defended his title 19 times in his seven-year reign—a record only topped by Joe Louis.

From his first professional match in March 1973, the son of a Georgia cotton-picker was known to insiders mainly as a reasonable sparring partner for Ali, Frazier, and others. His appearances on the undercard of great boxers were small tokens of gratitude for his courageous drudgery in the training ring. The talented boxer learned it all the hard way and with every completed round and every passing year he became an outstanding boxer in his own right. In June 1978, Holmes surprised the boxing world by outboxing the recently crowned WBC champion Ken Norton over 15 rounds. He then proceeded to astound them by successfully defending his title 16 times by the end of 1983. Blessed with superior reach and an exceptional jab, Holmes forced both unqualified and numerous better challengers—including Muhammad Ali and Ernie Shavers, for both of whom he had been a sparring partner in earlier years—to late stoppages or decision defeats. Even in moments of triumph, Holmes showed how humane he could be:

he often repeatedly called on the referee to stop the fight and take his inferior opponent out of the ring.

But for the majority of boxing fans, both these bouts and Holmes' public persona were just too unspectacular. But as long as he retained his title, the late starter couldn't have cared less. It was only when the world association refused to sanction a 17th title defense in a duel with Joe Frazier's son Marvis that the placid champion caused a sensation. He switched to the recently established International Boxing Federation (IBF) in December 1983 and was promptly ranked as its first world champion. He defended his new belt three times. Holmes was dethroned in September 1985 just one fight short of breaking Rocky Marciano's record of 49 victorious professional fights in a row when, aged almost 36,

he was unanimously outpointed by Michael Spinks. Despite the debates that followed the non-unanimous decision of the judges, the rematch in April of the following year confirmed that after 50 bouts in the ring, Holmes was past his best.

Once he had broken with the covetous promoter Don King, champion Holmes had enough money for a tranquil retirement. To this day, Holmes owns an entire shopping center, local administration building and penitentiary in his hometown of Easton, Pennsylvania. Nevertheless, until 1999, he kept returning to the ring. In 1988, Holmes was knocked out for the first time in his career by Mike Tyson. He also put up quite respectable, albeit limited sporting performances against world champions like Evander Holyfield and Oliver McCall in 1992 and 1995

respectively. These bouts are in sharp contrast to his bizarre match against former champion and one-time adversary James "Bonecrusher" Smith, which his promoters billed as a "Seniors' Championship." This was another warning sign for Holmes to stop ruining the memory of his outstanding career with mediocre appearances as an "old-timer" in shorts.

"I have enough common sense," Holmes once said with his typical sarcasm when asked about his addiction to comebacks, "I just don't use it." His dry humor and his winning jab remain unequalled to this day.

SPECIAL: 49 professional bouts won in direct succession
BORN: 11-02-1949, Cuthbert, Georgia (USA)
NICKNAME: The Easton Assassin
HEIGHT: 6'3"
LOWEST WEIGHT: 209 lbs
HIGHEST WEIGHT: 223.5 lbs
BOXING RECORD:
  73 professional bouts
  67 wins, 6 losses
  25 world championship bouts
FIRST WORLD CHAMPIONSHIP BOUT:
  1978 (win on points 15th round Ken Norton, WBC)
LAST WORLD CHAMPIONSHIP BOUT:
  1995 (loss on points 12th round Oliver McCall, WBC)
WORLD CHAMPIONSHIP TITLES: 1978–83 (WBC) 1983–85 (IBF)

GEORGE FOREMAN

SPECIAL: Boxer and minister; managed to reclaim the world championship title at the age of 46

BORN: 01-22-1948, Marshall, Texas (USA)

NICKNAME: Big George

HEIGHT: 6'3"

LOWEST WEIGHT: 217.5 lbs

HIGHEST WEIGHT: 256 lbs

BOXING RECORD:
81 professional bouts
76 wins, 5 losses
8 world championship bouts

FIRST WORLD CHAMPIONSHIP BOUT:
1973 (TKO win 2nd round Joe Frazier)

LAST WORLD CHAMPIONSHIP BOUT:
1995 (win on points 12th round Axel Schulz, IBF)

WORLD CHAMPIONSHIP TITLES:
1973–74 (WBA, IBF) 1994–95 (WBA, IBF)

Back home in Houston, Texas, the former KO king was a man of the cloth before he returned to the ring.

»MY DNA IS CHEESEBURGERS« GEORGE FOREMAN

Just how he managed to develop the physique he had is a miracle. As one of seven children in an impoverished Texan family, George Edward Foreman could only look forward to the bare necessities when he picked up his knife and fork at lunchtime. Nevertheless, standing 6'2" by the end of the 1960s, he was an amateur boxer bursting with power who could paralyze his opponents with the sheer force of his blows. The power he packed in his punches was the most impressive ever seen in a heavyweight since the introduction of boxing gloves in the ring.

In Mexico in 1968, the 19-year-old George Foreman knocked out his adversary to become Olympic champion. His subsequent successes at the professional level were just as impressive. Between 1969 and 1972, he took out 34 of his 37 opponents before the final bell. Then, in January 1973, he got the chance to challenge Joe Frazier for the world championship title. Ahead of the duel in Kingston, Jamaica, the challenger—who back then was considered taciturn—was still considered a rank outsider. At the weigh-in, champion Joe Frazier self-confidently announced that he would "floor him." But it turned out to be Foreman who floored Frazier six times in four and a half minutes and clinched an impressive victory. It could have been the start of an equally impressive reign as champion but Foreman was knocked out by his own incredible arrogance. After two low-risk title defenses against nameless victims, he completely overtaxed himself in October 1974 so that Muhammad Ali had no trouble knocking him out in the eighth round of their famous "Rumble in the Jungle" in Kinshasa, Zaire.

Two and a half years later, the Texan was dropped briefly by Jimmy Young and lost the match on points, ruining his chances of a planned rematch against Ali. But the disaster also lead to a new beginning: on that very evening, Foreman claims he had a religious experience in his changing room, as a result of which he retired from the ring. Until 1987, the former world champion stayed in his local parish in Houston working exclusively as a preacher and youth welfare worker. Then he started to train for a comeback in his spare time. What originally looked like a high-profile campaign to encourage the not-so-young to get fit, suddenly became serious business in November 1994 when Foreman knocked out the WBA/IBF champion Michael Moorer in the tenth round of their bout; only his third attempt at the title after his comeback. The sensational victory proved once again that "Big George" had outstanding puncher qualities and returned the title to the 46-year-old, twenty years after he had surrendered it.

Even the controversial decision over the German Axel Schulz in 1995 and the fact that he was subsequently stripped of his title for refusing a rematch could do nothing to dent the status of the all-American superstar. Whether as a burger-addicted grandfather ("My DNA is cheeseburgers."), a socially aware man of the cloth, or an eloquent guest commentator for boxing matches, Foreman will always be a humorous living legend for his generations of fans.

»HE IS A REAL,
REAL FIGHTER.
THE TOUGHEST MAN
IN THE WORLD.«

MUHAMMAD ALI

JOE FRAZIER

At his best, Frazier's upper body appeared to be mounted on the rolling wheels of a locomotive. But the real difference between Joe Frazier and the more cautious boxers of his day was the uncompromising way he marched forward. Standing no more than 5'9", Muhammad Ali's archrival perfected the high-pressure style of "bobbin' and weavin'" in the 1970s and is to this day considered one of the most imposing fighting spirits in the sport of boxing.

"Go on, Joe," his trainer and manager Yank Durham once called during a training session, "let us see the smoke rise from your gloves!" From that moment on, the nickname "Smokin' Joe" was like a quality mark for Frazier, the seventh of 13 children of a farm worker from South Carolina. Frazier—who had filled sandbags with moss and leaves as a nine-year-old—was twelve when he moved across the Cotton Belt to Philadelphia and only just 20 when he stepped in for an ill Buster Mathis and became the Olympic champion. A consortium of white businessmen called Cloverlay, Inc. supported the part-time professional in "Philly" and took a share in the earnings when Frazier usually sent his tune-up opponents crashing to the canvas before the final bell. Between 1965 and 1967, "Smoke" had notched up a perfect record of eleven stoppages and a decision over Oscar Bonavena. In March 1968, he took his revenge on Mathis for his only two amateur defeats with an impressive KO victory.

The triumph over the old rival from his amateur days meant that Frazier was recognized as champion when Muhammad Ali was stripped of his title for refusing induction into the U.S. Army. At least that was the ruling made by boxing commissions in New York and five other U.S. states and the associations in Mexico and South America. Other associations ranked Jimmy Ellis as champion in 1968 after he won an eight-man tournament that Frazier had refused to enter. But the "Philly Fighter" also put an end to this schism with the authority of his fists when he forced

Ellis to throw in the towel after four "smokin'" rounds of their 1970 bout. After successfully defending his title in two unspectacular bouts, the all-powerful world champion seemed to have run out of suitable opponents. With the return of Ali, Frazier appeared to have found a worthy adversary who would allow him to show his true colors.

It was the three legendary duels with Ali—one victory and two defeats—between 1971 and 1975 that have forever engraved Frazier's name on the collective boxing memory. But it was also his impressive victories over Jerry Quarry or George Chuvalo—the only one of Chuvalo's 91 adversaries to beat him before the final bell—that guaranteed Frazier a place in history as one of the all-time greats in a golden era of heavyweight boxing. In January 1973, Frazier was forced to surrender his title in Kingston, Jamaica, to the physically overpowering 3-1 outsider George Foreman. Foreman, who succeeded Frazier as Olympic champion, dropped Frazier a total of six times before referee Mercante waved off the fight. A rematch in 1976, which Foreman won by a KO in round 5, only proved that Frazier's smoke was all but gone. The final duel against Ali, the so-called "Thrilla in Manila" in 1975, took a lot out of the former champion.

Having retired from the ring, Frazier initially tried to start a second career as a popular entertainer. He eventually went back to his roots as a trainer and owner of a large gym in Philadelphia. It is here that Frazier, a religious man, is trying to offer his young protégés prospects for a life outside the ghetto. The motto in his gym is: "Sweat in the gym, don't bleed in the streets!"

SPECIAL: Ali's biggest opponent
BORN: 01-12-1944 in Beaufort, South Carolina (USA)
NICKNAME: Smokin' Joe, Philly Fighter
HEIGHT: 5'11½"
LOWEST WEIGHT: 203.5 lbs
HIGHEST WEIGHT: 217.5 lbs
BOXING RECORD:
  37 professional bouts
  32 wins, 4 losses, 1 draw
  12 world championship bouts
FIRST WORLD CHAMPIONSHIP BOUT:
  1968 (TKO win 11th round Buster Mathis, New York Titel)
LAST WORLD CHAMPIONSHIP BOUT:
  1975 (retirement loss 15th round Muhammad Ali)
WORLD CHAMPIONSHIP TITLES:
  1967 (WBC) 1970–73 (WBC, WBA)

There have just been too many outstanding athletes in modern professional boxing to say that Muhammad Ali was the best boxer of all time. It is, however, indisputable that this champion, whose legs were just as fast as his fists and tongue, electrified the boxing world in his day like no other. As presumptuous as he was charismatic, as egocentric as he was socially active, Ali became the most popular and enduring boxing icon to date in a professional career that spanned 21 years.

Born Cassius Marcellus Clay in January 1942, he had already created his own style by the time he won his Olympic gold medal at the 1960 Games in Rome. He dismissed his opponents with surprising combinations of unusual reflexes, almost dance-like footwork, highly creative intelligence, and the skillful way he dodged their counters. He also flirted with delusions of grandeur when he released a flood of rap-like rhymes about his adversary before each bout and painted a picture of himself as an unbeatable, almost astral figure. Since the days of Jack Johnson, no black boxer had demonstrated so little modesty. This is why a large part of the public longed for the bragging "Louisville Lip" from Kentucky to get a good thrashing in the ring. But at this stage, the middle-class kid knew how to avoid defeat every time.

His boxing carefully fine-tuned by coach Angelo Dundee, Clay usually made the first 17 opponents of his professional career look stupid. In 1963, he added to these strengths a dose of good luck when he managed to win a controversial decision over Doug Jones and picked himself up off the canvas in a match against Henry Cooper. The TKO over the brittle British boxer gave Clay the opportunity to challenge champion Sonny Liston in February 1964. His two surprising triumphs over the relatively unpopular world champion after the rematch in the following year would have reconciled him with the majority of his critics were it not for the fact that he joined the Black Muslims, as a result of which Clay changed his name to Muhammad Ali. Even after eight successful title defenses, the self-proclaimed "Greatest of 'em all" remained a suspicious character for a U.S. society that was dominated by white Protestants. Many fervent patriots saw their suspicions confirmed in the spring of 1967 when the champion refused to serve in Vietnam for religious reasons.

Convicted of draft evasion, Ali—who was now a world famous boxer—found himself temporarily out of work. The boxing commission stripped him of his title, withdrew his license, and only allowed him back into the ring three years later when it looked likely that he was to be granted a reprieve. Then, after only two tune-up fights, the 29-year-old dared to dance with the reigning champion Joe Frazier. In the first duel of a legendary series of three bouts, Ali lost a unanimous decision against "Smokin' Joe" in New York in March 1971. Three and a half years and 14 contests later, Ali took another shot at the world championship title by challenging George Foreman. Insiders held out little hope for him. But in the Rumble in the Jungle in Kinshasa, Zaire, on October 30, 1974, the underdog marched away with another remarkable victory: the challenger, who spent most of his time hanging on the ropes, let the powerful world champion waste his energy over seven rounds before hammering him down with a mighty combination in the eighth round.

The victory in this $10 million bout and his third and final grueling feud with Frazier one year later—which he won when Frazier retired in the 14th round—underpinned Ali's outstanding talent. But in doing so, he had used up almost all of his physical resources. Outboxed by Olympic champion Leon Spinks in February 1978, the ageing legend succeeded in putting on the champion's belt for the third time in a rematch that September. Ali immediately announced his retirement from the ring. By 1981, two unnecessary defeats at the hands of Larry Holmes and Trevor Berbick proved to him that further comeback attempts were futile.

Like no other sportsman before him, Ali used the mass media to portray a certain image of himself and combined his own interests with genuine involvement in social causes. Unlike his ego, this involvement has continued to grow. Despite being incapacitated by Parkinson's disease, Ali has continued to make charismatic use of his special status for the benefit of charity and his interest in international conflict resolution.

»HE IS AMERICA'S GREATEST EGO« NORMAN MAILER

Whether it was jogging with his twin daughters Jamillah and Rasheda (1971) or spending time with his third wife Veronica (1978), Ali's private life always fascinated the public. The star had to live with the fact that even the unsavory details of his private life were covered by the press.

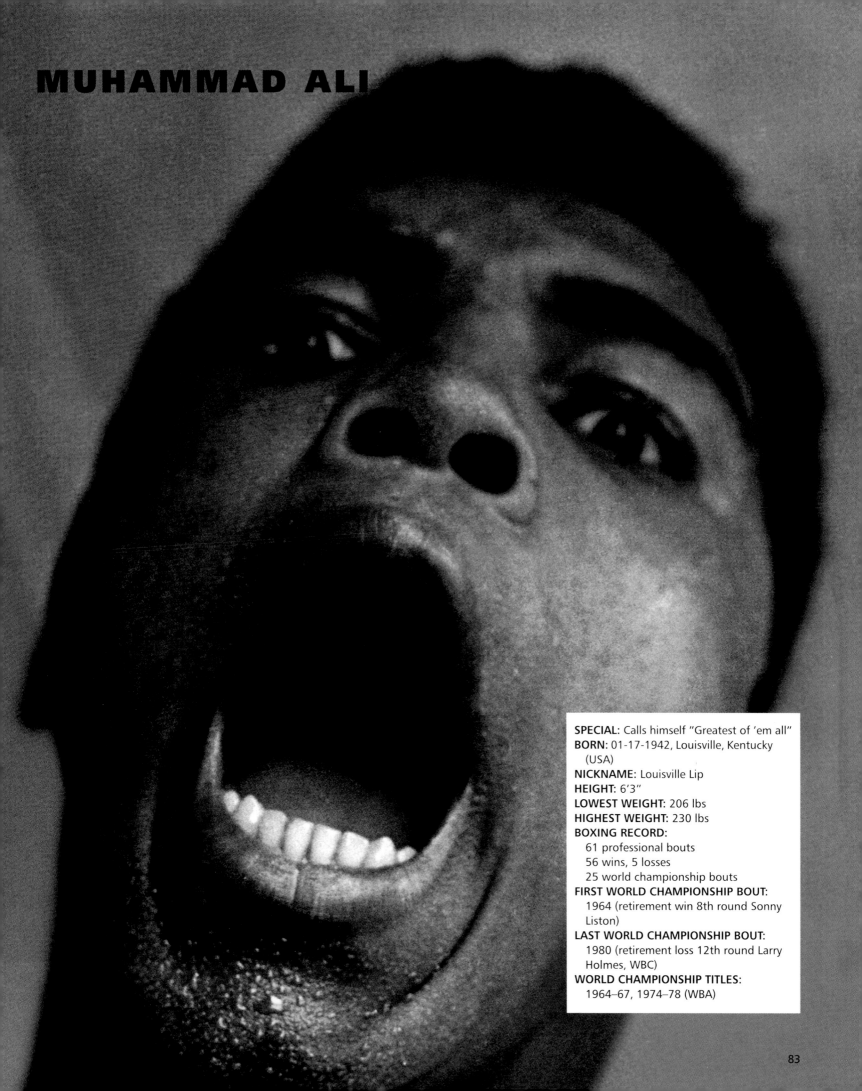

MUHAMMAD ALI

SPECIAL: Calls himself "Greatest of 'em all"
BORN: 01-17-1942, Louisville, Kentucky (USA)
NICKNAME: Louisville Lip
HEIGHT: 6'3"
LOWEST WEIGHT: 206 lbs
HIGHEST WEIGHT: 230 lbs
BOXING RECORD:
  61 professional bouts
  56 wins, 5 losses
  25 world championship bouts
FIRST WORLD CHAMPIONSHIP BOUT:
  1964 (retirement win 8th round Sonny Liston)
LAST WORLD CHAMPIONSHIP BOUT:
  1980 (retirement loss 12th round Larry Holmes, WBC)
WORLD CHAMPIONSHIP TITLES:
  1964–67, 1974–78 (WBA)

ROCKY MARCIANO

There have been greater natural talents and more elegant stylists than Rocky Marciano in modern heavyweight boxing. But when it comes to the determination with which a boxer lands his punches and takes those dealt out by his opponents, Marciano is surely the greatest of them all. As tough as the shoe leather his Italian father sewed together in the factories of Brockton, Mass., this late starter refused point blank to let himself be beaten in the ring. When he ended his professional career as world champion in 1956, he left with an unbeaten record of 49 bouts.

Rocco Francis Marchegiano, one of six children in a working class family, initially dreamt of becoming a basketball star to escape the modest circumstances in which he grew up. But he never made it past the tests for the Major League. Encouraged by several promising boxing matches contested during his time in the army and a brief amateur career, Marciano went to see the New York Manager Al Weill. When Weill signed Marciano and put him into the care of Charley Goldman, a former bantamweight professional, he was more impressed by the trial boxer's sheer will than his actual ability. Goldman declared that his protégé had "two left feet" and was not a great mover. Nevertheless, Marciano quickly learned the special dynamism that allowed him to translate his enormous power into lethal blows. When Marciano got the chance to challenge champion "Jersey" Joe Walcott, he had already won 39 of his 42 tune-up fights before the final bell, including one against Joe Louis.

In the bout against Joe Walcott in Philadelphia on September 23, 1952, "The Rock" was not only dropped by the champ, he lagged behind him on the judges' scorecards until the twelfth round. Then in round 13, the 5'8" athlete landed a perfect right on his opponent, who was both superior in reach and experience. Unable to defend himself, Walcott hit the deck. This punch heralded in the era of Marciano's dominance in the royal division. He then proceeded to confirm his superiority by successfully defending his belt in six championship bouts. With the exception of the first of two grandiose duels against the former champion Ezzard Charles, no one went the distance with the champion. Marciano quickly became the idol of the Italian-American community, which was already

Even when he visited the movie studios in Hollywood (seen here with Rock Hudson and Elizabeth Taylor, ca. 1955), Marciano was always the unaffected guy next-door.

"ROCKY MARCIANO STOOD OUT LIKE A ROSE IN A GARBAGE DUMP."

JIMMY CANNON

ecstatic following the astonishing successes of other boxing heroes like Rocky Graziano, Carmen Basilio, and Paddy DeMarco.

Six months after his triumph over Archie Moore, the unbeaten Marciano announced his retirement in April 1956. Marciano later explained that he had seen too many good boxers stay too long in the ring and contest one bout too many. He certainly didn't want the same thing to happen to him. Even purses of up to $2 million for a bout could not entice Marciano to step back inside the ropes one more time. The only place the public did see Marciano fight again was in two computer simulations: once in the final of a tournament in 1967, when he won a KO victory over former world champion Jack Dempsey, and two years later when he dropped

Muhammad Ali in the thirteenth round of their virtual bout.

Marciano's unequaled professional record was the result of a diligent athlete who worked on his weak points under the watchful eye of trainer Goldman in pre-match training camps that lasted up to three months. As a father and family man, the tight grip he kept on his assets was as firm as the stubbornness with which he believed in his chances of winning in the ring. His manager Al Weill is quoted as saying: "He wouldn't spend a penny to see an earthquake." It is ironic, therefore, that a catastrophe ended his life. In late August 1969—on the day before his 46th birthday—Marciano died when his private plane crashed on the way to a party arranged in his honor in Des Moines, Iowa.

SPECIAL: The only undefeated heavy-weight world champion
BORN: 09-01-1923 in Brockton, Massachusetts (USA)—died 08-31-1969
NICKNAME: The Rock
HEIGHT: 5'10¼"m
LOWEST WEIGHT: 184 lbs
HIGHEST WEIGHT: 189 lbs
BOXING RECORD:
  49 professional bouts
  49 wins, 0 losses
  7 world championship bouts
FIRST WORLD CHAMPIONSHIP BOUT:
  1952 (KO win 13th round "Jersey" Joe Walcott)
LAST WORLD CHAMPIONSHIP BOUT:
  1955 (KO win 9th round Archie Moore)
WORLD CHAMPIONSHIP TITLES: 1952–56

JOE LOUIS

The original plan was that Joseph Louis Barrow would grow up to be a good citizen with a decent job, maybe even a violinist in an orchestra. Instead he grew up to be Joe Louis, one of the best heavyweight champions in modern times and, what's more, the first black boxer to be accepted by everyone in the United States.

Initially, all Lilly Barrow wanted was for her seven children to have things a bit easier in later life. Just like thousands of other black families in the 1920s, the widow of an Alabama cotton-picker moved with her second, wealthy husband up north over the Cotton Belt. They settled in the flourishing industrial city of Detroit, where she sent her son Joseph to school in the mornings and to violin lessons in the afternoon. He soon began spending his time in the Brewster Recreation Center to learn the art of straights and hooks in the center's gym. This natural talent graduated from the gym in his own way: by 1934, Louis had won 50 of his 54 amateur bouts, 43 before the final bell. As a professional boxer, he won 21 fights over the course of the following two years—almost always by KO.

This could easily have been the end of the road for him because, since the days of Jack Johnson, no black challenger had been accepted for a world heavyweight championship bout. But acting on the advice of his manager John Roxborough—who even drew up seven commandments of good behavior for his protégé—the young Louis remained silent and taciturn. By doing so, he cleverly avoided any possible resentment. He preferred to let his powerful right hand do the talking for him in the ring.

It proved a good tactic: allowing him to drop ex-champions like Primo Carnera and Max Baer. Even his sensational KO defeat at the hands of Max Schmeling in New York in 1936 did not stop Louis. Having vented his frustration by defeating the former world champion Jack Sharkey in three rounds only two months later, the powers that be in boxing eventually granted him the chance to challenge champion James J. Braddock for the title on June 22, 1937.

In front of 45,000 spectators in Chicago's Comiskey Park, the "Brown Bomber" had to pick himself up off the canvas early in the fight before piling the pressure on his adversary and eventually forcing a TKO in the eighth round. But Louis refused to refer to himself as champion until he had finally exacted his revenge on Schmeling in a furious 121-second fight in New York in June 1938. The KO victory over the envoy from war-mongering Germany was viewed as symbolic. This, coupled with Louis' patriotic gesture of donating two complete purses to the Navy and Army relief funds in 1942, eventually turned the reserved athlete into an all-American hero. This unusual aura was further enhanced when he finished his stint in the army (1942–45), during which time his championship title had gone unchallenged. In athletic terms, however, Louis paid a high price for his sabbatical from the ring. When he came home from the war, he was unable to repeat his previous glorious performances. A rematch against the former light heavyweight champion Billy Conn, who had almost forced Louis to a defeat on points in 1941, turned out to be a double disappointment: neither boxer performed well. Of his two bouts against "Jersey" Joe Walcott, he won one on a split decision and the other with a late KO. In 1949, Louis announced his retirement from the ring. One year later he was back. Two crushing defeats at the hands of Ezzard Charles and Rocky Marciano in 1951 finally convinced him that the sun had set on his era. But that didn't change one fact: to this day, no champion in either this or any other weight division has equaled his long world championship reign of 11 years, eight months and 25 title defenses.

Louis did not remain wealthy throughout his retirement. The IRS held him in chancery for twenty years and several business enterprises failed. His own living legend, Louis worked for a time in the early 1970s as the official greeter in the luxury Las Vegas hotel Caesars Palace. He later suffered from Parkinson's disease and died in April 1981. His former adversary Max Schmeling considered him "a boxing genius."

> "THE SORT OF BOXING GENIUS THAT ONLY APPEARS ONCE IN SEVERAL GENERATIONS."
>
> MAX SCHMELING

SPECIAL: The first black all-American hero
BORN: 05-13-1914 in Lafayette, Alabama
(USA)—died 04-12-1981
NICKNAME: Brown Bomber
HEIGHT: 6'1½"
LOWEST WEIGHT: 197 lbs
HIGHEST WEIGHT: 213.5 lbs
BOXING RECORD:
  66 professional bouts
  63 wins, 3 losses
  25 title defenses
  27 world championship bouts
FIRST WORLD CHAMPIONSHIP BOUT:
  1937 (KO win 8th round James J.
  Braddock)
LAST WORLD CHAMPIONSHIP BOUT:
  1950 (loss on points 15th round Ezzard
  Charles)
WORLD CHAMPIONSHIP TITLES: 1937–48

JACK DEMPSEY

Jack Dempsey arrived on the scene at exactly the right time. In the Roaring Twenties, the era after the First World War that was characterized by dynamism and growth, America could not have found a more suitable sporting hero than Dempsey. The "Manassa Mauler" quite literally fought his way up from the bottom. He considered his steely fists and iron chin to be "the weapons God gave me to survive." This attitude reflected both his boxing style and the way he took both himself and his sport to new dimensions, becoming professional boxing's first national hero and major earner.

One of eleven children in an impoverished Mormon family of Irish, Scottish, and Native American descent, William Harrison Dempsey left his home in Manassa, Colo., at the tender age of 16. Earning a living as a hobo and casual laborer before turning to prizefighting and adopting the name "Kid Blackie," Dempsey was more interested in knowing where his next meal came from than in what bouts were lined up for him. This was before his uncompromising "you or I" mentality in the ring attracted the attention of the clever star manager Jack "Doc" Kearns. Kearns soon transformed the KO king of the undercard into a ranked boxer. In July 1919, he arranged a world championship bout against Jess Willard, who at that time had not fought in three years. It was to be Dempsey's hour of triumph: standing 6' tall, the challenger launched a furious attack on the champion, who was a whole five and a half inches taller than him. He not only succeeded in forcing Willard to retire in the break at the end of the third round looking very much the worse for wear, he also broke his jaw, two ribs and six of his teeth.

The new champion's will to attack in the ring and his genuine, mannerly behavior outside of it quickly made him an idol for the masses. Over the course of the eight years that followed, his manager Kearns and the promoter, Tex Rickard arranged seven world title fights with Dempsey. Five of them turned out to be the first million-dollar gates in the history of boxing. In July 1921, no less than 80,000 spectators—700 of which were newspaper reporters—packed into Boyle's Thirty Acres near Jersey City, N.J., to watch him fight against the French light heavyweight champion Georges Carpentier (Dempsey won

An unaffected rising star: Jack Dempsey became America's first sporting idol.

on a KO in the fourth round). In September 1923, his outstanding bout against the Argentinean Luis Angel Firpo (KO in the second round) attracted 82,000 spectators to the Polo Grounds in New York. But it wasn't all million-dollar gates: in the same year, the town of Shelby, Mont., went bankrupt when it guaranteed Dempsey $300,000 to defend his title against Tommy Gibbons (15 round decision) and just over 7,000 people turned up to watch the fight.

Dempsey's sporting boom came to an end in Philadelphia in 1926 when, after two years out of the ring, the world champion was outboxed by the undaunted stylish boxer Gene Tunney in front of a record crowd of 132,000 spectators. When he lost the rematch against Tunney in New York's Yankee Stadium

"HIS ONE AND ONLY AIM WAS TO DESTROY HIS OPPONENTS."

GRANTLAND RICE

—billed as the battle of the long count—in the following year, Dempsey went into retirement. If anything, his popularity was further enhanced by his unconditional acceptance of decisions that went against him. As a star performer and later as a referee for catch and boxing evenings, the national hero remained a big earner. Today, his total income is estimated to have amounted to $10 million: an astronomical sum for that era. The charismatic boxer was also a restaurateur until the 1970s. His establishment in the Brill Building on the corner of Broadway and 49th Street in Manhattan attracted more than just boxing enthusiasts. Dempsey's cheesecakes, which were even exported to Europe, were as soft and delicate as his left hook had been tough and fearful.

Dempsey made professional boxing a widely popular sport and himself an American icon whose popularity continued even after his death in May 1983.

SPECIAL: The first national hero and big earner of modern professional boxing
BORN: 06-24-1895 in Manassa, Colorado (USA)—died 05-31-1983
NICKNAME: Manassa Mauler, Steamhammer Jack, Kid Blackie
HEIGHT: 6'¾"
LOWEST WEIGHT: 185 lbs
HIGHEST WEIGHT: 192.8 lbs
BOXING RECORD:
　　80 professional bouts
　　60 wins, 8 draws
　　6 no-decision bouts
　　6 losses
　　8 world championship bouts
FIRST WORLD CHAMPIONSHIP BOUT:
　　1919 (retirement win 3rd round Jess Willard)
LAST WORLD CHAMPIONSHIP BOUT:
　　1927 (loss on points 10th round Gene Tunney)
WORLD CHAMPIONSHIP TITLES:
　　1919–26

JACK JOHNSON

Should a black man be allowed to hold a title as prestigious as "Heavyweight Champion of the World?" What's more, as champion, should he be allowed to display in public all the trappings of success—driving fast cars and being seen with beautiful white women? No other boxing champion in the 20th century has been the object of such unrefined hate and undiminished resentment as Jack Johnson, the "Galveston Giant" from the Texas coast. Similarly, none of his many successors have equaled his athletic ability.

Born Arthur John Johnson in Galveston in 1878, the 6-foot-tall dockworker combined power and excellent techniques to become a well-respected and equally well-avoided prize-fighter. His razor sharp jab was the model for later instruction books on boxing and his punch was both precise and lethal. He had completed 11 years as a professional boxer and contested 67 bouts in the ring without an

official title before he was finally permitted to take a shot at the world champion. Former world champion John L. Sullivan's refusal to step into the ring with black contenders had become a sort of gentleman's agreement in the world of boxing. Initially, starting in 1903, Johnson was described as the "Negro Champion." He had to follow the official titleholder, a moderately popular Canadian called Tommy Burns, half way around the world to finally get the chance to fight him in Sydney, Australia.

Weeks before the duel got underway in Rushcutter's Bay, racist remarks such as writer Jack London's call for Burns to "remove that golden smile from Jack Johnson's face" had already whipped up a one-sided ballyhoo. On December 26, 1908, Johnson belittled his opponent in front of 20,000 spectators. Burns, badly beaten and inferior to Johnson in every way, was eventually taken out of the fight by the referee in the 14th round at the instigation

of the police. Superiority of style was also characteristic of the way the first black heavyweight champion of the world dealt with his white challengers in the years that followed (the clever tactician carefully avoided other black boxers such as Sam Langford). But instead of earning him global recognition, Johnson's success was greeted with pogrom-like reactions in the United States. The news and first film coverage of his victories unleashed riots and isolated cases of lynching against blacks. As a result, film footage of the bouts was banned in many states for some time. The feverish search for the "great white hope," that would return the title to the Caucasian race, produced some strange characters.

Both the legendary, albeit lighter and smaller middleweight boxer Stanley Ketchel and the former champion James J. Jeffries, who returned to the ring after a six-year break, were all matched against Johnson and got a good

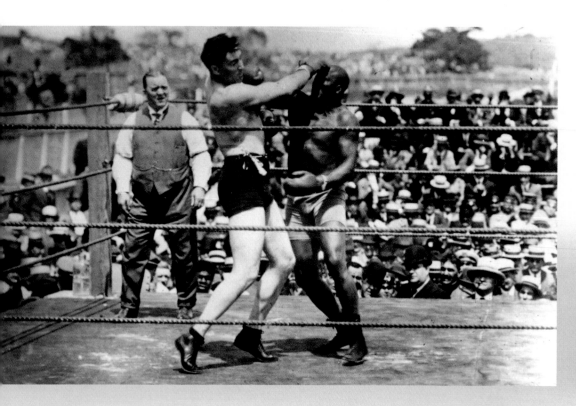

The end of an era: a question mark still hangs over Jack Johnson's defeat at the hands of challenger Jess Willard in the heat of the Havana sun in 1915.

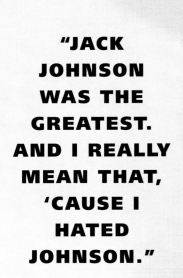

"JACK JOHNSON WAS THE GREATEST. AND I REALLY MEAN THAT, 'CAUSE I HATED JOHNSON."

TOM SHARKEY

thrashing for their trouble. Eventually, in 1913, the authorities used the Mann Act to punish this collector of cars and women for his flamboyant lifestyle. Johnson was sentenced to twelve months in prison for transporting a minor across state lines for "immoral purposes." In sporting terms, it was the beginning of the end for Johnson. The convict fled to Paris and defended his title there twice. But the lack of top competition and the fact that he was living the high life day after day took its toll on Johnson's athletic ability. "Papa Jack" was overweight and unfit when he stepped into the ring on April 5, 1915 at the age of 37 to fight the 6'5" Jess Willard. He was knocked out in the 26th round. His subsequent claims to have "thrown" the fight would appear at the very least debatable in view of his ever-diminishing efforts under the merciless Cuban sun.

Johnson returned to the United States in 1920 and served three-quarters of his sentence in Kansas. He continued to fight sporadically until he retired at the age of 50 and died in a motor accident in Raleigh, N.C., in June 1946.

SPECIAL: His wins triggered racial unrest and lynching of African Americans
BORN: 03-31-1878 in Galveston, Texas (USA)—died 06-10-1946
NICKNAME: Galveston Giant
HEIGHT: 6'1¼"
LOWEST WEIGHT: 192 lbs
HIGHEST WEIGHT: 221 lbs
BOXING RECORD:
  105 professional bouts
  68 wins
  10 draws
  16 no-decision bouts
  1 no bout
  10 losses
  8 title defenses
  8 world championship bouts
FIRST WORLD CHAMPIONSHIP BOUT:
  1908 (TKO win 14th round Tommy Burns)
LAST WORLD CHAMPIONSHIP BOUT:
  1915 (KO loss 26th round Jess Willard)
WORLD CHAMPIONSHIP TITLES:
  1908–1915

Brief product history
THE GLOVES

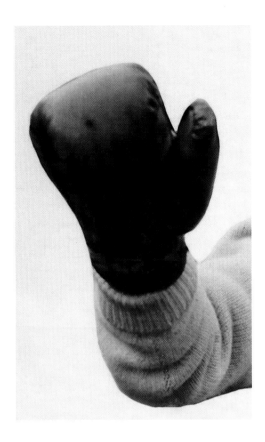

This 1920s model has a clearly extended thumb section, allowing for complete freedom of movement.

Modern competition gloves are much more padded: this cross section reveals the various foam layers in the lining and a pre-formed and virtually immobile thumb section.

Modern gloved prizefighting is usually considered to have been born in New Orleans on September 7, 1892: the day James J. Corbett and his adversary John L. Sullivan contested the very first "padded" heavyweight title fight. Corbett won. For many years, boxers had been using gloves to protect their sensitive fists during training. Here, too, the English boxing champion and trainer Jack Broughton was pioneering. The author of the first modern set of rules for boxing (The Broughton Rules, 1743) recommended that his protégés use so-called "mufflers" for sparring at his training center on Tottenham Court Road in London. These mufflers, which Broughton developed himself, were the forerunners of boxing gloves. However, use of these supposedly shock-absorbing pieces of equipment for official bouts was considered unmanly for many years. It was only in the second half of the 19th century that a more pragmatic attitude was adopted to the wearing of gloves as a result of countless hand injuries. Soon after, French leather gloves padded with felt or some other, similarly soft material began to be produced and used. The shock-absorbing

properties of these gloves was initially limited because they were almost all skintight, lightweight products weighing no more than two ounces, similar to the gloves used for training on equipment today. The first boxing boom was quickly followed in the early 20th century by the introduction of more generously padded, heavier models weighing between five and six ounces. While these gloves did absorb shocks to a certain degree, the thumb was still able to move freely, as was the case with all gloves. Over the decades that followed, generations of boxers suffered dangerous eye injuries caused either purposefully or accidentally by these freely moving thumbs.

The conspicuous number of retinal detachments and chronic cataracts that developed as a late consequence of thumbing lead to the rapid introduction of a thumbless glove in many areas in the early 1980s. The glove proved unpopular with many boxers and was very quickly replaced by an improved model: the thumb-attached glove. Here, the glove thumb is either stitched to the hand section or is formed in such a way that it is difficult to move. The weight of the glove—and, as

a result, its shock-absorbing properties—have since been increased again. In line with the regulations of the world's established boxing associations, today's professional boxers wear either eight-ounce (up to and including super middleweight) or ten-ounce gloves (light heavyweight to heavyweight) in competition. The rules for amateurs are slightly different: eight-ounce gloves are compulsory up to the welterweight division and ten-ounce gloves for the light middleweight class and above.

Despite costly and complex product research, the modern boxing glove is certainly not an optimum solution. In an article published in 1995, the respected American neurosurgeon and sports physician Robert C. Cantu described today's models as "archaic" and made an urgent call for the use of "space age materials and technology." He explained that during a bout, contact between the leather surface and water or sweat can significantly increase the weight of the gloves, causing the foam filling to shift considerably to the disadvantage of the knuckles.

In short, the high-tech era of boxing equipment has not even begun.

JACK ROOT · BOB FITZSIMMONS · "PHILADELPHIA" JACK O'BRIEN · JACK DILLON · GEORGES CARPENTIER · BATTLING SIKI · MIKE MCTIGUE · PAUL BERLENBACH · JACK DELANEY · TOMMY LOUGHRAN · MAXIE ROSENBLOOM JOHN HENRY LEWIS · BILLY CONN · GUS LESNEVICH · FREDDIE MILLS · JOEY MAXIM · ARCHIE MOORE · HAROLD JOHNSON · WILLIE PASTRANO · JOSÉ TORRES · DICK TIGER · BOB FOSTER · VICENTE RONDON · JOHN CONTEH

LIGHT HEAVYWEIGHT

VICTOR GALINDEZ · MATTHEW SAAD MUHAMMAD · MICHAEL SPINKS BOBBY CZYZ · VIRGIL HILL · PRINCE CHARLES WILLIAMS · ROY JONES · HENRY MASKE · MICHAEL MOORER · DARIUSZ MICHALCZEWSKI SUPER MIDDLEWEIGHT — **CHONG-PAL PARK · GRACIANO ROCCHIGIANI LINDELL HOLMES · MICHAEL NUNN · CHRIS EUBANK · NIGEL BENN JAMES TONEY · FRANK LILES · ROY JONES JR. · JOE CALZAGHE · SVEN OTTKE**

MORE THAN JUST HEROES ON THEIR WAY UP

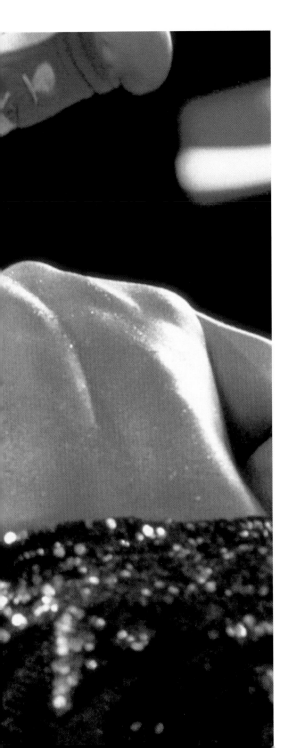

The public certainly doesn't handle light heavyweights with kid gloves. The champions in the 175 lb division are often described as tragic heroes on their way up, who consider their time in the second-highest of the eight classic weight divisions to be temporary and later come to nothing when they graduate to the heavyweight class. But this simplified view of things does not correspond to reality.

It is both correct and logical that future heavyweights often start their careers in the light heavyweight division. After all, boxers gain weight as they get older. Max Schmeling was crowned European professional champion in this division at the age of 21 while Cassius Clay won amateur gold at the Olympic Games in Rome at the age of 18. However, there are a whole series of other light heavyweight champions who suffered bitter defeats for their excursions into the heavyweight division. Georges Carpentier, Billy Conn, Archie Moore and Bob Foster, to name but a few,

were all frustrated in their attempts to become champion of the world in the royal division. Only Michael Spinks (1985) and Michael Moorer (1994) have succeeded in snatching the title in both divisions.

However, the majority of the light heavyweight limit's best boxers stay in this category, which was created in 1903, and have fought some of the most attractive boxing duels in the history of modern boxing. There are some genuine light heavyweight boxers who spend their entire boxing career in this division, even though the purses to be had there are comparatively modest. The cruiserweight class, in which title fights have only been contested since 1979, on the other hand, has really remained nothing more than a 'tween deck between two boxing floors: since Evander Holyfield moved up to the heavyweight division, there have been no outstanding and enduring champions in this class.

James Toney vs. Roy Jones Jr. (super middleweight), Las Vegas, 1994.

95

MICHAEL SPINKS

For many years, it looked as if Michael Spinks would never succeed in entirely convincing anyone of his outstanding qualities. In 1976, when the Golden Gloves champion won the middleweight gold medal at the Olympic Games in Montreal, his critics pointed to the absence of the Cubans and the Soviets, who had boycotted the Games, and the fact that he had drawn two byes in the tournament.

Then when he turned pro in 1977, it was his brother Leon who was in the limelight: three years Michael's senior, Leon Spinks became heavyweight champion of the world in 1978 when, to the amazement of the world, he defeated Muhammad Ali. But in the long run, it was the outsider Michael who went down in history as the greater of the two boxing brothers from an impoverished St. Louis family.

In 1981, Spinks II won a 15-round unanimous decision to gain the WBA light heavyweight title by outboxing Eddie Mustafa Muhammad with his two exceptional "weapons:" a reliable, precise jab and a brilliant right cross. Less than two years and five title defenses later, he became the last boxer in this weight division to unite the titles after winning a carefully fought match against WBC champion Dwight Muhammad Quawi in 1983. But his greatest hour was yet to come: after a 4,500-calorie diet, he moved up into the heavyweight division where he eventually outpointed the long-reigning champion Larry Holmes to become champion in September 1985. This victory made the eternally second Spinks brother the first boxer in his category to enhance his graduation to the royal division with the heavyweight crown.

A rematch against Holmes and a TKO over Steffen Tangstad confirmed Spinks as the IBF champion the following year. He was put out of action by being stripped of his title by the world association and then suffering a 91-second defeat at the hands of Mike Tyson. This disastrous showdown in June 1988 convinced the 32-year-old that it was time to retire; a decision he never reversed. By that time, one of the best technical boxers of his era and a casual man of independent means outside the ring had defied his detractors and already left a memorial to himself.

"ON THE WAY TO THE RING
I LEFT ALL MY FEARS BEHIND ME."

MICHAEL SPINKS

SPECIAL: First light heavyweight professional who also became heavyweight champion

BORN: 07-13-1956 in St. Louis, Missouri (USA)

NICKNAME: Slim

BOXING RECORD:
32 professional bouts
31 wins
1 loss
15 world championship bouts
(11 in light heavyweight,
4 in heavyweight)

FIRST WORLD CHAMPIONSHIP BOUT:
1981 (win on points 15th round Eddie Mustafa Muhammad)

LAST WORLD CHAMPIONSHIP BOUT:
1988 (KO loss 1st round Mike Tyson)

WORLD CHAMPIONSHIP TITLES:
1981–85 (light heavyweight)
1985–87 (heavyweight)

BOB FOSTER

SPECIAL: A sheriff turned boxing idol
BORN: 12-15-1938 in Albuquerque,
New Mexico (USA)
BOXING RECORD:
  65 professional bouts
  56 wins
  1 draw
  8 losses
  16 world championship bouts (1 in
  heavyweight, 15 in light heavyweight)
FIRST WORLD CHAMPIONSHIP BOUT:
  1968 (KO win 4th round Dick Tiger)
LAST WORLD CHAMPIONSHIP BOUT:
  1974 (draw 15th round
  Jorge Ahumada)
WORLD CHAMPIONSHIP TITLES:
  1968–74

"HE WAS PRACTICALLY UNBEATABLE IN HIS LIMIT."

THE RING

For many years, one man dominated the light heavyweight division: Bob Foster. He reigned supreme in his class between 1968 and 1974 with the authority of a world champion who has all the qualities a boxer needs. This gangly giant used his piercing jab to keep his opponents at a distance and make the most of his extensive reach. And if anyone dared come too close, he used his enormous power to bring the bout to an end. A sheriff by profession and hailing from Albuquerque, N.M., ten of his opponents failed to go the distance with him in the roped square. With 14 successful title defenses, he also set a record for his division that was to last until the 1990s.

For insiders, 29-year-old Foster was the hot favorite in May 1968 when he challenged champion Dick Tiger and inflicted on the aging Nigerian idol the only KO defeat of his career by landing a crushing blow in round 4. After this victory, the new champion roamed from Massachusetts to Montana like a traveling salesman, demonstrating his special talent in return for moderate purses. Foster impressed in world championship bouts against Mike Quarry, Chris Finnegan and Pierre Fourie, whom he succeeded in beating for a second time in a highly respected rematch in Johannesburg in 1973. What's more, he definitively confirmed his outstanding position in 1972 when he punished the recently declared WBA champion Vicente Paul Rondon for presumptuously claiming that he was the best by trouncing him in less than two rounds.

The more weighty purses offered in the top division repeatedly enticed Foster to try his luck as a heavyweight. These were the only times he blotted his almost perfect copybook record. In a title fight against Joe Frazier (KO defeat in 1970) and in matches with Doug Jones, Zora Folley, Ernie Terrell, and Muhammad Ali (KO defeat in 1972), it became clear that his physique was just not enough to withstand the top heavyweights. Back at light heavyweight level, however, the man with the lethal octopus arms remained unbeaten. Two months after a flattering draw in a world championship bout against Jorge Ahumada, the 35-year-old hung up his gloves in September 1974. By that time, he had long been elected to the International Boxing Hall of Fame in Canastota, N.Y.

ARCHIE MOORE

At the start of Moore's astounding professional career, Joe Louis was training for his first contest with Max Schmeling. At the end of it, Cassius Clay was already a ranked boxer. But Archie Moore did more than just experience boxing history during his career, he also wrote history as an outstanding light heavyweight champion. No world champion in this limit was ever crowned so late in life or stayed at the top as long as "The Ol' Mongoose."

Christened Archibald Lee Wright after his birth in Mississippi in December 1916 (some sources erroneously put this date at 1913), Moore learned everything the hard way. Adopted by an honorable uncle from St. Louis, he joined a gang and ended up stealing a driver's cash box from a streetcar at the age of 15. He was caught, brought before a court, and sentenced to three years in a penitentiary.

During the 22 months he actually spent there, he nurtured his talent for fistfighting. Of the 16 inmates that "Archie" beat in the correctional center's bouts, 15 were knocked out. This pattern was to continue when the hard-hitting young professional later took his sparring partners apart on a regular basis in Los Angeles. "Whenever I managed to put two or three punches together," he later recalled, "I was able to floor those guys."

But Moore was also an excellent defensive boxer. His arms crossed at chin level in the so-called shell style and his body constantly bobbing from side to side, he left his adversaries very few openings for attack. Nevertheless, or maybe because of this, the individual with no lobby had to fight well over one hundred opponents and cast off a total of six managers before he was at last given the

"HE'S THE SAME
AGE AS A LAWYER
WHO HAS BEEN
PRACTICING FOR
125 YEARS."

A. J. LIEBLING

chance to take a swipe at the title in the 17th year of his professional career. For years, Moore had been a top contender. Finally, in December 1952, at the age of 36, he faced champion Joey Maxim, nine years his junior, for the title and clearly outpointed his training partner. The triumph in the St. Louis arena was so long overdue that the new champion was almost incapable of celebrating as the world championship belt was fastened around his waist. "I could have got this thing twelve years ago," he said almost indignantly.

Moore then proceeded to hold on to "this thing" for exactly nine years and two months. About once a year, the aging world champion ran rings around his younger opponents. His victims included incredibly stylish boxers like Harold Johnson and dangerous punchers like

the Canadian Yvon Durelle, who Moore knocked out in 1958 in a memorable match. But he had already set his sights on the more lucrative bouts in the heavyweight division. But it wasn't to be: Moore never acquired the title. In 1955 and 1956, he was knocked out by both Rocky Marciano and Floyd Patterson in the fifth round despite getting off to a good start in both matches. In November 1962, aged almost 46, he finally realized that the end of his career was nigh when he failed to go the distance against an up-and-coming Cassius Clay. In March 1963, Moore took his leave from the ring with a TKO over Mike DiBiase. He had already been stripped of his title two years previously.

"He's the same age as a lawyer who has been practicing for 125 years," A. J. Liebling once

said. By the end of his career, Moore had over 200 professional fights under his belt, over 180 of which he won, at least 119 before the final bell. The exact data has never actually been compiled. Nevertheless, the old master never considered his profession to be a threat to his health. "It's not the length of a man's career that wears him down," was his motto, "it's the number of punches he takes." The sharp-minded and witty-tongued individualist even managed to prove this theory by leading an active public life after his fistic career. Moore took on countless roles as an actor and also spent time as an advisor to the Boy Scouts of America. Another youth initiative sponsored by him—Any Boy Can—continued to be the focus of his attention until his death in 1998.

TOMMY LOUGHRAN

He was hardly what the boxing world calls a feared puncher. Of the 173 professional fights he contested, Tommy Loughran only won 18 before the final bell. But what the Philadelphia-born descendant of an Irish immigrant lacked in punching power, he more than made up for with the stylish finesse that turned him into one of the most awesome technical boxers of his day.

His footwork allowed him to forestall almost all his opponents' attacks and his ability to determine the progress of a fight was phenomenal. Loughran regularly succeeded in coaxing his enraged adversary into his corner in the dying seconds of a round only to flop down on the stool that was whipped into the ring as soon as the bell went.

Loughran turned pro at the age of 17 and was soon running rings around both former and future champions like Harry Greb, Georges Carpentier, Max Baer, and James J. Braddock.

But almost eight years were to pass before he finally got the chance to challenge title-holder Mike McTigue in October 1927. Loughran outboxed both McTigue and the recognized NBA champion Jimmy Slattery in an equally superior manner and then went on to defend his united titles five more times, including once against the middleweight champion Mickey Walker.

He then renounced his title in the fall of 1929 to have a chance at the heavyweight championship.

Like almost every one of his successors who tried exactly the same thing, tricky Tommy was not able to transform his heavyweight ambitions into success. In his heavyweight debut fight, future world champion Jack Sharkey knocked out Loughran in the third round. In Miami, Fla., in March 1934, he lost a unanimous title challenge decision to the 86-pounds heavier Primo Carnera.

But these late defeats did nothing to diminish his outstanding status in light heavyweight boxing. What's more, thanks to his great talent for defensive boxing, his health remained virtually intact until his death at the age of 79.

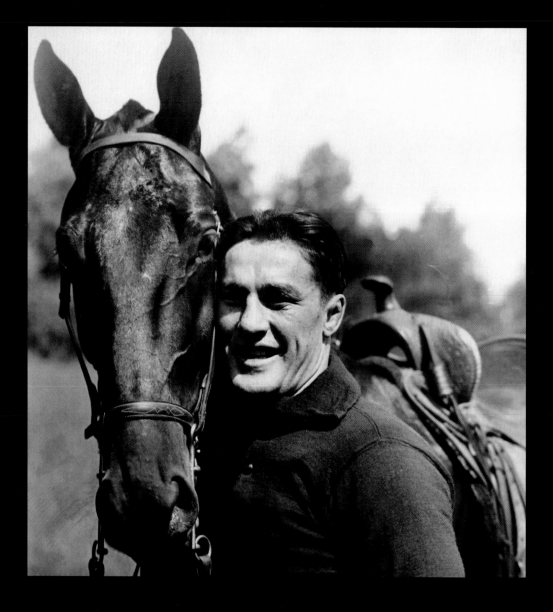

"ONE OF THE MASTER BOXERS OF ALL TIME."

PETER HELLER

SPECIAL: Star of the Roaring Twenties
BORN: 11-29-1902 in Philadelphia (USA)—died 07-07-1982
BOXING RECORD:
  175 professional bouts
  96 wins, 9 draws
  24 losses
  1 no-decision bouts
  45 no contest bouts
  world championship bouts (7 in light heavyweight, 1 in heavyweight)
FIRST WORLD CHAMPIONSHIP BOUT:
  1927 (win on points 15th round Mike McTigue, New York title)
LAST WORLD CHAMPIONSHIP BOUT:
  1934 (loss on points 15th round Primo Carnera)
WORLD CHAMPIONSHIP TITLES:
  1927–29

GEORGES CARPENTIER

The first European superstar, the best French boxer of all time and one of the most perfect light heavyweight athletes ever: whatever superlatives were conjured up to describe Georges Carpentier, they remain to this day almost entirely justified. In his 18-year professional career, the "Orchid Boy" collected national and international titles in five of the eight weight divisions. More than this, he was also a stylish and elegant pugilist whose punches were unusually—and often decisively—fast and powerful.

The graceful son of a miner from Lievin-les-Lens, Carpentier always exuded class when he stepped into the ringed arena. Initially his opponents were much older than him. This is why large numbers of women came to watch "Gorgeous George" fight, a first in professional boxing. And Carpentier didn't let the ladies down: Between the ages of 17 and 19, he won the European titles in the welterweight, middleweight and light heavyweight divisions in London, Monaco and Paris. He wasn't even 20 years of age when he wretched the European heavyweight title from "Bombardier" Billy Wells by knocking him out in Ghent in June 1913.

The most important and most peaceable phase of his career began after the First World War when the ubiquitous promoter Tex Rickard brought the charismatic "Croix de Guerre"-wearing war hero to America in 1920. Once there, the reigning European champion knocked out Battling Levinsky in the fourth round of their bout in October 1920 to become light heavyweight champion of the world. This was preparation enough. One year later, Rickard organized the incredibly hyped mismatch against heavyweight champion Jack Dempsey. It was dubbed the "Battle of the Century." But Carpentier just wasn't the right build and lost the bout in under four rounds. Nevertheless, the record gate of $1.8 million ensured both boxers colossal purses.

Carpentier still managed to pull in the crowds in Europe, even though Battling Siki relieved him of his light heavyweight crown in Paris in 1922. He remained a living legend and was regularly seen in his Paris bar long after his career ended in 1926.

"HE KNEW EVERY CORNER OF THE RING."

TOMMY LOUGHRAN

SPECIAL: The first European superstar
BORN: 01-12-1894 in Lievin-les-Lens (FRA)—died 10-28-1975
NICKNAME: Orchid Boy
BOXING RECORD:
  110 professional bouts
  88 wins, 6 draws
  15 losses
  1 no-decision bout
  world championship bouts (3 in light heavyweight, 1 in heavyweight)
FIRST WORLD CHAMPIONSHIP BOUT:
  1920 (KO win 4th round Battling Levinsky)
LAST WORLD CHAMPIONSHIP BOUT:
  1922 (KO win 6th round Battling Siki)
WORLD CHAMPIONSHIP TITLES:
  1920–22

NONPAREIL JACK DEMPSEY · BOB FITZSIMMONS · KID MCCOY · TOMMY RYAN
STANLEY KETCHEL · BILLY PAPKE · LES DARCY · MIKE O'DOWD · JOHNNY WILSON
HARRY GREB · TIGER FLOWERS · MICKEY WALKER · MARCEL THIL · FREDDIE STEELE
TONY ZALE · ROCKY GRAZIANO · MARCEL CERDAN · JAKE LAMOTTA · SUGAR RAY
ROBINSON · RANDOLPH TURPIN · CARL "BOBO" OLSON · GENE FULLMER · CARMEN
BASILIO · PAUL PENDER · DICK TIGER · JOEY GIARDELLO · EMILE GRIFFITH

MIDDLEWEIGHT

NINO BENVENUTI · CARLOS MONZON · RODRIGO VALDEZ · MARVIN HAGLER
MICHAEL NUNN · JULIAN JACKSON · JAMES TONEY · GERALD McCLELLAN · ROY JONES
BERNARD HOPKINS — LIGHT MIDDLEWEIGHT — DENNY MOYER · SANDRO
MAZZINGHI · NINO BENVENUTI · FREDDIE LITTLE · KOICHI WAJIMA · MAURICE
HOPE · WILFRED BENITEZ · MIKE McCALLUM · JULIAN JACKSON · DONALD CURRY
GIANFRANCO ROSI · TERRY NORRIS · JULIO CESAR VASQUEZ · FELIX TRINIDAD

TOP-CLASS BOXING

When boxing insiders talk about the great middleweights, their faces usually take on a strange transfigured appearance. They then say that such a terrific combination of punching power and dynamism is to be found in hardly any other weight division and that the number of outstanding champions and contenders is greater in this class (160–160 lbs) than in any other. While such lofty praise tends by nature to be rather euphemistic, it is certainly not far from the truth.

The successors of the very first middleweight champion, the unequalled Nonpareil Jack Dempsey, who was crowned in 1884, initially had a tough time of it. Popular, long-reigning champions like Stanley Ketchel (1908–13) and Mickey Walker (1926–32) were the exception rather than the rule. It was only in the 1940s that a whole battery of exceptional duels in the ring transformed the

middleweight category into the secret royal division for about twenty years. The magnificent bouts of Zale, Graziano, LaMotta, Basilio, and Sugar Ray Robinson almost effortlessly filled huge arenas and baseball stadiums. Later on, this era was relived for brief intervals with the arrival on the scene of Benvenuti, Monzon, and Hagler. Between 1945 and 1994, no less than 15 of the 50 "Fights of the Year" selected by the legendary magazine The Ring were middleweight bouts.

The splitting up of the classic limit into two or three categories (super middleweight since 1984 and light middleweight and super welterweight since 1962) significantly reduced the number of outstanding world championship bouts in this division. However, from time to time—and at the very least in unification bouts between rival champions—the middleweight division shows that it really is still top class.

Bernard Hopkins vs. Felix Trinidad, New York, 2001.

MARVIN HAGLER

It took the universally avoided Marvin Hagler 50 fights and the support of influential politicians in Massachusetts to eventually be given the deserved chance to take a shot at the world championship title. What's more, it took a questionable decision to eventually wretch the title from the long-reigning champion's grasp. Between these two bouts, the shaven-headed southpaw dominated the elite in his weight division in a steady and uncompromising manner that has never been repeated by any other boxer before or since.

For Hagler, the road to the top was quite literally rough and stony. As a junior, he hauled bricks and cement for the Petronelli Bros. construction company by day and trained under their supervision in their Brockton gym (Boston) by evening. His immense ambition drove him to work on his boxing in a serious and doggedly determined way right from the word go. A so-called converted southpaw, the young professional had such punching power in his fists that he became the best finisher of his day. "I call this one K and this one O," he once said of his hands, "they're my referees." Unbeknown to himself, these knockout fists later helped him avoid criticism generated by dubious decisions.

Hagler certainly cannot be said to have received preferential treatment when he lost two decisions against local heroes in Philadelphia. Similarly, his outstanding world championship title fight against champion Vito Antuofermo in November 1979 was declared a draw by officials. But this couldn't stop "Marvelous" Marvin. At his next attempt in 1980, he relieved Alan Minter of the title in only three furious rounds and defended his title twelve times over the six and a half years that followed. Eventually it was his TKO victories over Thomas Hearns and John Mugabi that brought Hagler the recognition he deserved.

Hagler was enjoying his reputation as unbeatable when he was outpointed by the reactivated Sugar Ray Leonard in April 1987 in his best-paid showdown. This loss confirmed the 33-year-old's embittered image of himself as being chronically underprivileged and he ended his career immediately. He moved to Italy, where he has been a successful actor and man of independent means since the 1990s.

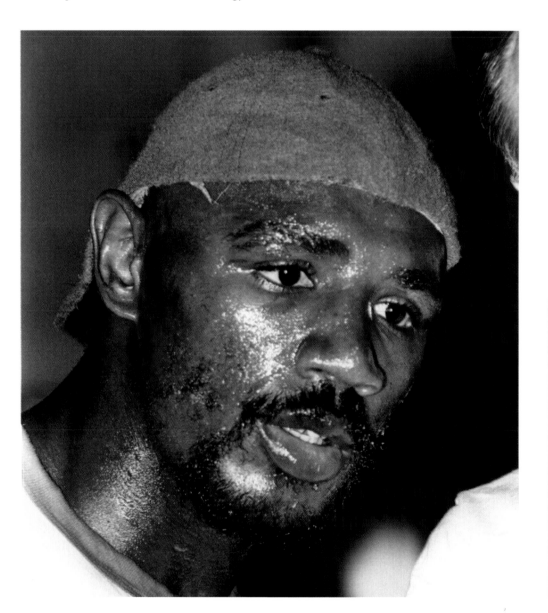

"MARVIN HAGLER STILL HATES ALL HIS OPPONENTS."

BOB ARUM

SPECIAL: An outsider turned all-time great
BORN: 05-23-1955, Newark, New Jersey (USA)
NICKNAME: Marvelous Marvin
BOXING RECORD:
  67 professional bouts
  62 wins
  2 draws
  3 losses
  15 world championship bouts
FIRST WORLD CHAMPIONSHIP BOUT:
  1979 (draw 15th round
  Vito Antuofermo)
LAST WORLD CHAMPIONSHIP BOUT:
  1987 (loss on points 12th round
  Sugar Ray Leonard, WBC/IBF)
WORLD CHAMPIONSHIP TITLES:
  1980–87

CARLOS MONZON

Whether it really was the Indian blood in his veins or quite simply his own highly ambivalent personality, Carlos Monzon had both the pride and the rage that gives a boxer that decisive edge in important bouts. Whether the mix was good or bad depends on the way you look at it: what was a benefit to this outstanding champion for his triumphs in the ring, proved tragically fatal for him in civilian life.

Despite having a record of only three lost decisions in a total of 86 professional fights, the wiry Argentinean from the province of Santa Fe was still considered a virtual nobody when he stepped into the ring to fight Nino Benvenuti for the world championship title in Rome in 1970. It was the first time that he had boxed outside the South American subcontinent. By knocking out the champion in round 12, the 28-year-old outsider made it quite clear to everyone in the Palazzo dello Sport that a new star had appeared in the middleweight sky. A hard jab with impressive reach and an authoritative right allowed him to dominate his duels both from the long and the half distance. This was certainly true of his record 14 successful title defenses in six and a half years.

Monzon confirmed his title victory in 1971 by quickly knocking out Benvenuti in a rematch and succeeded in keeping all world championship challengers at arms' length until mid-1977. Such challengers included Emile Griffith, Bennie Briscoe, José Napoles, and other usually top-class boxers. He also found time to enjoy living the high life of a celebrated hero everywhere from Buenos Aires to Paris. Monzon once again underlined his sporting status when he beat rival WBA champ Rodrigo Valdez in unification bouts in 1976 and 1977. However, it was when he retired as reigning world champion that things really took a dramatic turn.

It is likely that alcohol and drugs were involved when the retired boxer threw his third partner, Alicia Muniz, out the window in the heat of the moment. He was sentenced to eleven years in prison for manslaughter. The remainder of his sentence was to be suspended when Monzon was killed in a car accident when returning from a weekend furlough in early 1995.

> ## "EVEN AFTER HIS DEATH, MONZON REMAINED A CONTROVERSIAL PERSON."
>
> *THE RING*

SPECIAL: Holder of the record mark of 14 successful title defenses in 6½ years

BORN: 08-07-1942 in Santa Fe (ARG) —died 01-08-1995

BOXING RECORD:
- 101 professional bouts
- 89 wins
- 8 draws
- 3 losses
- 1 no-decision bout
- 15 world championship bouts

FIRST WORLD CHAMPIONSHIP BOUT:
1970 (KO win 12th round Nino Benvenuti)

LAST WORLD CHAMPIONSHIP BOUT:
1977 (win on points 15th round Rodrigo Valdez)

WORLD CHAMPIONSHIP TITLES:
1970–77

SUGAR RAY ROBINSON

Elegance and rhythm: Sugar Ray Robinson plays the piano in his London hotel room before his match against Terry Downes in 1962.

His European tours brought Robinson (seen here with his wife Edna Mae and son Ray Jr. in 1951) money and experience but also some unexpected defeats.

An instruction film about boxing attributes should just contain shots of his best fights. Sugar Ray Robinson is no less than the Picasso of boxing. More than anyone else in the 20th century, he celebrated his sport as an art form. A "puncher" as well as a technical and stylish boxer, the outstanding champion in two weight divisions knew how to combine the strategic means of the sweet science almost perfectly. What's more, he knew how to underpin his success effectively with equally elegant performances outside the ring.

Walker Smith Jr. was just eleven years old when he moved from Detroit to Harlem with his mother after her divorce. Once in New York he didn't box by this name for very long: as a junior he once adopted the name of his

training partner Ray Robinson to allow him to take part in an amateur tournament at the last minute. The name stuck. Soon afterwards, a journalist noted that the catlike, fast youngster's use of his fists was "sweeter than sugar." That is how he got his enduring nickname even before he turned pro in October 1940 after 85 victories in 85 official amateur bouts (including 40 first round knockouts). Some 91 matches later, the rare talent first became the undisputed champion in the welterweight division (1946–50) and then in the middleweight division, winning all but one non-title fight against Jake LaMotta.

Robinson was a past master at avoiding his opponents' attacks with nifty footwork and going into the offense with piecing combinations.

What drove him was the desire to outsmart his adversaries. "I like sussing people out and out-witting them," said Robinson, "but I still don't enjoy beating them up." Nevertheless, twice named "Boxer of the Year" by the legendary American magazine *The Ring*, Robinson was well able to destroy his opponents. His first challenger for the welterweight title, Jimmy Doyle, died in 1947 as a result of the injuries he sustained on the previous day in their world championship bout. Robinson's TKO over a completely demolished LaMotta in February 1951, which earned him the middleweight title for the first time, went down in boxing history as the "St. Valentine's Day massacre."

"Sugar" lost his title in July 1951 when at the end of an exhausting tour of Europe, he

SPECIAL: The perfect combination of
style and punching power
BORN: 05-03-1921 in Detroit (USA)—
died 04-12-1989
BOXING RECORD:
202 professional bouts
175 wins, 6 draws
19 losses
2 no-decision bouts
22 world championship bouts
(6 in welterweight, 15 in middleweight,
1 in light heavyweight)
FIRST WORLD CHAMPIONSHIP BOUT:
1946 (win on points 15th round
Tommy Bell, welterweight)
LAST WORLD CHAMPIONSHIP BOUT:
1961 (loss on points 15th round
Gene Fullmer, NBA title)
WORLD CHAMPIONSHIP TITLES:
1946–50 (welterweight), 1951–52,
1955–57, 1958–60 (middleweight)

was surprisingly outpointed by Randolph Turpin in London. But his revenge in their September rematch was indeed impressive: threatened with a stoppage in the 10th round of the fight as a result of a gaping eye wound, Robinson moved up a gear and launched a furious assault. This pattern was repeated until the end of the decade: whenever the master of the rematch's career was threatened by a defeat, he always hammered his successor in a rematch. These rematches, which were attended by massive crowds and included the series of duels with Gene Fullmer and Carmen Basilio, were the some of the best boxing had to offer in the 1950s. All told, Robinson contended 22 title bouts before 1961, losing only one before the final bell. This loss took

place in 1952, when he had to be taken out of the light heavyweight bout against champion Joey Maxim after 13 superior rounds because he was completely dehydrated. Robinson was able to translate his market value into handsome purses even without the aid of intermediary managers. His way of spending money was equally impressive. His preferred mode of transport for traveling around Harlem to check how his restaurants and laundries were doing was a pink Cadillac convertible. He even had a permanent hairdresser, masseur, and shoe cleaner on his rather extensive payroll. The egocentric's addiction to profit also kept Robinson from cooperating with the gangsters that virtually controlled professional boxing at the time

through the International Boxing Club in New York. They certainly tried to talk him around but Robinson wanted to be the only one to make money with Robinson. In his autobiography, Robinson claimed he even turned down an offer of $1 million to lose against Rocky Graziano in 1952.

When the 44-year-old announced his retirement in December 1965, he looked back on a professional career spanning 202 fights and 25 years. "I must have blown about $4 million," he once mused, "but I don't regret it." Muhammad Ali declared to his face: "You are really the greatest." And, well, Ali was always right! Robinson, who suffered from Alzheimer's and diabetes died in April 1989 shortly before his 68th birthday.

HARRY GREB

SPECIAL: True fighting spirit
BORN: 06-06-1894 in Pittsburgh, Pennsylvania (USA)—died 10-22-1926
NICKNAME: The Human Windmill
BOXING RECORD:
  299 professional bouts
  260 wins, 20 draws, 19 losses
  9 world championship bouts
FIRST WORLD CHAMPIONSHIP BOUT:
  1923 (win on points 15th round Johnny Wilson)
LAST WORLD CHAMPIONSHIP BOUT:
  1926 (loss on points 15th round Tiger Flowers)
WORLD CHAMPIONSHIP TITLES:
  1923–26

"NOT EVEN JACK DEMPSEY GAVE ME SUCH A HARD TIME."

GENE TUNNEY

He certainly wasn't a lesser boxer than Jack Dempsey; he was just smaller. And he was certainly more active than any other boxer in the 1920s. It is no surprise, therefore, that Harry Greb's interminable attacking style of fighting earned him the nickname "The Human Windmill."

Greb had obviously wiped the words "fear," "break" and "regular training" from his mind: he saw little point in practicing on sand bags when he could rush headlong into a real duel. After 13 years full of bouts, had an unbelievable 299 fights to his name.

"Not even Jack Dempsey gave me such a hard time," Tunney once said of him. The future heavyweight champion notched up the only defeat in his otherwise perfect career

in his first bout against the rough-and-ready boxer from Pittsburgh for the American light heavyweight title in May 1922. Other light heavyweights who later became world champions often fared no better against Greb: both Tommy Loughran and Maxie Rosenbloom were unable to escape his merciless attacks.

He felt most at home in the middleweight division. In August 1923, Greb became champion in this class when he outpointed Johnny Wilson in New York. He defended his title five times until June 1924. One of these matches saw him take on another attacker, Mickey Walker. For his performance in this bout he was voted "Fighter of the Year" by the recently established magazine *The Ring* later that year. But events took

a tragic turn in 1926: he was toppled from the throne by Tiger Flowers in two world championship bouts and later sustained serious injuries in a car accident. He died in Atlantic City in October of the same year after a nose operation to expand his respiratory tracts.

The ever-pugnacious star—who found it equally impossible to say no to a short-lived affair as to anyone in boxing gloves—had lived his short life of 32 restless, intense years in the same way he pursued his career in the ring: no hesitations; full risk. And the world sat up and listened once again when it posthumously became known that for the last five years of his life Greb had battled his opponents with sight in only one eye.

STANLEY KETCHEL

In the early 20th century, it was virtually impossible to ignore Stanley Ketchel. The outstanding middleweight boxer of the first decade of the century was not only blessed with spectacular punching power in his fists that almost always ensured him an early victory. As someone whose sporting successes transformed him from a hobo into a respected gentleman, he went down in history as the first great rags-to-riches story in modern prizefighting.

Stanislaus Kiecal was the descendant of Polish and Russian immigrants and spent his early life in Michigan before taking to the road as a teenager. The shorty with the cherub face soon demonstrated his talent for fistfighting in his first boxing booth

"ONE OF THE FIRST SUPERSTARS OF HIS SPORT."

THE RING

matches. His hyperactive style of fighting was attractive to watch and so successful that Ketchel chalked up 40 knockouts in 41 victories by the time he contested his first world championship bout. He seized the vacant title in May 1908 by knocking out Jack "Twin" Sullivan in the 20th round and then proceeded to beat all challengers that laid claim to the title in the same year, including Sullivan's twin brother Mike, Billy Papke and Hugo Kelly.

Known by this time as the "Michigan Assassin," the famous KO king temporarily lost his title to his archrival Billy Papke but managed to regain it from him in 1909. Ketchel beat Papke in three of their four encounters. He also beat another exceptional boxer of that era, Joe Thomas, by knocking

him out in round 32. But even heavyweights were not safe from him: the champion often anonymously took part in provincial tournaments in the guise of "Kid Glutz" and shook up some much heavier opponents. Ketchel secured himself a place in history when he challenged heavyweight champion of the world Jack Johnson in Colma, Calif., in 1909, and succeeded in downing him moments before he himself was knocked out.

With one eye on his dissipated, consuming lifestyle, the upstart once predicted his own fate: "I will never reach the age of 30," Unfortunately, Stanley Ketchel was right: In October 1910, the ex-boxer, who had just turned 24, was shot in the back by a farm hand on a ranch near Conway, Mo., probably out of jealousy.

SPECIAL: KO king and adventurer
BORN: 09-14-1886 in Grand Rapids, Michigan (USA)—died 10-15-1910
NICKNAME: Michigan Assassin
BOXING RECORD:
  66 professional bouts
  53 wins
  5 draws
  4 losses
  4 no-decision bouts
  8 world championship bouts
  (7 in middleweight, 1 in heavyweight)
FIRST WORLD CHAMPIONSHIP BOUT:
  1908 (KO win 20th round Jack Sullivan)
LAST WORLD CHAMPIONSHIP BOUT:
  1909 (KO win 12th round Jack Johnson)
WORLD CHAMPIONSHIP TITLES:
  1908–10

Brief product history
THE BOXING SHOES

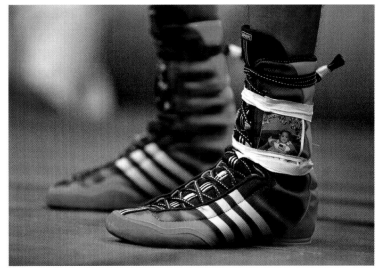

The traditional boxcalf leather boxing shoes *(above)* didn't cover the boxers' ankles. Modern boxing shoes have a higher shaft and leave room for personal embellishment. The American boxer Ricardo Williams wore a photo of his son on his shoes for his boxing final at the Sydney Olympics *(top right)*.

There are no special provisions governing the composition of the footwear that boxers are allowed to wear in the ring; just one strong recommendation: the soles should be clean and non-slip. To be unshakeable, a boxer needs a firm stance, while a good grip is essential for mobility. This is why the typical boxing shoes worn by athletes from the pioneer days until into the 1950s were made of fine boxcalf leather and had completely smooth soles. Before they entered the ring, they dipped their shoes into a small box of rosin near the steps. The rosin gave the soles even more grip. However, the powder contained magnesium and was aggressive and corrosive when it came in contact with the eyes. For this reason, the box of rosin was gradually done away with after the war.

Both amateurs and professionals have long since abandoned the practice of wiping their feet when entering the ring because the rubber soles of their modern fabric and synthetic shoes have a fine profile that virtually guarantees grip on the much improved ring canvas. However, the adhesive messages and advertising logos that are now attached to the ring floor are a new, additional threat: water and/or sweat on the smooth surface often does away with grip. If this happens and a boxer slips, it is up to the referee to point out that the slip was not caused by a scoring blow and ensure that the athlete

on the canvas does not lose a point for the round.

Modern boxing shoes are much lighter than their predecessors and cover much more of the boxer's calf. Boxers like to decorate the high shaft with all sorts of bits and bobs: colorful tassels, sparkly fringes and other similar things. After all, professional boxers are often eccentric. Here—as in other fashion and style trends—the retro look would definitely appear to be back. Heavyweight champion Mike Tyson, for example, purposefully wore for his brief world championship triumphs ankle-high black boxcalf shoes like the ones worn by his idol Jack Dempsey. It was the obsessive boxing historian's way of paying homage to Dempsey (Tyson can list the dates of records of the old boxing masters like no other). This gesture was soon copied by Lennox Lewis and others.

The rules of boxing decree that boxers must wear heelless shoes anytime they enter a ring for a fight. Well, almost everywhere. In May 1954, the officials made an exception for the bantamweight world championship between the Australian champion Jimmy Carruthers and Chamrern Songkitrat. Monsoon-like rain had flooded the ring in Bangkok's National Stadium and, as a result, the opponents were allowed to fight each other barefoot to avoid disappointing the 50,000 waiting spectators. After all, diving flippers would have made things a bit too awkward.

PADDY DUFFY · "MYSTERIOUS" BILLY SMITH · TOMMY RYAN · "JERSEY" JOE WALCOTT
HARRY LEWIS · JACK BRITTON · TED "KID" LEWIS · MICKEY WALKER · PETE LATZO
JOE DUNDEE · JACKIE FIELDS · BARNEY ROSS · HENRY ARMSTRONG · FRITZIE ZIVIC
SUGAR RAY ROBINSON · KID GAVILAN · JOHNNY SAXTON · CARMEN BASILIO · DON
JORDAN · BENNY "KID" PARET · EMILE GRIFFITH · CURTIS COKES · JOSÉ NAPOLES
BILLY BACKUS · CARLOS PALOMINO · JOSE PIPINO CUEVAS · SUGAR RAY LEONARD

WELTERWEIGHT

THOMAS HEARNS · DONALD CURRY · MILTON MCCRORY · MARK BRELAND · MELDRICK TAYLOR · IKE QUARTEY · PERNELL WHITAKER · OSCAR DE LA HOYA · FELIX TRINIDAD SHANE MOSLEY — LIGHT HEAVY WEIGHTS — **MUSHY CALLAHAN · JACK "KID" BERG TONY CANZONERI · BARNEY ROSS · CARLOS ORTIZ · NICOLINO LOCCHE · BRUNO ARCARI · ANTONIO CERVANTES · SAENSAK MUANGSURIN · AARON PRYOR · JUAN MARTIN COGGI · JULIO CESAR CHAVEZ · FRANKIE RANDALL · KONSTANTIN TSZYU**

EMERGING ELEGANCE

Elegance is the trademark of the slim and nimble stars in the under 147 lb weight class that has attracted insiders and admirers of beauty like no other. The issue of whether or not the history of these dynamic, ever-changing champions, which has been unfolding since the first title fight of the modern era in 1888, is comparable with the quality seen in the middleweight division will likely never be resolved, however. The world champions in this division have changed weight classes too frequently for that. They have been equally successful in their new divisions, however, and generated discussion as to which division they fought their best fights in that has far outlasted their career in the ring itself. This was the case for the legendary Henry Armstrong, who despite his still-valid record of 19 successive defending championships (1938–40) at times also held the championship belt in the featherweight and lightweight classes. This tradition was carried on by the two best-known "sweethearts" in the history of the welterweight class. Both Sugar Ray Robinson (1946–51) and Sugar Ray Leonard (between 1979 and 1983) used their dominance in this weight division as a springboard for collecting titles all the way up to the light heavyweight division.

This outstanding talent for historic changes in weight division and continual career leaps has most recently manifested itself in the current icon of the ring, Oscar De La Hoya. The megafights of this golden boy from East Los Angeles have also benefited from the virtually unending supply of top-rate rivals that is so essential for attaining athletic perfection in any class. "Ringsiders" already equate De La Hoya's welterweight fights with Ike Quartey, Felix Trinidad and Shane Mosley with those seen in the fantastic 1950s as well as with those which took place in the early 1980s when Leonard's duels with Thomas Hearns, Roberto Duran and Wilfred Benitez stole the show from even the heavyweights.

Shane Mosley vs. Oscar De La Hoya, Los Angeles, 2000.

PERNELL WHITAKER

SPECIAL: A stylist par excellence
BORN: 01-21-1964, Norfolk, Virginia (USA)
NICKNAME: Sweat Pea
HEIGHT: 5'9"
BOXING RECORD: 45 professional bouts,
  41 wins, 1 draw, 3 losses,
  23 world championship bouts
FIRST WORLD CHAMPIONSHIP BOUT:
  1988 (loss on points 12th round José
  Luis Ramirez)
LAST WORLD CHAMPIONSHIP BOUT:
  1999 (loss on points 12th round Felix
  Trinidad)
WORLD CHAMPIONSHIP TITLES:
  1989–91 (lightweight)
  1985–87 (light welterweight)
  1993–97 (welterweight)
  1995 (light middleweight)

"HIS EYES ARE MORE IMPORTANT THAN HIS LEGS OR HANDS."

SPORTS ILLUSTRATED

They call him "Sweet Pea," but "Houdini" would have been just as appropriate. In his 15 years as a professional boxer, the talented southpaw from Norfolk, Virginia, has evaded onslaughts from his opponents as skillfully and adeptly as an escape artist. "Probably the smoothest defense artist since Willie Pep," said Budd Schulberg in 1997. Whitaker may not always have satisfied the bloodlust of the most violent boxing fans in the process, however, as he usually completely outclassed his opponents in his victories, his boxing moves accompanied by amusing stunts that extended for the full allotment of rounds. Connoisseurs of the art of boxing, however, were often captivated by the stylistic repertoire of this fighter with such slick boxing techniques.

Taking the gold medal in 1984, the Olympic victor in the lightweight category soon began a triumphant march to the very top of the professional boxing sport. Seconded by star coach George Benton (until 1995), Whitaker took the lightweight titles from IBF champion Greg Haugen and WBC world champion José Luis Ramirez in 1989. He had already outboxed Ramirez once before a year earlier according to all the experts and the judges themselves. When he was able to defeat the highly respected WBA champ Azumah Nelson in May 1990, "Sweet Pea" became the titleholder in the three largest associations and in the years to follow the darling of the experts as well.

The "Fighter of the Year" in 1989, Whitaker led the ranking list of the best pound-for-pound boxers in the sports journals from thence forward and went on to collect more world championship titles as his weight increased. Whitaker became WBC light welterweight champion in 1992 and welterweight champion in 1993 by outpointing James "Buddy" McGirt. In 1995, an excursion in the light middleweight brought him a victory over Julio Cesar Vasquez and thus the fourth title of his professional career. The talented boxer nearly put himself out of business for lack of competition in "his" division, welterweight. All of his challengers appeared to have virtually no chance in the ring, and the involved managers never went through with the proposed *megafights*.

Such a fight finally took place in 1997, when the 33-year-old veteran entered the ring with the up-and-coming youngster Oscar De La Hoya in Las Vegas. Whitaker lost this important prestige fight on a decision to De La Hoya. Soon thereafter, a doping ban and a defeat against Felix Trinidad marked the end of this talented boxer's career.

JULIO CESAR CHAVEZ

SPECIAL: The boxing icon of Mexico
BORN: 07-12-1962, Ciudad Obregon (MEX)
NICKNAME: The Kid from Culiacan
BOXING RECORD: 110 professional bouts,
  103 wins, 2 draws, 5 losses, 37 world
  championship bouts (10 in super feather-
  weight, 3 in lightweight, 22 in light wel-
  terweight, 2 in welterweight)
FIRST WORLD CHAMPIONSHIP BOUT: 1984
  (KO win 8th round Mario Martinez, super
  featherweight)
LAST WORLD CHAMPIONSHIP BOUT: 2000
  (KO loss 6th round Konstantin "Kostya"
  Tszyu, light welterweight)
WORLD CHAMPIONSHIP TITLES:
  1984–87 (super featherweight)
  1987–89 (lightweight)
  1989–94,1995–96 (super featherweight)

"NEVER HAS A MEXICAN BOXER BEEN MORE ADMIRED THAN CHAVEZ."

THE RING

Ever since they began singing his praises, ringsiders have repeatedly compared Julio Cesar Chavez with boxing legends from the rough and distant past of the sport. And who would begrudge him the accolades? "The Kid from Culiacan" first established himself as the most exceptional fist fighter of his era in the 1980s with an attack style reminiscent of the most fearless of the first world champions of the 20th century. And just like these heroes of days gone by, he was never afraid to step into the ring with any of his serious opponents throughout his entire exceptionally active 20-year professional career.

The fourth of ten children of a railroad worker from the Mexican countryside Sonora went professional in Culiacan at just 17 years of age. Instead of continuing his engineering studies, the natural boxing talent found himself on the pay list of U.S. promoter Don King three years later. King arranged the first title fight for his undefeated protégé in 1984, a title bout with super featherweight champion Mario Martinez. Chavez won with a KO victory. A chin of solid steel and his powerful half-range punches aided the impressive attacker in further triumphs: In 1987 he took the lightweight title from WBA champion Edwin Rosario, and in 1988 from WBC world champion José Luis Ramirez. A year later, his status as the uncrowned king of all classes was impressively underscored by a TKO victory over Roger Mayweather (WBC titleholder in the super lightweight division).

Chavez had long since become a charismatic folk hero in Mexico and a crowd puller in the United States by the first time he nearly suffered defeat in 1990 in a match with competing IBF champion Meldrick Taylor. His desperate finish rendered him the winner on a technical knockout call by the referee two seconds before the end of the dramatic fight. He was saved once again in 1993 when a draw was called in his fight against welterweight champion Pernell Whitaker. His unparalleled string of victories finally ended in 1994, however, with a defeat on points against Frankie Randall during Chavez' 92nd professional fight. Chavez immediately regained the WBC title, but the high point of his incredible career was already behind him. Two defeats against Oscar De La Hoya (1996 and 1998) ushered in his gradual withdrawal from the sport.

He lost his last important match in 2000 against Konstantin "Kostya" Tszyu.

SUGAR RAY LEONARD

SPECIAL: A true superstar
BORN: 05-17-1956 in Wilmington,
South Carolina (USA)
BOXING RECORD:
40 professional bouts,
36 wins, 1 draw, 3 losses,
13 world championship bouts
(7 in welterweight, 2 in light middleweight, 1 in middleweight, 2 in super
middleweight, 1 in super middleweight
and light heavyweight)
FIRST WORLD CHAMPIONSHIP BOUT:
1979 (TKO win 15th round Wilfred
Benitez, welterweight WBC)
LAST WORLD CHAMPIONSHIP BOUT:
1991 (loss on points 12th round Terry
Norris, light middleweight WBC)
WORLD CHAMPIONSHIP TITLES:
1979–80, 1980–82 (welterweight)
1981 (light middleweight)
1987 (middleweight)
1988–89 (super middleweight and
light heavyweight)

Sugar Ray Leonard was predestined for the extraordinary as soon as he crowned his brilliant amateur career (155 victories in 160 fights) with Olympic gold in Montreal in 1976. The clever upstart from a large family in the state of Maryland could unleash his fists faster and more elegantly than any other boxer of his generation. And he possessed the charisma to turn a simple boxing king into a media darling with a stash full of advertising contracts in his pocket. Above all, Sugar Ray Leonard realized his full potential in the ring and at the cash register like no other boxer before him.

Once he had abandoned the idea of college studies, the freshly crowned Olympic victor began setting new standards as soon as he switched to the professional leagues. He ran a company he had founded himself, Sugar Ray Leonard Inc., and in this capacity hired a permanent trainer (Dave Jacobs) and a chief trainer (Ali's coach Angelo Dundee), who advised him at the ringside as well as in his choice of opponents. Instead of a manager, lawyer Mike Trainer seconded Leonard in contractual issues. The eloquent athlete had obviously mastered the arithmetic of the fighting world all by himself, however. Leonard pocketed what was then the record sum of 40,000 dollars for his debut fight in February 1977. Two million dollars in boxing purses came together less than three years later when he entered the ring with welterweight champion Wilfred Benitez.

So much cleverness paired with a healthy share of self-confidence did not always generate enthusiasm among the public. But when push came to shove in the ring, "Sugar" knew how to banish all skepticism in regard to his boxing talent with a convincing presentation of his fighting skills. "Sugar Ray Leonard can whip off your underwear with his tricks," chief coach Dundee once said of Leonard's astounding talent for movement. Those who assumed that Leonard did not have the necessary mental strength to compete with the best in his limit learned better in November 1979 in Las Vegas. There the 23-year-old challenger boxed fourteen and a half rounds with the previously undefeated WBC world champion and emerged the winner. This was the first of many classic Leonard fights that would go down in the annals of boxing history.

The new titleholder had just confirmed his reputation as a capable puncher with a spectacular KO victory over Dave Green when he took part in two legendary fights with his equally well-respected rival Roberto Duran in 1980. Leonard engaged in a fascinating yet for him unnecessary exchange of

punches over 15 rounds with this champion from Panama who had previously been categorized as a lightweight. In the end, he was narrowly defeated by Duran. Five months later, however, Leonard used his superior technique to taunt his opponent until Duran, completely nerve-wracked, walked away from the fight in the eighth round crying "No mas!" (No more!). This impressive revenge established Ray Charles Leonard, Sugar's real name, as the best professional pound-for-pound. His reputation was further confirmed in 1981 when he won the title in the light middleweight category (KO victory over Ayub Kalule).

"Sugar" appeared unstoppable in late 1981 with a hard-fought technical knockout win over Thomas "Hit Man" Hearns in yet another high-prestige megafight that united the welterweight titles. During training for

his next match, however, it suddenly became evident that he was suffering from detached retinas, which forced the 26-year-old into temporary withdrawal from the sport after his KO victory over Bruce Finch in the following year. Despite an operation, the wisdom of this withdrawal was further confirmed with a failed comeback attempt in 1984. Three years later, however, this exceptional boxer succumbed to more than just athletic temptation when he agreed to step in the ring with the dominating middleweight champion "Marvelous" Marvin Hagler for the guaranteed minimum purse of $11 million. To the great surprise of the bookies in Las Vegas, he won the hotly debated match by scoring the decision.

It could have been the *finale furioso* in Leonard's fascinating professional career. Unnecessary new revivals of his fights with

Thomas Hearns and Roberto Duran, as well as lucrative title bout challenges, always kept him from retiring, however. In November 1988 Leonard took possession of world championship belts no. 4 and 5, titles in the new super middleweight and light heavyweight categories, with a TKO victory over Don Lalonde. In February 1991, he was outboxed for twelve rounds by Terry Norris in a fight for Norris' WBC title in the light middleweight category. It was this event that brought about Leonard's realization: "I'm not from the 90s." In 1997, at nearly 41 years of age, he agreed to one more boxing spectacular with Hector Camacho Jr. in which Leondard was knocked out for the first time in his career and taken from the ring.

"Sugar" was, as he himself realized, a product of the 1980s. And the 1980s, in their sweetest moment, were made of "Sugar."

HENRY ARMSTRONG

"THE GREATEST BOXER WHO EVER LIVED."

BEAU JACK

achieved the unthinkable by 1938, taking the world championship titles in the featherweight, welterweight, and lightweight divisions within just ten months' time. "Hammerin' Hank" even risked a jaunt into the middleweight division in 1940, coming to a draw against champion Ceferino García. His true domain, however, was to be the welterweight division, in which he triumphed a total of 19 times—at up to five times per month. Armstrong's star first began to sink with two defeats against Fritzie Zivic in early 1941. His impressive career then finally ended four years later. Henry Jackson, Armstrong's real name, did not fade from the public eye, however. He starred as himself in a movie about his career and became a bar owner. Later he was forced into complete retirement by various illnesses, including the boxers' disease *pugilistica dementia*.

After his death in October 1988, doctors discovered that his heart was a third larger than normal. Few who had seen the "Hurricane" in action were surprised by this fact.

In our modern times, in which the opposing parties negotiate over the fighters' maximum winnings with the stamina of bazaar traders before a boxing contract is signed, Henry Armstrong's career in the ring must appear both astounding and prehistoric. "Hurricane Hank," as he was called, blew across the international boxing scene like a force of nature in the late 1930s, caring nothing for pounds as long as he was able to fight. And he could afford not to worry: His impressive, mobile attacking style was virtually irresistible in his day and brought him world championship titles in three different weight divisions.

According to the legend surrounding Armstrong, the young worker on the Missouri-

Pacific Railroad let the hammer fall the moment he heard of the fees being paid in prize boxing. His last purported words to his team were "I'll be back in a Cadillac." Then he left to fully concentrate on his sport. After an imposing career as an amateur (58 victories in 62 matches), this child of a multi-cultural family from the cotton plantations of Mississippi then suffered three losses in his first four professional matches and several lean years as a beginner. It was not until 1936 that he was discovered by the blues singer Al Jolson during a fight for the California featherweight championship. Under the singer's patronage, Armstrong became an exceptional boxer, who had

SPECIAL: A boxer with a big heart
BORN: 12-12-1912, Columbus, Mississippi (USA)—died 10-24-1988
NICKNAME: Hammerin' or Hurricane Hank
BOXING RECORD: 181 professional bouts, 152 wins, 8 draws, 21 losses, 26 world championship bouts (1 in featherweight, 2 in lightweight, 22 in welterweight, 1 in middleweight)
FIRST WORLD CHAMPIONSHIP BOUT: 1937 (TKO win 6th round Peter Sarron, featherweight)
LAST WORLD CHAMPIONSHIP BOUT: 1941 (TKO win 12th round Fritzie Zivic, welterweight)
WORLD CHAMPIONSHIP TITLES:
1937–38 (featherweight)
1938–39 (light welterweight)
1938–40 (welterweight)

BARNEY ROSS

**"HE COULD
MAKE YOU LOOK
AWFULLY CHEAP."**

JIMMY McLARNIN

The opponents faced off three times between 1934 and 1935 in front of a total of 90,000 fans in open-air arenas. And each time the decision was hotly contented. Ross was declared the victor in the first and third fight and was thus once again champion and "Boxer of the Year." By 1937 his exceptional reputation in the sport had been further underscored with title defenses against Izzy Jannazzo and Ceferino García. In the following year, however, Henry Armstrong ended Ross' reign as three-fold world champion to become the next great welterweight champion of the era. Physically in poor condition, Ross retired from the sport immediately after the painful decision defeat to "Hurricane Hank" (Henry Amstrong) at 28 years of age.

Ross received high honors for his service in World War II. He also suffered greatly when treatment of a wound left him with a temporary drug addiction. In the end it was cancer that would knock out the first light welterweight champion, however. Ross succumbed to the disease in 1967.

Just like the kosher meat Ross' father sold in his butcher shop in Chicago, Barnet Rosofsky always offered perfect quality during the nine splendid years of his professional career. And while the father was shot by robbers in his shop, the son always managed to elegantly extract himself from even the greatest dangers. Fighting under the name "Barney Ross," he was not once knocked out in 81 bouts and collected world championship titles in three weight divisions.

Always immaculate in appearance, the youngster's problem was that he fell exactly between the lightweight and welterweight classes when in ideal condition. In June 1933, however, this handicap became an advantage when the reigning lightweight champion Tony Canzoneri agreed to enter the ring with Ross in an in-between-division challenge. A better stylist, the challenger won two titles with a victory on points: the lightweight and the light welterweight title, the latter of which had been created only seven years previously. It was this light welterweight class on which Ross then concentrated. By 1935, Ross had won nine victories in the new division. He then continued his career in the welterweight division, going down in the annals of boxing history with a series of duels against Jimmy McLarnin that began in 1934.

McLarnin would become for Ross what Frazier was later to be for Ali—the ultimate incentive to fully develop his athletic potential.

SPECIAL: Champion between weight divisions
BORN: 12-23-1909 in New York (USA) —died 01-17-1967
NICKNAME: Pride of the Ghetto
BOXING RECORD: 81 professional bouts, 73 wins, 3 draws, 4 losses, 1 no-decision bout, 16 world championship bouts
FIRST WORLD CHAMPIONSHIP BOUT: 1933 (win on points 10th round Tony Canzoneri, lightweight and light welterweight)
LAST WORLD CHAMPIONSHIP BOUT: 1938 (loss on points 15th round Henry Armstrong, welterweight)
WORLD CHAMPIONSHIP TITLES:
1933 (lightweight)
1933–35 (light welterweight)
1934, 1935–38 (welterweight)

GEORGE "KID" LAVIGNE · FRANK ERNE · JOE GANS · OSCAR "BATTLING" NELSON · AD WOLGAST · WILLIE RITCHIE · FREDDIE WELSH · BENNY LEONARD · ROCKY KANSAS SAMMY MANDELL · TONY CANZONERI · LOU AMBERS · HENRY ARMSTRONG · SAMMY ANGOTT · LEW JENKINS · BEAU JACK · BOB MONTGOMERY · IKE WILLIAMS · JIMMY CARTER · JOE BROWN · CARLOS ORTIZ · ISMAEL LAGUNA · KEN BUCHANAN · ROBERTO DURAN · SUZUKI "GUTS" ISHIMATSU · ESTEBAN DEJESUS · JIM WATT · ALEXIS ARGUELLO

LIGHTWEIGHT

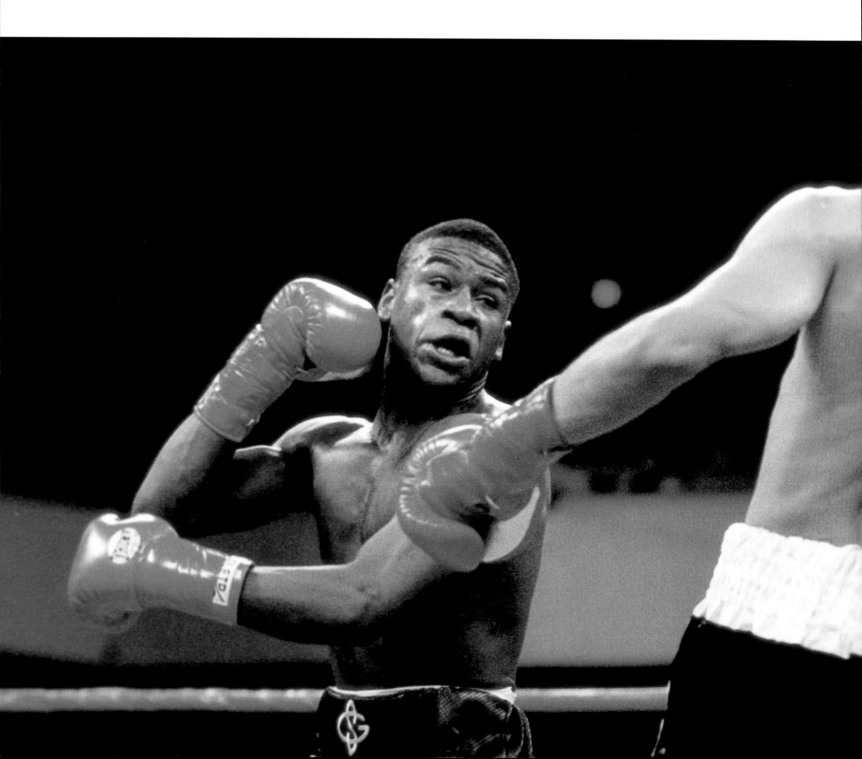

RAY MANCINI · LIVINGSTONE BRAMBLE · HECTOR CAMACHO · JULIO CESAR CHAVEZ PERNELL WHITAKER · MIGUEL ANGEL GONZALEZ · ORZOUBEK NAZAROV · STEVE JOHNSTON — SUPER FEATHERWEIGHT — JOHNNY DUNDEE · TOD MORGAN KID CHOCOLATE · GABRIEL "FLASH" ELORDE · HIROSHI KOBAYASHI · ALFREDO ESCALERA · SAM SERRANO · ALEXIS ARGUELLO · JULIO CESAR CHAVEZ · BRIAN MITCHELL AZUMAH NELSON · GENARO HERNANDEZ · YONG SOO CHOI · FLOYD MAYWEATHER JR.

TOUGH CHARACTERS

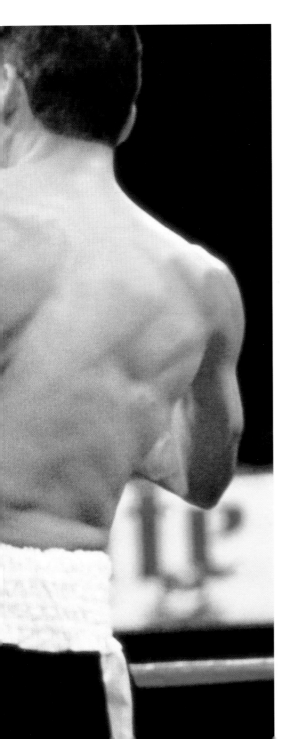

Small men must quickly learn how to make others respect them. It therefore comes as no surprise that lightweights were already an established concept at the beginning of the century, and that not just in the inner circle of the boxing world. The best athletes in this division up to 135 lbs were among the best prize boxers of that era and earned five-figure boxing purses of which most heavyweights could only dream. In the first decade of the 20th century, the marathon ring duels between Frank Erne, Joe Gans, Jimmy Britt, and Oscar "Battling" Nelson attracted audiences just as large as those for heavyweight fights. And it was in this decade that Benny Leonard, a "light" champion, advanced to become the most unanimously admired boxer in the sport.

Punches that fall like lightening and an unquenchable thirst for victory are the ingredients for the best title fights in this weight division, for which records have been kept since 1886. These fights were often turned into an extended series of battles with ever-changing victors, such as the bouts between Tony Canzoneri and Barney Ross (1933–35), Beau Jack and Bob Montgomery (1943–44) or Vinny Pazienza and Greg Haugen (1987–88). The temporary dominance of Latin American champions like Carlos Ortiz, Edwin Rosario, and the legendary Roberto Duran has now given way to truly multicultural competition with contenders and titleholders in the lightweight division meanwhile coming from every corner of the globe. The intermediate super lightweight or junior welterweight division up to 140 lbs, introduced back in 1921, has produced nearly exactly as many quality fighters. Exceptional boxers such as Wilfred Benitez, Aaron Pryor, and Julio Cesar Chavez fought their best fights in this class.

Floyd Mayweather vs. Angelo Nunez, Los Angeles, 1997.

121

ROBERTO DURAN

SPECIAL: Won titles in four different weight divisions between 1972 and 1990

BORN: 06-16-1951 in Guarare (PAN)

NICKNAME: Manos de Piedra

BOXING RECORD:
119 professional bouts, 104 wins, 15 losses, 22 world championship bouts (13 in lightweight, 2 in welterweight, 3 in light middleweight, 3 in middleweight, 1 in super middleweight)

FIRST WORLD CHAMPIONSHIP BOUT:
1972 (TKO win 13th round Ken Buchanan, WBA lightweight)

LAST WORLD CHAMPIONSHIP BOUT:
1998 (TKO loss 3rd round William Joppy, WBA middleweight)

WORLD CHAMPIONSHIP TITLES:
1972–78 (lightweight)
1980 (welterweight)
1983–84 (light middleweight)
1989 (middleweight)
1985–87 (heavyweight)

The people in his home country of Panama say he was born to box. And they say there is proof of it, too. But who needs proof after having once seen this four-time world champion in the ring?

Roberto Duran was not yet 14 when he managed to beat up adult opponents in semi-legal street fights in the *barrios* of Panama City. It was one of the many sources of cash, including shining shoes, begging and stealing, that the school dropout used to secure the basic survival of himself and his eight siblings. The rough and tumble youngster was soon given the nickname "Manos de Piedra," as it appeared he really did have hands made of steel. It is said that he once knocked a horse unconscious with his right fist. Usually, however, his victims were men—initially young amateurs then experienced professionals who were nearly always forced to relent to the anger and speed of his attacks before the final round. Viewed in retrospect this was no surprise. After all, Duran was well on his way to becoming a legend.

"I want to 'keel' him," was usually all that this dark horse uttered in broken English before his first big fights in the USA. A stereotypical macho, Duran anticipated the destruction of his opponents with something akin to glee in his pre-fight comments. And yet, he was not necessarily the type of boxer to fell his opponents with a single punch. Duran gradually pulled them into deep water with untiring attacks to the body, and then effectively finished them off in later rounds. "When the foundation crumbles," he once said with a grin, "then the building collapses." The high-handed athlete seldom felt pity for those he defeated. As one of his opponents was being carried out to the hospital on a stretcher Duran commented: "Next time I will send him to the grave!"

Anger alone could never have bought Duran far enough for the chance to fight against the reigning lightweight WBA world champion Ken Buchanan in June 1972, however. His manager Carlos Eleta had quickly hired two famous trainers, Ray Arcel and Freddie Brown, to polish this "diamond in the raw." The experts were thus not surprised when the 21-year-old dethroned the Scottish champion in Madison Square Garden in New York in the 13th round. Duran had not only acquired the title fair and square, he held on to it, too. By 1979 he had equaled the still valid record of 12 successful title defenses in his weight class and advanced

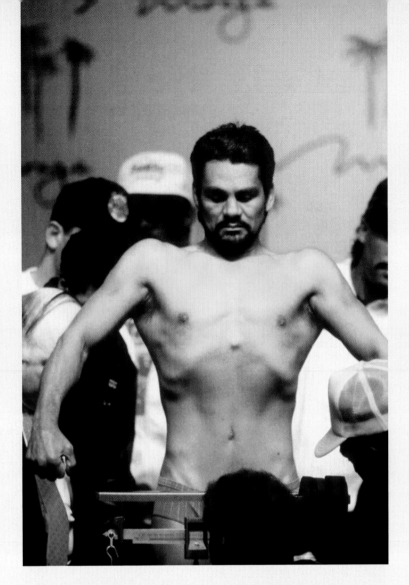

"HE WAS A FIGHTER FROM THE START."

JOHN SCHULIAN

to uncontested champion with a KO victory over Esteban DeJesus, who had previously been the first opponent to defeat Duran in a tune-up match. A mere one year later, he took the final step toward the Olympus of the boxing world, defeating the previously unbeaten welterweight world champion Sugar Ray Leonard on points.

Duran was at the high point of his much sought-after reputation as an exceptional boxer when, in a rematch five months later, he unexpectedly disappointed his fans. Frustrated by the more agile Leonard who was far outboxing him, Panama's icon of manliness gave up in the eighth round with the now-famous words "No mas!" (No more!). Following another points defeat in 1982 against light middleweight champion Wilfred Benitez and a lost

tune-up match, Duran's career appeared to be over. The Latino star reinvented himself, however, just in time for his 33rd birthday. A 5-to-2 outsider, he claimed an early victory over Davey Moore in June 1983, replacing Moore as the WBA champ in the light middleweight division. He proudly commented: "Now I am Roberto Duran again."

In the mid-1980s Duran once again appeared to be at the end of his career after defeats against Marvin Hagler and Thomas Hearns. And yet, he again returned as a champion. In February 1989, the 37-year-old Duran gave an astounded audience in Atlantic City an impressive demonstration in the fine art of boxing, outdoing the feared puncher Iran Barkley, WBC middleweight world champion, in 15 rounds. The rest of his unparalleled

career in the ring, which lasted until 2001, was a mixture of mediocrity and nostalgia. A third duel with Leonard in December 1989 provided little excitement and Duran lost it just as he did later fights with Hector Camacho Jr., Vinny Pazienza, and William Joppy, which the 47-year-old demanded in 1998 in an attempt to take the WBA middleweight championship title.

Duran did not last even last three rounds in the final fight. Duran had boldly demanded a monument to himself upon returning to Panama after his triumph over Barkley. But what was the point? For the people of Panama and boxing *aficionados* everywhere, this victor in more than a hundred professional fights will always remain what he was at the high point of his career—a man born to box.

ALEXIS ARGUELLO

Anyone who wants to be not just a world champion but also a true champ needs only to follow Alexis Arguello's recipe for victory. The first titleholder from Nicaragua was not only a charismatic athlete of extraordinary talents who became the king of three weight divisions—he also inevitably chose the most dangerous of all his challengers as his opponents. "Bring me the best," was his motto, "and I'll knock him out." For most, this would have led to being quickly dethroned. Arguello, however, managed to win a total of 19 of 20 title fights in eight years.

The child of a large family, Arguello began successfully fighting for boxing purses of under ten dollars at the age of 16. It was the same drive that several years later caused him to beg for the chance to spar with the reigning featherweight champion Ruben Olivares. The Mexican managed to send Arguello home with a black eye from this training duel. In November 1974, however, Arguello took his revenge in Inglewood, California, knocking Olivares out in the 13th round of their fight for the WBA title in the fully packed Great Western Forum. This was the dawn of a shining era for the telegenic victor who had been outpointed by Ernesto Marcel during his first attempt at the title in spring.

At 5'9", Agruello was exceptionally tall and always had the better range. By 1982 he had triumphed over all his rivals in title bouts and sailed upward in the weight divisions. He took the WBC junior lightweight title from Alfredo Escalera in 1978 and dethroned Jim Watt, lightweight world champion in the same association, in 1981. His feared hooks felled challengers such as Royal Kobayashi, Rafael "Bazooka" Limon, Bobby Chacon, and Ray Mancini. Arguello nearly took a fourth championship belt in title bouts with light welterweight champion Aaron Pryor in 1982 and 1983. On both occasions, however, he was bested by his contender's superior stamina.

In his 19 years as a professional before retiring in 1986, Arguello earned enough money to live in luxury in the location of his choice, Miami. The Sandinista regime soon confiscated the majority of his earnings, however, and the rest was consumed by three divorces. The ever-charming philanthropist thus made a short and disappointing attempt at a comeback at age 42. Since then, diverse drugs have become his new contenders.

"BRING ME THE BEST AND I'LL KNOCK HIM OUT."

ALEXIS ARGUELLO

SPECIAL: The first titleholder from Nicaragua
BORN: 04-19-1952, Managua (NCA)
BOXING RECORD:
88 Professional bouts, 80 wins, 8 losses, 22 world championship bouts (6 in featherweight, 9 in super featherweight, 5 in lightweight, 2 in light welterweight)
FIRST WORLD CHAMPIONSHIP BOUT:
1974 (loss on points 15th round Ernesto Marcel, WBA featherweight)
LAST WORLD CHAMPIONSHIP BOUT:
1983 (KO loss 10th round Aaron Pryor, WBA Light welterweight)
WORLD CHAMPIONSHIP TITLES:
1974–76 (featherweight)
1978–80 (junior lightweight)
1981–82 (lightweight)

For as long as he was active, Carlos Ortiz was regarded as an exemplary professional. When the purse was right, he would fight anyone, anywhere. This made him one of the most dangerous challengers in the late 1950s and an uncontested champion in the 1960s who took the title of world champion, literally. Tokyo, Manila, Mexico—Ortiz went anywhere a top-ranking challenger was to be found and risked his title to fight him.

The son of a Puerto Rican family that had immigrated to New York, Ortiz could afford risky duels. In his glory days, he was "a perfect fighting machine" with an optimal combination of speed, power, and strategic intelligence. Ortiz had begun his professional boxing career as an 18-year-old. His first 27 fights were a perfect success series. He even came out as TKO victor in an explosive match with Len Matthews in Philadelphia which he took part in without his manager's approval. A short while later a TKO victory over Kenny Lane in 1959 rendered him the world champion in the revived light welterweight division. Ortiz first experienced true recognition from 1962 onward after taking the lightweight title from long-standing champion Joe Brown in Las Vegas on a points victory.

By 1968, his ability to find the appropriate tactic for each opponent enabled Ortiz to dominate his division with only a short interruption. During this time period he successfully fought top-ranking boxers such as Flash Elorde and Sugar Ramos twice each and came out victorious in two of three fights with Ismael Laguna, who briefly took the title from him in their first fight in 1965.

Ortiz made nine successful title defenses in six countries before finally losing his world champion status on a decision to Carlos Teo Cruz in June 1968. A sudden comeback in 1971 ended with a TKO defeat to Ken Buchanan after ten victories. It was Ortiz' first and only TKO defeat in all of his 70 professional fights.

Ortiz was the established idol of the New York Puerto Rican community, which once convinced him to run for the Bronx City Council. As a retiree, he lost a large share of his fortune following a bout with alcohol and at one point made his living as a taxi driver. Finally, he began working as a trainer, an activity that allowed him to put his enormous knowledge to far better use—and enabled him to once again welcome every halfway decent boxer into his ring.

"IN TOP SHAPE HE WAS A PERFECT FIGHTING MACHINE."

THE RING

SPECIAL: A technician who managed to turn himself into a true fighter
BORN: 09-09-1936 in Ponce (PUR)
BOXING RECORD:
  70 professional bouts
  61 wins, 1 draw
  7 losses
  1 no-decision bout
  world championship bouts (5 in light welterweight, 13 in lightweight)
FIRST WORLD CHAMPIONSHIP BOUT:
  1959 (TKO win 2nd round Kenny Lane, light welterweight)
LAST WORLD CHAMPIONSHIP BOUT:
  1968 (loss on points 15th round Carlos Teo Cruz, lightweight)
WORLD CHAMPIONSHIP TITLES:
  1959–60 (junior welterweight)
  1962–65, 1965–68 (lightweight)

IKE WILLIAMS

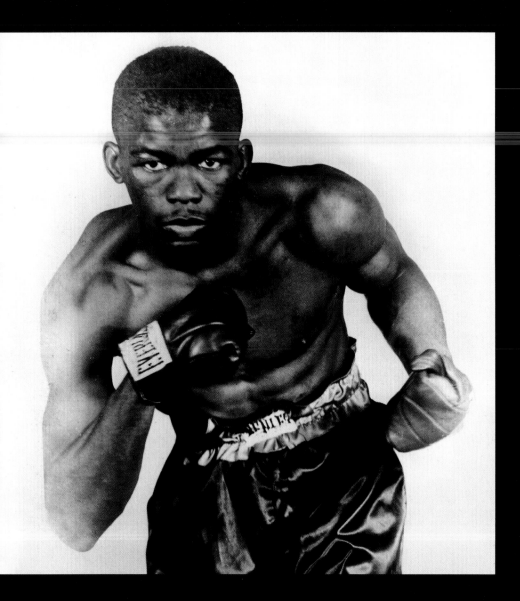

SPECIAL: A highly gifted outsider
BORN: 08-02-1923 in Brunswick, Georgia (USA)—died 09-05-1994
BOXING RECORD:
154 professional bouts
124 wins
5 draws
25 losses
10 world championship bouts
FIRST WORLD CHAMPIONSHIP BOUT:
1945 (KO win 2nd round Juan Zurita NBA title)
LAST WORLD CHAMPIONSHIP BOUT:
1951 (TKO loss 14th round Jimmy Carter)
WORLD CHAMPIONSHIP TITLES:
1945–47 (NBA)
1947–51

> ## "A DAMN GOOD BOXER, MAYBE THE BEST IN THE LIGHTWEIGHT DIVISION."
>
> BOB MONTGOMERY

Given the considerable number of his successes and the large boxing purses he collected, Ike Williams today appears as one of the greatest soldiers of fortune of his day. This outstanding lightweight of the post-war era held the world championship title in his class for four or six years, depending on interpretation. During this time, he was able to defeat opponents some of whose names would later become more respected than his own. For as long as he was active, however, Williams had to fight against opponents that lined up to meet him outside the ring. And those who helped him demanded a high price.

Born in Georgia as Isiah Williams, he became a professional in Trenton, New Jersey, at 16 years of age, demonstrating extraordinary talent early on. Williams had quick legs and moved fast. The hard series of lightening hits he landed with both fists made him look more like a middleweight. The Mexican Juan Zurita experienced just such an onslaught in April 1945, losing his world championship title, which was recognized by the National Boxing Association (NBA), to the 21-year-old in just two rounds. And this technique was still effective two years later when Williams won the title unification against his fierce mutual opponent Bob Montgomery, New York Boxing Association champion, with a TKO. Williams thus exacted impressive revenge for an earlier TKO defeat and remained uncontested world champion until 1951.

Such fights were first made possible, however, because Williams had himself represented by the influential mobster Blinky Palermo.

Williams had been forced into signing a pact with the mafia helper when he was threatened with a long-term ban from the ring for leaving his manager Connie McCarthy, an alcohol addict. Palermo's connections opened the door for Williams to important, lucrative fights in which he was able to defeat stars like Johnny Bratton, Beau Jack, and Kid Gavilan. Often, however, Palermo kept entire boxing purses that should have gone to Williams. He claimed to have strictly refused offers to purposely lose fights, such that in May 1951 when Williams risked his title against Jimmy Carter and, weakened by a weight loss regime, lost in the 14th round. It was the last title fight for Ike, who left the sport in 1955 after a total of 154 fights and lost his savings through poor investments. At the end of his life he was dependent on welfare.

BENNY LEONARD

We will never know whether he really engaged in regular sparring matches with a tomcat in his apartment to improve his reflexes. It is entirely possible, however, as Benny Leonard was willing to try anything that promised to perfect his movement in the ring during his active years as a boxer. In that early heyday of his sport, when champions like Jack Dempsey and Harry Greb sought fame and fortune in all-out slugfests, Leonard stood out as being one of the thinking boxers of his era—and was honored as a savvy and stylish boxer in Jewish circles and beyond with the nickname "Ghetto Wizard."

As a scrawny boy growing up on the Lower East Side in New York, the youngster born as Benjamin Leinert had to find a way to keep from becoming a favorite victim of bullies. His first boxing winnings, however, were kept a secret. His father Gershon Leinert, a candy dealer, and his family frowned upon boxing. Supposedly it was not until his son presented him with a 20-dollar bill after winning one of the professional fights he had been taking part in since he was 15 years old that his father was convinced. Several years later, manager Billy Gibson took notice of Leonard and provided him with the meticulous trainer George Engel. Under Engel's watchful eye, the youngster grew into an extremely fit, savvy boxer who was virtually impossible to beat.

Leonard acquired the world championship title in May 1917 with a TKO victory over Freddie Welsh and remained champion through four title defenses until 1925. His most fascinating duels were the no-decision bouts, fights without an official result, in which he outboxed well-known heroes of the ring such as Jack Britton, Johnny Dundee, Patsy Cline and Lew Tendler on what was sometimes almost a weekly basis. Leonard did lose one fight for the welterweight title with Jack Britton in 1922, but only because of being disqualified for hitting Britton when he was already down.

The "Wizard" led an exemplary life and had sufficient savings to retire on in 1925. The crash on the New York stock exchange in 1929 wiped out his savings, however, causing him to return to the ring for an additional 18 welterweight victories. Leonard finally retired for good in 1931 at the age of 36 after a TKO defeat against Jimmy McLarnin. Later an actor, a hockey team financer in Pittsburgh and a boxing referee, Leonard died in 1947 from a heart attack suffered while refereeing a fight in New York.

"LEONARD MADE BOXING LOOK ROMANTIC."

HERBERT G. GOLDMAN

SPECIAL: The first great methodical modern boxer
BORN: 04-07-1896 in New York, New York (USA)—died 04-18-1947
NICKNAME: Ghetto Wizard
BOXING RECORD:
   212 professional bouts
   184 wins, 6 draws, 22 losses
   8 world championship bouts
   (7 in lightweight, 1 in welterweight)
FIRST WORLD CHAMPIONSHIP BOUT:
   1917 (TKO win 9th round Freddie Welsh)
LAST WORLD CHAMPIONSHIP BOUT:
   1923 (win on points 15th round Lew Tendler)
WORLD CHAMPIONSHIP TITLES:
   1917–25

THE GROIN AND LOWER ABDOMEN PROTECTOR

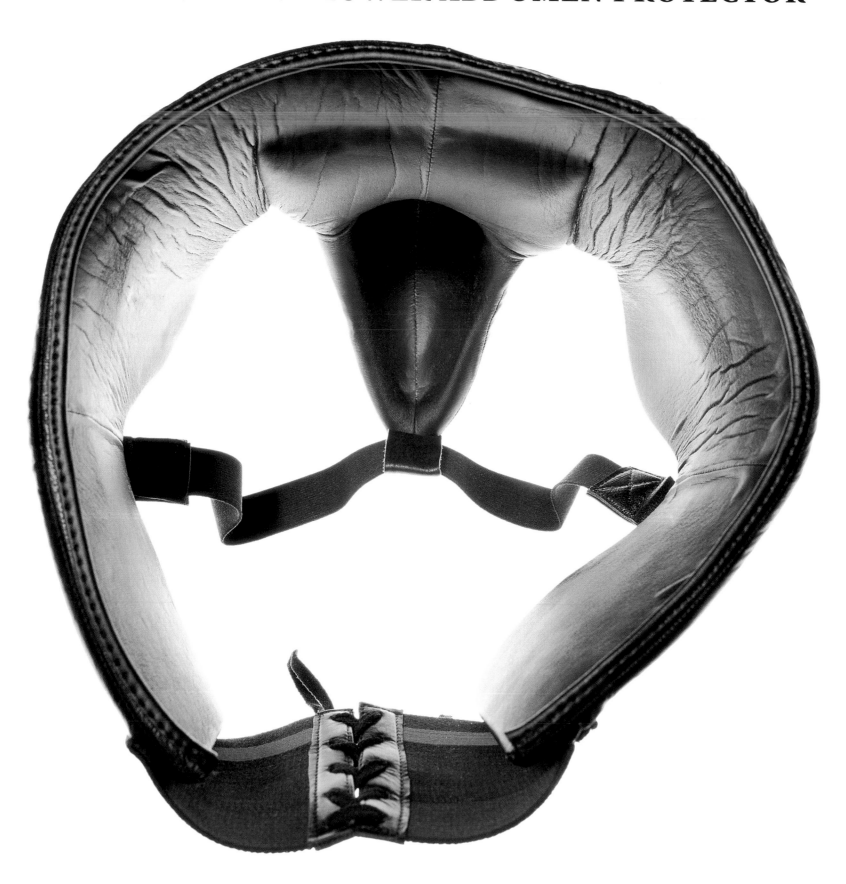

The modern successors of the old "Foul-proof Taylor" unite wearing comfort with a high level of protection *(above)*. Here, they offer a protective shield for Oscar De La Hoya *(right)* in a training fight.

Back when real and pretend hits below the belt were as common as other dirty tricks, groin and lower abdomen protection had a name all its own. Boxers did not wear a protective cup, but simply a "Taylor." It was toward the end of the Roaring Twenties that James P. Taylor, a New Yorker manufacturer of shoe soles, presented his invention to the world. In his store in Brooklyn, the cunning merchant produced the first models for a groin and lower abdomen protector that boxers could wear for sparring and fights. They were made of chamois and aluminum. He then took his prototype of patent number 1830572 to various boxing commissions and countless gyms, where he let himself be hit in the abdomen with a baseball bat and, to the astonishment of all, remained unharmed. The delicately built man soon acquired the nickname "Foul-proof Taylor" as a result of this impressive demonstration, but did not meet with immediate business success. Health protection measures were, at that time, regarded as unnecessary in men's sports.

The ongoing debate about interrupted fights reached its climax with Max Schmeling's disqualification victory over Jack Sharkey in June 1930. No one was particularly happy that the German had become the new heavyweight champion as a result of a low blow dealt by his opponent in the 4th round—after all, great fights were supposed to be won by means of athletic virtue and not disqualification. Taylor's invention arrived just in time for a new rule introduced three weeks later by the New York Boxing Commission. According to this "No-foul Rule," hits below the belt were no longer to be punished with immediate disqualification as the opponent could protect himself sufficiently with the new "foul-proof cup."

Taylor was thus finally able to market his patent and the sport of boxing was rid of at least one ignominious method of ending a fight early. The verdict of this leading boxing commission was quickly accepted elsewhere as well.

Today, groin and lower abdomen protection is an official requirement and the regulators for the established world associations have a standard catalog of disciplinary measures implemented when a boxer strikes another below the belt. The first low blow evokes a reprimand, the second a warning and deduction of points—not until the third low blow is the contestant disqualified. In the rulebook of the International Boxing Federation, specific note is made of the fact that "a championship fight cannot be ended with a hit below the belt" as the groin and lower abdomen protector offers "sufficient protection." A boxer who has taken such a hit is given up to five minutes time-out to recover from the low blow. If he afterwards refuses to continue the fight, he is disqualified by the referee without further ado. After all, as "Foul-proof-Taylor" already so effectively proved decades ago—not even a weapon far harder than a fist can do lasting damage to a well-made groin and lower body protector.

GEORGE DIXON · TERRY MCGOVERN · ABE ATTELL · JOHNNY KILBANE
JOHNNY DUNDEE · ANDRE ROUTIS · BATTLING BATTALINO · FREDDIE
MILLER · HENRY ARMSTRONG · KID CHOCOLATE · CHALKY WRIGHT
WILLIE PEP · SAL BARTOLO · SANDY SADDLER · DAVEY MOORE · ULTIMINIO "SUGAR"
RAMOS · VICENTE SALDIVAR · JOHNNY FAMECHON · ERNESTO MARCEL
RUBEN OLIVARES · BOBBY CHACON · DANNY LOPEZ · EUSEBIO PEDROZA

FEATHERWEIGHT

SALVADOR SANCHEZ · AZUMAH NELSON · BARRY MCGUIGAN · ANTONIO ESPARRAGOZA · JORGE PAEZ · KYUN-YUNG PARK · TOM JOHNSON ELOY ROJAS · LUISITO ESPINOSA · WILFREDO VASQUEZ · PRINCE NASEEM HAMED SUPER BANTAMWEIGHT — WILFREDO GOMEZ · DANIEL ZARAGOZA WELCOME NCITA · WILFREDO VASQUEZ · KENNEDY MCKINNEY · VUYANI BUNGU · MARCO ANTONIO BARRERA · ANTONIO CERMENO · ERIK MORALES

SMALL AND PUGNACIOUS

The best of them can throw punches like the big guys while dancing about the ring as though floating. The history of the featherweights is a complicated one nonetheless, for just as the greatest talents in this weight class present themselves so pugnaciously in the limelight, so the influential men in the background have often had to fight tooth and nail for recognition of their titles.

It began right from the start, with a historic duel between the New Zealander Billy Murphy and the "Belfast Spider" Ike Weir on January 13, 1890, in San Francisco. Murphy won the fight with a KO in the 12th round. Today, this fight is considered the first official title bout in the history of the featherweight division. The majority of the American reports on the fight regarded it as a British title bout only, however, and viewed their exceptionally talented compatriot George Dixon ("Little Chocolate") as

the true champion. This unfortunate dispute also extended to the issue of weight limits: Not until 1920 did the United States agree to the upper limit of 126 lbs which is still valid today.

The early high point of the sport at the start of the 1920s, in which heroes like Terry McGovern, Abe Attell, and Johnny Dundee fought furious bouts, thus did not receive the attention it should have. Nor did this change until the fights between Willie Pep and Sandy Saddler stole the show from the heavier classes in the 1940s. This weight division, as well the junior featherweight division (122 lbs) first established in 1976, has since been a fixed category in which many great bouts are fought. Duels such as those between Vicente Saldivar and Howard Winstone (1965–67) or Salvador Sanchez and Azumah Nelson (1982) have been among the best boxing has to offer.

Prince Naseem Hamed vs. Cesar Soto, Detroit, 1999.

EUSEBIO PEDROZA

SPECIAL: A perfect stylist and a quiet champion
BORN: 03-02-1953, Panama City (PAN)
NICKNAME: The Scorpion
BOXING RECORD:
  49 professional bouts
  42 wins
  1 draw
  6 losses
  22 world championship bouts
  (1 in bantamweight, 21 in lightweight)
FIRST WORLD CHAMPIONSHIP BOUT:
  1976 (KO loss 2nd round Alfonso Zamora, bantamweight)
LAST WORLD CHAMPIONSHIP BOUT:
  1985 (loss on points 15th round Barry McGuigan)
WORLD CHAMPIONSHIP TITLES:
  1978–85

"UNMATCHED ABILITIES AND FUROR"

THE RING

Panama's boxers had just immortalized themselves in the annals of the featherweight world championship with Ernesto Marcel and Rafael Ortega when the small isthmus republic outdid itself one more time in the late 1970s with a genuine masterpiece. Eusebio Pedroza was not just the undisputed world champion in the WBA records between 1978 and 1985, he was a veritable champion for fans and experts alike.

Polished to perfection in the legendary "Maranon Gym" in Panama City, the tall, young professional's complex talent soon set him apart from the rest. Pedroza could outbox his opponents when he wanted to or end the fight prematurely with a rain of hard punches. And he was nearly unbeatable in the final third of a ring duel. The champion

Alfonso Zamora had been able to stop the 22-year-old challenger in 1975 in two rounds in the bantamweight class, but as a featherweight Pedroza enjoyed an extended series of victories. After his triumph over title-holder Cecilio Lastra in April 1978, he successfully defended his championship 19 times in seven years. He thus came just one fight short of the record set in this weight class by Abe Attell.

Pedroza risked his title on four continents, often against top-ranking opponents. In the process he defeated Ruben Olivares, Juan LaPorte, and his countryman Jorge Lujan, all former world champions, as well as Rocky Lockridge (two points victories), who would go on to become a world champion. Only showdowns with the competing WBC

champions Danny Lopez and Salvador Sanchez could have further enhanced his reputation—but the promised title unifications never got past the planning stage. So, Pedroza continued his string of victories unabated until being outboxed by Barry McGuigan, another exceptionally talented boxer in his weight class, in June 1985 at the age of 32.

The decision victory coming after three knockdowns in the packed Queens Park Rangers soccer stadium in London was the *finale furioso* for the great champion, who immediately retired. In contrast to other world champions, Pedroza had saved enough money to quickly end a brief comeback attempt in lightweight. When last heard from, he was working as a detective in Panama City.

SPECIAL: A short life full of athletic triumphs

BORN: 02-03-1958 in Santiago (MEX) —died 08-12-1982

BOXING RECORD:
46 professional bouts
44 wins
1 draw
1 loss
10 world championship bouts

FIRST WORLD CHAMPIONSHIP BOUT:
1980 (TKO win 13th round Danny Lopez, WBC)

LAST WORLD CHAMPIONSHIP BOUT:
1982 (TKO win 15th round Azumah Nelson)

WORLD CHAMPIONSHIP TITLES:
1980–82

"ONE OF THE GREATEST FIGHTERS IN THE HISTORY OF MEXICAN BOXING."

THE RING

It was as if he sensed that he did not have much time left: Salvador Sanchez raced furiously to the top of the featherweight class in the late 1970s and left his lasting mark on the sport during his few professional years. The blond Mexican lost only one of 46 fights when he was outpointed by Antonio Becerra in a bout for the national title in 1977. He otherwise remained unbeaten until his early death in an accident, at which time experts already regarded him as one of the best boxers of all time in his weight class.

Could he have become the best of all? The only thing we can say for sure is that few boxers before or after could strike a punch as quickly and powerfully as Sanchez. The right-hander also had a reasonably good jab and amazing reflexes that allowed him to skillfully outbox his competitors for the full allotment of rounds. His special ability, however, lay in the explosive nature of his hits, which he landed with both fists. They took down the reigning WBC world champion Danny Lopez in 13 rounds when Lopez risked his title against Sanchez in 1980, as well as four of nine challengers who the new champion triumphed over the in next two years. Because of the larger boxing purses offered there, Sanchez defended his status exclusively in the USA and quickly become an idol for boxing Hispanics because of his impressive achievements in the ring between Arizona and California.

The ambitious champion faced some of the toughest opponents of his day, yet Sanchez rose to all challenges with bravura. He was named "Boxer of the Year" (together with Sugar Ray Leonard) in 1981 thanks to his TKO victory in the prestigious bout with the previously unbeaten junior featherweight champion Wilfredo Gomez. His TKO victory in the last round of his fight with the young Azumah Nelson one year later was one of the most thrilling bouts of the 1980s. Tragically it was also Sanchez' last. Just a few weeks after beating Nelson, the freshly confirmed champion died in an automobile accident in August 1982 when he collided head-on with an oncoming tractor on a country road north of Mexico City in his new Porsche. The investigating authorities established that Sanchez had been traveling at an extremely high rate of speed, an observation that had not infrequently occurred to his contenders in the ring as well.

WILFREDO GOMEZ

His strategy, like his personality, was uncomplicated. "I simply hit them until they can't take it anymore," Wilfredo Gomez once admitted, "and then they drop." Those who would believe that one of the most outstanding champions of his era relied on his immense striking power alone are mistaken, however. The greatest talent in the super bantamweight also handled everything else in the ring with ease—and usually better than his competitors as well.

The ambitious youngster had set his sights on a bantamweight title fight in 1977. But as there was no chance for a world championship in this weight class, Gomez shifted to the super bantamweight or junior featherweight class, which had been revived a year before. His KO victory over WBC champion Dong-Kyun Yum was the beginning of a long success story on two accounts: Just as the new weight class aided the challenger from Puerto Rico in becoming an international star, so Gomez helped this intermediate category to gain rapid prominence. Once he had become champion, Gomez held a long and lasting reign over the division. His 17 title defenses in nearly six years, all of which ended in TKOs, are a record even today.

From New York to Kitakyushu, but preferably in his hometown of San Juan, Gomez simply hit all of his challengers until they couldn't take it anymore—among them the excellent bantamweight champions Carlos Zarate and Lupe Pintor, who briefly switched into the higher weight limit to engage in lucrative bouts with him. His first excursion into higher divisions ended with catastrophe in 1981, however. Gomez suffered a fractured cheekbone just several seconds into a showdown with featherweight champion Salvador Sanchez. With his eye swollen shut and unable to fight, he was taken out of the fight in the eighth round. It was the first defeat for this exceptional boxer who remained unbeaten in his weight category.

Gomez later acquired the world championship belts in featherweight and super featherweight in 1984 and 1985, but was not able to successfully defend the titles. Wilfredo Gomez is still regarded as the as the best boxer to come from the island republic which has produced so many talents. His involvement in the drug business, for which he received a jail sentence in 1994, prevented Gomez from becoming an idol, however.

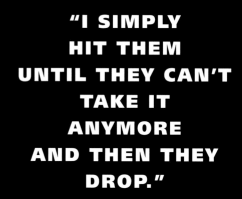

"I SIMPLY HIT THEM UNTIL THEY CAN'T TAKE IT ANYMORE AND THEN THEY DROP."

WILFREDO GOMEZ

SPECIAL: Super bantamweight star
BORN: 10-29-1956, Las Monjas (PUR)
BOXING RECORD: 48 professional bouts
44 wins, 1 draw, 3 losses
23 world championship bouts
FIRST WORLD CHAMPIONSHIP BOUT: 1977
(KO win Dong-Kyun Yum, WBC)
LAST WORLD CHAMPIONSHIP BOUT: 1986
(TKO loss 9th round Alfredo Layne, WBA)
WORLD CHAMPIONSHIP TITLES: 1977–83
(super bantamweight), 1984 (featherweight), 1985–86 (super featherweight)

SANDY SADDLER

rivals, Saddler stole the show from the heavier boxers in three additional, increasingly dirty duels. Due to the dubious nature of the fighting tactics used in them, the three victorious title fights between 1949–51 in the re-established super featherweight category were recognized by only a few commissions.

Saddler lost his title when Pep outboxed him in a rematch less than four months after the first fight. He nonetheless won the belt back with a TKO victory in 1950. It was the last halfway respectable duel between the two, who were initially banned from the sport in the following year after a wild match won early by the younger boxer of the pair. Only Saddler would later comeback as a champion—and would remain champion in name six years long. Several injuries, numerous showdowns against the best lightweights and nearly two years of military service enabled him to engage in only two more title defenses, against Teddy "Red Top" Davis and Flash Elorde. Both bouts were unconvincing.

As dubious as his performance may have been in the ring, Saddler's life between bouts was exceptionally clean: "I didn't drink, I didn't smoke—I lived for boxing," he once said. The aftermath of a taxi accident caused him to retire in 1957 after 162 fights. He soon took a job as a coach in the New York Maritime Union Gym. Alzheimer's disease has left him in need of constant nursing care since the 1990s.

With his towering, thin stature, Joseph "Sandy" Saddler appeared as fragile as if his creator had put him together with matches and chestnut halves. When he took his stance in the ring, however, his opponents nearly always came out the worse for wear. The power that lay in the speed of his unusually long arms made Saddler the hardest puncher in this history of his weight class. He was exceptional enough as it was, however.

Saddler learned the rough art of self-assertion early on in the streets of Harlem after having moved from Boston to New York with his Caribbean family. He was just 17 when he became a professional after a few amateur rounds in 1944. In the next few years he would knock out even stars such as Joe Brown. At age 22 he already had 94 bouts and a three-year waiting period as a trophy challenger behind him when we was finally allowed to box for the title. His unexpected KO victory over long-standing champion Willie Pep in August 1948 made him the star of Madison Square Garden overnight. Together with his arch-

SPECIAL: Greatest featherweight puncher
BORN: 06-23-1926 in Boston, Mass. (USA)
BOXING RECORD: 162 professional bouts, 144 wins, 2 draws, 16 losses, 9 world championship bouts (6 in featherweight, 3 in super featherweight)
FIRST WORLD CHAMPIONSHIP BOUT: 1948 (KO win 4th round Willie Pep)
LAST WORLD CHAMPIONSHIP BOUT: 1956 (TKO win 13th round Flash Elorde)
WORLD CHAMPIONSHIP TITLES: 1948–49, 1950–57

WILLIE PEP

"TRYING TO HIT HIM IS LIKE TRYING TO STAMP OUT A FLAME."

KID CAMPECHE

The poet Philip Levine once referred to him as "tiny, white perfection," while a journalist gave him the nickname "Will o' the Wisp." Taken together, the two compliments provide a fitting description of Willie Pep. Generally viewed as the best featherweight of modern times, Pep perfected a boxing style that blended all the virtues of a defense artist with the stamina of a fighter. "Hitting without being hit," he once explained, "is the object of the game." No one could turn this goal into reality with as much savvy as Pep. "Trying to hit him," said his opponent Kid Campeche after one fight "is like trying to stamp out a fire." The fire of enthusiasm had likely been burning in Guglielmo Papaleo, Pep's real name, since childhood—back when his nearly impoverished father had taken him to watch fights with Batt Battalino, the local hero in featherweight, in Hartford, Connecticut. "Peppie" acquired the needed drive as a teenager on the street, forced to take care of himself early on as a shoe cleaner or by means of other occasional jobs. Even as a young, hopeful amateur, Pep needed every nickel so badly that he once fought twice in one evening at an

amateur tournament in order to double the small sum he received for appearing. By the time he went professional in 1940, he had been beaten only three times in 65 fights. One of these losses was to the much heavier Walker Smith who would later, under the name Sugar Ray Robinson, become champion several times in two weight classes.

The young professional knocked out nearly the entire featherweight ranking list in less than three years with his bobbin' n' weavin' style, consisting of continual back and forth movement with the head and shoulders. Seconded by trainer Bill Gore, the 20-year-old stepped into the ring with titleholder Chalky Wright in November 1942 and became the youngest world champion in his weight class with a unanimous points victory. His untarnished victory series continued for 62 fights until March 1944, when Pep lost on points to the temporarily dethroned lightweight champion Sammy Angott in a non-title fight. Following this defeat, he embarked on an equally astounding series of 73 victories which held until late 1948. During this time period, Pep unified the title, which had been divided

for more than six years, with a TKO victory over NBA champion Sal Bartolo and dominated top caliber rivals such as Phil Terranova and Humberto Sierra. Even his military service in World War II and an airplane crash that forced him to take a five-month break to recover from his injuries in 1947 could not stop the world champion for long.

This became a privilege granted to Sandy Saddler, who stopped Pep cold in October 1948 in the fourth round of their title bout. It was the start of one of the bitterest series of duels in the post-war period. Three months later, Pep was able to take revenge with a points defeat. In September 1950, however, he had to admit he was beaten after seven sloppily boxed rounds. A fourth and final match was equally messy and ended with Pep giving up because one of his eyes was swollen shut. Both Saddler and Pep were suspended from the New York Boxing Commission as a result. He returned to the ring 20 months later, continuing to demonstrate his outstanding boxing skills in tune-up and show fights. One of his last great non-title fights against the reigning champion Hogan

SPECIAL: The model for all strategists in the ring
BORN: 09-19-1922 in Middletown, Connecticut (USA)
NICKNAME: Will o' the Wisp, Peppie
BOXING RECORD:
    242 professional bouts
    230 wins, 1 draw, 11 losses
    14 world championship bouts
FIRST WORLD CHAMPIONSHIP BOUT:
    1942 (win on points 15th round Chalky Wright)
LAST WORLD CHAMPIONSHIP BOUT:
    1951 (TKO loss 9th round Sandy Saddler)
WORLD CHAMPIONSHIP TITLES:
    1942–48
    1949–50

Battled out in four fights, the bitter rivalry with Sandy Saddler *(below right)* increased boxing fans' respect for Willie Pep. Pep won once on points.

"Kid" Bassey ended with the KO defeat of the 36-year-old in September 1958. As was usually the case, Pep had until that point been ahead on the jury's scorecards.

The 43-year-old Pep attempted a comeback in 1965, more as result of financial difficulties than from athletic ambition. This attempt was to end one year later. His passion for gambling and divorces repeatedly ate up the wealth acquired by the good-natured boxer. This retiree with a sense of humor has never lost his will to survive however, working at times as a second, ring referee and tax investigator. "I have a wife and a TV," he said many years ago signalizing inner harmony, "both of them function."

CHAPPIE MORAN · TOMMY KELLY · BILLY PLIMMER · PEDLAR PALMER
HARRY FORBES · FRANKIE NEIL · JIMMY WALSH · JOHNNY COULON · DIGGER
STANLEY · ABE GOLDSTEIN · PANAMA AL BROWN · SIXTO ESCOBAR · LOU
SALICA · MANUEL ORTIZ · VIC TOWEEL · JIMMY CARRUTHERS · EDER JOFRE
MASAHIKO "FIGHTING" HARADA · LIONEL ROSE · RUBEN OLIVARES · RODOLFO
MARTINEZ · ALFONSO ZAMORA · CARLOS ZARATE · JORGE LUJAN · LUPE PINTOR

BANTAMWEIGHT

JEFF CHANDLER · MIGUEL LORA · ORLANDO CANIZALES · RAUL PEREZ LUISITO ESPINOSA · JUNIOR JONES · MBULELO BOTILE · TIM AUSTIN JORGE JULIO · JOHNNY TAPIA — SUPER FLYWEIGHT — **RAFAEL ORONO · CHUL-HO KIM · JIRO WATANABE · KHAOSAI GALAXY · ELLY PICAL GILBERTO ROMAN · SUNG-IL MOON · ROBERT QUIROGA · JULIO CESAR BORBOA · HIROSHI KAWASHIMA · JOHNNY TAPIA · DANNY ROMERO**

TINY WARRIORS

The Spanish painter and playwright Eduardo Arroyo, who dedicated his 1986 play *Bantam* to the boxers in this category, referred to them as "a regiment of small, nervous men." And indeed this fits well with the image of the fighting cock that gave the bantamweight fighters their name and remains a valid image today as well. The best fighters in this class up to 118 lbs (formerly 110 lbs) unfailingly present themselves in just as uncompromisingly determined a manner as the miniature roosters from the district of Bantam on the island of Java. Boxing experts thus soon came to regard their duels as an athletic delicacy. Nor is this any wonder. The tiny athletes can throw lightening punches that both astound and enthrall their audiences.

The bantam boxers have always been regarded as the logical antipodes to the colossal but usually less dynamic heavyweights. With title bouts held since 1856, they were the second officially recognized weight category after the heavyweights. The debate over the recognition due the first champions was long just as combative in nature as the athletes themselves. Europe and America often had different world champions. The end of World War I ushered in the first boom for the small fighters, as stars like Kid Williams, Pete Herman, Joe Lynch and Abe Goldstein engaged in a series of exciting fights. In the long-term, however, the world championship titles became a contest between Latin American and Southeast Asian, regions of the world which later supplied the majority of dominating champions such as Manuel Ortiz, Eder Jofre, Fighting Harada, Carlos Zarate and Khaosai Galaxy (junior bantamweight).

The lack of their own candidates may have led to the decline in interest in this division still noticeable in Europe and the USA. The appeal of bantamweight duels remains undiminished, at least in the Southern Hemisphere, thanks to the continuing rivalry between the Latinos and the Asians.

Paulie Ayala vs. Johnny Tapia, Las Vegas 1999.

KHAOSAI GALAXY

SPECIAL: Champion of his weight division for many years
BORN: 05-15-1959 in Petchaboon (THA)
BOXING RECORD:
50 professional bouts
49 wins
1 loss
19 world championship bouts
FIRST WORLD CHAMPIONSHIP BOUT:
1984 (KO win 6th round Eusebio Espinal, WBA)
LAST WORLD CHAMPIONSHIP BOUT:
1991 (win on points 12th round Armando Castro, WBA)
WORLD CHAMPIONSHIP TITLES:
1984–92 (WBA junior bantamweight)

"MY BOY IS TOO STRONG."

MANAGER NIWAT LAOSUWANWAT

Khaosai Galaxy's goal of boxing like Pone Kingpetch (Thailand), the gifted technical boxer and his country's first world champion, was seldom evident in the ring. Thanks to his range and the uncomfortable southpaw stance, the former kickboxer from Petchaboon had a good chance of dominating his matches with his jab. But his strongest weapon remained his left hand, which was so effective it sometimes appeared to be on loan from much higher weight categories. Galaxy used it to help establish his seven-year reign as undisputed king in the recently established (1980) junior bantamweight division.

It was his mother who taught Khaosai and his twin brother Kaokor their first boxing maneuvers. Later he also admitted that he had learned to box "out of deep respect" for her. She did not live to see her sons' greatest

triumphs, however. These came in November 1984 in Bangkok when Khaosai outboxed Eusebio Espinal in a duel for the vacant WBA title—and then went on to outbox or knock out all of his challengers in 18 successful title bouts. In 1988 and 1989, Kaokor was also able to briefly twice become the WBA champion in the next highest division, but he was not to become a legend. Kaokor became a good professional, Khaosai an all-time great.

The gifted puncher usually engaged in defenses of his title in his home country of Thailand, although a hostile public in Korea or Japan did not really disturb him. Galaxy welcomed his opponents' attacks self-confidently, even with a smile, and then outboxed them in 15 of 18 cases with his superior stamina and excellent condition. According

to Khaosai, he never experienced any nervousness, as "my left hand, the power hand, won every fight for me."

It was to remain this way as well. As a young professional, Galaxy had lost only one tune-up fight, after which he triumphed without interruption. When he retired as the unbeaten world champion in January 1992 after exactly 50 professional fights, he had more or less beaten all of his serious competitors (including Kenji Matsumara and Armando Castro) at least once. Today the popular and deeply religious man of independent means owns a snooker club in Bangkok and has also established an excellent reputation for himself as a singer of Thai folksongs. Khaosai regarded his acceptance to the Boxing Hall of Fame in Canastota, New York, in 1999 as the "greatest honor in my career."

CARLOS ZARATE

Outstanding boxers usually have outstanding fight records. Carlos Zarate, however, had more than just that. When the tall professional challenged the WBC champion Rodolfo Martinez in May 1976, his perfect record encompassed 58 TKO victories in a total of 52 matches won against both amateurs and professionals. It was one of the most unusual success series in modern boxing and was continued almost as if it were matter of course. Zarate also became world champion with a TKO victory over Martinez and is of course regarded as one of the best bantam champions of all times in his home country of Mexico, a land which has produced many champions in this division.

The hard-hitting boy from the *barrio* was never really capable of anything else but boxing. In Ramos Millan, at the edge of Mexico City, he was continually being expelled from schools for fighting—much to the dismay of his single-parent mother. He was soon brought to the gym belonging to trainer "Cuyo" Hernandez, where Carlos ripened to an unbeaten young professional by sparring with the experienced champion Ruben Olivares, among other things. As a result of his enormous range, Zarate was able to "bore into" opponents with knife-sharp left jab before finishing them off at half range. The immense competition in his division, dominated by Latinos, also helped make him tough early on. Zarate remained world champion for three years and successfully defended his title nine times. His greatest triumph, however, was a non-title bout in which he took out his former stable mate and competing WBA king Alfonso Zamora in five rounds in 1977.

Zarate was later to himself become the victim of a younger stable mate in June 1979 with a questionable points defeat against Lupe Pintor. It was the end of a glorious reign that has yet to be successfully duplicated in the super bantamweight division. After suffering a TKO defeat against Wilfredo Gomez in 1978, Zarate lost additional title bout attempts to Jeff Fenech (1987) and Daniel Zaragoza (1988). His reputation as one of the best and most feared bantamweights of all times was not tarnished as a result, however. Zarate has today earned his place in the Hall of Fame as well as in the hearts of the many Mexicans who measure all up-and-coming talents against Zarate's abilities.

"A TRUE WORLD CHAMPION." HARRY MULLAN

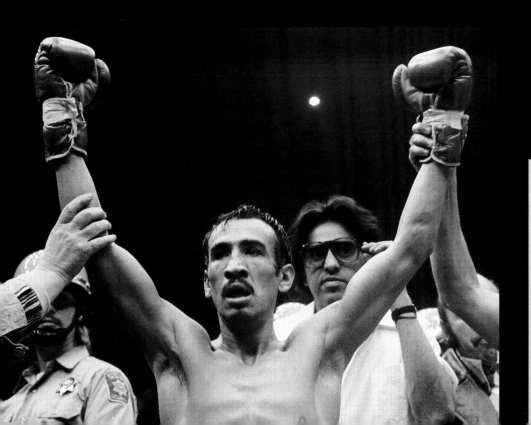

SPECIAL: KO king par excellence
BORN: 05-23-1951 in Tepito (MEX)
BOXING RECORD:
  65 professional bouts
  61 wins, 4 losses
  14 world championship bouts
  (11 in bantamweight, 3 in super bantamweight)
FIRST WORLD CHAMPIONSHIP BOUT:
  1976 (KO win 9th round Rodolfo Martinez, WBC bantamweight)
LAST WORLD CHAMPIONSHIP BOUT:
  1988 (TKO loss 10th round Daniel Zaragoza, WBC super bantamweight)
WORLD CHAMPIONSHIP TITLES:
  1976–79

Something truly unusual indeed must be afoot in the bantamweight class when a king in this division is treated as the best boxer pound-for-pound by the experts. Something like Eder Jofre, whose complex talents were viewed as excelling those of Dick Tiger, Emile Griffith, or Cassius Clay in the first half of the 1960s. The five-year champion first impressed the Brazilian titleholders in the modern history of his sport with outstanding techniques and immense power in both fists, making him a shining example of a boxer puncher. "[He] boxes like Sugar Ray Robinson and hits like a miniature Joe Louis," wrote the *New York Times* in 1960.

Jofre did not find it exactly easy being an international star. As a dedicated vegetarian and eloquent thinker, he set himself apart from the rest of the boxing scene soon after becoming a professional in 1957. The news of his perfect series of victories, which extended across 50 matches, had a long way to travel, however. At the start, Jofre fought only in Brazil, a true backwater of the boxing world at that time, and did not travel to the USA until 1960. He knocked out the Mexican ranking list competitor Joe Medel in the tenth round in Los Angeles Olympic Auditorium. The fight for the vacant NBA title took place in the same year, with Jofre winning with a KO victory over Eloy Sanchez in the same location. Universal recognition followed in January 1962, when the 25-year-old finished off the previously unbeaten European world champion Johnny Caldwell in the tenth round.

The triumph in the fully packed Ibirapuera stadium in São Paulo underscored the dominance of the new popular hero. And it turned the homeland patriot into a globe-trotter by force of necessity. In order to collect the large boxing purses that could not be paid in his home country, the world champion from then on preferred to defend his title elsewhere. He won against Herman Marquez in San Francisco, against the Filipino Johnny Jamito in Quezon City and against Bernardo Caraballo in Bogotá. Jofre's five title defenses ended in five TKO victories, as he always hit harder and more accurately than his contenders. The fight with his own body weight appeared at times to be a greater challenge to him than his opponents.

Jofre was not accustomed to saving his energy for the full number of rounds when he stepped into the ring with Masahiko "Fighting" Harada in May 1965 after 17 TKO victories. The tough fighter drove the champion to a points defeat by majority decision in his 51st professional fight and won the re match one year later in Tokyo. These were Jofre's only defeats in his impressive career, which was continued almost as impressively three years after his retirement in January 1967. The veteran then returned to the ring as a featherweight and was given a chance to fight WBC champion José Legra for the title in May 1973 after 15 victories. The unanimous points victory anchored the 37-year-old on his second throne. He triumphed over the equally legendary Vicente Saldivar in the same year.

The death of his father José, who had always been his "manager, trainer and best friend," in 1974 also represented the death of Eder Jofre's athletic ambitions. He took part in only a handful of fights after being divested of the title due to inactivity and then retired in late 1976. He remained a public personality, however, as a long-term congressional representative.

"ONE OF THE MOST UNDERRATED BOXERS IN HISTORY."

THE RING

His father José was Eder Jofre's mentor, manager, and trainer. Eder became a champion in two weight divisions under his guidance.

SPECIAL: The first Brazilian world champion
BORN: 03-26-1936 in São Paulo (BRA)
BOXING RECORD:
  78 professional bouts
  72 wins
  4 draws
  2 losses
  13 world championship bouts (11 in bantamweight, 2 in featherweight)
FIRST WORLD CHAMPIONSHIP BOUT:
  1960 (KO win 6th round Eloy Sanchez, NBA bantamweight)
LAST WORLD CHAMPIONSHIP BOUT:
  1973 (KO win 4th round Vicente Saldivar, WBC featherweight)
WORLD CHAMPIONSHIP TITLES:
  1960–65 (bantamweight)
  1973–74 (featherweight)

RUBEN OLIVARES

Ruben Olivares (*left, standing*) vs. Lionel Rose, Inglewood 1969.

SPECIAL: Master of the left hook
BORN: 01-14-1947 in Mexico City (MEX)
NICKNAME: Rockabye Ruben
BOXING RECORD:
  104 professional bouts
  88 wins, 3 draws
  13 losses
  13 world championship bouts (8 in bantamweight, 5 in featherweight)
FIRST WORLD CHAMPIONSHIP BOUT:
  1969 (KO win 5th round Lionel Rose, bantamweight)
LAST WORLD CHAMPIONSHIP BOUT:
  1979 (TKO loss 12th round Eusebio Pedroza, WBA featherweight)
WORLD CHAMPIONSHIP TITLES:
  1969–70, 1970–71 (bantamweight)
  1974 and 1975 (WBA, WBC featherweight)

"IF THE MONEY WAS RIGHT, I'D EVEN BOX AGAINST GEORGE FOREMAN."

RUBEN OLIVARES

Whenever talk between Tijuana and the Yucatán Peninsula turns to the left hook, Mexican boxing talent is presented with a truly unparalleled role model—Ruben Olivares and his 17 years as a professional. The three-fold world champion knew how to fell his opponents with a left hook like no other, and from 1964 to 1970 enjoyed an impressive success series spanning 60 fights (56 TKOs). As "Rockabye Ruben," he became the undisputed star of the Forum in Inglewood, California, where he often followed up his superb victories with large parties. "If the money was right, I'd even box against George Foreman," the small, loud man once boasted.

Naturally, he never stepped into the ring with Foreman. The son of a businessman from Mexico City instead fought for the right to challenge reigning world champion Lionel Rose after a victory over competitor Joe Medel in 1969. Olivares ended Rose's reign in five clear rounds and later won a TKO victor over his first challenger, Alan Rudkin. It was his next three world title bouts with his national archrival Jesus "Chuchu" Castillo in the fully packed Forum that would go down in history, however. Olivares was able to outpoint Castillo in the first fight despite a knockout, but an injury in the rematch forced him to abandon the fight. In the decisive third fight in 1971, "Rockabye" was able to take impressive revenge for the first defeat in his professional career. His second championship did not last long, however. In 1972 he was knocked out by Rafael Herrera, another rival from his home country.

Olivares became world champion for a third and fourth time in 1974 and 1975 with TKO victories over Zensuke Utagawa and Bobby Chacon, taking the WBA and WBC featherweight titles. But the loss of stamina from fighting demanding opponents and partying was beginning to take its toll. Alexis Arguello and David Kotey took the title belts away from him in each of his first title defenses. Five years later, he was so badly outboxed as a challenger in a fight against Eusebio Pedroza that the fight was stopped early. This was a clear sign to retire, which the popular hero then did—even though he did attempt a foolish comeback in 1986 at age 39. Today his memory is preserved in the Boxing Hall of Fame in Canastota, New York, just as it is in every gym in his home country of Mexico.

MANUEL ORTIZ

SPECIAL: The USA's greatest contribution to the bantamweight division
BORN: 07-02-1916 in Corona, California (USA)—died 05-31-1970
NICKNAME: Mannie
BOXING RECORD:
   127 professional bouts
   96 wins, 3 draws
   28 losses
   23 world championship bouts
FIRST WORLD CHAMPIONSHIP BOUT:
   1942 (win on points 12th round Lou Salica)
LAST WORLD CHAMPIONSHIP BOUT:
   1950 (loss on points 15th round Vic Toweel)
WORLD CHAMPIONSHIP TITLES:
   1942–47
   1947–50

Manuel Ortiz *(left, in robe)* and Vic Toweel after their title bout in 1950 in Johannesburg.

Willie Pep, who would later go on to become a ring legend himself, once said that just a few sparring rounds with Ortiz could quickly give contenders the idea "to hang up their boxing gloves right then and there." After all, Manuel Ortiz was a master of his sport. His effective uppercut enabled him to dominate nearly any infights while his boxing technique was always superior to that of his opponents in his glory days. As champion between 1942 and 1950, "Mannie" influenced the fates of his weight division as though it were his own private issue.

The son of Mexican immigrants took the hard way when he went professional after his first amateur title in 1938. He was promptly tested and outpointed in the flyweight division

in his debut fight with ranking list boxer Benny Goldberg. By late 1941 he had been defeated in nine of 43 additional fights by established stars such as Small Montana and Lou Salica and managed a draw against Little Dado, the reigning champion. This training began to pay off after a switch to the bantamweight division and to trainer and manager Tommy Farmer. Ortiz exacted convincing revenge in a title bout with Salica in 1942 and was defeated only twice in the next five years as bantam world champion in non-title bouts. He often triumphed effortlessly in 15 title bouts.

Long a celebrated icon of the new Hispanics on the West Coast, the Californian lost his title to Harold Dade in early 1947, only to win it back again two months later in a return

match. Four additional confirmations followed, until the South African Vic Toweel defeated Ortiz, who was meanwhile nearly 34 years old, in May 1950 in Johannesburg on points. This was the beginning of the end of his impressive career, during which Ortiz had defended the title 19 times over a total of eight years and 260 title bouts. He fought nine world champions in his 17 years as a professional and stepped into the ring 49 times on four continents with contenders from the world rankings list.

Mannie's retirement was somewhat less impressive by comparison. After failing as a farmer and nightclub owner, he died of a diseased liver in 1970—the outcome of a long-standing duel with alcohol that the enthusiastic partygoer had not been able to win.

"ONE OF THE BEST BANTAMWEIGHT CHAMPIONS."

HARRY MULLAN

Brief product history
THE MOUTHPIECE

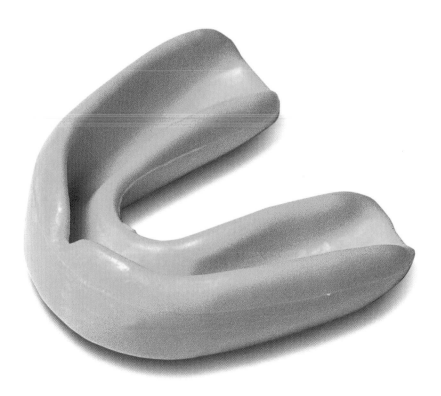

Perhaps it really was due to Ted "Kid" Lewis' crooked teeth that the mouthpiece became so popular early on in the history of boxing and was only made obligatory much later. According to tradition, the legendary British welterweight champion was the first prominent boxer in the modern era to wear the mouthpiece (there were several predecessor models in ancient times). As the story would have it, the Londoner had a friend who worked in a dental laboratory make him a small protective shield out of rubber after suffering numerous mouth injuries in earlier fights. Lewis wore this effective protection starting in 1913, although its use was occasionally disputed. Upon arriving in America in late 1914, the globetrotting professional learned that such devices were not permitted there. In those pioneer days Lewis and his American manager Jimmy Johnston were repeatedly involved in disputes with opponents and officials because of the mouthpiece.

Today the use of the protective device invented by British dentist Jack Marks in 1902 is not just permitted, it is required. The mouthpiece safeguards far more than

Bad omen: First Carl Daniels temporarily lost his mouthpiece in the duel with Terry Norris (1992) and later the title bout.

U.S. amateur Jose Navarro can't hear any better without his mouthpiece during the pause for his Olympic qualification in 2000—he can certainly breathe better though.

just the boxer's two rows of teeth. Its elasticity absorbs a great deal of the shock of a hit to the head. This shock-absorbing effect was further reinforced with the development of new models in the late 20th century incorporating plastic compounds such as kraton and vinyl. Today a general distinction is drawn between cheap standardized products made of rubber (and similar materials) and those formed of expensive, custom-made plastics. The difference in quality is enormous. Whereas the series production boil-&-bite models are adjusted to the boxer's teeth in a makeshift manner upon insertion in the mouth after being warmed in hot water, the custom-made models fit perfectly.

Every halfway ambitious professional now owns at least two such high-tech models. An additional coating of shockingly bright colors or a crowd-pleasing portrayal of the boxer's respective national flag is becoming ever more popular. For association officials, however, the only thing that counts is that the plastic protection device is in the boxer's mouth at the start of every round. Procedures differ if it should fall out during the exchange

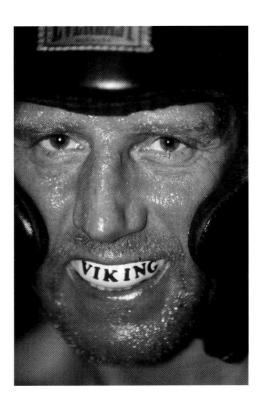

National colors or personal messages: There is always room for something, such as here on the mouthpiece of Englishman Steve Foster.

of blows. Some rule books call for the fight to be stopped until the boxer can replace the device, others forbid this, leaving the affected boxer to finish the round "unprotected." The deliberate "loss" of the mouth protector is thus not rewarded with a sought-after break, as such maneuvers are only all too common in the boxing ring.

A visible mouthpiece is often a sign of shortness of breath as a result of lack of stamina. When a boxer pushes his plastic protection piece forward during a fight, it is a clear sign to insiders that he is desperate for fresh oxygen. The poor out-of-breath boxer must be particularly careful on such occasions, however. If an opponent hits him in such a situation, his lips or mouth cavity could break open, resulting in serious injuries with an extremely heavy flow of blood.

FLYWEIGHT

FIDEL BASSA · DAVE MCAULEY · MUANGCHAI KITIKASEM · YURI ARBACHAKOV PICHIT SITBANGPRACHAN · SAENSOR PLOENCHIT · MARC JOHNSON LIGHT FLYWEIGHT — LUIS ESTABA · YOKO GUSHIKEN · HILARIO ZAPATA · JUNG KOO CHANG · MYUNG-WOO YUH · HUMBERTO GONZALEZ MICHAEL CARBAJAL · SAMAN SORJATURONG · PICHITNOI SITHBANGPRACHAN STRAWWEIGHT — RICARDO LOPEZ · PHALAN LUKMINGKWAN RATANAPOL SORVORAPHIN · CHANA PORPAOIN · ROSENDO ALVAREZ

EXOTIC MINIATURES

No matter how speedily these athletes let their fists fly at one another—when it comes to the distribution of boxing purses and attracting public favor, the flyweight almost always comes in last. This status is nothing less than traditional. The weight category up to 112 lbs was created in 1912 as an offshoot of the bantamweight division, well after the other seven traditional weight limits had been established. Two world wars would pass before international agreement on a universally recognized champions would be achieved.

Following Sid Smith's triumph over Eugene Criqui in the first title bout in 1913, boxing associations were in agreement as to who held the world championship title in the lightest of weight divisions for a mere 14 years. It was an era in which two of the greatest champions in this division, Jimmy Wilde and Pancho Villa, were already prospering. It was then followed by an intercontinental schism which essentially lasted until 1949

and prevented a number of exceptional title-holders such as Frankie Genaro, Midget Wolgast and in particular, Benny Lynch, from attaining the reputations they deserved. Not until Rinty Monaghan's triumphs did this weight division finally consolidate itself in the late 1940s. In the decades to come, this division was then also dominated by boxers of Latin American or Asian origin such as Pascual Perez, Pone Kingpetch, Miguel Canto, and Sot Chitalada.

This holds all the more true of the light flyweight division (up to 108 lbs) established in 1975 and the mini flyweight offshoot strawweight (up to 105 lbs), the title bouts in which are usually held somewhere between Caracas, Pusan and Osaka—but never in London or Las Vegas. Not until the past few years have the flyweights again begun to gain ground in the USA with the successes of Danny Romero, Mark "Too Sharp" Johnson and the extraordinary Ricardo Lopez.

Ricardo Lopez vs. Ratanapol Vorapin, Las Vegas 2000.

MICHAEL CARBAJAL

A long career at the very top of the sport is virtually impossible for fighters in the lower weight classes, where the continual drive to "keep off weight" exhausts professionals early and permanently. Yet, Michael Carbajal managed to achieve just that as a constant title contender or titleholder in the light flyweight division from 1990 to 2000. Whenever the *conoscendi* of the sport thought the last had been heard of him, this Hispanic from Phoenix, Arizona, returned with yet another brilliant triumph.

Carbajal ended his impressive amateur career in 1988 with the silver medal in Seoul and stepped into the ring for his first professional bout just a few months later. His highly effective body hooks and an unusually powerful punch in both fists quickly enabled him to leave the competition in the dust. Known as "Little Hands of Stone," he won the hearts of boxing fans, especially in the American southwest, and the 15th IBF championship (KO victory over Muangchai Kittikasem in July 1990). He defended the belt a total of six times, until meeting Humberto "Chiquita" Gonzalez, the competing WBC champion, in March 1993. Carbajal impressively demonstrated his ability to turn a precarious fight around with a single hit in this unification bout for two world championship titles. His TKO victory in the seventh round was soon chosen the "Fight of the Year" while he himself was elected "Fighter of the Year" by the boxing magazine *The Ring*.

This permanent guest in the pound-for-pound ranking lists appeared to be on the way out with defeats in two additional fights against Gonzalez (1994), but a diehard like Carbajal has several lives. Trained and managed by his older brother Danny, the talented "Banger" took back the vacant IBF belt in March 1996 with a victory over Melchor Cob Castro.

Eight months later he lost the title but not his extraordinary will to fight with a points defeat to Mauricio Pastrana. Carbajal retired from the ring in disappointment, however, when boxing referee Richard Steele stopped him in the middle of his feud with Jacob "Baby Jake" Matlala in July 1997 due to injuries. It was to be a temporary retirement.

Filled with renewed boxing spirit although no longer with reflexes as quick as they had once been, "Little Hands of Stone" began

"I AM A WARRIOR AND I NEVER GIVE UP."

MICHAEL CARBAJAL

slugging his way to the top of his division again in 1999. The 33-year-old veteran initially appeared to be the designated loser of the fourth fight after his two-year break, a title bout with the WBO champion Jorge Arce, who was twelve years his junior. Then, in the 11th round, a single effective hit was sufficient to turn the duel around for the marked challenger. Carbajal had once again proved that half a "fly" has more lives than a cat…

SPECIAL: World class for over a decade
BORN: 09-17-1967, Phoenix, Arizona (USA)
NICKNAME: Little Hands of Stone
BOXING RECORD: 53 professional bouts, 49 wins, 4 losses, 18 world championship bouts (light flyweight)
FIRST WORLD CHAMPIONSHIP BOUT: 1990 (TKO win 7th round Muangchai Kittikasem, IBF)
LAST WORLD CHAMPIONSHIP BOUT: 1999 (TKO win 11th round Jorge Arce, WBO)
WORLD CHAMPIONSHIP TITLES: 1990–94 (IBF), 1993–1994 (IBF, WBC), 1994 (WBO), 1996–97 (IBF), 1999 (WBO)

MIGUEL CANTO

Those who christened him on the Yucatán Peninsula in Mexico named him Miguel Angel Canto Solis. Those who witnessed his talents in the ring simply called him "El Maestro." This dominant flyweight of the 1970s knew how to evade attacks from opponents and skillfully counter them like lightening. And he knew how to masterfully assert himself as a champion for four years and in 14 title defenses—still the record in his division today—with excellent physical condition and superior boxing techniques. There may have been more spectacular Mexican boxers than this right-hander from Merida, but when it came to defense artists Miguel Canto was among the best.

Quickly successful on the streets of his hometown as well as in the amateur fights that followed, this fighter with an unusual talent for movement chose boxing as the way to earn his living after his father died when Miguel was only 19 years old. He became the champion of the Yucatán in his eleventh professional fight in 1970 and two years later was crowned champion of Mexico as well. After losing a decision to the Venezuelan Betulio Gonzalez in 1973, Canto took the world championship title on his second attempt by outboxing the favorite Shoji Oguma in Japan in January 1975 and winning a 2-to-1 decision. Canto went for the full allotment of rounds in an additional 13 of his 15 victorious title bouts held in places like Monterrey, Los Angeles and Tokyo, and was able to dominate highly favored contenders such as Ignacio Espinal, Antonio Avelar and Betulio Gonzalez, who he defeated in two additional fights.

The pinnacle of his career already behind him, Canto brought his belt to Pusan in Korea in March 1979 and was dethroned by Chan-Hee Park. Attaining only a draw six months later in Seoul, the disappointed ex-champion initially retired from the ring. One year later he attempted a comeback that got off to a promising start but ended with three TKO defeats. "El Maestro" had reached the end of his boxing career in mid-1982 and from then on embarked on a career as respectable businessman.

> ## "HE PROVED THAT DEFENSE IS JUST AS IMPORTANT AS OFFENSE."
>
> *THE RING*

SPECIAL: Strategist in the ring for 18 title bouts
BORN: 01-30-1949 in Merida, Yucatán (MEX)
NICKNAME: El Maestro
BOXING RECORD:
74 professional bouts, 61 wins, 4 draws, 9 losses, 18 world championship bouts
FIRST WORLD CHAMPIONSHIP BOUT:
1973 (loss on points 15th round Betulio Gonzalez, WBC)
LAST WORLD CHAMPIONSHIP BOUT:
1979 (draw 15th round Chan-Hee Park, WBC)
WORLD CHAMPIONSHIP TITLES: 1975–79

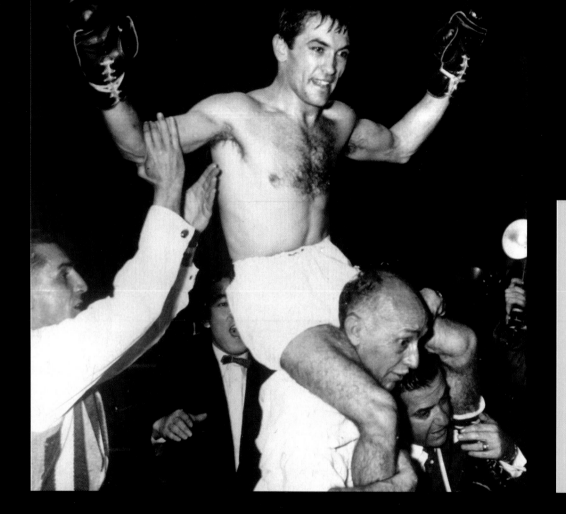

SPECIAL: The tough master of infighting
BORN: 03-04-1926 in Tupungate, Mendoza
(ARG)—died 01-22-1977
NICKNAME: El Terrier
BOXING RECORD:
92 professional bouts
84 wins
1 draw
7 losses
12 world championship bouts
FIRST WORLD CHAMPIONSHIP BOUT:
1954 (win on points 15th round
Yoshio Shirai)
LAST WORLD CHAMPIONSHIP BOUT:
1960 (TKO loss 8th round Pone
Kingpetch)
WORLD CHAMPIONSHIP TITLES:
1954–60

BENNY LYNCH

SPECIAL: Drank and boxed like no other
of his era
BORN: 04-02-1913, Clydesdale, Scotland
(GBR)—died 08-06-1946
BOXING RECORD:
111 professional bouts
83 wins
15 draws
13 losses
5 world championship bouts
FIRST WORLD CHAMPIONSHIP BOUT:
1935 (TKO win 2nd round Jackie Brown,
NBA/IBU title)
LAST WORLD CHAMPIONSHIP BOUT:
1938 (draw 15th round Peter Kane,
NBA/IBU title)
WORLD CHAMPIONSHIP TITLES:
1937–38

"IN HIS GLORY DAYS
HE WAS PERFECT."

RON OLIVER

He blossomed from the bleakest worker ghetto in Glasgow, the Gorbals, and once again lived in bitter poverty at the end his life. In between, however, Samuel Benjamin John Lynch spent a few glorious years showing the world just how good a flyweight boxer can be. Speedy leg work, well-balanced movements, enormous power, and keen boxing intelligence—they were all combined in Scotland's most important contribution to the sport, a true boxing ideal. It was only the quarrel between the competing associations in Europe and the USA that prevented the importance of this charismatic champion from being manifest in a long and adequate reign.

The former newspaper boy learned the sweet science in the difficult day-to-day life on the boxing booth circuit and thus already had experience in the ring before turning professional at 18.

He was crowned the Scottish champion three years later in 1934 and in just a year's time wrung a draw from British NBA world champion Jackie Brown in a non-title bout. In a rematch that took place that same year, he quickly outboxed his British rival as an official challenger in just one and a half rounds. Universal recognition as champion did not follow until early 1937, however, when Lynch took the starch out of the New Yorker Commission titleholder Small Montana in 15 rounds.

After ten confusing years, the widely popular and unfailingly polite athlete who helped downed opponents back to their feet was the first undisputed titleholder in his weight division. He had frequent bouts with alcohol even during his glory days, however, and aged quickly. After asserting himself with an impressive TKO victory over future champion Peter Kane in 1937, Lynch was clearly overweight for the title defense bout against American Jackie Jurich in June 1938. His KO triumph was therefore not recognized as a world championship title bout. He left the ring for good after two more defeats. His died eight years later at age 33 as the result of a bout with pneumonia against which the impoverished ex-champion was powerless.

Benny Lynch's fire burned out quickly, but in his most active phases it lit up the ring with its impressive intensity.

JIMMY WILDE

"THE BEST BRITISH BOXER OF ALL TIMES."

THE RING

SPECIAL: First star of his weight division
BORN: 05-15-1892 in Tylorstown, Wales (GBR)—died 03-10-1969
NICKNAME: The Mighty Atom
BOXING RECORD:
  145 professional bouts
  141 wins
  1 draw
  3 losses
  9 world championship bouts
FIRST WORLD CHAMPIONSHIP BOUT:
  1915 (TKO loss 17th round Tancy Lee)
LAST WORLD CHAMPIONSHIP BOUT:
  1923 (KO loss 7th round Pancho Villa)
WORLD CHAMPIONSHIP TITLES:
  1916–23

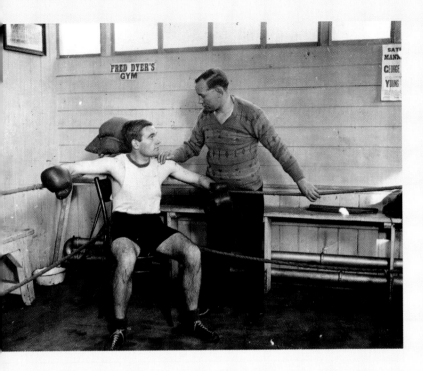

Wilde *(right)* visiting his son, who tried unsuccessfully to emulate him, in 1932.

Wilde relaxing at home with his wife Elizabeth, who was also his manager, in 1921.

With a somewhat anemic, youthful face and standing barely 5'2", Jimmy Wilde looked like a piano student or aspiring jockey at first glance. Those who underestimated Wilde in the boxing ring were ill advised, however. Just like how Clarke Kent turns into the omnipotent Superman in the comics, so this polite boy from the village of Tylorstown in Wales turned into a furious fighter with two gloves on his fist. Wilde was considered the ideal flyweight and became a boxing icon in Britain where he is still cherished today as the "the ghost with the hammer in his hand."

His maneuverability may have been innate, but his immensely powerful hits that could shake up even much heavier opponents were a result of professional "training" in the nearby coalmines where he worked since he was 14. Prizefighting thus literally offered Wilde a "way up," which he initially pursued with appearances at fairground booths. Wilde became a registered professional in 1910 at age 18. Apart from his home crowd in the small town of Pontypridd, virtually no one took note of the ensuing series of victories, however. The important National Sporting Club in London informed him that there were essentially no suitable opponents in his weight category. It thus took a total of 82 fights without a defeat (1 draw) until the fine gentlemen were willing

to invite the Welsh outsider to his first fight of real importance with the Frenchman Eugene Husson in March 1914.

Wilde won this duel with a TKO and was finally allowed to take part in fights with top-ranking contenders until he lost to the Scotsman Tancy Lee in the following year in an attempt to take the British and European belts. This defeat (fostered by an intestinal virus) was to be his last in the next six years—at the pinnacle of his abilities; the hard-to-corner Wilde was nearly unbeatable. A TKO victory over Joe Symonds in February 1916 brought him recognition, at least in Europe, as European world champion. International confirmation followed in December, when Wilde took down the American champion Giuseppe di Mefi, alias "Young Zulu Kid," in eleven rounds. Wilde had meanwhile taken successful revenge against Tancy Lee and had defended his title twice more by 1918. He was then slowed down for good by wartime military service.

Ambitious scientists in Great Britain had examined the exceptionally talented boxer in vain in an attempt to find a physiological explanation for his phenomenal talent for movement. On his six-month tour in 1920, veritable masses gathered in both the USA and Canada to see Wilde in demonstration fights against

usually much heavier opponents. The Welshman lost his last two official bouts, however. Back on the island in 1921, he was unable to withstand the superior stamina of the former bantamweight world champion, American Pete Herman. Above the bantamweight limit before this fight, Herman was supposedly only accepted by Wilde as a contender because the Prince of Wales was to be in the London audience. Two inactive years later, Wilde let himself be enticed into a title defense in New York without preparatory training. Wilde was beaten to a pulp by the legendary Pancho Villa in front of more than 40,000 viewers at the Polo Grounds until being carried out of the fight in the seventh round.

"I can't remember a thing," said Wilde later in his candid style, "until I woke up three weeks later and found myself in a bungalow on the coast near New York." The popular, aging star kept both feet on solid ground as an agile businessman and chairman of the National Union of Boxers until his death in 1969. The man known as the "The Mighty Atom" had officially reigned as champion for seven years and taken part in 145 professional fights, of which he lost only three. Wilde himself liked to also count the 719 victories in his 719 boxing booth appearances.

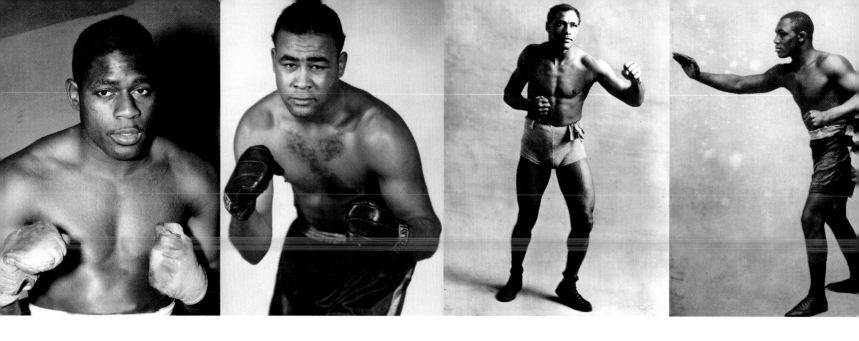

The best boxers of the 20th century who never got a chance at a title.

CHAMPIONS WITHOUT A TITLE

GEORGE BENTON

In his glory days, he was like a phantom: No matter where they hit, his opponents met only with thin air. George Benton, however, hit with great accuracy, enabling him to win 27 of his first 30 professional fights by the mid-1950s (1 draw). A hot world championship title candidate for several years, the showdown between Benton and Sugar Ray Robinson that insiders longed to see—or another well-deserved opportunity at the title—never materialized. A gunshot wound suffered in Philadelphia put an abrupt end to his active career (1969). "The uncrowned middleweight champion" retained his good reputation, however, by later helping many other professionals (including Leon Spinks, Mike McCallum, Meldrick Taylor) to world championship titles as a trainer.
Born May 15, 1933,
in Philadelphia (USA).
75 professional fights: 61 victories,
1 draw, 13 defeats.

CHARLEY BURLEY

There was nothing he didn't do well and virtually no one he didn't beat between 1937 and 1950: Fritzie Zivic in welterweight as well as the young Archie Moore in middleweight and another future champion Billie Soose—and occasionally a real heavyweight as well. The majority of his competitors avoided Charles Duane Burley "like the plague" because of his excellent combination of style and power. The toughest product to ever come out of Pittsburgh thus languished for much of 1940s on the world rankings list, unwillingly providing professionals such as Ezzard Charles with a career springboard with close, often disputable points defeats. Burley never suffered a TKO loss in his entire 89 matches and 14 years as a professional.
Born Sept. 6, 1917,
in Bessemer, Pennsylvania
(USA)—died Oct. 16, 1992.
98 fights: 84 victories, 2 draws,
11 defeats, 1 no-decision bout.

JOE JEANNETTE

Good physical condition and an unquenchable thirst for victory quickly helped Joseph "Joe" Jeannette advance to become the secret heavyweight favorite despite his late entry into the professional arena at age 25. It was the early 1920s, however, and he soon fell victim to the so-called color bar. White competitors refused to accept him as an opponent, and his former contender Jack Johnson, whom he had outboxed seven times between 1905 and 1906 (1 disqualification victory, 1 draw, 4 no-decision bouts) could earn far more as a champion fighting white challengers. Jeannette thus whiled away the time with duels against Sam Langford, Harry Wills, and Sam McVey, who he forced to declare defeat in a memorable ring feud in April 1909 after 49 rounds and 27 knockdowns. Jeannette boxed until he was 40 and took part in more than double his 157 officially registered fights.
Born August 26, 1879, in
North Bergen, New Jersey
(USA)—died July 2, 1958.
157 professional fights: 79 victories,
6 draws, 9 defeats, 62 no-decision
bouts, 1 annulled fight.

SAM LANGFORD

Even though he never gained an official world championship title on the way from lightweight to heavyweight, experts regard "The Boston Tar Baby" as the best boxer without a championship title. The racism and prejudice of two world champions (Jack Johnson and Jack Dempsey) prevented him from being able to take part in a heavyweight title bout in the 1920s and 1930s. "It is said that I feared no one," admitted Jack Dempsey later in retirement. "What nonsense! There was man I feared—Sam Langford!" The small fighter with the big reach fought just under 300 fights between 1902 and 1926, triumphing over current and future titleholders like Joe Gans and "Philadelphia" Jack O'Brien. Langford died nearly blind and entirely impoverished in January 1956 in Cambridge, Massachusetts.
Born March 4, 1883,
in Weymouth, Nova Scotia
(CAN)—died Jan. 12, 1956.
293 fights: 167 victories, 37 draws,
38 defeats, 48 no-decision bouts,
3 annulled fights.

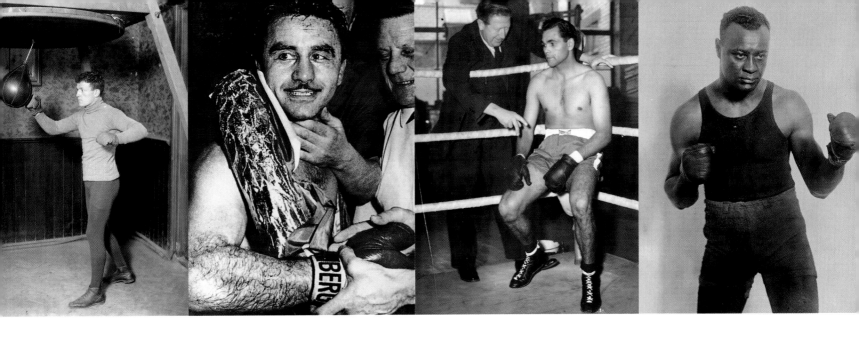

PACKEY McFARLAND

He triumphed over the best of the lightweights such as Benny Yanger, Tommy Kilbane, and the future champion Freddie Welsh—and knocked out former world champion Jimmy Britt. Yet, Packey McFarland never got a change to fight for the title. Titleholder Battling Nelson demanded that this bold professional from Chicago lose weight before the envisioned title bout while at the same time requesting the number of rounds be extended; others avoided him even more determinedly. Thus, all that remained to the well-mannered Packey was the satisfaction of having suffered only one defeat at the beginning stages of his career and otherwise remaining undefeated until its end in 1915. In his eleven years as a professional, he took part in 70 regular fights as well as 34 without an official result.
Born Nov. 1, 1888 in Chicago (USA)—died Sept. 23, 1936. 104 fights: 64 victories, 5 draws, 1 defeat, 34 no-decision bouts.

LÁSZLÓ PAPP

Hungary's greatest boxer of all times had won three gold medals at three Olympic games by the time the socialist government allowed him to become professional in 1956 at age 31. The talented and savvy boxer then summarily outclassed Europe's middleweight elite between Vienna, Dortmund, and Madrid, although he was repeatedly slowed by his fragile punching hand. After being the European champion in 1962, the southpaw defended his title a total of six times until 1965. His government then forbid him to take part in a planned title bout with the reigning champion Joey Giardello. This result was doubtless beneficial to both Giardello and Hungary: The unbeaten professional later became chief trainer for the Hungarian amateur team.
Born March 25, 1926, in Budapest (HUN). 29 fights: 26 victories, 3 draws.

DAVE SANDS

His career began brilliantly and ended in tragedy. One of five boxing sons of a Puerto Rican father and an Aborigine mother, Dave Sands (who was born as Ritchie Sands) quickly ascended to became Australian champion in the middle and light heavyweight classes in the 1940s. After moving to Great Britain, he triumphed over well-respected middleweights such as Robert Villemain, Dick Turpin, and later Carl "Bobo" Olson. Even a brief excursion into the heavyweight division was rewarded with yet another Australian title. Sands ranked number one on the middleweight ranking list and was already regarded as a candidate for a title fight with Sugar Ray Robinson when he suffered a fatal crash in a truck at just 26 years of age in 1952. One can only speculate what he might have been able to achieve with his immense potential.
Born Feb. 4, 1926, in Burnt Ridge (AUS)—died Aug. 11, 1952. 104 fights: 93 victories, 1 draw, 8 defeats, 2 no-decision bouts.

HARRY WILLS

They called him the "The Black Panther" or "Dempsey's dark shadow." After all, Harry Wills was long considered the only serious contender for the heavyweight throne. The tall model athlete who began as a dockworker in New Orleans had outclassed respected rivals like Fred Fulton and Luis Angel Firpo as well as the legendary Sam Langford in 16 of 18 fights by 1924. The title bout with Dempsey planned by the New Yorker Boxing Commission never materialized, however. On one occasion Wills refused to fight with other contenders who aspired to the title and on another promoter Floyd Fitzsimmons was not able to gather the necessary sum of money in time for the deadline. The first payment on his mega purse enabled Wills to easily retire to Harlem in New York at the end of his ring career in 1932.
Born May 15, 1889, in New Orleans (USA)—died Dec. 21, 1956. 97 fights: 80 victories, 4 draws, 9 defeats, 4 no-decision bouts.

THE TRAINING

GYMS AND CAMPS

3 MINUTES

As long as he is in the gym, a boxer's life runs in a precise, unrelenting tact: three minutes' work, one minute break, three minutes' work, one minute break—that is the ever-repeating rhythm of his exertions. This holds true of work at the punching ball and the heavy punchbag, for shadow boxing and for sparring. And it influences the limits of his physical stamina as well, for it is the same rhythm found in serious, real-life situations in the ring: three and one and three and one …

"The absolute authority of time" (according to Joyce Carol Oates) can be exercised by means of the gong or the whistle, or simply with the famous call "Time!" In general, however, time does not stop for exceptions or interruptions, or at best only for those that serve to increase the torture. It is not rare for trainers to let their charges slave away for four minutes instead of three or to shorten the break—the oasis of the tormented—to 30 seconds.

Such perfidious maneuvers are intended to prepare the athletes for the enormous demands the sport places on their stamina. In the world of the ring, the three-and-one tact calls the ultimate shots for all male boxers (women have two-minute rounds).

Sweat and pain form a common bond between all kinds of athletes. *1st row:* Lennox Lewis stretching *(right)* Jack Dempsey with Trainer Ernie Dusek *(center)* and Ignacio Zurda Pina doing a headstand *(far right)*. *2nd row:* Terry Norris out of breath *(right)* Kevin Lueshing throwing punches *(center)* and Muhammad Ali taking a break *(far right)*. *3rd row:* Nigel Bennan takes it to the limit *(right)* Alan Minter *(center)* trains his jaw while Larry Gains trains his neck muscles *(far right)*.

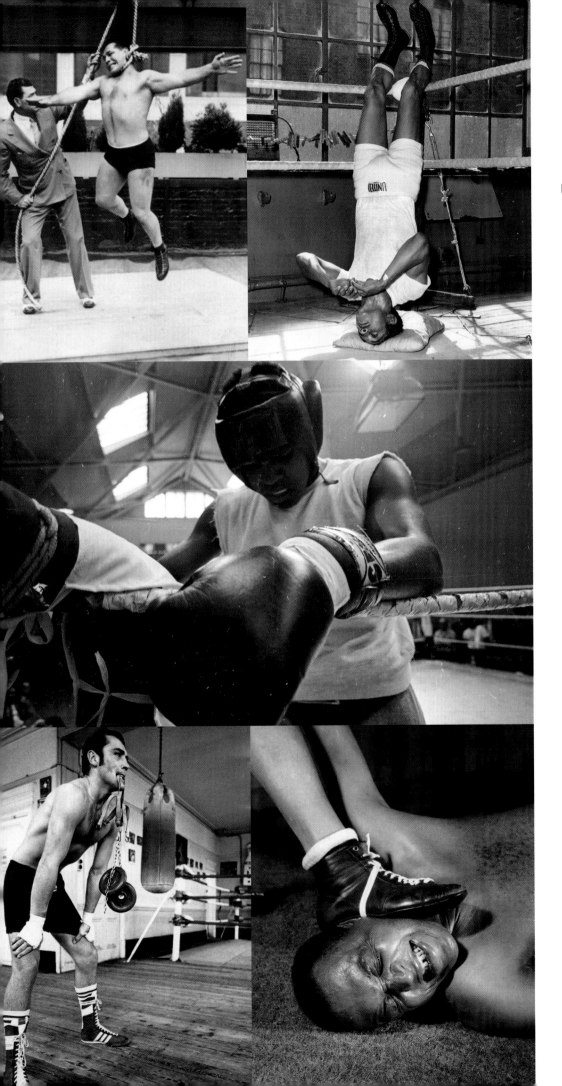

THE HARDER THEY COME

"WORK! NO ONE EVER
SAID IT WAS EASY.
IF IT WAS EASY
EVERYBODY WOULD DO IT."
RON STANDLER

"TRAINING BOXERS
IS LIKE TRYING TO
CATCH A FISH.
IT IS TECHNIQUE,
NOT STRENGTH THAT
IS IMPORTANT."
ANGELO DUNDEE

"WHEN YOU GET YOUR
BODY IN SHAPE
YOU HAVE EVERYTHING
THAT YOU NEED.
YOU HAVE POWER,
YOU HAVE GRACE,
YOU HAVE EVERYTHING."
BEAU JACK

"IT IS ALL ABOUT
GETTING YOUR BOXER
IN TOP SHAPE AT JUST
THE RIGHT TIME.
YOU DON'T WANT TO GET
HIM THERE TOO EARLY
OR TOO LATE.
HOPEFULLY YOU GET HIM
THERE ON THE EVENING
OF THE FIGHT."
GOODY PETRONELLI

"WHEN YOU BRING
A PIECE OF GOLD OUT OF
THE GROUND YOU KNOW
THAT IT IS GOLD. BUT
YOU HAVE TO CLEAN IT.
YOU HAVE TO POLISH IT.
YOU HAVE TO
GIVE IT FORM."
RAY ARCEL

"MANY HAVE THE TALENT
FOR MOVEMENT
BUT NOT THE HEART;
MANY HAVE THE HEART
BUT NOT THE TALENT
FOR MOVEMENT;
BRINGING THE TWO
TOGETHER IS SOMETHING
MYSTERIOUS,
LIKE WORKING ON
A PIECE OF ART."
CUS D'AMATO

"I LOVE BOXING.
EVERYTHING ELSE
IS SO BORING."
MIKE TYSON

HOPE AND SWEAT

Every champion's biography starts here. The gym, as the training room is known around the world in the universal jargon of boxing, is the inescapable starting point for all ambitions. This is where the first steps and punches are practiced. This is where work with the various training devices begins and eventually progresses to sparring with a real opponent. There is no other place to learn the art of boxing.

Did Menander, Pythagoras, and the "coaches" who came after them already use such training rooms back in antiquity? No concrete evidence of such rooms has yet surfaced. Established in the 18th century,

the London "academies" of the British boxing pioneers James Figg and Jack Broughton are regarded as the first boxing schools. There, gentlemen of the upper classes tried their hand at the "noble arts"— boxing, fencing, and wrestling. And yet, the so-called academies were not housed in magnificent institutional buildings but were typically found in a small hall or floor attached to a pub.

Today's common term for the training site came onto the scene with the Americanization of the sport: The Anglo-American term "gymnasium" simply became the "gym."

Generations of reporters and authors have since untiringly sung the praises of the unmistakable (and hard to ignore) smell of sweat, leather and rubber particles—and with it the unique patina of worn-out training devices and aging buildings. It is the occasionally somewhat nostalgic account of an extraordinary and generally unromantic world suffering from a noticeable lack of oxygen and investment. For many, however, old equipment and rotting floorboards are just as indispensable to the general aura as are the ringside guests—teens and dreamers, former boxers and know-it-alls. The true *aficionados* of the boxing world like to wrinkle their noses

Opposite page: Ex-WBO champion Tommy Morrison prepares for his duel with Lennox Lewis in October 1995 in the Main Street Gym in Tulsa,

Oklahoma. Brief pause for a female boxer: Bonnie "The Cobra" Canino *(above)* during her training program in the Gym in Dania, Florida, in 1996.

not at these cramped, old halls, but at the spacious, new gyms they regard as so sterile.

As training methods become more scientific and prosperity increases in many locations, the old and dilapidated boxing gyms are increasingly giving way to modern, well-lit training halls. Here, athletes train just as intensely as before—but these buildings are no longer homes. Existences such as that of the legendary coach Cus D'Amato, who lived in his New York gym with a pay phone and several hundred woodworms for company are a thing of the past. And those who would wax nostalgic for such days have also long since departed this life.

The industry surrounding boxing has simply become more realistic, the number of training facilities has been reduced almost everywhere. Whereas more than 80 gyms once existed in a boxing stronghold like Philadelphia, that number has today decreased to just a little over 20. The situation is similar in most large American cities, as well as in those in Europe and Latin America. In keeping with the laws of economic consolidation, it is generally only the most successful of these breeding grounds for new talent that have survived the downward economic tendencies.

The social side effects of boxing have remained virtually unaltered, however, despite

all the changes. Just as Jack Broughton once sought to train both the fists and the character of his mostly aristocratic athletes, so committed trainers now dedicate their lives to the descendents of immigrants and the underprivileged.

Getting the boys "off the streets," giving them a sense of direction and removing them from the temptations off violence-prone, drug-filled neighborhoods—many coaches see these educational goals as being of equal importance to physical training in their gyms. And of course they wouldn't exactly mind if one of these boys turns into a future champ either.

FAMOUS GYMS

Gleason's Gym has meanwhile become a historic institution of the New York boxing world, even though it has now moved location twice. Robert Galiardi, who soon changed his name to Bobby Gleason, established the gym in 1937 on the corner of 149th Street and Westchester Avenue in the heart of the Irish neighborhood of the South Bronx. Despite the cramped quarters, it soon became the training center for Phil Terranova, Jake LaMotta, Jimmy Carter, and other champions. Coaching legends such as Ray Arcel and Chickie Ferrara formed their protégés here. Innumerable world champions from other locations set up their final training camp at Gleason's before their title defenses in New York, especially when Gleason was able to offer more spacious quarters after moving to a more central location in Manhattan on the corner of 30th Street and Eighth Avenue in 1974. Seven years after Gleason's death, Ira Becker and the current managing director Bruce Silverglade expanded again

in 1986 with a move to the 15,000-square-foot factory floor on Front Street in Brooklyn. Since then, no less than 200 professionals, 200 hobby boxers, 150 amateurs and 80 women have been brought to their full potential here.

Ever since it began producing one world-class athlete after another in 1980s, the red and gold colors of the professionals from the **Kronk Gym** in Detroit have been a symbol of success. This is primarily attributable to the trainer, who grew up together with his athletes in a lower-class neighborhood of the Motor City. Emanuel Steward was a former bantamweight Golden Gloves Champion and electrician when he assumed responsibility for the training of his half-brother and other juniors in the training rooms of the Kronk Center, a youth facility named after local politician John F. Kronk, in the 1970s. Steward made nationally respected amateurs out of many of the youngsters and turned the

best of them into professionals. The first generation of champions included Milton McCrory, Duane Thomas and in particular Thomas Hearns. Later, equally successful generations were to follow. Today the gradually modernized gym is regarded as one of the best American boxing addresses where aspiring amateurs and established champions (Lennox Lewis, Oscar De La Hoya) peacefully coexist in keeping with Steward's precise scheduling plans.

To call the **Ringside Gym** in Las Vegas just a "gym" would come close to being an insult. The old-fashioned institution on Charleston Boulevard has offered its customers a home away from home for as long as champions and challengers have been coming to the gambling metropolis. This is especially attributable to the charisma of a certain Johnny Tocco, who opened the gym in the heart of the old "downtown" section of the city in 1955 and managed it as a gentle dictator until

his death in 1997. Tocco, who was originally from St. Louis, accepted all serious training guests and let them pay whatever they could afford. Some nobodies gave him a single dollar, while some champions gave him thousands. But they all returned here whenever they could—including the likes of Sonny Liston, Larry Holmes, Marvin Hagler, Mike Tyson, and many others. Nor did anything change after Tocco's death and despite competition from the new Top Rank Gym run by promotion tsar Bob Arum. The new owner Luis Tapia has modernized the furnishings and equipment, but left the historic photos and the name untouched.

There may be far many older gyms in Europe and perhaps a few larger ones as well, but when it comes to productivity, none can hold a candle to the **Universum Gym** in Hamburg. The important German promoter Klaus-Peter Kohl built his a modern training hall to house his many professional charges in the city

district of Wandsbek in 1922. It even featured two rings and comfortable stands for the public. Ever since, champions have seemed to shoot out the blue ring floor like crocuses in the springtime under the guidance of Fritz Sdunek and two additional trainers. The long-standing world champions Dariusz Michalczewski and Regina Halmich were followed by titleholders such as the cruiserweight Juan Carlos Gomez, lightweight Artur Grigorian, and the heavyweight Klitschko brothers Vitali and Vladimir who attained worldwide recognition. Kohl's investment, which was in part attributable to lucrative TV contracts, thus paid off. With nine world champions, including three female champions, the stable belonging to the former fast-food stand and casino tycoon has become the most successful boxing operation on the continent.

Japan's most traditional boxing gym, the **Teiken Gym** is located in the heart of the

chic Tokyo business district of Shinyuku-kyu. Opened back in 1925, generations of future national and Asian champions such as flyweight Masao Ohba (WBA, 1970–73), light heavyweight Tsuyoshi Hamada (WBC, 1986–87) and two welterweight champions have shed their sweat on the spacious 3,230 square feet around the ring. Under the guidance of the important promoter Akihiko Honda, the gym is now once again a genuine breeding ground for ambitious athletes in this sweet science. No less than 30 professionals and some 200 amateurs share the punchbags, punching balls and tight practice schedules in the sparring ring. Regardless of their performance, these athletes are consistently encouraged and trained by the young head coach Yuichi Kasai and seven additional trainers. The flow of customers remains steady at Japan's top boxing address, as the sport of boxing now enjoys immense popularity in the capital city and beyond.

CAMP DAYS

The moment of truth may usually arrive in the noise and artificial light of an overfilled world of luxury hotels and casinos, but the prize boxer prepares himself for the big moment in an entirely different environment. The tough preparation work usually begins in the seclusion of the gym and typically climaxes before important duels in the so-called training camp. There the aspiring champion can concentrate on his athletic task with no distractions and, for the most part, surrounded only by those there to help him achieve his goal: trainers, sparring partners, masseurs, physical therapists and other helpers. Whatever may appear interesting or tempting in the outside world is fully blocked out here.

The boxer moves into his camp just like a monk going into seclusion. And just like a monk, he lives according to a schedule that starts early in the day: up at dawn and in bed as soon as it grows dark. This virtuous nature of this undertaking is nearly always underscored by the choice of location. Camps are usually situated in the mountains, in forests or near lakes. Floyd Patterson bunked down in a camp in Highland Mills, New York, before his fights, while Archie Moore fled to his own private refuge on the outskirts of San Diego. Even the highly public Muhammad Ali later swore by his spartan camp in the Poconos, a chain of hills on Highway 61 in Pennsylvania. He dubbed it "Fighter's Heaven" and once said that he felt more at home in the wooden barracks here than in his house in Cherry Hill.

This undertaking is also a way of paying tribute to earlier generations of champions, as an appreciation of the hard, healthy country life style is as old as the use of gloves at the world championships—and possibly even older. At the turn of the century, Professor Mike Donovan, a boxing coach at the New York Athletic Club, recommended that professionals seek a training camp "in a mountainous or hilly region of the country, where one is certain to find fresh air and no dust." Out in the country, world champions from Dempsey to Foreman have ardently devoted themselves to such pursuits as chopping wood, which trainers today still regard as an ideal form of strength training for boxers.

Modern sports psychologists like to point out the mental benefits of the camp. In those undisturbed weeks of cooperation, the team can develop what is known as "confluence"—a feeling of unity shared by all team members that further strengthens their collective confidence. Again and again, champions have described how the positive team spirit in their inner circle has given them additional inspiration and courage. On the flip side, helpers have often been sent home if they poisoned the positive atmosphere with doubts about an upcoming victory. This, too, is in keeping with the rules of the monastery—in order to protect the group's concentration and ability to focus, the unbeliever is banned from its midst.

In his training camp in Reno, Nevada, light heavyweight Virgil Hill added several additional weight units before his eleventh title defense (WBA) against Thomas "Hit Man" Hearns. Here, he is pictured during barbell training in his hotel room in 1991.

WHISKY 'N

The more intensively a boxer prepares for his next fight in the gym or in a camp, the more his interest in the temptations of urban life wanes. At least this is what is supposed to happen during that phase of intensive training in which complete abstinence is the hard and fast rule. This is hard enough when it comes to alcohol and tobacco—as evidenced by several prominent exceptions: champion Sonny Liston still permitted himself very generous rations of bourbon during his training periods and Roberto Duran was apt to grab a pack of cigarettes as soon as no one was looking. But it would appear that no form of asceticism is so strongly called for —and so remorsefully trespassed against— than sexual abstinence.

In Leonard Gardner's famous boxer novel *Fat City* (1969), young Ernie Munger is plagued by a bad conscience before his first professional fight. In the changing room, he confesses to one of his stable mates that he picked up a lady on the evening before the fight. Now he hopes "that I haven't ruined the fight in bed." This is a prototypical fear that is more widespread in the boxing world than in almost any other sport. According to traditional opinion, "the female" is a potential thief. Sexual contact with her will rob the fighter of a large portion of the energies he needs in the ring—and of the aggression that results from the frustrations of abstinence.

This idea is linked with the concept of women as fatal seductresses, such as seen in the antic legend of Odysseus' crew and the sirens who tried to lead them off their course. An

WOMEN

Women at close range. *1st row:* Marcel Cerdan *(far left)* and Mike Tyson (left) with female fans. *2nd row:* Playboy bunny girls carry John Conteh *(far left)*, Art Aragon with Marilyn Monroe and Mickey Rooney (center) and Terry Norris with his wife. *3rd row:* Frank Bruno with his daughter and wife *(far left)* and Alan Minter in the firm grip of Diana Dors (left).

in-depth psychological interpretation could thus keep whole battalions of analysts enthralled for months. In the eyes of scientists, however, the concept of robbed energy would not hold up under more detailed examination. Many modern trainers and managers still recommend abstinence before fights to their charges, but this has more pragmatic reasons. "It is not the act in and of itself," star coach Angelo Dundee once explained to reporters: "It is about going looking for it and the wine and late hours." This lifestyle, according to Dundee, prevents boxers from "mentally preparing."

Dundee liked to say that his protégés—including Muhammad Ali and Sugar Ray Leonard—were adult men. When in doubt, however, he was willing to place guards in front of their hotel rooms' doors before important fights to keep them completely isolated. This was also the method followed by the seconds of those legendary champions of the early 20th century who presented themselves as explosive double talents. To be just as fearless of a go-getter in the ring as in the pub or the saloon—this was the ideal at the heart of a sport bursting with manliness. It logically gave birth to a hero with two faces: the ascetic who could temporarily deny himself in order to reach his athletic goals and the pleasure-hungry, polygamous sinner.

The boxer thus shows what extremes a human is capable of achieving and is a symbol of a never-ending fight. And it is an entirely different fight from the one that Ernie Munger loses early on in the start of his professional career in Gardner's *Fat City*.

TRAINING METHODS

Los Angeles is still asleep on this morning in 1992, but Olympic medallist and new professional Oscar De La Hoya is already on the go, doing his roadwork.

MORNING AGONY

This is usually the first endurance test for the mind and legs on the morning of a demanding training day. Both would prefer to go back to bed, but the morning run cannot be put off. It typically takes place before breakfast, some time between five thirty and nine o'clock, ten o'clock at the very latest. Appropriately dubbed "roadwork," the number of boxers who truly look forward to running at this hour of the morning is few indeed.

The former light heavyweight champion Willie Pastrano dreamed of a pill that would render this arduous, compulsory exercise unnecessary. It would function as follows: "You get up in the morning, swallow the pill, eat breakfast, take a deep breath—and there you go, you've run five miles." Had he been able to patent an invention to accompany the idea, Pastrano would certainly have become a rich man. The majority of boxers share his aversion to running. Despite the variety of passing landscapes, boxers often regard running as boring and simply not much fun.

Running is essential, however, as it forms the foundation for training in the gym and the upcoming fight. The athlete's running performance also provides the coach with a clear indication of his trainee's level of aerobic stamina. In the acute training phase before the fight, many coaches are apt to brag to journalists about the terrific times their boxers have just made—and boxers being among the most talented endurance athletes around, this bragging is usually not entirely unjustified either.

Before boxing developed into a modern competitive sport, however, running was seldom part of the training regime. This comes as no surprise, considering the more or less stationary boxing style, focused on nearly continual confrontation with little necessity for footwork, preferred by the dominating professionals at the start of the 20th century. The development of a more mobile, strategically oriented style as well as the gradual lowering of the maximum number of rounds (initially 15, now 12) demanded ever-greater mobility and stamina, however. The ideal boxer now has great endurance and relies on his quick legs and lightening reflexes to skillfully control a fight rather than merely trying to knock his opponent down.

The round of morning agony is thus becoming harder and harder for current and future champions to avoid. Old-timer George Foreman is certainly not among their number, however. In his last active years, the two-time ex-champion coasted on the level of fitness he had previously established and which progressively began disappearing. In his own words, he now gauges his running tempo "according to how far away the refrigerator is."

Jump roping champion: super middleweight world champion James "Lights Out" Toney in the Outlaw Gym in Los Angeles, 1994.

JUMP TILL YOU DROP

It appears so playful and casual that observers tend to view it as a warm-up exercise only. In fact, however, jump roping has many different training advantages. Those who hop in time to the rope's beat are strengthening their leg and stomach muscles, improving their speed and promoting balance and mobility as well. This dance-like exercise also hones reflex coordination and the sense of balance. These units, which are usually broken down into several three-minute rounds or extend up to 10 or 15 minutes with no breaks, are also excellent endurance training. They provide a steady and grace-ful form of what sports experts term "sub-maximal exertion."

Ambitious professionals jump the rope, which is adjusted to their height and now made of leather or rubber rather than hemp (the swing is more even and stabile with heavier materials), more than 1,000 times.

When they are talented enough or in the right mood, they may even vary the performance a little. They may skip with crossed arms and varying leg positions (rope crossing), swing the rope twice around on each jump, thus reaching top speeds (double jumping) or jump backwards and forwards over the "halved" rope. In the process they fall into certain rhythms that they then maintain or alter. Correspondingly, the use of music (e.g., rap, ska or reggae) in the gym is more popular here than with any other exercise. Sonny Liston's rope skipping sessions, for example, became famous after his death. The boxer would synchronize his skipping feet with the rhythms of a fast-moving soul ballad such as Jimmy Forrest's "Night Train" sung by James Brown.

Boxers like Sugar Ray Robinson or Floyd Patterson with excellent motor skills were great fans of jump roping. The opportunity

to watch them was always a special treat. Reporters, spectators and notorious fight fans traditionally measure the quality of an athlete's footwork on his performance with the jump rope. Less well-coordinated boxers, on the other hand, take the jump rope in hand with an obvious sense of duty. Their interaction with the whirring rope lacks that certain touch of elegance that makes jump roping a true demonstration of physical skill. Virtually no one forgoes the exercise, however. Jump roping drives the blood into the muscles at the beginning and end of a training session better than any other exercise. It is indeed an excellent warm-up, but it is so much more as well.

For boxers around the world, the motto thus continues to be: Jump till you drop.

CUSTOM-TAILORED MUSCLES

Back when the number of rounds was not yet limited and gloves were considered training devices only, the methods for building strength were much simpler. Valiant title contenders lifted railroad ties and chopped down entire forests with an ax to strengthen the muscles in their arms and shoulders. Push-ups and dumbbell training were soon added. Since the advent of modern sports psychology, however, boxing trainers have been able to define training goals with far greater precision. An athlete's overall power now encompasses three different components: maximum strength, speed, and endurance. Professionals must have a well-balanced combination of all three.

Just how much static muscle build-up is beneficial for a boxer is still a subject of heated controversy today. There is general agreement, however, that weight and machine training should be carefully limited. Only muscle mass which can be transformed into dynamic power is important in the ring, and optimal performance that peaks quickly and then fades is of little use. This is why only laypersons are impressed by boxers with bulging, well-defined muscles, while *aficionados* of the sport remain more skeptical. They have all too often seen such bodybuilders hit the canvas early on in a real fight.

Sensible strength training thus seeks to achieve the optimal combination between muscle mass, condition and dynamics. This means that, when in doubt, lower weights with a larger number of rapid repetitions are preferable even when using modern equipment (e.g., bench presses). Targeted strength training works exactly the other way around. In strength training with dumbbells, for example, very heavy weights are used and the number of repetitions is kept low. This exertion level may be increased in several phases during pyramid training. High-tech, pioneering machines for strength training now make it possible to build up almost any conceivable muscle group more accurately than previously thought possible. In the early 1990s, cruiserweight champion Holyfield took advantage of this development to purposely and permanently bulk up on mass before switching to the heaviest weight division.

Holyfield also hired a ballet trainer, an endurance expert, and other advisors to help perfect his boxing skills. He thus became the prototype of a training philosophy that combined a wide variety of elements. Scientific findings on biorhythms were also called into play to ensure that all aspects of training were implemented at the optimal time point. Strength training, for example, is best in the morning hours when the strength-sensitive testosterone level reaches its peak. In keeping with this finding, professionals, and amateurs everywhere now pump iron before lunchtime.

Despite all of the scientific methods, a number of simple exercises used for centuries remain in the training plan virtually unaltered. The many variety of push-ups are a recognized method of promoting dynamic strength, just as is throwing practice punches with small, hand-held dumbbells. At an advanced age, George Foreman still swore by his preferred method of arm muscle training—chopping wood.

Specialist Lee Haney directs the extensive strength-training program for the multiple heavyweight world champion Evander Holyfield in Houston, Texas, in 1994.

FLEXIBLE STRATEGIES

They are called "gymnastic" or "free exercises," which brings to mind limbering or warm-up activities. Exercises without equipment have multiple training goals, however, ranging from dexterity training to targeted muscle build-up. They are focused on building a body that is optimally suited to the complex demands of the sport from head to toe. Flexible, highly trained muscles are especially needed in the stomach, back and neck regions. In principle, however, not a single area of the body should be left out.

Circular training has long since become the preferred method for building up the key muscle groups. Alternation between sit-ups, jackknives, relaxation exercises in the prone position, the wrestler's bridge and other exercises produces a cycle of dynamic torture in which flexible strength is trained in the most important muscle groups. Special attention has always been devoted to the stomach area, which is understandable considering the strain to which it is subject during a fight. As a target for body punches in the ring, the

boxer's entire upper body must function as a muscular shield that effectively absorbs the effect of the blows.

The stories of uncompromising trainers dropping medicine balls on their trainees' stomachs is an established part of boxing mythology. Although these tales are often exaggerated, most trainers did in fact push their charges to the limit of agony, as can be seen in the photos and reports in Joe Frazier's "Workout." Medicine balls are also popular aids for lengthening and stretching various muscles groups in less spectacular exercises (pulling them towards the body from an overextended position, placing them to the side, pushing them away, etc.) and are also used for training resilience.

The general trend in gymnastic exercises has long been to executions with shorter weight movement distances and very specific focus on certain muscle groups. Instead of sit-ups, which exert a great deal of pressure on the spine, short crunches are now being recommended. Instead of the brute wrestler's bridge,

some athletes now prefer isometric exercise for strengthening the neck muscles. These isometric exercises (calisthenics) demand great expenditure of strength with virtually no weight movement distance by building up resistance against a stationary blockade (e.g., arm pressed against the wall). This trains tonic strength. Nor is it seldom for top-ranking professionals to add a special gymnastics trainer to their team nowadays.

In the broader sense of the word, the boxer is also doing "gymnastics" when he kneads small rubber balls in his hands or chews gum. The rubber balls are used to strengthen the finger muscles and the gum has replaced the plug of tobacco often seen in old boxer films for training the chin muscles. The more developed the muscles of the lower jaw, the more effectively they can absorb the shock of a hit to the chin—or at least so the theory goes. Whether this is really scientific fact or not is debatable. It is, however, a prime example of how meticulous boxers work to get in shape for their sport.

Lennox Lewis gets some help stretching from Courtney Shand in Madison Square Garden in New York during a public training session there in April 2000.

INVISIBLE OPPONENTS

The opponent is always there—invisible but moving about nonetheless. So the boxer gives him room, evades, feints and counters. Two jabs followed directly by a cross with the right fist. Now the legs are called into play, a quick step to the side and put your guard back up. Keep your reach, stand firm, circle the opponent, or draw him along behind you—even though no one else in the gym can see him. The boxer takes the centuries-old pantomime of shadow boxing entirely seriously during his training. In this simulation he is alone with himself and his ghosts, and yet those who watch him long enough suddenly find they are able to see his partner, too.

On a more fundamental level, however, the boxer's attention is focused inward. Just as the karate enthusiast goes through the various hand and foot techniques in the ritual individual Kata exercises, so the boxer practices his entire repertoire of movements when boxing with the shadow. He does not put all of his strength into the punches or take them to their full extent, as the focus of this exercise is the technical accuracy of the various blows and steps, not the effects they produce. Errors in the pattern of movement can thus be corrected and precise execution of moves internalized until the boxer has the entire choreography down pat—even though it can never be truly perfected. The shadow boxer harmonizes his performance by looking inward, one could almost say by meditating.

The boxer appears lost in his movements for good reasons. The dance with the invisible foe demands a high level of concentration, especially when the boxer is carrying out this exercise in front of a mirror. As unerring as a camera, the mirror reveals even his smallest errors. After all, there simply aren't that many ways to execute an uppercut, to be precise there is really only one. This is why shadow boxing is used as training for fighters of all levels of expertise: The novice learns the first steps and punches, while the champion perfects the details. The boxer thus mentally anticipates the situations he might face in a real fight, similar to a high jumper mentally reviewing each step before making a jump.

The exercise retains its esoteric character even when the boxer's fists are closed around two small, handheld barbells. After all, mental preparation for a fight is just one of the aspects being trained here, another is building up speed in the fists. The boxer will need both, as an evening will eventually arrive on which his opponent is no longer invisible to him or anyone else.

James Salava uses the mirror in the changing room of the Blue Horizons in Philadelphia, Pennsylvania, for the last limbering exercises before a fight in 1997.

GYM WARS

The purpose of sparring is obvious. As a training fight between two well-padded opponents, sparring is a simulation of a real ring duel. Complete movement patterns and tactical behaviors which the boxer is trying to learn can be practiced with an intensity similar to a real fight but without the same results. These include entire sequences of punches and steps designed to improve the boxer's overall performance or perfect specific strategies for the next bout. Sparring matches can serve as both an educational and preparatory instrument.

Sparring between equals, in which both opponents derive the same amount of benefit from the experience, is seldom, however, especially during preparations for an upcoming fight. Such simulations generally have very set characters. There is a main fighter, usually of superior skill, and a training partner who has been assigned to him. The more skilled fighter's task is to land scoring blows on his opponent. He must carefully measure his attacks, however. They should neither be too harmless nor so strong that they intimidate or dupe the

boxer in training. The typical sparring partner is like an extra at a dress rehearsal. The focus is not on his performance, but on that of his counterpart. Nor should he use his own style in the sparring match, but instead adopt the style of the boxer whom the trainee is actually going to fight.

Whole armies of mediocre professionals without especially bright perspectives have uncomplainingly assumed the role of the trial horse. Others, usually ambitious youngsters, have taken advantage of the training matches with their betters as an opportunity from which they have much to learn. The young Larry Holmes learned so much from sparring with Muhammad Ali and George Foreman that he became a champion himself several years later—and left Ali with no chance of victory in a title defense. When just a teenager, Alexis Arguello sparred with world champion Ruben Olivares during the latter's training sessions in Managua. Arguello received quite a beating but did manage to land a few good blows. Just a few years later he dethroned Olivares. The older man then told Arguello

that he had sensed this would happen, but hadn't told Arguello at the time, as "it would have driven you mad."

Sparring reveals a boxer's true potential to the trained eye. When ambitious enough, it is here in this carefully gauged test of strength that he can prove his true worth to trainers and managers alike. It was thus that Oliver McCall advanced to become a title contender (and brief WBC champion) after supposedly once knocking Mike Tyson to the canvas. In most cases it is impossible to establish the truth of such unofficial reports—in keeping with the unwritten laws of their creed, sparring partners are obligated to silence.

Impressive sparring triumphs can cause dramatic shifts in the gym hierarchy. Which is why some half-serious matches have gradually turned into bitter fights for hotly disputed rankings. The so-called gym wars may initially spur the contestants on to top performance, but in the long-term they can destroy their physical stamina. Those who waste all their ammunition in minor skirmishes seldom have much left for the real "war."

Lennox Lewis simulates a fight scene with his sparring partner in a training camp in Scotrun, Pennsylvania, in 2000. Headguard and cup protector act as a protective shield during gym wars.

THAT'S A WRAP

Two hands wrapped in white bandaging say volumes more about a boxer's work and the risks he takes than any gloved poses ever could—which is why they have remained a favorite motif for photographers to this day. For active boxers, however, protecting the more than 20 individual knucklebones is a simple necessity. Not a working day goes by on which these brave men do not carefully wrap their two most important weapons. Preparation of the hands is an extensive procedure carried out with meticulous attention to detail when they are facing their next important bout or critical sparring match. It is not seldom for the trainer or assistant entrusted with this responsibility to devote 20 minutes or more to the task.

Careless sports reporters have grown accustomed to referring to the cumbrous-looking procedure as "bandaging" or "taping." The two terms so often used as synonyms refer to two entirely different steps, however. Step 1: The hand is wrapped with thin roles of gauze and an elastic dressing (bandaging). Step 2: The bandaged hand is further stabilized with medical tape (taping). The complete procedure is not necessary, or even permitted, in every situation. Depending on the professional coach's viewpoint, taping may or may not be necessary for a training match in which gloves with thicker padding are usually used. Taping is not allowed for amateurs, who are permitted only to affix the wrapping with tape in the wrist area.

Ideally, a good wrapping is a small work of art, providing protection for the knuckles and joints without excessively limiting the mobility of the thumbs and fingers. It is therefore not seldom for specialists to be called in to perform the procedure before important fights. They are not free to wrap as they please, however. All national and recognized world associations limit the length and width of the wrapping in two categories (up to super middleweight and light heavyweight and up) with a degree of nitpicking that far surpasses even the strictest government regulations. Nor may the tape be applied "closer than 1 inch to the knuckles" according to the rulebook of the International Boxing Federation (IBF).

Adherence to these regulations can be checked several times before a real fight. A boxer's team has the right to inspect the contender's bandaging before the fight. The referee or another official also checks to make sure everything is in proper order. A monogram applied to the wrapped hands with a marker is used as a non-reproducible seal of approval. Considering this level of transparency, stories of horseshoes, iron rings, and other items being hidden in boxing gloves can once and for all be relegated to the realm of myth and slapstick film scenes where they originated. Even the best wrapping handiwork is no guarantee that a boxer's career may not be hindered by a capsular tear, fatigue fracture or other type of fracture. After all, as David James, the former coach for the British Olympic team once said: "The human hand was actually designed more for grasping than for hitting."

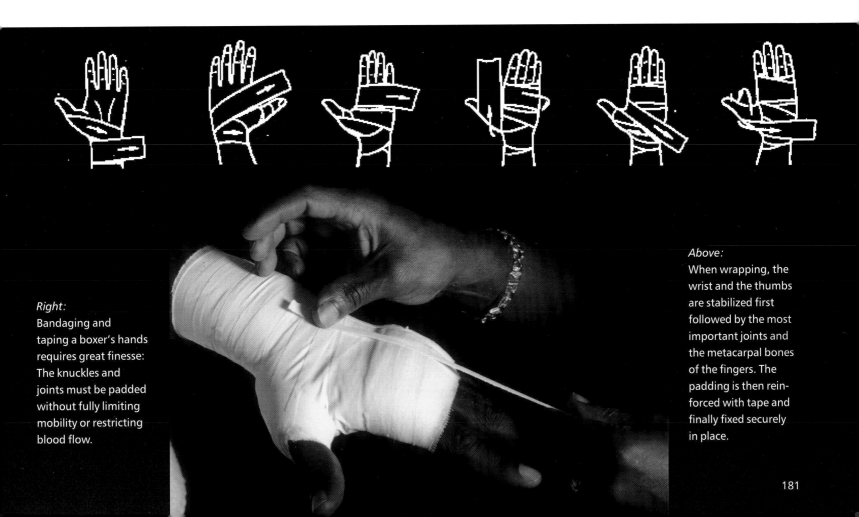

Right:
Bandaging and taping a boxer's hands requires great finesse: The knuckles and joints must be padded without fully limiting mobility or restricting blood flow.

Above:
When wrapping, the wrist and the thumbs are stabilized first followed by the most important joints and the metacarpal bones of the fingers. The padding is then reinforced with tape and finally fixed securely in place.

THE PUNCHBAG

Or heavy bag

"Always hit the punchbag like you were trying to knock a hole straight through it," an old boxing trainer once said to the young Cassius Clay. No one has yet succeeded in knocking a hole in the cylinder filled with horsehair, felt or foam, but this advice does summarize the main purpose of the exercise in a nutshell. The heavy bag is well suited for improving the sense of correct distance to an object and learning completely new series of hits. (Some trainers affix notes with entire combination sequences for their charges to follow on the heavy device.) The wearing of well-padded bag gloves weighing ten ounces and up is now mandatory.

Mike Tyson takes a shot at the heavy bag during show training in 1995.

PUNCHBAG & CO.

Nothing is better for practicing real punching and hitting than a stationary or moving target, which is why punchbags, speedballs, etc. are part of the standard equipment of any gym. This is where the boxer trains the force, timing, and accuracy for his repertoire of blows, tests his technique and his sense of distance. It helps him develop the necessary arm strength for accomplishing his goals in the ring. The equipment workout is thus "specific training," as methodological experts would call it.

It is hard to tell how long the basic concepts for today's equipment have actually been around. In British boxing halls of the 18th and 19th century, fine gentlemen concentrated primarily on boxing and sparring gymnastics. Bareknuckle champions refused to accept any scientifically grounded methods until the early 20th century. Practicing throwing punches with the aid of equipment was made mandatory at the very latest when boxing became a professional sport, however. And it is amazing to see how little the inventory of equipment has changed since then. Apart from the variety of new fillings and suspension techniques, one can definitely say that nearly everything now used by Lennox Lewis was once available to Jack Dempsey as well.

THE SPEEDBALL

The even "ratataratata" sound is an art to beginners and the result of being able to maintain a steady punching rhythm for experts. In addition to refining the motoric skills, it improves strength endurance in the shoulders and arms and helps build up the muscles of the forearm. Just like a soccer ball is made of an inflatable rubber skin and leather hull, so the double-suspension technology assures a high level of mobility. Coaches like to remind their charges that alternating footwork should not be forgotten at the ball either. An occasional change of tempo is also considered beneficial.

Lennox Lewis in a one-on-one dialog with the speedball in 1999.

FLOOR-TO-CEILING BALL

Hitting the rubber and leather ball, which is suspended on both the top and bottom and springs backward and forward, is an art in and of itself. And that is precisely why the floor-to-ceiling ball exists. The boxer uses it to train both his timing and accuracy, as well as to hone reaction skills and coordination. The ever-varying position and movement of the ball makes this activity especially difficult. The exercise is regarded as excellent counterattack training because the boxer must react to the ball as it springs back towards him. The boxer circles the ball in a clockwise or counterclockwise direction.

Fernando Vargas trains on the floor-to-ceiling ball in front of the press in 2000.

MAIZE BALL

Hung on a chain, the maize ball serves as a small target for point landings with the fist. Individual and double hits can be executed with great accuracy here, making this exercise highly beneficial for beginners and experts alike. The maize ball (which used to be filled with corn) is disappearing from modern gym inventories nonetheless.

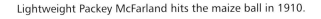

Lightweight Packey McFarland hits the maize ball in 1910.

MITTS

Padded punching mitts in which trainers or teammates can insert their hands have made it possible to simulate certain fight situations and combinations with greater accuracy than ever before. The coach acts like a real opponent, a moving partner who can evade or press in on the trainee. Short, set commands or signals indicated the types of hits called for, which are then executed as rapidly as possible. Working with mitts requires dynamic movement and quick, mid-movement reactions, which is why it is often used as a warm-up before the fight.

Coach George Francis trains Frank Bruno with mitts in 1996.

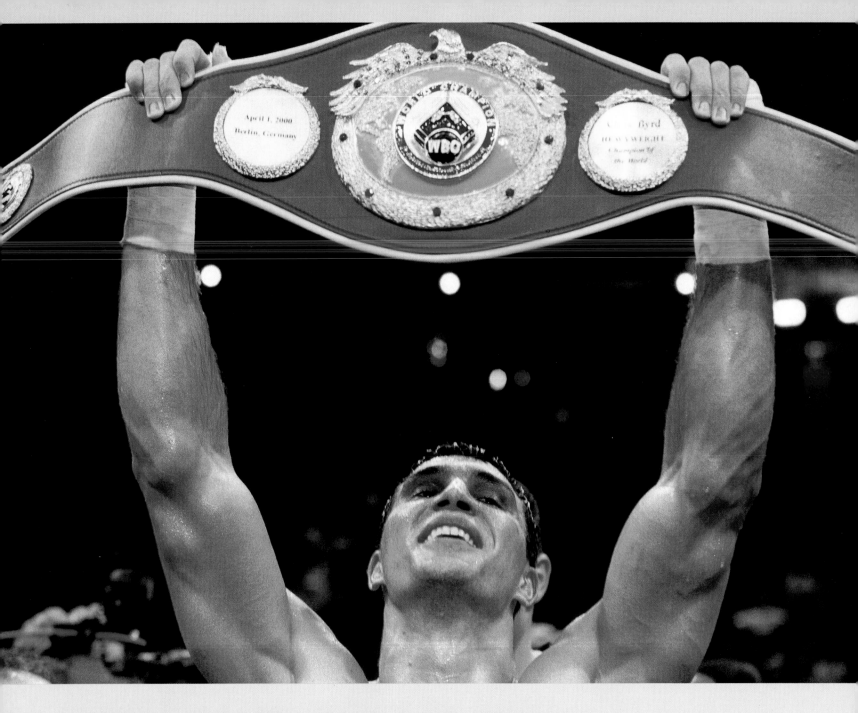

PREPARING TO TAKE THE TITLE

**VLADIMIR KLITSCHKO'S PREPARATION WORK
FOR THE HEAVYWEIGHT WBO WORLD CHAMPIONSHIP BOUT AGAINST CHRIS BYRD**

How professional boxers go about doing their work in the ring is easy enough to see. What they do in training, however, remains a mystery to most. And yet preparations or the build-up for an upcoming fight usually follow a meticulous plan designed to optimize all athletic performance parameters by the day of the fight. The German star coach Fritz Sdunek, who trained the Ukrainian challenger Vladimir Klitschko in fall 2000 for his bout with WBO heavyweight champion Chris Byrd followed just such a meticulous

plan. The coach from former East Germany and his model athlete spent a total of ten weeks in Kiev, Hamburg, and Cologne bringing the 1996 Olympic gold medallist in top form. Their efforts, chronicled on the following page, were not in vain: The younger of the Klitschko brothers defeated the champion on October 14, 2000, in Cologne by unanimous decision, becoming the new heavyweight titleholder.

Vladimir Klitschko completed a detailed, ten-week training program in Hamburg and Kiev before taking the WBO champion belt on October 14, 2000. Trainer Fritz Sdunek meticulously prepared the Ukrainian for his bout with the American titleholder Chris Byrd in Cologne. Their efforts were rewarded.

OVERALL PREPARATORY WORK:
AUGUST 7TH TO OCTOBER 14TH, 2000

AUG. 7TH–20TH (1ST–2ND WEEK):
Individualized preparatory training in Kiev.
General athletics: strength and endurance
6 training units (TU) per week. Strength
training with weights, shadow boxing.

AUG. 21ST–SEPT. 10TH (3RD–5TH WEEK):
General and specific strength and endurance
training in Hamburg with a technical, tactical
emphasis.
10 TU per week. Endurance runs, strength
training with weights, exercises with the
medicine ball, circular training, shadow boxing,
jump roping, equipment training, video
studies of opponents, tactical adjustment
with mitt training.

SEPT. 11TH–OCT. 8TH (6TH–9TH WEEK):
Honing special physical and technical/tactical
skills.
10 TU per week. Individualized sparring, equipment training, shadow boxing, jump roping,
endurance runs with sprints, jumps, video
feedback studies of own training performance.
Stress test on Sept. 13th: 12 sprints of over
800 meters (2,625 feet) in 3 minutes each,
1 minute break.
Stress test on Sept. 20th: 12-minute endurance
run ("Cooper Test").

9th week: 1 sparring unit of more than
12 rounds.

OCT. 9TH–14TH (10TH WEEK):
Stabilization phase: Honing technical and
tactical skills, attaining optimal physical and
psychological stability.
6 TU per week. Mitt training, shadow boxing,
endurance runs, reaction and speed training,
Discussion of tactics.

TOTAL PREPARATION EFFORTS FOR THE BOUT:
76 sparring rounds of 3 minutes a piece;
540 rounds of 3 minutes a piece with
equipment, strength training, etc.;
143 miles run.

TRAINING METHODS

Stopping a right-hand cross counter to head with left to follow, with inside left hook to jaw.

The Solar Plexus Punch

How to feint your opponent into leaving an opening for it.

Blocking a right swing & sending a right uppercut to the chin.

The Safety Block

Pulling down an opponent's guarding hand to make an opening.

Pinning your opponent's hands, as you draw out for a clinch.

The Corkscrew Blow.

Blocking a left lead to the body and countering with left hook to the face.

Guard out & Right ready for action.

Crouching and sending the left straight to body.

Drawing away from a right swing, to counter with straight right to the face

Sparring for an Opening.

Stepping outside of a straight right to the face, shoving it over left shoulder with left hand and standing ready to face the body.

Avoiding a straight right to the face by stepping to the right & sending over a right chop to the face

Blocking an opponent's High left swing for the head & standing ready to block his Right Jab to body

BOXING BASICS

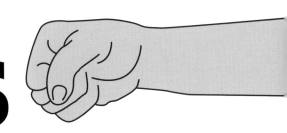

I. STARTING POSITION

In order to simplify the following presentation, all positions are described from the point of view of a right-handed person; i.e., left-handers should perform the movements in the exact opposite direction.

The feet are planted approximately shoulder-width apart. The left foot is positioned slightly forward and flat on the floor. The right foot may be lifted off the floor slightly at the heel. The body weight is evenly distributed on both legs. The knees are slightly bent.

The upper body is turned slightly inward in order to minimize the attack surface and protect the chin with the forward shoulder. The torso remains upright.

The half-bent arm of the left leading hand is stretched out at shoulder height. It is used to prepare a hit with the striking hand (for right-handers this is usually the right hand) resting in a bent position at collarbone height. The elbows are pointed inward. The head remains upright; the chin pulled in slightly.

II. FOOTWORK

The legs act as a flexible foundation for the boxer. They should enable him to move in any direction without losing his balance. The feet should therefore always shift position in a gliding motion, i.e. near to the floor, before being set back down again.

The impulse for forward movement comes from the ball of the rear foot. The body's center of gravity is then shifted to the front foot.

When moving backwards, the rear foot should always be moved to the back first. The body's center of gravity is then shifted to the rear foot.

During side steps, the weight is initially shifted to the rear foot. Body weight is not shifted back until the front foot has been moved back to the side.

It is especially important to take care never to cross the feet at any time during any of these maneuvers.

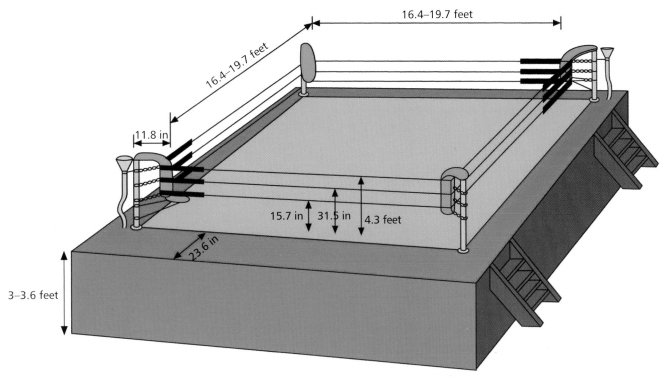

III. PUNCHING TECHNIQUES

1. THE LEFT JAB (STRAIGHT LEFT)

The straight left with the outstretched leading hand (the left jab) is the most common punch, as it can be thrown very quickly from the starting position. It may be an effective single or double hit (double jab) or prepare a path for the striking hand by tearing open the opponent's cover. This holds especially true of the jab to the body that pulls the opponent's hands downwards.

Movement sequence: The left arm shoots out to the opponent's head or body with a certain amount of pressure from the hips and shoulders. It clearly rotates inwards, i.e. clockwise, during this motion. The arm snaps back from the punch in the same manner. The left foot is moved slightly forward before the punch. The right fist continues to cover the chin.

III. 1

2. STRAIGHT RIGHT (RIGHT JAB)

The straight right provides the boxer with the greatest amount of punching power, making it his most effective and often most crucial weapon. An attacker exposes himself during this move, however, so it should be used only sparingly and with great care. The groundwork for this punch is usually laid with jabs.

Movement sequence: The right arm shoots forwards while simultaneously rotating inwards. The shoulders stay as straight as possible. The left fist remains raised to protect the upper body and chin.

The rear right foot, the hips and the shoulders press the body, which is rotating on its axis, forwards and the body weight is clearly shifted to the front left foot.

III. 2

3. THE LEFT HOOK

Landed suddenly outside of the opponent's field of vision, the left hook is one of the most dangerous boxing punches—regardless of whether it comes as a blow to the head (e.g., tip of the chin) or as a blow to the body (e.g., solar plexus). Boxers like to use this as a counter punch.

Movement sequence: The body weight is initially shifted to the rear right foot while the shoulders and hips dynamically pull the left half of the body forwards. At the same time, the bent left arm is pushed forward in a curving movement. The right fist remains close to the head for cover. The rotation of the body is supported by the front left foot, which turns inward on the ball of the foot. In a hook to the opponent's body, the boxer's upper body also bends forward slightly.

III. 3

4. THE RIGHT HOOK

The right hook with the striking hand must travel farther than the left hook with the leading hand before connecting with its target. It is therefore seldom used as a single punch.

It can also be highly effective when thrown from half range or up close as a follow-up punch.

Movement sequence: The movement is similar to a left hook, only the boxer turns on the ball of his rear right foot in this case.

III. 4

5. THE UPPERCUT

There is no better weapon against an opponent churning his way forwards during infights or at half range than an uppercut. It breaks open the opponent's cover and is extremely effective as a blow to the chin. The uppercut is usually executed with the striking hand as it can be thrown quickly and securely from the starting position.

III. 5

Movement sequence: The inside of the striking fist is facing the boxer's own body, while the back of the fist is facing the opponent. The upper body is slightly bent toward the right hip.

The right striking arm, which has previously remained bent, shoots upwards out of this movement to the opponent's head or body. The leading hand remains near the chin while the arm stays close to the body for cover.

6. THE CROSS

As a reaction to an opponent's attempt to strike a blow, the cross is usually executed with the left jab. It takes advantage of the fact that the opponent's head and the left side of his body are exposed while he attacks.

Movement sequence: The upper body is bent slightly outward to evade the opponent's blow. At the same time, the boxer's arm (usually the left) pushes across and under the opponent's arm and strikes him in a cross to the body. The rear right leg supports the upper body and presses it forwards. The hips and shoulders are turned inward in the direction of the blow.

Ill. 6

7. DOUBLE HITS

Double hits are landed with the same fist and are aimed first at the opponent's head and than at his body (or vice versa) directly one after the other. The first blow opens the opponent's cover enabling the second, stronger blow to connect with the exposed body region.

Movement sequence: Following a punch such as a hook to the head, the right fist then immediately strikes an uppercut to the body.

Another possible double hit combination would be an uppercut to the body with the left hand followed by a hook from the side to the head.

Ill. 7

8. SERIES OF PUNCHES

A series of punches is a sequence of two or more hits with the striking or leading hand combining various techniques. In training, specific combinations of blows are practiced until the boxer can execute them automatically in a fight.

Movement sequence: Left jab and straight right, e.g., to the head, followed by two uppercuts to the body and then a jab to the head.

IV. DEFENSIVE TACTICS

9. BLOCKING

A good boxer's skill is reflected not only in the number of hits he lands but also in the use of quick evasion tactics and effective protective postures such as those seen during blocking.

The opponent's blow is blocked with a less sensitive body region where a hit does not have any effect nor does it bring the opponent any points. Such regions include the shoulders, the upper arms and forearms, the fists and the open hand.

Ill. 9

10. PARRYING

The opponent's blow is deflected with the inside of the fist or the underarms in such a manner that it misses its target.

Ill. 10

11. SLIPPING

An opponent's attempt at a blow to the body is evaded by bending the upper body and head forwards and to the left or right. The knees bend only slightly or not at all.

Ill. 11

12. BOBBING

Bobbing is an ideal method for evading an opponent's jabs. The boxer "shrinks" by suddenly bending at the knees. The head is thus removed from the blow zone as the boxer slips under the punch.

Ill. 12

13. ROLLING

Rolling helps the boxer evade hooks from half range.

The upper body follows the direction of the blow from the attacker, avoiding contact with the glove or softening its impact (rolling with the punches). This is a good starting position for throwing counter hooks.

Ill. 13

14. EVADING

When under attack, the boxer can take a step backwards or to the side (side step), bringing his head and body out of his opponent's striking range. This move requires

excellent reaction abilities in a real fight situation. It is also important not to move too far away from the opponent.

Ill. 14

15. COUNTERING

The boxer prepares his own blow even while evading that of his opponent. If a boxer can broadly deduce what type of hit his opponent is going to try and use, a counter move can help prevent its execution.

Ill. 15

V. PROTECTIVE POSTURES

16. HALF COVER

In the half-cover position, the left shoulder is pulled up slightly to protect the chin. The left arm, bent at a right angle, covers the body while the bent right arm with the fist

held at face level protects the head. The weight is on the rear leg. The half-cover position is highly effective and thus the preferred protective posture at the ropes.

Ill. 16

17. DOUBLE COVER

In the double-cover position, the upper body is bent to make it shorter. The right and left forearms are folded across the body while the elbows are positioned parallel to each other at the same height. The fists are held tightly together directly in front of the face to protect the head. This position is considered especially effective as a defensive strategy at the ropes or in the corner of the ring.

Ill. 17

18. CROSS ARM GUARD

When using the cross arm guard, the arch of the boxer's right, half-lifted arm protects the chin while the left arm is kept close to the body to act as a shield. The upper body bobs continually from right to left to avoid the opponent's blows. Very rapid and effective hooks can be thrown as counter punches from this bobbing cross arm guard position.

VI. ILLEGAL BLOWS

19. PUNCHING SURFACES

Boxing rules clearly define which parts of the human body can be used as targets for blows. These include the front of the upper body above the beltline as well as the sides and front of the neck and facial regions.

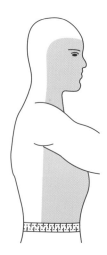

Ill. 19

The unavoidable blows to the arms and shoulder regions which occur during a fight because of blocking and evasion maneuvers are not regarded as hits. If one of the boxers purposely lands a blow outside of the accepted striking surface, the referee can warn or in some cases disqualify him.

20. HEAD BUTT

The opponents' heads are often dangerously close to one another, such as during a dynamic infight. Not infrequently, this situation results in intentional and unintentional collisions. Both forms of fouls can lead to the fight being stopped early, such as when one of the boxers is critically injured in the eye region.

The call, however, can vary greatly. If the blow was unintentional, a "technical decision" is announced after a certain number

Ill. 20

of rounds, whereas the offending boxer will be disqualified if the move was intentional.

21. LOW BLOW

Punches to the body can sometimes land under the beltline, whether on purpose or by accident. The first case is referred to as an intentional foul, the second as an unintentional foul. Modern cup protectors are robust enough to prevent a serious injury that could cause the fight to be stopped. The boxer who was been struck by a low blow is therefore given several minutes to recover before the fight continues.

If he does not continue the fight, he will be disqualified. The same holds true even if the blow was intentional.

Ill. 21

22. TURNING AWAY

Quickly turning the body on its axis or moving to the side is often sufficient to evade an opponent's blow. What was then intended as a legal punch to the head or body then becomes an "illegal blow" to the shoulders or back. This intentional turning away is then considered a foul. After all, the boxer is supposed to defend himself from his opponent's attack frontally with the permitted defensive techniques (blocking, evading, bobbing, etc.) instead of moving out of the line of fire by turning away. He is supposed to "face the fight." As is the case with other fouls, if the boxer continues to avoid confrontation, he will receive an initial warning and then be disqualified.

Ill. 22

THE FIGHTS

THE WHOLE DRAMA

THE HYPE

Boxing events require extensive preparations. Weeks, even months before the evening of the big duel, a fight of equal or greater importance is taking place outside the ring. It is the battle for the public attention, the fight to lure spectators into the arena or in front of the TV set. It is fought by the organizers and promoters and its outcome plays a crucial role in determining the financial success of the endeavor as a whole. Profit and loss depend, among other things, on how important or attractive the potential boxing spectators regard in particular the main fight to be. It is a well-known fact, however, that a certain amount of influence can be exercised in this matter.

Long before the introduction of modern promotional strategies, impresarios such as the legendary Tex Rickard already knew how to create hype for their events. Some of their tricks and techniques are still used in almost exactly the same manner today. Rickard was the first to coin the term "Fight of the Century" for Jack Johnson's title bout against James Jeffries 1910. The use of this term has been increased exponentially ever since. Rickard also took full advantage of social, ethnic and national differences between opponents, presenting their sporting matches as symbolic prestige duels between blacks and whites, the Old and the New World, etc. Former world champion Riddick Bowe used the same technique in 1995 to make a national affair of his fight with the exiled Cuban Jorge Luis Gonzales. "First I'm going to beat you up, then I'm going after Castro," Bowe threatened his opponent at a press conference.

And of course boxers have likewise always been obliged to help generate publicity for their fights. All public events, from the signing of the contract to diverse media appointments, are used to build the level of expectations to a seething crescendo. Nothing is more effective than a certain atmosphere of animosity between the opponents, whether real or pretend. Disrespectful remarks, arrogant predictions and mutual threats ranging from implied to actual violence—a general rule of thumb is that the more negative the opponents' attitude towards one another, the better the ticket sales. TV stations now add to this hype by giving fights mottos such as "The Uncivil War" or "Unfinished Business."

Whether one regards this as dubious manipulation of human curiosity or an inherent aspect of this spectator sport—it is highly effective either way. "Give the people what they want, how they want it," boxing promoter Tex Rickard once said, "and not how you think it should be."

Charles Brewer takes everything off in Düsseldorf in 1998 in order to stay within the super middleweight limit. Fernando Vargas, Peter McNeeley, …

THE WEIGH-IN

From a formal perspective, it is an unexciting and unspectacular event. A few boxers in their underpants climbing onto a scale, surrounded by numerous officials wearing more or less important expressions—that is just about all there is to see at this obligatory weigh-in ceremony. A group of journalists and hard-core fans gathers at these events nonetheless, following the action with fervent intensity. For this inner circle the whole process represents far more than meets the eye.

Just like gamblers sizing up horses at the track before the race begins, so the self-proclaimed and genuine boxing insiders, the connoisseurs of the sport, attempt to judge the athletes' condition during the weigh-in. What they can more or less determine is the degree of physical fitness revealed by the scantily clad fighters, whether they appear

to be optimally trained. Should this not be the case, there may be minor or even major alterations in the odds and betting quotas for the fight. This was exactly what happened in October 1990 when the new heavyweight champion James "Buster" Douglas presented himself before his first title defense against Evander Holyfield in Las Vegas as an overweight pizza lover. The betting odds changed within just a few seconds.

The athletes' psychological condition is of equal or greater importance to their physical

condition, however. Of course, a fighter's state of mind is not visible at first glance, but most observers are convinced that it can be ascertained by careful scrutiny nonetheless. The boxers' behavior during this ritual is thus monitored with great intensity. Who appears stabile and self-confident, who avoids glances from whom? The last meeting before the fight gives both opponents a final opportunity "to strike a few mental blows at one another," as American author George Plimpton once put it. And the best athletes in the sport

Same scale, same facial expression: Before the welterweight championship at the Staples Center in Los Angeles in June 2000, Oscar De La Hoya presents himself just as telegenic and relaxed as…

… Frank Bruno, Bruce Seldon, and Mike Tyson *(from left)* take advantage of their appearance on the scale to demonstrate their confidence and determination.

have surely taken ample advantage of this opportunity.

Archie Moore always fixed his challengers with a frozen stare on the scale, while Chris Eubank punished them with demonstrative ignorance. Still others attempt to intimidate their adversaries with words or disparage them as failures, cowards, etc. This practice took a dangerous turn when Benny "Kid" Paret taunted his opponent Emile Griffith as a homosexual during the weigh-in before their third title bout in March 1962. This created an animosity in the fight that would prove deadly. Griffith landed so many hard blows to his opponent's head that Paret fell into a fatal coma in the twelfth round.

No one took these psychological skirmishes as far as the young Cassius Clay in February 1965, however. On the morning before his title bout with Sonny Liston, the challenger staged a chaotic incident during the weigh-in at the Miami Beach Convention Hall, hysterically deriding the title defender as an idiot and threatening to attack him then and there in pretend rage. This unseemly show achieved the desired effect: Liston was irritated and the press pack was convinced that Clay was a crazy show-off trying to hide his own fear and had no chance of winning the fight.

Scenarios such as this are rare exceptions, but the air is always heavy with potential psychodrama during a weigh-in. Even when everything remains peaceful, the weigh-in represents a relatively uncomplicated opportunity for getting up close and personal with the stars of the ring. The visitor feels like an insider, and may even return home with autographed gloves or photographs. A sense of anticipation spreads before the impending event—just a few more hours and then it will all begin. Organizers and TV shows thus tend to make the most of the weigh-in—news and photographs of professionals on the scale are effective publicity for the big show.

…does his opponent "Sugar" Shane Mosley. Only Mosley was left smiling at the end of this world-class match, however. He won on points to become the new WBC champion.

THE WALK-IN

"They came swaggering down the aisle, a seething current of heads." This was how the American author David Remnick describes the entry of heavyweight world champion Floyd Patterson and his entourage in *King of the World* (1999). The two statements accurately reflect the charged atmosphere and movement patterns during the so-called walk-in. The knot of confidants pushes their way forward to the ring with a dancing figure in their midst, half-hidden under the hood of his fighting robe. It is the boxer on whom all their hopes are pinned, and this electrifying moment ushers in the start of the spectacle itself.

Some boxers claim that the reactions of the masses, who have meanwhile been whipped into a frenzy, no longer penetrate their tunnel of concentration. Others claim they can sense the adrenalin pumping through their veins and feel like "Spartacus, entering the arena to fight to the death," as former supper middle-weight champion Nigel Benn once phrased it. They are indeed presented just like the gladiators of ancient days, merely with modern lighting and sound effects. It is no longer possible to conceive of the walk-in to a title bout anywhere in the Western world without accompanying theme music. (The main fighters in bouts in Thailand and other Southeast Asian countries are lead to the ring bedecked with garlands of flowers and other ornaments while accompanied by the chiming bells.)

Tina Turner's "Simply the Best," George Thorogood's "Bad to the Bone" and other thematic hymns provide the carpet of sound on which ring heroes everywhere are swept before the spectators. Additional special effects serve to further intensify the grandiose aura of the scene. Naseem Hamed, also known as the "Prince," once had himself carried to the edge of ring on a shimmering, gold-colored litter in his native Britain. His compatriot Chris Eubank roared up a ramp to the ring on a motorcycle. Light heavy-weight champion Dariusz Michalczewski, nicknamed "Tiger" in Germany, was lower-ed into the ring in a cage through the roof of a Hamburg auditorium. What holds true for the catwalks at big fashion shows now plainly holds true for the walk-in as well: "Anything goes!"

Hector Camacho Jr. *(top left)*, Prince Naseem Hamed *(top center, bottom left)*, Oscar De La Hoya *(top right)*, Frank Bruno *(center)*, and Anthony Mundine *(bottom right)* make their spectacular entries. The only rule of the show: "Anything goes!"

Opposite page:
Entry of the gladiator: Champion Michael Moorer and his entourage make an impressive entry into the ring in Las Vegas in November 1994. The heavyweight world champion lost his title to George Foreman in a KO defeat there.

THE STAREDOWN

One doesn't have to be a psychologist to sense the explosive nature of this moment. When the referee calls the opponents to the center of the ring for final instructions (which usually run something along the lines of "I want a clean fight, no holding, no hitting after the break"), they suddenly find themselves standing directly across from one another—and can look critically into the other's eyes. It is a psychological test of strength, as the look says volumes about the boxer's state of mind: up close and personal, his eyes often reveal determination or doubt, self-confidence or fear. This can create an advantage for at least one of the two adversaries even before the

ritual ends with the traditional touch gloves. Some are convinced that the fight is decided in this very moment.

Reporters and spectators in particular thus never tire of trying to read the exchange of glances like some read palms. And their interpretations are often confirmed when the boxer who appears uncertain actually does lose later on. Floyd Patterson stared embarrassedly down at his shoes when facing Sonny Liston and there was panic evident in Bruce Seldon's frozen stare just before his duel with Mike Tyson. Weren't those clear signals?

Team members and athletes are often more careful in applying such "kitchen sink

DaVarryl Williamson *(top left)* and Michael Bennett *(above)* during the U.S. Olympic qualification in Tampa Bay, February 2000. The seconds in which the referee rattles off his instructions provide an ideal opportunity for intimidation or psyching out.

Oscar De La Hoya *(top right)* stares at the auditorium ceiling in concentration, not in fear. Here, he is pictured at the lightweight title bout in Las Vegas in 1995. The challenger Genaro Hernandez had no chance to undermine his opponent with angry glances before the fight.

psychology." The boxer who appears to be the most confident is not always the winner. And of course, there are those fighters who purposely avoid the other's glare, not because of insecurity but in an attempt to maintain their concentration. Oscar De La Hoya, for instance, fixed his gaze at the auditorium hall during the staredown to focus his energies before a fight. No one would have ever dared to take this as a sign of cowardice on his part!

There are more than enough battles of words in the run-up to the fight, however, even when this is not exactly in keeping with regulations. These exchanges range from

James Toney's rather prosaic "Your ass is mine!" to the more linguistically complex aphorisms of Muhammad Ali. In Kinshasa, Ali referred to George Foreman as a chump rather than a "champ" and informed Foreman "You're going to get thrashed tonight in front of all these Africans!" during the referee's opening words. If this psyching out is not followed by a corresponding boxing out after the first gong sounds, however, even the most sophisticated intimidation maneuvers prove worthless.

"Boxing is like nothing else," the famous ring physician Ferdie Pacheco liked to say, "they'll knock you flat on the floor."

THE EXCHANGE OF BLOWS

When the signal for the first round is given, all conjectures and predictions are suddenly just so much hot air. Now it is time for the fight itself, pure action that tells "a unique and highly condensed drama without words" as the American author Joyce Carol Oates once put it. After all, "even when nothing sensational happens: then the drama is 'merely' psychological."

Here, the punches that are landed or miss their mark count like relevant and irrelevant arguments at a trial in a court of law. And just like in a court of law, the judge passes a verdict in the end: victor on points or on a KO, old champion or new one. The idea is to influence the course of the debate in one's own favor—to impose one's own

concept, as the trainers say, on the opponent's concept. "Whatever the other guy wants to do," advised boxer Sam Langford, "don't let him do it."

The number of hits exchanged by opponents can vary greatly. The record is still ascribed to Zack Padilla, who hit challenger Ray Oliveira exactly 207 times in the final

It was blow for blow as Tommy Morrison and ex-champion George Foreman boxed for the WBO heavyweight title on June 7, 1993, in Las Vegas. Morrison, the more mobile of the two adversaries, was awarded the well-deserved victory on points at the end of twelve action-packed rounds. The title had become vacant when Michael Moorer stepped down as champion.

round of his WBO light welterweight title defense in December 1993 according to computer statistics. This corresponds to a rate of 1.15 hits per second. Padilla threw 1,596 punches in this fight. Heavyweight boxers look like they are moving in slow motion by comparison: During the return bout between Lennox Lewis and Evander Holyfield in November 1999, Lewis registered a total of 490 punches (195 of them hits), while Holyfield registered 416 (137 of them hits). The record for the lowest number of blows is held by heavyweight Trevor Berbick, who threw just four punches during the first round of his duel with Carl Williams in 1988.

A boxer must punch. The rulebook stipulates that an inactive fighter be declared the loser on a TKO defeat. The referee must signal the end of the unequal duel when he establishes that one of the boxers is too groggy or injured and, therefore, unable to continue the fight. The drama has then reached its conclusion.

THE BREAK

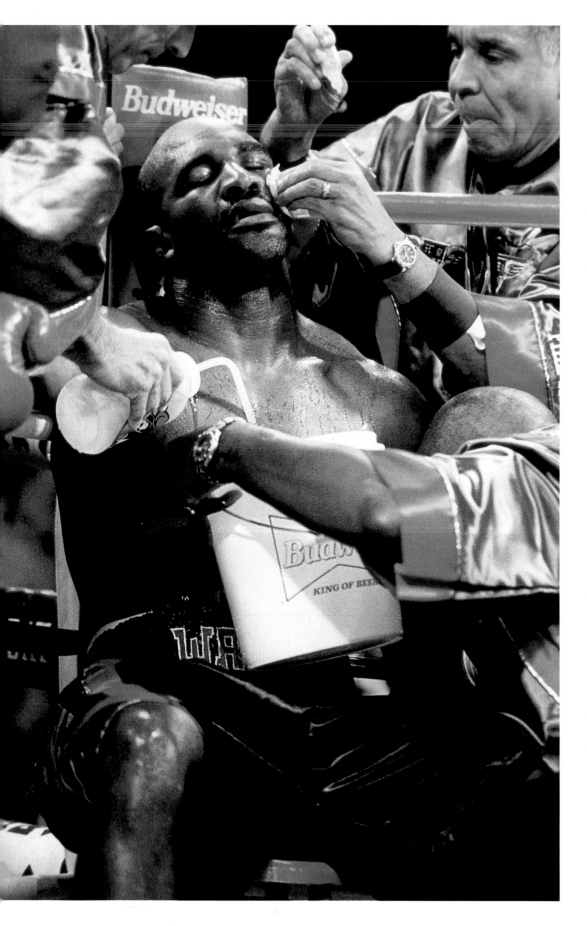

It may not last much longer than the blink of an eye, but a lot can happen in the ring break nonetheless. Once the main characters have retired to their respective corners to recover in a sitting or (less frequently) in a standing position, their team members begin working full speed. The trainer, assistant, and cut-man now pack tactical discussion, therapy, and medical treatment into a precisely one-minute "pit stop." Strategies are altered, motivational seminars held and wounds cared for a best as possible. Then the neck is massaged, the mouthpiece cleaned, and the spittoon filled—a complete repair job in 60 seconds.

The team members' actions are usually conducted simultaneously in a well-oiled routine—anything hectic that could disturb the boxer is avoided. A good cut-man practices subtle understatement, even when the boxer comes "out of the round" with gaping laceration wounds. The trainer is the only one not to put on a continual display of the we'll-fix-that-in-a-jiffy attitude. In the critical phases of a ring duel he must also criticize, shake up and re-motivate his charge to save the fight or "turn it around." This is the psychologically interesting aspect of the pause and is accordingly surrounded by innumerable tales of sudden and unexpected miracles.

"You're blowing it, son," coach Angelo Dundee once warned Sugar Ray Leonard during a pause in Leonard's fight with Thomas Hearns. This lit the fuse for a furious finish in which "Sugar" stopped his opponent Hearns in the second-to-last round. Other trainers have appealed to their charges' sense of manliness, reminded them of beloved family members or painted bright pictures of what they would be able to buy after winning the title.

The "Tomorrow You'll Cry" speech with which trainer Teddy Atlas inspired Michael Moorer to dethrone champion Evander Holyfield in 1994 is already a classic. When Moorer retired to the corner, Atlas sat down in Moorer's chair and suggested they either exchange places or Moorer finally pick up the pace a little.

The break is about more than just hand towels and Vaseline; it may decide the outcome of the fight itself.

Patching up and refreshing: Lots of busy hands care of Evander Holyfield *(opposite page)* and Felix "Tito" Trinidad *(right)* during the brief one-minute break.

TEDDY ATLAS' WORDS TO TITLE CONTENDER MICHAEL MOORER ON APRIL 22, 1994, IN LAS VEGAS

"Do you want me to trade places with you—is that what you want? Listen, this guy is at the end of his rope. There comes a time in a man's life when he has to decide if he wants to live, survive or win. You're doing just enough to keep him away from you and hope that he leaves you in peace. You're lying to yourself, but tomorrow you'll be crying! You're lying to yourself and I would be lying to you too if I let you get away with it! But tomorrow you'll be crying over it. Do you want to cry tomorrow? Then don't lie to yourself!"

207

THE KNOCKDOWN

A quick end to a European championship: British heavyweight Richard Dunn is knocked out by his countryman Joe Bugner in the first round of this fight in 1976.

Some swear they saw the punch coming as if in slow motion. Others claim they didn't notice a thing. Later they sit in the locker room and ask their coach what happened. Obviously there are as many ways of perceiving a knockdown as there are boxers who have experienced one. Only its effect remains more or less the same. It is, after all, the most visible form of humiliation there is in sports.

This is likely one of the reasons that only few of those who have experienced a knockout have later tried to describe the experience, which is actually a "neurological short circuit" in the brain. Victors like to talk about having "flattened" their opponent and "knocking his lights out"—losers prefer to remain silent. The highly detailed description that dethroned world champion Floyd Patterson once gave a friend who happened to be a reporter for the *New York Times* is thus the lone classic in this field. It is "not a 'bad' feeling," Patterson said of his KO experience, but "actually (...) a 'nice' feeling (...) It doesn't hurt, you're just unbelievable groggy, (...) like floating on a pleasant cloud." Then, however "a confused pain" sets in, linked with anger and shame, "and then you just want to disappear through a trap door that opens up in the ring floor (...) and drops you into the locker room (...)."

And yet a knockdown is not always a knockout. Experienced professionals take their time when the referee begins to count over them. They get back on their feet just in time to continue the fight after the obligatory eight count and passing the referee's test ("What is your name?" "How many fingers am I holding up?"). Despite the deduction of points at the end of the round, knockdowns do not have to mean defeat. Again and again, unshakable boxers have returned to the fight and managed to "turn it around." In the eyes of the fans, "picking oneself up off the ring floor" even has something heroic about it. Several knockdowns in the same fight, however, usually lead to the stopping of the duel, the TKO (technical knockout). The various boxing association usually stipulate stoppage of the fight after three knockdowns in the same round. After all, on occasion it really is better when the fight ends before the lights "get knocked out!"

THE TRIUMPH

The gesture in which athletes raise their arms in triumph after a hard-fought victory is by no means exclusive to the world of boxing. The Monday issue of newspapers all over the world feature cheering soccer and baseball players, weightlifters and swimmers in this exact same position. But only in boxing does the announcement of the judges' decision regularly result in main characters and spectators conglomerating in and around the ring in a seething mass of humanity. Swept up in its own dynamics, this crowd often effortlessly flattens barricades and security guards alike.

"Suddenly the ring was flooded with people," said Max Schmeling of the minutes following his KO victory over Joe Louis in Yankee Stadium in New York. Even on the way to the locker room, the surprise victor registered "faces distorted with joy." "Some of the members of the stumbling, screaming crowd clutched at me as if they just wanted to touch me somewhere, others tore scraps of the bandages off my fists as if they were relics." Not until decades afterwards had Germany's only heavyweight champion digested the "outpouring of emotions" and "irrational needs" that takes place in "these minutes of ecstatic satisfaction."

Perhaps more so than any other types of sports enthusiast, the boxing fan seeks direct contact to the victorious boxer. And the boxer in turn seeks universal recognition when he, as is currently the fashion, climbs onto all four ring posts one after the other and greets fans on all sides. These triumphant gestures may be executed in a true wave of euphoria, such as when the victor has himself carried out by his supporters or draped in his country's flag. They can often take on a demonstrative, egomaniacal character seen among victorious outsiders, however. Cassius Clay's spontaneous words after his surprise victory over clear favorite Sonny Liston are a perfect example. "Eat your words!" "Eat your words!" Clay screamed loudly to the reporters in the first rows who had given him no chance of victory before the fight.

And they took it back. After all, boxing triumphs have something irresistible about them.

Heavyweight Ezra Sellers appears to reach for the ceiling of the Foxwoods Resort Casinos in Ledyard, Connecticut, after his KO victory over John McClain in 1997.

THE RECONCILIATION

Of course there are exceptions when boxers have not been willing to limit their rivalry with opponents to the fight in the ring. Such extended animosity is usually the result of degrading comments and behavior from the opponent before the fight. As a rule, however, the "war" usually ends with the final gong and the two fighters, who were relentlessly pummeling one another mere moments ago, wrap their arms around each other and may even call upon the audience to applaud one another.

And they have good reason to do so. As long as the fight is on, the opponents share the enormous pressures that come with it —they experience pain, stress, and agony together. Despite their continued efforts to do one another in, this subconsciously creates

a feeling of connectedness and mutual respect such as that experienced by Muhammad Ali and Joe Frazier in their three epic ring duels. Looking back later, Ali commented that he and his archrival were a "pretty good team." "Without him I couldn't have become what I am and without me he couldn't have become what he is," said Ali.

Today Ali is a close friend in particular with Ken Norton, who once broke Ali's jaw. Friendships also developed between Joe Louis and Max Schmeling, Beau Jack and Bob Montgomery—and many other former rivals. This phenomenon is also to be found among amateurs, an excellent example of which is the comradeship between the German Dieter Kottysch and the Pole Wieslaw Rudkowski. Kottysch, the only German gold medallist at

the 1972 Olympic tournament in Munich, took his final-round opponent to a wild celebration party on the evening after their bitter fight in the ring. The two happily caroused through Munich's bars until morning—and have remained friends from that day forward, visiting each other at least once a year.

"You have to understand that boxing is just a game that we play," the former light heavyweight and heavyweight champion Michael Spinks once said. This enlightening comment was addressed to his opponent Dwight Braxton, who wanted to attack his conqueror after their bout for the light heavyweight title in March 1983. Fortunately, boxers usually view their sport just as did Spinks, while fighters such as Braxton remain the rare exception.

THE FIGHT AFTERWARDS

For *aficionados* and officials, it is all over as soon as the ring announcer proclaims the result. For the boxers themselves, however, it is now that the fight first really begins to take effect. Pain and exhaustion begin to make themselves felt as the body is gradually released from the numbing mercy of endorphins. Some fighters already need a shoulder to lean on just to get down from the ring, others manage to make it to the locker room before collapsing, where they quickly transform from heroes into helpless convalescents.

"We pulled him after us like a drunkard," said Muhammad Ali's personal physician Ferdie Pacheco of the minutes after Ali's first duel with Joe Frazier (1971). Down the hall a few feet away, his defeater was busy burying his mangled face in a shower drain full of ice cubes, as Dave Wolf one of Frazier's coaches, later confirmed. "Can't somebody do something here?" yelled Frazier in between holding his face to the ice, "it hurts." The two later briefly landed in Flowers Fifth Avenue Hospital in Manhattan to be examined for fractures and possible latent injuries. This fact was initially kept secret and later played down—neither of the two bitter rivals wanted to admit that the other had

The reality after the fight begins to set in for Jo Weidin *(above)*, Antoine Byrd *(left)*, Dick Richardson *(opposite page, top)* and Vitali Klitschko *(opposite page, bottom)*.

"HIS ENTIRE BODY WAS COVERED WITH WELTS AND INJURIES AND THERE WERE LARGE BRUISES ON BOTH HIPS—CONTUSIONS WHERE FRAZIER HAD HIT HIS HIP JOINTS. HIS FACE WAS PUFFED UP (...) HE LATER SAID THAT THIS FIGHT WAS THE CLOSEST THING TO DEATH HE HAD EVER EXPERIENCED."
FERDIE PACHECO on Muhammad Ali (after Ali's third fight with Joe Frazier)

"THE NEXT DAY IT HURT AS THE MUSCLES STRETCHED AND PRESSED

fought well enough to have sent him to the emergency room.

It is always better to take precautionary measures, however. From a medical standpoint, the boxer is in an extremely critical situation after every halfway energetic fight. His physical reserves have been used up by the great exertion; there may be dramatic fluid loss or dehydration. Both can cause his vital systems to collapse, with symptoms ranging from temporary faintness to a life-threatening coma. Added to this is the danger of an acute but latent blood clot *(haematoma)* in the brain: Without rapid computer-aided tomography (CAT scan) of the skull it is impossible to tell whether or not some of those hard hits may have caused more damage than just a disfigured face.

CAT scans and temporary fighting bans have meanwhile been made obligatory, at least after KO defeats, in all major arenas of the boxing world. Voluntary precautionary hospital admissions, in which the boxer is monitored during a brief in-patient stay of 12 to 24 hours after hard fights, are becoming ever more common. Pain is matter-of-course, however, and often lasts several days. This is, after all, what is sometimes referred to as the "hurt business."

"AND THEN I PASSED OUT BECAUSE THE PAIN WAS SO BAD (...) I WOKE UP IN AN AMBULANCE. MY WIFE CAROLYNE WAS AT MY SIDE, CRYING HER EYES OUT. MY BODY WAS IN TORTURE WITH THE PAIN, BUT SOMEHOW I MANAGED TO TURN TO HER AND SMILE. 'WOULD YOU LIKE TO GO TO A PARTY?'"

NIGEL BENN
(after his fight with Gerald McClellan)

"MY FACE LOOKED LIKE A PIECE OF LIVER THAT A BUTCHER HAD LAID ON A BLOCK AND WORKED OVER WITH A WOODEN HAMMER."

JAKE LAMOTTA
(after his fight with Nate Bolden)

THE WHOLE DRAMA

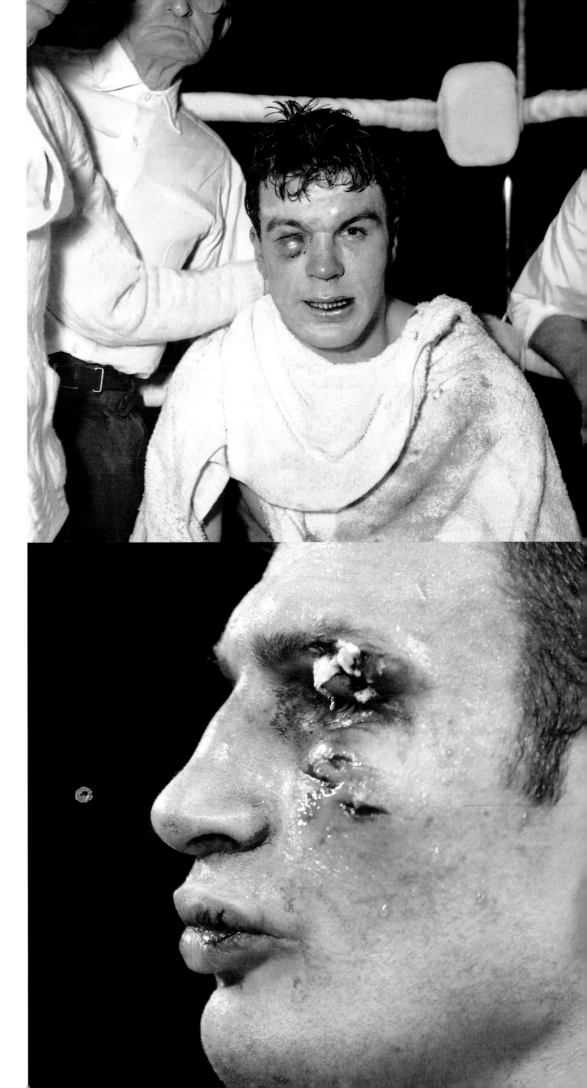

Henry Maske beforehand

Henry Maske after his victory

The German photographer Gordian Heinrichs captured the faces of amateur and professional boxers before and after their fights in the early 1990s.

Alexander Boy beforehand

Alexander Boy after his defeat

THE FIGHTS

Heiko Schütz beforehand

Heiko Schütz after his defeat

Robert Johnson beforehand

Robert Johnson after his defeat

THE WHOLE DRAMA

ROUND TRIP:

USA—NORTH-EASTERN COAST

by Steve Farhood

Steve Farhood, born in 1957, made a name for himself as the chief editor of *The Ring*, a position he held until 1997. Today, the New Yorker works as a TV commentator and freelance author. He is also the spokesperson for the Boxing Writers Association of America.

At the beginning of the modern boxing era, the biggest fights on American soil took place in California and Nevada. Boxing was forbidden in many of the eastern states or limited exclusively to a few private sports clubs. As the moralists finally gave way, the focus of boxing attention shifted to the densely populated harbor cities of the northeast—Boston, Philadelphia, Baltimore, and New York—home of Irish, Italian and Eastern European immigrants. And as has been the case for centuries, these economically underprivileged groups were also more than ready to try their luck in the ring at the beginning of the 20th century. One of their number was John L. Sullivan, heavyweight world champion and the first American boxing superstar, who came from a family of Irish immigrants that had settled in the Boston area around 1750.

In the early 1920s the promoter Tex Rickard commissioned the construction of the new Madison Square Garden and boxing—which had first been officially legalized in New York in 1920—became a synonym for the Roaring Twenties. In 1923 Jack Dempsey defended his heavyweight title against Angel Luis Firpo in front of more than 80,000 at the Polo Grounds, a baseball stadium in New York City. Three years later, in 1926, he lost the belt to Gene Tunney in the rain-drenched Sesquicentennial Stadium in Philadelphia—this time in front of a record-breaking audience of 120,000.

New York and Chicago were the capitals of American boxing during the 1930s and 1940s and until well into the 1950s, when the revenues generated by ever more popular TV broadcasts gradually became more important than earnings from admission fees. Madison Square Garden was known as the "mecca of the boxing world," and all of the most famous champions from this era stood in the ring here at least once. Additional important event locations of this era were the Madison Square Garden Bowl (New York), Yankee Stadium (New York), Boston Garden (Boston) and Municipal Stadium (Philadelphia). Fights between various ethnic groups were the biggest crowd pleasers, with Irish (Jimmy McLarnin, Billy Conn, Mickey Walker), Italians (Rocky Graziano, Willie Pep, Jake LaMotta, Rocky Marciano, Lou Ambers) and Jews (Benny Leonard, Barney Ross, Maxie Rosenbloom) as the most frequent opponents.

Many black families left the American South in the 1940s and 1950s and went north in search of work in the industrial centers there. Some of them settled in the northeast and produced boxers like Sugar Ray Robinson (New York), Ike Williams (Trenton, New Jersey) and Sandy Saddler (Boston).

The 1950s could be viewed as the Golden Age of boxing, with fight events taking place five and six times a week in cities like New York. But the sport was dominated by criminals, and the all-powerful International Boxing Club (IBC) controlled nearly all world champions of that day. Jim Norris, the IBC president, acquired a controlling interest in Madison Square Garden (MSG) and for all practical purposes held a boxing monopoly in the United States until his organization was broken up by the American federal government.

Since the beginning of the 1960s, only a small number of fights have been held in large track-and-field or baseball stadiums. Madison Square Garden, on the other hand, retained its importance for the boxing world. The fights there were meanwhile being arranged by the legendary Teddy Brenner. The first encounter between Muhammad Ali

and Joe Frazier—the much-anticipated greatest boxing bout of all times—took place in the "new Garden" (it had been renovated in 1968) in 1971. Other talented boxers who appeared at MSG include Roberto Duran, George Foreman, Sugar Ray Leonard, Marvin Hagler, Carlos Monzon, Bob Foster, Salvador Sanchez, Larry Holmes, Julio Cesar Chavez, Mike Tyson, Oscar De La Hoya, Roy Jones Jr. and Felix Trinidad.

Madison Square Garden no longer has its own boxing division, but important boxing events still do take place there. The boxing scene shifted to the casino mecca of Atlantic City, located on the seacoast of New Jersey, toward the end of the 1970s. The casinos on the Indian reservations in Connecticut now offer regular boxing events as well. It thus remains to be seen if the large urban centers of the American northeast will ever regain their original status as the center of the boxing world.

Opposite page: Madison Square Garden in New York was the epicenter of Big Business for many decades. Open-air arenas such as Yankee Stadium *(above)* were also used for historic duels such as that between Ali and Norton III. Here, the opponents chase each other around the stadium after signing the contract in 1976.

TOP TEN OF THE NORTHEASTERN COAST:
1. Willie Pep
2. Benny Leonard
3. Mickey Walker
4. Sugar Ray Leonard
5. Joe Gans
6. Rocky Marciano
7. John L. Sullivan
8. Gene Tunney
9. Tommy Loughran
10. Marvin Hagler

HISTORY

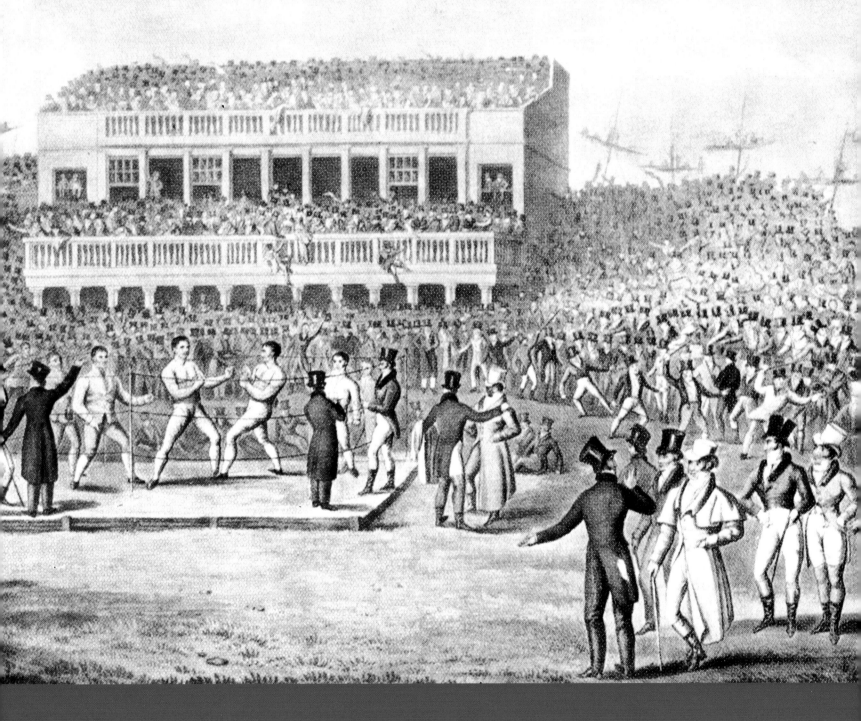

Antiquity
SOLDIERS AND GLADIATORS

In terms of cultural history, many different types of boxing have been in existence ever since humans discovered that their balled fist serves as a natural weapon. Early evidence proves that boxing matches were carried out as a form of leisure-time activity over 8,000 years ago in the Nubian valley of what is now Ethiopia. In the 5th century B.C., the area was invaded by the Egyptians, who took

all the advanced civilizations of the Eurasian region during that era. Chalk drawings dating back to approximately 2000 B.C. and featuring boxing youths with gloves and protective helmets were later also found on Crete.

A number of different types of boxing matches were fought in front of spectators in ancient Greece between 800 and 400 B.C. In one particularly brutal version promoted by

however, a defeat was a public catastrophe. During the 71st games (496 B.C.), Kleomedes of Astypalaia killed his opponent Ikkios of Epidaurus after being granted the jury's approval.

The boom continued unabated, however. Aspiring future champions trained with head-guards and the forerunners to the modern punchbag. These were athletic professionals in

Portrayal of boxing youth from the pre-Greek era, approximately 1600 B.C.

Antique mosaic from the Neptune Baths at the Roman harbor of Ostia.

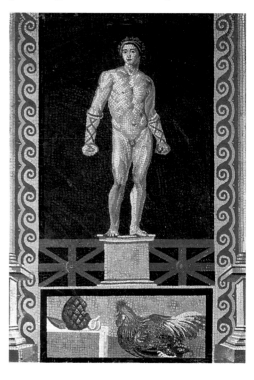

A gladiator with bandage-wrapped fists strikes a pose fit for an ancient deity in this mosaic.

the sport back with them to their homeland on the banks of the Nile. Hieroglyphs from that era describe fights between soldiers, who typically fought their boxing duels exclusively for the entertainment of pharaohs and kings. The bandages they wore were made of leather wrappings extending from the knuckles to the elbows and were likely used to protect the delicate bones in the hands and forearms. The exact same type of construction is also pictured in approximately 5,000–6,000-year-old depictions of boxing fights such as those found near Baghdad, which was at that time the center of Mesopotamia. It is possible that boxing existed in

King Theseus in the 9th century B.C., two persons engaged in a boxing match while in a seated position. The two boxers sat within arm's reach of each other on flat stones and hit each other with metal-reinforced leather bandages until one of the two contestants died (on good days, loss of consciousness was sufficient to end the fight). A more civilized type of boxing was introduced at the 23rd Olympic games in 688 B.C., with Onomastos from Smyrna becoming the first champion. The athletic skills of the naked boxers attracted great attention, drawing cultural praise in the form of poetic verses, pottery, and sculpture. For the loser of the match,

the truest sense of the word, receiving support from the city, region, etc. Sticks were used to mark off the ring and boxing stars such as Theagenes of Trakea (5th century B.C.) and the supposedly undefeatable Cleitomachus (3rd century B.C.) were referred to as "world champions." The most prestigious honors, however, were reserved for Olympic double victors in boxing and a significantly more brutal discipline called *pancratium*. Virtually anything was permissible in the attempt to defeat opponents in this blend of wrestling and boxing. The sport of boxing had the same spectacular, Circensian flavor in the Roman Empire, with gladiators recruited from the

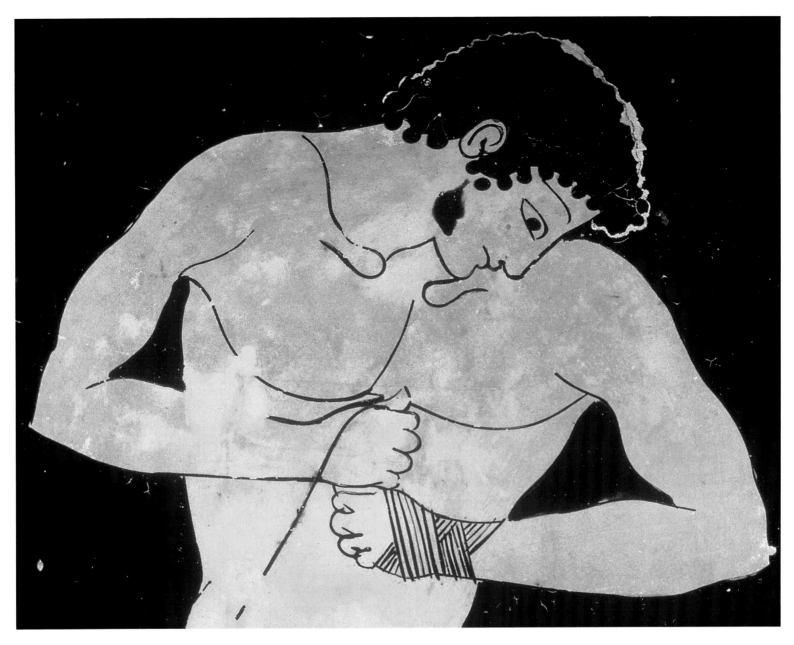

An athlete protects his hands with leather straps on this Greek vase (5th century B.C.). Created some 400 years later, this Hellenistic gladiator made of bronze wears *caestus,* metal-reinforced bandages.

ranks of prisoners and slaves fighting for freedom or death with thorn-lined bandages know as *caestus.* Rulers such as Caligula, who was a great boxing enthusiast, had athletes imported from Africa, promising them marriage with young Roman woman as an extra reward for victory.

Early forms of boxing had meanwhile also been established in other Asian cultures. In China, Buddhist monks developed a complicated system of precise movement patterns similar to the choreographies seen in other ritualized martial arts such as Tai Chi and Kendo. The first boxing schools were founded in the 6th century A.D. Athletes in India had

likely been proving their athletic prowess in boxing and wrestling matches long before this, however. The Indian national epic, the *Bhagavad-Gita,* mentions boxing fights, as do the great poetic verses of European antiquity such as Homer's *Ilias* and *Odyssey* as well as Vergil's *Aeneis.*

As a result of the dramatic injuries they caused, fights with *caestus* were soon banned in the Roman Empire, however. The ancient heyday of the sport was brought to a close for at least the next 1,000 years when Emperor Theodosius forbid the continuation of the Olympic games, which had last taken place in 393.

KO IN THE 1st ROUND

HOW ULYSSES WON
A BOXING MATCH INCOGNITO

The stranger didn't look intimidating and he was obviously elderly as well. It thus didn't take much courage for the highwayman Irus, the community beggar, to toss a few insults the strangers' way on that evening in Ithaca. Irus barks at the stranger to get away from the palace gates immediately, "or you shall be dragged out neck and heels." Then he adds: "up then, and go of yourself, or we shall come to blows." So begins the 18th book in Homer's "Odyssey," which describes a public fistfight in great detail. But the old man is no one other than Ulysses himself, transformed by the goddess Athena, and he has no intentions of letting himself be driven from the gates of his own palace. One threatening word

quickly follows the next, until those gathered at the gates, the princes and suitors, anticipate an entertaining spectacle. "This is the finest sport you ever saw," exclaims the leader Antinous in delight, "the stranger and Irus have quarreled and are going to fight, let us set them on to do so at once." A prize is quickly set for the winner. The one of the two social underdogs to come out on top is promised his choice of a freshly roasted, stuffed goat stomach and will be the uncontested city beggar from thence on. "He shall be free of our table and we will not allow any other beggar about the house at all."

As is the case with so many ancient fistfights, the showdown between Irus and Ulysses represents the fight of the underprivileged for their very existence. There is something to be won and even more to be lost as it

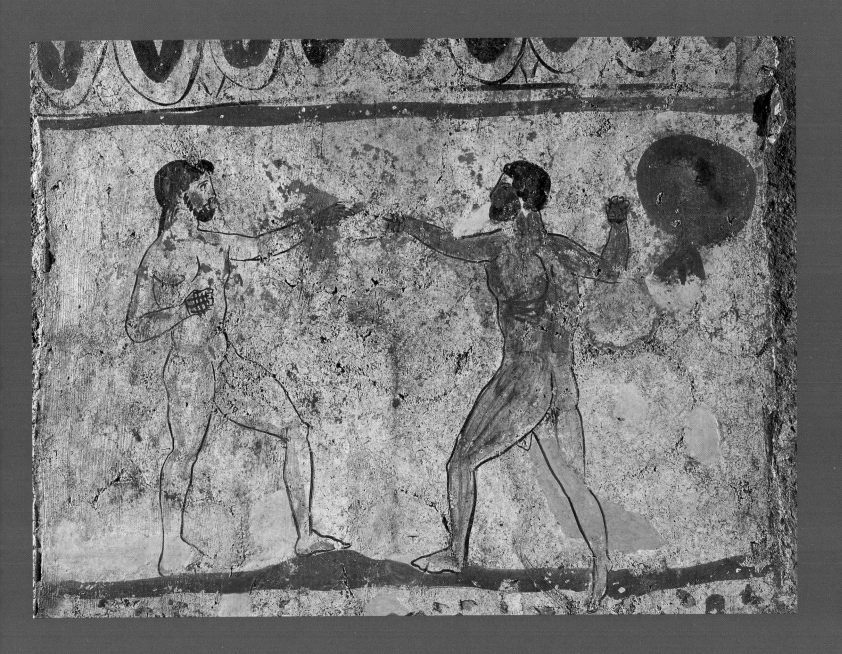

Opposite page: The Greeks also expressed their admiration for boxing in their pottery, as can be seen on this amphora from the 6th century B.C. The memorial slab with scratch drawings and paintings on plaster *(above)* shows that the naked fighters also suffered severe bodily injuries.

soon turns out. When Irus catches a glimpse of the "old man's" athletic body while putting on the leather bandages (which are not described in greater detail) he decides he would rather skip the whole affair.

But Antinous refuses to be denied the pleasure of the spectacle and threatens to hand Irus over to the cruel king Echetus, who "will cut off your nose and ears, and draw out your entrails for the dogs to eat." A prizefight such as this can't simply be cancelled once it has awakened the curiosity of a ruler. And thus "they brought him into the middle of the court, and the two men raised their hands to fight."

The subsequent exchange of blows in Ithaca proves just as one-sided as a title bout with the young Mike Tyson in Las Vegas. Irus throws a harmless punch to the right shoulder, while Ulysses lands "a blow on the neck under the ear" (likely referring to the edge of the jaw line). Unrecognized, Ulysses "deemed it best to give the lighter blow for fear the Achaeans should begin to suspect who he was." But even the softened punch breaks Irus' bones and leaves him bleeding and unconscious. "He fell groaning in the dust, gnashing his teeth and kicking on the ground, but the suitors threw up their hands and nearly died of laughter."

The invitation to the communal evening banquet is a symbol of the social advancement possible for the victors of such fights even back then. Before dinner, however, the victor brings the defeated Irus outside the courtyard and thus out of range of the ruler's random whims. Ulysses is a fair sportsman par excellence; he will later revenge himself on the princes who have made themselves at home in his court by other means.

The Bareknuckle Era
ON THE EDGE OF LEGITIMACY

the prowess of the best fighters in their district with those of fighters from other locations. The boxing business also thrived in traveling booths, however. The staff that operated such boxing booths at fairs challenged the spectators to duels. If no one volunteered, they demonstrated the art of bareknuckle fighting among one another in exhibition fights. Wrestling moves intended to force the opponent to the canvas and thus end the round were also permitted. The boxers had 30 seconds to appear on the middle line that divided the ring, an action referred to as coming up to scratch, to signify they were ready to participate in the next round. Not until the practice halls known as "boxing academies" were erected in the 18th century did boxing begin to attract enthusiasts from more elevated social circles. The small "amphitheater" built by James Figg in the heart of London in 1719 had a great influence on boxing style. As an active champion and master of the noble science of defense, Figg was a pioneer of his sport. His

It is generally unknown in what form boxing was practiced after gladiatorial fights were banned by the Christian emperor around A.D. 500. It is likely that the sport survived the Middle Ages primarily as part of the curriculum in fencing schools as well as in various forms not entirely distinguishable from wrestling. Albrecht Dürer's fencing illustrations, published in 1512, also picture a dozen boxing techniques, while the introductory wrestling book by the Dutchman Nikolaus Petter, published in 1674, features a separate chapter with the first written boxing instructions. There is also evidence of public boxing matches in England during approximately the same period. The famous literary diarist Samuel Pepys described a "prize fight (…) between a Mathews (…) and a Westwicke, who was injured in several places on the head and legs" in his diaries in 1662. In January 1681, the London-based "Protestant Mercury" became the first newspaper to report on a "boxing fight (…) before his lordship, the Duke of Albemarle, between one of the duke's servants and a butcher. The latter won the prize (…)."

Boxing matches for prizes were often initiated by noble landowners, who wanted to test

Jack Broughton and James Figg *(top)* were the first recognized boxing teachers in London. The duels between Daniel Mendoza and Richard Humphries *(above)* created increased interest in boxing in England.

public influence was soon surpassed by that of his trainee Jack Broughton, however.

Broughton became champion in 1734 and established a well-respected reputation for both himself and his sport. A ferryman by trade, Broughton opened his own boxing school with the help of a loan from his protégé, the Duke of Cumberland, and published the first rulebook in 1743. He also introduced defensive and countering techniques to method training, as well as the predecessors to modern boxing gloves, known as mufflers. In 1750, however, he was defeated by a lucky punch in a duel with Jack Slack. This drew the wrath of the duke, who had invested a great sum of money in the fight and now arranged for Broughton's boxing school to be closed. From then on the championship title changed hands repeatedly under rather dubious conditions, until the end of the 18th century when Daniel Mendoza and Richard Humphries became true stars of the sport and attracted general public interest. It would still take some time, however, before the sport attracted truly large audiences.

More than 20,000 curious onlookers were on hand when Henry Pearce stepped into the ring with Jem Belcher in 1805 in Blyth and again

when Tom Cribb fought the former American slave Tom Molineaux in the county of Leicester in 1811. More than 30,000 spectators made the pilgrimage to the horseracing track in Worcester in 1824 for Tom Spring's fight with Jack Langan (the weight of the audience caused part of the stands to collapse). Boxing fans were willing to undertake even the most arduous of journeys, as the officially banned fights were held out in the countryside, far away from

the long arm of the law. The Protestant Pietism of the Victorian era and rigid authoritarian powers greatly damaged the sensitive betting business, however. In April 1860, the last great bareknuckle fight between Sayers and Heenan was stopped by the police. Like Jem Mace and Tom Allen, many of England's best boxers soon immigrated to Australia or the United States to continue their careers there. The island was no longer the epicenter of the sport.

Tom Spring *(top)* from Townhope was one of the first great stars of the ring. His first duel with Irishman Jack Langan *(above)* in Worcester in January 1824 lasted more than two and a half hours.

HEENAN vs SAYERS

THE LAST GREAT BAREKNUCKLE FIGHT

This form of boxing was officially banned, just as were all other types of prizefighting at the time, but what could the authorities possibly do to prevent such fights from taking place? Scheduled to take place on April 17, 1840, anticipation of the fight between Tom Sayers, the best man England had to offer, and American boxing champion John Carmel Heenan, reached a fever pitch for the first time in boxing history as soon as the news of the coming fight spread to both sides of the Atlantic. Reporters from New York, Paris, and a variety of other locations traveled to London to report on the duel for the "world championship title" for their respective papers. Famous personalities from the world of literature, such as Charles Dickens and William Thackeray, as well as representatives of the aristocracy and members of parliament, had announced they would attend the event. After all, this was a true megafight before the word had even been invented.

Great care had to be taken in making preparations, however, as the London authorities had declared they would prevent the fight from taking place. The two opponents thus trained outside of the city in secret locations in the surrounding counties and did not make the journey to Farnborough in Hampshire until the morning of the fight. Sayers managed to reach Farnborough undiscovered in a box used to transport horses, but Heenan was initially detained and only released on bail. He arrived at Farnborough in disguise. Also making their way to Farnborough were entire trainloads of curious spectators, who had purchased tickets "to nowhere" for three pounds each at the London Bridge station. The city police followed these crowds suspiciously to the limit of their jurisdiction, but did not interfere. The field in which the ring had been marked off was

Opposite page: The illegal bareknuckle championship "Heenan vs. Sayers" attracted international attention in 1860. *This page:* Heenan greets the cartoonist Thomas Nast, who is to document the fight for the *New York Illustrated Newspaper.* The call to start came immediately after the two opponents formally greeted each other in the ring. The merciless fight lasted for 42 rounds over 2 hours and 20 minutes until being broken up by the police. The outcome was judged as a draw, but it is doubtful whether the championship belt officially changed hands at the fight location considering the police intervention.

only nine miles away. There the Anglo-American duel to which the *Times* devoted an entire special edition began unfolding, initially undisturbed.

The exchange of blows did the preceding hype justice. Again and again, the stocky Sayers besieged his opponent, who was 16 centimeters taller, with effective hits to the eye area. But the American used his physical superiority to send the man from Bristol tumbling to the canvas in round after round. After seven rounds Sayers was left batting about with only one arm, as he had injured the other while blocking a punch. One round later Heenan also suffered a hand injury. But neither one of the boxers was willing to relent until Sayers' seconds intervened in the 37th round when Heenan had pressed Sayers to the ropes so forcefully by the neck that they feared his back would break.

This was precisely the moment that the referee wanted to end the fight with a victory decision for the American. He suddenly found himself overruled by the onlookers, who had by now been whipped into a state of frenzy, and was carried from the ring. So, the half-strangled Sayers and Heenan, with his face swollen almost beyond recognition, continued to swing at each other for another five rounds until the fierce match was finally ended by the arrival of the police. It was the signal for everyone present (including the loudly protesting Heenan, who wanted to continue the duel in another location despite his injuries) to disperse in every possible direction. The excited public pushed the stranger into the first train to London, however, and collected a total of 3,000 pounds for their brave hometown favorite, but not before extracting a promise from him never to enter the ring again.

The bout in Farnborough, which was regarded as a draw, was in fact Tom Sayers' last fight. First and foremost, however, it was a final fantastic and dramatic high point at the end of the bareknuckle boom.

ROUND TRIP:

USA— WEST COAST

by Ivan G. Goldman

Ivan G. Goldman, born in 1942, reports from Los Angeles about the boxing scene on the west coast for *The Ring, KO Boxing* and other magazines. The author of a non-fiction book and a crime novel, he also works for daily newspapers like the *New York Times* and the *Washington Post*.

Due primarily to its large Hispanic population, the West Coast of the USA was the epicenter of one of the most important professional boxing scenes in the world for the entire 20th century. Boxing is the most popular sport after soccer for Americans of Latin American heritage, and many Americans of other descents were infected with boxing fever by their Hispanic neighbors, especially in Los Angeles. The city was probably the most popular event location for boxing fights in the USA around 1950. Frank Sinatra, Bob Hope, William Holden, Al Jolson, and many other Hollywood stars— the true royalty of American society—held their glamorous court in the sold-out boxing arenas. And boxing fans of the time were enthusiastic, tough, and well informed.

Opened in 1924, the Olympic Auditorium served not just as an event location but also as a backdrop for nearly every Hollywood movie every made about boxing. It looked exactly like moviemakers pictured a boxing arena: raw, common, steely, and merciless. Even the concrete walls of the changing rooms contributed to the oppressive atmosphere. The classics "Requiem for a Heavyweight" and of course "Rocky," the most successful boxing movie of the 20th century, are among the movies filmed here.

Movie stars and gangsters like Mickey Cohen (himself a former boxer) and Frankie Carbo rubbed shoulders in the Olympic and other city event locations such as Hollywood Legion Stadium and Ocean Park Arena. The mobsters

managed many boxers, held the reigns behind the scenes, and controlled the illegal betting surrounding professional boxing, thus making a decisive contribution to the sport's "bad boy" image. For the most part, however, this image was naturally created by the boxers them-selves—tough young men from a wide variety of social backgrounds. Nearly all of them came and went virtually unnoticed, if they were lucky earning a few days in spotlight before disappearing from the scene. Among the boxing greats who made the west coast their home were James J. Jeffries (heavyweight world champion 1899–1905), Art Aragon, Henry Armstrong, Jerry Quarry, Bobby Chacon and the superstars Oscar De La Hoya and Shane Mosley in the late 20th century.

TICKETS

One of the most resplendent figures among the boxing promoters was Aileen Eaton, who put her razor-sharp instinct to good use arranging the fight evenings for the Olympics from 1942–80. The clever businessman George Parnassus, who was once her matchmaker, soon came to be regarded as her most intense rival. He organized hundreds of boxing events, many of them featuring world champions, at the Great Western Forum which had opened in 1968.

By 2000, however, business was slowing down for nearly all of the large boxing arenas in Southern California. The big events now take place 310 miles to the east in Las Vegas. The casinos there pay the promoters high fees to attract rich gamblers to their tables with boxing events. Jerry Buss, the last boxing promoter at the Great Western Forum, claimed he lost $7 million in 17 years. And yet, more boxing matches took place in California in 1999 than in almost any other American state. Most of these matches were between boxers at the very start (or end) of their career. Despite the economic realities, the American west coast has retained its enthusiasm for the sport of boxing.

Boxing history was written at the Great Western Forum in Inglewood *(opposite page)* and the Olympic Auditorium in Los Angeles *(above)*.

TOP TEN OF THE WEST COAST:
1. Manuel Ortiz
2. Bert Colima
3. Art Aragon
4. Enrique Bolanos
5. George Latka
6. Fred Apostoli
7. Richie Lemos
8. Shane Mosley
9. Oscar De La Hoya
10. Baby Arizmendi
Honorable mention: Carlos Chavez

The Start of the Modern Era
FROM SPECTACLE TO GREAT SPORT

By the early 19th century, prize boxing had been introduced to the United States with the arrival of British and Irish immigrants passing through the country's large harbor cities. In their ranks, the rough-and-tumble sport first prospered on both the Atlantic and Pacific coasts as a tolerated form of public entertainment only. Tom Beasley's victory over Jacob Hyer in New York (1816) is regarded as the first truly notable boxing fight to be held in the New World. Some 33 years later, Hyer's son Tom took part in the first duel for the American title and defeated Yankee Sullivan in 16 rounds. All in all, the scene was developing into a state of increasingly dynamic chaos. Championship titles passed hands repeatedly, primarily between British professionals such as Jem Mace and Joe Goss who had immigrated to the USA and descendents of Irish immigrants. Unclear jurisdictions completed the confusion.

Boxing matches in public were prohibited after Tom McCoy was killed in 1842 during a 120-round marathon with Englishman Chris Lilly. From then on, the preferred locations for ring duels were remote towns or small offshore islands. Towards the end of the century, however, the ban was eased without being totally lifted. Whenever a big fight was planned, the authorities simply looked the other way. John L. Sullivan was thus able to publicly establish himself as the last hero of the bareknuckle era with a reputation surpassing all who had preceded him. A man well able to hold his drink, Sullivan had mowed down Paddy Ryan in Mississippi City in 1882 in just ten minutes, and proved to be an absolute master of the sport over the next few years. His loud boast that he "could beat up anyone in the joint" could be heard resounding in even the lowest of dives.

After requiring more than 2 hours and 75 rounds to defeat Jake Kilrain in 1889, however, the "Boston Strong Boy" finally called for the introduction of the more modern "Queensberry Rules" in boxing. This rulebook, commissioned by the Marquis of Queensberry and drawn up by the Englishman John Graham Chambers in 1867, stipulated the three-minute fight and one-minute break intervals, which are still in effect today. It furthermore called for "new boxing gloves of the best quality" and prohibited all wrestling techniques.

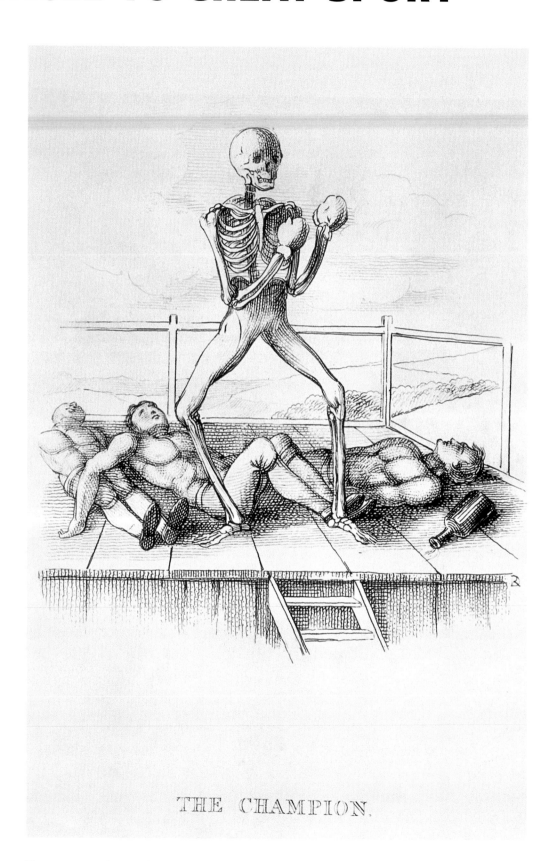

THE CHAMPION.

Illustrators soon began taking advantage of the symbolic power of boxing for all sorts of topics and motifs. This lithograph entitled *The Champion* (dated approximately 1850) is a vivid *memento mori*.

such as Joe Gans or Jack "The Giant Killer" Dillon actually sometimes managed to come out the winners of such bouts. Conflicts with the authorities likewise continued unabated. In England and in America, active boxers and officials repeatedly had to answer to the courts for fatal accidents in the ring. In the changing rooms, the police informed the fighters that they would be held personally responsible for severe injuries to their opponents. Boxing had become an indoor sport for the upper classes in England by the time the National Sporting Club, founded in 1891 in London, began advertising most of the fights carried out on its premises as exclusive club events. In New York, the "Horton Law" permitted boxing events starting in 1896, but four years later, the law was revised. In 1911, the new "Frawley Law" ushered in the so-called no-decision era. In an attempt to prevent popular betting on the fights, this law permitted only ten-round duels without a point decision in the state of New York. Boxers defending their championship titles in the new mecca of the sport could thus only be dethroned with a TKO defeat. And a number of the best boxers in the ranking lists had no real chance at a title at all as a result of the exclusion of blacks from title bouts, the so-called color bar that was soon in place in all of America as well as England.

The first world championship after the introduction of the modern rulebook turned into a personal disaster for Sullivan, however. His opponent James J. Corbett proved to be a technically far superior boxer, knocking Sullivan out in the 21st round of their match in New Orleans in September 1892.

The bareknuckle era thus faded into history, while the start of a new boom would soon run into old obstacles. The number of active boxers had significantly increased, not least due to the introduction of seven additional weight classes between 1856 (bantamweight) and 1909 (flyweight). No agreement on universally valid limits could be reached between the Old and the New World, however, and the best of the lighter weight boxers often had to fight with much heavier opponents for the chance to earn lucrative boxing purses. It was a true indication of their great talent that exceptional boxers

As popular as it may have appeared in these pioneer days, the rough-and-tumble sport was nonetheless in a phase of stagnation. And this stagnation was followed by World War I.

During the American Civil War, sparring matches among soldiers were part of everyday life *(top)*. John L. Sullivan *(above left)* was the last bareknuckle champion, the sport was then dominated by Robert Fitzsimmons *(center)* and James J. Corbett *(above)* until the turn of the century.

JOHNSON vs JEFFRIES

SHOWDOWN IN RENO

George "Tex" Rickard knew how to make money. The cunning businessman was always interested in new, spectacular sources of income—first as a gold miner and hotel owner in Alaska, then as a casino owner in Nevada. The boxing boom at the start of the new century was the perfect opportunity for him. In 1906 Rickard had, without hesitation, paid out $30,000 in boxing purses and had an arena built to lure the lightweight world championship between Joe Gans and Battling Nelson to his hometown of Goldfield, Nevada. His loud ballyhoo for the "Duel of the Races" ensured him a full house—and a full wallet. Four years later, Rickard began working on his largest project to date, drumming up interest in the most important title bout to have been held for many years. This time, however, it was to be the war of the races.

Jack Johnson had obviously inflicted a blow to the ego of white Americans by taking the heavyweight title in 1908. Ever since he had begun his showy reign as champion, the duped "superior" race had been feverishly seeking a white hope, an opponent who could wipe the "golden grin" off Johnson's face, as the author Jack London phrased it. After several fruitless attempts, a potential opponent appeared in the form of former champion James J. Jeffries, who had given up his title in 1905. And Rickard offered $101,000 for the right to promote the match, more than any other promoter. Rickard sold the film rights to the fight for the same amount and had a new arena built in Reno, Nevada. The rest was easy. Spurred on by racist propaganda and the atmosphere of carefully contrived animosity between the opponents, a total of 16,000 spectators attended the fight on America's national holiday, the 4th of July, 1910, generating a record take of $270,000.

After a few restrained rounds in the afternoon sunlight, however, it soon became clear that the 36-year-old Jeffries, the betting favorite,

was no longer in any shape to take on the well-trained Johnson. After being hard hit by Johnson in the 6th round, the boilermaker was left with only one open eye. His best attempts all missed, while punches thrown his way landed with great success. As the fight continued, both Jeffries and his second, ex-world champion James J. Corbett, were heckled by the spectators. So was Johnson, when not busy waving to the public. Finally, Johnson brought his opponent to the canvas in the 15th round after a double blow to the chin. When Jeffries got back on his feet, the world champion promptly repeated the performance. Tex Rickard, who also served as referee, was only able to count to "7" however, before angry fans began slipping through the ropes of the ring. They wanted to prevent the man who represented the hopes of white America from being left down for the count. The fight ended in a KO defeat for Jeffries nonetheless.

The news of Jeffries' humiliation spread throughout the United States and triggered public displays of triumph or bitter disappointment, depending on skin color, and civil war-like attacks. Numerous deaths and severe injuries were the result. Never before had a sporting event shaken the continent as deeply as this boxing match, and its aftermath was extremely wide-ranging. The authorities forbid the public showing of the film footage in an effort to prevent further racial conflict, and began closely scrutinizing Johnson. One year later, they authorized his criminal prosecution under false pretences. Determined whites continued searching for a new "hope" and even proclaimed a "Heavyweight Caucasian Champion" in the meantime. On his part, Jeffries regretted ever leaving his farm near Los Angeles for the foolish comeback attempt.

In the end, the cunning businessman Tex Rickard was the only one to emerge from this memorable afternoon as a real winner.

Opposite page: Before their duel in Reno, Jack Johnson *(left)* and James Jeffries *(far left)*, pictured here with his trainer Sam Berger *(center)*, start off on a training run for publicity.

Johnson's athletic victories and elegant appearance was a thorn in the eye of white America *(far left)*. James J. Jeffries *(left)* was regarded as the great "white" hope to win the championship belt. The 36-year-old suffered an embarrassing defeat in the ring, however. Many white racists were thus greatly satisfied when the world champion Jack Johnson was forced to appear at one of many court hearings *(below)*.

ROUND TRIP:

CENTRAL AMERICA— MEXICO

by Eric Armit

Eric Armit, born in 1940, has been writing about the international boxing scene for 40 years. His works have appeared in such publications as the British *Boxing News.* An expert on Latin America, Armit is also a member of the Ranking List Committee for the European Box Union (EBU).

Although the sport of boxing enjoys unabated popularity in Mexico, the boxing scene there has generally suffered as a result of the country's direct proximity to the USA. Year after year, the best Mexican fighters follow the call of U.S. dollars to California and Nevada, thus considerably depleting the Mexican boxing scene.

There were times in which at least three fight evenings per week took place in the capital of Mexico City and small arenas like the Coliseo became the homes of the best boxers in the world. Boxing greats such as Ruben Olivares, Carlos Zarate and Lupe Pintor made their most important appearances here. The Coliseo has now closed its doors for good, however, and no more than three or four boxing events per month are held in the large cities. The fact that even this many fights now take place is primarily attributable to Salvador Lutteroth,

the country's leading promoter whose family has been organizing boxing fights in Mexico since 1937. Also located in Mexico City is the Aztec Stadium, in which more than 130,000 spectators watched Julio Cesar Chavez triumph over Greg Haugen in 1993. The size of this impressive crowd will, in all likelihood, never be seen here again.

The timeframe between 1965 and approximately 1985 can be viewed as the golden age of Mexican boxing. Every list of the ten best Mexican fighters of all times contains several boxers from this era, such as Ruben Olivares, Carlos Zarate, Salvador Sanchez, Miguel Canto and Vicente Saldivar. In the Mexican countryside, however, boxing remains just as popular as ever. Cities like Guadalajara, Juarez, Mexicali, Ciudad Obregón, Los Mochis, and Tijuana regularly offer exciting fight evenings in their local boxing arenas.

After the passing of the old guard—men like Cuyo Hernandez and Lupe Sanchez—the modern generation of boxing managers are more reminiscent of tough businessmen than the "fatherly" figures who used to occupy the corner of the ring. Ricardo Maldonado, Fernando Beltran, and Nacho Huizar currently run the best boxing stable and employ top trainers like Ignacio Beristan and Jose "Olivares" Morales. Beristan is regarded as the "Angelo Dundee" of Mexican boxing. Managers bring their fighters to him when they need to be prepared for important matches. Morales has built up a strong boxing stable in the past few years together with his sons Erik and Diego.

The Mexican boxing scene is not romantic. The arenas are small and the training conditions are usually poor. That doesn't matter to the local boxing fans, however. They regard

boxing as a kind of bullfighting with gloves, and demand that their fighters face danger unafraid. A boxer lacking in courage can expect to face a wave of scorn, mockery, and beer. It is poverty that drives these men into the ring, and their *machismo* won't let them give up. It is a hard life, and one that produces equally hard boxers.

Boxing was never able to attain widespread popularity in the rest of Central America, although there were repeated phases in which the sport experienced a short-lived heyday in the various individual countries. Panama is the exception to this rule. This Central American country produced an entire string of world-class boxers during the 1960s and 1970s, among them Roberto Duran, Ismael Laguna, Eusebio Pedroza and Hilario Zapata. Today there are only a handful of professional boxers in Panama, none of whom have yet

earned a reputation for being "world class." Only approximately ten fight evenings are held in the entire country each year, mostly in Panama City and Colón. Luis Spada, the most famous promoter and manager in the history of Panamanian boxing, now maintains only a very small boxing stable.

Despite the success enjoyed by Alexis Arguello, boxing remains a mere peripheral phenomenon in Nicaragua, although it did experience a brief upsurge in popularity thanks to Antonio Adonis Rivas' victory in the WBO super flyweight championship in 1999. And while regular fight evenings are held in El Salvador and Costa Rica, boxing is virtually non-existent in Guatemala, Honduras, and Belize.

Opposite page: Native Mexican champions like bantam king José Becerra are enthusiastically celebrated.

They serve as role models for the boys in the gym at Tepito *(above)*, a district of Mexico City.

TOP TEN OF MEXICO:
1. Julio Cesar Chavez
2. Ruben Olivares
3. Ricardo Lopez
4. Miguel Canto
5. Carlos Zarate
6. Lupe Pintor
7. Joe Medel
8. Erik Morales
9. Marco Antonio Barrera
10. Daniel Zaragoza

Between the Wars
A SPORT IN ITS HEYDAY

The highly emotionally charged duel between Jack Johnson and Jess Willard in 1915 in Havana was one of the first megafights of the modern era.

After champions like James J. Corbett and Robert Fitzsimmons became the first stars of modern boxing, the sport produced its first icon in the Roaring Twenties. And who could have been more ideal to trigger a true boom for all those involved than a charismatic heavyweight world champion?

Under the assumed first name "Jack", William Harrison Dempsey became the new titleholder in the heaviest of all classes in 1919 and was soon the uncomplicated hero of the social classes striving for betterment. His brilliant TKO victories in the ring and his continual striving for dignity made the upstart from a poor background the symbol of a dynamic industrial society. Naturally, Dempsey also became a magnet for the public, breaking the so-called million-dollar barrier for live appearances in his five world championship bouts between 1921 and 1927. By the time

the "Manassa Mauler" from Colorado retired after his second defeat against Gene Tunney in 1927, he had earned what was for that time the absolutely astronomical sum of over $3.5 million for his appearances, including the fights he refereed. Dempsey and his business partners also benefited from the fact that the sport had meanwhile acquired a halfway solid foundation, even though still lacking international standardization. The "Walker Law" adopted in New York in 1920 permitted boxing matches with and without point decisions, as long as a boxing commission was there to supervise the fight, and active fighters and officials had the appropriate licenses. Other U.S. states quickly adopted these guidelines as well. The National Boxing Association (NBA) was formed as an umbrella organization for the various commissions in the same year. Several states, including New York,

insisted on independence, however. The ranking lists introduced by the new boxing publication *The Ring* in 1925 also helped to make the competition more transparent.

The International Boxing Union (IBU) was formed in Paris in 1920 as an initial group of 13 member countries on three continents. It was to be the foundation stone for an international controlling body in the sport, but the most important boxing markets—the USA and Great Britain—soon pulled out. In the lower weight limits, competing world champions recognized only by the IBU, the NBA, or the New York Commission frequently existed side by side. But even this confusion of titles couldn't stop the boom. Outstanding champions like Tommy Loughran, Mickey Walker, Harry Greb and Benny Leonard illuminated the scene with their talent. Gyms in the large cities of Los Angeles, New York,

London and everywhere in between were practically bursting at the seams with ambitious new title challengers. Hardly a day of the week went by without another well-attended fight night.

The beginning of the Great Depression in the late 1920s lowered a few purses, but was unable to reduce the popularity of the sport of boxing itself. A record of 230 title bouts was registered in the 1930s, as compared to the 117 that were held between 1910 and 1920. And the business was becoming ever more international. In addition to the new American stars (Tony Canzoneri, Lou Ambers, Barney Ross and Henry Armstrong), Europeans like Max Schmeling, Marcel Thil, Baltazar Sangchili, and Benny Lynch were also able to occasionally make their mark as well. Boxers from more "exotic" geographic locations, such as Kid Chocolate from Cuba, Sixto Escobar from Puerto Rico and the bantam king Al Brown from Panama went from being mere curiosities to titleholders. The glamorous scene was admittedly often influenced by dubious characters, as evidenced by the unstoppable career of the boxing colossus Primo Carnera, who was

elevated to the world championship throne by mobsters. A new icon was soon found for the most important weight division in the sport, however, in the form of Joe Louis.

The "Brown Bomber" from Detroit dominated the sport between 1937 and 1948, and that not just in the heavyweight division alone. Despite continuing racial segregation, he also became the first dark-skinned all-American hero. Coming out a victor in the rematch with Max Schmeling, the patriotic soldier who donated several boxing purses to the war fund became a figurehead for an America united in a time of danger. Louis lowered the color bar in the sport of boxing once and for all. He was also the last world champion to take part in a title bout of more than 15 rounds, agreeing on 20 rounds with his challenger Abe Simon in 1941. Louis had already won the match in the 13th round, however, with a TKO victory.

World War II permanently slowed the careers of Louis as it did those of countless other professionals. The heavyweight title did not change hands from 1942 to 1946, nor did the title in any division above lightweight. Only two title bouts took place in the entire world in 1945. The international political catastrophes hit the sport of boxing in its heyday.

The Italian-American lightweight champion Lou Ambers, "The Herkimer Hurricane," helped the lighter weight divisions achieve true recognition in the 1930s. Ambers won 90 of his 104 professional fights.

At the same time, immigrants like Kid Chocolate from Cuba brought new blood to boxing.

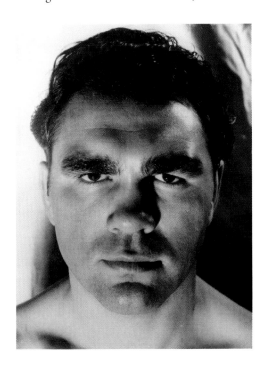

Europeans like Max Schmeling enriched the more international boxing scene between the wars.

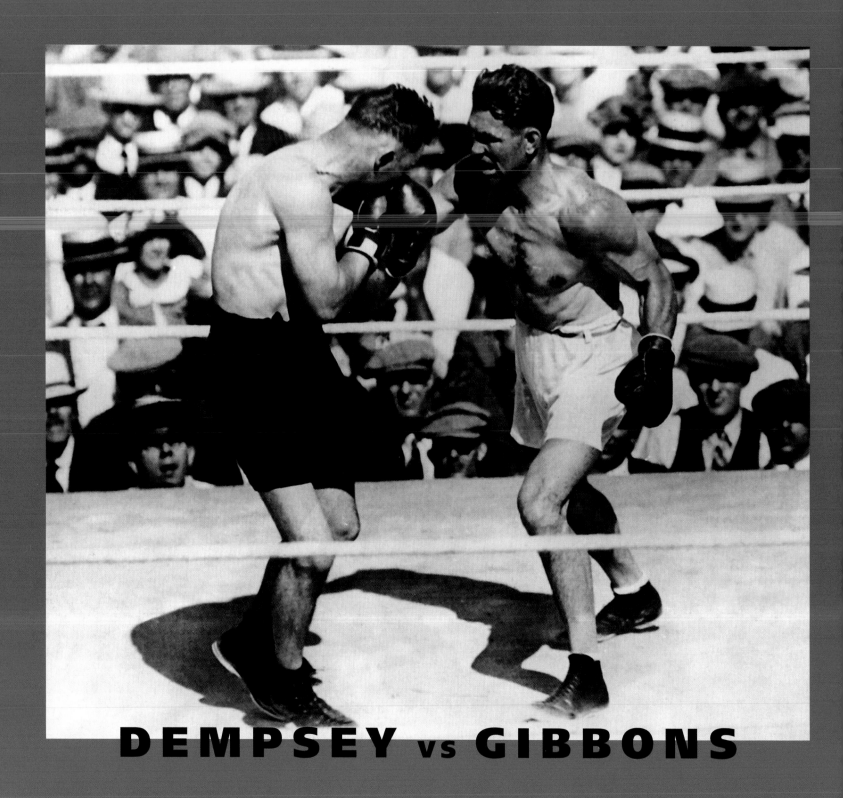

DEMPSEY vs GIBBONS

BIG FIASCO IN THE LITTLE BOOM TOWN

Virtually nothing could go wrong in those golden years of boxing once heavyweight world champion Jack Dempsey had been booked as the main attraction for a boxing event. The extremely popular champion guaranteed a full house and a healthy bank account. In the summer of 1923, however, several inexperienced businessmen from the state of Montana somehow managed to turn a Dempsey appearance into a flop. It must have been truly hard work.

The presence of oil had made the small town of Shelby, numbering just 2,000 inhabitants, rich nearly overnight, and boxing was now to finally put it on the map of the United States. At least that is how a few oil entrepreneurs and city officials pictured it in a meeting with Dempsey's manager Jack "Doc" Kearns. By the time they parted company, the sharp impresario had extracted a large guarantee purse from them. His protégé would receive a total of $300,000, payable in three installments before the day of the fight on which he would defend his title against a certain Tommy Gibbons. To be sure, Gibbons was more a plumped-up ex-light heavyweight than a dangerous challenger, but Dempsey's name was sure to fill the arena for 40,000 spectators to be constructed for the event.

Not long after the contract had been signed, the business leaders of Shelby discovered that they had less green cash than black gold.

Although they managed to scrape the first rate together on time, the second was already impossible to finance. Doc Kearns turned down the offer to pay in sheep instead of dollars without blinking an eye. Several oil concessions thus had to be sold, and a few mortgages taken out to ensure that the manager received his two-thirds on time. This wreaked havoc on the calculations for the price of admission, however, which suddenly rose from the planned $10 to $50. Such prices prevented many interested potential spectators from purchasing a ticket, no matter how much they would have liked to see Dempsey. The catastrophe on Independence Day was soon inevitable.

No more than half of the planned 40,000 spectators appeared in the wooden arena on July 4th, and in turn half of them had simply charged the admission gates without paying for a ticket. They witnessed a more or less boring fight in which a carelessly prepared Dempsey struggled with his agile opponent for the full allotment of twelve rounds. Nor were the guileless people of Shelby permitted much contact with the boxing icon after the point decision had been announced. Doc Kearns was quick to grab the victorious Dempsey and the $60,000 purse, jump into a train chartered exclusively for the purpose, and disappear. The challenger, Gibbons, who had expected a share of the takings, was left with pockets as empty as those of the organizers of this memorable world championship bout.

Hardest hit, however, was Shelby's financial community. Four banks went under on the Monday after the world championship bout. Several businesspeople and creditors who had been involved in the fight were also forced to declare bankruptcy. For thoughtful observers, the fiasco in the little boomtown was a warning not to lose all touch with reality in the general euphoria surrounding the sport.

In the fast-paced 1920s, the name Jack Dempsey was long a synonym for world-class sport (above). *Opposite page:* The idol's performance in Shelby, however, was dubious at best (right).

The unsung Tommy Gibbons thought the fight with Dempsey would help him to the top, but his big payday and ensuing fame never materialized.

ROUND TRIP:

CARIBBEAN —PUERTO RICO

by Mario Rivera Martino

Mario Rivera Martino, born in 1924, has spent the past 50 years reporting on boxing in Latin America for *The Ring* and the local *San Juan Star* (Puerto Rico). He is also the press spokesperson for the World Boxing Organization (WBO).

Probably no country on earth has produced more professional boxers per square mile than Puerto Rico. By the end of the century it had already generated more than 30 world championship titleholders—no small feat for an island a mere 93 miles long and 34 miles wide. Mexico, another Central American country, has given birth to a great number of boxing world champions, but also has a population of 80 million, compared to just 4 million Puerto Ricans. The natives of the island can be especially proud of light middleweight Felix Trinidad, regarded by many experts as the best boxer in all weight divisions until his KO defeat in fall 2001. In addition to this exceptional athlete, the island also laid claim to two other world champions in the large boxing associations in 2000, Daniel Santos and Eric Morel. There have been times in which no less than seven Puerto Rican world champions adorned the world champion lists of the four large boxing associations. And Felix Trinidad, Wilfredo

Gomez, Wilfredo Benitez, Carlos Ortiz, Wilfredo Vasquez, and Daniel Jimenez all held titles in at least two different weight divisions.

With the exception of Cuba, none of the other neighboring Caribbean islands can boast of so many boxing successes. They do offer a few truly unforgettable stars, however. Among their number are Emile Griffith from the Virgin Islands, who fought furious duels with Nino Benvenuti in 1967 and 1968, and his countryman Julian Jackson, two-time world middleweight champion (1990, 1995, WBC). Teo Cruz, lightweight world champion from 1968–69 who came from the Dominican Republic, was also a boxer of exceptional talent. The real number of Caribbean champions is actually much larger, however, as several of the better-known boxers from the islands held an American or Commonwealth passport (e.g., Mike McCallum and Lennox Lewis).

Puerto Rico's unusual position within the professional boxing scene is likely a result of

the fact that the island is politically linked to the USA and that its citizens have had unrestricted US citizenship since 1917. It therefore comes as no surprise that boxing has been legalized in Puerto Rico since May 16, 1927—precisely during the golden age of boxing brought about by men like Jack Dempsey and Gene Tunney.

Sixto Escobar became Puerto Rico's first boxing world champion when he won the bantamweight title from the Mexican Baby Casanova in Montreal in 1934. Sixto's most important title defenses all took place in New York, however, he fought only three times in Puerto Rico, having to go the full allotment of rounds with Lou Salica, Harry Jeffra and Kayo Morgan (1937–39).

On Puerto Rico, the sport of professional boxing thrives not least thanks to the public subsidies which is provided to the majority of the island's approximately 40 gyms. The 67 municipalities on the island have repeatedly

demonstrated their generosity in purchasing equipment, covering running expenses, etc. The gym owned by the family Trinidad is currently the most popular of all training centers, and does not need such donations, however. The Trinidad clan has been financially well off since its son Felix attained fame and fortune as a professional boxer while simultaneously achieving the status of national hero. The island's many boxing *aficionados* have already placed "Tito" in the same category as legends such as Carlos Ortiz, José Torres, Wilfredo Gomez, and Wilfred Benitez.

When Trinidad Jr. returned from the USA after his points victory over Oscar De La Hoya in 1999, he was met at the San Juan airport by thousands of fans celebrating their elation at his victory in the surrounding streets. The wild victory celebration continued for days on end, as a triumph over a star from the United States is still associated with high prestige on the island. A good deal of patriotism also came into play two years later when Trinidad's designated opponent for the united middleweight championship title, Bernard Hopkins, made derogatory comments about Puerto Rico during a press conference. The American thus so enraged his opponent's fans that the public appearance had to be brought to an early and chaotic close. Hopkins won the duel for the title in New York's Madison Square Garden, forcing "Tito" to suffer the first defeat in his brilliant career. Hopkins' arrogance won him few fans among Puerto Ricans, however. Their hearts continue to belong to Trinidad, Wilfredo Rivera, Juan Molina, and other representatives of the current generation of boxers from the island.

Opposite page: Felix Trinidad is the latest idol from Puerto Rican boxing fans.

Sixto Escobar (*top left,* with Mario Rivera Martino *2nd from left, and above*) is the island's oldest boxing icon and still a frequent guest of honor at ringside although now in retirement.

TOP TEN OF PUERTO RICO:
1. Wilfredo Gomez
2. Felix Trinidad
3. Carlos Ortiz
4. Wilfred Benitez
5. Edwin Rosario
6. Esteban DeJesus
7. Alfredo Escalera
8. Pedro Montanez
9. Sixto Escobar
10. José Torres

ON THE WAY TO A GLOBAL MATCH

Following the end of World War II, the business with the sweet science in America was picked up again as if it had never been left off. Some of the most spectacular series of duels in the modern history of professional boxing (Zale vs. Graziano, Pep vs. Saddler, Robinson vs. LaMotta) occurred in these first years after the war. Exceptionally talented boxers such as Willie Pep, Sandy Saddler, Ike Williams, Kid Gavilan, and Archie Moore were able to establish themselves as universally respected champions in the 1950s. The crowd-puller for white Americans was heavyweight world champion Rocky Marciano, while black Americans celebrated the brilliant rise of a man who was perhaps the best athlete of the modern era—Sugar Ray Robinson. A number of Hispanics (Manuel Ortiz, Pascual Perez) and exotic boxers from other continents (Yoshio Shirai, Hogan "Kid" Bassey, Jimmy Carruthers) were likewise able to earn membership in this distinguished club. All in all, however, the championships were held exclusively between Chicago and New York.

This was in part attributable to the fact that the world market was more concentrated in the United States at the beginning of the TV era. Weekly live broadcasts like the extremely popular Friday night fights helped the best professionals (and only the best) to boxing purses

After the war, New York's Madison Square Garden once again became the center of the boxing universe. English middleweight champion Randolph Turpin *(above right)* parades with his manager and two brothers before his return bout with Sugar Ray Robinson.

Extroverted promoters like Jack Solomons felt right at home in the boxing scene of the 1960s.

and a degree of renown that would otherwise have hardly been possible. It was also the result of an equally diligent and dubious promotion cartel which had complete say in the allocation and organization of title bouts. The commando headquarters of this cartel were located in the International Boxing Club in New York, founded in 1949, whose president Jim Norris played a shady game with the most important boxing managers and the most greedy members of the mob. Anyone who wanted to box for a world championship title had to accept one of the IBC managers, and usually found himself fighting in one of the several arenas in which Jim Norris held a large stake—New York's Madison Square Garden (third version), the Chicago Stadium or the Detroit Olympia.

This situation continued for nearly ten years, until Norris' boxing club was broken up by order of the Supreme Court in 1958.

Young Cassius Clay's swing at the Beatles, who are promptly all left seeing stars, could almost be regarded of a foretaste of things to come. Under the name Muhammad Ali, Clay would soon turn the boxing scene into an intercontinental pop arena.

The dirt kicked up during the investigations damaged the image of the highly popular sport, just as did the findings of the "Kefauver Hearings," a sub-committee established by the U.S. Senate in 1958. This committee investigated manipulation in the boxing business and exacted several confessions. Criticism was further intensified as a result of the fatal boxing accident suffered by Benny "Kid" Paret, who fell into a deadly coma during his world championship bout with Emile Griffith in March 1962, while millions of TV viewers watched. The loud, self-proclaimed rise of Cassius Clay, who later called himself Muhammad Ali, came just in the nick of time. Thanks to his unexpected victory over the universally feared Sonny Liston and his notorious criminal record, the charismatic Ali, who had taken Olympic gold in Rome in 1964, began a whole new empire in dialog with the mass media.

Equally articulate and pugnacious, but always offensive and with a flexible range of gestures, Ali staged himself as the sport's first pop star from the mid-1970s onward, leveling ethnic, religious and political barriers. His victories in the ring appeared to raise the triumph of the intelligent athlete to an art form and, together with his opinionated appearances, helped him go from being a "mere" heavyweight champion to the most prominent star of his era. Next to Ali, all of the other outstanding boxers of the 1960s, such as a Bob Foster, Carlos Ortiz, Eder Jofre, and Vicente Saldivar, were just ordinary sports heroes. When Ali, who meanwhile had his title suspended for refusing to enter into military service, stepped into the ring with his successor Joe Frazier in March 1971 (and lost), half of the world was watching the live broadcast.

By 1975 Muhammad Ali had made even more exciting boxing history with two victories over Joe Frazier and a sensational triumph over George Foreman. His loss of physical stamina was becoming ever more apparent, however. When he turned in his WBA title in the fall of 1978, most of the champions of his sport bore Latin American names such as Corro, Cuevas, Arguello, Pedroza, Gomez, and Canto, and they benefited greatly from the increasing globalization of the TV era. Power had slipped from the New York IBC and the dubious men behind the scenes there to a handful of internationally operating major-league promoters, and to the broadcast stations of NBC, CBS, and others. From then on it was only the boxers themselves who were important, and their fights were followed with great interest by the sharp eyes and cameras of the new boxing powers.

ALI vs FOREMAN

RUMBLE IN THE JUNGLE

Considering the duel between George Foreman and Muhammad Ali to be just another heavyweight world championship is now thought akin to blasphemy. Entitled "Rumble in the Jungle" and preceded by previously unprecedented ballyhoo, the fight which took place on October 30, 1974, is regarded as an *opus magnum* by *aficionados* of modern boxing. Still others see it is much, much more. Never before had a showdown between two boxers occurred within such a provocative social and cultural context.

Muhammad Ali, a former champion and the forerunner of a new "black" self-confidence, was symbolically returning to the continent of his ancestors, to become king a second time. At least that is how the industrious organizers of his title bout presented it—the media company Video Techniques, the soon-to-be notorious impresario Don King, and not least, the government of Zaire led by President Mobutu Sese Seko—along with the undefeated world champion George Foreman. With the support

of a British company, they had collected an unparalleled total purse of $10 million to lure the opponents to Kinshasa. And once that was successfully accomplished, they set about turning the fight into a signal of African-American independence by garnishing it with numerous cultural extras.

The division of sympathies quickly became clear. Ali was the romantic favorite of the people of Zaire. Wherever he met them, he took the time for a small gesture or a brief exchange of words. Foreman, on the other hand, remained largely secluded, introverted, and silent. The bookies in Las Vegas and the majority of the journalists who had traveled to Zaire from all corners of the globe regarded the title defender as the designated victor, however. After all, Foreman had a short time ago easily demolished Joe Frazier and Ken Norton, two boxers to have formerly defeated Ali, just as he had 37 of his 40 less capable opponents.

And even though Ali's camp promised a repeat of his triumph over the equally powerful and muscular Sonny Liston ten years before, few experts really expected a new miracle. On the morning of October 30, however, more than five weeks after the original date was postponed due to a training injury suffered by Foreman, a miracle was precisely what occurred.

In the fight with Liston, Ali had danced and countered with effortless ease. On the soft floor of the ring in Kinshasa, however, he stood virtually still after the second round, letting himself be pummeled by Foreman's heavy punches and frequently using the elasticity of the rope to help absorb part of the impact of the hits. Ali would later refer to this tactic as "rope-a-dope," but his coach Angelo Dundee simply labeled it "insanity" during the breaks between rounds. This strategy, an invented impromptu in the ring, soon paid off. Ali absorbed his opponent's hardest hits and then let loose his own series of punches. In the 8th round, one of these caught the completely exhausted title defender hard enough to bring him to the canvas—and keep him there until the count was over. A total of 60,000 spectators in the Stade du 20 Mai in Kinshasa as well as millions of TV viewers all over the world got the sensational fight they had been hoping for.

At nearly 33 years of age, and with 46 professional fights behind him, Muhammad Ali had once again told his fans and skeptics alike the story of the clever, fearless man who defeats the foolish giant. It has been the favorite story in this sentimental sport ever since, and this time it literally traveled around the globe—at least until a lightening storm cut the line of communication between Kinshasa and the rest of the world.

In Kinshasa, the challenger Muhammad Ali used every available opportunity to present himself as the charismatic hope of the Black Continent *(top left)*. In contrast, George Foreman's public appearances seemed much more contrived *(above)*. In the ring, however, the powerful titleholder initially seized all the initiative *(left)*. He didn't realize that this was part of his opponent's strategy.
Opposite page: The population celebrates Ali's sensational victory in the ring with unabashed euphoria.

The Postmodern Period
VARIETY OR CHAOS

The slow decline of Muhammad Ali may have robbed the boxing world of its most charismatic active personality in the early 1980s, but by no means left the sport in an athletic crisis. On the contrary, never before had there been so many enthralling duels in virtually all of the weight divisions; never before had so many professionals been so well technically and physically trained. Sugar Ray Leonard, Roberto Duran, Thomas Hearns and Marvin Hagler—no less than four all-time greats, battled it out with each other in truly classic duels. Other exceptional champions included Aaron Pryor, Wilfred Benitez, Donald Curry, Azumah Nelson, Julio Cesar Chavez, and Jeff Chandler. The center of the boxing universe had shifted from Chicago and New York to the desert of Nevada, however, where casino hotels hosted world championship bouts as a way of luring guests to their tables and because more money could be brought into the coffers here than anywhere else. On the east coast, Atlantic City soon

followed suit. Boxing had become a form of entertainment controlled by event managers and TV directors.

Every great fight needs to be for a title, and thus the number of champions began sky-rocketing. Between 1975 and 1988, six of what would eventually become nine new interim divisions were added to the eight traditional weight limits. In some places they were known as "super lightweights," in others as "junior welterweights," which didn't exactly help clarify matters any. On top of it all, the world associations were split several times. Whereas the World Boxing Association (WBA) and the World Boxing Council (WBC) had been able to agree upon joint titleholders at least part of the time since their establishment in 1962 and 1963 until well into the 1970s, several simultaneous champions per limit now became standard procedure. In 1983 a third association, the International Boxing Federation (IBF), split off from the WBA. In 1988 it was followed by the World Boxing Organization (WBO), which is recognized primarily in Europe. By the late 1980s, this situation had given rise to 68 "world champions" (four associations with 17 titles each) in professional

Show elements abound today: Roy Jones Jr. *(top)* poses with dancers in the New York Radio City Music Hall before a title defense in December 2000. Michael Moorer *(above left)* and Evander Holyfield use the Universal Studios backdrops for a press conference in October 1997.

Personality cult is a matter of course when eccentric featherweight Prince Naseem Hamed appears at his title bouts. Here, he is lowered into the Olympia in London in March 2000 to defeat the South African Vuyani Bungu in four rounds.

boxing (another five associations were not able to gain a strong enough foothold by the millennium).

The methods with which the experts from the four established associations, referred to as the "alphabet soup boys" in boxing jargon, used to determine the rankings soon appeared equally questionable. Each association simply ignored many of the best boxers if these athletes didn't happen to be contracted to a promoter linked with their organization, instead listing far less talented title hopefuls who were managed by the "right" business partners. The corruption in the associations became all too clear towards the end of the millennium, when several promoters admitted to having paid the IBF up to $100,000 to have the desired opponents for their title-holders briefly listed in the rankings.

Given this situation, nothing could have been more ideal in the world of professional boxing in 1986 than the rise of a mere 20-year-old to become the youngest world champion in the history of the heavyweight division— especially considering that he was able to unify the titles of the three largest associations with impressive authority within just nine months' time. Only it soon became apparent that Mike Tyson was not exactly the role model type. The "controversial champion" led such a notorious life outside of the ring that his escapades rapidly made him one of the most disreputable and scandalous characters worldwide. The more impressively Tyson mowed down his opponents in the ring until his sensational defeat by Buster Douglas in February 1990, the more his prison sentences and frequent disqualifications encouraged the all-to-familiar prejudices against the sport.

It took honorable athletes like Evander Holyfield and Lennox Lewis to provide this especially important division with a new reputation in the mid-1990s. The most exceptional stars like Oscar De La Hoya, Felix Trinidad, Shane Mosley, Roy Jones Jr. and Prince Naseem Hamed came from other weight classes, however. Their exclusive contracts with leading pay TV stations guaranteed them extremely lucrative purses, while at the same time preventing a number of highly attractive duels—the undefeated star of Home Box Office was naturally to be spared the humiliation of a defeat against the undefeated favorite from Showtime and vice versa. The old, shady business has thus remained unchanged, even if wrapped in more modern packaging, and its appeal to the masses is as strong as ever.

THE LAST GREAT GALA IN THE MIDDLEWEIGHT DIVISION

If he had announced that he was going to walk on water, a few thousand curious onlookers would doubtless have appeared to watch. After all, fans had meanwhile come to expect the unexpected from the two-time champion Sugar Ray Leonard. In the summer of 1986, however, the former Olympic gold medalist and professional world champion set a goal that appeared to be outside of even his reach. After having been absent from the sport for nearly three years, Leonard wanted to return to the ring and take on the undisputed middleweight champion Marvin Hagler, perhaps the best active boxer at the time. This impossible showdown, scheduled to take place on April 6, 1987, quickly became the most talked about megafight of the decade.

Could a 30-year-old ex-professional now working as a TV commentator stand his ground against a champion who had been undefeated for eleven years? This was the question around which the ballyhoo for the fight, started months beforehand, centered. The two opponents were sent on a promotional tour through twelve American cities, but the title-holder left the tour early shortly before Christmas after visiting just nine cities—in the battle of words with the always eloquent public darling Leonard, Hagler always came in second. The majority of experts agreed, however, that it was Hagler who would have the greatest advantage in the ring at Caesar's Palace in Las Vegas. Regardless of the outcome, both opponents would walk away as financial winners with a record purse of $12 million for Hagler and $11 million for Leonard—not to mention their share of the TV earnings. The 15,400 seats in the open-air arena were sold out four months in advance and the TV broadcast was watched by an estimated 300 million viewers. Never before had a duel outside of the heavyweight division captivated the attention of so many people.

Those who expected to witness a slaughter were soon disappointed, however. With a few exceptions, Leonard allowed his opponent to land only a few scoring blows and demonstrated clever defensive tactics.

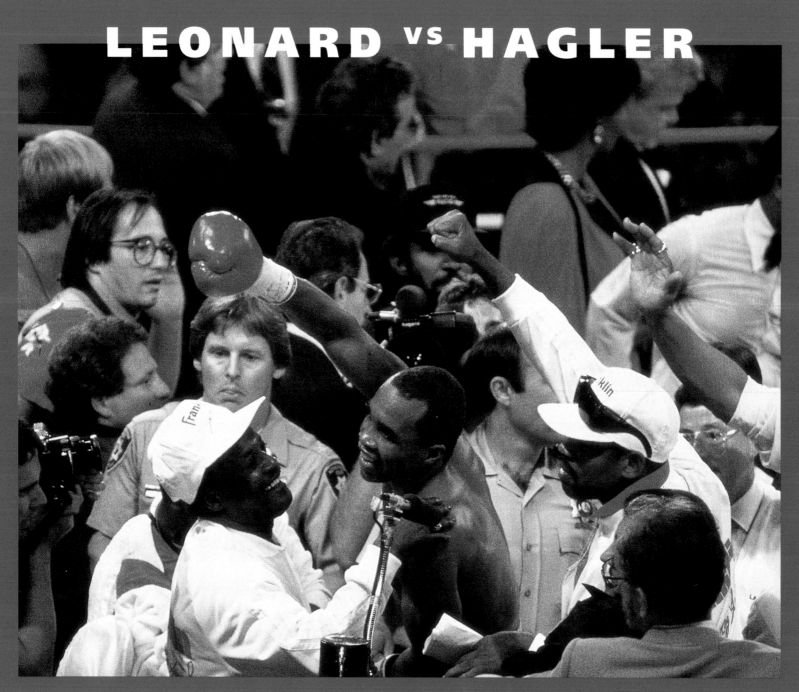

LEONARD VS HAGLER

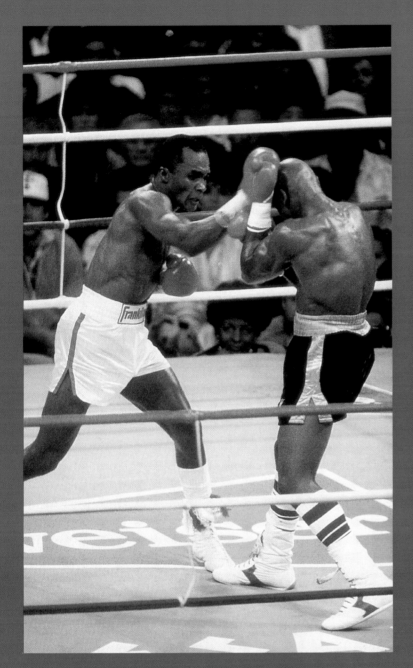

Sugar Ray Leonard's strategy of selective offensive punches enabled him to steal the points for many of the twelve rounds from his physically superior adversary Marvin Hagler *(above left)*. Leonard had frequently predicted his much celebrated points win *(opposite page)* during press appearances *(above)*.

Hagler, meanwhile, began the match with such reserve that it appeared he wanted to outbox his adversary rather than simply knock him out in order to compensate for his own lack of reputation as a skilled technical boxer. "Marvelous" Marvin was nearly always able to land his hardest hitting punches, however, and shook Leonard badly in the second third of the duel. A furious exchange of blows from both fighters brought the fans to their feet in the 9th round and left Leonard gasping tiredly for air. "Sugar" now once again demonstrated that he was much more than a smug dancer and returned to the fight. Foot to foot and shoulder to shoulder, Leonard braced himself against the physically stronger titleholder in an explosive final round and was once more sent tumbling back on the rope. Then the megafight was over.

Did Leonard's fists hit often enough, or was Hagler not sufficiently dominant? The three judges were of varying opinions. Two awarded the

victory to the challenger, one of them with the scandalous point ratio of 118 to 110. The third member of the jury awarded the victory to the title defender. The crowning of Sugar Ray Leonard as champion, which should have by all rights been a shining and joyous occasion, thus acquired a somewhat bitter aftertaste. There was a difference of ten points between the votes, unusual for such a close match. Leonard understandably let himself be celebrated as a victor against all odds, but equally understandable was the resentment that drove Hagler to step back from professional boxing following this decision.

Even Leonard had no desire to prolong his comeback, so the titles, which had until then been united, once again became free. They would not become the exclusive property of any of the subsequent champions until the next millennium. The memorable evening in Las Vegas was thus the last great gala in the middleweight division so rich in talented boxers.

ROUND TRIP:

SOUTH AMERICA— ARGENTINA

by Carlos Irusta

Carlos Irusta, born in 1948, has been writing about boxing and other popular sports since he was 16. The renowned sports journalist works for the Argentine weekly paper *El Grafico*.

South American boxing got its start in New York, of all places, with the Argentinean Luis Angel Firpo. Dubbed the "Wild Bull of the Pampas" by the journalist Damon Runyon, Firpo proved himself worthy of this nickname when he stepped into the ring with Jack Dempsey on September 14, 1923, at the Polo Grounds. Although he tumbled to the canvas nine times in front of the 80,000 spectators, Firpo indeed fought like a wild bull, defeating the famous champion with a right hook to Dempsey's chin that certainly represents one of the truly great moments in the history of boxing.

Boxing had previously been banned in Buenos Aires, but was finally legalized soon after this fight. The English had introduced this sport to Argentina, just as they had soccer, rugby, tennis, and polo. Boxing was regarded as a sport for the upper classes, with matches occurring exclusively in private clubs. Just like the tango, the music of the suburbs, the popularity of boxing soon exceeded these tight boundaries. Two Argentine boxers were able to attain great success abroad during those years: Carlos Gardel in Paris and Firpo in New York. The two men were linked by a strong friendship.

In 1932, the large stadium known as Luna Park opened its gates to the public, and Justo Suarez was the first native Argentine boxing idol able to lure masses of spectators there. Due to the many European immigrants in Argentina, the boxing promoters Ismael Pace and Pepe Lectoure sent for the first boxers from Italy and Spain with calculated caution.

Juan Domingo Perón made the acquaintance of the young starlet Eva Duarte, who would later become famous as "Evita," in Luna Park in the 1940s. The pair regularly occupied seats in the front row of the stadium to watch important attractions such as the boxing matches between Jose Maria Gatica and Alfredo Prada.

Pascual Perez won the flyweight title in Tokyo in 1954, making him the first Argentine world champion. In 1957, Juan Carlos Lectoure organized his first fight evenings in Luna Park at age 21. Thanks to Lectoure's efforts, Horacio Accavallo (1965) and Nicolino Locche (1966) both became world champions in Tokyo, followed by middleweight Carlos Monzon in Rome in 1970 and Victor Galindez in Luna Park itself in 1974. A whole series of popular boxers, including heavyweight Oscar "Ringo" Bonavena in particular, turned the regular Saturday fight evenings into top social events. Lectoure decided to close Luna Park in 1988, however, when the average number of spectators slipped below 15,000. Without this center of activity, boxing developed into a TV sport. The age of Osvaldo Rivero began, and with him champions like Juan Martin Coggi (world championship title in Mar del Plata), Jorge Castro (Tucumán), Julio Cesar Vasquez Buenos Aires), Marcelo Dominguez (Paris) and Carlos Salazar (Mar del Plata).

To date, Argentina has currently produced 23 boxing world champions: Monzon and

Perez were the most successful and Locche the most popular, while Corro, Castellini, and Ballas held the title for the briefest period of time. Two professionals, Santos Laciar and Juan Martin Coggi, were even able to attain three world championship titles.

Nor does the international boxing scene suffer from a lack of representatives from other South American countries. Columbia has produced no less than 27 world champions to date, including Antonio Cervantes, alias "Kid Pambele," the best Columbian boxer of the 20th century, Rodrigo Valdez (who was twice defeated by Carlos Monzon), Miguel "Happy" Lora, and Mauricio Pastrana. Other famous Columbian boxers include Fidel Bassa and Bernardo Caraballo, a boxer and an artist.

The Venezuelan boxing promoter Rafael Otazo organized many fight evenings in Caracas in the 1920s, frequently pairing black and white boxers as opponents. Among Venezuela's most famous and most popular

world champions are Carlos Morocho Hernandez, Vicente Paul Rondon, Alfredo Marcano, Antonio Gomez, Betulio Gonzalez (three-time world champion in the flyweight division, 15 world championship fights) and Lumumba Estaba.

The Brazilian Eder Jofre was regarded as one of the best boxers in the world in the 1960s, and the junior lightweight Acelino Freitas is gaining a reputation as a true KO artist.

Chile has also produced several impressive boxers like Arturo Godoy, who are among the hardest fighters in the world.

Uruguay has meanwhile brought forth excellent stylish boxers such as Dogomar Martinez, who fought the bout of his life against Archie Moore in Luna Park. Also worthy of mention are Jupiter Mansilla, Coco Peralta and Santos Pereyra, one of the most charismatic boxers in South America who is also known as "Joe Louis" because of his similarity to the American heavyweight of the same name.

Promoter Juan Carlos Lectoure in the Luna Park Gym *(opposite page)*, which was part of the Luna Park Stadium complex in Buenos Aires *(top left)*. The funeral of ex-champion Carlos Monzon in Santa Fe was attended by thousands *(above)*.

TOP TEN OF SOUTH AMERICA:
1. Carlos Monzon (ARG)
2. Pascual Perez (ARG)
3. Nicolino Locche (ARG)
4. Eder Jofre (BRA)
5. Antonio Cervantes (COL)
6. Betulio Gonzalez (VEN)
7. Santos Laciar (ARG)
8. Victor Galindez (ARG)
9. Rodrigo Valdez (COL)
10. Luis Angel Firpo (ARG)

COACHES ...

... AND HANDLERS

THE LEGENDARY
TRAINERS OF THE 20TH
CENTURY

THE EMERGENCY DOCTOR
IN THE CORNER

ROUND TRIP:
GREAT BRITAIN

THE CORNERMEN

The trainers
COACHES ...

If boxing is a science, then trainers are professors of this discipline. They are masters that pass on the art of the right steps, movements and punches as if they were teaching a student to speak a new language. After all, what are their protégés initially if not students? The young boy who arrives at the gym for the first time with his bag and towel might well have muscles and enthusiasm, but he certainly cannot yet express himself well in the language of the sweet science. Gil Clancy, for many years one of the most respected trainers in the USA, once summed it up as follows: "You have to be taught how to box." The reason being that: "Boxing is not about power, it's about skill." Some trainers prefer to stay with their charges from the moment they deliver their very first blow to a punch bag (known in the business as "from the scratch") to the peaks of their professional careers. Detroit's Emanuel Steward entered into one such model coach-boxer relationship with five-time world champion Thomas Hearns. The same can be said for Brockton's Petronelli brothers, Goody and Pat, who turned Marvin Hagler into one of the greatest middleweight champions of modern times. In both cases, the trainers attached great importance to "getting the boys off the streets" and a close, personal relationship developed between the gurus and their disciples.

Other trainers consider themselves above all "polishers" whose job it is to take a trained youngster—for example, at the end of his amateur career or after his first few professional bouts—and bring him to the peak of his abilities. Still others are considered makers of champions, who only appear on the scene when the professional boxer is preparing for his title fights. These trainers can also build up a relationship of trust with their charges. However, the main focus here is undoubtedly on fine-tuning styles and developing concrete strategies. Regardless of the style of teaching they prefer, trainers are indispensable at all stages of a boxer's career because, as coach Kevin Rooney once put it, "every boxer needs someone to tell him he's making mistakes." But trainers have not always been considered vital in modern-day boxing. In the early days of pugilism there were indeed teachers like the famous Pythagoras of Samos, who made a name for himself as a trainer of Olympic champions. But with the re-emergence of the sport at the start of the bareknuckle era in Great Britain (and later in the United States), specific training was initially considered dispensable for fearless men. It is not known whether methodical training was the norm in the intervening period. It was only with the establishment of the so-called academies in London that preferably active boxers became popular trainers in this sport in the 18th century. They were the forerunners of those authoritarian masters on both sides of the Atlantic in the middle of the 20th century who became everything to their boxers: crafty strategists, tough but loyal foster fathers, cooks and self-made psychologists rolled into one.

The complex requirements of modern boxing demand a more intimate or even obsessive type of trainer, the sort that would be unthinkable in other sporting disciplines. Especially in the critical weeks of preparation leading up to a bout, ambitious coaches would ideally like to control every aspect of their protégés' existence: nutrition, rest and even their love lives. This sometimes leads to bizarre situations. Trainer Ray Arcel (1899–1994) often shared a hotel room with his protégés to prevent them from eating and drinking on the sly and, if necessary, often looked after them in the same room for several days after the bout if the boxer was too messed up to make the return journey. Others—like Muhammad Ali's coach, Angelo Dundee—organize night shifts for their helpers to ensure that their boxers do not waste their energy on women in the run-up to the big fight.

While the symbiotic relationship between trainers and boxers may still exist in some cases today, they are increasingly developing into sober business relationships. In view of this fact, it is true what boxing journalist Dave Anderson wrote about the major trainers in the *New York Times* in 1991: "Fighters come and fighters go, but coaches are the boxing constant."

Vinnie Veccione watches Peter McNeeley warming up, 1995.

Assistants help contender Michael Grant stretch, 2000.

Coach Teddy Atlas with his protégé
Michael Moorer, 1994.

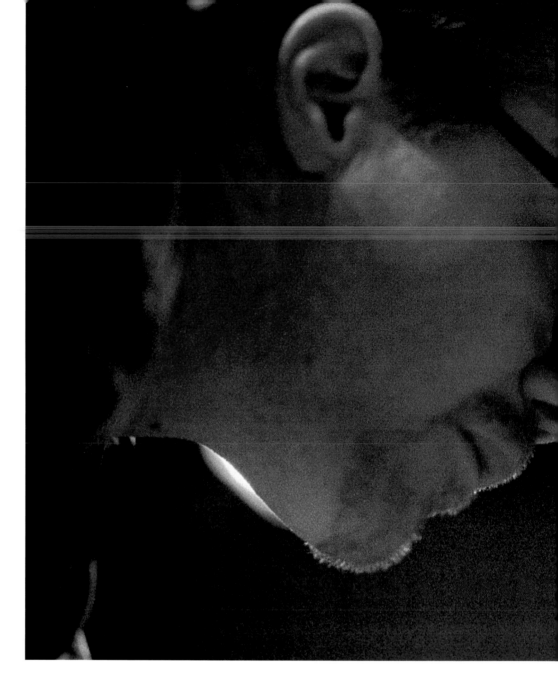

Eyeball to eyeball: Lucia Rijker *(right)* receives close attention from her trainer Freddie Roach during a break, 1998. Jeremy Williams *(below)* listens intently to what his coach has to say in between rounds, 1995.

When it really comes down to it, the close emotional relationship between the boxing trainer and his protégé can be more intense than coach-athlete relationships in other sports. The reason for this is the very special type of drama that pervades pugilism. In a title fight lasting twelve rounds, there can be up to eleven breaks; eleven chances for the boxer's chief adviser to offer tactical and strategic advice. At times such as these, trainers become a sort of inner voice for their boxers. As coach Richie Giachetti once said to his protégé Larry Holmes: "I can't fight for you, but I can tell you what you're doing wrong and tell you what you should be doing instead."

Some trainers identify themselves so closely with their athletes during the bout that they think they feel the opponent's punches on their own bodies. Many well-known trainers have experienced this phenomenon first hand. Generally speaking, however, the coach must keep cool and not lose sight of what is going on. If,

... AND

for example, he sees that the agreed game plan is not panning out, he has to set about changing it for the better in the corner. What's more, if his assistants tell him that their boxer has fallen hopelessly behind on points (or if the fight is about to be waved off due to injury), the coach has to try to get his man to knock out his adversary in the remaining minutes of the match, regardless of whether the boxer is a talented puncher or not.

In the so-called later rounds, the coach has to be much more to his boxer than just a strategic adviser. The more the boxer's physical power wanes, and the more injuries hinder his progress, the more vital it is to tap into

A victorious Kevin Kelley *(below)* shares his world featherweight champion title with his trainer Phil Borgia in July 1993 while a beaten Gregorio Vargas is comforted by his coach.

Holyfield. At the end of the eighth round, Atlas sat down on Moorer's stool and enacted the following role reversal: launching into an impressive monologue for the benefit of his oftentimes lethargic professional boxer, he berated Moorer: "You're gonna cry like a baby tomorrow. Is that what you want?" But when the situation is hopeless, the trainer also has to be able to recognize this fact and indicate it by throwing in the towel. It is a painful decision because, just like his charge, every coach hopes that the match will be turned around at the last minute. But when the point of no return has been reached, it is up to the handler to protect his boxer without reserve. This is exactly what Eddie Futch did in 1975 when he took Joe Frazier out of the murderous rubber match with Muhammad Ali ("Thrilla in Manila") before the final round. The experienced trainer has since then often been asked whether Frazier would not have survived the last three minutes. And every time he replies: "I'm not a time-keeper. I'm a handler of fighters."

HANDLERS

and mobilize his mental reserves. An emotional reference to the mega bucks that are waiting for the boxer if he wins or what he owes to his fans or relatives is often much more effective than the straightforward instruction to throw a double jab.

The various psychological tricks used by trainers to really shake up their charges in the breaks between rounds are well documented in the anecdote archives of the sport. But it was Teddy Atlas who in April 1994 really set the standard: with a performance that was worthy of a Hollywood film, he sufficiently fired up contender Michael Moorer to win a points victory over heavyweight champion Evander

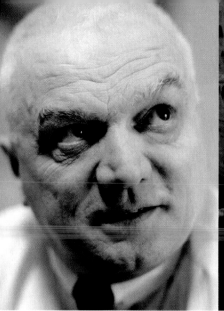

THE LEGENDARY TRAINERS

CUS D'AMATO

(1908–1985)

A resolute work ethic and unconditional devotion to his protégés are characteristic of the style of this unconventional New Yorker who, after a deprived childhood in the Bronx, spent 50 years working as a manager and trainer. His school—which for many years was also his home—was the Gramercy Gym in downtown Manhattan, which opened in 1930. Here, the loner and patriarch trained both highly talented amateurs and subsequent professional world champions like Floyd Patterson and José Torres. He taught his own, very mobile style of fighting and preached an ascetic lifestyle. Throughout his entire life, D'Amato was always reluctant to work with the shadier characters in the business. Long after he moved from the city to the Catskill Mountains, D'Amato took a young delinquent called Mike Tyson under his wing in the 1980s. Tyson became his foster child and late masterpiece. D'Amato followed his protégé's meteoric career with new enthusiasm right up until his death in 1985.
Champions: Floyd Patterson, José Torres, and Mike Tyson, among others.

RAY ARCEL

(1899–1994)

Christened the "Doyen of American boxing trainers" by *The Ring*, Ray Arcel only contested a few bouts before starting work as coach Dai Dolling's assistant in New York in the roaring twenties. He soon became one of the most prolific and widely respected trainers of all in Stillman's Gym in Manhattan. From Abe Goldstein and Ezzard Charles to Roberto Duran, Arcel, a meticulous worker and crafty strategist, perfectly prepared hundreds of boxers for their bouts in his sixty years as a trainer. His list of charges includes almost 20 world champions. He taught his boxers attributes that they would need not only for the ring but also for life. For both, Arcel was convinced that boxers required a minimum of intelligence. He often said: "If you can't think, you're nothing but a bum in the park." In 1988 Ray Arcel was named "Boxing Man of the Century."
Champions: Abe Goldstein, Charlie Phil Rosenberg, Frankie Genaro, Jack "Kid" Berg, James J. Braddock, Tony Zale, Ezzard Charles and Roberto Duran, among others.

GEORGE BENTON

(born 1933)

While he was still an uncrowned middleweight boxer in Philadelphia, stars like Sugar Ray Robinson studiously avoided George Benton. After an ominous shooting incident, which injured him and ended his career, all this changed: the best boxers on America's East Coast now flocked to his door. Benton adapted the psychological capacity for understanding he learned from his own coach Joe Rose and learned how to gain respect from his charges during his time as Eddie Futch's assistant. For many years, Benton was head coach for the Duva clan's boxing stable and regularly turned successful amateurs into renowned professional world champions. His greatest gift was his talent for identifying the little weaknesses of his boxers' opponents. It was this gift that provided the boxing world with Leon Spinks' sensational victory over champion Muhammad Ali in 1978. This victory also proved Benton's theory that "styles beat styles!"
Champions: Leon Spinks, Pinklon Thomas, Rocky Lockridge, Mike McCallum, Meldrick Taylor and Evander Holyfield, among others.

ANGELO DUNDEE

(born 1921)

The only reason Angelo Dundee followed his brother Chris to New York and Miami was to help him manage boxers. But it didn't take long for the Philadelphia-born college graduate to lose himself more in the sweet science than anyone else in the Dundee family. Taught by the legendary Charley Goldman, Dundee became a widely respected cornerman in the 1960s and soon opened his own Fifth Street Gym in Miami. For many years, Dundee was coach to both Muhammad Ali and the well-established Sugar Ray Leonard and the most popular trainer in boxing. This energetic encourager and passable cut-man remains to this day modest in the public eye. For Dundee, the boxer is always the winner; he just does his bit ("shtick") and puts his heart and soul into his work.
Champions: Carmen Basilio, Willie Pastrano, Luis Rodriguez, Sugar Ramos, Muhammad Ali, Sugar Ray Leonard and Slobodan Kacar, among others.

OF THE 20TH CENTURY

EDDIE FUTCH

(1911–2001)

For as long as he could remember, Eddie Futch was surrounded by champions. As a promising lightweight boxer, he sometimes sparred with Joe Louis. As a trainer of amateurs, he seemed to be able to churn out tournament winners like a machine. But it took him decades to be able to live off being a coach. This is what makes it all the more astounding that the former post office sorter trained over 20 world champions in his time: from Don Jordan in 1958 to Wayne McCullough in 1995 and is today considered "the most respected guru in his sport" (Harry Mullan). With his quiet voice but unmistakable authority, "Papa Smurf" coached his protégés until his retirement in 1996 and gave them the ability to win the big fights even as outsiders: a talent illustrated by Joe Frazier and Ken Norton against Muhammad Ali. For the clever tactician, sorting his boxers' strengths from their opponents' weaknesses was "just like working at the Post Office."
Champions: Don Jordan, Bob Foster, Joe Frazier, Alexis Arguello, Michael Spinks, Marlon Starling and Riddick Bowe, among others.

CHARLEY GOLDMAN

(1888–1968)

Israel "Charley" Goldman didn't visualize a specific ideal boxer in his head, he had a much more individual concept: everyone who trained with him should work meticulously on perfecting their own talents. Born in Warsaw and raised in Brooklyn, the bantamweight boxer had contested about 400 official and not-so-official bouts by 1914. Then he joined forces with manager Al Weill and began training younger boxers. After five year's abstinence from the sport, Goldman became a widely respected institution in the legendary Stillman's Gym in the 1930s. In 1936, Goldman led Lou Ambers to a lightweight world championship title. But undoubtedly his greatest coup came in the 1950s when he tirelessly transformed the initially technically deficient Rocky Marciano into the unbeaten heavyweight champion of the world. As far as Goldman was concerned: "He must be good because he beats all the others."
Champions: Al McCoy, Lou Ambers, Joey Archibald, Marty Servo, and Rocky Marciano, among others.

BRENDAN INGLE

(born 1941)

Even though he is driven by motives that are more characteristic of a social worker than a coach, Brendan Ingle has long enjoyed a reputation in the boxing world as the most influential coach in Great Britain. Ingle has been teaching a blend of orthodox and unorthodox styles, at his gym in St. Thomas Club For Boys And Girls in Sheffield since the 1970s. In this way, the former professional boxer has turned adolescents like Herol Graham, Johnny Nelson and, most recently, Naseem Hamed, into internationally respected champions. Since these boxers turned champions, his dilapidated training center has been valued in Britain as "an academy for boxing excellence" (*Boxing Monthly*). Despite this success, Ingle insists that educating his boxers for life is and always has been the main focus of his training plan: "Helping problem kids turn their lives around is still more rewarding than producing however many world champions."
Champions: Herol Graham, Johnny Nelson, Herbie Hide, and Prince Naseem Hamed, among others.

EMANUEL STEWARD

(born 1944)

The hotplates he brings everywhere with him to prepare nutritious food for his protégés are famous the world over. But even more famous than his hotplates is the man himself: Emanuel Steward. Better than anyone else in the younger generation of coaches, Steward can ignite the flame in his charges and has already worked with over 20 champions including Thomas Hearns, Oscar De La Hoya, and Lennox Lewis. In the 1970s, he transformed the inconspicuous Kronk Gym in Detroit into a breeding ground for excellent amateurs. With Hearns, he switched to the professional sport in 1977 where he is now a specialist for established greats with minor stylistic weaknesses. The tireless perfectionist considers his job to consist of "bringing the boxer to his emotional and physical peak on exactly the right day." To this end, he is rewarded with lucrative shares of earnings and a relatively free hand in the training camp.
Champions: Thomas Hearns, Duane Thomas, Dennis Andries, Michael Moorer, Graciano Rocchigiani and Lennox Lewis, among others.

Cut-man

THE EMERGENCY DOCTOR IN THE CORNER

"You must be perfectly clear about what you have to do and concentrate on that (…). Above all, you cannot allow yourself to be shocked. As soon as you think 'Oh, how awful,' you're finished."

This was how Londoner Dennie Mancini once described the mental attributes required for his job, which goes unnoticed by the majority of boxing spectators. After all, boxing enthusiasts devote their attention to the boxers and the bout. But what happens when a cut bursts open or an eyebrow swells so much that the boxer can only see with one eye? This is where the cut-man comes in. At best, they

remain as calm and collected as Mancini. And as quick: the time allocated to them is strictly limited. Whatever damage has been caused, the cut-man has to reduce it or patch it up as well as he can in only 60 seconds.

With a blob of petroleum jelly on the back of his hand and swabsticks at the ready between his teeth or behind his ear, the cut-man waits in his boxer's corner for the next break. Once the bell rings, he is usually the first into the ring to treat the boxer's face with towel, water, and skin cream. He tries to reduce swelling by applying an enswell or a chilled drink can to the afflicted spot. He treats cuts by absorbing the blood

with swabs and then applying the only clotting mixture permitted by the regulations of the major associations: an adrenalin 1:1000 solution. If he is found to have used anything else—like the infamous Monsel's Solution, also known by insiders as "Elephant Shit"—the boxer he treated is disqualified immediately.

Dubious magic solutions comprising ash and honey are a thing of the past. They belong to an era in which trainers assumed responsibility for the toolbox that quite literally saved their boxers' faces during the 60-second break. The boxers often paid a high price for this when the skin around their eyes was disfigured

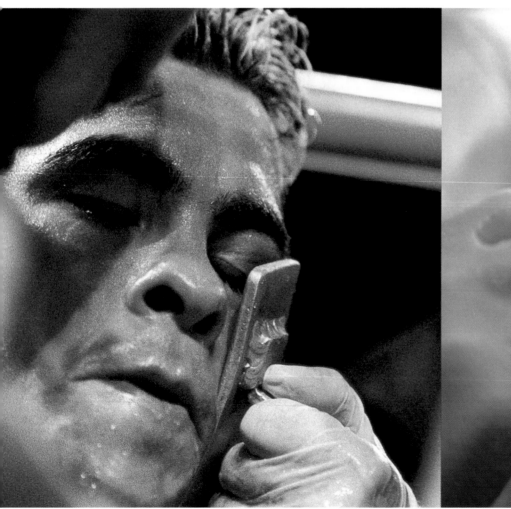

Former world champion and unconditional fighter Arturo Gatti needed an enswell to combat the swelling on his face in his match against Ivan Robinson in 1998; Gatti eventually lost when the match was stopped.

Swabsticks are used to absorb blood, keep Nestor Lopez' nose free and allow him to breathe. Soon after this photo was taken in Los Angeles in June 2000, he was knocked out by his opponent Carlos Navarra.

and became as thin as parchment. Nowadays, the cut-man is a specialist and a obligatory member of the team for all important matches. The $500 to $5000 he earns for his services is nothing compared with the financial damage against which he protects the boxer, his promoter and manager. If the boxer is no longer able to continue the fight because of an unintentionally sustained injury, he is—according to international rules—declared the loser by TKO after round 4. If this happens, all dreams of lucrative title bouts go up in smoke.

This is exactly what happened in February 1990 when Mike Tyson was impeded by several swellings during his title fight against Buster Douglas and was knocked out in the tenth round. Immediately after this sensational defeat, Tyson's cut-man was fired. The same thing happened in June 1996, when the legendary Julio Cesar Chavez had to retire in the fourth round of his welterweight title fight with Oscar De La Hoya because of a gaping cut: without thinking, Chavez' handlers had decided to dispense with the cut-man in the corner. And who knows, maybe Henry Cooper might have achieved something more surprising than a defeat at the hands of Cassius Clay if the British bleeder with the snow-white skin had not been stopped in the fifth round by blood pumping out of his wounds.

In view of these facts, it is not hard to understand why the best cut-men in this bloody business—"stars" like Ralph Citro, Freddie King, Chuck Bodak, Alan Toweel, and Dennie Mancini—are specialists who are held in high esteem around the world. They can save the skin of people who want to go back into the ring for more.

Arturo Gatti also needed swabs to stem the flow of the blood that was hampering his vision. Once blood vessels burst, however, there is usually nothing more that can be done.

Soothing and pampering often go hand in hand when a champion like heavyweight Evander Holyfield turns to his cornermen for the 60 seconds between rounds. This photo was taken in 1997.

ROUND TRIP:

GREAT BRITAIN

by Glynn Evans

Glynn Evans was born in 1965. He boxed as an amateur in London and has been writing for all well-known British boxing magazines for about ten years now.

The cradle of civilized pugilism has gone down in boxing history for two things: its classic, stylish boxers and its predilection for chivalrous losers that go down with their flags flying. Following a landmark case in the Old Bailey (Britain's supreme criminal court), boxing was legalized in Great Britain in 1901. After four deaths at a boxing event, eight members of the National Sporting Club (NSC)—which was the self-appointed supreme body of British boxing from 1891 to 1929—were charged with manslaughter. They were acquitted on the grounds that a coincidental death at a properly monitored sporting event is not a crime.

In 1909, the introduction of the sumptuous Lord Lonsdale Belt for the winner of British title bouts attracted champions like Ted "Kid" Lewis and ensured that the NSC organized all British championships until 1929. At this time, only "pure-blooded" natives with white parents were allowed to contend for the title: a disgraceful color bar that was only abolished in 1947. Around the same

time, some London business men, above all Harry Jacobs, began meeting the steadily increasing working class demand for bouts by holding boxing evenings in larger, public arenas like the ring in Blackfriars, the Wonderland and the Premierland.

A short time later, provincial England saw its first boxing contests in Liverpool Stadium, which had been erected over a burial ground. As a result of the almost tragic fate met by numerous defending champions in this arena (many lost there belts there), it was nicknamed the "Graveyard of Champions." The steady stream of Celts that had been toughened up by work in the shipyards and coal-mining villages produced a string of Welsh and Scottish boxing legends like Benny Lynch, Freddie Welsh, Jim Driscoll, and Jimmy Wilde.

In 1929, the authority of the NSC passed to the recently established British Boxing Board of Control (BBBC). Despite occasional time-honored spectacles—like the fact that the referee decides the match and not the

judge—this board of control earned itself an outstanding reputation for its work and efficiency and served as a model for other boxing control boards around the world.

The years immediately following World War II, when over 2,000 active boxers tried their luck in the ring, can safely be considered the golden era of British boxing. It was the era of Jack Solomons, boxing promoter extraordinaire, who fed the boxing-hungry fans with regular boxing events in open-air stadiums like the White City Stadium and various football stadiums. The number of spectators regularly passed the 40,000 mark. Moreover, "Jolly Jack" made halls like the Haringay Arena, the Empire Pool and Earls Court—where Randolph Turpin shocked the world by defeating Sugar Ray Robinson on points in 1951—popular. Solomons organized 16 world championship bouts between 1946 and 1968. But his greatest hour undoubtedly came in 1963 when Henry Cooper's outstanding hook sent Cassius Clay crashing to the floor of Wembley Stadium.

Starting in 1965, Solomon's dominance began to be undermined by a London cartel headed by Harry Levene and later Mickey Duff. With the help of an exclusive contract with the BBC, control rights to the most important London locations and the strangely restrictive practice of banning all rival boxers from any sort of advertisement for the 14 days preceding their bout, the consortium succeeded in exercising a boxing monopoly until the early 1980s. In the intervening twenty years, the cartel organized over 20 world championship bouts in the Royal Albert Hall and Wembley Arena.

After a century of more or less undisputed boxing monopoly, the British event scene has over the past fifteen years witnessed a bitter struggle for dominance between Frank Warren, Frank Maloney, and Barry Hearn. Through regular appeals to the courts, Warren succeeded in getting most of the restrictions abolished. He forced the abolition of the ban on live transmissions and established a boxing empire whose most famous fighters included Frank Bruno, Nigel Benn, and Naseem

Hamed. Hearn derived the most benefit from the public and financial pulling power of the eccentric Chris Eubank and built up a network of regional entrepreneurs with the help of whom he took the major events out of the capital city and into provincial centers. Maloney, head of Panix Promotions, helped Lennox Lewis to his status as undisputed heavyweight champion of the world.

The huge influence of cable television in the late 1980s and early 1990s managed to boost TV viewer ratings into the realm of eight digits and transformed talented boxers into stars. All of the three top promoters have recently concluded exclusive contracts with the pay TV channel Sky Sports, which now practically controls the entire British boxing scene. Even though this arrangement has resulted in unprecedented, regular transmission of bouts, the sport is now, unfortunately, only accessible to a much smaller number of people.

The British boxing business has a long tradition of elegance and sophistication: teatime boxing *(opposite page)* the World Sports Awards ceremony in the Royal Albert Hall with Lewis and Audley Harrison *(top left)* and a tournament in St. George's Hall in Liverpool *(above)*.

TOP TEN OF GREAT BRITAIN:
 1. Jimmy Wilde
 2. Robert Fitzsimmons
 3. Ted "Kid" Lewis
 4. Jim Driscoll
 5. Jack "Kid" Berg
 6. Naseem Hamed
 7. Lennox Lewis
 8. Nigel Benn
 9. Ken Buchanan
10. Benny Lynch, Randolph Turpin

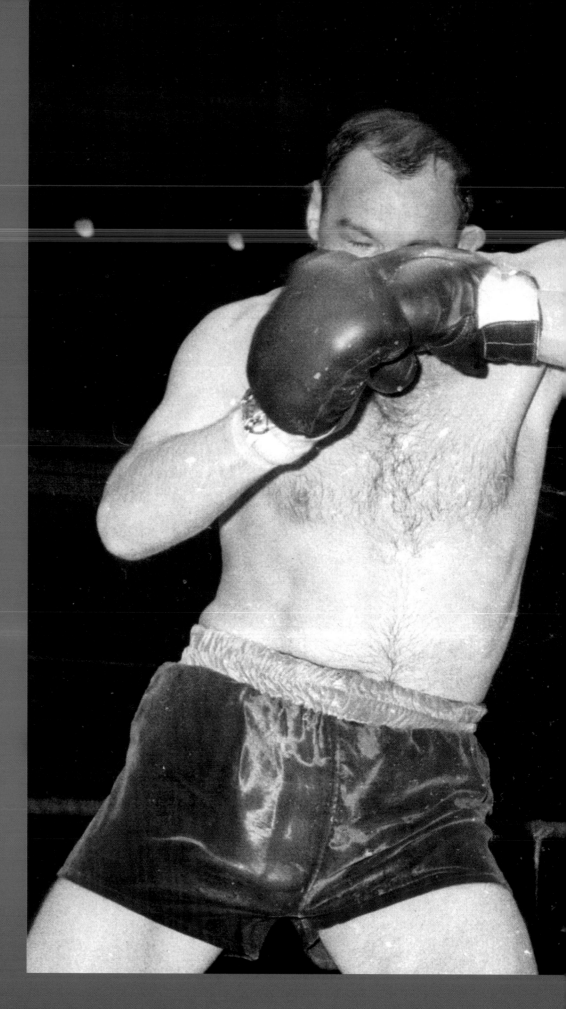

THE OFFICIALS

The world boxing associations
SUPERVISION, INSIGHT, OVERVIEW

Just like every other umbrella organization for sporting disciplines, the sanctioning bodies in professional boxing all assume binding controlling tasks from the application of rules and regulations to the monitoring of championships. Various committees compile contender rankings, recognize champions and their opponents, set deadlines for duels, grant licenses for boxers, managers, etc., and nominate delegates and officials. This is how the autonomous athletic commissions operate in the federal states of the USA and this is how the national and continental controlling bodies operate around the globe. They all determine the fate of boxing more of less as effectively as a single legitimate authority would.

It is only at the top and most important level, where there are several world associations, that this principle does not work in professional boxing. While in soccer about 203 member states accept the decisions made by FIFA and about 210 track and field athletic associations trust the IAAF on international matters, the control over what happens in boxing has been split up between four well-known and a plethora of lesser-known associations. These associations almost always have their own world champions and contender rankings in all weight limits, and they also have their own officials and rules that deviate from those of other associations in several aspects. There is a long tradition of this organized chaos in the sweet science: one single, globally acknowledged body has never succeeded in establishing itself for any length of time.

This is why boxers, their trainers, promoters, and officials move into unknown territory before every new match and have to meticulously examine the relevant rules and regulations of the appropriate association.

WBA: World Boxing Association, est. 1962

WBC: World Boxing Council, est. 1963

THE RULES EXPLAINED

Ever since John Graham Chambers published the Queensbury Rules in 1867, the first rules for gloved prizefighting, the task of refining and amending the regulations has been assumed by national and international associations. The result is relative chaos: while the regulations published by Chambers have for the most part been retained, numerous ways of dealing with specific provisions have evolved. Depending on where a fight takes place, the active participants, officials, and assistants have to adapt to different rules.

Some of the key terms from the traditional set of rules are explained briefly below:

STANDING EIGHT COUNT
A groggy boxer is taken out of the fight and is counted to eight while he is still standing.

MANDATORY EIGHT COUNT
A boxer who has been knocked down is always counted to at least eight.

SAVED BY THE BELL
A boxer who has been knocked down is not counted out if the round ends during the count (this usually applies in the final round only, when the fight is then considered over).

3 KNOCKDOWN RULE
If a boxer is knocked down three times in one round, the fight is stopped and he automatically loses.

10-POINT MUST SYSTEM
The boxer who wins a round must always be awarded 10 points. The boxer who loses the round usually gets 9 points or, in cases where the losing boxer is much weaker than his opponent, 8 points. Deductions for knockdowns and warnings are made in the final tot up.

TECHNICAL DECISION
If the fight has to be stopped due to an unintentional foul (such as a head butt), the result is declared a "technical draw" up to a specific round (usually between the fourth and the sixth). After that, the points allocated are used to determine the winner.

This is also why many spectators who do not know the ins and outs of the rules are confused when the same situation results in different decisions, e.g., stoppage as a result of an accidental foul. Neither this nor other similarly confusing situations nor the way the associations deal with their rankings is good for a sport that is suspected of being notoriously easy to influence. Even experts are often confounded by the criteria according to which the rating committees proceed in this matter. More than once, the associations have been suspected of giving preference to the protégés of their most important promoters while at the same time purposefully ignoring other boxers.

Playing the organizers' and managers' game in this way is lucrative for the associations: they usually receive between two and four percent of the total purse as their sanctioning fee for authorizing and monitoring title fights. However, this concealed compliance is so damaging for the reputation of professional boxing that journalists who have been following the sport for many years vent their frustration with a healthy dose of cynicism. "The rumor that the officials accepted bribes under the table is false," an anonymous critic once joked, "They take bribes over the table, around the table and sometimes they even take the table itself too." Just how accurate this statement is came to light in the summer of 2000 at the end of the case brought against the IBF in New Jersey. Here, promoters admitted making generous donations to the IBF to ensure that certain boxers were included in the rankings and title fights sanctioned. IBF President Bob Lee Sr. was found guilty on six points and had to face a civil action in late 2000. Various authorities now control the business of this world association.

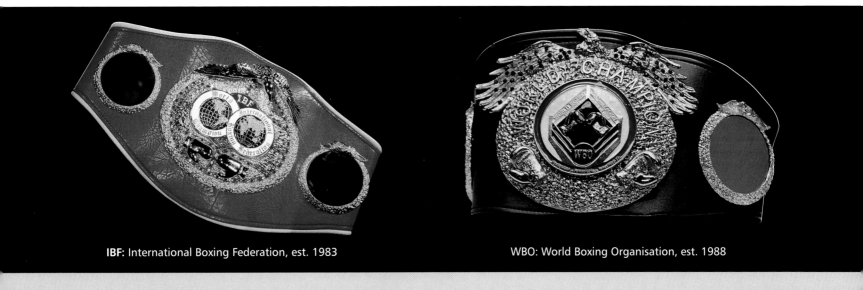

IBF: International Boxing Federation, est. 1983

WBO: World Boxing Organisation, est. 1988

UNIFORM RULES FOR TITLE FIGHTS
To at least limit the confusion and disputes about the rules to be used, the three most renowned world associations—the WBA, WBC, and IBF—drafted a uniform set of regulations a few years ago.
This set of rules is used for all American and international title fights that are supervised by a boxing commission in the USA.
Since their introduction, these rules are also being used to judge an increasing number of title fights outside the United States. The most important rules are outlined as follows:

NO STANDING EIGHT COUNT
There is no standing eight count.
NO 3 KNOCKDOWN RULE
This means that as long as the boxer is willing to continue the fight, the match is not automatically stopped when a boxer is knocked to the floor three times in one round.
FIGHTER CANNOT BE SAVED BY THE BELL IN ANY ROUND
A boxer who has been knocked down can be counted out even if the round is ended during the count.
10-POINT MUST SYSTEM
The 10-point must system is used to score the fight.

The only person permitted to stop the fight is the referee.
If a match has to be stopped because of an unintentional foul, the match is ruled a "technical draw" up to and including the fourth round; after the fourth round, the points (technical victory) are counted to determine the winner.

THE SCHISM OF THE ASSOCIATIONS

The co-existence of several rival world associations may appear to today's observers to be the result of an increasingly lucrative and therefore increasingly corrupt boxing business. But the history of the disputes surrounding the recognition of titleholders is as long as the history of the sport itself. Unlike earlier eras and conflicts, however, these differences are now institutionalized. Whereas in the past, decisive bouts determined the legitimacy of champions, we now have a permanent schism of the associations.

In the early 20th century, the recognition of world champions was based on the agreement reached by a handful of office holders and the reporters they worked with. In 1911, the International Boxing Union (IBU) was established in Europe. Initially, this was intended to be an alliance for all countries involved in boxing. Instead, however, two independent control bodies were established in the USA nine years later: the National Boxing Association (NBA)

and the influential Boxing Commission of the State of New York. Conflicts soon regularly erupted between these three umbrella organizations. In the weight divisions below heavyweight in particular, these disputes led to the recognition of different titleholders.

Precarious situations were not, therefore, unusual. In 1927, for example, the NBA recognized Benny Bass as the new world featherweight champion while the New York Commission initially recognized Tony Canzoneri. The same thing happened in 1932 when the IBU ranked Frenchman Marcel Thil as middleweight champion while the NBA and New York Commission held fast to titleholder Gorilla Jones, who had been defeated by Thil. Such differences lasted months or even years. Eventually, a sporting contest between the rival boxers or a joint resolution clarified the matter. In 1938, the IBU finally decided to withdraw its recognition of its champions to bring an end to a schism that has lasted several years.

The prospects further improved when the IBU's successor—the European Boxing Union (EBU), which was founded in 1948—joined forces with the NBA, the New York Commission, and the British Association to establish a joint World Championship Committee. Things augured well for a short period.

But the committee didn't work. Instead, the NBA reformed itself as the World Boxing Association (WBA) in August 1962 and initially counted 51 different member associations. Six months later, the World Boxing Council (WBC) was set up in Mexico City. The two associations cooperated reasonably well until the 1970s when they both preferred to maintain their own lists of titleholders and contenders. This dual system soon sank into limited chaos with the arrival on the scene of the International Boxing Federation (IBF), which was founded in 1983, and the World Boxing Organization (WBO), which was established in South Africa in 1988. Where once there had

been eight titleholders in the traditional weight divisions, four boxers were now entitled to call themselves champions in each of 17 weight classes. Excluding the more recently established associations, this means that there are a total of 68 champions! The flood of world champions and title fights is not least the result of a collective greed for significance. Just as the viewers and powerful television channels are calling for great duels for great titles of honor, organizers and managers are doing everything within their power to provide them, whatever the cost. But the quality of the fights on offer suffers as a result because instead of competing against one another, top professional boxers coexist alongside one another beneath the protective glass domes of the various world associations. Every now and then, luxurious purses are used to entice rival champions out from beneath these domes into unification bouts for several world title belts. Generally speaking, the major TV channels are beginning to catch on to the idea of quality boxing. Ratings and buy rates have proven that it is not so much the title but more the reputation and the sporting potential of the boxers that matters to the majority of boxing fans.

Champions like Roy Jones Jr. *(opposite page)* and Lennox Lewis *(top)* enjoy the prestige that comes with victories in the ring. This is no surprise considering the rarity of unification bouts such as the middleweight world title fight between Felix Trinidad and Bernard Hopkins *(above)* in 2001.

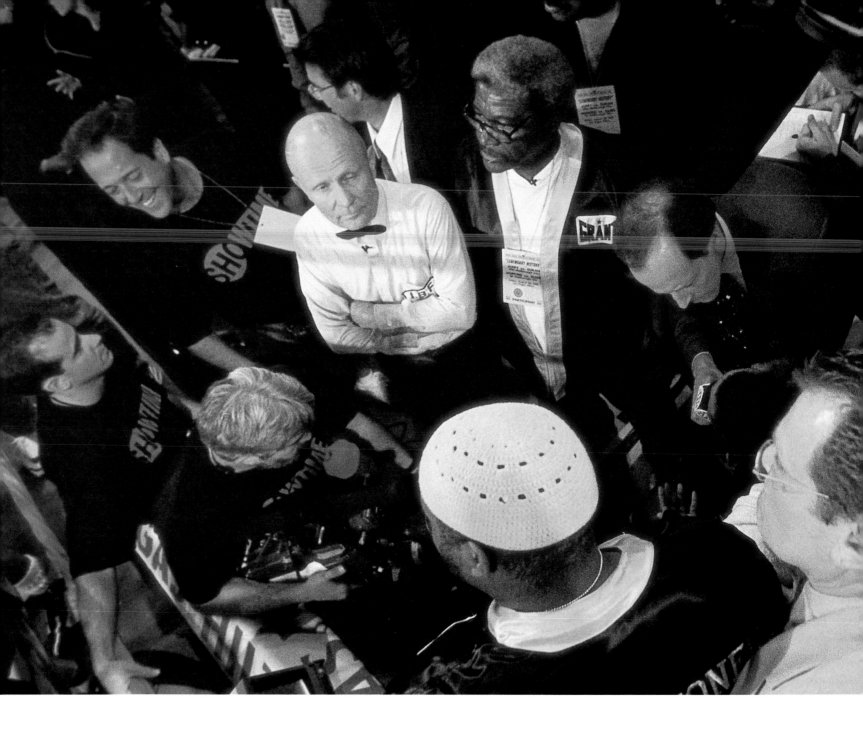

The unbiased officials

CAUGHT IN THE CROSSFIRE OF CRITICISM

They are collectively known as the officials, the unbiased officials, or the umpires, without any differentiation between the tasks they have to complete. They are just a group of sober gentlemen who either sport a dickie bow or an embroidered coat of arms on their lapels. Be that as it may, the tasks at a contemporary professional bout are divided up as strictly as possible between the officials. While in the past, two spectators were selected from the audience to act as umpires and regulate the half-legal bareknuckle bouts, an entire team of specialists is on hand to do the job nowadays. Referees and judges, timekeepers, delegates and ringside physicians are the authorized personnel that oversee matters either in the ring or at the ringside, and decide whether the match should be continued or stopped and decide what the outcome will be. Moreover, because millions of dollars—and not just three and a half guineas or five pounds—are at stake here, the unconcealed criticism of their performance has not exactly abated down through the years.

The decisions made by the officials in boxing are based on a definite set of rules that are clearly implemented by the national or international associations. The validity and applicability of these rules is discussed and explained to everyone involved at a rule meeting, which is usually convened on the eve of a big fight. But the rules and provisions are "only" the notes: like the notes on a sheet of music, they have to

This illustration shows the usual arrangement of officials in and around the ring. Small deviations in order are possible depending on the occasion and the number of title fights (possibly involving several world associations).

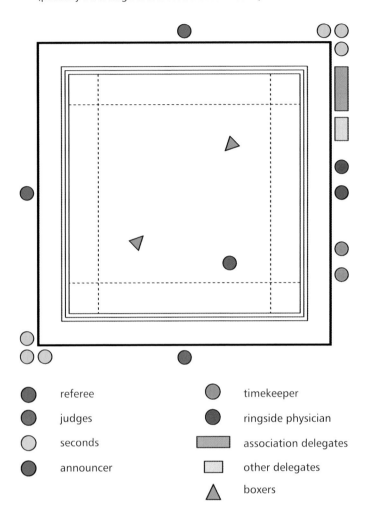

●	referee	●	timekeeper
●	judges	●	ringside physician
○	seconds	▬	association delegates
●	announcer	▭	other delegates
		△	boxers

Left: Referees like Mills Lane *(center)* are the center of attention in the run-up to big bouts (here, Joppy vs. Duran, August 1998) and are watched very carefully.

be interpreted. And the interpretation of rules is always a wonderful opportunity for a dispute in the world of martial arts. Hardly a month goes by without either the involved parties or media representatives crying foul about a new scandal or, at the very least, a blatant disadvantage. After all, in almost every contest, there is always someone who thinks that the fight was stopped either too early or too late, or the count was too long or too slow. And as far as the scoring is concerned: well that was just plain madness! The difference between these complaints and those made in other sports is that prizefighting has fanned the flames of suspicion and mistrust more than any other sport.

A round in a title fight that was ended ten seconds too early or a full minute too late; an unintentional head butt that was judged an intentional foul and lead to disqualification; an incorrect decision that transformed the obviously inferior house fighter into a winner—all of this and more happens in the ring in different ways again and again to this day. And it happens just often enough to discredit the decision-makers in this sport almost as a single body. However, this is unfair to those incorruptible officials who make their decisions to the best of their knowledge and belief. As the renowned New York author and Muhammad Ali biographer Thomas Hauser once said: "Some of the best people I have ever met are in boxing and some of the worst people I have ever met are in boxing."

The referees

ADJUDICATORS AND DIRECTORS

"Okay. I want a clean fight. Listen to my instructions at all times. No head butting. No holding. No punching after the break. And now touch gloves and box!"

Nowadays, the referee usually directs these or other similar words at the boxers in the moments before their bout when they and their seconds are called into the middle of the ringed arena. This ritual address during the so-called "touch gloves" ensures that the third man is the only authority in the ring over the boxers and their trainers. Both sheriff and judge rolled into one, he monitors the way the bout is fought, administers disciplinary punishment, and decides spontaneously (or in consultation with the ringside physician) whether a boxer should be taken out of the fight because of either inferiority or injury. He is the director of the performance and, in the event that someone is unable to rise from the canvas, also acts as an emergency helper by removing the injured athlete's mouthguard to allow him to breath more easily.

As the world famous referee Mills Lane once joked, you need a healthy portion of understatement and irony to consider the job a "chance to get the best seat in the house without having to pay for a ticket, even though you have to stand throughout the fight!" After all, the unbiased umpire has to make every single one of his decisions in the blink of an eye, leaving no room for either himself or the association that has hired him to reverse this decision later on. In 1999, Lane's colleague Elmo Adolph wrote an article for the magazine *Fight Game* in which he stated, "it would be nice to have the time to consider before we act,

as all our critics inevitably do." Adolph quoted star referee Richard Steele, who responded to the criticism of a television reporter following a controversial decision to stop the fight with the following words: "Unfortunately, I wasn't able to see the television recording of the incident before I made up my mind."

However, no one is seriously calling into question the necessity of having neutral adjudicators. This necessity was recognized over 250 years ago by the British boxing pioneer Jack Broughton. Paragraph VI of his first set of boxing rules, the Broughton Rules, dating from 1743, decreed that "to prevent Disputes, in every main Battle the Principals shall, on coming on the Stage, choose from among the gentlemen present two Umpires, who shall absolutely decide all Disputes that may arise about the Battle." Broughton also made allowances for the eventuality that this might not always be enough: "and if the two Umpires cannot agree, the said Umpires to choose a third, who is to determine it." This third party, the referee, was only permitted to make a decision in the event of a dispute. But he was not a referee in the modern sense of the word and remained outside the ring. Down through the years, his powers increased. In England, however, the rules of the National Sporting Club decreed until the early 20th century that he remain outside the ring.

Until that point in time, the "third man" was the only judge who could decide in the event of a decision on points. The heavyweight title bout between Jack Johnson and Jim Johnson in Paris in 1913 was the first time two judges—Franz Reiche and Marcel Oudin—were hired

for a boxing match. Only if these two judges could not agree on the outcome was referee Emile Maitrot's judgment to be decisive. Ironically, the result was a draw. This jury structure still applies today with the exception of Great Britain, where the BBBC (British Board of Boxing Control) still adheres to the sole authority of the referee and point judge for almost all bouts, at both national and regional level. For international title fights, on the other hand, the referee has long since been relieved of the task of awarding points, allowing him to focus his entire attention on refereeing the bout. He now only collects the scorecards from the jury of three between the rounds to pass them to the supervising delegates from the relevant association.

Eminent referees such as Arthur Donovan, Arthur Mercante Sr. or Richard Steele were masters in the art of balancing their egos while in the ring. In other words, they were able to exercise sufficient authority and decisiveness without giving themselves unnecessary airs in the process.

Be that as it may, they were not infallible. To this day, Richard Steele is still criticized for a controversial decision he made during the world title bout between Julio Cesar Chavez and Meldrick Taylor in 1990. Steele took Taylor, who was badly punched up but leading on points, out of the fight two seconds before the end of the last round to protect him against any further hard blows. To this day, he stands behind his decision. He reasons: "one wrong decision in this business and you are playing with someone's life. You've got to remember that."

INTERNATIONAL RING COMMANDS

"STOP!"	– to interrupt a fight	Boxers are counted or counted out
"BOX!"	– to restart a fight	(to "8" or "10"). While they are not
"BREAK!"	– to separate boxers from a clinch	obliged by the rules to do so, referees
"TIME!"	– at the start and end of rounds and temporary stops (timeouts)	may issue exact instructions to the boxer
"OUT!"	– at the end of a fight by KO or TKO	such as "no holding please!" or
"(NAME OF THE BOXER)"	– caution in the event of a rule infringement	"step back!"

Whether it means instructing the boxers prior to the bout *(top left)*, taking an injured athlete out of the fight *(top right)*, sending a boxer to a neutral corner *(center left)* or counting a boxer out *(center right and above)*, the "third man" always plays a dominant role in a boxing match.

HALL OF FAME OF REFEREES

STAN CHRISTODOULOU

(born 1944)

You have to be as outstanding as Stan Christodoulou to earn yourself a solid international reputation as an unbiased referee from South Africa. Encouraged by boxing mentor Willie Toweel, the young man from Johannesburg refereed his very first title bout in his hometown in 1973: the bantamweight world title fight between Romeo Anaya and Arnold Taylor. This was followed by so many other title fights that Christodoulou was probably the first umpire to have refereed world championship bouts in all 17 weight divisions. He is also doing marvelous work in several capacities in national associations in South Africa and its neighboring countries.

JOE CORTEZ

(born 1943)

The US-born Joe Cortez has used exemplary determination and physical fitness to separate even the most colossal opponents and has earned himself respect with his unerring performances. After about 30 years in the business, he has gained a vast amount of experience, which stands him in good stead when it comes to stopping fights before the final bell. Matches refereed by Cortez last as long as he considers justifiable without restrictions—and not a single second longer. And, as the boxing magazine *The Ring* puts it: "if anything, this makes him even better."

ARTHUR DONOVAN

(died 1980)

As the son of an American middleweight champion and boxing teacher at New York's Athletic Club, Donovan ended his unspectacular career as a professional boxer to become one of the best referees in his profession between the two world wars. Donovan's presence during major heavyweight title fights—especially those involving Joe Louis—were notorious. The incorruptible neutral umpire's employment at the Athletic Club kept him independent. He was elected to the Boxing Hall of Fame in Canastota in 1993.

RUBY GOLDSTEIN

(1907–1984)

As a lightweight boxer, he was one of those professionals that stayed in the rankings for a long time without ever winning the title. He gained his first experience as an unbiased official by refereeing army boxing matches. This induced the New Yorker to change jobs in the ring and become one of the most respected referees in the business after World War II. Goldstein only had to bow out once: he fainted as a result of the extreme temperatures during the Maxim vs. Robinson light heavyweight world title bout in 1952. However, his overly restrained refereeing of the fatal world championship bout between Emile Griffith and Benny Paret prompted him to retire as early as 1962.

MILLS LANE

(born 1937)

A brief tap to the side of his nose and the obligatory "Let's get it on!" were the trademarks of this "third man," who umpired over 100 title fights in the 1980s and 1990s. The former amateur boxer, prosecuting attorney, and judge from Reno, Nev., passed judgment and weighed up the options in the ring with unmistakable authority and was never intimidated by big names when making his decisions. Host of his own courtroom television show, *(Judge Mills Lane),* he retired from the ring in 1999.

ARTHUR MERCANTE SR.

(born 1920)

The former Golden Gloves finalist and university graduate from New York began refereeing Navy boxing matches while serving under Gene Tunney during the war. He earned himself an outstanding reputation as a licensed professional referee in the mid 1950s. Between 1960 and 1999, Mercante was the universally respected neutral party in over 110 title fights including Frazier vs. Ali I. Although retired from active duty in the ring, he sometimes commentates fights on TV and coordinates officials at the WBC.

LARRY O'CONNELL

(born 1938)

By the time he gained his first referee's license in 1976, Larry O'Connell already looked back on an impressive amateur career and several years as a trainer. This stood him in good stead when it came to allowing a boxing match "to flow" while at the same time exercising the necessary authority. The man from Kent is able to "read" a duel in the ring and is a popular choice for umpiring bouts in the top weight division because of his robust constitution. Since 1985, England's No. 1 unbiased official has been traveling the world as an incorruptible referee and judge. To date, he has worked on three of the five continents.

RICHARD STEELE

(born 1944)

Of all the recent living legends in this guild, Steele was certainly the most popular. The man from Nevada has been hired more than any other referee for title fights. When he retired in 2002, the number of world championship bouts refereed by Steele had well exceeded 150. The subject of intermittent criticism over the years, this star referee made up for any errors with countless convincing performances. A gentleman with iron authority in the ring, Steele refereed his matches with unparalleled superiority. He now runs a gym in Las Vegas.

The judges

A VERDICT AFTER EVERY ROUND

There is nothing either complex or stressful about their task; in fact, it isn't even difficult. "In most matches," says the New York boxing writer Thomas Hauser, "75 percent of the rounds could easily be scored by someone who knows boxing and watches carefully." Nevertheless, the work of the three judges at the ringside is called into question more often and more intently than that of any of the other officials. There is one simple reason for this: if neither of the boxers is knocked out and the fight isn't stopped before the final bell, it is the

three judges. For all other bouts, there are usually two judges who, together with the referee (who also scores in this case), form a jury of three. This means that at the end of all professional duels, there are three votes. Together, these votes can produce one of three possible results: a unanimous decision or a split decision in favor of one of the two adversaries, or a draw. This, at least, is true of the vast majority of national associations. In Great Britain, on the other hand, the referee is responsible for both refereeing and scoring

American judge Eugenia Williams came under suspicion when to universal dismay she ruled Evander Holyfield the winner of the heavyweight world championship fight against Lennox Lewis (the final decision was a draw). Mrs. Williams had been instated as a judge for the match upon the intervention of Holyfield's promoter Don King and is alleged to have received financial support from him a short time previously.

One of the deadly sins of a judge has always been to take to heart how important victory

The area that counts for scoring blows is limited to the upper body and the head.

The judge fills out a scorecard at the end of each round ...

... and hands it to the referee, who passes it on to the sanctioning body for their records.

judges who decide the outcome of the match. And this outcome can make or break entire careers and business partnerships.

Since they were introduced to relieve the workload of the referees, the judges take their seats directly at three different sides of the ring. From there, they observe what goes on and score each round according to the so-called "10-point must system". If they are judging an international title fight, there are

at national championships and matches where a title is not involved. It must be said, however, that many neutral parties are unhappy with this status quo.

It is not surprising, therefore, that people often assume that the members of the jury of three are selected and paid by the organizers. While this is naturally the task of the sanctioning bodies, appearances are often deceptive. In March 1999, for example, the

would be for one of the two combatants. This is why Joe Louis' comment about the judging referee Ruby Goldstein would be a huge compliment for any jury member. In Louis' first title fight against "Jersey" Joe Walcott in 1947, Goldstein contradicted the two judges who ruled in favor of Louis by declaring his opponent the winner. Louis wasn't in the slightest bit bothered by this decision: "I know Ruby," said Louis, "He calls 'em like he sees 'em."

THE 10-POINT MUST SYSTEM

Every round is scored in such a way that the better boxer is awarded 10 points and his opponent 9. This means that if one boxer wins all twelve rounds of a title fight, the score at the end of the match will be 120:108 in his favor.

For a title fight in which each boxer wins an equal number of rounds (six each), the score will stand 114:114 at the final bell. A draw for a round is scored 10:10. When it comes to title fights, however, the judges are encouraged to decide each round in favor of one of the boxers where at all possible.

From these scores, deductions are made for knockdowns or blatant inferiority. This means that the score for a round can be 10:8 or even 10:7. In addition, the referee deducts one point for every warning from the total score of the appropriate boxer at the end of the bout.

The scores noted by the judges for each round are only accessible to the delegates of the sanctioning body. Their three final tallies are called out by the announcer as the "official result."

IBF/USBA INTERNATIONAL BOXING FEDERATION
UNITED STATES BOXING ASSOCIATION

City_____ Date_____

Club_____

_____ Vs _____

Corner Points	Round	Corner Points
	Official's Signature	

The judges enter their score on the scorecard (above) at the end of each round. This score is then entered in the overall scorecard of the sanctioning body (below).

IBF/USBA INTERNATIONAL BOXING FEDERATION/UNITED STATES BOXING ASSOCIATION
REFEREE:

CLUB_____ CITY_____ DATE_____

_____ VS:_____ WEIGHT CLASS_____

JUDGE (white)

NAME:			NAME:	
Score	Total Points		Score	Total Points
		1		
		2		
		3		
		4		
		5		
		6		
		7		
		8		
		9		
		10		
		11		
		12		
		13		
		14		
		15		
	Less Points Deducted			
	Net Score			

JUDGE (blue)

NAME:			NAME:	
Score	Total Points		Score	Total Points
		1		
		2		
		3		
		4		
		5		
		6		
		7		
		8		
		9		
		10		
		11		
		12		
		13		
		14		
		15		
	Less Points Deducted			
	Net Score			

JUDGE (red)

NAME:			NAME:	
Score	Total Points		Score	Total Points
		1		
		2		
		3		
		4		
		5		
		6		
		7		
		8		
		9		
		10		
		11		
		12		
		13		
		14		
		15		
	Less Points Deducted			
	Net Score			

BOUT WON BY_____ REMARKS:_____

_____

_____ (SIGN)_____

The timekeeper
EVERY SECOND COUNTS

The bell operated by timekeeper Joe Palmer (above) during the Peterson vs. Harvey bout in 1936 is almost clerical in appearance. Today's equipment is much more high tech (below).

Two large stopwatches within view and a gong or a unit that generates an optical signal within reach: this is the rudimentary arsenal at the disposal of the honorary ringside timekeeper. With these tools, the timekeeper must indicate the start and the end of each three-minute round (first stopwatch) and the one-minute break in between (second stopwatch). On top of this, there are the knocking or pounding signals that are made to remind the helpers in the corner that only ten seconds of the break remain and that they must leave the ring immediately. This sound, which also comes ten seconds before the end of a round, indicates to the referee that he must soon end the boxing for that round.

The timekeeper also knocks when one of the boxers hits the canvas. From this point on, his signs indicate the passing seconds and help the referee give the boxer a count. The referee generally follows this rhythm as soon as the other boxer has gone into the neutral corner. If the boxer delays for a few seconds, it is not the fault of the referee. In the famous "battle of the long count" against Gene Tunney in 1927, Jack Dempsey was very reluctant to go into the corner. In doing so he gave his opponent—who went on to win the fight—14 seconds instead of 10 to recover from his knockdown. The referee Dave Berry had acted entirely in accordance with the rules.

The timekeeper also provides assistance in the event of a knockdown or any other temporary stoppage by stopping the clock for the count. He records down to the second when and for how long the fight was interrupted or when it was stopped. Because of the number of tasks that have to be completed, it is almost always the case today that two officials are employed to tackle all time-related matters: the timekeeper and his assistant, the knockdown timekeeper. You would think that with all these people and equipment, nothing could possible go wrong. But it sometimes does.

After Muhammad Ali had knocked down Charles "Sonny" Liston during their bout in Lewiston, Maine, in May 1965, timekeeper Frank McDonough gave the signal for 20 seconds before referee "Jersey" Joe Walcott reacted to it. Walcott was too busy ordering Ali into the neutral corner. When he did begin counting, Liston got up and continued the fight. Things became chaotic when Walcott listened to the shouts of other officials and declared Liston KO. Similar chaos occurred in South Africa's Sun City during a WBA heavyweight title fight in 1984: the timekeepers overlooked the end of the eighth round and watched while Gerrie Coetzee was counted out after a punch from Greg Page 50 seconds later. Despite protests, the decision was not overruled.

In the computer era, there have been many attempts to replace the work of the timekeeper with electronically controlled computer systems or to synchronize the time shown to the delegates of the sanctioning body and the time shown on television screens. But the organizers and associations protect the men at the bell as if a piece of boxing history would disappear forever were their positions to be abolished. To save them, they are willing to accept a few occupational accidents from time to time.

The ringside physician
ROUTINE AND EMERGENCY TREATMENT

Of all the officials at a boxing event, the job of the ringside physician comes closest to that of a firefighter. If nothing unforeseen happens, their tasks are all routine. But if something out of the ordinary does happen, they have to be on the spot immediately offering emergency treatment. Like many other medics, they are either a safety net or the patient's last hope.

Part of the routine is the brief check at the weigh-in during which the physician, who is licensed and hired by the relevant boxing association, examines the boxers to ensure that they are fit enough to fight. The "doc," as he is universally known in the business, checks the athletes' pulse, breathing, pupillary reflexes and examines their hands for any possible fractures. To date, a physician has never been known to prevent a champion or a contender from taking part in a bout because of a finding at the weigh-in. However, a ringside physician did forbid the Berliner Graciano Rocchigiani from taking part in his 1998 WBC light heavyweight title fight against Michael Nunn only a few hours before it was due to begin because the boxer was feverish with flue. The entire boxing evening was postponed for six weeks as a result.

Another part of the routine is the post-match check during which the ringside physician examines the boxers for any possible damage. This check encompasses initial treatment of wounds—above all the stitching or clipping of cuts—and is all part and parcel of the everyday work of a sports physician. If there are any signs of long-term damage, the "doc" will recommend that the boxer be brought to hospital for observation and comprehensive treatment.

Things are much more acute, however, if a boxer is so badly injured that it doesn't look as if the fight can go on. In this case, the referee will ask the ringside physician to enter the ring either during the break or a temporary stoppage so that he can briefly examine the boxer and make a diagnosis. While the doctor's opinion is not binding, it is generally respected. But because his diagnosis can decide the result of the fight, the ringside physician is often the subject of fierce criticism. It goes without saying that the "doc" recommended stoppage either much too early or much too late,

depending on who is doing the criticizing. This was exactly the case with trainer Lou Duva in 1985 when he let off steam in front of the press about how the badly punched up Ray Mancini had been left in the world lightweight championship title bout against his protégé Livingston Bramble only to lose later by a whisker. "Who are these doctors," he complained, "where do they come from? For all we know, they could be vets."

However, everyone agrees on one thing: in the event of a serious knockout, the "doc" must be on hand to help the boxer. Because once the unconscious boxer cannot be revived with smelling salts, things really get serious in the ring. The British boxing association has learned from experience and numerous accidents in the ring and now insists that an anesthetist is present at the ringside. Other commissions should follow this example as soon as possible.

Ringside physician and referee attend to Dan Sherry in Brighton in 1991 *(above)*. World championship contender Billy Schwer's bad cuts are seen to immediately *(below)*, Las Vegas in 1995.

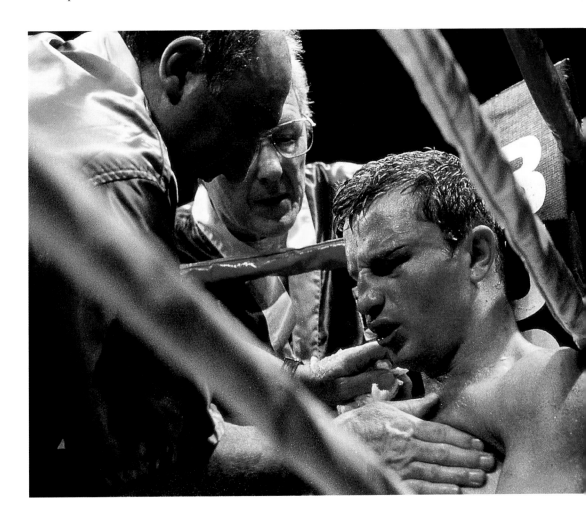

ROUND TRIP:

CONTINEN-TAL EUROPE

by Per-Ake Persson

Per-Ake Persson was born in 1958. He has spent ten years traveling around half of Europe from his native Sweden to report for America's *Boxing Update* and other international periodicals.

In Europe, boxing was initially considered a sport that was mainly practiced in the English-speaking world. In the early 20th century, a mixture of "English" boxing and Savate (a martial art that was also known as *la boxe française* [French boxing]) was still more popular in France. Then the significance of "English" boxing began to grow around the world. The sport's first stars hailed from America: the black heavyweight fighter Sam McVey settled in France and contested the majority of his bouts there. Jack Johnson, heavyweight champion of the world, also felt very much at home in France because there was less racial discrimination there than in the USA.

France's first home-grown boxing star was Georges Carpentier. Carpentier became an international star after grasping the world light heavyweight belt in 1920. Another French war hero was Eugene Criqui who made a name for himself in the flyweight, bantamweight and featherweight divisions during the boxing boom of the 1920s. Charles Ledoux also won international acclaim in the bantamweight and featherweight divisions.

During the depression of the 1930s, which also led to a decline in boxing, a young welterweight boxer called Marcel Cerdan began to build up his reputation in North Africa. In 1948, Cerdan—who had since switched to the middleweight division—snatched the world champion's belt from Tony Zale only to lose it again a year later to Jake LaMotta. Cerdan died tragically in a plane crash while traveling to the USA to contest a rematch against LaMotta. In the 1950s, French professional boxing set the tone at European level even though only very few of the continent's boxers were a match for America's best fighters. Promoters and managers like Jean Bretonnel,

José Jover, and Roger Bensaid ran major boxing stables and together with Charles Legrain, regularly organized boxing evenings at locations such as Cirque d'Hiver and Port de La Versailles in Paris. The New-York based agent George Kanter brought both a large number of American boxers to Europe and a large number of Europeans to the States. Today, the country's best boxers are under contract to Louis Acaries and his brother Michel, who himself was once a good middleweight boxer. Alongside Great Britain, France is the only country where professional bouts are held every weekend in small halls around the country. Moreover, the French boxing association has enjoyed great success with a system of tournaments for boxers of all classes.

Boxing became a very popular sport in **Italy** in the early 20th century and the sport's first Italian umbrella organization was established

in 1916. The country's first famous boxer was the heavyweight Pietro Boine, who was also a successful athlete and fencer. Giuseppe Carpegna became Italy's first major boxing promoter and was involved in every big Italian bout that took place in the country between 1920 and 1945. With the support and backing of the dictator Benito Mussolini, many Italian boxers succeeded in holding their own among Europe's best in the 1930s.

Even after World War II, Italy repeated its pre-war successes. Rosario Busacca managed stars like Franco Festucci and Duilio Loi, while promoters like Umberto Branchini or Renzo Spagnoli were in demand at international level. Nino Benvenuti, Sandro Mazzinghi, Bruno Arcari and Sandro Lopopolo all won world championship titles while Italy's attractive tax laws made the country an extremely popular location for boxing events.

Even though the 1980s produced a string of good Italian world champions (Nino LaRocca, Patrizio Oliva, Maurizio and Loris Stecca and Sumbu Kalambay), interest in boxing slowly began to dwindle. When the sponsors began to desert the sport in the 1990s, the television channels soon followed suit. Today, it is mainly the sons of Sabbatini and Spagnoli who are working hard to reverse the sport's fortunes in Italy.

The first ever boxing match in **Spain** took place in Barcelona in 1903. However, it was only much later that the sport became more popular in this country. In 1935, the bantamweight boxer Baltazar Sangchilli became world champion and the heavyweight Paolino Uzcudun, who was discovered while chopping wood, twice fought Primo Carnera: once in Barcelona in 1930 in front of a crowd of 81,000 (to this day the largest crowd ever recorded

Marcel Cerdan *(opposite page, center)* seen here with Edith Piaf *(left)* Mauricio Stecca *(top left)* Tony Ortiz *(top);* and Laurent Boudouani, *(above)* succeeded in working their way up from being hopefuls to being champions.

at a bout in Europe) and against an equally impressive backdrop in Rome in 1933.

At the end of World War II, several Spanish boxers became European champions. However, very few succeeded in repeating this success at international level like José Legra, the Spaniard who lived in Cuba and held onto the featherweight belt from 1968 to 1969. After this, interest in boxing continued to decline until it reached its lowest point in the late 1980s. Since then, the sport has once again gained in popularity in Spain. Javier Castillejo recently conquered a WBC title while Tundra Promotions has developed into a boxing stable full of Spanish and Russian fighters that is well renowned around Europe. Established in the 1970s by Enrique Soria Jr. under the name Madrid Boxing Club, Tundra Promotions focuses on Eastern Europe, where, in the opinion of many experts, the future of boxing lies.

Boxing was introduced into **Denmark** in 1896 and began gaining in popularity when promoter Mogens Palle organized his first fights in the 1950s. Tom Bogs, Jorgen Hansen, Ayub Kalule, Gert Bo Jacobsen, Johnny Bredahl and Jesper D. Jensen were all considered outstanding European boxers in their day. To this day, Palle still organizes events. The only difference is that he now has a strong partner at his side: his daughter Bettina is also a highly successful promoter.

In **Norway,** professional boxing was banned in 1980. The main reasons for doing so were the dangers usually associated with the sport and a generally poorly considered attitude to boxing. Although the ban is still in place, Norwegian boxing fans can follow the progress of their idols abroad more comprehensively than ever before thanks to cable television and pay TV. In the 1980s, heavyweight boxer

Steffen Tangstad twice won the EBU title and also contended a world title. The cruiserweight boxer Ole Klemetsen also became a superstar in the 1990s.

Even though the first bouts in **Sweden** were held in 1890, it was only French boxing hero Georges Carpentier's visit to Stockholm in 1921 that boosted the popularity of the sport. Sweden's first great boxer was the heavyweight Harry Persson who fought both during and after World War II. The 1950s was the start of the Ingemar Johansson era. He became European champion in 1956 and won his first world heavyweight championship bout against Floyd Patterson in 1959. Of his successors, three really stand out: Bo Hoegberg, Lennart Risberg and Bo Pettersson. But interest in boxing began to wane more and more until professional boxing was eventually banned in 1970. By that time, however,

Swedish boxing had long passed its peak. Today, cable television and pay TV provide boxing fans with broad coverage of professional bouts. Moreover, there are more Swedish professional boxers on the circuit than ever before: George Scott, Armand Krajnc and Fredric Alvarez, to name but a few.

Germany was the only other country in continental Europe where boxing became really popular. The first boom began in the 1950s and 1960s when Erich Schöppner, Gustav "Bubi" Scholz and Karl Mildenberger battled it out for European or even world titles in front of capacity crowds in Dortmund and Berlin. The second boom followed in the 1990s when rival promoters Wilfried Sauerland and Klaus-Peter Kohl succeeded in establishing generally acknowledged champions in the form of light heavyweight champions Henry Maske (IBF 1993–96), Dariusz Michalczewski

(WBO, since 1994) and Sven Ottke (IBF, since 1998) and the heavyweight Vladimir Klitschko (WBO, since 2000).

In smaller nations like Austria, Switzerland, Belgium and the Netherlands, however, sporting potential and infrastructure were simply not enough developed to ensure true and long-term peaks of popularity for professional boxing.

European champion Ole Klemetsen of Norway, *(opposite page, far left)* and Swedish world champion Ingemar Johansson *(opposite page, left)* did the honors for Scandinavia while Max Schmeling *(top left)* and Henry Maske *(above)* respectively dominated entire eras in Germany.

TOP TEN OF CONTINENTAL EUROPE:
 1. Marcel Cerdan (FRA)
 2. Max Schmeling (GER)
 3. Nino Benvenuti (ITA)
 4. Bep van Klaveren (NED)
 5. László Papp (HUN)
 6. Ingemar Johansson (SWE)
 7. Ayub Kalule (DEN)
 8. Sandro Mazzinghi (ITA)
 9. Duilio Loi (ITA)
10. Henry Maske (GER)

GREAT DUELS

BLOW BY BLOW

What is the best thing about a top-class, well-matched boxing contest? You can run it all over again, and the remake will fill the coffers of the promoters as much as it fires the imagination of boxing enthusiasts.

A change of tactics, a new trainer—and the second fight, the rematch, can have a completely different outcome to the first. And then, of course, there has to be a third fight, a decider, the rubber match. This will prove which of the adversaries is really the better fighter.

Sometimes that is what happens, sometimes not. And what then …? Fight series are dramaturgical high points in the fight business: they establish a rivalry in a series of set-piece confrontations. And rivals who for the course of these feuds become involuntary companions may then find themselves inextricably and permanently linked. This was very much how Sugar Ray Robinson viewed himself and his archrival Jake LaMotta, whom he encountered six times in the ring: "We were almost married to each other." But they did not even come close to setting records in this respect: in the early years of the twentieth century, due to racial discrimination, black prize-fighters, for lack of other opponents, were all too often compelled to fight each other over and over again. The high number of eighteen fights that the perpetual world championship contenders Harry Wills and Sam Langford fought in the years between 1914 and 1922 was not regarded at the time as particularly sensational.

Today it is above all those series of fights which made champions and indeed legends of their rival pairs that have remained engraved on the collective memory of the sweet science: Louis and Schmeling, Ali and Frazier, Holyfield and Bowe. At the time, these bitter adversaries unwittingly provided mutually beneficial publicity and in their trails of strength created virtuoso masterworks—pain-filled symphonies reverberating with speed and passion. However, it was usually much later that the participants realized that they had fundamentally been working in cooperation all along. "Tony and me, we earned good money," said Rocky Graziano once, in reference to the three brutal ring duels that he and Tony Zale delivered in the years between 1946 and 1948. There is no higher praise that one boxer can accord to another.

November 11, 2000, Mandalay Bay Resort & Casino, Las Vegas. Just before the world championship contest between Lennox Lewis and David Tua, the very air seems to vibrate with tension, as it often does at great boxing events. And when the end result is close, fans and *aficionados* demand at least one rematch.

TED "KID" LEWIS
vs. JACK BRITTON

On the prizefighting scene of the early twentieth century, rivalry had a name all of its own, or rather two specific names—those of Jack Britton and Ted "Kid" Lewis. These two bitter competitors, who during their long careers boxed in almost all the available weight divisions of the time, fought each other in 20 official duels between 1915 and 1921—and unofficially apparently even more often. They took their turn as champion so regularly over their six world title fights that it seemed as if they regarded the welterweight world title as their own personal affair.

They enlivened an epoch in boxing that due to the large number of "no-decision" bouts and World War I was not exactly rich in high points. When Gershon Mendeloff, who fought under the ring name Kid Lewis, came to the USA from London in 1914, in many areas of the country boxing was compelled to live with a restrictive handicap: in order to prevent fixing and speculative betting in this dubious sport, the referee was forbidden to announce a definitive result for a fight. Initially the European welterweight champion also participated in several of the exhibition bouts of the time, and thus in August 1915 first fought William J. Breslin alias Jack Britton, a combative, hard-hitting pro from Clinton, New York. Lewis, a tireless attacker with a repertoire of fast punch combinations was in the opinion of the ringside reporters the better man in this match and he thereby earned the chance five months later to box against Britton for the world title.

Lewis won this bloody duel in Boston as well as the rematch, both on points. Then Britton turned the tables, "won" their next two no-decision fights and finally, in New Orleans in April 1916, took the world title. This points victory over 20 rounds was confirmed by a similar result six months later, in Boston. What was more important, at least from the point of view of the promoters, was that Lewis and Britton were by now established as archrivals.

The English Jew from London's East End and the Irish Catholic from rural New York State—they were two adversaries whose ethnic origins and religious differences were aggravated by the publicity for their fights. At some point, even the boxers began to believe in the dubious hype: Britton complained loudly about Lewis' alleged dirty tricks, and for some time both had refused the obligatory handshake before the fight. This open animosity between the two fighters only served to heighten the atmosphere at their well-attended fights. In June 1917, Lewis took the world title back from the American on a points decision; in March 1919, in Canton, Ohio, Britton had his revenge with the only knockout victory (in the ninth round) in their series of contests. "Dumb" Dan Morgan, the manager of the victor on this occasion, later that evening sent cables out to the world declaring: "Irishman kayoes Englishman on St. Patrick's Day!" In between times, there were several "no-decision" bouts, whose unofficial results are difficult to confirm: In the time-honored tradition, both Dan Morgan and Lewis' manager Jimmy Johnston filed partisan reports on the fights through the telegraph offices, and in such a way that their men seemed to come out in the end almost as good as even.

In February 1921, this time in New York, Britton prevailed once again when he defended his title against Lewis in 15 rounds. Shortly thereafter, the two who had become archrivals over the years turned to other opponents in higher weight divisions and fought on until 1929 (Lewis) and 1930 (Britton), although neither succeeded in taking further world titles.

Neither Jack Britton *(far left)* nor Ted "Kid" Lewis were prepared to back off in their pro fights. This guaranteed a unique series of at least 20 duels in the welterweight division.

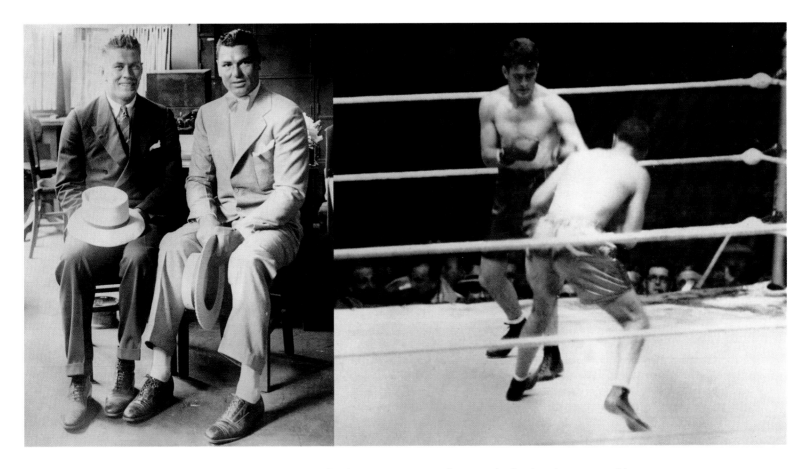

Tunney *(above left)* and Dempsey *(above right)* respected each other. However, once they were in the ring they gave nothing away.

GENE TUNNEY
vs. JACK DEMPSEY

They were both sons of the working class before they rose to become American sporting icons of the "roaring twenties." However, Jack Dempsey and Gene Tunney were such fierce adversaries in the ring that their two title fights projected an aura of symbolic antagonism—so much so that it seemed as if much more was at stake than the sporting controversy over who was the better man at heavyweight.

Since 1919, when he demolished titleholder Jess Willard in just four rounds, Dempsey had become a potent identity symbol for the mass of industrial workers. This former hobo and day laborer set little store by finely honed technique; instead he relied on his extremely high punch rate and his will to win. After a fast and furious stoppage victory over Luis Angel Firpo (1923) the popular "Manassa Mauler" gradually began to run out of high-grade opponents. A proposed showdown with "Black Panther" Harry Wills fell through after Wills refused to fight a qualifying bout for the world championship against Gene Tunney, a former US champion at light heavyweight.

So Tunney became the challenger: he was a former Marine from New York, who also shone outside the ring with his elegant appearance and fondness for Shakespeare quotations. The "Fighting Marine" was regarded as the "thinking man's champion." He was a cool but determined strategist and in September, 1926, made optimum use of his advantages in the title fight that had been heralded with so much bally-hoo. More than 120,000 spectators in Philadelphia's Sesquicentennial Stadium witnessed the 29-year-old challenger dominate Dempsey, rusty after a three-year break from the ring, punishing him with un-relenting jabs and fast punch series. At the end of ten one-sided rounds, Tunney received the unanimous approval of the points judges. His opponent later confessed to his wife: "Honey, I forgot to duck!"

The popular interpretation of the result, that Dempsey had lost the fight mainly because of his long period of inactivity boosted expectations of a rematch. The way was cleared when "Steamhammer Jack" won a world championship qualification bout against Jack Sharkey in July 1927. In September of the same year 104,500 boxing fans streamed in to Soldier Field on the shores of Lake Michigan, Chicago; they were to pay out enough to ensure the first ever two million dollar gate ($2.66 million, to be more precise), of which Tunney received $990,000 and his challenger $ 450,000. The great revenge, however, did not quite come off.

In a similar fashion to the first duel, Tunney again initially called the shots. After six rounds he had inflicted cuts over both Dempsey's eyes and shaken him once. But then in the seventh round, Tunney was caught by a brilliant cross, which left him open to a hail of ferocious hooks. With his left arm clinging on to the middle rope, Tunney slumped in a daze to the canvas. And this is where he was given time: before referee Dave Barry could begin the count he had to enforce the rules by maneu-vering the reluctant Dempsey into a neutral corner. Thus, instead of the officially registered nine seconds, apparently fourteen seconds ticked by before Tunney once again got to his feet. Dempsey's last chance had gone. For the remaining three rounds, he was once again out-boxed by the "Fighting Marine."

Was Dempsey cheated of victory by the delayed count? An exemplary loser, Dempsey was much more cautious than others in his comments on the "Battle of the Long Count": "He wasn't that hard hit, he could still stand up."

JOE LOUIS vs. MAX SCHMELING

Could two great boxing matches be more different? The two historic heavyweight duels between Joe Louis and Max Schmeling could hardly be beaten in this respect. They both took place against the same backdrop, the New York Yankee Stadium and were controlled by the same referee, Arthur Donovan. However, apart from these two identical features, there was a whole world of difference between the two events.

Schmeling could not have been more of an outsider when in June, 1936, he fought the young Louis for the right to challenge James J. Braddock for the world championship. The German seemed destined to be the third ex-champion after Primo Carnera and Max Baer to be laid low by the "Brown Bomber" on his rapid rise to the top. After 23 wins within the distance in 27 victorious pro fights, the 22-year-old Louis was considered almost unbeatable. Nevertheless, his opponent, with 32 more fights and nine years more experience behind him was adamant: he had spotted a weakness that made Louis' defense vulnerable. Almost all the experts smiled indulgently. They assumed that the veteran fighter, who had already suffered seven defeats, was sentenced to imminent execution. On the evening of the fight, they were to discover what Max had meant. Louis had a habit of letting his left lead hand drop slightly after delivery of one or two jabs—and at precisely this moment he left himself open to a right counter punch. In the fourth round, the German was able to land this punch so hard and so accurately that for the first time in his career the "Bomber" was knocked to the canvas. Visibly shocked, thereafter he continued to box on courageously but mechanically and took increasing numbers of hits to the left side of his face. In the twelfth round, a second knockdown set him up for the deciding right that Schmeling threw shortly after. This time, Louis was irretrievably knocked out.

This sensational victory over the black favorite was celebrated by the Nazi regime as proof of the superiority of the Aryan race. Hitler personally saw to it that the film of the contest that Schmeling brought back with him was shown with great success in cinemas throughout Germany. However, the less Schmeling himself participated in the symbolic exaltation of his success, the more he seemed to run up against the circles that controlled boxing in America at that time. Their influence ensured that it was Louis and not Schmeling who finally got the chance to challenge Braddock. But after he had grasped this opportunity, Louis himself consistently pushed for the rematch. As long as he still had "Smelling" to beat, the new title-holder indicated, he could not yet consider himself to be the champion. Two years after his great victory, a strong police presence lined the ring on that night in 1938 as the once so highly rated contender from Brandenburg walked in for the rematch under a barrage of missiles and insults from the hostile mob (there was a live audience of 75,000 spectators in total). This opportunity for sporting revenge had been transformed into "a confrontation between two political systems", as Schmeling later wrote in his memoirs. In contrast to the broader conflict that followed, the contest in the ring turned out to be extremely short-lived. From the first bell, Louis fell upon his challenger and peppered him with innumerable punishing blows. Before Schmeling even had time to collect his thoughts, he had been decked three times. In addition, one of Louis' punches cracked one of his vertebrae. After exactly 124 seconds of the battle, Schmeling's coach Max Machon signaled his already overdue surrender.

The best German heavyweight of all time never again fought for the world championship crown. "The bitterest and most painful defeat of my life" also meant that Schmeling was relieved of at least one burden on his return: he was finally free of the unwanted role of model Aryan.

Opposite page: By signing the fight contract in 1938, Joe Louis *(2nd from left)* cleared the way for his revenge on Max Schmeling *(left)*
Above: Posing for the camera at the weigh-in took longer than the contest itself. In New York, the German challenger was knocked out after just 124 seconds in the ring *(right)*.

SUGAR RAY ROBINSON vs. JAKE LAMOTTA

There was hardly ever a title at stake when they fought each other, but who cared about that anyway? When Sugar Ray Robinson and Jake LaMotta met up, a brilliant duel could be guaranteed. In one corner was the elegant stylist with an all-round command of boxing skills, in the other the relentless infighter with a will and a chin hewn from granite—they matched each other so perfectly that boxing fans followed their duet six times in eight years, every time with the same delight. "Sugar" vs. "The Bronx Bull" became an evergreen on the fight cards of the 1940s, even though as far as results were concerned there was really only one genuine surprise.

When they met for the first time in October 1942, they were both hopeful contenders: Robinson as a welterweight and LaMotta at middleweight. But what the black star from Harlem lacked in weight he made up for over ten rapid-fire rounds by his technical advantage. Robinson was mostly able to prevent LaMotta from storming forward and boxed him to a unanimous points victory. However, in Detroit in February, 1943, the courageous Italian-American demonstrated his explosive athleticism when he almost sent "Sugar," the 3:1 favorite, tumbling through the ropes—and he dominated the later rounds of this second duel with his persistent attacks. LaMotta's points win was the first defeat for Robinson, an exception among boxers, who had been unbeaten in his previous 125 fights, 40 as a pro and 85 as an amateur.

And for the next eight years it was also to be his only defeat. Exactly three weeks later, Robinson won a bitterly contested rubber match at the same venue on a split points decision. Was there perhaps a suspicion of a gift to his opponent? They had to wait until 1945 until they could once again astound the world of boxing with the fourth and fifth episodes in this series of duels. In February of that year, in New York's Madison Square Garden "Sugar", who had in the intervening period become the official challenger for the welterweight crown, convincingly outpointed his arch-rival yet again. But in September, before a delighted crowd at Comiskey Park in Chicago, LaMotta, still waiting for a chance at the middleweight title, overwhelmed the out of condition favorite in the later rounds. Robinson was nevertheless given the majority decision points verdict.

Over five years later, on Valentine's Day 1951, the stage was set for their final duel in Chicago. As by then both Robinson and LaMotta had become world champions in their respective divisions, the fight was billed as "The Battle of the Champions." However, some eloquent eyewitnesses to the battle spontaneously renamed it "The St. Valentine's Day Massacre." Robinson was then at the peak of his abilities, while LaMotta suffered from chronic problems trying to make the weight. The result was a brutal slaughter that became increasingly one-sided as LaMotta's strength drained away. Only his superhuman endurance allowed the "Bronx Bull" to remain standing until referee Frank Sikora waved him out of the fight in the thirteenth round.

Afterwards Robinson said in amazement: "That guy, you hit him with everything you got and he just keeps right on as if you were a crazy man." For his part, LaMotta returned the compliment: for him, Robinson was "the only one that I could never put just where I wanted him." Unlike his conqueror, LaMotta was soon obliged to let up in order to avoid further harm. Typically, he joked later that he had boxed against "Sugar" so often that "it's a wonder I don't have diabetes."

For LaMotta, destined to lose his sixth and last duel with Sugar Ray Robinson *(left),* the 1951 battle turned into the so-called "St. Valentine's Day Massacre."

Whenever Bob Montgomery *(above right)* from Philadelphia fought the New Yorker Beau Jack for the title, it was sure to be a terrific contest.

BEAU JACK
vs. BOB MONTGOMERY

In some inexplicable fashion, two attendant circumstances remained constant for all four fights of this series. On every occasion that the legendary lightweights Beau Jack and Bob Montgomery squared up to each other in New York's Madison Square Garden they delivered extraordinary fights to their enthusiastic public. And each time, the fighter considered to be the outsider in the build-up to the fight was the victor on the night.

Popular sentiment favored Beau Jack to win on the night in May 1943 when he set out to defend his lightweight world championship title (New York version) against the aggressive challenger from Philadelphia. With a fighting style that was as skillful as it was striking, the former shoeshine boy from Georgia had become a resident attraction at Madison Square Garden; in all he fought 21 fights at this venue during his professional career. But the "Bobcat", as Montgomery was known in the steel towns near his home, was this time able to withstand Jack's first aggressive onslaught and then unsheathed his own claws, gradually imposing his dominance over the fight. At the end of fifteen classic rounds his points victory was uncontested. He became the new champion with immediate effect—and six months later the favorite for the rematch, a duel between two extraordinary pros.

On this occasion, however, Jack kept his adversary busy for almost the entire distance, with sharp jabs from his lead hand, only beginning to ease off rapidly in the last two of the fifteen rounds of the contest. An impressive final burst from Montgomery wreaked havoc on the New Yorker's eye area, but not on the final result. Jack was once again world champion. His reign was not to last long. Less than five months later,

in April 1944, the "Bobcat" once more clawed the title from his grasp. To the delight of the 19,000 fascinated spectators in Madison Square Garden, the adversaries fired off countless punches at each other, but on this occasion, Montgomery clearly registered a greater number of effective hits. Nevertheless, the margin was narrow and the verdict was split. Two of the three judges had the "Philly Fighter" ahead, while the third gave the New York local hero the fight.

When these evenly matched competitors met for a final duel in August of the same year, for the first time there was no championship belt at stake. But who among the almost 16,000 spectators paid any mind to that? This time it was all about the two fighters' own private and personal championship, not to mention the welfare of the entire American nation. The sale of war bonds that was linked to ticket sales for the fight brought in a record $35.8 million. And when it was announced that the guests of honor in the VIP seats were disabled war veterans, there was an ovation that lasted several minutes. Against this patriotic backdrop, Beau Jack's eventual second place almost seemed an irrelevance. In the eyes of the crowd, both men were victorious. Shortly after this event, with a total of 55 rounds of ring combat behind them, both adversaries were drafted into the same army unit on the same day. Photographs showed them standing peaceably side-by-side, united by their uniforms.

Neither Jack nor Montgomery ever managed to become undisputed world champion of all the sanctioning bodies of the time. Nevertheless, between them, in their four classic duels they kept a total audience of well over 60,000 live spectators spellbound; in 1944, Jack was honored as "Fighter of the Year." Today, both men are recognized as all-time greats of their weight limit and have been inducted into the International Boxing Hall of Fame in Canastota, New York.

TONY ZALE
vs. ROCKY GRAZIANO

There may well have been boxing matches with more finesse than the three battles of the ring fought by Tony Zale and Rocky Graziano. But as far as the popular elements of a fist-fight are concerned, the merciless trading of blows, the dramatic twists of fortune in the course of events and that extra incalculable dash of spectacular violence—nothing else even comes close to these legendary middleweight title bouts. They were fights that the renowned boxing journalist Jimmy Cannon once criticized as "fights that the reformers could cite as grounds for driving this business out of the arenas and ballparks." But they were also classics of their kind that were twice honored with the title of "Fight of the Year."

Concentrated action was a pre-programmed component of these two adversaries, both considered as diehards who pulled no punches. By 1941, Tony Zale, the man with the iron fists, had boxed himself up and out of the steelworks of Gary, Indiana and had become world champion. War service in the US Navy compelled his lay-off from pro boxing until 1946. At 33 years old, when he faced a challenger nine years his junior he was judged to be the outsider. Graziano, a reformed delinquent from New York's Lower East Side had wide charismatic appeal, and not least because of the best right in his weight division, he was heralded as the coming man.

Although Graziano was briefly knocked down in the first round, the 38,000 spectators who crowded New York's Yankee Stadium soon began to believe they were witnessing the predicted result: from the second to the fifth round, "Rocky" let loose with a barrage of effective punches which the champion laboriously but consistently fended off. At the end of the fifth round, Zale's seconds had to steer the champion, by now barely standing on unsteady legs, into his corner. The "Man of Steel" was obviously completely disoriented. Then the tide turned: as if working on subconscious guidance, the battered world champion powered one of his much-feared body hooks into the solar plexus of his opponent and followed up with a left to the chin. The referee had already counted Graziano out long before he began slowly to drag himself up off the canvas.

In Chicago in July, 1947, the role of the all-but beaten loser who is suddenly transformed into the victor fell to Graziano. Injured above one eye right from the start of round one and practically blinded in the other by swelling, towards the end of the fifth "The Rock" produced a furious attacking burst. In the sixth he pounded the champion backward and almost through the ropes, then punched on until referee Behr waved the dazed Zale out of the fight. This wild exchange of blows in the stifling summer heat of the arena had drained both fighters of their last reserves of strength. However, a conclusion to their rivalry had not yet been reached: one year later, in June, 1948, in Rupert Stadium in Newark, New Jersey, Graziano and Zale faced each other yet again.

And yet again, each drove forward against the other for the entire length of two brilliant rounds, taking a round apiece; then in the third round the 35-year-old Zale landed two knockdown punches. The second of these led to the early stoppage of the fight and for the final time confirmed a victory for the "Man of Steel", who had earlier predicted a KO win in the third round. Three months later, after a defeat by Marcel Cerdan, Zale retired. Graziano, on the other hand, who later collapsed again while still in the dressing room, was to box on for a further four years. Later, after he had seen film of the fight, he said: "If I'd known what was going on there, I'd have given up in the first round." But neither of these heroes of the ring appeared to know when it was time to stop.

Opposite page: Former steelworker Tony Zale *(far left)* and reformed delinquent Rocky Graziano had both experienced tough conditions. At their first meeting, Zale was first knocked down before he won in round six *(right)*. At the third meeting *(below)* he kayoed his opponent three rounds sooner.

SANDY SADDLER
vs. WILLIE PEP

One thing is for sure; they would never win a trophy for the cleanest fight of all time. Despite this, these four merciless ring duels between Sandy Saddler and Willie Pep mark an epoch during which the feather-weight division aroused more excitement and interest than ever before—and more than it is ever likely to again.

Willie Pep was a master of the noble fistic art, who could demonstrate with speed and finesse how to hit and not get hit himself. He was a convincing champion with a run of 73 consecutive wins; he was also the favorite to win this bout, his seventh title defense in six years. But in October 1948, when he met the hard-hitting Saddler (56 KOs in 85 wins, 2 draws and 6 defeats), something was wrong from the start. The dangerous banger from Harlem caught Pep in the very first round with a punch that opened up his nose. In the third, he floored the shaken champion twice, before finally putting him out for the full count in the fourth round. The crowd in the sold-out Madison Square Garden was just as disappointed with the performance of the dethroned champion as he was himself. "I just didn't take him seriously enough," confessed "Will o' the Wisp" later.

Less than four months later, on what he himself described as "the greatest night of my life," he was to deliver the best performance in his 26-year career. Pep, bursting with energy, threw so many fast punches that at first Saddler scarcely had a chance to launch his own attack; in the first round alone, Pep scored 27 lead hand punches in quick succession. He stayed so close inside that his opponent had no opportunity to take advantage of his longer reach—even though by doing so he took punches that opened up cuts above and below his eyes. Saddler only began to rediscover his rhythm in the later rounds, when he was able to shake his challenger visibly on more than one occasion. But on that night Pep simply refused to be knocked down: he managed to withstand a final furious attack and, even though badly marked, was awarded a unanimous points victory.

His unexpected revenge was later designated "Fight of the Year" by *The Ring*. This high standard was not to be achieved in the remaining two fights in their series of duels. Where the rivals had resorted to the occasional dirty trick in their two fights at Madison Square Garden, this was merely a foretaste of what was to come in New York's Yankee Stadium in September, 1950—and even more so one year later at the Polo Ground. The two constantly trod on each other's feet in retaliation when they thought they were the victims of holding, shoving or thumbing (gouging an opponent's eye with the thumb). All too often it seemed as if there was urgent need for more than one referee at a time. On both these world championship occasions the result itself was less than satisfactory: in 1950, Pep had to give up the fight because of a dislocated shoulder, while in 1951 he was again forced to pull out because of injury, this time a badly swollen eye.

After their final clash, both Saddler and Pep were temporarily suspended. There were to be no more title fights in their division for the next three and a half years. This was not least a result of the questionable example set by these two rivals, the greatest fighters in their weight limit, in the course of their four increasingly dirty fights. As far as the many clinches and fouls were concerned, at least Willie Pep made some kind of attempt at an explanation. "You mustn't forget that we were fighting for the title," said Pep later, after he had retired. Their mutual animosity was later to be replaced by friendship.

A few days before their second fight in February 1949, Willie Pep and Sandy Saddler size each other up again.

Ezzard Charles and Rocky Marciano show their determination at the weigh-in for their rematch in September, 1954.

ROCKY MARCIANO
vs. EZZARD CHARLES

In his 49 professional fights, Rocky Marciano all too often met opponents who were his superior as far as technique was concerned —Joe Louis, "Jersey" Joe Walcott and Archie Moore to name but a few. But none of these presented him with as great a challenge as Ezzard Charles, a much-underrated boxer-puncher from Cincinatti. For this reason their two duels for the right to the heavyweight crown are legendary highpoints in their sport. In 1997, *The Ring* counted both fights among their list of the greatest title fights of the modern era.

Marciano had already successfully defended the title he won in 1952 twice when he came up against this ex-world champion in June 1954. And as Charles had lost two of his last four fights, the titleholder was the clear betting favorite. But once they were in the ring at the New York Yankee Stadium, Charles impressively demonstrated to the 47,000 spectators why they called him the "Cincinnati Cobra." Although the former middleweight and light heavyweight fighter initially used clever footwork to avoid direct confrontation, he then went on the attack with just as much lack of compromise.

A brilliant and at times brutal exchange of blows developed, during which both Charles' hook and Marciano's right clearly left their mark: the world champion had a deep cut on his left eye, while his challenger had numerous swellings. But in the later rounds only one of the adversaries was able to pile on more pressure— and that man was Marciano. So, as Marciano had been able to demonstrate a greater head of steam, the final decision of the judges was close but unanimous. Two of them gave the titleholder

8 and the third 9 of the 15 rounds of the contest. Later, the legend of the ring frankly admitted: "This was the hardest fight of my career." And barely three months later he then had to get through the rematch.

At the same venue, this time in front of 34,000 spectators, "The Rock" put his opponent under pressure from the outset—and a well-aimed blow put him down for a short time in the second. But the "Cobra" was not slow to strike back. Marciano was soon once again bleeding from his eyebrow and from his nose, split in the sixth round by a double hit from his opponent (although Marciano claimed he was elbowed). It seemed as if a stoppage in favor of the challenger was in the air. But at this critical point Marciano shifted up a gear— and roused "Suzy-Q", as he called his lethally powerful right. The first appearance of this punch, in the eighth round, floored Charles and the second, set up by a left hook, took care of the rest before the gong: by the time the glassy-eyed challenger struggled to his feet referee Al Berl had already completed a count of ten. Thanks to his unbending will—and to "Suzy-Q"—Rocky Marciano had once again prevailed against his stubborn adversary. Two fights and twelve months later he retired, still unbeaten, a fighter born to win, who simply rejected defeat.

Ezzard Charles was to continue a professional career that had been punctuated by no less than 13 world championship fights for a further five erratic years. Until the fall of 1959 from Tacoma to Syracuse and back he fought another 23 pro contests but won only ten of these. The "Cobra" from Cincinnati was never again to challenge for the world championship in the top weight limit, nor for any other significant title.

In their rematch toward the end of 1955 in Boston, Carmen Basilio once again defeated his opponent Tony DeMarco by a KO in the 12th round.

CARMEN BASILIO
vs. TONY DEMARCO

It should not really be possible for two boxing matches between the same two opponents to be so similar that the second is a replica of the first. But Carmen Basilio and Tony DeMarco came close with their action-packed duels for the welterweight crown. In 1955, within a period of five months both contests served up the same dramatic course of events with the same eventual victor—and but for a tiny difference their duration was almost identical.

When these two Italian-Americans met for the first time in June 1955, a fierce trading of blows guaranteed to please the public was in prospect. Neither the challenger Basilio nor DeMarco, who had become champion after a KO victory over titleholder Johnny Saxton, were known as great stylists or for their mastery of defensive skills. They both preferred to rely on the power of their fists, their stamina, and their readiness to withstand whatever amount of punishment was rained down on them. The War Memorial Auditorium in Syracuse was therefore a particularly fitting venue for their clash. In a place built to commemorate the brave fallen in historic battles, right from the signal for the first round an unreserved exchange of blows developed. Initially Basilio, the homeboy from the nearby onion fields around Canastota, had the worst of it; DeMarco, the champion, allowed him no respite. But the challenger held his ground at the half-distance and gave back hook for hook. By the mid-point of this 15-round contest both fighters were already badly marked, Basilio above both eyes and on the upper lip and DeMarco by a gaping cut over the right eye. From round eight Basilio's strategy of attrition, to wear down the champion with blows to the body, began to pay dividends. With each

minute that passed, DeMarco grew more tired and was knocked down twice in the tenth. Two rounds later, one minute and fifty two seconds into the twelfth, the champion, by now barely able to stand on unsteady legs and already well on the way to defeat, was taken out of the fight by referee Harry Kessler. The triumph at the War Memorial was a spectacular confirmation for a talented fighter who had survived 63 pro fights thus far on the difficult path to the top. Basilio embodied the principle of mind over matter rather than mastery of finely honed technique. "When he hits you, you know you've been hit," said Basilio about DeMarco. All you had to do was ignore the effects: "If you think it's going to hurt, then it will hurt."

In November 1955, in the rematch the "Upstate Onion Farmer" again had no time to feel pain. In front of his home crowd in Boston Gardens, filled that night to capacity with 13,300 spectators, DeMarco attacked even more fiercely than before. The ex-champion was obviously going for victory within the scheduled distance. In round seven he visibly rocked Basilio with a powerful left hook. But the new titleholder was able to withstand the onslaught in this and in the following round by keeping moving—and thanks to his better condition was gradually able to regain the upper hand. DeMarco took two counts in the twelfth round before referee Mel Manning waved him out of the fight one minute and fifty four seconds into the round.

The second dramatic episode in the feud between these two punchers from America's East Coast had lasted exactly two seconds longer than the first. And it had produced the same winner—a master of pain who in the future was to fight out yet more historic series with Johnny Saxton, Sugar Ray Robinson, and Gene Fullmer.

FLOYD PATTERSON
vs. INGEMAR JOHANSSON

Neither of them may have belonged to the phalanx of the best heavyweight champions of all time, but in dramatic terms, the feud between Floyd Patterson and Ingemar Johansson for the title of world champion lacked for nothing. Thirteen knockdowns in a total of fourteen rounds, two outsider victories and the overturn of a historic curse—that was the considerable credit balance of their duels in a period in the sport with few other high points.

Few were delighted by the way in which Floyd Patterson clung on to the world title that he won as a 21-year-old in 1956. His trainer Cus D'Amato, who was also his mentor and manager, steadfastly refused to cooperate with the mafia-operated International Boxing Club (IBO) that controlled the majority of contenders. And in any case, he was cautious in his selection of potential opponents. Because of this, according to the renowned boxing essayist A.J. Liebling, his protegé soon began to seem like "a Delacroix who had run out of canvas." Could Ingemar Johansson be the guy for Patterson to prove himself against? The experts doubted it. In a public training session before his rendezvous with the world champion, the European champion from Gothenburg in Sweden seemed hulking and sluggish; his much-vaunted right was nowhere to be seen.

So, New York's Yankee Stadium was not exactly full to overflowing in June 1959 when the European met the favored world champion. The latter still seemed so confident after two restrained rounds that he began to close the distance from his opponent. Then Johansson feinted with his left and in the next moment as his opponent moved to avoid the blow, landed a right full on his head—and the next that Patterson was to remember was a request from referee Ruby Goldstein to go to a neutral corner. This request was however not directed at him, as he lay dazed on the canvas—and he later fought on guided only by his subconscious. In this third round Patterson struggled back to his feet six times in all, before Goldstein finally took him out of the fight.

It was to be a year before the humiliated Patterson got a chance to avenge his defeat. This time, watched by more than 45,000 spectators around the ring of the New York Polo Grounds, the former Olympic gold medallist at middleweight abandoned his cross-armed "peek-a-boo" style in favor of a more conventional stance. He initially employed skillful footwork to avoid "Thor's Hammer" as Johansson's right had been dubbed. In the second round, when a direct hit did nevertheless put him down, this had no lasting effect. Three rounds later, Patterson's superior boxing skills allowed him to set the tone. A first left hook took the legs from the Swede and floored him briefly; a second conclusively ended the fight for Johansson. Thus, Patterson succeeded where so many other heavyweight champions had so often tried and failed: he ascended to the throne of the so-called "World Champion of all Divisions" for a second time. Until then, the accepted rule had been: "They never come back."

Patterson's triumph had been so clear-cut that for their third fight in March 1961, few gave his opponent any chance at all, so the meeting in the Miami Beach Convention Center was another box-office flop. From a sporting point of view, however, it was the most interesting of their duels. In the very first round, the Swede had his adversary down twice, before he himself took a count. Then it became increasingly clear that Patterson was out-boxing him. The fight came to its painful end in round six: Patterson landed two rights to the head and Johansson landed on the deck. By the time he got to his feet, referee Billy Regan had just finished the count. It was a dramatic end to a series of fights packed with surprises.

In the rematch in the summer of 1960 Floyd Patterson clearly dominated the Swede Ingemar Johansson— and won within the distance.

ROUND TRIP:

SOUTH AFRICA

by Bert Blewett

Bert Blewett was born in 1933 and is the most prominent South African voice on the theme of boxing. He is editor of the South African magazine *Boxing World,* a TV commentator, columnist for the *Sunday Tribune* and author of the standard work *The A—Z of World Boxing.*

Although the country enters the third millennium with twelve internationally recognized "world" champions, the sport of boxing has reached a low point in its history—thanks to a great extent to policies that the South African minister for sport Ngconde Balfour has described as "maladministration."

The decline began at the end of the 1990s when internal disputes among South African boxing functionaries led to irregularities in betting offices and to waning interest in the sport. In their disappointment, not only the print media but large numbers of boxing fans turned their attention to other forms of sport and in a very real sense gave boxing the boot.

As boxing in South Africa is controlled by legislation, the government set up a special commission to establish a new basic structure for the sport. Since then a further commission was set up by the government to administer the sport on a temporary basis until a new law could be introduced by parliament. "Boxing South Africa," as this association founded in the summer of 2001 is called, took up its duties at the beginning of 2001.

"My intervention in the sport of boxing will undoubtedly be regarded as deliberate interference," said Balfour, "but I could not stand by and watch such a popular sport be destroyed by egoism and the selfish deeds of a few individuals."

When one bears in mind that boxing has existed as a sport in South Africa for around 120 years, this is the least the Minister can do. Although fist fighting was first legalized on the continent in 1923, both bareknuckle fights and contests under the Queensberry rules had been taking place on South African soil since about 1880, including the longest bareknuckle fight in the history of Africa. In 1890, in the Kimberley diamond fields,

Barney Malone and Jan Silberbauer squared up to each other and fought 212 rounds over five hours and two minutes, until Malone was declared the victor.

Although heavyweights have undoubtedly dominated the boxing scene in South Africa, the first South African world champion was a bantamweight. Willie Smith took the title of the British version of the world championship in London in October 1927, when he defeated Teddy Baldock on points. The first undisputed South African world champion was another bantamweight, Vic Toweel, who won a points decision over Manuel Ortiz in Johannesburg in May 1950. At this time the sport was still segregated along racial lines, and another 23 years were to pass before the first officially approved "mixed race" fight was staged. In Johannesburg in December 1973, Bob Foster and Pierre Fourie fought not just for the light

heavyweight title—with this fight they also overcame the strict boundaries of apartheid that for almost a hundred years had kept black and white boxers apart.

In 1979, the last racial restrictions in sport were abolished and sports fans in South Africa were at last able to enjoy what many today regard as a golden age of boxing. The heavyweight division was generally the most popular (in September, 1983, Gerrie Coetzee won the WBA version of the world championship), although increasingly the best South African boxers have fought in the lighter weight divisions. Brian Mitchell was the first of these great little boxers—he won the WBA junior light-weight title in September 1987. More outstanding boxers such as Welcome Ncita, Jacob "Baby Jake" Matlala, Vuyani Bungu, and Lehlohonolo Ledwaba then carried on the tradition. Many experts are of the opinion

that Vuyani Bungu, who was IBF champion at junior featherweight from 1994 to 1999, is by far the best boxer that South Africa has ever produced.

Strong competition and the influence of television has had such an effect that the number of first class South African promoters has slumped so far that they can now easily be counted on the fingers of one hand. The best known of these is Rodney Berman of Golden Gloves, closely followed by Branco Milenkovic, Mike Segal, and Mzi Mnguni. Carnival City, the new Sun International casino near Boksburg has over a very short time become South Africa's largest and most significant venue, and not only for boxing. And the only truly unique cultural feature remaining in connection with boxers from South Africa is that they have their own personal announcers to proclaim their entrance to the ring.

Before his world championship fight in Carnival City, Lennox Lewis visited Nelson Mandela's former home in Soweto *(opposite page, top)*.
The president's guests of honor also included Vuyani Bungu *(opposite page, bottom)*, Michael Spinks, and Joe Frazier *(above)*.

TOP TEN OF SOUTH AFRICA:
1. Vic Toweel
2. Vuyani Bungu
3. Brian Mitchell
4. Gerrie Coetzee
5. Jacob Matlala
6. Welcome Ncita
7. Pierre Fourie
8. Dingaan Thobela
9. Jake Tuli
10. Laurie Stevens

DICK TIGER
vs. GENE FULLMER

When their career paths crossed, they were both well on the way to becoming legends of the middleweight division; and the determined challenge that each presented to the other was to prove to their mutual advantage in confirming that status. However, only in boxing could there be such wide diversity as that which characterized the three duels in the feud that Dick Tiger and Gene Fullmer fought within the space of ten months at the start of the 1960s.

In 1959, Fullmer became the National Boxing Association titleholder with a memorable stoppage victory over Carmen Basilio. No less significant was the unofficial title of "crowd-pleaser" that the strong-willed fighter from Utah was accorded by insiders in the fight game. Fullmer did not waste much time on technical finesse; he headed straight for direct confrontation in an attempt to wear down his opponents. This was how he achieved his two victories over Sugar Ray Robinson and the seven successful defenses of his NBA world championship. However, when he fought Dick Tiger in Candlestick Park, San Francisco in October 1962, the talented slugger came up against a challenger who was both his technical and his physical superior.

Tiger, who came into the world 33 years earlier in Nigeria as Richard Ihetu, took on the fight from the first gong. Standing toe-to-toe with the champion, the unshakeable fighter from the Igbo people gave back as good as he got in hard-hitting hooks. It became clear in the later rounds that this man from West Africa, who had developed his skills in England, was in much better physical condition. The champion was particularly prone to cuts and by the tenth round Tiger's punches had opened up both of Fullmer's eyebrows. While Tiger's condition enabled him to press on with the attack, in the remaining rounds the titleholder, by then much the worse for wear, had to shift down a gear. The judges' decision was unanimous, and a new star, later named "Boxer of the Year" for 1962, was born.

Four months later in the rematch in the Las Vegas Convention Center, Fullmer changed his strategy in an attempt to avoid the painful experience of another clear defeat. The already twice-dethroned ex-champion largely avoided direct confrontation but landed a few surprises and kept moving. On this occasion, at the end of 15 close rounds, both fighters were badly marked and shared a draw. It was a decision that seemed more flattering to Tiger and gave rise to some doubt. This doubt was to be banished later that same year in a third, decisive match in the world champion's own "living room."

More than 30,000 spectators were there when the rivals met up once again in the ring of the Liberty Stadium in the Nigerian city of Ibadan. And this time, in his home country, Tiger transformed the contest to unify the world championship titles into his own personal party. In a fight that seemed to be the quintessence of all previous experience, the new champion systematically out-boxed his predecessor, leaving him not even the ghost of a chance. Fullmer, badly damaged under and above both eyes, was taken out of the fight after seven one-sided rounds by his manager Marv Jensen. He frankly admitted later: "My mother and my father could've been the referee and the judges, and I still wouldn't have won a single round."

That long night in Ibadan marked the end of the career of the courageous Mormon. In contrast, the hero from Nigeria, two years his senior, continued to go into the ring until 1970 and in 1966 was also to move up a division to become world champion at light heavyweight.

At their first meeting in October 1962, Dick Tiger took the title from Gene Fullmer *(bottom left)* and later enjoyed well-earned congratulations from his fans.

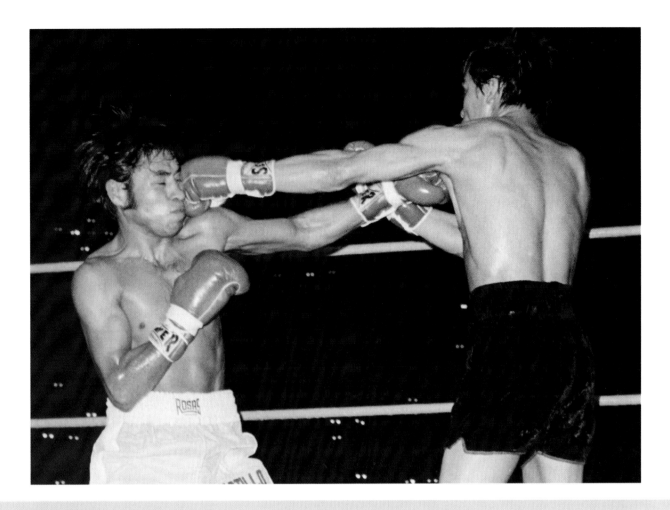

There was always an even balance of give and take in the fights between the Mexican bantamweights Jesus "Chuchu" Castillo *(right)* and Ruben Olivares.

RUBEN OLIVARES VS. JESUS "CHUCHU" CASTILLO

In boxing, as in other matters, Latin America does not end at Tijuana and Mexicali. In Inglewood, California, immigrant hispanics have done much to determine the atmosphere and flavor of pro boxing events staged in the giant arena of the Forum. The *cholos* (guys) have always required their favored boxers to be warriors contemptuous of pain, and at the end of the 1960s, this was why they took one fighter in particular to their hearts—Ruben Olivares, the KO king of the small realm of the bantamweights.

It was in front of this crowd in August 1969, that the 22-year-old businessman's son from Mexico City chopped down the reigning champion Lionel Rose in less than five rounds. It was Olivares' fifty-first knockout win in a series of 52 unbeaten appearances so far (there was one draw)—and impressive proof of why his brown-eyed fans called him "El Puas", the spike. (His blue-eyed fans named him "Rockabye Ruben.") A second Mexican title contender, Jesus "Chuchu" Castillo thought the ebullient champion was overrated and by no means unbeatable. He gave notice that he intended to knock the braggart from his throne in his second title defense in April 1970. The fuse had been lit for a local rivalry that was to pack the Forum to the doors three times in the space of twelve months.

At first, Olivares tried as usual to overwhelm his opponent with his brilliant hook. But Castillo, a clever strategist, dodged these murderous blows and landed some effective counter punches of his own on the titleholder. One of these temporarily downed Olivares in the third round. From then on "El Puas" concentrated more on his considerable reserves of boxing skill and used his spike with more restraint. He now shook Castillo thoroughly several times, but was unable to knock him out. In the end, he could not be denied a unanimous points victory—and the confirmation of his world champion's title. This enthralling exchange of blows had been at times so evenly balanced that the internal Mexican on Mexican duel was repeated six months later. "Rockabye Ruben" was reminded of this right from the outset. In the very first round, Castillo landed a punch that opened a gaping wound above the title-defender's left eye. It was to be a continuing handicap: although Olivares fought on trading blow for blow equally with his opponent, his sight was increasingly hindered by the unstoppable flow of blood. Referee Dick Young was finally unable to avoid stopping the fight in the fourteenth round because of injury. Olivares had been defeated for the first time in 62 professional bouts—but the dethroned world champion still did not consider himself fundamentally defeated.

Would Castillo finally be able to convince him of this in the rubber match? In April 1971, the new world champion once again briefly put his archrival on the canvas. Thereafter, however, Olivares gave him scarcely a chance. For this third duel, the feared power-puncher had transformed himself into a clever all-rounder, who blended skillful defense with occasional attacking moves. Although this was clearly less thrilling than the previous gripping fights, along with an impressive final burst in the later rounds it allowed him to regain his title. Commenting on the unanimous points decision in his favor, Olivares said that this time he had "used his head."

The hot-blooded rivalry between "El Puas" and "Chuchu" attracted 53,000 boxing fans to the Forum. It seems unlikely that two bantamweights will ever again be able to sell so many tickets, either in Inglewood or elsewhere for that matter.

They had plenty time to get to know one another: after Griffith won their rematch *(above)* in 1967, they met again in 1968 for the rubber match *(opposite page)*.

NINO BENVENUTI
vs. EMILE GRIFFITH

What do you get when you match two top class boxers who are both as strong-willed as they are experienced against one another? In the best case you get unforgettable thrilling duels like the three middle-weight title fights in a mere eleven months that Nino Benvenuti and Emile Griffith delivered in Madison Square Garden, New York.

Emile Alphonse Griffith was a great all-rounder with an obvious weakness for the sweet things in life: when the Caribbean-born New York resident was at his peak, he did not always take his training program and his next opponent with due seriousness. Between 1961 and 1963, Griffith lost his welterweight crown to both Benny "Kid" Paret and Luis Rodriguez, only to return triumphant in the eventful rematches. Four years later it seemed as if this pattern was set to be repeated at middleweight—only this time there was to be no happy end for Emile.

Griffith should have taken a warning when he was challenged in April 1967 by Giovanni "Nino" Benvenuti. The fisherman's son from Trieste had won the welterweight gold medal at the Rome Olympics in 1960, and as a charismatic and unshakeable pro had become the idol of his fellow Italians. A former world champion in the little-regarded light middleweight division, Nino had also already taken the European champion's belt in the limit above when he met Griffith in their first world championship duel. Added to this was a stiff lead hand, which the 19,000 spectators in New York's Madison Square Garden rarely saw his adversary able to avoid. It was the fourth round before Griffith could floor the taller Italian, who also had a longer reach. But Benvenuti got to his feet and continued to dominate the fight.

At the end of the 15 exciting rounds that *The Ring* was later to designate "Fight of the Year," all three points judges voted unanimously in favor of the Italian.

Five months later when the new champion entered the ring in the Shea Stadium in New York for the rematch, he had a cracked rib. And as he so often did in return fights, Griffith put on a simply brilliant performance. The result was an impressive revenge. Griffith set about Benvenuti with telling jabs and punch combinations that inflicted damage on his opponent's chin, nose and eye area, and in the fourteenth round knocked him to the canvas. Nevertheless, Benvenuti made it through to the final gong. Two of the three judges gave Griffith the fight on this occasion (the third went for a draw). So there had to be a deciding rubber match. The date for this great duel was set for March 1968 at the opening of the new Madison Square Garden. It was to be a *finale furioso:* yet again Griffith and Benvenuti threw their best punches and the tide of battle turned several times over the course of 15 top-class rounds. Benvenuti set his seal on the first and third quarters of the fight by briefly putting his rival on the canvas, but Griffith was able to pile on the pressure in the second quarter and in the final stages. But by then it was too late: the national icon from Trieste was awarded the victory by an extremely narrow margin. Had the great Emile once again been too self-confident? According to his trainer Gil Clancy, he had brought his tuxedo with him to the dressing room, ready to change into for his victory celebration. This most recent loss of the world championship proved to be a defining moment for the rest of his 19-year professional career. After this fight, Griffith tried on four more occasions in all to regain the world title—each time in vain. Benvenuti, on the other hand, was to retain his title until his defeat by Carlos Monzon in 1970.

MUHAMMAD ALI
vs. JOE FRAZIER

The boxing match that took place on March 8, 1971, was not simply just one more heavyweight world championship bout. It was the greatest event that had taken place since two men had walked on the surface of the moon three years before. And once again, it seemed as if the eyes of the whole world were focused on one tiny spot—this time it was the ring in Madison Square Garden, New York, where two highly contrasting characters were to meet for the first time.

During the 1960s, Muhammad Ali and Joe Frazier had clearly established themselves as the two dominant alpha males in the pack of world-class heavyweights. But a direct confrontation between the two had foundered on the suspension that was meted out to the reigning champion Ali for his refusal of the draft. During this compulsory three and a half year lay-off, Frazier had moved up to become undisputed world champion. The showdown in New York was to bring the reactivated and the reigning champions together: the narcissistic, elegant "Greatest of 'em all" and the tireless but taciturn fighter "Smokin' Joe." And one of two spotless records (31 and 26 straight wins respectively) would be ruined. Ali had his moments when his superior reach allowed him to land accurate jabs and rapid punch combinations on his opponent. But for almost all of the total of fifteen rounds Frazier stayed inside and landed increasing numbers of his feared hooks from the half-distance. With each and every punch he landed, the angry titleholder seemed to be taking his revenge for the insults of his challenger, who had caricatured him before the fight as the white man's dumb favorite. "Smoke" shook Ali in the eleventh round and knocked him down so hard that the end of the thrilling contest seemed in sight. But the "Louisville Lip" got back on his feet. It was in the end to be in vain. Finally, all three points judges had Frazier ahead, although both fighters were badly bruised.

Bitter feelings were still very much to the fore in January 1974, when Ali and Frazier, who had in the meantime been deposed by George Foreman, met for a rematch at the same venue. Five days before the fight itself, during a chaotic live broadcast by the ABC network, the two all but came to blows. But the smoke was followed by very little fire: At this meeting, Ali managed to avoid infighting with all the legal, and some illegal, tactics at his disposal, and to score points at every available opportunity. Frazier lacked the dynamism (and the imagination) to rewrite the script for this qualifying fight for a chance to challenge for a world championship bout with Foreman. This time the unanimous points decision went to Ali.

The rubber match in September 1975, in Quezon City, a suburb of Manila, capital city of the Philippines, was every bit as extraordinary as the rematch had been ordinary. Here, both adversaries drained the last resources from their bodies to produce one of the most exciting battles in the history of boxing. This time, after his defeat of George Foreman, Ali was the reigning champion and Frazier the challenger, who initially could only take his punishment. But from the fifth round, once "Smoke" had warmed up, he began to take the initiative. But then Ali came back into the fight and proceeded to beat Frazier into an unrecognizable, swollen mass of bruises, until the challenger's trainer Eddie Futch pulled him out of the fight before the start of the final round.

Did Futch only forestall Ali in his task, as some were soon to speculate? The end of the last and most renowned part of this trilogy almost seemed closer to a coma for two players than the triumph of an undisputed victor. For both participants the "Thrilla in Manila" had been, as Ali later formulated it, a borderline experience that was "next to death."

Opposite page: In the final round of their first contest in 1971, Joe Frazier knocked Muhammad Ali down for the first time in his career. After Ali succeeded in taking his revenge in 1974, in 1975 promoter Don King brought the adversaries together for a third time *(above)*. The unforgettable "Thrilla in Manila" was to be a near-death experience for both men.

With his extraordinarily long reach, Thomas Hearns *(left)* was able to control the start of his first duel against Sugar Ray Leonard in September 1981.

SUGAR RAY LEONARD vs. THOMAS "HIT MAN" HEARNS

As a young boxer, Sugar Ray Leonard had expressed doubts that any fight would ever be worth paying $1,000 for a ringside seat. But even he was to concede later that he would have paid that much for a close-up view of a fight that took place in September 1981. In the event, this would have been a practical impossibility: during the bout billed as "The Showdown," the former Olympic victor and reigning WBC champion was himself in the ring at Caesar's Palace in Las Vegas—and opposite him was the as yet unbeaten WBA titleholder Thomas "Hit Man" Hearns.

This meeting of these two megastars, who could scarcely have been more different in their approach, had been heralded with much ballyhoo. Leonard, the smart golden boy, was regarded as a clever all-rounder, who would rather outclass his rivals technically than go straight for a knockout at any price—even though he showed he had the heart of a fighter when matched against Roberto Duran and Wilfred Benitez. Hearns, on the other hand, the "Motor City Cobra" from the Kronk Gym in Detroit, had lethal venom in his right fist. Whenever this rangy man with the tentacular arms of a sea-monster hit his target, his opponents dropped as if paralyzed. It was no wonder then that even up against the master boxer Leonard, Hearns still seemed a credible favorite to the bookmakers.

On the most exciting night for boxing of the 1980s, the WBA champion was at first content to pursue the agile Leonard with his long-reaching lead hand. And sometimes he was on target, sometimes not. In any case, he certainly did enough to assert his dominance over the first third of the fight. In the sixth and seventh rounds Leonard found a way to move closer inside under the jabs of his opponent and to shake him through with lightning-swift punch combinations. From then on the roles were suddenly reversed: the feared banger Hearns became a stylishly accomplished dancer, scoring well from the outside but himself remaining elusive, while the stylist Leonard went after him aggressively but often in vain. Until the thirteenth, at least: then "Sugar" found his target and with powerful and effective blows pounded the "Cobra" through the ropes. Hearns, who had clearly been ahead on points, survived a count and what was left of the round, only to be taken out of the fight in the next round, by then completely drained of strength, by referee Davey Pearl.

His first defeat in this prestigious duel was still on the mind of this outstanding boxer as he, like Leonard, then moved up through the weight limits, winning four further world titles on the way. Eight years were to pass before he got the chance to take his revenge. In the intervening period Leonard, by then 33 years old and with two long lay-offs behind him, had gone on to become IBF champion at super middleweight and light heavyweight, while Hearns was almost 31 years old and super middleweight titleholder of the recently formed WBO. But who paid any heed to these titles when the main issue in June, 1989, was a decider between two legends of the ring? In the course of "The War," as the fight had been officially designated, these experienced pros once again delivered a formidable battle, fought at a very high technical level. Only now it was Hearns who was clearly dominant for much of the time. The "Cobra" downed his opponent in both the third and the eleventh rounds and rocked him on several other occasions. But "Sugar" stole the show with a furious final phase. The final analysis of the judges' points cards after the full 12 rounds resulted in a draw. While it was by no means a fully satisfactory outcome for Thomas "Hit Man" Hearns, for the spectators it was another great experience—although not at quite the same pace as the first. And there were certainly no complaints from the ringside about the ticket price.

AARON PRYOR
vs. ALEXIS ARGUELLO

Alexis Arguello had a dream. Between 1974 and 1981, the star from Nicaragua, who was as smart as he was outstanding as a boxer, succeeded in winning the title in three separate weight limits—on each occasion beating the best champions there were from featherweight to lightweight. All he lacked now was something that would truly put him in a class of his own: a world championship belt in a fourth weight limit. So once more "Flaco de Explosivo" as he was called challenged the best fighter in the next division up.

But Aaron Pryor too had a dream—or at least an aim in life. The underdog who was raised in the poorer districts of Cincinnati intended to defend his WBA junior welterweight championship for at least as long as it took to make him financially secure. For him there was indeed a great deal at stake when he agreed to meet Arguello in September 1982 in Florida for summit of world champions. "Alexis will always be a champion," commented Pryor, "but for me this is all about either four dollars ninety an hour or being world champion."

23,800 live spectators thronged into Miami's Orange Bowl to encircle the "Ring of Fire," as the fight had been officially dubbed. And not one of them was to be disappointed. From the outset, both these artists of offense maintained a blistering pace, although Pryor was initially in control—in the first round alone the "Cincinnati Hawk" registered 130 punches. Then, after five rounds, Arguello seized the initiative and landed a succession of hard, accurate rights on his target. But it was obvious that nothing was going to faze Pryor. He was even able to shrug off with relative ease a fierce hail of blows in the thirteenth and go on to finish off his drained opponent. A mighty hook sent Arguello reeling into the ropes, where he was able to offer no defense against a further barrage of more then 20 punches. The 2–1 favorite in the betting then lay senseless on the canvas for four minutes, and collapsed again later in the dressing-room. Arguello came to grief in what experts were later to call "the best boxing match of the 80s" against a great, although possibly illegally stimulated adversary. Rumors of a very special water bottle used to refresh Pryor in the rest periods between rounds continued to circulate for some considerable time afterwards. But the 30-year-old champion had to acknowledge a second handicap in his contest with Pryor, who was three years younger as well as physically superior: the hard-hitting power of his punches that had brought him so many early victories in the lower weight divisions seemed to be drained of their effect in this higher limit. "I hit Pryor with everything," said Arguello, "and it seemed like my punches couldn't even break an egg."

The steely chin of his adversary was again to prove an insoluble problem for Arguello ten months later in the rematch. In this second contest in Caesar's Palace, Las Vegas, Arguello again managed to land several hard hits on his forcefully attacking opponent. But Pryor once more brought his stronger physique into play. Pryor was, so to speak, at home in the junior welterweight limit, while Arguello was not. In the tenth, the "Hawk" swooped down on his prey and knocked out the three-times champion.

Arguello's dream of a fourth title was to remain just a dream, while Pryor's attainment of a better life proved to be merely a brief *intermezzo*. After his ring career came to an end this outstanding pro drifted temporarily into the drugs scene in his hometown, where he struggled to survive as a social welfare case. These days, however, he works training youngsters in Cincinnati.

Here, at their first meeting in Miami in 1982, Aaron Pryor keeps the tireless Alexis Arguello *(right)* busy with a body blow.

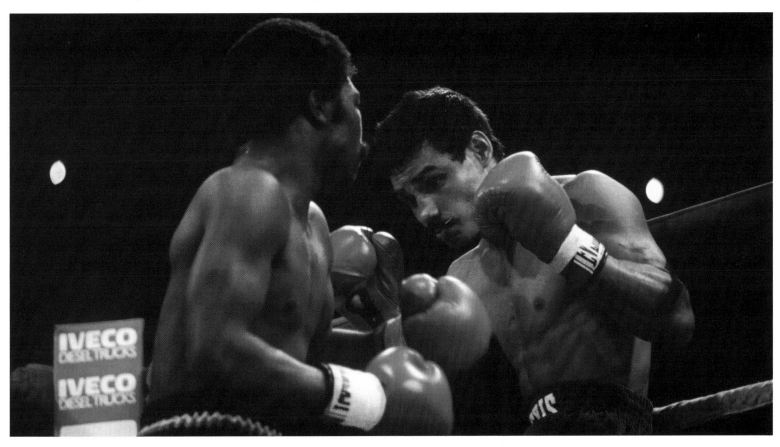

CHRIS EUBANK
vs. NIGEL BENN

It may seem barbaric that boxing contests gain added pulling power from openly acknowledged animosity between the adversaries—but it is nevertheless true. When a sporting rivalry apparently or actually spills over into real life, and it becomes "personal," the expectations of the average fans are significantly raised. And this is further enhanced when both the men in the ring, like Chris Eubank and Nigel Benn, have the same nationality.

Along with Michael Watson, these two English pros had established themselves as members of the world middleweight elite. But in their overall approach, they could hardly have been more different. While Benn as the "Dark Destroyer" rose to become a furious KO king, Eubank presented himself as a dandified peacock who made no secret of his inner aloofness from the fight business. The "Brighton Braggart" dismissed his sport as a mug's game and Benn as an opponent with no class. So, it was no surprise that the aura of mutual contempt surrounding their long-awaited duel for Benn's World Boxing Association title in November 1990 was, according to the champion, "one hundred percent genuine."

The Birmingham National Exhibition Centre was packed full when, from the outset, Benn went on to the attack in his uncompromisingly aggressive style. The blows he landed visibly shook Eubank. "I didn't know that people could have such strength," admitted the challenger afterwards. But the "Brighton Peacock" paid him back in the same coin. There then developed a highly dramatic exchange of blows, in the course of which Benn's appearance began to deteriorate critically. From the middle rounds on, Benn fought with a badly swollen eye, and soon

began to run out of gas. After taking several hard, effective punches and what was to be a final hail of blows, he was taken out of the fight by referee Richard Steele just before the end of the ninth round. This experienced referee had presided over two champions in an absolutely top-class world championship bout.

In the summer of 1991, Eubank relinquished this title and moved up to super middleweight where he also ruled as WBO world champion until 1995. After concluding a lucrative TV deal he became increasingly cautious in his choice of opponent. So, it was to be three years before he finally agreed to the long-awaited rematch with Nigel Benn, who had by now become the WBC titleholder in the same division. The title defense took place in October 1993 in the famous Old Trafford football stadium in Manchester and earned record purses for both fighters.

Surrounded by the deafening roar of more than 40,000 spectators, Eubank had the better start. After two rounds, however, Benn began to assert himself. In the fourth, the "Dark Destroyer" caught the WBO champion with a combination that sent him staggering into the ropes. But his considerable resilience saved Eubank yet again. Two rounds later, referee Larry O'Connell handed out a warning to Benn for low punching, a warning that led to a points penalty that was to have serious consequences. The adversaries continued an exchange of blows that was as exciting as it was evenly balanced, until the final round, which was dominated by Eubank. Despite this, the final result was a draw that seemed to flatter Eubank more than Benn. Either way, as *The Observer* declared on the following day: "The conclusion should encourage both of them to dilute their notorious mutual hostility with a large injection of respect." But there was later to be as little chance of a genuine reconciliation between the two as there was of a deciding rubber match.

Opposite page: In Birmingham Benn *(left)* did not hit Eubank *(far left)* often enough to win. In Manchester *(above)* his commitment was rewarded by a draw.

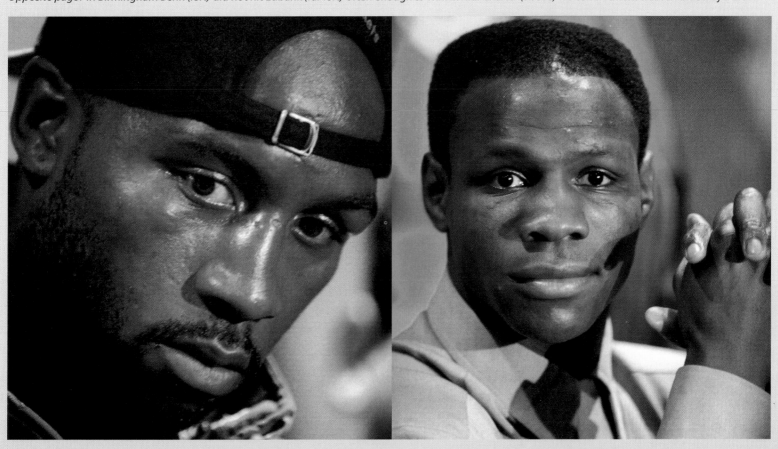

In their first fight, in Las Vegas in 1991, Jeff Fenech *(right)* was able to make an impression on Azumah Nelson, but not on the judges.

AZUMAH NELSON
vs. JEFF FENECH

By the end of the 1980s they were both already heroes of the ring in their home countries—and it almost goes without saying that they were also universally respected world champions. Azumah Nelson, the doubly gifted boxer-puncher from Accra in Ghana, had been impressively dominant as WBC world champion at both featherweight and super featherweight. And by 1989 Jeff Fenech, a former juvenile delinquent from Sydney, Australia, had already stormed with undiminished aggression through three weight limits and had become champion in each of them. While there was a certain logical inevitability about the dramatic intensity of their two summit meetings, their outcome was surprising in two respects.

When he met Fenech in the arena of the Mirage Hotel, Las Vegas in June 1991, Nelson was the clear favorite. "Ghana's 'King of the Ring,'" as *The Ring* called him, could fight just as well as he could feint and had remained unbeaten in the six years and twelve title fights since his first world championship triumph. On the other hand, although the likewise unbeaten Australian was respected as a genuine fighter who imposed confrontation on his opponents in masterly fashion, during his drive forward "The Thunder from Down-Under" always remained vulnerable to counter punches. And after a long lay-off between fights, was his physique really up to the move to a higher fourth weight limit?

Whatever reservations the experts may have had about him, Fenech swept them away that night. For 12 rounds the tireless challenger stayed close enough in on Nelson to entangle the titleholder in what seemed a never-ending series of exchanges. Fenech was clearly the more active of the two in this high-class contest, but there were no knockdowns. This thrilling battle between the two super featherweights stole much of the show from the fight at the top of the card that night, the rematch between Mike Tyson and Donovan "Razor" Ruddock, men who were almost double the weight of their smaller colleagues. At the end of their fight, the resulting controversial draw did more to save the reigning champion than to confirm his right to the title. While still in the ring, the normally hard-boiled Fenech broke down in tears of disappointment.

While it was quite conceivable that promoter Don King had left the mark of his greedy hands on this contest, this could be totally ruled out in the rematch the following year, in March, 1992. This time on his home ground, the Australian was the host to his rival; he was the bookmakers' favorite and had given advance notice that he would send the Ghanaian back for his return trip in a body bag. All this packed out the Princess Park in Melbourne with 37,000 avid spectators, but Azumah Nelson refused to be impressed. That night the by now 33-year-old "Professor" of the boxing ring delivered an impressive and painful lecture on the counter punch. Time after time, he broke through Fenech's onslaughts with effective, lightning-swift punches that had the Australian on the deck in both the first and second rounds. When Fenech was knocked down once more in the eighth round, referee Arthur Mercante took him out of the fight.

This demolition in his own back yard must have hit the 28-year-old Fenech pretty hard. After a further defeat within the distance by Calvin Grove, he retired from boxing for a time. In contrast, with this fight the old-timer Nelson established a reputation as the king of the rematch and continued his impressive career. In 1995, in his seventeenth year as a professional boxer, he once more regained the title that he had lost in the intervening period, and in the following year won a rematch against the former champion Jesse James Leija. He was not finally dethroned until 1997, when he lost to Genaro Hernandez.

HUMBERTO GONZALEZ
vs. MICHAEL CARBAJAL

It is no easy task for a prizefighter in a division with a top weight-limit of barely 49 kilograms to win a reputation as a warrior in miniature—or any other significant degree of recognition, for that matter. But in March 1993, when Humberto "Chiquita" Gonzales and Michael Carbajal touched gloves for the first time, the entire world of boxing watched the title unification bout between these two light flyweights. Both the Mexican WBC champion Gonzalez and Carbajal, the undefeated IBF titleholder from Phoenix, Arizona, were notorious for the unusual power in their small fists. The fact that their aggressive style occasionally left little room for defensive tactics only added to the attraction of their duel.

And no one in the Hilton Center in Las Vegas that night was to be disappointed. From the sound of the very first bell, the two competing titleholders slugged it out with speed and determination. Initially it was Gonzales who landed the more effective punches. In the second round he knocked his taller opponent to the canvas, and in the fifth appeared to have completely demolished him with a heavy barrage of punches. But Carbajal came back. With his eyes still glazed over, he survived several more attacks until the end of the round, and went on after the pause to demonstrate exactly why he was known as "Little Hands of Stone." A shower of powerful head and body blows now began to take their toll on Gonzales, and finally, in the seventh, Carbajal administered the *coup de grace:* a brutal left hook put the battered Mexican out of the fight well before the distance.

This action-packed showdown was the first light flyweight duel to be awarded the title of "Fight of the Year" by *The Ring,* and it later appeared in that magazine's list of "The 100 Greatest Fights of All Time"

in seventeenth position. And it was of course the forerunner of two more fights. In February, 1994, in the sold-out Forum in Inglewood, California, it seemed as if events would follow a similarly explosive course, when Gonzalez, already bearing the marks of a couple of injuries, finally heeded the warnings of his coach Nacho Beristain and from then on chose a considerably more cautious approach. The new strategy was successful: as a boxer, "Chiquita" was superior to his opponent and, almost unnoticed, managed to take several rounds. For his part, Carbajal seemed to have left his most powerful weapons at home. At the end of the fight, two of the three points judges had Gonzalez ahead on their scorecards.

But those who believed that Carbajal, who received his first ever defeat in this fight, would approach the rubber match in his usual explosive manner were to be disillusioned nine months later. In a bullfight arena in Mexico City, the two rivals met as experienced but only moderately aggressive combatants. What had been hyped as the definitive duel in the feud between the two pint-sized heroes of the Hispanic ring ran its uneventful course more like a ballet, completely devoid of knockdowns. "'Chiquita' persuaded Carbajal to box like a gentleman," reported *World Boxing* magazine. "This turned 'the little hands of stone' into 'few punches of significance.'" Under the circumstances, the result was predictable: as in February, Gonzalez was once again the beneficiary of a points decision.

In a broader sense, however, both fighters reaped the benefits. After their highly regarded series of duels, "Chiquita" and "Little Hands of Stone" suddenly became familiar names even to those fight fans who had never previously even been aware of the existence of a light flyweight title in professional boxing.

In their first duel Carbajal was first knocked down, before he finally won. WBC president Suleiman was one of the first to congratulate him *(bottom right).*

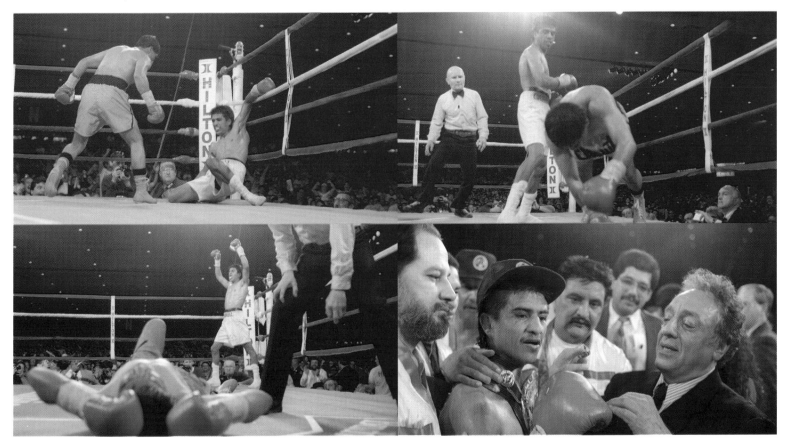

RIDDICK BOWE
vs. EVANDER HOLYFIELD

In the last decade of the twentieth century, this series of three fights almost seemed born of necessity. It was certainly a necessity for heavyweight boxing, which had provisionally lost its figurehead when Mike Tyson went in to jail on March, 1992, just as it was for the two antagonists involved, whose championship caliber had for a variety of reasons long been in doubt. So just who was Evander Holyfield before he came up against Riddick Bowe for the first time in November 1992? A cruiserweight from Georgia, pumped up by weights and diets; a champion who after his victory over the Tyson-conqueror James "Buster" Douglas had brought little credit to the titles of the three most significant sanctioning bodies—of this much at least the majority of experts were convinced. And what of the challenger Bowe, whose fans liked to call him "Big Daddy"? At 1.96 meters tall, and weighing in at a good 110 kilograms, he was undoubtedly a colossus of a man. But as yet, this sometimes-gluttonous upstart from a large family in Brownsville, Brooklyn's most disreputable neighborhood, had failed to show that he had the heart of a fighter.

So, in Las Vegas on that fateful Friday in November 1992, neither fighter was regarded as a clear favorite in the betting. Nevertheless, what then unfolded before the eyes of 17,000 spellbound spectators in the Thomas and Mack Center became "The Fight of the Year." Maintaining a constant fast pace the physically superior Bowe pounded the champion with painfully accurate jabs and brutal hooks, but even at his opponent's most brilliant moments, Holyfield knew where to find the right counter punch combinations. This culminated in a furious tenth round as "Big Daddy" first used punishing blows to drive his adversary back, only to become the object of a final attack from Holyfield. Bowe then ensured that the judges' decision went in his favor with a knockdown in the eleventh and by demonstrating his dominance in the twelfth and final round. But Holyfield also earned much respect for his limitless strength of will. As the British sports journalist Hugh McIlvanney declared: "He is the kind of man who makes you feel it is a privilege to share the same planet."

Holyfield's will to win was still as strong when the two met again a year later, in November 1993, in the open-air arena of Caesar's Palace, Las Vegas. This time the god-fearing Holyfield took a more prudent approach—and Bowe had gained almost five kilograms. So, after "The Real Deal" had repulsed Bowe's initial attack, he began to take control of the fight. Then, in the seventh round, an uninvited guest in the form of a parachutist landed in the ring, forcing a 20-minute break in the fight, and causing the pregnant Mrs. Bowe to faint. After the fight resumed, there was no decisive change in the course of events. Two of the three points judges had Holyfield ahead at the final bell, a decision that meant that he became only the fourth heavyweight in history to regain his championship title (the WBA and IBF versions).

Two years later, neither Holyfield nor Bowe wore the insignia of a world champion when they went into the ring at the same venue for their rubber match. But none of the 13,000 spectators seemed disturbed by that. They all got their money's worth from a fight that saw Holyfield, by now 33 years old, knock down his opponent and junior by five years in the sixth round of this top-class duel—and, despite this setback, the well-conditioned Bowe come back to win within the distance two rounds later. "I fought with everything I had," Holyfield said after the fight, "but everything wasn't enough." And his adversary told him, "I love you, man!" It was a fitting finale to a series of duels that saw two good boxers mature into true champions.

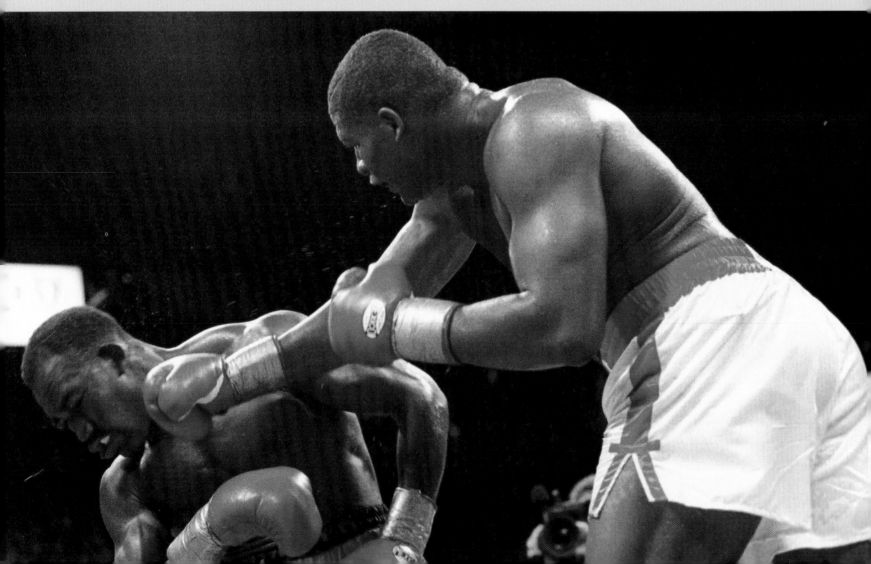

Opposite page: In 1992, Riddick Bowe *(left)* was able to dominate the first episode of their rivalry due to his superior physique. In the second, in 1993, Holyfield won by a very narrow margin *(above)*. In the decider in 1995, he then had to bow to the unfettered power of his adversary before the full distance *(right)*.

ROUND TRIP:

AFRICA—GHANA

by Christian Abbew

Christian Abbew was born in 1954 and for 30 years has been writing from Ghana about boxing in Africa. He writes regularly for the *Ghanaian Times* and the *Evening News* as well as for several weekend magazines.

Seldom has a sport been adopted with more enthusiasm by a local population than boxing has in Ghana. The reason for this is that long before the introduction of the sport of boxing as governed by the Marquess of Queensberry Rules, unregulated fist-fights took place in Ghana—both in the form of single combat and as group battles *(asafo atswere)* that took place among members of the Ga tribe in the capital city of Accra. Thus, when Edward Bannerman brought the sport of boxing back with him in 1924 after a long stay in England, he was welcomed with open arms.

The very first fight night took place in Nsawam, in the east of Ghana. The organizer was Mr. William, who was the area chief of police. One year later, Edward Bannerman staged the first boxing match in Accra, and in later years made the names of such boxers as Charleston Sykes and Surpriser Sowah. Sowah also played a major role in the subsequent development of the sport: he trained other boxers, who in their turn were to train

future world champions and master trainers. By 1941 professional boxing had also won a large following in the south of the country, and in large and small towns such as Kumasi, Sekondi, Tarkwa and Dunkwa, regular fight nights were staged. Within the next decade the boxers mentioned above and other Ghanaian fighters appeared in the ring in the United Kingdom. Among their number was Roy Ankrah, the first Ghanaian to win a title in England. Ankrah, the "Black Flash", won the Commonwealth championship title at featherweight. Fighters such as David "Poison" Kotey, who won the world featherweight championship in 1975, followed in his footsteps. Azumah Nelson held the WBC world titles at featherweight and junior lightweight that he won in 1984 and 1988 respectively for a total of thirteen years. In 1988, he was followed by Nana Yaw Konadu who defeated the Mexican Gilberto Roman. The next Ghanaian world champions were to be Ike Quartey, who won the WBA welterweight crown in 1994, and

Alfred Kotey, who became WBO flyweight world champion in 1995. Many Ghanaian boxers were originally under contract to stables like the state-supported Ghana Management and Promotion Syndicate, which brought on David Kotei Poison to become world champion. Later, champions such as Azumah Nelson, Ike Quartey, and Nana Yaw Konadu were represented by the Ringcraft Promotion and Boxing Syndicate. Today, the best known promoters are Ambition and Nii Armah Promotions, Lionheart, Prince and Baseline International Promotions, and Despite. Currently, Ghana's favorite boxing arena is the Kaneshie Sports Complex, the "Madison Square Garden of Ghana," with two rings that, according to specific event requirements, can seat 200 to 500 and 500 to 1,000 spectators respectively. Other venues include the Accra Sports Stadium, the Prempeh Assembly Hall, and Lebanon House.

Boxing spectators in Ghana make their own unique contribution to the sport by spurring on their favorites with drumming

and songs—and after a fight has been won, they like to storm the ring itself to continue their celebrations there. The musical backing often begins in the boxers' training camps and continues throughout the day.

As in any other sport in Ghana, pro boxers have to overcome many difficulties. Boxing schools are poorly equipped and there are often long gaps between fight nights, so much so that boxers are compelled to go abroad for financial reasons. In addition, the purses offered are so small that many boxers are forced to seek support from promoters to finance their fight training. The three major international boxing events to have taken place in Ghana, Robertson vs. Ramos (1964), Nelson vs. DalRovere (1987) and Konadu vs. Polanco (1988) all resulted in quite significant financial losses.

Among the best-known Ghanaian boxers currently active are S.K. Armah, Commonwealth champion at lightweight; James Agbeko, African champion at bantamweight,

and high on the WBC ratings list; Steve Dotse; Kofi Jantuah, Commonwealth welterweight champion and high on the WBC ratings list, and Napoleon Tagoe, a cruiserweight who is also on the WBC ratings list.

Other West African states have produced world champions in professional boxing. From Senegal, there was Battling Siki, who took the Africa, Commonwealth and world titles in light heavyweight in 1922. In 1966, the Nigerian Dick Tiger won the world championship at light heavyweight. Those West African states such as Togo, Côte d'Ivoire, Benin and Burkina Faso that have not yet produced a boxing world champion have good boxing arenas and a lively boxing scene, so the future of the sport in the south of the region seems secure. Another positive indication for the future is that a number of new boxing promoters and event organizers have come on to the scene, and there are already plans to stage a series of fight-nights at 14-day intervals.

As seen here in Mathare Valley, near the Kenyan capital Nairobi, African boxing talent develops under the most basic of conditions. All too often, the infrastructure for staging international fights is inadequate

TOP TEN OF AFRICA:
 1. Azumah Nelson (GHA)
 2. Dick Tiger (NGR)
 3. Hogan "Kid" Bassey (NGR)
 4. David "Poison" Kotey (GHA)
 5. Ike Quartey (GHA)
 6. Ayub Kalule (UGA)
 7. Battling Siki (SEN)
 8. John Mugabi (UGA)
 9. Sumbu Kalambay (ZAI)
10. Cornelius Boza-Edwards (UGA)

SENSATIONS

THE TRIUMPH OF THE UNDERDOG

Just as each sport has its own rules, so it also has its own very specific dramaturgical conventions. This is probably particularly true for single combat, in the course of which fortune can change sides, often several times and in a wide variety of ways, turning literally on a single, sudden blow. Boxing duels remain undecided right up to the very end, and are thus thrilling and often enough even more than that. The uncertainty about who will be declared the victor in the dramatic finale after the fight has gone its distance can occasionally make a contest seem like a mystery play.

The more unforeseeable its triumphs and humiliations, the more existential is the effect of this sport: in the astonishing victory of the outsider, in the final blow for freedom of the underdog, in the lucky punch and even in the wrong decision, the nature of life is revealed in all its unpredictability. The sensations in boxing therefore always act as additional stylistic devices, because the only moral of this small, violent drama is that, in the words of the popular saying, "it's not over until the fat lady sings."

At the beginning of 1990, when Mike Tyson, champion of all the significant sanctioning bodies, was matched against one James "Buster" Douglas, the bookmakers of Las Vegas made no profit. Since "Iron Mike" had established his reign of terror, heavyweight title fights had been more like predictable spectaculars than genuine duels. The previous six challenges together had lasted twenty rounds in total, and the seventh provided him with an opponent scorned by the *Los Angeles Times* as "the number one challenger in the *Mad* magazine rankings." So, it was little wonder that in all the many bookies' offices on the Strip, just one solitary bet on the result of this fight was taken.

However, on February 11, 1990, Buster Douglas appeared in front of 20,000 spectators in the Tokyo Dome as a fearless, totally prepared opponent. The 42–1 underdog from Columbus, Ohio, until then more likely to have been a spectator on the fringes of the world elite rather than a part of it, seized his chance at the world championship as a unique opportunity. After all, what were the blows of the hardest puncher when compared with

The outsider Hasim Rahman assumes a resolute pose in the All-Star Gym in Johannesburg, in front of the newspaper poster of the words that the title defender, Lennox Lewis, had boastfully used to belittle him a few days before their duel in April 2001—"I'll whip the bum."

But on fight night in Carnival City, near Johannesburg, there is a total sensation in round 5: the challenger Rahman triumphs as the new heavyweight champion of the world by a stoppage victory over the under-trained Lennox Lewis. The latter got his revenge in the rematch.

the illness and death that had recently afflicted his family?

From the outset Buster scored thanks to the superior reach of his lead hand and, inflicting painful uppercuts at will, put the brakes on the storming attacks of his opponent. Tyson, until then considered almost unbeatable, was thrown into a state of mild panic: his handlers, who seemed little more than a sycophantic entourage, had no advice to give.

Was a small miracle developing here? The ringside experts were already beginning to believe in this possibility when, in round eight, Tyson landed a punishing uppercut. The downed challenger cleverly used referee Octavio Meyran's tentatively begun count to lift himself off the canvas on the count of nine—then calmly proceeded with his mission. Heavy blows once again shook Tyson to the core until, after a series of four hooks, for the first time in his boxing career he was down

on the canvas. As he struggled to his feet, Meyran signaled the end of the turbulent contest. The greatest upset in the modern era of professional boxing was concluded in the tenth round, after precisely 1 hour and 23 minutes. It is triumphs such as this, of the unknown journeyman from Ohio, that enhance the attractions of boxing. When long-reigning champions and previously unbeaten KO kings suddenly lie helpless on the canvas, the fall of the favorite becomes a symbolic expression of the greatest intensity. Be it Joe Louis at his first encounter with Max Schmeling in New York in 1936 or George Foreman against Muhammad Ali in Kinshasa in 1975—a knocked-out boxer is always more visibly and utterly beaten than any other sportsman. And the more unexpected the event, the greater the renewal of belief in a kind of social justice inherent in this bloody sport. The victory of the

underdog does indeed openly demonstrate that anyone, no matter what their rank or skin color, still has a chance.

Outside his native Sweden, Ingemar Johansson was considered as no more than a clumsy pseudo-pro when, in 1956, he knocked out the reigning heavyweight champion Floyd Patterson. In 1962, while still a minor, Japan's hero of the ring, Fighting Harada, as a substitute challenger, took the flyweight title from the highly regarded Pone Kingpetch—only to lose his own bantamweight belt six years later to yet another "teen-aged sub," the Australian aboriginal Lionel Rose. So the victory of the complete outsider is the constantly renewed triumph of the individual who clings unwaveringly to his self-belief. But the wheel of a boxer's life turns mercilessly onward: sooner or later, the man who is unexpectedly victorious will, either more or less unexpectedly, himself in due course be beaten.

THE LUCKY PUNCH

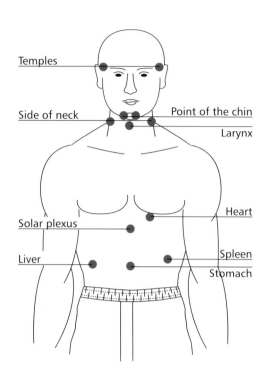

The illustration above shows the classic knockout points. A single blow to any of these points can be enough to render an opponent unfit to fight on.

In a combat sport, anyone clearly inferior in all significant aspects to their opponent will, sooner or later and in line with their staying power and personal pain threshold, inevitably succumb. And yet, relatively often, and against all expectations, a small, thrilling wonder takes place in boxing. It happens in a flash and in the fight game is known as the "lucky punch."

Just such a stroke of fortune happened unexpectedly in a dramatic world championship contest on June 6, 1988. It was on this fateful evening that Thomas Hearns, the already legendary "Hit Man," risked his first defense of the WBC middleweight crown that he won the previous year. His challenger in the ring of the Las Vegas Hilton Center was Iran Barkley, known to be a hard-hitting, but predictable, banger. Hearns immediately showed himself to be a master boxer, able to connect at will with the contender from New York's South Bronx. Hook, jab, cross, uppercut, every punch possible in the sport landed mercilessly and accurately on the face

of the outsider. In fact, it was so battered after the first two rounds that an imminent stoppage of this totally one-sided duel seemed inevitable.

"You're bleeding," his handlers told Barkley during the pause, as they examined his split lip and the cuts above both eyes. The man who liked to be called "The Blade" responded, "I got no time to bleed!"

As the third round began, Barkley, once again tormented by blows, suddenly countered with a swinging right. This unorthodox punch, born of desperation, caught Hearns so hard that his knees buckled. Then a second wild right powered in, propelling the dismayed favorite through the ropes. The "Hit Man" got back on his feet just in time to continue the fight, but was unable to defend himself as an unavoidable hail of blows from the challenger rained down, and the referee signaled an early end to the contest. The Detroit superstar had, in the short space of a single careless second, and against all expectation, lost his champion's belt in the fourth weight division.

Iran "The Blade" Barkley had simply "refused to go down" as American sports journalist Jimmy Cannon once described the instinct for survival in the ring. This was how Cannon described the tireless fighting spirit of Tony Zale, an earlier middleweight legend, who in 1946, 42 years before Barkley, brought off a similar coup. Clearly outclassed and visibly battered, in the sixth round of his first duel with Rocky Graziano, Zale, the reigning champion, suddenly landed a blow square to the solar plexus of the challenger. He had already put his opponent out of the fight before he followed up with a hook to the chin that lifted Graziano clear off his feet. Thus, Zale held on to the crown in the same way that Barkley won his: as a tireless worker whose ring ethics transformed him into a fighter scornful of pain. "You're sent in there to fight," wrote Cannon of Zale, "and that's what you do, for as long as you can, whatever happens." Because there is always that one chance for a single winning punch—even when it seems scarcely less likely than a miracle.

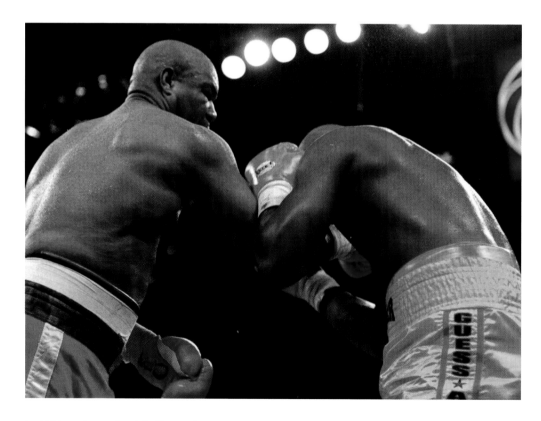

In 1994, a picture-book bull's-eye hit on title defender Michael Moorer transformed the apparently defeated George Foreman into the victor by a knockout, and world champion at the age of 46.

KO IN THE LAST SECOND

Runners can be overtaken in the last 10 meters of a 10,000-meter race. Basketball players can still lose a game by a score in the final second. But for boxers a late defeat does not just inflict emotional pain: right up to the very end, as a result of a direct hit, they can not only lose a fight they have been convincingly winning but also completely lose conscious control. In 1990, this was the fate of junior welterweight champion Meldrick Taylor when he risked his IBF title in a bid to add to it the WBC crown of his opponent Julio Cesar Chavez.

For eleven long rounds Taylor stood toe-to-toe with the legendary Mexican in the ring of the Hilton Center, Las Vegas—and landed most of the really telling blows in this brilliant duel. The former Olympic champion from Philadelphia was far enough ahead on all three of the points-judges' scorecards that he could have relied on dancing and evasive tactics for the duration of the final round. Instead he chose to continue the confrontation without let-up—until in the very last minute he first lost control of his legs, then finally of everything.

Sixteen seconds before the final gong, Taylor was floored by a hard right from Chavez. With eyes glazed over, he got to his feet on a sixcount from referee Richard Steele. However, instead of allowing the exchange of blows to continue, two seconds before the full distance the experienced referee took the beaten fighter out of the contest. Was his intention to protect Taylor from further damaging blows? Or was it to protect the aura of Chavez, undefeated in a run of 68 professional fights and managed by the influential promoter Don King? Speculation about the contest, dubbed the first megafight of the 1990s, spread like wildfire: some remaining doubts could only be silenced some three and a half years later, in 1994 to be exact, when Chavez decisively won the rematch, again in Las Vegas, with a knockout in round eight.

Chavez' feat of will in stubbornly holding on to the end in search of the winning chance won him even greater respect, despite all the turbulence surrounding the decision itself. He joined distinguished historic company: ring legends such as Jake LaMotta and Archie Moore had also succeeded in turning round almost lost battles into victorious stoppages in the final minutes. In September, 1950 LaMotta had clung on with what strength he had left to his middleweight championship when he knocked out the clear points leader, Laurent Dauthuille, 13 seconds before the final gong. In August 1954, Moore succeeded in achieving a very similar feat; in the fourteenth round, he struck out repeatedly at his archrival Harold Johnson, until that point in the lead, until the referee finally delivered Johnson from his torment.

Last minute triumphs such as these are prime examples of the tireless fighting spirit that fans and observers take delight in discovering in their heroes of the ring—and they illustrate the fact that perseverance and the will to keep on to the end of a long and difficult road sometimes pay off. As the New York boxing reporter Ed Sullivan wrote with unrestrained intensity in 1950, after LaMotta's knockout victory over Dauthuille, "of such deeds are champions made."

Visibly the worse for wear after his unlucky knockout defeat by Julio Cesar Chavez in March 1990, Meldrick Taylor watches a video recording of the fight. Due to lack of caution in the eleventh round, he lost his world title one minute before the gong.

THE WRONG DECISION

It was just as it so often is in this attractive but occasionally dubious sport. When, for once, all the world is looking on, something goes wrong. March 13, 1999 should have gone down as a red-letter day in the history of modern professional boxing. In the persons of Evander Holyfield and Lennox Lewis, the two champions of the three great world-sanctioning bodies were to compete in Madison Square Garden for the undisputed title of heavyweight champion of the world. For seven long years there had not been a duel like this. But a contest which should have at last restored a long-lost clarity and order to the pugilistic class of kings ended before the watching eyes of a worldwide television public in a new kind of fiasco.

Over 21,000 spectators present in the historic arena looked on as the British WBC world champion, using only his leading hand and a few sporadic rights, kept his clearly physically inferior opponent at a respectful distance. It was rarely spectacular but always effective. WBA and UBF titleholder Holyfield, for his part, still had to deliver not only the knockout punch in the third round that the gods had apparently promised him in a dream, but also any evidence of the necessary fitness and ultimate will to win. However, the points judges did not permit him to lose. Their overall decision was declared to be draw, an announcement met with loud protests from the fans, and not only those from Britain.

"A draw!?!?!" demanded the U.S. *Boxing Digest* sarcastically in its post-fight issue—and pointed to computer statistics that were so clear, "more so than ever seen before between the two top fighters in the same limit" (348 hits were registered for Lewis, and 130 for Holyfield.) *The Ring* called the result "The crown of betrayals" and many official bodies, including the New York State District Attorney's Office and the Senate Investigating Committee announced inquiries. Only the omnipresent promoter and tycoon Don King appeared to be in good spirits at the prospect of a rematch—and a second big payday. All evening he kept repeating his mantra of greed: "Let's do it again, let's do it again!" A return bout did in fact take place in Las Vegas in November 1999; and this time the points victory was awarded to Lewis.

It is evenings such as this that have all too often sullied the reputation of prize fighting and have become almost a tradition in themselves. One-sided favoritism and manipulation have stuck so closely to the modern history of this performance-sport that it seems they are indispensable ingredients. In 1933 Max Schmeling was deprived of victory when Jack Sharkey was declared the winner in their second world championship bout. "Jersey" Joe Walcott was cheated in 1947 when a questionable points decision awarded the champion's belt to his aging opponent Joe Louis. Decades later, Schmeling's "grandson" Axel Schulz was similarly outmaneuvered. In an IBF title contest in 1994, the "oldie" George Foreman, whom he had battered, was given the victory instead of him.

Often enough a flattering draw is used as a way to protect an established titleholder. Ceferino García was shielded in this way against the young contender Henry Armstrong (1930), Vito Antuofermo against Marvin Hagler (1979), Julio Cesar Chavez against Pernell Whitaker (1993)—and, of course, Holyfield against Lewis. The unacknowledged "shadow" statistics of other wrong decisions that are in themselves barely contentious are, however, considerable. In the undercard fights, considered of little interest by the wider public, often incomprehensible decisions that favor home fighters have become so commonplace that spectators react as citizens do to political corruption scandals. They are so used to them that they no longer even remember to protest.

Lennox Lewis *(opposite page, left)* believes himself the winner, Evander Holyfield does not. At the end of the attempt to unify the heavyweight titles (March 1999) to general consternation the judges in Madison Square Garden declared the match a draw. Lewis was to win the rematch.

THE STOPPAGE

And then there are the fights that end before going the full distance, without either of the contestants being knocked out. These are the most troublesome events in the pro-boxing calendar because, from an emotional perspective, a sporting result based on a stoppage cannot provide a satisfactory alternative. A contest not fought to its natural conclusion leaves active participants and spectators alike with unsettling perceptions of unfulfilled promise.

In earlier, semi-legal times, boxing bouts were often forcibly cut short. When the police raided isolated open-air venues, spectators and officials fled at lightning speed into the undergrowth. With the beginning of the modern era of boxing, an early stoppage was, as a general rule, the result of a disqualification, as befell Jack Sharkey for a low punch on Max Schmeling during their world championship bout in 1930. Debates in the aftermath of such decisions damaged the reputation of the sport and strenuous attempts were made to avoid this. In the 1990s, however, several such incidents led top author Budd Schulberg to fear that "bizarre climaxes to the bigger fights 'had become' the rule rather than the exception."

Mexico City, November, 1994: In the fifth round of his title defense against Luis Santana, the renowned junior middleweight champion Terry Norris hits his opponent after the referee has ordered a break—and loses his WBC title through disqualification. The rematch in April 1995 ends in a similar way; on this occasion, Norris fouls in the third round. Atlantic City, July/December, 1996: Norris' "record" is beaten by Andrew Golota. The heavyweight, originally from Poland, is disqualified twice in five months in two separate attention-grabbing showdowns with former champion Riddick Bowe, both times for repeated low punches.

Las Vegas, February 1997: In a return fight for the WBC heavyweight title, the psychologically distressed Oliver McCall refuses to fight his opponent Lennox Lewis. After he

The heavyweight summit in Las Vegas on June 28, 1997 was meant to be the fight of the year. And judged by the public reaction it aroused, it certainly was. At any rate, the seats in the MGM Grand Garden (above) were sold out soon after the details of this rematch between WBA world champion Evander Holyfield and his challenger Mike Tyson were announced. There had, after all, been a sensation seven months earlier. The outsider in the betting, Evander Holyfield had stood firm against "Iron Mike" and had finally been declared the victor after the fight was stopped in round eleven.

suffers a nervous collapse in the fifth round, he is taken out of the fight by the referee. Atlantic City, March, 1997: the previously unbeaten light heavyweight champion Roy Jones Jr. temporarily loses both respect and his WBC title when he mercilessly continues to pound the exhausted Montell Griffin, who is huddled on the canvas.

Las Vegas, June, 1997: Frustrated by the way the fight is going, in the third round of their rematch the challenger Mike Tyson savagely bites off part of the right ear of WBA world champion Evander Holyfield. This attack, which provokes disgust world-wide, leads to disqualification and a one-year ban for "Iron Mike."

Lake Tahoe, July, 1997: Lennox Lewis' opponent Henry Akinwande offers him no fight whatsoever: after the beanpole-tall challenger spends four rounds clinging to his compatriot, referee Mills Lane finally takes him out of the fight for persistent passivity.

Passivity and fouls are the most likely reasons for a bout to be stopped by the officials. However, an unintentional injury can also be the reason for a stoppage. In such cases, in accordance with the different rules of the major sanctioning bodies, the resulting decision is called either a "technical draw" or a "no contest." However, after completion of a specific minimum number

of rounds (four in the case of the WBC) the points scores registered thus far are used to come to a "technical decision."

A decision of this kind was the outcome of a bout in Fargo, North Dakota in February 1993, when challenger Adolpho Washington was taken out due to a cut in the penultimate round of his title fight with Virgil Hill. The badly bleeding wound had not been inflicted by the WBA champion, but by an over-assertive TV cameraman. Always, when one finally believes that all possible reasons for a stoppage are already known, it can be guaranteed that the very next day something absolutely and completely unimaginable will happen.

The new champion *(above)* appears at the weigh-in for the rematch, here next to promoter Don King *(center)*, unfazed by his opponent's attempt to rattle him. *Next double page:* Once in the ring, the defending champion quickly took control of the situation. Soon frustrated, Tyson knocked his opponent down from behind and in round three bit him, first on the shoulder then on the ear. This incredible chain of events caused Holyfield to lose part of his ear—and Tyson to lose this tumultuous fight through immediate disqualification.

ROUND TRIP:

JAPAN

by Joe Koizumi

Joe Koizumi was born in 1947. At the age of seventeen he began to write from Japan for *The Ring* and other magazines. He also works as a TV commentator, manager, trainer, promoter, and matchmaker.

In 1921, Yujiro Watanabe brought the noble art of self-defense with the fists to Japan. Watanabe had gone to California in 1906 to seek his fortune. During his fifteen years in the USA, he learned the basics of boxing in Roof Turner's San Francisco gym and even contested several fights—at this time the state of California operated a strict prohibition on all professional fights longer than four rounds. After his homecoming, the 33-year-old lightweight opened his own gym in Tokyo. Watanabe's Nippon Boxing Club was the first boxing academy to make this martial art, previously completely unknown in Japan, available to the general public.

In 1924 Watanabe staged the first Japanese championship contest, in Tokyo; in this bout Kintaro Usuda gained a points victory over his opponent Kiyoshi Kawakami in eight rounds. At that time there was no official distinction between amateur and professional boxing, so that, in 1928, Usuda (a student at Meiji University) was able to reach the quarterfinals of the ninth Olympic Games

in Amsterdam, although he had previously fought as a semi-pro.

At that period Shanghai was the mecca of pugilism in Asia—and a city where many Filipino fighters, influenced by American culture, found fame and honor. Watanabe, too, called in Filipino boxers from Shanghai for his first international boxing events. They showed great class in their bouts against Watanabe's students, thus giving a boost to the sport and the constantly growing community of Japanese boxing fans.

In the years that followed, more private boxing clubs in the style of Watanabe's boxing school sprang up, and in 1933 the daily newspaper *Yomiuri Shimbun* hit upon the idea of inviting world-class boxers from France to Japan, to be matched against the best local fighters. Elimination bouts were organized to select Japan's representatives for this international contest. During these proceedings there appeared as if from nowhere an as yet undefeated novice by the name of Tsuneo "Piston" Horiguchi, who beat Kaneo Naka-

mura on a TKO decision in the second round —this was the same Nakamura who was reckoned to be the best featherweight of his time.

On July 3, 1933, in a real battle of the ring, Horiguchi fought the former flyweight world champion Emile "Spider" Pladner to an eight-round draw. By the time this bout took place, Horiguchi was already known as "Piston"—he had been given this English nickname because the constant battering of his punch combinations was like the motion of a mechanical piston, to the Japanese fans an apt simile for fistfighting. Horiguchi, still considered today to be the best Japanese fighter of the pre-World War II period, registered 47 consecutive victories and in Hawaii won the highly regarded Asian championship title. However, "Piston" was to the end denied a chance at the world championship belt, because the Japanese, European, and American boxing organizations did not at this time maintain official links.

During World War II boxing was banned in Japan, but in December, 1945, the first

post-war fights had already taken place. This led to a development unique in the history of pugilism. The first world champion fighter that Japan ever produced was trained and managed by an American. Dr. Alvin R. Cahn, who made Yoshio Shirai a world champion in 1952, was not even a boxing trainer. He was an American biologist who supervised the provision of food supplies to the Japanese population on behalf of the government of occupation during the difficult post-war period.

After Shirai finally lost his world championship belt to the Argentinean Pascual Perez in 1954, after four successful title defenses, Japanese boxing fans were forced to wait until the appearance of Masahiko "Fighting" Harada before they could once again celebrate a world champion. Harada, who captured the flyweight title in 1962 by a knockout victory over the Thai Pone King-petch, is reckoned to be one of the greatest boxers of the post-war era—partly because in 1965 he also won the world title at

bantamweight from the previously undefeated Brazilian Eder Jofre.

Since the time of Shirai, Japan has produced more than 40 world champions, not least as a result of economic growth and the continuing commercialization of the country. Japanese television companies collaborate with local boxing promoters to stage regular world title fights. Due to this, and because of strict training conditions, several ambitious Japanese challengers have become world champions.

Usually numbered among the outstanding and best-known Japanese world champions are Hiroshi Kobayashi (junior lightweight 1967–71), Masao Ohba (flyweight 1970–73), Kuniaki Shibata (featherweight 1970–71), Koichi Wajima (junior middleweight 1971–74 and 1976), Yoko Gushiken (junior flyweight 1976–81) and Jiro Watanabe (bantamweight 1982–86).

Today Japan is at the very center of the Asian boxing scene—a country with a huge number of boxing fans that constantly produces new heroes of the ring.

Top Left: 45,000 spectators surrounded the ring in Tokyo in 1952 for the Shirai vs. Marino flyweight world championship.

Huge crowds of spectators streamed in to the title fights of Fighting Harada *(above)* in the 1960s.

TOP TEN OF JAPAN:
1. Fighting Harada
2. Kuniaki Shibata
3. Yoko Gushiken
4. Jiro Watanabe
5. Masao Ohba
6. Yoshio Shirai
7. Hiroshi Kobayashi
8. Guts Ishimatsu
9. Koichi Wajima
10. Shozo Saijo

FATEFUL FIGHTS

The Fate of Gerald McClellan

NINE AND A HALF ROUNDS

Nobody could claim that Gerald McClellan did not know the risks inherent in his sport. On the contrary, the hard-hitting American middleweight champion from Freeport, Illinois emphasized at every opportunity and with almost too much enthusiasm the cruel nature of pugilism. Just a few weeks before his thirty-fourth professional fight, a super-middleweight world championship bout against the British Nigel Benn, the self-styled "G-Man" (short for Gunman) talked to a journalist from

drove his British adversary through the ropes with a barrage of hard, scoring punches, forcing him to take a count. But by the second round, Benn was paying him back in the same coin. There followed ever more intense, volatile exchanges of blows that increasingly and for longer periods visibly sapped the strength of the American more than that of his opponent. Then in the tenth round it happened: having twice already taken the count, McClellan, on his knees for a third time, was finally taken out

Above: In the London Arena in 1995, the stage-managed animosity between Gerald McClellan *(opposite page)* and Nigel Benn *(right)* culminated in a brutal exchange of blows.

the English *Boxing Monthly* and compared himself to the pitbull terriers he bred at home. He claimed that in the ring, just like his fighting dogs, he glared at "this guy that I hate so much, that I really want to knock unconscious." Late in the evening of February 25, 1995, however, after nine and a half dramatic rounds in the London Arena, he himself plunged into a mental darkness, from which to this day he has not fully awakened.

It all began in almost exactly the same way as it always did when this explosive pro entered the ring. The signal for the start of the first round had barely sounded when McClellan

of the fight by referee Alfred Azaro—and collapsed while still in his corner under the care of his handlers.

McClellan, from 1993 to 1995 an uncompromising WBC champion at middleweight, survived the final duel of his career thanks to rapid medical intervention. Neurosurgeons in the Royal London Hospital that same night removed a blood clot from his brain and snatched him back from imminent death. But the father-of-three has never fully returned to his previous life. Since his return to America, almost blind, unable to speak, and with severely impaired hearing, he has been confined

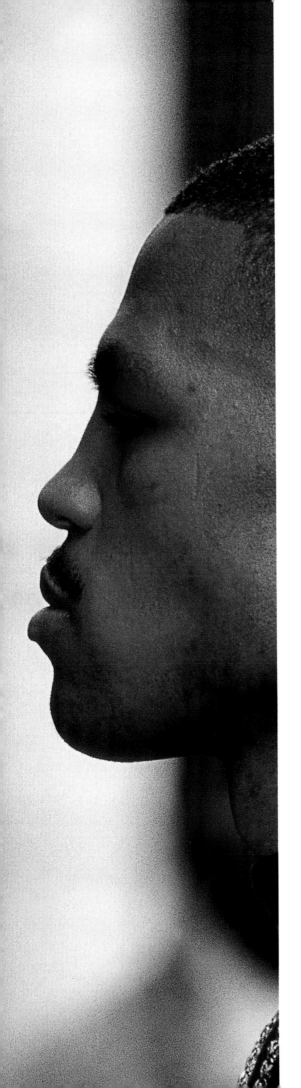

to a wheelchair and is profoundly mentally disabled. The only thing fully revived in the aftermath of this tragic case is a debate that is almost as old as boxing itself.

Here, the argument is more concerned with ethical rather than medical considerations: can a sport that, in spite of all possible preventative measures, must at all times reckon with such fateful consequences even hope to be tolerated by society? The devotees of this at times terrible sport have for many decades rebutted calls for a

ever really be when its strategic object is to damage the opponent's physical well-being?

In fact, from a medical point of view, the provision for the contest between McClellan and Benn was exemplary. Four doctors and an anesthetist were present. An emergency medical vehicle was on standby to rush the unconscious fighter to the nearby hospital, which had already been alerted to receive him. The whole scenario was, in the words of co-promoter Frank Warren next best to "having an operat-

Seconds, security staff and officials tend to the unconscious McClellan after his KO defeat and collapse *(above)*: he has never fully recovered from his injuries.

ban on boxing with the claim that their athletes willingly expose themselves to the sport's intrinsic risks. And they believe that in borderline cases it is more constructive to minimize the chance of future accidents in the ring by the introduction of new safety measures, as has happened so often in the past. After all, with the reduction of the number of rounds in title fights to twelve and the requirement in industrialized countries for a compulsory time-out from competition, coupled with brain tomography (CAT scan) after a knockout, there have been significantly fewer fatalities than in previous decades. But how safe can a contact sport

ing theater at the ringside." Despite all this, none of the fateful consequences except actual clinical death could be prevented. Thus February 25, 1995 was, for acclaimed sports columnist Hugh McIlvanney, "a dramatic reminder of something about which the most ardent defenders of boxing should never have been able to delude themselves—that when one man is landing full-blooded punches on another man's head, nothing done during the intervals in the action, or when it is over, can remove the risk of severe and perhaps fatal brain damage."

And this risk remains.

LIVING WITH THE RISK

The sensational deaths and disabling injuries suffered in boxing have, with astonishing regularity, given rise to repeated short-lived debates about the right of boxing to exist as a sport. Whenever an athlete participating in any halfway meaningful, possibly televised, contest falls into a potentially life-threatening coma, the demands for the abolition of professional boxing increase in volume. And just as regularly, opponents counter the indignant campaigns of doctors' organizations such as the American Medical Association (AMA) with facts that put the dangers of combat sports disciplines into relative perspective. The risk of life-threatening injury in boxing is 1.3 cases for every 10,000 participating athlete, which is significantly less than the comparative rates for deep-sea diving (11 cases), mountain-climbing (51 cases) or horse-racing (128 cases). According to an evaluation in the American *Sports Illustrated* magazine, in the

years from 1918 to 1983, worldwide, 645 amateur and pro boxers were fatally injured, which represents an annual average of 8.6 cases. There is a continuing downwards trend, according to Robert Cassidy, writing in *The Ring* in 1994, as "the rules of boxing have changed dramatically, wiping out many of the dangerous, macho practices of the Golden Era."

The discussion around the pros and cons of the sport sometimes carries with it more cultural preconceptions than real attempts at debate, and is a diversion from the crucial topic of the long-term health risks to athletes. No one today seriously disputes that each boxing contest brings with it for its active participants the potential hazard of lasting effects on brain function.

A variety of medical studies, carried out using widely different statistical criteria, all lead to the general conclusion that the risk of permanent head injury increases in relation

to the number of fights contested, or rather, the number of effective punches sustained. By 1970, an analytical evaluation of all the available specialist literature on this topic, carried out by Friedrich Unterharnscheidt, ended conclusively in the unambiguous summary that "every boxer must recognize the possibility of permanent traumatic injury, which is correspondingly greater the earlier he begins to box, the more regularly he participates and the longer his career lasts."

In 1928, in an early study in this field, Dr. Harrison Martland introduced the term "punch drunk" to refer to this particular syndrome, a term which is still used in everyday speech today. Contemporary medical science, on the other hand, has for some considerable time used the term *dementia pugilistica* and includes under this heading a wide variety of symptoms: motor disorders, loss of co-ordination, partial reduction of muscle

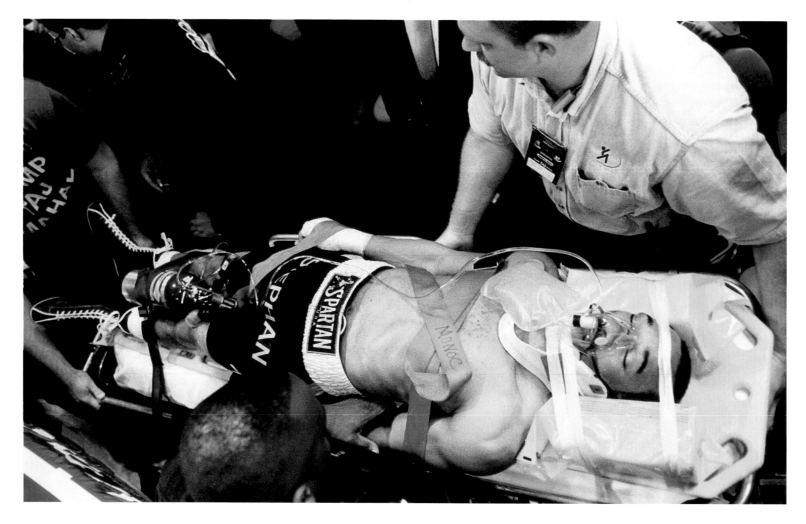

Even immediate admission to a hospital failed to prevent the death of Stephan Johnson after a fight in Atlantic City in 1999.

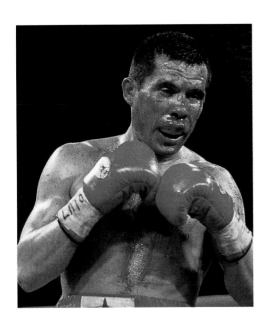

Heavily bleeding wounds (*shown here:* Julio Cesar Chavez) are the dramatic side of boxing. More serious, however, is neurological damage.

control, speech and memory disorders, and emotional instability, including depressive and/or aggressive phases.

This leads to the conclusion that tremors caused by blows received can not only give rise to dangerous blood clots (*hematoma*) in various parts of the brain, that in acute accidents in the ring lead to collapse—the constituent parts of the brain itself, its cells, nerves (transmitters) etc. are permanently changed, or even deformed, by constantly repeated shocks.

This is presumably what the former heavyweight champion Sonny Liston attempted to express when he tried to explain the possible long-term effects of his sport to a close friend. He used an image of the various parts of the brain resting in their respective "cups." "If you take a bad hit, your brain flops out of its cups—plop! and you're KO. Then your brain goes back into the cups, and you come

around. But if it happens often enough, sometimes even just once, if the punch is hard enough, then your brain never goes right back into the cups, and then you need other people to help you through your life." We do not know exactly what Liston meant by the "cups." And we know just as little today about the details of how neurological defects arise through boxing. What is the role played by dehydration caused by the need to "make the weight," a fluid loss that naturally also affects the head? And is there really a causal link between *dementia pugilistica* and syndromes such as Alzheimer's and Parkinson's, that have suspiciously afflicted many boxers in their retirement e.g., Joe Louis, Rocky Graziano, Sugar Ray Robinson and Muhammad Ali? It seems much more constructive to pursue such lines of enquiry when dealing with the darker side of the sport, rather than to remain fixated on a basic debate on fatal accidents.

MEMENTO MORI—DEATHS IN BOXING

Year	Number of Deaths	Year	Number of Deaths	Year	Number of Deaths	Year	Number of Deaths
1918	3	1939	3	1960	12	1981	7
1919	5	1940	5	1961	11	1982	7
1920	3	1941	8	1962	16	1983	10
1921	9	1942	8	1963	16	1984	6
1922	19	1943	5	1964	17	1985	7
1923	15	1944	7	1965	13	1986	3
1924	16	1945	10	1966	12	1987	4
1925	13	1946	17	1967	6	1988	4
1926	6	1947	11	1968	6	1989	4
1927	7	1948	18	1969	7	1990	4
1928	12	1949	20	1970	9	1991	5
1929	16	1950	14	1971	12	1992	3
1930	23	1951	15	1972	12	1993	1
1931	8	1952	19	1973	5	1994	2
1932	21	1953	25	1974	11	1995	10
1933	10	1954	7	1975	12	1996	7
1934	6	1955	11	1976	6	1997	8
1935	9	1956	15	1977	9	1998	2
1936	6	1957	13	1978	10	1999	4
1937	8	1958	9	1979	11	2000	6
1938	7	1959	14	1980	5	2001	6

Source: Joseph A. Svinth, 2001.

Can boxing be made "safer"?

RESEARCH AND REGULATION

For a long period, in pro boxing as in other hazardous contact sports, it was an accepted although generally regretted fact that even the most skilled of doctors could not look into the interior of the human brain. But in recent decades, this is exactly what the apparatus of modern neurological science has made possible. Since these advances, methods for early diagnosis of brain damage in boxers have progressed greatly. Ever more frequently, an increasing number of both pro and amateur boxers have been prevented from continuing their sporting careers due to medical decisions based on initial signs of functional disorders. In addition, there is a growing trend amongst all participants towards improvement in the provisions made in case of accidents in the ring. Even taken together, however, these

Twice world championship contender at heavyweight Jerry Quarry became increasingly disabled and by the time of his premature death was completely dependent on the help of others.

factors have done little to reduce the inherent dangers of the sport, but have somewhat lessened the careless attitude to safety standards.

The key to this new responsibility lies particularly in two high-tech medical procedures that allow detailed examination of the brain, micro-section by micro-section—computed axial tomography (CAT scan) and the even more precise magnetic resonance scan (MR-scan). Unlike earlier procedures such as air encephalography, these scanning methods are painless and risk-free for the subject. Any halfway serious boxing organization has made such examinations a precondition of issuing or renewing a boxing license. In an increasing number of countries, in the event of a knock-out defeat, an immediate CAT scan of the loser's head is compulsory; in addition, a period of suspension of from four to twelve weeks is obligatory. A file available on the Internet, the Suspension List, gives details of all currently suspended boxers, as long as their national organizations have lodged this information. Only a very few promoters and managers have the nerve to simply disregard this.

Disturbing findings in routine scans have on more than one occasion led to well-known pros at the peak of their careers being compelled to retire. Among their number are the American Michael Bentt, who was discovered to have an abnormal decline in brain cells after the loss of his WBO heavyweight crown in 1994, and the Irish world championship challenger Ray Close, whose third title bout with WBO champion Chris Eubank (scheduled for February 1995) was called off after a CAT scan at the Royal Victoria Hospital in Belfast. This examination showed abnormal changes in his brain, and caused the British umbrella organization to ban him from fighting. The world championship event in the King's Hall, Belfast had to be cancelled, as did a TV contract for a minimum of four fights that would have made Close a millionaire.

The former flyweight champion Dave McAuley should also have joined their ranks. However the Scottish pro did not accept the verdict of an initial CAT scan and took a second test in Chicago—this time without giving any cause for concern. Accordingly, the British organization once again gave him the

Years after his final fateful contest, the disabled ex-boxer Michael Watson appears in public for the first time at a football match.

green light to go ahead with his forthcoming defense of the IBF title.

The world sanctioning bodies, in particular the WBC, make their contribution to the dissemination of knowledge gained from the latest research in neurophysiology and other relevant fields by organizing international congresses for ringside doctors and medics. The more progressive national commissions have, in the meantime, attached to the sanctioning of professional boxing events new standards in obligatory safety provision (ambulances on standby at the venue, anesthetist at the ringside, etc.). This is of course still no guarantee against fatal accidents. Even if the annual worldwide number of deaths (currently around four to six per annum) has fallen, and pros with early signs of brain damage are occasionally filtered out of active participation, by its very nature, fistfighting remains hazardous to health—and potentially life threatening.

Before the bout between Tommy Morrison and Marcus Rhode in Tokyo in 1996, the referee also donned protective gloves.

Boxing and Aids
THE STATISTICAL RISK

By the end of the last century, there had been not one single proven case of an athlete being infected by any of the variants of HIV during competition. Nevertheless, there is no question that in a discipline with the ever-present possibility of a direct exchange of blood, precautionary measures are necessary. For some years, prejudices fed by ignorance and a bizarre kind of machismo delayed the introduction of regulations to deal with this situation. However, since they have been overcome, the provision of a negative Aids-test result has become an essential precondition almost everywhere for the granting of professional licenses and the sanctioning of title fights.

Since the 1990s, not least due to some sensational cases involving infected pro boxers

there have been improved levels of awareness of this problem. Notable amongst these was the case of featherweight Eduardo Castro, 21 years old at the time, who despite a positive test result by the Nevada State Athletic Commission afterwards fought two bouts in California. In 1993, the Colombian featherweight Ruben "Hurricane" Palacios was the first world champion to be prevented from defending his WBO title due to a positive HIV test a few days before his defense; Palacios had to surrender both his title and his license. In the mid 1990s, Paul Banke, the California-born former super bantamweight champion (WBC) made a public announcement of his retirement on the same grounds. But no case aroused as much attention as that of Tommy Morrison. In February

1996, shortly before a scheduled bout in Las Vegas, this internationally known heavyweight, who had been WBO champion for a short time in 1993, and had played himself in the Sylvester Stallone movie epic *Rocky* announced that he had tested positive. Despite this, in November of the same year the tough guy from Oklahoma was matched in Tokyo with the unranked Marcus Rohde.

Rohde had been fully informed of the residual risks of contracting the virus (a chance of some 85 million to one), but as it turned out there was very little violent physical contact: he was knocked out almost immediately by Morrison after only a few exchanges of blows.

ACCIDENTS AND REGULATIONS
RECORD OF A CONTINUING DEBATE

February 17, **1741** In a bareknuckle championship bout in London, lasting 35 minutes, George Stevenson from Yorkshire is defeated by the reigning titleholder Jack Broughton, and dies a few days later as a result of injuries from the duel. Deeply affected by this death, Broughton, a pioneer of modern professional boxing, develops a set of rules for the sport. In *Broughton's Rules*, published on August 16, 1743, downed boxers are explicitly protected: hitting an opponent when he is down is forbidden, as is holding "by the hair, the breeches or any part below the waist." A downed fighter is allowed 30 seconds to recover. September 13, **1842** After a fight near Yonkers, New York, lasting 120 rounds or some 160 minutes, the American Tom McCoy is knocked out by his British adversary Chris Lilly and dies while still in the ring. This tragic accident gives grounds for banning prize fighting in the United States and forces it on to the wrong side of the law. In addition, Lilly's second, the boxer Yankee Sullivan, is jailed for two years. December 6, **1897** In London, the British bantamweight champion Walter Croot dies as a result of the knockout in the sixteenth round of a world championship contest against the Chicagoan Jimmy Barry. Croot strikes his head with such force on the floor of the ring that he suffers a brain hemorrhage. Barry and the presiding officials of the National Sporting Club are charged with manslaughter, but in a trial that attracts much publicity, they are eventually acquitted. Similar procedures are applied in London in 1901, when, after a fatal victory over Billy Smith, Jack Roberts is brought to trial on charges of "culpable homicide and manslaughter." May 24, **1913** A public favorite perishes in the Canadian city of Calgary when, in the very first round of his contest with Arthur Pelkey, the 21-year-old Luther McCarty falls to the ground and never regains consciousness. After the death of the young Nebraskan heavyweight, captured on photographic film and widely publicized, there are demands for the abolition of boxing. However, a deeper investigation reveals a previous injury to be the cause of death: in a riding accident several weeks before the fight, McCarty had apparently broken his collarbone and, it was suspected, a cervical vertebra. August 25, **1930** Heavyweight Frankie Campbell collapses in the fifth round of his fight with the future world champion Max Baer and dies several hours later in hospital. Baer is later exonerated in court of any contributory responsibility. March 24, **1962** A nationwide audience of television viewers is shocked as the live broadcast of the "rubber match" between Benny Paret and Emile Griffith in New York's Madison Square Garden ends in tragedy. In the twelfth round, the challenger Griffith has the welterweight champion on the ropes and overwhelms him with a barrage of blows, until referee Ruby Goldstein finally steps in. It is too late: Paret falls, slips into a coma and dies ten days later. His death provokes New York's Senator Max Turshen and other political figures to call for a law (never formally introduced) on the abolition of professional boxing. March 21, **1963** Exactly a year after the death of Paret, the next tragedy occurs in Los Angeles. During a bout that ends in his stoppage defeat by world champion Sugar Ramos, featherweight Davey Moore hits the base of his skull against the bottom rope but fights on. He later collapses in the dressing room and dies four days later in hospital. Officials lose little time in rushing through new safety standards. To prevent accidents of the Paret and Moore type, by July of the same year, the number of ring-ropes is increased from three to four in New York State. In September, the (long-despised) "safety count" is provisionally introduced: this allows the referee to enforce an eight-count on a downed boxer, even when he is ready to fight on. July 19, **1978** In Bellária, Italy, after a knockout defeat in the twelfth round by European champion Alan Minter, middleweight Angelo Jacopucci falls into a coma and dies. After a second fatal accident in the space of seven months (on December 17, 1977) the German Jörg Eipel, the European welterweight champion, remains unconscious for several days after he is knocked out in the fourteenth round of his fight with Alain Marion, the European Boxing Union (EBU) is the first international body to reduce the number of rounds in title fights from 15 to 12. November 13, **1982** After withstanding an immense number of scoring punches, the Korean Deuk Koo Kim is taken out of the fight in the fourteenth round of his contest in Las Vegas against WBA lightweight champion Ray Mancini. He immediately falls into a coma and dies five days later. The rival WBC organization reacts by reducing the length of its title fights: henceforth fights under their sanction last for 12 rather than 15 rounds. In 1987 and 1988 respectively, the WBA and IBF come into line. September 21, **1991** The bitter contest for the vacant WBO super-middleweight crown between Chris Eubank and Michael Watson ends in catastrophe: Watson becomes unconscious in the twelfth round, then lapses into a coma. With around half of his brain function destroyed and paralyzed on one side of his body, years later and still confined to a wheelchair, the ex-pro sues the British regulatory body for negligence in its duty to ensure adequate medical provision. In December 1999, at the end of a high-profile test case, the High Court in London rules for the complainant (Watson) and orders the British Boxing Board of Control (BBBC) to pay £1 million damages. Faced with bankruptcy, the Board lodges an appeal against this decision.

Andrew Golota vs. Riddick Bowe

NEW YORK CITY, JULY 11, 1996

The intention in itself was admirable. "Boxing Returns to the Mecca" was the slogan for a new offensive started by the management of New York's Madison Square Garden in the winter of 1995: fistfighting, which had in the meantime migrated to the sphere of the hotel casinos, was to make a comeback in seriously staged spectaculars to one of the most significant boxing arenas in the world, back to where Fullmer and Robinson had boxed, where Benvenuti met Griffith and not least where Frazier and Ali fought. This was the guiding spirit behind the fourth night of the new campaign, when, in the shape of ex-world champion Riddick Bowe and the yet undefeated Andrew Golota, two famed heavyweights were matched at the top of the card. But a night that had been hyped as the biggest-ever gala of the revived sport ended late in the evening of July 11, 1996 in a giant-sized fiasco: instead of two athletes fighting it out between themselves, suddenly, hundreds of over-excited opposing supporters slugged it out in a brutal mass brawl.

Events spun out of control in the seventh round, when Golota, clearly in the lead despite several warnings, was disqualified for persistent low blows. While Bowe was still writhing in pain on the canvas, his manager Rock Newman and several of Bowe's entourage, until then sheltering in the ring security zone, jumped into the ring and, as self-appointed avengers, lit into Golota and his handlers. The Olympic bronze medallist from Warsaw was injured on the head by a blow from a cell phone; his trainer Lou Duva suffered a heart attack, was given emergency oxygen and had to be carried from the ring on a stretcher. By this time, the Polish fans

Three months later, there was a repeat performance of these ugly scenes in the ring. In the replay of the fight, in the Atlantic City Convention Center …

In July 1996 in his bout with ex-world champion Riddick Bowe, the punches of Andrew Golota landed below the belt. This caused the Pole from Chicago first to be warned and finally to be disqualified. Immediately after, a feud broke out in Madison Square Garden, spreading from the ring out into the auditorium seating. The security staff was late in arriving.

had also stormed the ring to challenge Bowe's powerful entourage. And before the spectators realized what was happening, the scuffle erupted beyond the confines of the ring into the rows of seating and turned into a full-scale racially motivated brawl: 24 people (15 spectators and 9 police) subsequently needed treatment in New York hospitals, and 16 participants were temporarily arrested.

The horrific scenario in the arena was not least due to the disastrous security provision. The 120 security guards and ushers,

some of them elderly, were physically overwhelmed by the aggressive supporters. The police presence was limited to 18 uniformed officers standing at the entrances: 30 minutes were to go by before a further 150 police officers arrived.

"Security? What security?" was how the magazine *Boxing Monthly* portrayed this organizational chaos. But this most scandalous of the boxing incidents of the 1990s yet again caused the reputation of the sport to suffer an even greater battering worldwide —if this was indeed possible after similarly

catastrophic events in Stuttgart and elsewhere. This might well beg the additional question: "Reputation? What reputation?"

However, the management of Madison Square Garden did not allow themselves to be diverted from their planned course by what their president, Dave Checketts called "the actions of a few despicable people," and continued to put on boxing events. And Andrew Golota remained similarly set in his ways: in the rematch with Riddick Bowe in Atlantic City in December of the same year, he was once again disqualified for low blows.

…Golota again caused a sensation due to his crude low blows. In the ninth round, the referee intervened and disqualified Golota once again.

ROUND TRIP:

AUSTRALIA

by John Hogg

John Hogg was born in 1946. As a journalist and boxing historian, he has followed the Australian boxing scene for 30 years. He is the editor of the annual *Record Book* for that continent and writes regularly for the Australian magazine *The Fist*.

The visit of Jem Mace, world champion in all classes under the *London Prize Ring Rules*, to Australia in 1877 was a milestone in the development of Australian boxing. After April 17, 1884, the day that Alick Agar died as a result of his bout against James Lawson in Randwick, bareknuckle fighting was officially banned on the fifth continent. However, the first title fight for the Australian championship at heavyweight took place two months later, in the Victoria Hall in Melbourne. In this bout, Bill Farnan knocked out the Caribbean-born Peter Jackson in the third round. While boxing in Melbourne enjoyed a real boom, in Sydney, after two deaths in 1893, it continued to be banned for some years. It was only at the turn of the century that regular fight-nights, which took place in sporting clubs such as the Golden Gate and the Gaiety, were resumed. As the authorities kept a very close

eye on events of this kind, it was common for boxers' contracts to include a clause that stipulated the decision in the event of "police intervention."

The year 1908 introduced the Golden Age of Australian boxing. Promoter Hugh D. McIntosh erected a large open-air arena at Rushcutters Bay, Sydney for the world heavyweight championship contest between Tommy Burns and Bill Squires. Appropriately on December 26, Boxing Day, of the same year, the American Jack Johnson seized the world champion's belt from Burns, and in the aftermath boxing fever swept across the whole country. In 1912, the Sydney Stadium was roofed over and McIntosh sold his share to R. L. "Snowy" Baker, whose company Stadiums Ltd. shortly afterwards gained control of the most important arenas in the three largest cities—Sydney, Melbourne, and Brisbane.

On October 3, 1913, Baker convened a meeting where the rules of boxing were finally standardized and the weight divisions fixed. Stadiums Ltd. was taken over in 1915 by John Wren, and remained the most important promoter of major boxing events until well into the second half of the twentieth century.

The period 1911 through 1916 was the time of the great Les Darcy, who defeated every opponent and was considered the uncrowned king of the middleweights. Unhappily, his brilliant progress came to an abrupt end when he died on May 24, 1917 in the USA.

During the economic crisis of the 1930s, boxing began to flourish once more. In the many small arenas in and around Sydney, an average of ten boxing evenings a week took place, and in both Melbourne and Brisbane, two events per week were the norm, while even in smaller towns it was possible to see

regular fights. Jack Carroll, Ron Richards, Fred Henneberry, and Ambrose Palmer were the big names of this time.

The 1940s were dominated by Vic Patrick, Tommy Burns, and Dave Sands. On February 2, 1946, Patrick beat Burns in front of 13,000 spectators at the sold-out Sydney Stadium, while outside the doors stood yet more crowds who had been unable to get tickets. In 1947 Patrick was himself defeated in a great fight with the American Freddie Dawson.

On November 15, 1952, in South Africa, Jimmy Carruthers took the world title at bantamweight from Vic Toweel; other greats of that time were Elley Bennett and George Barnes.

After a slack period in the 1960s, boxing enjoyed a revival with the help of television, which broadcast fights three times per week. Lionel Rose (1968–69, bantamweight) and John Famechon (1969–70, featherweight) succeeded in taking world titles, while Anthony Mundine and Hector Thompson both made it as far as a world title challenge.

In more recent times, the successful promoter Bill Mordey made champions of Jeff Fenech (1985), Jeff Harding (1989), and Kostya Tszyu (1995). Nevertheless, even these successes have been unable to halt the gradual decline of Australian boxing. Over the last two decades, public interest in the sport has been waning. Whereas in 1970 there were 378 boxing events, by 1999 the number had fallen to only 63 in all. Today boxing has the status of a marginal sport, taken seriously neither by public-service television nor by the press. Only on pay TV is it still possible to experience boxing in one's own home, and the future of Australian boxing must therefore be viewed with a deal of skepticism. Perhaps the stars of tomorrow can change this.

Top left: The Sydney Convention Center was the venue for the Olympic Boxing Tournament in 2000. *Above:* The former bantamweight champion Lionel Rose, in 1968 the first Aborigine to win a professional world championship, carries the Olympic torch.

TOP TEN OF AUSTRALIA:
1. Les Darcy
2. Jack Carroll
3. Jimmy Carruthers
4. John Famechon
5. Lionel Rose
6. Ambrose Palmer
7. Dave Sands
8. Ron Richards
9. Jeff Fenech
10. Hector Thompson, Anthony Mundine

ONLY IN BOXING

CURTAIN UP!

Roll up, ladies and gentleman, roll up and be amazed! Muhammad Ali, the best boxer in the world matched in single combat against the famed wrestler Antonio Inoki! West meets East in the "World Championship of the Martial Arts"! Now surely that would be a must-see event for any even halfway curious person—either at the venue or on screen? By the end of the fifteen confusing rounds of this spectacular, staged with the maximum possible ballyhoo in the Tokyo Korakuen Dome on June 26, 1976, the disappointed witnesses had learnt better of it. A match that Ali had, with his usual modesty described as "the greatest single sporting event in the history of the world" turned out to be "the dullest event in sports history" (John Stravinsky). For fifteen endless action-starved rounds, Inoki squatted close to the canvas like a sand crab and used kicks to fend off Ali's half-hearted attacks. At the end of the farce, the combatants were given a draw, and considerably smaller purses than the total of $8.2 million originally offered. In all respects the evening was a dud.

Time after time spectacular events of an unorthodox kind are dreamed up in the show business world of pro boxing—and sometimes they even actually take place. Duels such as that between Muhammad Ali and the gigantic basketball star Will Chamberlain, or a showdown between an Ultimate Fighting Champion and light heavyweight world champion Roy Jones Jr. thankfully remained just circus-ring fantasies. Other apparently unlikely events did, however, take place—like the unofficial fight-night in Toronto in April, 1976, when George Foreman finished off a total of five nameless opponents, or the woman against man contest—a so-called intergender bout—in Seattle in October, 1999, when a 36-year-old woman with a criminal record, Margaret MacGregor outboxed the harmless part-time jockey Loi Chow over four rounds.

Only in boxing, or so it seems, things can happen that would occur in no other sport. After all, in the era of the boxing booth, men squared up to bears, or one man fought several adversaries. Yes, ladies and gentlemen, just step right on in: The show goes on and on …

Above: In Berlin in the mid-1920s, August the boxing bear successfully lands a knockout blow.
Right: The same kind of circus-style curiosity was aroused by Hughes Boxing Pavilion, a boxing booth touring England around 1945.

GIANTS AND COLOSSI

It is a traditional axiom in the performance sport of prizefighting that the imposing physical presence of the athletes boosts public interest in a fight. During the nineteenth century in Great Britain and in the United States bareknuckle heroes fought successfully under nicknames such as "The Bristol Bull," "The Great Gun of Windsor," or "The Irish Giant" that emphasized their physical bulk. The admiration attracted by modern-era heavyweight pros such as Jess Willard (6'5") and Fred Fulton (6'4") was also enormous. Willard, known after his birthplace as the "Pottawatomie Giant," held the championship for two years after his stoppage victory over Jack Johnson (1915), while Fulton was reckoned to be a possible title contender. But then within the short space of a year, the fate of so many other boxing giants overtook them: they were outclassed by the visibly smaller but much more dynamic Jack Dempsey. While Willard, Fulton and later the South African Ewart Potgieter (7'2") could at least demonstrate real athletic skills, with the regrettable career of Primo Carnera the sport came dangerously close to becoming something of a fairground sideshow. The 6'5"-tall, big baby of a stonemason, from Sequals in Italy, was discovered in a traveling circus by the French manager Léon See, and built up by him in Europe into a well-protected pro boxer. But by the time of his first appearance in America, it was obvious that Carnera had very little talent. His backers, reckoned to be connected to the world of organized crime, succeeded in building him up into a title contender with the nickname "The Ambling Alp." Fitted up with an oversized mouthguard that was supposed to make him seem more intimidating, in 1933 Carnera won a doubtful stoppage victory over Jack Sharkey and actually held the world championship, until one year later, in eleven totally one-sided rounds, Max Baer punished him for his presumption. At the end of his career in the ring (1945), Carnera went on to join the more appropriate Show-Catch scene, one that would also have best suited Tony Galento. With his height of 5'7" and body weight of 234 lbs, "Two Ton Tony" was a special phenomenon, even for professional boxing. This former doorman from New Jersey gained dubious fame in 1939 when, after ten only moderately impressive years as a pro, he became yet another victim of world champion Joe Louis. In this glorious stoppage defeat, Galento was made to pay, and not only for the lucky punch that allowed him briefly to drop his legendary opponent—his taunts and insults had obviously annoyed the champion even before the first bell sounded. There in the New York Giants Stadium, "Two Ton Tony" was knocked out

In the 1950s, South African Ewart Potgieter showed off his gigantic stature.

In the 1930s, Primo Carnera caused a similar furor.

so convincingly in the fourth round that observer Bugs Baer later claimed "they could have counted him out while he was still on his way down." Size alone cannot guarantee class. But it can mean cash when an ample physique is stage-managed into cult status. And this is precisely what one Eric Esch, better known by his ring name of "Butterbean," did during the closing years of last century. This one-time factory worker from Alabama moved over after 45 wins in 47 fights on the Tough Man contest circuit to professional boxing, where with his full weight of 300 lbs he rapidly became an almost self-parodic celebrity. As the so-called "King of the Four Rounders," "Butterbean" advanced to the dizzy heights of champion of the low-rated International Boxing Association (IBA), whose "title defense" bouts were crowd-pleasers on the undercard of promoter Bob Arum's boxing galas. As in the boxing booths of times past, big Eric always came speedily to the point in the space of a few rounds, with the public's favorite usually triumphing in a KO victory. Even Bob Arum's statement to a corruption investigation that some of these victories were bought did little to harm the status of this cult figure.

Every so often, flashes of the sideshow still break through.

In the 1990s, The American Eric Esch, aka "Butterbean," appeared to be largely inescapable.

TALES OF THE TAPE—WHAT THE TAPE MEASURE REVEALS

Name	Height (feet/inches)	Weight (lbs)	Reach (inches)	Neck (inches)	Chest (inches)	Waist (inches)	Biceps (inches)	Fist (inches)	Thigh (inches)
JACK JOHNSON	6-1¼	192	74	17½	37½	36	16	14	22½
JACK DEMPSEY	6-0¾	187	77	16½	42	33	16¼	11¼	23
PRIMO CARNERA	6-5¾	260	85½	20	48	38	18½	14¾	30½
JOE LOUIS	6-1½	197	76	17	42	36½	15	11¾	22½
ROCKY MARCIANO	5-10¼	184	68	16¾	39	32	14	11½	22
MUHAMMAD ALI	6-3	210½	82	17½	43	34	15½	12½	25
JOE FRAZIER	5-11½	205	73½	17½	42	34	15	13	26
GEORGE FOREMAN	6-3	217¾	82	17	42	34	15	12	25
MIKE TYSON	5-11½	218	71	19¾	43	34	16	13	27
BONECRUSHER SMITH	6-4	230	82	18	42½	38	18	13¾	29
EVANDER HOLYFIELD	6-2	215	77½	19½	43	32	16	12½	22
LENNOX LEWIS	6-5	245	84	18½	44	34	17	12	26

Comeback after Retirement
A DANGEROUS GAME WITH AGE

Particularly for those possessed of a fighting spirit, there must be a unique attraction in the idea of staving off the first signs of physical decline by asserting oneself once again in competitive combat. It is the particular misfortune of boxers that an over-optimistic estimate of their own resources will be much more cruelly punished in the ring than it would be, let us say, on the tennis court—and their "expiration date" can fall due between one fight and the next. "You always tell yourself 'I'll quit when I start to decline," said Sugar Ray Robinson on one occasion, describing the boxer's battle with himself, "and then you wake up one morning and it's already happened." Naïveté, over-confidence, and simply lack of money are the main reasons why the greats of the ring carry on beyond the zenith of their careers. All too soon most of them are left in no doubt of their "sell-by date" by younger opponents, as was the 37-year-old Joe Louis by Rocky Marciano (1951), the 33-year-old Nino Benvenuti by Carlos Monzon (1971) and the 38-year-old Muhammad Ali by Larry Holmes (1980). All three of these meetings were out-and-out executions that brought the rapid retirement of the defeated "oldies" in their wake. This is an inevitable result of the unstoppable ticking of the clock. "Horses get old, cars get old, even the pyramids in Egypt crumble." (Muhammad Ali).

In 1995, the "old-timer" George Foreman once again became heavyweight world champion.

In 1997, Hector Camacho (left) put an end to Sugar Ray Leonard's last comeback.

But occasionally it is necessary to administer more than one beating to knock the desire to flirt with a comeback out of some incorrigible veterans. In 1988, Larry Holmes was overtaken by the same fate as his predecessor Ali, when, at the age of 38, he was taken to pieces over four rounds by Mike Tyson, 17 years his junior. Nevertheless, he persisted, and in 1992 against Evander Holyfield and again in 1995 against Oliver McCall, twice challenged in vain for the world heavyweight title. In March, 1997, after six years in retirement, Sugar Ray Leonard stepped back into the ring: once there, the 40-year-old grandfather was thrashed by Hector Camacho Jr., and for the first time, unprecedented in his career, the fight was stopped before the full distance. His former rival Roberto Duran fared no better in 1998 when, at the age of 47 years, he tried his luck against William Joppy, the WBA middleweight champion. The boxing icon from Panama did not even last three full rounds—and continued his career against less significant opponents.

Why does the duel between the aging and the up-and-coming star continue to be a classic draw for fans and matchmakers alike? Presumably because showdowns of this kind symbolize the war between the generations—and from time to time, just often enough, they end in an unexpected victory of experience over youth. An example of this occurred in 1952 when Archie Moore, at that time 36 years old, became the oldest "freshly-minted" world champion of the modern era; from then until 1960, he successfully defended his title six times against significantly younger rivals. Similarly, in November, 1994, heavyweight George Foreman caused one of the greatest sensations of the decade: hopelessly behind on points, the ex-world champion, at nearly 47 years of age, pulled off a knockout over Michael Moorer and once more took possession of the champion's belt (WBA and IBF versions).

But when two senior athletes clash in the ring, the occasion is likely to be bizarre rather than brilliant. This was demonstrated in Fayetteville, North Carolina in June 1999 when James "Bonecrusher" Smith and his opponent Larry Holmes boxed for the newly created "Legends Title." In this slow-motion duel the two dinosaurs of the heavyweight division, whose ages totaled 97 years, attempted to conjure up memories of their Las Vegas world championship bout of almost 15 years back, when Holmes won on a narrow points decision. But as the exhausted "Bonecrusher" was taken out of the fight in the eighth round, the spectators felt more relief than enthusiasm. This slow waltz by Smith and Holmes was to have been the first in a series based on the pattern of the "Seniors' Tour" in tennis. However, from time to time it really is an advantage that, in boxing, not all much-hyped events actually take place.

Ex-champion Larry Holmes fended off the threat of retirement for many years.

Triumph over Disadvantage
CAREERS AGAINST THE ODDS

Mario D'Agata could only guess at rather than hear the acclaim for his success achievements in the ring. D'Agata, born deaf-mute, was, despite his disability, world champion for a short time in 1986.

When the referee took his badly marked opponent out of the fight in the sixth round, Mario D'Agata suddenly found himself hoisted shoulder-high by his enthusiastic fellow-countrymen. The 30-year-old bantamweight from Arezzo was acclaimed in a spontaneous collective outburst of jubilation in the Foro Atletico stadium in Rome, because his victory over Robert Cohen gained him the world championship (New York and EBU version). The noise of the crowd of tens of thousands on that June night could at best only be guessed at by the courageous Tuscan. And he expressed his own personal emotions in those minutes not with words, but in his usual manner, with gestures and looks. Born deaf-mute, D'Agata could use neither voice nor ears. However, he was well able to match the best of his era in the skilful and determined use of his fists. Taking the world title was the ultimate confirmation of D'Agata's courage in ignoring his inborn sporting disadvantage. And the world of boxing gained another classic example for the claim that anyone, whatever their apparent limitations, can fight to improve their chances.

This was precisely what the Frenchman Eugene Criqui did 33 years earlier, when he became world champion in the same weight division as D'Agata, although his jaw had been shattered by a bullet during military action at Verdun. Since then, his jaw had been held together by a structure of metal plates and animal bone. Then there was the Hawaiian-born American Tami Mauriello, who despite a stiff knee-joint made it as far as a title fight with Joe Louis (September, 1946)—even though he only lasted two minutes in the ring. Boxing fans in the Netherlands in the 1920s and 1930s greatly admired the lightweight Cornelis "Battling" van Dijk, who only had the sight of one eye. The man from Rotterdam was famed for sending his twin brother Gideon as his stand-in to a pre-fight medical examination, to avoid a possible ban. In Spain in the 1970s, another deaf-mute fighter, José Hernandez, triumphed as national and European champion at middleweight. The Catalan even challenged for Cornelio Bassi's world title in April 1971 and missed the championship by a narrow points margin over 15 rounds.

However, the most remarkable comeback for a boxer after a physically disabling injury happened in the chosen homeland of limitless opportunity. Craig Bodzianowski was a promising American cruiserweight from South Chicago with a record of 13 professional wins, when in the summer of 1984, while on a motor-cycle tour, he was involved in an accident with serious consequences. The lower part of his right leg had to be amputated. Through the exercise of supreme willpower—and with the aid of a cutting-edge prosthesis—he returned to the ring in December 1985. He soon appeared on several ratings lists, and after 28 contests (24 wins, 1 draw), in July 1990 he got a chance at the title. In this contest Bodzianowski clearly lost on points to WBA champ Robert Daniels. However, he made an impressive mark as a courageous fighter who did not permit two broken ribs to stop him fighting on.

Such incredible stories are sentimental favorites in the chronicles of a sport where everything is geared to the principle of self-assertion. And who better personifies the motto "Never quit!" than a successful athlete who has been disadvantaged from the very start?

A stiff knee-joint did not hold the Hawaiian Tami Mauriello back from a career in the ring.

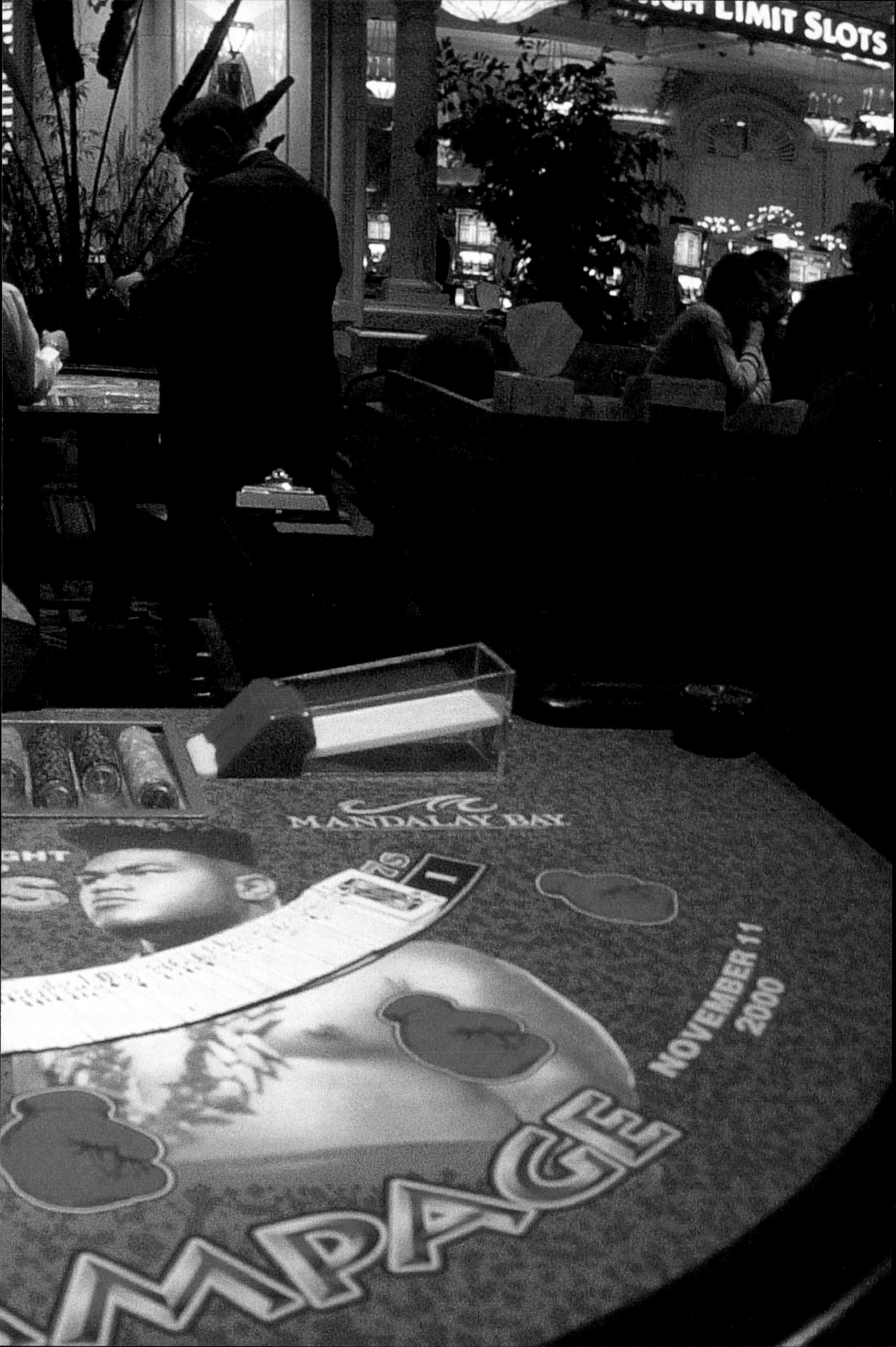

THE BUSINESS

THE IMPRESARIOS

The art of presentation: promoter Don King in 1996, with a cardboard figure of Mike Tyson *(above)*, Lennox Lewis and Michael Grant in 2000 *(opposite page)*.

"Never say 'No' before you hear the price"

HYPE AND GLORY

"The next fight is always the greatest, the most important, the decider, the fight not to be missed on any account." This the evergreen publicity for prize-boxing that in earlier times was spread by barkers, and is now circulated by fax or on the Internet. It does not matter that the ballyhoo and *bragadoccio* only communicate a vague promise. In show business, the publicity is the seduction process: it is what transforms the fight into a major public occasion. The hype creates the radiance in which victors shine and glitter like heroes. Today, this hype is the sum of the efforts of many who pull the strings in boxing. There are the managers who build their fighters up into larger-than-life figures, apparently sprung from the world of comic book superheroes—people with evocative and menacing names such as "Bonecrusher," "Lights Out," "The Blade," or "Razor." There are the promoters who stylize the duel of the fighters at the top of the card into a summit meeting of embittered rivals—a showdown that can leave the road to the top open for only one of the two adversaries. And then there are the TV stations, both public-service and commercial, that have for some time now presented these events with flashy advertising and just as highly-charged catch-phrases ("The Challenge," "Risky Business," "For Pride and Country"). They, along with their partners and co-workers, the matchmakers, booking agents and event managers in the halls and hotel casinos, form the hard core of a business where strident come-ons and gigantomaniac projections are the stuff of everyday life. The talk is always of the rising superstar, the next megafight, cross-road fight or, at the very least, "the fight of the century." And this is not so much an option as an obligation in a sport that more than any other has dedicated itself to sensation—and where the advice still holds good, as the promoter Pete Ashlock once said, "never say 'No' before you hear the price."

Jack Solomons Promotion.
FOR THE LIGHT HEAVYWEIGHT CHAMPIONSHIP OF THE WORLD.
WHITE CITY JULY 26TH 1948

The Promoters

CRANKING UP THE CASH

"Sitting behind a desk, smoking a fat cigar and drinking whiskey all night long" This was how the former light heavyweight champion Mike Rossman, who should have known better, described the accepted idea of the average working day of a boxing promoter. The widely believed cliché of the laid-back, pleasure-loving cynic persists today, because it goes along with naïve perceptions of the influential stringpuller in this sport, and because the at times grandiose appearances of earlier successful personalities, from James W. Coffroth ("Sunny Jim"), by way of Herman "Muggsy" Taylor to the British promoter Jack Solomons obviously reinforce this image.

The daily schedule of the modern boxing promoter leaves little time for casual whiskey consumption. As the organizer of professional boxing events, the impresario, in co-operation with others, or with members of his own organization, must concentrate on planning and arranging these occasions—even when the details are delegated to technical directors or managerial staff. In addition, he must take care of the promotion of the event itself, which means ensuring a high public interest and awareness. The ballyhoo created by press conferences, poster campaigns etc. is in the final analysis a major influence on the popular success of the night. This is reflected in the "live gate," the total take from ticket sales at the venue that usually constitutes the only source of finance for a fight-night when no TV broadcasters are involved.

For long-term success, he must be prepared to take risks and to have a considerable fund of PR ideas and skills. The pioneers of the modern boxing business possessed both these qualities in good measure. The legendary Tex Rickard (1871–1929), a former gold prospector and gambler, succeeded in creating spectacular publicity for his first fight-night. In 1906, when he brought Joe Gans and Battling Nelson to the mining town of Goldfield in Nevada to contest the world lightweight championship for an astounding joint purse of $30,000, he put the entire amount on display in business premises in the town, stacked up in piles of $20 gold coins.

This attracted huge attention, and 8,000 spectators turned up for the event, which earned Rickard a record take for that time of $70,000.

It rapidly became a tradition in boxing promotion to talk long and loud about the huge sums at stake in an event. Another such tradition was started by Sunny Jim Coffroth, who gave the fighters at the top of the fight-card a cut of the gate-money. Both Coffroth and Rickard understood that as long-term a relationship as possible with an attractive titleholder was good insurance for their business. Just as Tex Rickard became boxing's first tycoon in the years after World War I through an exclusive partnership with Jack Dempsey, so Mike Jacobs prospered in the 1930s through the efforts of his crowd-puller Joe Louis and the International Boxing Club dominated the 1950s with the rise of Rocky Marciano. Those who really want to be big in boxing must sign up great fighters and then build them into larger-than-life champions.

It has become standard practice for promoters to tie future stars and their managers to long-term contracts. Because of this, they often maintain their own stables of boxers, financed by the take from events and any potential TV deals. And in the main, they are not inclined to overmuch modesty, and usually beat the drum loudly for their own enterprise. They announce lucrative deals that do not always materialize, or stage-manage dramatic public appearances for their hopefuls. Much more often than strictly necessary, however, promoters such as Don King, that most famous of boxing tycoons, relate wild tales from their own personal path to success. That truth occasionally comes second to the compulsion to gain attention was once verified by King's rival, Bob Arum. "Yesterday I was lying," Arum corrected himself to the press: "Today I am telling the truth." Arum and King represent the circus ringmaster tendency in boxing promotion. More recent success stories, such as those of the South African Cedric Kushner, the German Wilfried Sauerland, or Frank Warren in Britain show that, even in the brash world of the sweet science, quieter approaches can be successful, too.

Boxing promoters like the British Jack Solomons *(opposite page)* and the American Russell Peltz *(above)* come across as self-made men who are also men of the world.

TEX RICKARD
THE FIRST TYCOON

He was an adventurer with solid principles, a gambler and a pioneer—and it is precisely this blend that allowed him and his sport to prosper in a pioneering era. "Tex", as everyone called him, was not just simply the dominant promoter of his time. He was also the first real tycoon, who helped pro boxing progress to a completely new dimension. Whatever successes were achieved in the sport in the first three decades of the twentieth century, in one way or another they always had something to do with Rickard.

Born in 1871 in Missouri, and raised in West Texas, George Lewis Rickard quit school early to work as a stockman and contribute to the support of his family. He then tried his luck as a young rancher in Brazil, as a town marshal in Texas and as moderately successful gold prospector and hotel owner in Alaska. Shortly after this, he also opened a hotel and gaming hall in Goldfield, Nebraska, and let it be known that he was ready to put on a "fight-night" to increase the status of the small town. Rickard did this in fine style: in 1906 he used the handsome sum of $30,000 to attract the lightweight champion Joe Gans and his challenger Battling Nelson to Goldfield, enthusiastically drummed up publicity and finally achieved a record-breaking take at the event itself of $70,000. Four years later, in Reno, he set a new gate record of $270,000 for the heavyweight world championship bout between James J. Jeffries and Jack Johnson.

Rickard had minimized his personal financial risk by selling advance film rights to the fight and by borrowing money together with other business partners. In this way, he was able to outdo all competitors to his offers. And just as he had done earlier in Goldfield, in Reno he exploited racist tendencies for his own ends, by setting up the duel as a matter of honor between men of different skin colors.

Tex Rickard found both the money and the arguments to persuade the champion Jess Willard (top far left, with Rickard) to a risky title defense against his protégé Jack Dempsey. The last photo taken before his death in 1928 shows the crafty businessman as a jovial family man.

His skillful, sometimes uninhibited orchestration of public expectations then took Rickard with his megastar Jack Dempsey to the championship. Having meanwhile moved to New York, in 1921 Rickard set up an unequal duel between "Steamhammer Jack" and the European lightweight champion Georges Carpentier as a symbolic war of the continents. Over 80,000 spectators came to the fight in Jersey City; they bought tickets to the total value of $1.8 million. This was to be the first of a total of five seven-figure takes that the promoter was to achieve by 1927 with the help of his main crowd-puller.

Rickard never actually concluded a contract with Dempsey, a fact that the boxer later confirmed in his memoirs. The correct payment of the purse and the share of the gate was a matter of honor for the promoter. The more consistently Rickard increased his ticket prices, the more time he had to devote to the magazine *The Ring* that he co-founded, and its ratings lists that he personally compiled from 1925 on. As the leaseholder of Madison Square Garden, in the very same year he invested in a new arena, constructed on a different site; this was "The house that Tex built" (Madison Square Garden, version two). The tireless impresario constantly cultivated his contacts in leading social circles, without at any point losing his feel for the mood of the average boxing fan. His creed was: "Give folks what they want, how they want it, and not what you think they want." Towards the end of his glory years in the 1920s, Rickard concentrated on persuading Jack Dempsey to make a comeback, and on extending his business interests to Florida and Great Britain. But on January 6, 1929, in Miami, he died of peritonitis. By this time, boxing had become established as a socially acceptable and lucrative public sport in the grand style—Rickard's style.

At the news of Rickard's death in 1929, all the flags on his building, Madison Square Garden —popularly known as "The house that Tex built"— were lowered to half-mast. The entry of his coffin into the arena in New York was attended by thousands.

TOP DOGS AND GLOBAL PLAYERS

THE EIGHT TOP PROMOTION ORGANIZATIONS

AMERICA PRESENTS, INC.

In the 1990s, in a relatively short space of time, the former media manager Mat Tinley and his partner Dan Goosen, already experienced in the fight game, joined the big players in the boxing business in America. Determination and a generous financial cushion allowed the young Denver-based company to buy in a whole stable of boxers from athletes who had taken part in the 1996 Olympic Games in Atlanta (David Reid, later David Tua) and from the ranks of already developed champions (Miguel Angel Gonzalez, Bernard Hopkins, Mike Tyson). Their residual risks were secured by an exclusive contract with the U.S. broadcasting network Fox Sports. After Goosen left the company (in 2001), Tinley's organization ran into difficulties.

DON KING PRODUCTIONS

Often regarded with hostility and from time to time linked with shady maneuvering behind the scenes, Don King can nevertheless claim to be in the top rank of his business. The best known promoter in the world, he has presented more than 300 title fights since the 1970s, including innumerable classics with such stars as Ali, Holmes, Foreman, Chavez and Tyson, and he has staged dazzling landmark events with as many as six world title bouts and 130,000 spectators. In 1999, King almost compensated for the loss of Tyson by staging the two multi-million dollar Lewis vs. Holyfield title fights, and by the rise of his protégé Felix Trinidad to the rank of best boxer pound-for-pound.

CEDRIC KUSHNER PROMOTIONS

During the final decade of the twentieth century, Cedric Kushner advanced with relative calm and considerable diligence to become one of the major players. A resident on Long Island, the South African originally managed Fleetwood Mac and other pop music acts, before gaining his first sports successes with boxing shows in Chicago and through the IBF heavyweight champion Tony Tucker. His excellent international connections have brought him co-promotion shares in over 150 title fights. He has marketed these at intercontinental level through his own television company, CK Sports Network, as he did with his USA-wide fight series of heavyweight bouts, the *Heavyweight Explosion*.

MAIN EVENTS, INC.

An aura of fairness and decency surrounds the boxing organization that the Duva clan took to the top over a period of four decades. Until very recently, the driving force of this family-led company was the patriarch Lou Duva, a former amateur pugilist and trucker, who early on in his career as a manager and trainer hit upon the idea of signing the best talent from the Olympic Games. The breakthrough came with the class of 1984, from which four students (Mark Breland, Meldrick Taylor, Pernell Whitaker and Evander Holyfield) became champions. Further outstanding amateurs, namely Vernon Forrest, Zab Judah and Fernando Vargas, were brought on to join the world professional elite. However, Lou and his son Dino left the business in 2001, and Gary Shaw now runs the company.

SPORTS NETWORK LTD.

Like almost no other promoter in the younger generation, the Londoner Frank Warren has profited from the new spirit of the times. A substantial deal in the 1980s with the private television company ITV allowed this businessman to enjoy a meteoric rise almost without parallel in the boxing business. In the 1990s, Warren surpassed his sometimes elderly competitors within the UK, and put on several WBO title-fight shows to popular acclaim. The legal consequences of his dispute with his former partner Don King, and the loss of his star Prince Naseem Hamed caused him to falter for a short time. But the "Comeback Kid" came back into the game at the end of the 1990s with Mike Tyson's British appearances and his first engagements in the USA.

TEIKEN PROMOTIONS, INC.

On the extremely lively South-East Asian boxing scene, there are a number of hard-working promoters. But there is only one tycoon—Akihiko Honda. This always eloquent manager and promoter has more than 30 pros in his Teiken Gym stable in Tokyo, and his promotion company stages the majority of high-end boxing events in Japan, including many international title fights. The influence and contacts of this "finest gentleman in boxing" (*Boxing Digest*) extend over the whole of the Pacific region (Thailand, Philippines) and as far as America. There, not least because of the lucrative Japanese TV deals that he can facilitate, he has become a most favored business partner. An end to his privileged position is apparently not in sight.

TOP RANK

Throughout decades of constant rivalry, Bob Arum, Harvard graduate and former lawyer, has risen to become Don King's closest competitor. This sharp-witted New Yorker founded his promotion company in 1986, in the early days of Las Vegas' role as the new boxing Mecca. It was here that he served up to a discerning public a regular feast of the best and most charismatic boxers, from Sugar Ray Leonard to Oscar De La Hoya. His sure showman's instinct led him to enjoy particularly popular success in the 1990s, staging the "oldie" George Foreman and the overweight four-round Champ "Butterbean." Despite the loss of his star of many years' standing, Oscar De La Hoya, Arum continues to do good business with Floyd Mayweather Jr. and Diego Corrales.

UNIVERSUM BOX-PROMOTION

Unlike his perennial rival Wilfried Sauerland, Klaus-Peter Kohl, a German businessman involved in mass-market catering, decided to pursue a determinedly international concept after securing long-term television contracts. Since then, it seems that boxers from half the United Nations gather in his Hamburg gym, and Kohl can draw upon the stars among them (Artur Grigorian, Istvan Kovacs, Dariusz Michalczewski, Juan Carlos Gomez and the Klitschko brothers) to stage big fights month after month. As a result, this ambitious self-made man, who also looks after the interests of the three women world champions Michele Aboro, Regina Halmich, and Daisy Lang, has become the most influential promoter in Europe.

HOW A FIGHT IS MADE

Promoter Jack Solomons *(center back)* and his partners watch as Bos Murphy *(left)* and Lew Lazar sign their fight contracts in 1955.

It usually starts with a promoter hiring a matchmaker to put together the pairings for a pro-boxing night—this might be George, a matchmaker from London who now has the job of finding a couple of genuine touchstones, and several possibly less genuine, for from four to seven of the promoter's protégés. George then calls all the gyms he knows, from Glasgow down to Brighton, hoping to strike paydirt quickly. If he is lucky in his prospecting, he then has to cut the manager of the gym and the boxer's personal manager—and they are not necessarily the same person—in on the purse. When he chases after overseas opponents, George will usually link up with a local insider, a booking agent, to act for him. The booking agent can then go to a local promoter, personal manager, or even both, to find the right boxer. And once again, this means George must in

some cases find from his agreed purse cuts for three, maybe four middlemen—and this does not take into account any shares for trainers or other handlers.

The so-called fight contract is then concluded between the promoter and, if appropriate, the booking agents and management of the boxer, and together with all necessary documentation, such as licenses or permissions from an overseas organization, HIV-test, and other medical certification, it is submitted to the regulatory body by the weigh-in at the very latest. This body must then approve (in technical terminology "sanction") the fight. The contract can set upper weight limits, that is, a heavyweight can be required to appear at the weigh-in with a bodyweight between specific limits. In the case of title-fight contracts, it is usual to include a rematch

clause, and for there to be covert agreements, so-called options. For example, it is possible to have a contractual requirement that when a titleholder is defeated, his management will receive a cut of the take from a number of the new champion's future fights. Without agreeing to such options, a challenger may never get a chance at the title, at least in the case of voluntary title defense. In cases of a compulsory title defense against the number one contender from the applicable rankings list, only the right to promote the event is at stake. If both promoters want to stage the fight independently, they must enter a bidding war, to provide the best guaranteed purse to both fighters. This means that whoever offers the most gets the promotion rights and, of course, the opportunity to earn big bucks.

DON KING

ONLY IN AMERICA

An electrifying artwork of a shock of hair, baroque burlesques of public appearances, draped in gold jewelry, and an ongoing weakness for hidden treachery—these are the few stylistic tricks that Donald "Don" King has played up to the hilt over the past three decades on his way to becoming the most significant, most influential and the most hated promoter of his time. Wherever the most famed impresario in the world bobs up, he personifies the world of this at times dubious multi-million dollar sport. His career has been a classic of the "Only in America" brand, as he himself never tires of pointing out.

After graduating from high school in the 1950s, he became one of the major figures on the gambling scene in the East Side ghettos of his hometown Cleveland, Ohio. "Donald the Kid" was a powerful numbers racket "czar," who did not shrink from violence to protect his interests. In 1954, he shot dead in a dispute a certain Hillary Brown, and in court successfully pled self-defense against an armed intruder. However, twelve years later, out on the street, he kicked to death Sam Garrett, who owed him money. King had already served three and a half years of his sentence for this homicide when in 1971, while in the Marion State Correctional Institution, he heard a radio report of the first duel between Joe Frazier and Muhammad Ali. His enthusiasm for boxing was immediately kindled, as was his desire to become the czar of this business too, once he was released.

Good friends in the entertainment industry helped smooth the way for the ex-con to meet Ali—and this led indirectly to his first boxing presentation. In 1972 the former world champion starred in a couple of exhibition sparring bouts at a charity gala organized by Don King. Shortly afterwards, King became the manager of his first ranking pro, Ernie Shavers, a world title contender. His real international breakthrough came in 1975, when the underrated outsider was able to pull in from organizations close to the Mobutu regime in Zaire a record purse of $10 million for a world title bout between George Foreman and Ali. This megaevent in Kinshasa established King as a new big player in the business, a position that was soon secured by the rise of his protégé Larry Holmes, who became champion in 1978.

Like so many pros who came after him, Holmes one day discovered massive fraud in the calculation of his purse. But even the world champion, a feared figure in the ring, decided against legal action and allowed himself to be bought off on the installment plan. The same or similar experiences were to be relived later by Tim Witherspoon, Terry Norris, Julio Cesar Chavez, and last but not least, Mike Tyson, who were all snared by the promoter's persuasive

rhetoric and tempting promises. King's political pose as a soul brother serving the interests of his fellow African Americans was a means to an end. If the payoff was big enough, he was prepared to take his reigning champions to South Africa in defiance of the international anti-apartheid boycott. Dollars rather than political principles were the deciding factor. "When you've got a quarter, he wants the first 26 cents of it," said the ex-pro Tex Cobb once, speaking of King.

The obsessively hardworking promoter has, over the years, bought himself a rich collection of boxing talent and knows how to boost them up through the ratings lists of the world sanctioning bodies. His charges have more than

once been the beneficiaries of controversial decisions in title bouts. After the loss of his imprisoned golden goose Mike Tyson, it seemed for a time in the 1990s as if his grip on the business was slackening. Then this wizard of survival managed to conjure up two new heavyweight champions, Oliver McCall and Bruce Seldon, who allowed him to stay in the game. However, his situation soon became precarious once again. For his comeback, Tyson broke with

King, and, with the exception of Felix Trinidad, the promoter's stable contained no up-and-coming superstars in the lower weight limits.

With more than 300 title fights behind him, one might think that by the end of his seventh decade (in 2001) Donald "Don" King might just have earned enough to retire. But this workaholic has still not even begun to slacken off. Neither have the investigators from the tax authorities and the FBI, who have this manipulator, who was granted a pardon for earlier misdemeanors, in their sights on suspicion of several cases of evasion and deception. Like highly focused boxers in the ring, they are ready and waiting to pounce on his next mistake.

True to his jovial image: "Teflon Don" and the entourage of the light middleweight champion Keith Holmes.

The Managers
SHARKS AND PATRIARCHS

The most popular argument for the need for managers in boxing is the un-worldliness of their charges. In a business world dominated by sharks and hyenas, so it is argued, there is a need for professional negotiators who are fluent in shark and hyena. The assistance of these mediators allows the athletes to concentrate on the sport itself, without worrying about the business details. Bill Cayton, who with his partner Jim Jacobs looked after the careers and bank accounts of Wilfred Benitez, Vinny Pazienza, and the young Mike Tyson, was convinced that "hardly any guys under thirty understand anything about money." He also firmly believed that "a boxer who thinks he can be his own manager is his own worst enemy."

The most popular argument against the need for managers in boxing is a long tradition of bad experiences, closely followed by the desire of some enlightened boxers to take their fate into their own hands. All too often, simpler-minded boxers have suffered as a result of large or small maneuvers used

British managers such as Frank Maloney *(above, with Lennox Lewis)* and Bill Faversham *(below)* always figure in the ranks of loyal supporters.

by their managers to cheat and exploit them. Even Jack Dempsey, at the peak of his career, split with Jack "Doc" Kearns, as crafty as he was notorious, because he felt he had been taken for a sucker. Managers are keen to hug their boxers as long as they are successful, but once their protégés lose their titles, those same managers rapidly disappear, never to be seen again. This is how the cliché of the disloyal exploiter who only subscribes to his own self-interest has developed. "Never have so few taken so many for so much," as the former junior welterweight Saoul Mamby once put it.

In real life, both managerial extremes exist—as does a broad spectrum in between. Which is why a young professional might get lucky and be snapped up by one of the "good" sharks. François Descamps was a manager and partner of great integrity who looked after the French boxing hero Georges Carpentier for more than 18 years of his professional boxing career. The New Yorker Gil Clancy looked after Emile Griffith as a coach and manager for all of his 109 pro fights (1958–77). Cus D'Amato acted like an adoptive father in the same capacity for José Torres and Floyd Patterson. And when the legendary manager Bob Foster died in 1994, he left everything he had to his former star pupil and sole heir, Jimmy McLarnin, who had been world champion at welterweight from 1933–35. All these men, and many other stringpullers, saw themselves part of a symbiotic success relationship with their charges, and felt a corresponding sense of duty.

"The best possible for my boy, and 20 (or 25) percent of that for me." This is the motto guiding managers when they negotiate deals for their boxers with event organizers, promoters and where appropriate, with television networks.

Sometimes the manager and the promoter, or as previously mentioned the trainer, are one and the same person. And as far as the "better" sharks in the business are concerned, they all have the same aim as Frank Maloney, partner of the heavyweight champion Lennox Lewis. In an interview, the inimitable Londoner

At the side of James Toney, Jackie Kallen became a rare example of a successful woman in professional boxing management.

The eloquent Shelly Finkel worked discreetly in the background for Mike Tyson.

declared that he had "two ambitions: to make Lennox Lewis the most successful sportsman of all time, and to see Lennox retire unbeaten."

Maloney is a prime example of how managers of today no longer feel the need to present themselves as the patriarchs of their athletes. Several of the more experienced successful pros are now looking for a different kind of business relationship. In the 1990s, Roy Jones Jr., a superstar in both middleweight and light heavyweight divisions, hired a lawyer to represent him in contract negotiations, rather than a manager. In recent years, Evander Holyfield, Oscar De La Hoya and other intelligent champions have acted in a similar manner. As in the past, however, it is important to choose the right people for the job—no matter what they are called.

THE MOB IN THE FIGHT BUSINESS

They use a piece of water pipe (…) and they take just an ordinary piece of newspaper, you know, newspaper don't show no fingerprints (…) and they try to hit you twice, and they finish you with two if they can. Anyway, they give you two and split you, break your skull."

This was how the go-between William Daly described to the promoter Jackie Leonard in Los Angeles in May 1959 what happened to "naughty boys" who would not cooperate with people in certain circles. Mr. Daly knew what he was talking about: he was a member of the International Boxing Club (IBC) in New York, dissolved because of its illegal monopoly, and was a close confidant of the Mafia capo Frankie Carbo. In April 1959, Carbo had sent Virgil Akins, a boxer controlled by one of his frontmen, to the West Coast to defend his title against Don Jordan. On this occasion, Jordan, who was backed by Leonard and his friend Donald Nesseth, won the fight, and neither of the victor's backers now wanted to remember the pre-fight agreement—that if his boy lost the title, Frankie Carbo was to get a cut of Jordan's purse.

Daly was completely unaware that his detailed report of his employer's methods was being taped with the assistance of a concealed microphone. In the end, it was this involuntary statement that helped to break

Promoter Jackie Leonard *(left)* and manager Don Nesseth were threatened at the end of the 1950s by the Mafia. They refused to cut Frankie Carbo in on Don Jordan's purse. The middleman William Daly *(below)* was severely beaten up. He is shown here in hospital being questioned by reporters.

one of the most unscrupulous and powerful rings in modern boxing history. Four months after this recording was made, the State Attorney's Office in Los Angeles brought charges against Carbo and his accomplices for conspiracy to extort. One and a half years later, severe prison sentences took the leaders of these illegal cartels out of the game. Never before had it been possible to demonstrate so clearly the infiltration of the sport by the mobsters.

The maneuvers described were, however, no novelty. Ever since the time that the business of betting on the results of important fights began to flourish in parallel with the sport itself, dubious tie-ups and arrangements between groups have continued to come to light. The kings of this shadowy world were in sympathy with the boxers, who, like them, were almost complete social outcasts, and they also scented the possibility of vast profit margins. In 1933, with the giant-sized Primo Carnera, the Mafiosi first succeeded in developing a heavyweight world champion. Two frontmen for the feared mobsters Owen "Owney" Madden and Dutch Schultz persisted in pushing the only moderately talented Italian onward to the championship through a string of fixed fights and unusual disqualification victories.

The mob only developed a controlling interest with the appearance of Paul John

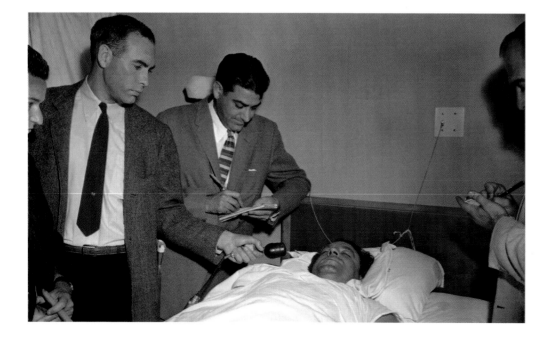

"Frankie" Carbo, also known as "The Gray" or "The Underworld Commissioner for Boxing." Carbo, an upstart from the Lucchese family in New York, controlled through his enforcer Frank "Blinky" Palermo and other frontmen almost all the champions and title contenders from lightweight through to light heavyweight. In this enterprise, he also worked with the equally avaricious James Norris, who was chairman of the International Boxing Club and had considerable interests in various arenas. Norris, with the protection of his silent partner Carbo, built up a monopoly position through the IBC, which in effect made his club the only organizer of title fights and the sole organization to profit from lucrative broadcasting rights. In the 1950s, anyone who wanted to fight for a world title had to do so in arenas controlled by Norris, and with a manager from Carbo's clique—or there would be no championship bout.

This rigged game was upset in 1952 when the anti-trust authorities in New York moved against the IBC's practices. But two years later, a district court declined to open proceedings. After a long wrangle over areas of judicial competency, Norris' club was eventually convicted of persistent offenses against the right to free competition and its previously overweening powers were reduced to

a bare minimum. In 1960–61, the hearings of a U.S. Senate sub-committee on corruption in boxing, the so-called Kefauver Hearings, did what remained to be done to make the abuses of power in the sport public knowledge. Former champions such as Jake LaMotta and Ike Williams testified that they had been respectively successfully and unsuccessfully offered bribes by Carbo's middlemen to deliberately lose fights.

In February 1961, Frankie Carbo was sentenced to 25 years imprisonment for his attempted extortion in connection with the Akins vs. Jordan world championship fight. Palermo got 15 years, two-thirds of which he actually served, and their accomplices received similar terms. At least for a short time thereafter boxing was granted a breathing space.

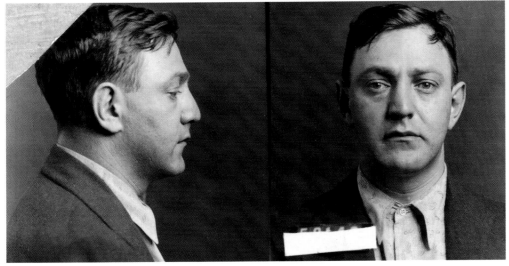

Proceedings in a New York district court should have put Frankie Carbo (top) behind bars. In earlier years, Dutch Schultz (above) had manipulated the boxing business. Police photo, 1935

SONNY, BLINKY, PEP AND THE OTHERS

A CHAMPION IN THE HANDS OF THE MAFIA

In retrospect, it is difficult to know if he ever had a chance of a different kind of life. Charles "Sonny" Liston could not really have imagined so, anyway. The future world champion became so quickly and unwittingly a part of the underworld around him that there could have been no question of a more honorable option. And as he had risen under these conditions, even had he wished to, he could not have shaken off his minders. The case of Liston became a lesson in how a boxer can fall into the hands of the mob.

Few people were waiting for the illiterate young delinquent in 1952 on his release from the State Prison in Jefferson City, Missouri. Only a boxing trainer in his home town of St. Louis, and one Frank W. Mitchell, editor of the *St. Louis Argus,* a man at home in all spheres of society. This notorious gambler used his secret links to local mobster John Vitale to get work for Sonny. But soon Vitale and the equally dubious underworld king "Big" Barney Baker were also using the bull-like strength of the amateur boxer to carry out leg-breaker

Above: *Blinky Palermo* (left) *had already looked after the career of welterweight Johnny Saxton, before he found Sonny Liston.*
Left: *Sonny's manager Pep Barone (with Liston) was Palermo's frontman.*

jobs—to jog the memories of certain people about overdue payments or other kinds of debt. Not long after, Liston, who had recently crossed over to the ranks of pro boxers, became the property of those moving in Mafia circles.

Vitale had forced Mitchell out of his contract with his protégé and had carved up the Liston cake among his associates: 52 percent for the inevitable Frankie Carbo, 24 percent for Joseph "Pep" Barone, who was to be Liston's manager, and 12 percent each for Carbo's close associate Frank "Blinky" Palermo and for Vitale himself. With the boxer's move to Philadelphia in 1958, Palermo got the job of looking after Liston on behalf of the other shareholders. Blinky did this so well that he soon won the trust of the pro. Whenever the occasionally volatile Liston came into conflict with the law in Philadelphia, Palermo and his friends helped him out of tight corners. This is why Sonny, who paid little mind to the financial details of his contracts, was happy to be associated with them. Later, when the Senate Investigating Committee asked if he knew Frank Palermo, Liston denied this firmly on several occasions, and it was only after continued persistent questioning that a light seemed to come on for Liston:

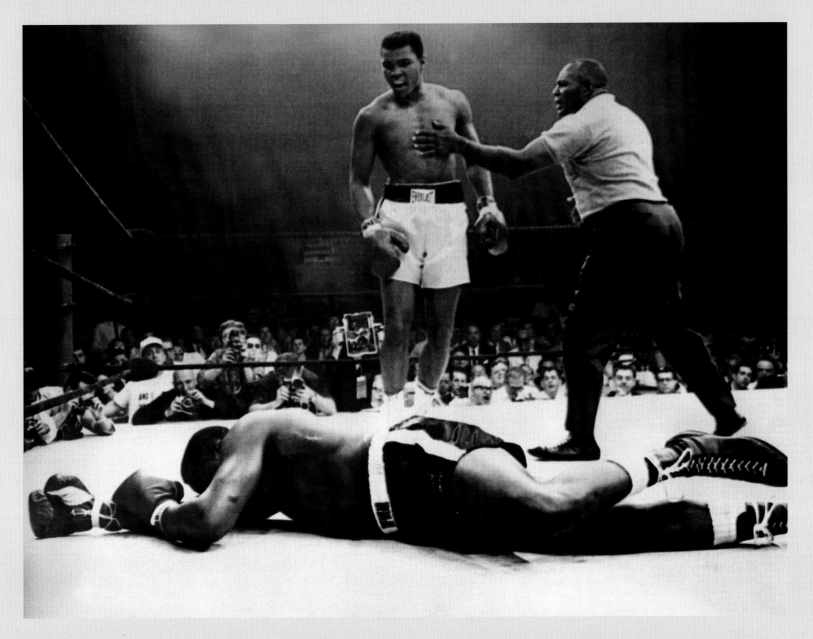

When Liston was knocked out in the first round of his return fight with Muhammad Ali in Lewiston in 1965, there was widespread speculation about fixing. To this day, however, there has been no conclusive evidence for this.

"You mean Blinky. Yeah, I know Blinky. Everybody knows him." With the clean-up in boxing, Liston's shady connections soon became obsolete. To get a professional license from the Pennsylvania Boxing Commission, the pro had to officially change over from Pep Barone to a licensed boxing manager. When he applied for permission for a world title fight against Floyd Patterson in New York in the spring of 1962, the application was rejected. The authorities there had good reason to doubt that he had cut himself free from his old ties. The fight was staged in Chicago instead, and Liston won by a KO in the first round. At last, the Mafia owned the most prestigious of all the boxing

champions, even if they did have to control him indirectly, through middlemen. Meanwhile, Frankie Carbo had been jailed for 25 years and Palermo was to follow him soon after. Both continued to issue their directives, but now from their prison cells.

Their grip on the world champion loosened a little after Liston lost his title to Muhammad Ali in 1964, and a year later lost the rematch. The circumstances surrounding this second defeat gave rise to much speculation, which has never been cleared up, about fixing and manipulation. The only sure thing afterwards was that without his title, Liston became just one

of the many boxers who continue to fight purely for the sake of the money, in his particular case right up until 1970. In 1966, he moved to Las Vegas, where he gathered round him the usual mix of gamblers, big shots, and dreamers. On the evening of January 5, 1971, his wife Geraldine found him dead in their bedroom. The scenario seemed very like that of a fatal drug overdose, but rumors of a hushed-up killing went around. Whatever actually happened, the mystery of his demise seemed fitting. "He was riding a fast, dark train to nowhere," wrote Nick Tosches in his biography of the tragic champion, "and at the end of the line, it tipped him out down this slope."

Al Weill's *(left)* skillful matchmaking was his personal contribution to world champion Rocky Marciano's impeccable career.

Matchmakers and Booking Agents
THE ARCHITECTS

In the red corner, we have the former champion of the United States of America (or the Italian master), and in the blue corner the youngster from Puerto Rico (or the experienced Slovakian)—announcements such as these ring out on fight-nights everywhere, from Miami to Marsala. Behind this façade is concealed the painstaking and wearisome work of the matchmakers and booking agents. They are the architects of this multi-national business: whatever the program offers, they have designed and laid the foundations for it.

It all starts when a matchmaker is hired by a promoter, or by a local impresario to put together pairs of fighters, or matches. As a rule, he has to find opponents for boxers in his client's "stable" or from the territory of the impresario. And, of course, he must find suitable pros to match the development levels of the "house fighters." So, he will not, for instance, match a world-class pugilist against

a novice, or a title contender with a fighter who is over the hill. Along with the caliber of an opponent, his style must also be taken into account—and the question of whether such a duet will deliver an attractive and not too one-sided fight.

Notable matchmakers like Al Weill or the unsurpassable Teddy Brenner had a gift for long-range spotting of a potential match and the chutzpah to keep in mind not just the interests of their clients, but those of the public as well. "Brenner worked with managers, but never for them," was how *The Ring* once hailed the king of Madison Square Garden. "He didn't protect the boxers, and dozens of hopefuls who sought the spotlight in the end wished they had never jumped into the most famous ring in the world."

As even the wiliest of insiders could not know all the pro boxers in the worldwide fight game, nor be in a position to engage

them directly, matchmakers often enlist the help of booking agents. At least within their own countries, booking agents can draw on invaluable stores of local knowledge and contacts with managers and trainers that enable them to identify opponents of the required quality. By the time a fight contract is concluded, it is not unusual for three, four or even more middlemen to be involved, and they all have to get their percentage. Entire chains of such working relationships exist, developed over vast distances and over many years and even decades, and based entirely on trust. No other business in the world of competitive sport is more old-fashioned and laborious in its methods, but none is more dependent on personal relationships than the boxing business, where verbal agreements and contracts sealed with a handshake still count for as much as those with official stamps and signatures.

TEDDY BRENNER

STYLES MAKE FIGHTS

As is the case in any other trade, in pro boxing there are moderate, good and very good matchmakers—and Teddy Brenner, their undisputed king. For twenty years this gifted boxing expert pulled together the bill of fare for the fight cards in New York's Madison Square Garden, using a simple but effective method: he first asked himself if he personally would like to see this or that fight. He thought like a fan, and for other fans and served up with particular relish "close-run" contests between opponents of almost equal standing. His motto for this skillful craft—styles make fights—still prevails today.

Born in New York in 1917, the former shirt salesman quickly became involved in the world of boxing, which in the period immediately after the end of World War II was straining at its seams with activity. From 1947 on, Brenner put together fights in New Jersey for his friend, the manager Irving Cohen; in Manhattan he helped the Madison Square Garden matchmaker Al Weill. In addition, he booked boxers for the St. Nicholas Arena on the West Side, which soon, and not least due to his efforts, won the unofficial title of "House of Upsets." His great era really began in 1957, when he became chief matchmaker for Madison Square Garden—where he was to remain for the next twenty years, until 1978.

Whether it was Floyd Patterson, Cassius Clay, Joey Giardello, Nino Benvenuti, or Roberto Duran—Brenner found opponents for these boxing greats who offered them a real challenge rather than an easy ride. In the person of Joey Banks he served up to the young Cassius Clay for his eleventh professional bout a young, dangerous puncher, who even managed to put Clay on the canvas in the very first round. Just as boldly, he matched the universally highly rated contender Benny Huertas against another title contender, Roberto Duran, to see who would come out on top. His judgment on the talent of boxers was "unequalled," according to *The Ring*. "He was the best matchmaker there has ever been," said his pupil and admiring successor, Bruce Trampler. In his own estimation, Trampler profited greatly from Brenner's experience, as it was simply impossible not to learn when in his presence.

Brenner continued his career in the 1980s as a partner in the sports broadcasting company ESPN, which transmitted weekly fights he had arranged. Then he was forced, first by treatment for cancer and then by the pernicious onset of Parkinson's syndrome, to withdraw for longer and longer periods to his New York apartment. In the 1990s, in poor health and confined to a wheelchair, he was seen less and less frequently in public. He permitted only old friends of many years standing to visit him occasionally. Teddy Brenner died at 83 years of age on January 7, 2000 in a New York hospital. He was the father of two children, had five grandchildren, and in the words of American boxing promoter Bob Arum was "a fantastic boxing expert," a fact that he could acknowledge without fear of contradiction.

The next night is always the best: Teddy Brenner in his office at Madison Square Garden.

HIGH ROLLERS AND COMPLIMENTARY SUITES

Wherever enough people pursuing quick success gather together, boxing prospers as a business, especially among like-minded people. At the time of the gold rush in Nevada at the beginning of the twentieth century, the first regional boom of the century got under way. A second boom, this time international in scale, which grew in parallel with the transformation of Las Vegas into the Eldorado of gaming, seemed only logical. Fight fans and gamblers together formed such a significant and economically powerful target group that the desert metropolis was easily able to overtake the previous boxing Mecca of New York. Today, when big title fights are being set up, Las Vegas almost automatically gets first option.

This was by no means clearly predictable in 1955 when the first fight-card worthy of the name was staged, with a fight between Archie Moore and Nino Valdes, at the top of the bill. Up until the mid-1960s, Las Vegas was a small town of some 100,000 citizens and a handful of hotels like the Dunes, the Desert Inn, and the Thunderbird—spaciously constructed hostelries which could from time to time afford to put on worthwhile but not too costly fight-nights. Soon, however, with the rise of Caesar's Palace and other such gigantic complexes came a new generation of resort hotels, which offered organizers a complete event infra-structure package under one roof. Press conferences and weigh-ins could be held here, as could public training rounds and last but by no means least, the fight itself.

Impresarios could in this way save on extra expenses, while the hotel managers gained a new argument in the contest to attract those most high-powered of guests, the so-called high rollers, to their casinos. And lo and behold! Fights drove customers for their hotel beds and their baccarat tables straight into their open arms. And it came to pass that the laws of Nevada specifically allowed for intensive betting activity round the sport. Thus by the end of the 1980s at the latest, boxing world championships had built up cash flow levels that were unachievable anywhere else. The extra revenue directly generated in the greater Las Vegas area by the megafight between Sugar Ray Leonard and Marvin Hagler in April 1987 was calculated at $90 million. The total economic value of the event amounted to an estimated $300 million.

For a considerable time, the MGM Grand, the Mirage, and now also the Mandalay Bay, alongside Caesar's, have become important co-promoters of fight-nights, their long-term planning carried out by highly-paid sports events managers. An example of the fierce ambition which drives the fight for advantage in this area was provided in 1995 by the MGM Grand. The largest hotel resort in Vegas concluded a costly exclusive contract with Mike Tyson just after his release from prison for his next six fights.

But the time of unlimited growth was coming to an end. The once so committed Mirage had to cut back on the extent of its boxing program, and it was not alone. Involvement in the East Coast casino town of Atlantic City began to decline as the Trump Plaza and other hotel giants began to consolidate their position after many years of booming expansion. At the same time, from the mid-1990s on, in Connecticut and elsewhere a whole phalanx of casinos has been set up on the reservation territories of various American Indian Nations. Among these, Foxwoods Resort and Casino, the Mohegan Sun and other hotel complexes run by Native Americans have become widely known as venues for second-ranking title fights. The synergetic attractions of boxing and the gaming tables, at least in America, remain hand in glove.

In 1989, the sold-out open-air arena of the Mirage attracted fans and gamblers to the third fight between Leonard and Duran. Since then, the Mandalay Bay *(top)* and the MGM Grand *(opposite, top)* have generally called the shots on the Las Vegas scene.

CUMULATIVE EFFECTS
THE FINANCIAL DIMENSIONS OF A FIGHT NIGHT IN LAS VEGAS

For the *aficionados* the showdown between middleweight champion "Marvelous" Marvin Hagler and his prominent challenger Sugar Ray Leonard was a long-awaited megafight. But for the organizers and for the Las Vegas area as a whole it also meant megabucks. In cooperation with the event organizer, Caesar's Palace, the promoter at Top Rank and the local tourist authority, *The Ring* magazine put together a breakdown of the expected total revenue generated by the fight.

Ticket sales for the outdoor arena (15,400 seats):	7,9 Mio. $
Betting revenue (34 licensed betting offices):	20–25 Mio. $
Total proceeds from direct sources (tickets, pay-per-view showings, TV broadcasting rights, etc.):	100 Mio. $
Total proceeds from indirect sources (visitor spending in hotels, restaurants and food outlets, casinos, etc.):	300 Mio. $

Scantily clad round card girls in high heels and star announcers with powerful voices, such as Michael Buffer *(opposite page, right)* and Mike Goodall *(opposite page, far right),* have long been indispensable elements of major boxing.

FINE LADIES—HONORABLE GENTLEMEN

The live spectacle of boxing is almost like a trip back in time to a world of yesteryear. However obsolete or bizarre the rituals around the ring may seem, they are always unique. On the giant stage of boxing, pre-ordained conventions and outmoded role models are part of the protocol, so that spectators are almost against their will surrounded by an atmosphere of unavoidable nostalgia. This ambience is all part of the special attraction of a sport that with a light touch succeeds in linking showmanship with tradition.

Great dignity and a sense of ceremony are essential requirements in order to fit the job profile for the live announcer as the highest expression of cultivated manhood. As master of ceremonies, wearing a bow tie and fine tailoring, it is no coincidence that he stands at the very center of events when he announces the main fight. The unchanging salutation to the public ("Ladies and gentlemen …"), the introduction of the officials and the adversaries, along with their fight records and weights, and at international title fights the request to stand for the national anthems—all these contribute elegantly and effectively to the build-up of public suspense.

When the world-famous American Michael Buffer intones his own personal copyright-protected exhortation "Let's get ready to rumble!" the crowd in the arena goes wild.

Announcers made their debut in the ring long before the arrival of the microphone. One somehow knew of the legendary Joe Humphreys that throughout his 50 years of service and with just his own penetrating tones, his voice could fill the arena with sound. After this legend died in 1936, his footsteps were followed by several well-known but lesser figures, such as Harry Balogh, Johnny Addie, Jimmy Lennon Sr., and others. Only in the post-modern TV age have such outstanding announcers as Buffer and Jimmy Lennon Jr. been able to establish themselves as real stars, able to win attractive advertising contracts. Buffer, who has even released his own CD, has become a highly paid advertising partner for the beer giant, Budweiser.

In comparison to this, the attention achieved by the so-called round card girls is fleeting. At the end of the 1950s, these scantily clad models holding their cards up high became a fashionable spot of color, as the glamorous style of Las Vegas began to spread over the rest of the boxing world. Purists in the

sport and feminists have persistently attacked the flirtatious parade of the round card girls, who are usually recruited from model agencies or strip shows. But today what Thomas Hauser wrote specifically of the USA may also be applied to other countries: "Where the country as a whole has become more open to feminism, boxing has gone in entirely the opposite direction." Hauser was reporting on the failed attempt of a promoter to attract the internationally famous models Fawn Hall and Donna Rice with the offer of $25,000 each if they would act as round card girls for the heavyweight world championship contest between Michael Spinks and Gerry Cooney in 1987. In the normal run of events, and at best, things turn out the other way round: the round card girls may possibly attract offers for better-paid engagements in fashion or show business. At least that is the hope that drives many beauties in the United States to enter round card girl contests, sometimes held several days before a fight, in an attempt to win what is only a moderately paid job. In the end, these blondes, brunettes and redheads merely fill the modest role that the male-dominated world of boxing has cast them in—the saucy stunner in high heels.

THE PUBLIC

SPECTATORS AND AFICIONADOS

In the public perception, there are two widely different notions of the average boxing fan. One version has this figure as an endearing, loyal, if somewhat cranky oddball on the wrong side of 40, who fills in the time between fight-nights collecting signed gloves and autograph cards, reading dog-eared illustrated books and the like. He is probably a little out of date, often lower middle-class and most likely to be mild-mannered. In the second version, he is a dubious, sensation-seeking voyeur, whose "eyes light up and neck hair

training sessions and is tolerated as part of the scenery. And then there are the women of all age groups, who in recent years have frequently and unequivocally made their presence felt and often heard. It would, therefore, be a mistake to see the boxing public as a homogenous male grouping of like-minded onlookers. In its striking multi-layered variety, it displays as many social and cultural facets as society itself, and is as temperamental (and often as opportunistic) in its reactions as one could possibly imagine.

to their origins, become symbols of hope for a particular town or region, or even for a whole state. The native Australian Lionel Rose, who from 1968–69 was the first champion to emerge from his race was considered to be punching for all Aborigines, while the American Virgil Hill's long reign as light heavyweight world champion between 1987–91 and 1992–97 unleashed a completely unprecedented wave of boxing euphoria in his sparsely-populated home state of North Dakota. At home in Bismarck, Grand Forks or Rapid Falls, Hill's title defenses regularly turned into public holidays for the "Buffalo State." The largest available venues were sold out in a matter of days, and regional television viewing figures were simply astounding. No less important for Hill was the small but faithful troop of guys from home who followed their local world champion to unfamiliar and sometimes far distant proving grounds. In June 1997, when Hill lost his title to Dariusz Michalczewski in Oberhausen, Germany, later that same night he apologized for his defeat in a speech to the fans who had traveled with him—and thereby earned much acclaim.

However, for some considerable time now, the reactions of disappointed devotees have by no means always been so moderate. In Mexico and elsewhere, victors over local favorites are regularly pelted with drinks cans and other missiles on their way back to the dressing rooms. In October 2000, in Auburn Hills, Detroit, there was a hailstorm of beer glasses when Polish-born Andrew Golota threw in the towel after only three rounds of his duel with Mike Tyson. And toward the end of 1980, the legendary Roberto Duran was forced to discover how rapidly euphoric affection can tip over into unbridled rage. After he had refused to continue the fight during his second contest with Sugar Ray Leonard, in New Orleans, on his return to Panama City his enraged followers smashed the windows of his house and called him a coward and a homosexual. Duran was well aware of the ambivalent nature of the average boxing fan, and therefore had little difficulty in rationalizing these incidents. As the legendary boxer later said: "That's how boxing fans are, today, tomorrow and forever."

In 1996, in the MGM Grand in Las Vegas, British fans show their support for Frank Bruno.

stands on end at the prospect of seeing someone else beaten to a soufflé," as the American journalist Irving Cobb once put it. Of course, these stereotypes do exist in the ringside world, both the calm and steady *aficionado* and the raucous, bloodthirsty rowdy; but they keep company with all conceivable variations in between—the dandy with an enthusiasm for the sport and a penchant for the smoky atmosphere of the smaller venues, the upstart with a retinue from the shadier sectors of society, the aging has-been, the so-called gym rat, who constantly mooches around at

As an audibly present crowd, for the boxer his fans are an integral part of his social identity, as well as a direct stimulus. Their partisan support is rousing, their encouragement inspires. "You'll never know what it's like, if you haven't been in the ring yourself, and the roar is just for you," enthused Sugar Ray Robinson, talking of the following wind he benefited from as the public's favorite. Conversely, the athlete also grants his identity to his supporters, and they see themselves confirmed in his success. This is particularly evident in the case of those pros who, due

The emotions of the spectator make no distinction between "important" and "less important" fights. The young woman (above) at a fairground boxing booth in Newbury, England is just as involved as the crowd in the Welsh capital city, Cardiff in 1994, applauding the ostentatiously staged walk-in of super middleweight champion Chris Eubank. Eubank was to win the contest against his Irish challenger Sam Storey after the fight was stopped in the seventh round— thereby successfully defending his WBO belt for the twelfth time.

WANNABES AND VIPS

Even from its earliest years when prize fighting had a reputation as a spectacle for the common people as well as for the more dubious sectors of society, there have been those among the wealthy and famous who have consistently sought out close contacts with the sport. In England, for instance, sensation-seeking aristocrats mixed with ordinary people at the officially banned bareknuckle fights, held outside the town boundaries; and often it was only their high status that protected them from arrest. In America, respectable business people laid their bets

the heir to the throne: "Pleased to meet you, Prince. If you're ever in Boston, just drop by!"

In the first great boxing boom in the Roaring Twenties, it became the height of fashion just to "drop by." Senators and actors lined the ringside at the fights of the new idol Jack Dempsey. Rudolph Valentino squared up to Dempsey for the photographers, just as the Beatles posed with Muhammad Ali in later years. And the American President Franklin D. Roosevelt made a habit of visiting world championship contenders like Jack Sharkey and Max Schmeling in their training camps. The VIP

the con artists, all prepared to pay sweetly for the opportunity to rub shoulders with the famous. Who else was in a position to pay anywhere from a couple of hundred to several thousand dollars for a seat for an evening—not counting the small change for the stretch limo and a few rounds of sparkling wine or champagne? And not least, it has now become a matter of status to be able to mix with the VIPs at megafights. In this respect, the first showdown between Joe Frazier and Muhammad Ali set new standards. World-class stars like Diana Ross, Dustin Hoffman, and many

In 1996, the soccer star Diego Maradona (right) rounds off his appearance at the General Paz Junior's Club in Cordoba, Argentina in an appropriate manner. Maradona had earlier fought a three-round charity exhibition bout against Santos Lanciar, an ex-champion at flyweight.

Hollywood actor and boxing fan Mickey Rourke (left) tried in 1990 to play an active part in the ring. Despite gaining a degree of respect, his talents do not fit him for a starring role in the sport.

at the ringside along with day laborers and gamblers. The situation in South Africa and Australia was much the same. For many, even before the dawn of the modern era, the world of boxing exerted an attraction even more powerful than all the social restrictions and conventions put together.

This was the case for example with His Majesty King Edward VII, who as the young Prince of Wales invited the reigning world champion John L. Sullivan, on tour in England during the winter of 1887, to demonstrate his pugilistic art in St. James' Barracks. After the rough diamond American and his partner Jack Ashton had boxed a few sparring rounds, he paid his respects in a forthright manner to

area around the ring became larger, and despite the need for more security precautions, the fight organizers welcomed this—after all, to be honored by the presence of such pillars of society meant social acceptability.

The advent of television gave a further boost to the status of the front rows. Genuine boxing fans like Alain Delon and Frank Sinatra used their fame to indulge their taste for the fight game. On the other hand, those with less dedication to pugilism used the publicity at these sporting gala events and hoped to revive their own popularity through walkabouts and other close contacts with the crowd. All these celebrities trailed in their wake a perfumed cloud of the wealthy, the *nouveaux riches,* and

others were literally falling over each other's feet in New York's Madison Square Garden on the evening of March 8, 1971. Burt Lancaster was hired as co-commentator for the live closed-circuit transmission; and Frank Sinatra, alongside all the ringside press photographers, took pictures for *Life* magazine. The whole scenario was "like a combination of New Year's and an Easter Parade," said John Condon, at that time head of PR for the Garden, describing the scene later for Ali's biographer Thomas Hauser. "It was one of those nights when anybody who was anybody was there." The ability to stage such evenings is a social characteristic and privilege of a sport that remains as debatable as it is charismatic.

Stars at the ringside are an integral feature of big fights: Jean Simmons, Stewart Granger and Michael Rennie at the Savold vs. Woodcock fight *(top left)*; Malcolm X, Yoko Ono and John Lennon with Muhammad Ali's boxing shorts *(above)* and actress Paulette Goddard, wearing a white coat *(top right)*.
Robert De Niro talks shop with Jake LaMotta *(left),* while the Duke of Windsor and the singer Jane Pickens obviously feel for Floyd Patterson *(right).*
Greta and Gregory Peck at the Mills vs. Maxim duel in London *(bottom left);* Rudolph Valentino is photographed here alongside Jack Dempsey *(below)* and Frank Sinatra, together with Ava Gardner, follows the Turpin vs. Humez bout in White City Stadium *(bottom right).*

Boxing Bars—Meeting Places for Insiders

LOCAL HEROES

Just ask for Jimmy, that's Jimmy Glen. Everybody on the East Coast of America who has ever seen a boxing match knows him. In the days when America was still bursting at the seams with talent, Jimmy was there in the middle of it all—he helped Joe Louis, he was a buddy of Sugar Ray Robinson. And now he is the owner of Jimmy's Neutral Corner, a small bar on 43rd Street West, in the center of Manhattan. It is one of the last of its kind, just like Jimmy himself. Because the people who want to yarn about boxing get fewer and fewer, as the rents go up and up.

So those who still meet, meet here: Bert Randolph Sugar, also known as "The Hat," the eccentric ace reporter *par excellence,* and Johnny Bos, a booking agent who works on a world-wide scale, and many others. The framed photos of fights on the wall are mainly in black and white, but the drinks are more colorful and after the fifth round they may go over the same stories yet again. Did Dempsey really lose to Harry Wills, why Ike Williams got involved with the Mafia, how often Riddick Bowe won

the Golden Gloves—all these and more are tossed into the mix along with the latest news.

And it sometimes happens that for several nights in a row, boxing does not come into the conversation at all, because in a general way, Jimmy's Neutral Corner is a bar for all possible (and some impossible) kinds of people. This openness follows tradition, for meeting places for *aficionados* of the sport have never been cliquey, exclusive places, as the term "boxing bar" might lead you to expect. The close connection with the catering trade is historic: the first training halls in England were in the upper rooms of popular hostelries, or off their back courtyards, and naturally, in an era without mass media, the pubs and taverns were also places to exchange the latest news. It was here that bets were laid, deals were made and tales retold—and if space permitted, bouts were boxed. Later, meeting places for fans developed on the way to the arenas, when they were not actually a part of them, or came to life in establishments run by retired participants in the sport. In the Manhattan of the 1950s, after the

fight shows in Madison Square Garden the aficionados made pilgrimages to the bars of Mickey Walker, Tony Canzoneri, and others, or to Jack Dempsey's extensive restaurant on the corner of 49th and 7th. In Europe too, former stars lined up to open their own bars, with widely varying degrees of success. But for the most successful of today's pros, this way of life long since became a rare exception—the amounts of their lucrative purses allows the champions to undertake much larger enterprises in their retirement from the ring.

So maybe there are still a couple of "mine hosts" from the "KO Nation" out there somewhere in the world who have papered the walls of their bars with memories. There are former athletes like the WBO ex-champion at cruiserweight Ralf Rocchigiani, for instance, who runs Rocky's Bar in Berlin's Charlottenburg district, and of course living boxing encyclopedias like Jimmy Glenn. So ask for Jimmy. And if he hasn't just that minute gone off to be the man in the corner for some young pro, then Jimmy will be right there.

Jack Dempsey's Restaurant and Bar on Broadway in Manhattan was a long-time favorite destination for boxing fans and show-business personalities. The former heavyweight champion himself was often to be found there.

The International Boxing Hall of Fame
LAURELS COME LATER

The idea is much older than the building itself. American experts and insiders in specific sports have enrolled their greatest baseball stars and the best football players in the so-called "Halls of Fame" of their sports. Polish and Italian immigrant communities list their most praiseworthy fellow countrymen and countrywomen—including singers, actors and even boxers—in halls of fame which exist in readable form only. This was also what Nathaniel S. Fleischer, the legendary founder and publisher of *The Ring* did from 1954 on: he inducted the best of the "pioneers," "old-timers" and modern champions of the pugilistic arts into a highly regarded, ever-increasing roll of honor in his illustrious journal.

But some decades later Edward S. Brophy, a boxing fan with a fine feel for the economic value of nostalgia acquired a piece of solid ground as a real location for this castle in the air. In 1984 in his hometown of Canastota, in New York State, he began to make preparations to establish a real museum of boxing. In 1990 it was officially opened as the International Boxing Hall of Fame (IBHOF) and along with innumerable items of memorabilia and the history of Madison Square Garden, it features a wall of plaques with portraits and short, written tributes that immortalize both great boxing champions and outstanding figures directly associated with the sport (ring announcers, promoters etc.). Dempsey and Duran, Ali and Frazier, the trainers Angelo Dundee and Eddie Futch—many greats of the fight game have been given their place here.

The annual high point for the IBHOF is without doubt the "Induction Weekend" held in early summer. During this long weekend thousands of fans stream into this small town, just off the New York State Thruway to celebrate the official induction of the newly immortalized. For these four days, legendary figures gather here, and it is possible to reach out and make personal contact with them, and to ask for autographs. The opening dinner that takes place late on Thursday evening and the workshops, presentations and celebrity boxing bouts on the Friday are the first opportunities

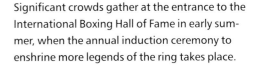

Significant crowds gather at the entrance to the International Boxing Hall of Fame in early summer, when the annual induction ceremony to enshrine more legends of the ring takes place.

for contact with the stars. These are followed on the Saturday by the traditional golf tournament, a big memorabilia auction and a banquet, on the Sunday by a breakfast organized by the fire-fighting service and finally by an auto-cavalcade—the Parade of Champions on their way to the official ceremony. On these occasions one can see the heroes of old in some neutral corner, if only for as long as it takes for a snapshot. Thus it might happen that "Marvelous" Marvin Hagler, out on the parking lot of Graziano's Motorlodge and Restaurant, an official center for the events, would hear, "Hey, Marvin, you were the best! In my opinion you even beat Sugar Ray Leonard!" And the question of whether this admirer really did have Hagler ahead on points has no real significance, as by the time that these most special of days come to an end, everyone is a winner.

Fists and photos behind glass: inside the Hall of Fame the former champions of the sport of boxing coexist peacefully side-by-side in eternal youth.

The history of boxing in the media
FROM RECORD BOOKS TO PAY TV

Would a boxing bout be anything other than a brawl of no importance if reports of it were not spread countrywide and across continents? It is the mass media that creates real public significance for this sport, for only by gaining wider recognition can athletes and their duels be accorded any recognizable status. Fame must have a basis of tradition, and for this reason the technical development and distribution of the various media have always had a decisive influence on fortunes in boxing.

The record books that gave details of the careers of the best of the bareknuckle fighters were the earliest means which helped the sport to gain objective public recognition. Pierce Egan's *Boxiana*, published in England from 1818, the American *Fistiana and Boxiana*, issued from 1841 and its successor the *New York Clipper Annual* which appeared from 1869 are the earliest periodicals of this type. Not long afterwards, fight reports became popular features in American newspapers, particularly in Richard Kyle Fox's

Like so many other promoters of his time, the industrious Jack Solomons studied the latest international boxing news the moment it came off the telegraph machine.

Police Gazette. As boxing duels acquired greater significance, there was a correspondingly greater need for chroniclers of the sport, and ringside journalists were treated almost as fight officials. When New York State ushered in the so-called "no-decision" era with the Frawley Law of 1911, the published verdict of the representatives of the press became an unofficial surrogate for the officially prohibited on-the-spot points decision.

Wily managers and promoters rapidly recognized the advantages of enthusiastic cultivation of press relations; their post-fight race to the nearest telegraph office to pass on glowing descriptions of the latest triumphs of their boys to the newspapers and press agencies became for a time a real competition in itself. From 1897, the fight organizers increasingly began to make filmed recordings, charging admission for showings in cinemas, thereby winning wider exposure for their fighters—and a lucrative extra earner for themselves. The powerful effect of screening

LANDMARKS IN LIVE BROADCASTING
TELEVISION AND BOXING

AUGUST, 1933, London. For the first time ever, a television camera films an exhibition bout (Johnny Curley vs. Harry Corbett). **APRIL, 1938** The first live boxing contest to be televised was the British light heavyweight championship bout between Len Harvey and Jock McAvoy at Harringay Arena, London. **FEBRUARY, 1939** In London, for the first time ever, a live television transmission of a boxing contest is broadcast to the general public. The fight between Eric Boon and Arthur Danahar is shown live on screen in three cinemas. **MAY, 1941** Live broadcasting is tested in the USA. The middleweight championship fight between Billy Soose and Ken Overlin is shown in the Guild Theater in New York. **SEPTEMBER, 1944** Promoter Mike Jacobs and the TV network NBC conclude the first TV contract, to screen a series of 51 fights, sponsored by the Gillette Safety Razor Company, in Madison Square Garden in New York. The premiere: Willie Pep's featherweight title defense against Chalky Wright. **JUNE, 1951** The first closed-circuit televised event, Joe Louis' title defense against Lee Savold is screened in eight cinemas in all, in six cities. **MAY, 1965** The first intercontinental live satellite broadcast of a fight marked the return match between Muhammad Ali and Sonny Liston in Lewiston, Maine, USA. **DECEMBER, 1965** The welterweight world title fight between Emile Griffith and Manuel Gonzalez is the first boxing contest to be broadcast in color.

demand beyond national borders to other countries and continents.

But it was the income from live broadcasts to cinemas, using the closed-circuit format that was soon to win huge profit margins for the big promoters and their major fighters. And it was the wide reach and penetration of the medium that was to make the best and most charismatic of the titleholders—above all Muhammad Ali—into world-famous sporting icons. Since then, paydays that during the reign of Ali seemed so enormous have been easily and frequently surpassed in the post-modern era of the megafight, due to the quantum shift experienced in the international TV market with its private cable networks and various forms of pay TV. Due to these developments, however, this once freely available sport is now well on the way to becoming as exclusive as it was in its pioneering days—the intermittently interested spectator is once again forced to rely on newspaper reports for information.

these films was amply demonstrated in 1910 in the USA, where after a film of the fight between Jack Johnson and James J. Jeffries in Reno was shown in cinemas, racially motivated riots broke out in several cities across the country. Thereafter, the transporting and screening of such films were prohibited for a time.

While films and newspaper reports could only relay accounts of events after they had happened, from the 1920s on, for the first time, the dramatic atmosphere of the sport could be transmitted over the live medium of radio. The radio stations and their best live commentators brought the action in the ring directly into the living rooms of their listeners and thus made a large contribution to the first great boxing boom.

After the end of World War II, the wide impact of boxing was reinforced by the advent of television. In America, live broadcasts sponsored by financially powerful companies now went out on air several times a week. Elsewhere in the world, in Europe and Japan, boxing contests were occasional high points in the TV schedules. The development of satellite technology quickly made it possible for big title fights to be broadcast according to

Early film of a bout staged in a television studio at Crystal Palace in London in 1935 *(top)*. It was only after the end of World War II that live transmissions of title fights were beamed into British and American living rooms. It was the start of the era of free TV *(above)*.

The involvement of television

BROADCASTERS AND AUDIENCES

An action zone tailor-made for the geometry of the TV screen, a drama with only two main characters and regular breaks that cry out to be filled by advertising—these are the inherent characteristics that have predestined boxing to be an ideal TV spectacle. It is no wonder then that the volatile marriage between this medium and the sweet science was contracted early and still survives in a modified version until today.

Television films of boxing duels were experimented with in Great Britain and later in the USA by the 1930s. Shortly after, the network broadcasters in the USA, who used relay masts, enthusiastically fell upon the booming sport. The "Friday Night Fights" from New York's Madison Square Garden, presented by NBC and sponsored by Gillette soon became

so popular that other regular programs followed. Up until the mid-1950s, the four big U.S. networks showed five live broadcasts per week between Monday and Saturday. This allowed the bigger boxing presenters a degree of independence from their spectators, as the live gate was no longer their main source of income; however, the fan base for smaller club-based live shows was badly affected. The new medium had an obvious downside.

By the end of the 1950s, it was plain that the first flush of TV frenzy would soon be over. While television transmissions were now gaining in popularity in Europe, Japan and Mexico, the networks in the United States were gradually cutting back. The big fights were no longer concentrated almost exclusively in the Chicago–Philadelphia–New York

triangle and the prestige of the sport had obviously been hard hit by corruption scandals and several serious accidents. With the end of the "Friday Night Fights" in 1964, everyday television had to a great extent bidden farewell to boxing. Its role was taken on by the more flexible techniques of closed-circuit shows (large-screen TV transmissions), which thanks to satellite technology could soon be broadcast across and beyond whole continents. The global high point for this technology was reached in March 1971 with the first duel between Joe Frazier and Muhammad Ali that was watched worldwide by 1.3 million people in 320 cinemas and other venues.

But just as the powers of the charismatic worldwide star Ali gradually waned, so did

Boxing experts employed by British Sky TV feed information into computers on punches and connecting hits scored by the fighters in the ring in the Cardiff International Arena in 1999. The resulting computer-supported statistics were used to aid an objective post-fight analysis of events.

The broadcasters' production teams are faced by ever-greater challenges as the requirements for live transmission of fight-nights continue to escalate. A growing number of fixed and mobile specialist cameras deliver pictures from all possible angles of the ring itself and of the spectator stands. And this, of course, means enormous increases in production costs.

the financial strength of closed-circuit TV. In the 1980s new television formats were developed, specifically by the commercial broadcasters and specialist sports channels distributed by cable networks such as USA, ESPN or Eurosport, whose programs were more effectively aimed at a boxing clientele, which in terms of numbers, had been significantly reduced. And from there it was only a small step to the current variants of subscription television and pay TV, or pay-per-view, through which broadcasting revenue can be significantly increased.

Today, the American market is dominated by two established and competing brands, the subscription channel HBO, part of the Time-Warner group, and its pay-per-view subsidiary TVKO, as well as the equivalent Viacom companies, Showtime and Set. In Europe, their example is followed by ITV or Sky (United Kingdom), Canal plus (France), Telepiú (Italy), Premiere and Premiere World (Germany) and others.

The considerable economic power of the subscription television channels has in many cases ensured for promoters and the star fighters who are contractually bound to them bigger purses and shares than any other TV format. Thus by as early as 1988 the television and casino bosses could guarantee Mike Tyson, the first superstar of this new era, a cool $20 million for his world

championship bout with Michael Spinks in Atlantic City.

The once independent medium had become de facto a co-promoter, from time to time neglecting the journalistic virtues of distance and neutrality in reporting events. There is more than a little food for thought in the

fact that the annual list of the "50 Most Influential People in Boxing" compiled on a basis of inside information and published by the American specialist magazine *Boxing Digest* regularly features three or four decision-makers from HBO and Showtime in its top ten rankings.

Three former world champions, *(from left to right)* Barry McGuigan, Jim Watt and Steve Collins, are together in the studio in Cardiff in 1999, to help presenter Paul Dempsey commentate on the fights.

Astonishment in the Paramount Theater in New York: the cinema audience was unprepared for the time-lapse direct transmission of a live U.S. Navy boxing tournament. There was a delay of exactly sixty six seconds while the original live television pictures were transferred to 35mm film stock, dried and then projected on to the large screen. Experiments such as this prepared the way in the USA for the forthcoming era of closed-circuit shows in public venues and arenas.

The first big-screen TV
CLOSED-CIRCUIT

To serve up on screen to as many people as possible in as many venues as possible the live action from an event—that is the simple idea behind the so-called closed-circuit shows, also known as theater-TV. It is a concept that is almost as old as the electronic medium itself, and in boxing functioned more successfully and profitably than in any other sphere.

The men from Gaumont-British Corporation had initially only had a test-run of broadcasting technology in mind when in February 1939 they broadcast the first live television transmission of a boxing duel (Eric Boon vs. Arthur Danahar) to three different cinemas from London's only transmitter at Alexandra Palace. In America, too, the first live broadcasts of fights were publicly performed experiments. The telephone networks used on these occasions were not suitable for regular intensive transmission use, and the first boxing programs of the commercial television networks (from 1944 on) meant that the commercial potential of this format lay dormant for some time.

It was not until 1951 that the first major title fight, between Joe Louis and Lee Savold, was broadcast live exclusively in the closed-circuit format; in all, eight cinemas across six major cities were linked up to the event. Only a couple of years later it became clear that the large networks with their many boxing programs had been overtaken, and boxing organizers were just as happy to count on the guarantees offered them by the closed-circuit operators. Theater-TV had developed into a real alternative. The fight between Rocky Marciano and Archie Moore generated $1.125 million in revenue—the medium's first million-dollar gate.

During the 1960s, satellite technology expanded the market for closed-circuit TV into neighboring countries and other continents, so that this format was in a position to compete with the more usual home TV. Quite frequently, a combined solution was devised for the trade in international television rights—as was the case with Joe Frazier's title defense against Muhammad Ali in 1971, when in some European countries the fight was shown in closed-circuit format and in others broadcast over national television networks. Worldwide for this "fight of the century," a total of 320 cinemas and other venues were linked to the closed-circuit network. Thereafter it was never again to be as significant or as impressive in scope. On the contrary, the usual closed-circuit audiences became more renowned for raucous, volatile and occasionally abusive behavior.

Until well into the 1980s closed-circuit remained a popular institution and an extra earner, but was then rapidly superseded by more modern forms of television and changes in social habits. Pay TV and pay-per-view took the experience of the great events out of the boozed-up collective sphere and placed it firmly in the more intimate domestic environment of the viewers' own four walls. Here, consumers can—although admittedly for a many times larger fee—make their own choice of viewing companions.

THE 10 MOST SUCCESSFUL LIVE BROADCASTS

Fight	Date	Price(US$)	Purchasers	Revenue(US$)
Evander Holyfield W disq Mike Tyson	28.06.1997	49.95	1.90 Mio	99.6 Mio
Evander Holyfield TKO 11 Mike Tyson I	09.11.1996	49.95	1.60 Mio	79.9 Mio
Mike Tyson W disq 1 Peter McNeeley	19.08.1995	44.95	1.58 Mio	67.9 Mio
Felix Trinidad W 12 Oscar de la Hoya	18.09.1999	49.95	1.25 Mio	62.4 Mio
Mike Tyson TKO 3 Frank Bruno	16.03.1996	44.95	1.40 Mio	55.9 Mio
Evander Holyfield D 12 Lennox Lewis	13.03.1999	49.95	1.10 Mio	54.9 Mio
Evander Holyfield W 12 George Foreman	19.04.1991	39.95	1.36 Mio	48.9 Mio
Mike Tyson TKO 1 Bruce Seldon	07.09.1996	44.95	1.00 Mio	46.0 Mio
Mike Tyson W 12 Donovan Ruddock	28.06.1991	34.95	1.20 Mio	42.0 Mio
Evander Holyfield KO 3 Buster Douglas	25.10.1990	35.95	1.06 Mio	38.6 Mio

Source: Showtime Event Television and Multichannel News, 28.3.2001

Radio and the golden era of boxing

RADIO YEARS

Up until the 1920s, it was only possible to directly follow the action of a boxing bout at the venue itself. Newspaper reports and film shows were only able to relate events after they had occurred, and could not fully convey the highly charged atmosphere on the spot. With the advent of radio, however, fans who had been unable to buy a ticket for the fight could nevertheless experience the fight live. And this benefited both the first big broadcasting companies and the sport that they enabled their listeners to hear. Contrary to skeptical forecasts, the new medium did not draw interested people away from attending in person—in fact, because of the vivid impressions that were created of the incomparable atmosphere of the fights, hosts of new fans were attracted.

In April 1921, KDKA, the local radio station in East Pittsburgh, Pennsylvania successfully completed a pilot project by broadcasting a no-decision lightweight bout between Johnny Dundee and Johnny Ray. International recognition for the effectiveness of radio followed in July of the same year with the world championship duel between Jack Dempsey and Georges Carpentier, hyped as the "Fight of the Century." Julius Hopp, the concert manager of Madison Square Garden, initiated an operation that was carefully planned and prepared over the weeks and months preceding the fight, to transmit the event from an open-air arena in New Jersey (Boyle's Thirty Acres) over a radius of 250 miles to thirty official receiving stations. This was only achieved thanks to authorization by one Franklin D. Roosevelt, at that time president of the Navy Club, to use a powerful 3.5-kilowatt naval transmitter, borrowed to set up a broadcasting station in the railroad station at Hoboken, two and a half miles away from the arena. On the evening of July 2 the fight commentary of amateur radio enthusiast J. Andrew White went on air on a long-wave frequency: "The Frenchman is down! The referee is counting—three, four … Carpentier makes no effort to rise … six, seven … he's sinking to the mat … nine, ten! The fight is over!"

Dempsey, radio, and professional boxing—in the next few years all three were to experience a brilliant upswing in their careers, based on mutually beneficial support. Three years after Dempsey's knockout victory over Carpentier, NBC initiated its extraordinarily popular program of "Friday Night Fights," which made their commentator Sam Taub the first star reporter of the sport. This former newspaper journalist was a master of the art of describing events in the ring in such a way that his listeners felt as if they themselves had actually seen the fight; in addition, he was the host of the talk show "The Hour of Champions" for the New York station WHN for 24 years. There were soon almost as many radio stations in America as there were fight-nights to report—and whenever and wherever there was boxing, the excitable gents in the glass-fronted boxes erected for their benefit behind the press area very soon became an accepted fixture.

Just as Taub and his successor at NBC, Don Dunphy, became famous on one side of the Atlantic through their blow-by-blow commentaries, in Europe, the best voices in boxing also began to make a name for themselves. This also applied to boxers, who were able to boost their popularity quite significantly by appearances on radio shows. To be on air meant popularity; there was scarcely a pro who neglected to give the obligatory radio interview after a fight. The reach of radio spanned continents: in 1934, with the heavyweight world championship won by Max Baer over Primo Carnera, for the first time a boxing contest was broadcast live throughout the entire world. Unfortunately, there was a regrettable technical glitch on this occasion, when during the final interview the sobs of the defeated Carnera in the background were also relayed across the airwaves to the listeners.

The glory years of radio were to last well into the post-World War II years, when a second boxing boom was making its presence felt. But the more the Western television networks expanded, the weaker the radio signal became.

A break to honor a champ: In August, 1937, in Tonypandy, Wales miners wait by a radio for the result of the heavyweight world championship contest in New York's Yankee Stadium between Joe Louis and their hero Tommy Farr.

The print media and their journalists
ORACLES AND CHRONICLERS

In ancient times there were epic poets such as Homer and Virgil to compose verse in praise of the great sporting deeds of fistfighters and wrestlers, for heroes never remain unsung. In the modern era there are both principled chroniclers with elegant writing styles and vain, self-satisfied, opinionated writers to provide written testimony of the dramatic events in modern prizefighting. Since the pioneering era of the sport, newspaper reporters who perform this function have become a conduit for information and indispensable peripheral figures in the world of boxing. "It was the writers that made George Foreman great," Foreman knew enough to admit, because "they tell folks about you. Without these guys, you're dead."

The semi-legal duels of the bareknuckle era in Great Britain were not least publicized by the tireless efforts of Pierce Egan, who is generally acknowledged to be the first boxing author worthy of the name. In the early nineteenth century this playwright and poet described for the London *Weekly Dispatch* with loving attention to detail the social background and course of events of fights, and in 1812 published the first of his five record books *Boxiana*. The first boxing magazine *Boxing Reviewed* was published by Thomas Fewtrell in 1790. In the United States a regularly published boxing forum did not appear until the last quarter of the nineteenth century, when Richard K. Fox's *Police Gazette* began to print fight reports. Fox, an immigrant adventurer from Dublin, quickly recognized that the circulation of his populist newspaper would be boosted by regular reports of boxing bouts, and in return, he assisted the careers of several active participants in the sport. In the shape of the *Police Gazette* Diamond Belt he donated the first significant championship belt of the modern era.

Once again, England was ahead by a short nose in publishing the first specialist boxing magazine, *Boxing,* in 1909; its name was changed in 1946 to *Boxing News* and under this name, and now published at fortnightly intervals, it is still going strong today. Thirteen years later, in the USA, Nat Fleischer and Ike Dorgan, at that time the press representative for the preeminent promoter Tex Rickard, founded the now legendary monthly magazine *The Ring.* In a time before worldwide organizations and

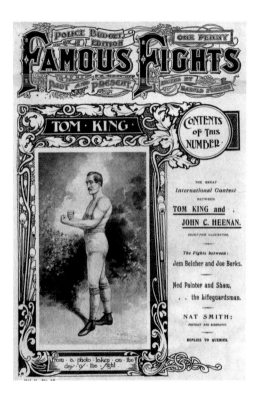

disputes over the recognition of champions and challengers, these and other serious specialist publications brought to international events a certain amount of objectivity. The ratings lists published from 1925 on in *The Ring* were accepted as a definitive and independent barometer of the respective worth of professional fighters; anyone not mentioned there was not considered for a title fight.

For those with only a casual interest in the sport as well as for those organizing fights, the

boxing scribes of the influential dailies are today still considered a vital factor. While the specialist magazines are targeted at an inner circle of already highly motivated regular supporters, the editors of the daily press reach a wider public. In the main, it is for them that the press conferences, training-camp visits and other events in the run-up to big fights are organized. For the better in their number, their job has always been much more than "the best way to be a jerk and earn your living" as the legendary boxing author Damon Runyon once disparagingly described sports journalism. There is no dispute that at one time a whole army of low-paid hacks stood in line every Saturday morning at Madison Square Garden to pick up envelopes stuffed with dollar bills left for them by promoters—as thanks for expansive and none too critical reports. But at the very same time, incorruptible spirits such as Dan Parker of the New York *Daily Mirror* campaigned through their articles against the Mafia entanglement in the sport. This uncompromising attitude is also found in the commentaries of the pugnacious Michael Katz, whose articles spanning many years in the *New York Times*, the *Daily Mirror* and latterly for the *House of Boxing* Web site have been the scourge of the infamous maneuvers of promoters and the various world boxing organizations. Aristocrats of the pen and jerks, chroniclers and moralists—they all belong to a world of words that boasts as wide a range of quality as the athletes in the ring.

Top: In the United Kingdom, early periodicals such as *Famous Fights* functioned both as listings magazines and as specialist journals. *Left:* In 1928, the retired heavyweight world champion Gene Tunney grants an audience to reporters on the roof of the Savoy Hotel in London.

The first issue of The Ring *was published on February 15, 1922, and was sold for 20 cents.*

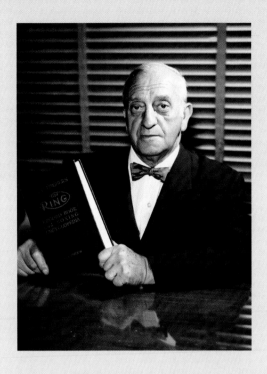

As founder, publisher, and editor-in-chief, Nat Fleischer led the magazine for fifty years.

His successor Stanley Weston collected memorabilia like the shorts of Rocky Marciano (white) and Joe Lewis.

THE RING

POINTS VICTORY FOR A LEGEND

In 1920, when the so-called Walker Law once again made prize fighting legal in the State of New York, and big fights acted like magnets on the public, Nat Fleischer had what was initially a relatively modest idea. The much-traveled boxing fan and sports editor of the New York *Evening Telegram* decided to found a regional news-sheet for the growing numbers of ringside enthusiasts, to keep them and the inner circle on the boxing scene up to date with current events. Somehow or other, however, he was overtaken by events and the original idea grew into a much larger phenomenon: the small leaflet rapidly expanded into a major publication of world-wide renown, and is today the oldest sports periodical in the USA. This "Bible of boxing" as its subtitle has it, has gone beyond being merely an institution and has now assumed mythological status, and even now, at the beginning of the twenty-first century, it is still as challenging as the proudest of boxers.

By 1921, Fleischer had already found a powerful financial backer for his project, in the person of promoter Tex Rickard, who had recently become wealthy through the

heavyweight world championship contest between Dempsey and Carpentier. On February 15, 1921, together with Rickard's press chief Ike Dorgan, he published the first issue of *The Ring*, soon introduced monthly ratings lists, and from 1928 on recognized the best boxer over all divisions by awarding him the title of "Fighter of the Year" and an accompanying champions belt. This specialist publication soon became the independent conscience of a sport that was all too vulnerable to corruption—and Fleischer, its publisher and editor-in-chief, and occasional official at title contests, became a respectable institution.

For the four decades from 1932 until his death in 1972, Fleischer, by now without the help of Dorgan, led the famous magazine as a benevolent dictator. Based in the offices of the old Madison Square Garden, he was surrounded by all the best gyms on Broadway and on Times Square and the market for pro boxers was determined by his ratings lists. They were more objective and less prone to corruption than the lists of today. After Fleischer's death, there was a gradual shift in the focus of power in the sport towards the

casinos of Las Vegas and the executive suites of the television networks, and the two competing world sanctioning bodies, the WBA and WBC, introduced ever greater numbers of weight divisions and champions. At this period even *The Ring* found itself beaten and staggering on to the ropes: it passed along a series of owners until in 1989 it finally fell into the hands of Fleischer's former partner (and later rival) Stanley Weston. "I couldn't let the old lady die," declared Weston. Today, this venerable magazine with its subscribers on five continents is published by Kappa Publishing, to whom Weston sold his rights, as did the producers of *KO Boxing* and *World Boxing*. Reduced revenue has meant a corresponding temporary reduction in print quality, a phenomenon all too common in specialist boxing magazines published in the USA today. But the small team of editorial staff in its offices in Ambler, a suburban town on the northern fringes of Philadelphia, is by no means ready to throw in the towel yet. On the contrary: surprisingly, when the December 2000 edition of the *The Ring* appeared, it was printed in full color.

Ringside photographers
A THOUSAND EYES

In this age of computer-enhanced picture technology, it is almost a truism that photographs can be manipulated, and therefore have only limited use as historic documents. But for the average sports enthusiast, as much as for the athletes themselves, a photo of a fight has now, as it has always had, a dual purpose—as both collective memory and public proof. And it is for this reason that boxing photographers have always been accepted as indispensable ringside chroniclers. Their cameras take visual "transcripts" of the history of a sport that could hardly have more dramatic brilliance.

"For a sports photographer boxing means as much as a car crash for a film director," the photography critic Richard B. Woodward once confirmed, that is to say it is "graphic dynamite, thrilling and easy to manage." In contrast to other forms of sport, like basketball or hockey, the drama of boxing is played out on a relatively small stage. Only two adversaries make their entrances and under the supervision of an impartial moderator, perform their intrinsically symbolic playlet of victor and vanquished. The strikingly simple graphic language of the triumphantly upright victor and his destroyed opponent, literally beaten to the ground, is according to Woodward a universal "Esperanto for victory and defeat."

At the start of the modern era, press photographs provided the only visual evidence of the boxing contests that fascinated ever-greater numbers throughout the twentieth century. But even well after the advent of the television age, they remained an indispensable element of the sports pages of the more significant daily newspapers. All fans, no matter whether they had been ringside on Friday night or had watched on television, by Monday at the very latest scanned the sports pages of their favorite newspaper for an attractive photo of the big fight—a thrilling, sometimes harsh black-and-white shot that condensed the essence of the whole fight into a single moment. Time after time, this was precisely what the very best of these artists of the medium-format camera managed to achieve. Despite the laborious processes involved in taking pictures, conditions for press photographers at that time were favorable. As a general rule, the fight organizers reserved for their use two of the four rows of ringside seats, where their view was interrupted at that time by three rather than four ropes. The invention of stroboscopic flash technology in 1938 gave them a dazzling supplementary light source that allowed them to use the most rapid of shutter speeds to "freeze" even the quickest movements of the protagonists in the ring. The "only" challenge now was to anticipate the ideal moment in an exchange of blows to capture the agony, the contempt for pain, and the unfettered energy of the action. There is no pause to allow for reaction time in boxing.

"You can't watch and then shoot," acknowledged Charles Hoff, for thirty years the renowned ringside photographer for the *New York Daily News.* "You have to learn to shoot instinctively. While it's happening." Initially, during the middle years of the twentieth century it was little-recognized American sports photographers like Hoff or William Klein who shot these outstanding boxing pictures, many of which have since been bought up by large museums and galleries. They were succeeded in the more recent era of color photography (and of Muhammad Ali) by Neil Leifer, Ken Regan from the USA and others, photographers who see themselves in the first instance more as highly skilled craftspeople. In parallel, conditions for photographers at the ringside became less favorable. The introduction of the fourth ring rope and the presence of TV-camera operators placed considerable restrictions on stills photographers; their dazzling flashguns have been superseded, as they are a disruptive factor for television filming. However, the demand for outstanding pictures of this sport will flourish for as long as it can continue to produce both impressive fights and fascinated spectators.

A press photographer from the British magazine *Picture Post* as he closely follows the action in the finals of the Miners Amateur Boxing Club tournament in Murrayfield Ice Rink, Edinburgh, in 1955.

APPENDIX

THE WORLD CHAMPIONS OF OUR TIME

D = draw
disq = disqualified
KO = knockout
Pts = points
ret = retired
rsf = referee stops fight
splt = split decision
td = technical decision
TKO = technical knockout
W = win

IBF = International Boxing Federation
IBU = International Boxing Union
NBA = National Boxing Association
NY = New York State Boxing Commission
WBA = World Boxing Association of America
WBC = World Boxing Council
WBO = World Boxing Organization

The country abbreviations follow the three-letter code used by the International Olympic Committee. For identification of the abbreviations, please refer to the table on page 420.

HEAVYWEIGHT

08-29-1885 Cincinnati (USA): **John L. Sullivan** W 6 Dominik McCaffrey
09-07-1892 New Orleans (USA): **James J. Corbett** KO 21 John L. Sullivan
03-17-1897 Carson City (USA): **Robert Fitzsimmons** KO 14 James J. Corbett
06-09-1899 Coney Island (USA): **James J. Jeffries** KO 11 Robert Fitzsimmons
05-13-1905 *Jeffries retires from professional sport.*
07-03-1905 Reno (USA): **Marvin Hart** TKO 12 Jack Root
02-23-1906 Los Angeles (USA): **Tommy Burns** W 20 Marvin Hart
12-26-1908 Sydney (AUS): **Jack Johnson** TKO 14 Tommy Burns
04-05-1915 Havana (CUB): **Jess Willard** KO 26 Jack Johnson
07-04-1919 Toledo (USA): **Jack Dempsey** ret 3 Jess Willard
09-23-1926 Philadelphia (USA): **Gene Tunney** W 10 Jack Dempsey
07-31-1928 *Tunney retires from professional sport.*
06-12-1930 Bronx (USA): **Max Schmeling** disq 4 Jack Sharkey
06-21-1932 Long Island (USA): **Jack Sharkey** W 15 Max Schmeling
06-29-1933 Long Island (USA): **Primo Carnera** KO 6 Jack Sharkey
06-14-1934 Long Island (USA): **Max Baer** TKO 11 Primo Carnera
06-13-1935 Long Island (USA): **James J. Braddock** W 15 Max Baer
06-22-1937 Chicago (USA): **Joe Louis** KO 8 James J. Braddock
03-01-1949 *Louis retires from professional sport.*
06-22-1949 Chicago (USA): **Ezzard Charles** W 15 Jersey Joe Walcott
07-18-1951 Pittsburgh (USA): **"Jersey" Joe Walcott** KO 7 Ezzard Charles
09-23-1952 Philadelphia (USA): **Rocky Marciano** KO 13 "Jersey" Joe Walcott
04-27-1956 *Marciano retires from professional sport.*
11-30-1956 Chicago (USA): **Floyd Patterson** KO 5 Archie Moore
06-26-1959 New York (USA): **Ingemar Johansson** TKO 3 Floyd Patterson
06-20-1960 New York (USA): **Floyd Patterson** KO 5 Ingemar Johansson
09-25-1962 Chicago (USA): **Sonny Liston** KO 1 Floyd Patterson
02-25-1964 Miami (USA): **Cassius Clay** ret 6 Sonny Liston
Sept. 1964 *The WBA strips Clay of his title for failing to defend.*
03-05-1965 Chicago (USA): **Ernie Terrell** W 15 Eddie Machen (WBA)
02-06-1967 Houston (USA): **Muhammad Ali** W 15 Ernie Terell (WBA/WBC)
April 1967 *Ali is stripped of his title because he refuses to join the U.S. Army.*
03-04-1968 New York (USA): **Joe Frazier** TKO 11 Buster Mathis (NY)
04-27-1968 Oakland (USA): **Jimmy Ellis** W 15 Jerry Quarry (WBA)
02-16-1970 New York (USA): **Joe Frazier** KO 5 Jimmy Ellis (WBA/WBC)
01-22-1973 Kingston (JAM): **George Foreman** TKO 2 Joe Frazier (WBA/WBC)
10-30-1974 Kinshasa (ZAI): **Muhammad Ali** KO 8 George Foreman (WBA/WBC)
02-15-1978 Las Vegas (USA): **Leon Spinks** W 15 Muhammad Ali (WBA/WBC)
03-18-1978 *The WBC strips Spinks of his title for failing to defend.*
06-10-1978 Las Vegas (USA): **Larry Holmes** TKO 15 Ken Norton (WBC)
09-15-1978 New Orleans (USA): **Muhammad Ali** W 15 Leon Spinks (WBA)
06-27-1979 *Ali retires as WBA champion.*
10-20-1979 Pretoria (RSA): **John Tate** W 15 Gerrie Coetzee (WBA)
03-31-1980 Knoxville (USA): **Mike Weaver** KO 15 John Tate (WBA)
12-10-1982 Las Vegas (USA): **Michael Dokes** TKO 1 Mike Weaver (WBA)
12-11-1983 *Holmes relinquishes the WBC title and is instead recognized by the IBF.*
09-23-1983 Richfield (USA): **Gerrie Coetzee** KO 10 Mike Dokes (WBA)
03-09-1984 Las Vegas (USA): **Tim Witherspoon** W 12 Greg Page (WBC)
08-31-1984 Las Vegas (USA): **Pinklon Thomas** W 12 Tim Witherspoon (WBC)
12-01-1984 Sun City (RSA): **Greg Page** KO 8 Gerrie Coetzee (WBA)
04-29-1985 Buffalo (USA): **Tony Tubbs** W 15 Greg Page (WBA)
09-21-1985 Las Vegas (USA): **Michael Spinks** W 15 Larry Holmes (IBF)
01-17-1986 Atlanta (USA): **Tim Witherspoon** W 15 Tony Tubbs (WBA)
03-22-1986 Las Vegas (USA): **Trevor Berbick** W 12 Pinklon Thomas (WBC)
11-22-1986 Las Vegas (USA): **Mike Tyson** TKO 2 Trevor Berbick (WBC)
12-12-1986 New York (USA): **James "Bonecrusher" Smith** TKO 1 Tim Witherspoon (WBA)
02-19-1987 *Spinks is stripped of the IBF title for not defending.*
03-07-1987 Las Vegas (USA): **Mike Tyson** W 12 James "Bonecrusher" Smith (WBA)
05-30-1987 Las Vegas (USA): **Tony Tucker** TKO 10 James "Buster" Douglas (IBF)
08-01-1987 Las Vegas (USA): **Mike Tyson** W 12 Tony Tucker (WBA/WBC/IBF)
05-06-1989 Syracuse (USA): **Francesco Damiani** KO 3 Johnny Du Plooy (WBO)

02-11-1990 Tokyo (JPN): **James "Buster" Douglas** KO 10 Mike Tyson (WBA/WBC/IBF)
10-25-1990 Las Vegas (USA): **Evander Holyfield** KO 3 James "Buster" Douglas (WBA/WBC/IBF)
01-11-1991 Syracuse (USA): **Ray Mercer** KO 9 Francesco Damiani (WBO)
12-24-1991 *Mercer is stripped of his title because he does not defend it against Michael Moorer. The WBO title is declared vacant.*
05-15-1992 Atlantic City (USA): **Michael Moorer** TKO 5 Bert Cooper (WBO)
11-14-1992 Las Vegas (USA): **Riddick Bowe** W 12 Evander Holyfield (WBA/WBC/IBF)
12-14-1992 *The WBC withdrew recognition from Bowe for failing to negotiate terms for a title defense against Lennox Lewis.*
02-03-1993 *Moorer relinquishes the WBO title.*
05-08-1993 Las Vegas (USA): **Lennox Lewis** W 12 Tony Tucker (WBC)
06-07-1993 Las Vegas (USA): **Tommy Morrison** W 12 George Foreman (WBO)
10-29-1993 Tulsa (USA): **Michael Bentt** TKO 1 Tommy Morrison (WBO)
11-06-1993 Las Vegas (USA): **Evander Holyfield** W 12 Riddick Bowe (WBA/IBF)
03-19-1994 London (GBR): **Herbie Hide** KO 7 Michael Bentt (WBO)
04-22-1994 Las Vegas (USA): **Michael Moorer** W 12 Evander Holyfield (WBA/IBF)
09-24-1994 London (GBR): **Oliver McCall** TKO 2 Lennox Lewis (WBC)
11-05-1994 Las Vegas (USA): **George Foreman** KO 10 Michael Moorer (WBA/IBF)
03-04-1995 *Foreman is stripped of the WBA title for refusing to defend against Tony Tucker.*
03-11-1995 Las Vegas (USA): **Riddick Bowe** KO 6 Herbie Hide (WBO)
04-08-1995 Las Vegas (USA): **Bruce Seldon** TKO 7 Tony Tucker (WBA)
06-28-1995 *Foreman relinquishes the IBF title.*
07-01-1995 *Bowe vacates the WBO title.*
09-02-1995 London (GBR): **Frank Bruno** W 12 Oliver McCall (WBC)
10-31-1995 *Bowe requests reinstatement as WBO champion.*
12-09-1995 Stuttgart (GER): **François Botha** W 12 Axel Schulz (IBF)
01-11-1996 *Bowe is stripped of the WBO title.*
03-27-1996 *Botha is stripped of the IBF title after testing positive for doping.*
03-16-1996 Las Vegas (USA): **Mike Tyson** TKO 3 Frank Bruno (WBC)
06-22-1996 Dortmund (GER): **Michael Moorer** W 12 Axel Schulz (IBF)
06-29-1996 Indio (USA): **Henry Akinwande** KO 3 Jeremy Williams (WBO)
09-24-1996 *Tyson is stripped of the WBC title for not defending.*
09-07-1996 Las Vegas (USA): **Mike Tyson** TKO 1 Bruce Seldon (WBA)
11-09-1996 Las Vegas (USA): **Evander Holyfield** TKO 11 Mike Tyson (WBA)
02-01-1997 *Akinwande relinquishes the WBO title to fight Lennox Lewis for the WBC title.*
02-07-1997 Las Vegas (USA): **Lennox Lewis** TKO 5 Oliver McCall (WBC)
06-28-1997 Norwich (GBR): **Herbie Hide** TKO 2 Tony Tucker (WBO)
11-08-1997 Las Vegas (USA): **Evander Holyfield** TKO 8 Michael Moorer (WBA/IBF)
06-26-1999 Millwall (GBR): **Vitali Klitschko** KO 2 Herbie Hide (WBO)
11-13-1999 Las Vegas (USA): **Lennox Lewis** W 12 Evander Holyfield (WBC/WBA/IBF)
Feb. 2000 *The WBA withdraws recognition of Lewis because he fails to defend.*
04-01-2000 Berlin (GER): **Chris Byrd** ret 9 Vitali Klitschko (WBO)
08-12-2000 Las Vegas (USA): **Evander Holyfield** W 12 John Ruiz (WBA)
10-14-2000 Cologne (GER): **Vladimir Klitschko** W 12 Chris Byrd (WBO)
03-03-2001 Las Vegas (USA): **John Ruiz** W 12 Evander Holyfield (WBA)
04-22-2001 Brakpan (RSA): **Hasim Rahman** KO 5 Lennox Lewis (WBC/IBF)
11-17-2001 Las Vegas (USA): **Lennox Lewis** KO 4 Hasim Rahman (WBC/IBF)
2002 *The IBF strips Lewis of the title for failing to defend.*
12-14-2002 Atlantic City (USA): **Chris Byrd** Pts 12 Evander Holyfield (IBF)
03-01-2003 Las Vegas (USA): **Roy Jones Jr.** W 12 John Ruiz (WBA)
03-08-2003 Hanover (GER): **Corrie Sanders** TKO 2 Vladimir Klitschko (WBO)

CRUISERWEIGHT

03-31-1980 Las Vegas (USA): **Marvin Camel** W 15 Mate Parlov (WBC)
11-25-1980 New Orleans (USA): **Carlos DeLeon** W 15 Marvin Camel (WBC)
02-09-1982 Johannesburg (RSA): **Ossie Ocasio** W 15 Robbie Williams (WBA)
06-27-1982 Cleveland (USA): **S.T. Gordon** TKO 2 Carlos DeLeon (WBC)
05-21-1983 Billings (USA): **Marvin Camel** KO 9 Ric Sekorski (IBF)
07-17-1983 Las Vegas (USA): **Carlos DeLeon** W 12 S.T. Gordon (WBC)
10-06-1984 Billings (USA): **Lee Roy Murphy** TKO 14 Marvin Camel (IBF)
12-01-1984 Sun City (RSA): **Piet Crous** W 15 Ossie Ocasio (WBA)
06-06-1985 Las Vegas (USA): **Alfonso Ratliff** W 12 Carlos DeLeon (WBC)
07-27-1985 Sun City (RSA): **Dwight Muhammad Quawi** KO 11 Piet Crous (WBA)
09-21-1985 Las Vegas (USA): **Bernard Benton** W 12 Alfonso Ratliff (WBC)
03-22-1986 Las Vegas (USA): **Carlos DeLeon** W 12 Bernard Benton (WBC)
07-12-1986 Atlanta (USA): **Evander Holyfield** W 15 Dwight Muhammad Quawi (WBA)
10-25-1986 Marsala (ITA): **Rickey Parkey** TKO 10 Lee Roy Murphy (IBF)
05-15-1987 Las Vegas (USA): **Evander Holyfield** TKO 3 Rickey Parkey (IBF)
08-15-1987 St. Tropez (FRA): **Evander Holyfield** TKO 11 Ossie Ocasio (WBA/IBF)
04-09-1988 Las Vegas (USA): **Evander Holyfield** KO 8 Carlos DeLeon (WBA/WBC/IBF)
Nov. 1988 *Holyfield relinquishes all titles to fight at heavyweight.*
03-25-1989 Casablanca (MAR): **Taoufik Belbouli** TKO 8 Michael Greer (WBA)

05-17-1989 London (GBR): **Carlos DeLeon** TKO 9 Sammy Reeson (WBC)
06-03-1989 Stanley (GBR): **Glenn McCrory** W 12 Patrick Lumumba (IBF)
 Aug. 1989 *Belbouli relinquishes the WBA title due to a knee injury.*
11-28-1989 Nogent-Sur-Marne (FRA): **Robert Daniels** W 12 Dwight Muhammad Quawi (WBA)
12-03-1989 Copenhagen (DEN): **Boone Pultz** W 12 Magne Havnaa (WBO)
03-22-1990 Gateshead (GBR): **Jeff Lampkin** KO 3 Glenn McCrory (IBF)
05-17-1990 Aars (DEN): **Magne Havnaa** TKO 5 Boone Pultz (WBO)
07-27-1990 Capo d'Orlando (ITA): **Masimiliano Duran** disq 11 Carlos DeLeon (WBC)
03-09-1991 Atlantic City (USA): **Bobby Czyz** W 12 Robert Daniels (WBA)
07-20-1991 Palermo (ITA): **Anaclet Wamba** TKO 11 Masimiliano Duran (WBC)
 July 1991 *Lampkin relinquishes the IBF title.*
09-06-1991 Salemi (ITA): **James Warring** KO 1 James Pritchard (IBF)
07-25-1992 Manchester (GBR): **Tyrone Booze** KO 7 Derek Angol (WBO)
07-30-1992 Stanhope (USA): **Al Cole** W 12 James Warring (IBF)
02-13-1993 Hamburg (GER): **Marcus Bott** W 12 Tyrone Booze (WBO)
03-26-1993 Hamburg (GER): **Nestor Giovannini** W 12 Marcus Bott (WBO)
 Sept. 1993 *WBA strips Czyz of his title due to inactivity.*
11-06-1993 Paris (FRA): **Orlin Norris** TKO 6 Marcelo Figueroa (WBA)
12-17-1994 Hamburg (GER): **Dariusz Michalczewski** TKO 10 Nestor Giovannini (WBO)
March 1995 *Michalczewski relinquishes the title to fight at light heavyweight.*
06-10-1995 Manchester (GBR): **Ralf Rocchigiani** TKO 11 Carl Thompson (WBO)
07-22-1995 London (GBR): **Nate Miller** KO 8 Orlin Norris (WBA)
April 1996 *Marcelo Dominguez is declared world champion by the WBC after Anaclet Wamba is stripped of his title because he fails to make weight. Cole is stripped of the IBF title because he fails to make the weight.*
08-31-1996 Palma de Mallorca (ESP): **Adolpho Washington** W 12 Torsten May (IBF)
06-21-1997 Tampa (USA): **Uriah Grant** W 12 Adolpho Washington (IBF)
10-04-1997 Hanover (GER): **Carl Thompson** W 12 Ralf Rocchigiani (WBO)
11-08-1997 Las Vegas (USA): **Imamu Mayfield** W 12 Uriah Grant (IBF)
11-08-1997 Las Vegas (USA): **Fabrice Tiozzo** W 12 Nate Miller (WBA)
02-21-1998 Mar del Plata (ARG): **Juan Carlos Gomez** W 12 Marcelo Dominguez (WBC)
10-30-1998 Biloxi (USA): **Arthur Williams** TKO 9 Imamu Mayfield (IBF)
03-27-1999 Derby (GBR): **Johnny Nelson** TKO 5 Carl Thompson (WBO)
06-05-1999 Biloxi (USA): **Vassiliy Jirov** TKO 7 Arthur Williams (IBF)
12-09-2000 Villeurbanne (FRA): **Virgil Hill** TKO 1 Fabrice Tiozzo (WBA)
02-13-2002 Marseille (FRA): **Jean-Marc Mormeck** TKO 9 Virgil Hill (WBA)
 2002 *Juan Carlos Gomez relinquishes the WBC title.*
10-11-2002 Campione d'Italia (ITA): **Wayne Braithwaite** TKO 10 Vincenzo Cantatore
02-21-2003 Miami (USA): **Wayne Braithwaite** TKO 4 Ravea Springs (WBC)
03-08-2003 Marseille (FRA): **Jean-Marc Mormeck** TKO 9 Alexander Gurov (WBA)

LIGHT HEAVYWEIGHT

04-22-1903 Detroit (USA): **Jack Root** W 10 Kid McCoy
07-04-1903 Fort Erie (CAN): **George Gardner** KO 12 Jack Root
11-25-1903 San Francisco (USA): **Robert Fitzsimmons** W 20 George Gardner
12-20-1905 San Francisco (USA): **"Philadelphia" Jack O'Brien** KO 14 Robert Fitzsimmons
05-28-1912 Indianapolis (USA): **Jack Dillon** KO 3 Hugo Kelly
10-24-1916 Boston (USA): **Battling Levinsky** W 12 Jack Dillon
10-12-1920 New York (USA): **Georges Carpentier** KO 4 Battling Levinsky
09-24-1922 Paris (FRA): **Battling Siki** KO 6 Georges Carpentier
03-17-1923 Dublin (IRL): **Mike McTigue** W 20 Battling Siki
05-30-1925 New York (USA): **Paul Berlenbach** W 15 Mike McTigue
07-16-1926 Brooklyn (USA): **Jack Delaney** W 15 Paul Berlenbach
 June 1927 *Delaney relinquishes the title to fight at heavyweight.*
08-30-1927 Hartford (USA): **Jimmy Slattery** W 10 Maxie Rosenbloom (NBA)
10-07-1927 New York (USA): **Tommy Loughran** W 15 Mike McTigue (NY)
12-12-1927 New York (USA): **Tommy Loughran** W 15 Jimmy Slattery
 Sept. 1929 *Loughran relinquishes the title to fight at heavyweight.*
02-10-1930 Buffalo (USA): **Jimmy Slattery** W 15 Lou Scozza (NY)
06-25-1930 New York (USA): **Maxie Rosenbloom** W 15 Jimmy Slattery
 June 1931 *Rosenbloom is stripped of the title for not defending.*
03-18-1932 Chicago (USA): **George Nichols** W 10 Dave Maier (NBA)
03-01-1933 West Palm Beach (USA): **Bob Godwin** W 10 Joe Knight (NBA)
03-24-1933 New York (USA): **Maxie Rosenbloom** KO 4 Bob Godwin
11-16-1934 New York (USA): **Bob Olin** W 15 Maxie Rosenbloom
 Aug. 1935 *The IBU strips Olin of the world championship title.*
09-17-1935 Vienna (AUT): **Hein Lazek** disq 13 Merlo Preciso (IBU)
10-31-1935 St. Louis (USA): **John Henry Lewis** W 15 Bob Olin (NY/NBA)
09-01-1936 Vienna (AUT): **Gustav Roth** W 15 Hein Lazek (IBU)
03-25-1938 Berlin (GER): **Adolf Heuser** KO 7 Gustav Roth (IBU)
 May 1938 *The IBU strips Heuser of the world championship title with the intention to unify the titles.*
 July 1938 *The New York State Boxing Commission strips Lewis of his title.*
02-23-1939 New York (USA): **Melio Bettina** TKO 9 Tiger Jack Fox (NY)
07-13-1939 Pittsburgh (USA): **Billy Conn** W 15 Melio Bettina (NBA/NY)

 Dec. 1940 *The NBA strips Conn of his title for changing to heavyweight. In March, the New York State Boxing Commission also withdraws recognition of Conn.*
01-13-1941 Cleveland (USA): **Anton Christoforidis** W 15 Melio Bettina (NBA)
05-22-1941 New York (USA): **Gus Lesnevich** W 15 Anton Christoforidis (NBA/NY)
06-20-1942 London (GBR): **Freddie Mills** KO 2 Len Harvey (NBA)
07-26-1948 London (GBR): **Freddie Mills** KO 2 Gus Lesnevich (NBA)
01-24-1950 London (GBR): **Joey Maxim** KO 10 Freddie Mills (NBA)
12-17-1952 St. Louis (USA): **Archie Moore** W 15 Joey Maxim (NBA)
 Oct. 1960 *The NBA strips Moore of his title for not defending.*
02-07-1961 Miami (USA): **Harold Johnson** TKO 9 Jesse Bowdrey (NBA)
 Feb. 1962 *Moore is stripped of the NY title for not defending.*
06-01-1963 Las Vegas (USA): **Willie Pastrano** W 15 Harold Johnson (NBA)
03-30-1965 New York (USA): **José Torres** W 15 Willie Pastrano (NBA)
12-16-1966 New York (USA): **Dick Tiger** W 15 José Torres (NBA)
05-24-1968 New York (USA): **Bob Foster** KO 4 Dick Tiger (NBA)
 Dec. 1970 *The WBA strips Foster of his title for not defending.*
02-27-1971 Caracas (VEN): **Vicente Rondon** TKO 6 Jimmy Dupree (WBA)
04-07-1972 Miami Beach (USA): **Bob Foster** KO 2 Vicente Rondon (WBA/WBC)
 Aug. 1974 *Foster is stripped of his title for not defending and retires.*
10-01-1974 London (GBR): **John Conteh** W 15 Jorge Ahumada (WBC)
10-07-1974 Buenos Aires (ARG): **Victor Galindez** ret 12 Len Hutchins (WBA)
 May 1977 *Conteh is stripped of the WBC title for not defending.*
05-21-1977 Monte Carlo (MON): **Miguel Cuello** KO 9 Jesse Burnett (WBC)
01-07-1978 Milan (ITA): **Mate Parlov** KO 9 Miguel Angel Cuello (WBC)
09-15-1978 New Orleans (USA): **Mike Rossman** TKO 13 Victor Galindez (WBA)
12-02-1978 Marsala (ITA): **Marvin Johnson** TKO 10 Mate Parlov (WBC)
04-14-1979 New Orleans (USA): **Victor Galindez** ret 9 Mike Rossman (WBA)
04-22-1979 Indianapolis (USA): **Matthew Saad Muhammad** TKO 8 Marvin Johnson (WBC)
11-30-1979 New Orleans (USA): **Marvin Johnson** TKO 11 Victor Galindez (WBA)
03-31-1980 Knoxville (USA): **Eddie Mustafa Muhammad** TKO 11 Marvin Johnson (WBA)
07-18-1981 Las Vegas (USA): **Michael Spinks** W 15 Eddie Mustafa Muhammad (WBA)
12-19-1981 Atlantic City (USA): **Dwight Braxton** TKO 10 Matthew Saad Muhammad (WBC)
03-18-1983 Atlantic City (USA): **Michael Spinks** W 15 Dwight Muhammad Quawi (WBC/WBA)
12-10-1985 Los Angeles (USA): **J.B. Williamson** W 12 Mama Muhammad (WBC)
12-12-1985 Pesaro (ITA): **Slobodan Kacar** W 15 Eddie Mustafa Muhammad (IBF)
02-09-1986 Indianapolis (USA): **Marvin Johnson** TKO 7 Leslie Stewart (WBA)
04-30-1986 Edmonton (GBR): **Dennis Andries** W 12 J.B.Williamson (WBC)
09-06-1986 Las Vegas (USA): **Bobby Czyz** TKO 5 Slobodan Kacar (IBF)
03-07-1987 Detroit (USA): **Thomas Hearns** TKO 10 Dennis Andries (WBC)
05-23-1987 Port of Spain (TRI): **Leslie Stewart** KO 9 Marvin Johnson (WBA)
 Aug. 1987 *Hearns relinquishes the WBC title to fight at middleweight.*
09-05-1987 Atlantic City (USA): **Virgil Hill** TKO 4 Leslie Stewart (WBA)
10-29-1987 Las Vegas (USA): **Charles Williams** ret 9 Bobby Czyz (IBF)
11-27-1987 Port of Spain (TRI): **Donny Lalonde** TKO 2 Eddie Davis (WBC)
11-07-1988 Las Vegas (USA): **Sugar Ray Leonard** TKO 9 Donny Lalonde (WBC)
 Leonard relinquishes his title.
12-03-1988 Cleveland (USA): **Michael Moorer** TKO 5 Ramzi Hassan (WBO)
02-21-1989 Tucson (USA): **Dennis Andries** TKO 5 Tony Willis (WBC)
06-24-1989 Atlantic City (USA): **Jeff Harding** TKO 12 Dennis Andries (WBC)
07-28-1990 Melbourne (AUS): **Dennis Andries** KO 7 Jeff Harding (WBC)
April 1991 *Moorer relinquishes the WBO title to fight at heavyweight.*
05-09-1991 Leeds (GBR): **Leeonzer Barber** ret Tom Collins (WBO)
06-03-1991 Las Vegas (USA): **Thomas Hearns** W 12 Virgil Hill (WBA)
09-11-1991 London (GBR): **Jeff Harding** W 12 Dennis Andries (WBC)
03-20-1992 Las Vegas (USA): **Iran Barkley** W 12 Thomas Hearns (WBA)
April 1992 *Barkley relinquishes his title to concentrate on the fight for the IBF super middleweight title.*
09-29-1992 Bismarck (USA): **Virgil Hill** W 12 Frank Tate (WBA)
03-20-1993 Düsseldorf (GER): **Henry Maske** W 12 Charles Williams (IBF)
07-23-1994 Bismarck (USA): **Mike McCallum** W 12 Jeff Harding (WBC)
09-10-1994 Hamburg (GER): **Dariusz Michalczewski** W 12 Leeonzer Barber (WBO)
06-16-1995 Lyon (FRA): **Fabrice Tiozzo** W 12 Mike McCallum (WBC)
11-23-1996 Munich (GER): **Virgil Hill** W 12 Henry Maske (IBF/WBA)
 Feb. 1997 *Tiozzo is stripped of the WBC title for not defending.*
03-21-1997 Atlantic City (USA): **Montell Griffin** disq 9 Roy Jones Jr. (WBC)
06-13-1997 Oberhausen (GER): **Dariusz Michalczewski** W 12 Virgil Hill (IBF/WBA/WBO)
 June 1997 *Michalczewski relinquishes his titles.*
07-19-1997 Indio (USA): **William Guthrie** TKO 3 Darrin Allen (IBF)
08-07-1997 Ledyard (USA): **Roy Jones Jr.** KO 1 Montell Griffin (WBC)
09-20-1997 Aachen (GER): **Lou Del Valle** TKO 8 Eddy Smulders (WBA)
02-06-1998 Uncasville (USA): **Reggie Johnson** KO 5 William Guthrie (IBF)
07-18-1998 New York (USA): **Roy Jones Jr.** W 12 Lou Del Valle (WBA/WBC)
03-08-2003 Marseille (FRA): **Mehdi Sahnoune** TKO 9 Bruno Girard (WBA)
03-29-2003 Hamburg (GER): **Dariusz Michalczewski** KO 9 Derrick Harmon (WBO)

SUPER MIDDLEWEIGHT

03-28-1984 Atlantic City (USA): **Murray Sutherland** W 15 Ernie Singletary (IBF)
07-22-1984 Seoul (KOR): **Chong-Pal Park** KO 11 Murray Sutherland (IBF)
Dec. 1987 *Chong-Pal Park relinquishes the title to fight for the WBA title.*
12-06-1987 Seoul (KOR): **Chong-Pal Park** TKO 2 Jesus Gallardo (WBA)
03-12-1988 Düsseldorf (GER): **Graciano Rocchigiani** TKO 8 Vincent Boulware (IBF)
05-23-1988 Chungju (KOR): **Fulgencio Obelmejias** W 12 Chong-Pal Park (WBA)
11-04-1988 Las Vegas (USA): **Thomas Hearns** W 12 James Kinchen (WBO)
11-07-1988 Las Vegas (USA): **Sugar Ray Leonard** TKO 9 Don Lalonde (WBC)
05-27-1989 Seoul (KOR): **Inchul Baek** TKO 11 Fulgencio Obelmejias (WBA)
Sept. 1989 *Rocchigiani relinquishes his title because he fails to make weight.*
01-27-1990 New Orleans (USA): **Lindell Holmes** W 12 Frank Tate (IBF)
03-30-1990 Lyon (FRA): **Christophe Tiozzo** TKO 12 Inchul Baek (WBA)
Aug. 1990 *Leonard relinquishes the WBC title.*
12-15-1990 Monte Carlo (MON): **Mauro Galvano** W 12 Dario Matteoni (WBC)
April 1991 *Hearns relinquishes the WBO title to fight at light heavyweight.*
04-09-1991 Marseille (FRA): **Victor Cordoba** TKO 9 Christophe Tiozzo (WBA)
05-18-1991 Verbania (ITA): **Darrin Van Horn** KO 11 Lindell Holmes (IBF)
09-21-1991 London (GBR): **Chris Eubank** TKO 12 Michael Watson (WBO)
01-10-1992 New York (USA): **Iran Barkley** TKO 2 Darrin Van Horn (IBF)
09-12-1992 Las Vegas (USA): **Michael Nunn** W 12 Victor Cordoba (WBA)
10-03-1992 Marino (ITA): **Nigel Benn** ret 3 Mauro Galvano (WBC)
02-13-1993 Las Vegas (USA): **James Toney** ret 9 Iran Barkley (IBF)
02-26-1994 London (GBR): **Steve Little** W 12 Michael Nunn (WBA)
08-12-1994 Tucuman (ARG): **Frank Liles** W 12 Steve Little (WBA)
11-18-1994 Las Vegas (USA): **Roy Jones Jr.** W 12 James Toney (IBF)
03-18-1995 Millstreet (IRL): **Steve Collins** W 12 Chris Eubank (WBO)
03-02-1996 Newcastle (GBR): **Sugarboy Malinga** W 12 Nigel Benn (WBC)
07-06-1996 Manchester (GBR): **Vincenzo Nardiello** W 12 Sugarboy Malinga (WBC)
10-12-1996 Milan (ITA): **Robin Reid** KO 7 Vincenzo Nardiello (WBC)
March 1997 *Jones relinquishes the IBF title because he has won a light heavyweight title.*
Sept. 1997 *Collins retires from professional sport.*
10-11-1997 Sheffield (GBR): **Joe Calzaghe** W 12 Chris Eubank (WBO)
12-19-1997 London (GBR): **Sugarboy Malinga** W 12 Robin Reid (WBC)
03-27-1998 Telford (GBR): **Richie Woodhall** W 12 Sugarboy Malinga (WBC)
06-21-1998 Tampa (USA): **Charles Brewer** TKO 15 Gary Ballard (IBF)
10-24-1998 Düsseldorf (GER): **Sven Ottke** W 12 Charles Brewer (IBF)
06-12-1999 Wilmington (USA): **Byron Mitchell** TKO 11 Frank Liles (WBA)
10-23-1999 Telford (GBR): **Markus Beyer** W 12 Richie Woodhall (WBC)
04-08-2000 Paris (FRA): **Bruno Girard** W 12 Byron Mitchell (WBA)
05-06-2000 Frankfurt (GER): **Glenn Catley** TKO 12 Markus Beyer (WBC)
09-01-2000 Beakpan (RSA): **Dingaan Thobela** KO 12 Glenn Catley (WBC)
12-15-2000 Montreal (CAN): **Davey Hilton** W 12 Dingaan Thobela (WBC)
07-10-2001 Montreal (CAN): **Eric Lucas** TKO 7 Glenn Catley (WBC)
03-15-2003 Berlin (GER): **Sven Ottke** splt 12 Byron Mitchell (WBA)
Ottke unifies the IBF and WBA super middleweight titles.

MIDDLEWEIGHT

07-30-1884 Staten Island (USA): **Nonpareil Jack Dempsey** KO 22 George Fulljames
01-14-1891 New Orleans (USA): **Bob Fitzsimmons** KO 12 Nonpareil Jack Dempsey
Fitzsimmons relinquishes his title to fight at heavyweight.
03-02-1896 Long Island City (USA): **Kid McCoy** KO 15 Tommy Ryan
McCoy relinquishes the title.
10-24-1898 Coney Island (USA): **Tommy Ryan** W 20 Jack Bonner
Ryan retires from professional sport.
05-09-1908 Colma (USA): **Stanley Ketchel** KO 20 Jack "Twin" Sullivan
09-07-1908 Los Angeles (USA): **Billy Papke** KO 12 Stanley Ketchel
11-26-1908 Colma (USA): **Stanley Ketchel** KO 11 Billy Papke
Jan. 1910 *Ketchel relinquishes his title because he fails to make weight.*
03-19-1910 Paris (FRA): **Billy Papke** KO 3 Willie Lewis
Ketchel is determined to reclaim the title.
05-27-1910 Colma (USA): **Stanley Ketchel** KO 3 Willie Lewis
Oct. 1910 *Ketchel is shot.*
06-08-1911 London (GBR): **Billy Papke** ret 9 Jim Sullivan
03-05-1913 Paris (FRA): **Frank Klaus** disq 15 Billy Papke
10-11-1913 Pittsburgh (USA): **George Chip** KO 6 Frank Klaus
01-01-1914 Sydney (AUS): **Eddie McGoorty** KO 1 Dave Smith (Australian World Title)
03-14-1914 Sydney (AUS): **Jeff Smith** W 20 Eddie McGoorty (Australian World Title)
04-06-1914 Brooklyn (USA): **Al McCoy** KO 1 George Chip
11-28-1914 Sydney (AUS): **Mick King** W 20 Jeff Smith (Australian World Title)
12-26-1914 Sydney (AUS): **Jeff Smith** W 20 Mick King (Australian World Title)
05-22-1915 Sydney (AUS): **Les Darcy** disq 2 Jeff Smith (Australian World Title)
11-14-1917 Brooklyn (USA): **Mike O'Dowd** KO 6 Al McCoy
05-06-1920 Boston (USA): **Johnny Wilson** W 12 Mike O'Dowd
1921 *Wilson loses the title because he fails to make weight.*
08-14-1922 New York (USA): **Dave Rosenburg** W 15 Phil Krug
11-30-1922 Brooklyn (USA): **Mike O'Dowd** disq 8 Dave Rosenburg
March 1923 *O'Dowd relinquishes the title after a knockout in the first round of a non-title bout.*
08-31-1923 New York (USA): **Harry Greb** W 15 Johnny Wilson

02-26-1926 New York (USA): **Tiger Flowers** W 15 Harry Greb
12-03-1926 Chicago (USA): **Mickey Walker** W 10 Tiger Flowers
1931 *Walker relinquishes the title.*
01-25-1932 Milwaukee (USA): **William "Gorilla" Jones** KO 6 Oddone Piazza (NBA)
The NBA strips Jones of his title after he loses against Marcel Thil.
06-11-1932 Paris (FRA): **Marcel Thil** disq 11 William "Gorilla" Jones (IBU)
01-13-1933 New York (USA): **Ben Jeby** TKO 12 Frank Battaglia (NY)
08-09-1933 New York (USA): **Lou Brouillard** KO 7 Ben Jeby (NY/NBA)
10-30-1933 Boston (USA): **Vince Dundee** W 15 Lou Brouillard (NY/NBA)
09-11-1934 Pittsburgh (USA): **Teddy Yarosz** W 15 Vince Dundee (NY/NBA)
09-19-1935 New York (USA): **Ed "Babe" Risko** W 15 Teddy Yarosz (NY/NBA)
07-11-1936 New York (USA): **Freddie Steele** W 15 Ed " Babe" Risko (NY/NBA)
Sept. 1937 *Thil retires from professional sport.*
04-07-1938 Berlin (GER): **Edouard Tenet** ret 12 Josef Besselmann (IBU)
The IBU strips Tenet of his title to unify the world championship titles.
May 1938 *Steele is stripped of the title for not defending.*
07-26-1938 Seattle (USA): **Al Hostak** KO 1 Freddie Steele (NBA)
11-01-1938 Seattle (USA): **Solly Krieger** W 15 Al Hostak (NBA)
11-18-1938 New York (USA): **Fred Apostoli** KO 8 Young Corbett III (NY)
06-27-1939 Seattle (USA): **Al Hostak** KO 4 Solly Krieger (NBA)
10-02-1939 New York (USA): **Ceferino Garcia** TKO 7 Fred Apostoli
05-23-1940 New York (USA): **Ken Overlin** W 15 Ceferino Garcia (NY)
07-19-1940 Chicago (USA): **Tony Zale** ret 13 Al Hostak (NBA)
05-09-1941 New York (USA): **Billy Soose** W 15 Ken Overlin (NY)
Soose is stripped of his title for not defending.
11-28-1944 New York (USA): **Tony Zale** W 15 Georgie Abrams
09-27-1946 New York (USA): **Tony Zale** KO 6 Rocky Graziano
07-16-1947 Chicago (USA): **Rocky Graziano** TKO 6 Tony Zale
06-10-1948 Newark (USA): **Tony Zale** KO 3 Rocky Graziano
09-21-1948 Jersey City (USA): **Marcel Cerdan** ret 11 Tony Zale
06-16-1949 Detroit (USA): **Jake LaMotta** ret 10 Marcel Cerdan
02-14-1951 Chicago (USA): **Sugar Ray Robinson** TKO 13 Jake LaMotta
07-10-1951 London (GBR): **Randolph Turpin** W 15 Sugar Ray Robinson
09-12-1951 New York (USA): **Sugar Ray Robinson** TKO 10 Randolph Turpin
Dec. 1952 *Robinson announces his retirement from professional sport.*
10-21-1953 New York (USA): **Carl "Bobo" Olson** W 15 Randolph Turpin
12-09-1955 Chicago (USA): **Sugar Ray Robinson** KO 2 Carl "Bobo" Olson
01-02-1957 New York (USA): **Gene Fullmer** W 15 Sugar Ray Robinson
05-01-1957 Chicago (USA): **Sugar Ray Robinson** KO 5 Gene Fullmer
09-23-1957 New York (USA): **Carmen Basilio** W 15 Sugar Ray Robinson
03-25-1958 Chicago (USA): **Sugar Ray Robinson** W 15 Carmen Basilio
May 1959 *Robinson is stripped of his title for not defending.*
08-28-1959 San Francisco (USA): **Gene Fullmer** TKO 14 Carmen Basilio (NBA)
01-22-1960 Boston (USA): **Paul Pender** W 15 Sugar Ray Robinson (NY)
07-11-1961 London (GBR): **Terry Downes** ret 9 Paul Pender (NY)
04-07-1962 Boston (USA): **Paul Pender** W 15 Terry Downes (NY)
10-23-1962 San Francisco (USA): **Dick Tiger** W 15 Gene Fullmer (NBA)
Nov. 1962 *Pender relinquishes his title.*
08-10-1963 Ibadan (NGR): **Dick Tiger** TKO 7 Gene Fullmer
12-07-1963 Atlantic City (USA): **Joey Giardello** W 15 Dick Tiger
10-21-1965 New York (USA): **Dick Tiger** W 15 Joey Giardello
04-25-1966 New York (USA): **Emile Griffith** W 15 Dick Tiger
04-17-1967 New York (USA): **Nino Benvenuti** W 15 Emile Griffith
09-29-1967 New York (USA): **Emile Griffith** W 15 Nino Benvenuti
03-04-1968 New York (USA): **Nino Benvenuti** W 15 Emile Griffith
11-07-1970 Rome (ITA): **Carlos Monzon** KO 12 Nino Benvenuti
April 1974 *Monzon is stripped of the WBC title for not defending.*
05-25-1974 Monte Carlo (MON): **Rodrigo Valdez** KO 7 Bennie Briscoe (WBC)
10-05-1974 Buenos Aires (ARG): **Carlos Monzon** KO 7 Anthony Mundine (WBA)
06-26-1976 Monte Carlo (MON): **Carlos Monzon** W 15 Rodrigo Valdez (WBC/WBA)
Aug. 1977 *Monzon retires from professional sport.*
11-05-1977 Campione d'Italia (ITA): **Rodrigo Valdez** W 15 Bennie Briscoe
04-22-1978 Buenos Aires (ARG): **Hugo Corro** W 15 Rodrigo Valdez
06-30-1979 Monte Carlo (MON): **Vito Antuofermo** W 15 Hugo Corro
03-16-1980 Las Vegas (USA): **Alan Minter** W 15 Vito Antuofermo
09-27-1980 London (GBR): **Marvin Hagler** TKO 3 Alan Minter
Feb. 1987 *Hagler is stripped of his title for not defending.*
04-06-1987 Las Vegas (USA): **Sugar Ray Leonard** W 12 Marvin Hagler (WBC/IBF)
April 1987 *The IBF strips Leonard of the title.*
June 1987 *Leonard relinquishes the WBC title.*
10-10-1987 Las Vegas (USA): **Frank Tate** W 15 Michael Olajide (IBF)
10-23-1987 Livorno (ITA): **Sumbu Kalambay** W 12 Iran Barkley (WBA)
10-29-1987 Las Vegas (USA): **Thomas Hearns** KO 4 Juan Roldan (WBC)
06-06-1988 Las Vegas (USA): **Iran Barkley** TKO 3 Thomas Hearns (WBC)
07-28-1988 Las Vegas (USA): **Michael Nunn** TKO 9 Frank Tate (IBF)
02-24-1989 Atlantic City (USA): **Roberto Duran** W 12 Iran Barkley (WBC)
March 1989 *Kalambay is stripped of the WBA title for not defending.*
04-18-1989 Atlantic City (USA): **Doug DeWitt** W 12 Robbie Sims (WBO)
05-10-1989 London (GBR): **Mike McCallum** W 12 Herol Graham (WBA)
Jan. 1990 *Duran is stripped of the WBC title for not defending.*

04-29-1990 Atlantic City (USA): **Nigel Benn** TKO 8 Doug DeWitt (WBO)
11-18-1990 Birmingham (GBR): **Chris Eubank** TKO 9 Nigel Benn (WBO)
11-24-1990 Benalmadena (ESP): **Julian Jackson** KO 4 Herol Graham (WBC)
05-10-1991 Davenport (USA): **James Toney** TKO 11 Michael Nunn (IBF)
July 1991 *Eubank relinquishes the title to fight at super middleweight.*
11-20-1991 London (GBR): **Gerald McClellan** TKO 1 John Mugabi (WBO)
Dec. 1991 *The WBA withdraws recognition of McCallum because of his upcoming fight for an IBF title.*
04-22-1992 East Rutherford (USA): **Reggie Johnson** W 12 Steve Collins (WBA)
Feb. 1993 *Toney relinquishes the IBF title after he has become IBF super middleweight champion.*
March 1993 *McClellan relinquishes the WBO title.*
05-08-1993 Las Vegas (USA): **Gerald McClellan** TKO 5 Julian Jackson (WBC)
05-19-1993 Leicester (GBR): **Chris Pyatt** W 12 Sumbu Kalambay (WBO)
05-22-1993 Washington (USA): **Roy Jones Jr.** W 12 Bernard Hopkins (IBF)
10-01-1993 Buenos Aires (ARG): **John David Jackson** W 12 Reggie Johnson (WBA)
1994 *McClellan relinquishes the WBC title to fight at super middleweight.*
1994 *Jones relinquishes the IBF title to fight at super middleweight.*
May 1994 *The WBA strips Jackson of the title because he fought in an unauthorized non-title bout.*
05-11-1994 Sheffield (GBR): **Steve Collins** TKO 5 Chris Pyatt (WBO)
08-12-1994 Tucuman (ARG): **Jorge Castro** W 12 Reggie Johnson (WBA)
March 1995 *Collins relinquishes the WBO title to fight at super middleweight.*
03-07-1995 Worcester (USA): **Julian Jackson** TKO 2 Agostino Cardamone (WBC)
04-29-1995 Landover (USA): **Bernard Hopkins** TKO 7 Segundo Mercado (IBF)
05-19-1995 Jaen (ESP): **Lonnie Bradley** TKO 12 David Mendez (WBO)
08-19-1995 Las Vegas (USA): **Quincy Taylor** TKO 6 Julian Jackson (WBC)
12-19-1995 Tokyo (JPN): **Shinji Takehara** W 12 Jorge Castro (WBA)
03-16-1996 Las Vegas (USA): **Keith Holmes** TKO 9 Quincy Taylor (WBC)
06-24-1996 Yokohama (JPN): **William Joppy** TKO 9 Shinji Takehara (WBA)
1997 *Bradley relinquishes the WBO title due to an eye injury.*
06-28-1997 Sheffield (GBR): **Otis Grant** W 12 Ryan Rhodes (WBO)
Grant relinquishes the title to fight at light heavyweight.
08-23-1997 New York (USA): **Julio Cesar Green** W 12 William Joppy (WBA)
01-31-1998 Tampa (USA): **William Joppy** W 12 Julio Cesar Green (WBA)
05-02-1998 Villeurbanne (FRA): **Hassine Cherifi** W 12 Keith Holmes (WBC)
01-30-1999 Cottbus (GER): **Bert Schenk** KO 4 Freeman Barr (WBO)
04-24-1999 Washington (USA): **Keith Holmes** TKO 7 Hassine Cherifi (WBC)
Nov. 1999 *The WBO strips Schenk of his title due to inactivity.*
11-27-1999 Lübeck (GER): **Armand Krajnc** TKO 8 Jason Matthews (WBO)
04-14-2001 New York (USA): **Bernard Hopkins** PS 12 Keith Holmes (WBC)
05-13-2001 New York (USA): **Felix Trinidad** TKO 5 William Joppy (WBA)
07-21-2001 Bayamon (PUR): **Harry Simon** W 12 Hassine Cherifi (WBO)
2001 *The WBO strips Simon of his title due to inactivity.*
09-29-2001 New York (USA): **Bernard Hopkins** TKO 12 Felix Trinidad (WBA, WBC)
11-03-2001 Lübeck (GER): **Armand Krajnc** W 12 Paolo Roberto (WBO)
04-06-2002 Copenhagen (DEN): **Harry Simon** W 12 Armand Krajnc (WBO)
03-01-2003 LasVegas (USA): **Ronald Wright** W 12 J.C. Candelo (IBF)
03-29-2003 Philadelphia (USA): **Bernard Hopkins** TKO 8 Morrade Hakkar (WBC/WBA/IBF)
04-26-2003 Mashantucket (USA): **James "Lights Out" Toney** W 12 Vassily Jirov (IBF)

JUNIOR MIDDLEWEIGHT
10-20-1962 Portland (USA): **Denny Moyer** W 15 Joey Giambra (WBA)
04-29-1963 New Orleans (USA): **Ralph Dupas** W 15 Denny Moyer (WBA)
09-07-1963 Milan (ITA): **Sandro Mazzinghi** KO 9 Ralph Dupas (WBA)
06-18-1965 Milan (ITA): **Nino Benvenuti** KO 6 Sandro Mazzinghi (WBA)
06-25-1966 Seoul (KOR): **Kim Ki-Soo** W 15 Nino Benvenuti (WBA)
05-26-1968 Milan (ITA): **Sandro Mazzinghi** W 15 Kim Ki-Soo (WBA)
Jan. 1969 *The WBA declares the title vacant because Mazzinghi refuses a rematch against Freddie Little.*
03-17-1969 Las Vegas (USA): **Freddie Little** W 15 Stan Hayward (WBA)
07-09-1970 Monza (ITA): **Carmelo Bossi** W 15 Freddie Little (WBA)
10-31-1971 Tokyo (JPN): **Koichi Wajima** W 15 Carmelo Bossi (WBA)
06-04-1974 Tokyo (JPN): **Oscar Albarado** KO 15 Koichi Wajima (WBA)
01-21-1975 Tokyo (JPN): **Koichi Wajima** W 15 Oscar Albarado (WBA)
1975 *The WBA withdraws recognition of Wajima.*
05-07-1975 Monte Carlo (MON): **Miguel de Oliveira** W 15 Jose Duran (WBC)
06-07-1975 Kitakyushu (JPN): **Jae Do Yuh** KO 7 Koichi Wajima (WBA)
11-13-1975 Paris (FRA): **Elisha Obed** ret 10 Miguel de Oliveira (WBC)
02-17-1976 Tokyo (JPN): **Koichi Wajima** KO 15 Jae Do Yuh (WBA)
05-18-1976 Tokyo (JPN): **Jose Duran** KO 14 Koichi Wajima (WBA)
06-18-1976 Berlin (GER): **Eckhard Dagge** ret 10 Elisha Obed (WBC)
10-08-1976 Madrid (ESP): **Miguel Angel Castellini** W 15 Jose Duran (WBA)
03-05-1977 Managua (NCA): **Eddie Gazo** W 15 Miguel Angel Castellini (WBA)
08-06-1977 Berlin (GER): **Rocky Mattioli** KO 5 Eckhard Dagge (WBC)
08-09-1978 Akita (JPN): **Masashi Kudo** W 15 Eddie Gazo (WBA)
03-04-1979 San Remo (ITA): **Maurice Hope** ret 8 Rocky Mattioli (WBC)
10-24-1979 Akita (JPN): **Ayub Kalule** W 15 Masashi Kudo (WBA)
05-24-1981 Las Vegas (USA): **Wilfred Benitez** KO 12 Maurice Hope (WBC)
06-25-1981 Houston (USA): **Sugar Ray Leonard** TKO 9 Ayub Kalule (WBA)

July 1981 *Leonard relinquishes his title to fight at welterweight.*
11-07-1981 Rochester (USA): **Tadashi Mihara** W 15 Rocky Fratto (WBA)
02-02-1982 Tokyo (JPN): **Davey Moore** TKO 6 Tadashi Mihara (WBA)
12-03-1982 New Orleans (USA): **Thomas Hearns** W 15 Wilfred Benitez (WBC)
06-16-1983 New York (USA): **Roberto Duran** TKO 8 Davey Moore (WBA)
June 1983 *Duran relinquishes the WBA title to challenge WBC champion Hearns.*
03-11-1984 Atlantic City (USA): **Mark Medal** TKO 5 Earl Hargrove (IBF)
10-19-1984 New York (USA): **Mike McCallum** W 15 Sean Mannion (WBA)
11-02-1984 New York (USA): **Carlos Santos** W 15 Mark Medal (IBF)
Feb. 1986 *Santos is stripped of the IBF title for not defending.*
06-04-1986 East Rutherford (USA): **Buster Drayton** W 15 Carlos Santos (IBF)
Sept. 1986 *Hearns relinquishes the WBC title because he fails to make weight.*
12-05-1986 Las Vegas (USA): **Duane Thomas** TKO 3 John Mugabi (WBC)
06-27-1987 Montreal (CAN): **Matthew Hilton** W 15 Buster Drayton (IBF)
07-12-1987 Bordeaux (FRA): **Lupe Aquino** W 12 Duane Thomas (WBC)
Sept. 1987 *McCallum relinquishes the WBA title to fight at middleweight.*
10-02-1987 Perugia (ITA): **Gianfranco Rosi** W 12 Lupe Aquino (WBC)
11-21-1987 Las Vegas (USA): **Julian Jackson** TKO 3 In Chul Baek (WBA)
07-08-1988 San Remo (ITA): **Don Curry** ret 9 Gianfranco Rosi (WBC)
11-04-1988 Las Vegas (USA): **Robert Hines** W 12 Matthew Hilton (IBF)
12-08-1988 Detroit (USA): **John David Jackson** ret 7 Lupe Aquino (WBO)
02-05-1989 Atlantic City (USA): **Darrin Van Horn** W 12 Robert Hines (IBF)
02-11-1989 Grenoble (FRA): **Rene Jacquot** W 12 Donald Curry (WBC)
07-09-1989 Paris (FRA): **John Mugabi** TKO 1 Rene Jacquot (WBC)
07-15-1989 Atlantic City (USA): **Gianfranco Rosi** W 12 Darrin van Horn (IBF)
03-31-1990 Tampa (USA): **Terry Norris** KO 1 John Mugabi (WBC)
Sept. 1990 *Julian Jackson relinquishes the WBA title to fight at WBC middleweight.*
02-23-1991 Point-a-Pitre (FRA): **Gilbert Dele** TKO 7 Carlos Elliott (WBA)
10-03-1991 Providence (USA): **Vinnie Pazienza** TKO 12 Gilbert Dele (WBA)
Pazienza relinquishes the title due to injuries after a car accident.
12-21-1992 Buenos Aires (ARG): **Julio Cesar Vasquez** TKO 1 Hiroshi Kamiyama (WBA)
July 1993 *John David Jackson relinquishes the WBO title to fight at middleweight.*
10-30-1993 Phoenix (USA): **Verno Phillips** TKO 7 Lupe Aquino (WBO)
12-18-1993 Puebla (MEX): **Simon Brown** KO 4 Terry Norris (WBC)
05-07-1994 Las Vegas (USA): **Terry Norris** W 12 Simon Brown (WBC)
09-17-1994 Las Vegas (USA): **Vincent Pettway** KO 4 Gianfranco Rosi (IBF)
11-12-1994 Mexico City (MEX): **Luis Santana** disq 5 Terry Norris (WBC)
03-04-1995 Atlantic City (USA): **Pernell Whitaker** W 12 Julio Cesar Vasquez (WBA)
March 1995 *Whitaker relinquishes the WBA title to defend his welterweight title.*
05-17-1995 Perugia (ITA): **Gianfranco Rosi** W 12 Verno Phillips (WBO)
Rosi is stripped of his title title after testing positive for doping.
06-16-1995 Lyon (FRA): **Carl Daniels** W 12 Julio Cesar Vasquez (WBA)
08-12-1995 Las Vegas (USA): **Paul Vaden** TKO 12 Vincent Pettway (IBF)
08-19-1995 Las Vegas (USA): **Terry Norris** TKO 2 Luis Santana (WBC)
11-22-1995 Sheffield (GBR): **Paul Jones** W 12 Verno Phillips (WBO)
12-16-1995 Philadelphia (USA): **Terry Norris** W 12 Paul Valden (IBF/WBC)
12-16-1995 Philadelphia (USA): **Julio Cesar Vasquez** TKO 11 Carl Daniels (WBA)
Feb. 1996 *Jones is stripped of the WBO title for not defending.*
03-01-1996 Indio (USA): **Bronco McKart** TKO 9 Santos Cardona (WBO)
05-17-1996 Monroe (USA): **Ronald Wright** W 12 Bronco McKart (WBO)
08-21-1996 Le Cannet (FRA): **Laurent Boudouani** TKO 5 Julio Cesar Vasquez (WBA)
March 1997 *Norris relinquishes the IBF title.*
04-12-1997 Las Vegas (USA): **Raul Marquez** TKO 9 Anthony Stephens (IBF)
12-06-1997 Atlantic City (USA): **Keith Mullings** TKO 9 Terry Norris (WBC)
12-06-1997 Atlantic City (USA): **Luis Ramon Campas** TKO 8 Raul Marquez (IBF)
08-22-1998 Hammanskraal (RSA): **Harry Simon** W 12 Ronald Wright (WBO)
12-12-1998 Atlantic City (USA): **Fernando Vargas** TKO 7 Luis Ramon Campas (IBF)
01-29-1999 Madrid (ESP): **Javier Castillejo** W 12 Keith Mullings (WBC)
01-30-1999 Leganes (ESP): **Javier Castillejo** W 12 Keith Mullings (WBC)
03-06-1999 Atlantic City (USA): **David Reid** W 12 Laurent Boudouani (WBA)
03-03-2000 Las Vegas (USA): **Felix Trinidad** W 12 David Reid (WBA)
12-02-2000 Las Vegas (USA): **Felix Trinidad** TKO 12 Fernando Vargas (WBA/IBF)
06-23-2001 Las Vegas (USA): **Oscar De La Hoya** W 12 Javier Castillejo (WBC)
2001 *De La Hoya relinquishes the WBC title.*
09-21-2001 Las Vegas (USA): **Fernando Vargas** KO 7 Shibata Flores (WBA)
10-12-2001 Indio (USA): **Ronald Wright** W 12 Robert Frazier (IBF)
03-16-2002 Las Vegas (USA): **Daniel Santos** TKO 11 Luis "Yory Boy" Campas (WBO)
09-14-2002 Las Vegas (USA): **Oscar De La Hoya** TKO 11 Fernando Vargas (WBA)
05-03-2003 Las Vegas (USA): **Oscar De La Hoya** TKO 7 Luis "Yory Boy" Campas (WBC/WBA)

WELTERWEIGHT
10-30-1888 Fort Foote (USA): **Paddy Duffy** KO 17 William McMillan
July 1890 *Duffy dies and the title is claimed by Tommy Ryan and "Mysterious" Billy Smith.*
08-09-1891 Richardson (CAN): **Tommy Ryan** KO 3 William McMillan
12-14-1892 San Francisco (USA): **"Mysterious" Billy Smith** KO 14 Danny Needham
07-26-1894 Minneapolis (USA): **Tommy Ryan** W 20 "Mysterious" Billy Smith
1895 *Ryan is stripped of his title because he fails to make weight.*
03-17-1897 Carson City (USA): **George Green** KO 12 "Mysterious" Billy Smith

08-26-1897 San Francisco (USA): **"Jersey" Joe Walcott** KO 18 George Green
08-27-1898 New York (USA): **"Mysterious" Billy Smith** W 25 Matty Matthews
04-17-1900 New York (USA): **Matty Matthews** KO 19 "Mysterious" Billy Smith
06-05-1900 Brooklyn (USA): **Eddie Connolly** W 25 Matty Matthews
08-13-1900 Buffalo (USA): **Jim "Rube" Ferns** ret 15 Eddie Connolly
10-16-1900 Detroit (USA): **Matty Matthews** W 15 Jim "Rube" Ferns
05-24-1901 Toronto (CAN): **Jim "Rube" Ferns** KO 10 Matty Matthews
12-18-1901 Fort Erie (CAN): **"Jersey" Joe Walcott** TKO 5 Jim "Rube" Ferns
11-29-1906 Chelsea (USA): **Honey Mellody** TKO 12 "Jersey" Joe Walcott
04-23-1907 Los Angeles (USA): **Mike "Twin" Sullivan** W 20 Honey Mellody
April 1908 *Sullivan relinquishes the title because he fails to make weight. Harry Lewis is later recognized as champion.*
02-19-1910 Paris (FRA): **Harry Lewis** W 25 Willie Lewis
Feb. 1911 *Lewis relinquishes the title to fight at middleweight.*
11-09-1911 Liverpool (GBR): **Dixie Kid** KO 2 Johnny Summers
10-04-1912 Paris (FRA): **Marcel Thomas** W 15 Dixie Kid (IBU)
07-22-1913 Boston (USA): **Mike Glover** TKO 4 Marcel Thomas
01-01-1914 Melbourne (AUS): **Waldemar Holberg** W 20 Ray Bronson (Australian World Title)
01-24-1914 Melbourne (AUS): **Tom McCormick** disq 6 Waldemar Holberg (Australian World Title)
03-21-1914 Sydney (AUS): **Matt Wells** W 20 Tom McCormick (Australian World Title)
06-01-1915 Boston (USA): **Mike Glover** W 12 Matt Wells
June 1915 *Glover loses his claim for the title after he is defeated by Jack Britton.*
04-24-1916 New Orleans (USA): **Jack Britton** W 20 Ted "Kid" Lewis
06-25-1917 Dayton (USA): **Ted "Kid" Lewis** W 20 Jack Britton
03-17-1919 Canton (USA): **Jack Britton** KO 9 Ted "Kid" Lewis
11-01-1922 New York (USA): **Mickey Walker** W 15 Jack Britton
June 1923 *Walker is stripped of the New York title for not defending.*
07-27-1923 Boston (USA): **Jimmy Jones** W 10 Dave Shade (NY)
New York withdraws recognition of Jones.
06-02-1924 Philadelphia (USA): **Mickey Walker** W 10 Lew Tendler
05-20-1926 Scranton (USA): **Pete Latzo** W 10 Mickey Walker
06-03-1927 New York (USA): **Joe Dundee** W 15 Pete Latzo
Sept. 1928 *Dundee is stripped of his title for not defending.*
03-25-1929 Chicago (USA): **Jackie Fields** W 10 Young Jack Thompson (NBA)
05-09-1930 Detroit (USA): **"Young" Jack Thompson** W 15 Jackie Fields
09-05-1930 Cleveland (USA): **Tommy Freeman** W 15 "Young" Jack Thompson
04-14-1931 Cleveland (USA): **"Young"Jack Thompson** ret 12 Tommy Freeman
10-23-1931 Boston (USA): **Lou Brouillard** W 15 "Young" Jack Thompson
01-28-1932 Chicago (USA): **Jackie Fields** W 10 Lou Brouillard
02-22-1933 San Francisco (USA): **Young Corbett III** W 10 Jackie Fields
05-29-1933 Los Angeles (USA): **Jimmy McLarnin** KO 1 Young Corbett III
05-28-1934 Long Island City (USA): **Barney Ross** W 15 Jimmy McLarnin
09-17-1934 Long Island City (USA): **Jimmy McLarnin** W 15 Barney Ross
05-28-1935 New York (USA): **Barney Ross** W 15 Jimmy McLarnin
05-31-1938 Long Island City (USA): **Henry Amstrong** W 15 Barney Ross
10-04-1940 New York (USA): **Fritzie Zivic** W 15 Henry Amstrong
07-21-1941 Newark (USA): **Freddie "Red" Cochrane** W 15 Fritzie Zivic
02-01-1946 New York (USA): **Marty Servo** KO 4 Freddie "Red" Cochrane
Sept. 1946 *Servo retires from professional sport.*
12-20-1946 New York (USA): **Sugar Ray Robinson** W 15 Tommy Bell
Feb. 1951 *Robinson relinquishes the title to fight at middleweight.*
03-14-1951 Chicago (USA): **Johnny Bratton** W 15 Charley Fusari (NBA)
05-18-1951 New York (USA): **Kid Gavilan** W 15 Johnny Bratton
10-20-1954 Philadelphia (USA): **Johnny Saxton** W 15 Kid Gavilan
04-01-1955 Boston (USA): **Tony De Marco** TKO 14 Johnny Saxton
06-10-1955 Syracuse (USA): **Carmen Basilio** TKO 12 Tony DeMarco
03-14-1956 Chicago (USA): **Johnny Saxton** W 15 Carmen Basilio
09-12-1956 Syracuse (USA): **Carmen Basilio** TKO 9 Johnny Saxton
Sept. 1957 *Basilio relinquishes the title after he has become middleweight world champion.*
06-06-1958 St. Louis (USA): **Virgil Akins** TKO 4 Vince Martinez
12-05-1958 Los Angeles (USA): **Don Jordan** W 15 Virgil Akins
05-27-1960 Las Vegas (USA): **Benny "Kid" Paret** W 15 Don Jordan
04-01-1961 Miami Beach (USA): **Emile Griffith** KO 13 Benny "Kid" Paret
09-30-1961 New York (USA): **Benny "Kid" Paret** W 15 Emile Griffith
03-24-1962 New York (USA): **Emile Griffith** TKO 12 Benny "Kid" Paret
03-21-1963 Los Angeles (USA): **Luis Rodriguez** W 15 Emile Griffith
06-08-1963 New York (USA): **Emile Griffith** W 15 Luis Rodriguez
April 1966 *Griffith relinquishes the title after he has become middleweight world champion.*
08-24-1966 New Orleans (USA): **Curtis Cokes** W 15 Manuel Gonzalez (WBA)
04-18-1969 Inglewood (USA): **José Napoles** TKO 14 Curtis Cokes
12-03-1970 Syracuse (USA): **Billy Backus** TKO 4 José Napoles
06-04-1971 Inglewood (USA): **José Napoles** TKO 8 Billy Backus
May 1972 *New York withdraws recognition of Napoles because he fails to defend the title.*
06-16-1972 Syracuse (USA): **Hedgemon Lewis** W 15 Billy Backus (NY)
08-03-1974 Mexico City (MEX): **José Napoles** TKO 9 Hedgemon Lewis
Napoles keeps his WBC title and relinquishes the WBO title.

06-28-1975 San Juan (PUR): **Angel Espada** W 15 Clyde Gray (WBA)
07-12-1975 Mexico City (MEX): **José Napoles** W 15 Armando Muniz (WBC)
12-06-1975 Mexico City (MEX): **John H. Stracey** TKO 6 José Napoles
06-22-1976 London (GBR): **Carlos Palomino** TKO 12 John H. Stracey (WBC)
07-17-1976 Mexicali (MEX): **Jose Pipino Cuevas** TKO 2 Angel Espada (WBA)
01-14-1979 San Juan (PUR): **Wilfred Benitez** W 15 Carlos Palomino (WBC)
11-30-1979 Las Vegas (USA): **Sugar Ray Leonard** TKO 15 Wilfred Benitez (WBC)
06-20-1980 Montreal (CAN): **Roberto Duran** W 15 Sugar Ray Leonard (WBC)
08-02-1980 Detroit (USA): **Thomas Hearns** TKO 2 Pipino Cuevas (WBA)
11-25-1980 New Orleans (USA): **Sugar Ray Leonard** ret 8 Roberto Duran (WBC)
09-16-1981 Las Vegas (USA): **Sugar Ray Leonard** TKO 14 Thomas Hearns (WBA/WBC)
Nov. 1982 *Leonard retires from professional sport.*
02-13-1983 Fort Worth (USA): **Donald Curry** W 15 Junsok Hwang (WBA)
08-13-1983 Las Vegas (USA): **Milton McCrory** W 12 Colin Jones (WBC)
12-06-1985 Las Vegas (USA): **Donald Curry** KO 2 Milton McCrory (WBC)
09-27-1986 Atlantic City (USA): **Lloyd Honeyghan** KO 6 Donald Curry
Dec. 1986 *Honeyghan is stripped of the title for not defending.*
02-06-1987 Atlantic City (USA): **Mark Breland** KO 7 Harold Volbrecht (WBA)
02-22-1987 London (GBR): **Lloyd Honeyghan** TKO 2 Johnny Bumphus (WBC/IBF)
08-22-1987 Columbia (USA): **Marlon Starling** KO 11 Mark Breland (WBA)
10-28-1987 London (GBR): **Jorge Vaca** TKO 8 Lloyd Honeyghan (WBC/IBF)
The IBF does not recognize Vaca's title because the bout lasted only 12 instead of 15 rounds.
03-29-1988 London (GBR): **Lloyd Honeyghan** KO 3 Jorge Vaca (WBC)
04-23-1988 Berck-Sur-Mer (FRA): **Simon Brown** TKO 14 Tyrone Trice (IBF)
07-29-1988 Atlantic City (USA): **Thomas Molinares** KO 6 Marlon Starling (WBA)
Jan. 1989 *Molinares is stripped of the title because he fails to make weight.*
02-05-1989 Las Vegas (USA): **Marlon Starling** TKO 9 Loyd Honeyghan (WBC)
02-05-1989 Las Vegas (USA): **Mark Breland** TKO 1 Seung Soon Lee (WBA)
05-08-1989 Santa Ana (USA): **Genaro Leon** KO 1 Danny Garcia (WBO)
Oct. 1989 *Leon relinquishes the WBO title.*
12-15-1989 Yabucoa (PUR): **Manning Galloway** W 12 Al Hamza (WBO)
07-08-1990 Reno (USA): **Aaron Davis** KO 9 Mark Breland (WBA)
08-19-1990 Reno (USA): **Maurice Blocker** W 12 Marlon Starling (WBC)
01-19-1991 Atlantic City (USA): **Meldrick Taylor** W 12 Aaron Davis (WBA)
March 1991 *Brown relinquishes the IBF title to fight for the WBC title.*
03-18-1991 Las Vegas (USA): **Simon Brown** TKO 10 Maurice Blocker (WBC)
10-04-1991 Atlantic City (USA): **Maurice Blocker** W 12 Glenwood Brown (IBF)
11-29-1991 Las Vegas (USA): **Buddy McGirt** W 12 Simon Brown (WBC)
10-31-1992 London (GBR): **Crisanto Espana** TKO 8 Meldrick Taylor (WBA)
02-12-1993 Randers (USA): **Gert Bo Jacobson** W 12 Manning Galloway (WBO)
03-06-1993 New York (USA): **Pernell Whitaker** W 12 Buddy McGirt (WBC)
06-19-1993 San Diego (USA): **Felix Trinidad** KO 2 Maurice Blocker (IBF)
Oct. 1993 *Jacobsen relinquishes the WBO title.*
10-16-1993 Belfast (GBR): **Eamonn Loughran** W 12 Lorenzo Smith (WBO)
06-04-1994 Levallois-Perret (FRA): **Ike Quartey** TKO 11 Crisanto Espana (WBA)
Quartey is stripped of the WBA title.
04-13-1996 Los Angeles (USA): **Jose Luis Lopez** TKO 1 Eamonn Loughran (WBO)
Oct. 1996 *Jose Luis Lopez is stripped of the title after testing positive for doping.*
02-22-1997 Hamburg (GER): **Michael Loewe** W 12 Santiago Samaniego (WBO)
04-12-1997 Las Vegas (USA): **Oscar De La Hoya** W 12 Pernell Whitaker (WBC)
1997 *Loewe relinquishes his title due to injuries.*
02-14-1998 Stuttgart (GER): **Ahmed Katajev** W 12 Leonard Townsend (WBO)
10-10-1998 Paris (FRA): **James Page** KO 2 Andrei Pestraiev (WBA)
09-18-1999 Las Vegas (USA): **Felix Trinidad** W 12 Oscar De La Hoya (WBC/IBF)
05-06-2000 Neuss (GER): **Daniel Santos** KO 5 Ahmed Katajev (WBO)
06-17-2000 Los Angeles (USA): **Shane Mosley** W 12 Oscar De La Hoya (WBC)
2001 *Trinidad relinquishes the IBF title.*
02-17-2001 Las Vegas (USA): **Andrew Lewis** TKO 7 James Page (WBA)
05-12-2001 New York (USA): **Vernon Forrest** W 12 Raul Frank (IBF)
2001 *Daniel Santos relinquishes the WBO title.*
01-26-2002 New York (USA): **Vernon Forrest** W 12 Shane Mosley (WBC/IBF)
2002 *Vernon Forrest relinquishes the IBF title.*
03-16-2002 Las Vegas (USA): **Antonio Margarito** TKO 10 Antonio Diaz (WBO)
01-25-2003 Temecula (USA): **Ricardo Mayorga** TKO 3 Vernon Forrest (WBA/WBC)
02-08-2003 Las Vegas (USA): **Antonio Margarito** TKO 2 Andrew Lewis (WBO)
03-22-2003 Campione d'Italia (ITA): **Cory Spinks** W 12 Michele Piccirillo (IBF)

JUNIOR WELTERWEIGHT
02-18-1930 London (GBR): **Jack "Kid" Berg** ret 10 Mushy Callahan
04-24-1931 Chicago (USA): **Tony Canzoneri** KO 3 Jack "Kid" Berg
01-18-1932 Philadelphia (USA): **Johnny Jadick** W 10 Tony Canzoneri
02-20-1933 New Orleans (USA): **Battling Shaw** W 10 Johnny Jadick
05-21-1933 New Orleans (USA): **Tony Canzoneri** W 10 Battling Shaw
06-23-1933 Chicago (USA): **Barney Ross** W 10 Tony Canzoneri
June 1935 *Ross relinquishes the title to fight at welterweight.*
04-29-1946 Boston (USA): **Tippy Larkin** W 12 Willie Joyce
06-12-1959 New York (USA): **Carlos Ortiz** W 2 Kenny Lane
09-01-1960 Milan (ITA): **Duilio Loi** W 15 Carlos Ortiz

09-14-1962 Milan (ITA): **Eddie Perkins** W 15 Duilio Loi
12-15-1962 Milan (ITA): **Duilio Loi** W 15 Eddie Perkins
Jan. 1963 *Loi retires from professional sport.*
03-21-1963 Los Angeles (USA): **Roberto Cruz** KO 1 Battling Torres
06-15-1963 Manila (PHI): **Eddie Perkins** W 15 Roberto Cruz
01-18-1965 Caracas (VEN): **Carlos Hernandez** W 15 Eddie Perkins
04-29-1966 Rome (ITA): **Sandro Lopopolo** W 15 Carlos Hernandez
04-30-1967 Tokyo (JPN): **Paul Fuji** KO 2 Sandro Lopopolo
The WBC withdraws recognition of Fuji because he does not defend his title.
12-12-1968 Tokyo (JPN): **Nicolino Locche** ret 9 Paul Fuji (WBA)
12-14-1968 Quezon City (PHI): **Pedro Adigue** W 15 Adolph Pruitt (WBC)
01-31-1970 Rome (ITA): **Bruno Arcari** W 15 Pedro Adigue (WBC)
03-10-1972 Panama City (PAN): **Alfonso Frazer** W 15 Nicolino Locche (WBA)
10-28-1972 Panama City (PAN): **Antonio Cervantes** KO 10 Peppermint Frazer (WBA)
Aug. 1974 *Arcari relinquishes the WBC title because he fails to make weight.*
09-21-1974 Rome (ITA): **Perico Fernandez** W 15 Lion Furuyama (WBC)
07-15-1975 Bangkok (THA): **Saensak Muangsurin** ret 8 Perico Fernandez (WBC)
03-06-1976 San Juan (PUR): **Wilfred Benitez** W 15 Antonio Cervantes (WBA)
06-30-1976 Madrid (ESP): **Miguel Velasquez** disq 4 Saensak Muangsurin (WBC)
10-29-1976 Segovia (ESP): **Saensak Muangsurin** TKO 2 Miguel Velasquez (WBC)
Dec. 1976 *Benitez relinquishes the WBA title because he fails to defend the title against Cervantes.*
06-25-1977 Maracaibo (VEN): **Antonio Cervantes** TKO 5 Carlos M. Giminez (WBA)
08-03-1977 New York (USA): **Wilfred Benitez** TKO 15 Guerrero Chavez (NY)
12-30-1978 Seoul (KOR): **Sang Hyun Kim** TKO 13 Saensak Muangsurin (WBC)
02-23-1980 Seoul (KOR): **Saoul Mamby** KO 14 Sang Hyun Kim (WBC)
08-02-1980 Cincinnati (USA): **Aaron Pryor** KO 4 Antonio Cervantes (WBA)
06-26-1982 Highland Heights (USA): **Leroy Haley** W 15 Saoul Mamby (WBC)
05-18-1983 Las Vegas (USA): **Bruce Curry** W 12 Leroy Haley (WBC)
01-22-1984 Atlantic City (USA): **Johnny Bumphus** W 15 Lorenzo Garcia (WBA)
01-29-1984 Beaumont (USA): **Bill Costello** TKO 10 Bruce Curry (WBC)
06-01-1984 Buffalo (USA): **Gene Hatcher** KO 11 Johnny Bumphus (WBA)
06-22-1984 Toronto (CAN): **Aaron Pryor** W 15 Nicky Furlano (IBF)
07-21-1985 Campione d'Italia (ITA): **Ubaldo Sacco** TKO 9 Gene Hatcher (WBA)
08-21-1985 New York (USA): **Lonnie Smith** TKO 8 Bill Costello (WBC)
Dec. 1985 *Pryor is stripped of the IBF title for failing to defend.*
03-15-1986 Monte Carlo (MON): **Patrizio Oliva** W 15 Ubaldo Sacco (WBA)
04-26-1986 Lucca (ITA): **Gary Hinton** W 15 Antonio Reyes Cruz (IBF)
05-05-1986 Los Angeles (USA): **Rene Arredondo** TKO 5 Lonnie Smith (WBC)
07-24-1986 Tokyo (JPN): **Tsuyoshi Hamada** KO 1 Rene Arredondo (WBC)
10-30-1986 Hartford (USA): **Joe Manley** KO 10 Gary Hinton (IBF)
03-04-1987 Basildon (GBR): **Terry Marsh** TKO 10 Joe Manley (IBF)
07-04-1987 Ribera (ITA): **Juan Coggi** KO 3 Patrizio Oliva (WBA)
07-22-1987 Tokyo (JPN): **Rene Arredondo** TKO 6 Tsuyoshi Hamada (WBC)
Sept. 1987 *Marsh retires from professional sport.*
11-12-1987 Los Angeles (USA): **Roger Mayweather** TKO 6 Rene Arredondo (WBC)
02-14-1988 Corpus Christi (USA): **James "Buddy" McGirt** TKO 12 Frankie Warren (IBF)
09-03-1988 Atlantic City (USA): **Meldrick Taylor** TKO 12 Buddy McGirt (IBF)
03-06-1989 Reno (USA): **Hector Camacho Jr.** W 12 Ray Mancini (WBO)
05-13-1989 Inglewood (USA): **Julio Cesar Chavez** KO 10 Roger Mayweather (WBC)
03-17-1990 Las Vegas (USA): **Julio Cesar Chavez** TKO 12 Meldrick Taylor (IBF/WBC)
08-17-1990 Nizza (FRA): **Loreto Garza** W 12 Juan Coggi (WBA)
02-23-1991 Las Vegas (USA): **Greg Haugen** W 12 Hector Camacho Jr. (WBO)
March 1991 *Haugen is stripped of his title after testing positive for doping.*
April 1991 *Chavez relinquishes the IBF title and keeps his WBC title.*
05-18-1991 Reno (USA): **Hector Camacho Jr.** W 12 Greg Haugen (WBO)
06-14-1991 Sacramento (USA): **Edwin Rosario** KO 3 Loreto Garza (WBA)
12-07-1991 Reno (USA): **Rafael Pineda** TKO 9 Roger Mayweather (IBF)
March 1992 *Camacho is stripped of the WBO title because he does not defend his title.*
04-10-1992 Mexico City (MEX): **Akinobu Hiranaka** TKO 1 Edwin Rosario (WBA)
06-30-1992 Los Angeles (USA): **Carlos Gonzalez** TKO 2 Jimmy Paul (WBO)
07-18-1992 Las Vegas (USA): **Pernell Whitaker** W 12 Rafael Pineda (IBF)
09-09-1992 Tokyo (JPN): **Morris East** TKO 11 Akinobu Hiranaka (WBA)
01-13-1993 Mar del Plata (ARG): **Juan Coggi** TKO 8 Morris East (WBA)
March 1993 *Whitaker relinquishes the IBF title after he has become WBC welterweight champion.*
05-15-1993 Atlantic City (USA): **Charles Murray** W 12 Rodney Moore (IBF)
06-07-1993 Las Vegas (USA): **Zack Padilla** W 12 Carlos Gonzalez (WBO)
Padilla retires from professional sport.
01-29-1994 Las Vegas (USA): **Frankie Randall** W 12 Julio Cesar Chavez (WBC)
02-13-1994 Atlantic Ctiy (USA): **Jake Rodriguez** W 12 Charles Murray (IBF)
05-07-1994 Las Vegas (USA): **Julio Cesar Chavez** Tech Dec 8 Frankie Randall (WBC)
09-17-1994 Las Vegas (USA): **Frankie Randall** W 12 Juan Coggi (WBA)
01-28-1995 Las Vegas (USA): **Konstantin "Kostya" Tszyu** TKO 6 Jake Rodriguez (IBF)

02-20-1995 Inglewood (USA): **Sammy Fuentes** TKO 2 Fidel Avendano (WBO)
01-13-1996 Miami (USA): **Juan Coggi** Tech Dec 5 Frankie Randall (WBA)
03-09-1996 Milan (ITA): **Giovanni Parisi** TKO 8 Sammy Fuentes (WBO)
06-07-1996 Las Vegas (USA): **Oscar De La Hoya** TKO 4 Julio Cesar Chavez (WBC)
08-16-1996 Buenos Aires (ARG): **Frankie Randall** W 12 Juan Coggi (WBA)
01-11-1997 Nashville (USA): **Khalid Rahilou** TKO 11 Frankie Randall (WBA)
05-31-1997 Atlantic City (USA): **Vincent Phillips** TKO 10 Konstantin "Kostya" Tszyu (IBF)
05-29-1998 Pesaro (ITA): **Carlos Gonzalez** TKO 9 Giovanni Parisi (WBO)
10-10-1998 Paris (FRA): **Sharmba Mitchell** W 12 Khalid Rahilou (WBA)
02-20-1999 New York (USA): **Terron Millett** TKO 5 Vincent Phillips (IBF)
05-15-1999 Miami (USA): **Randall Bailey** KO 1 Carlos Gonzalez (WBO)
02-20-1999 New York (USA): **Terron Millett** TKO 5 Vincent Philips (IBF)
05-15-1999 Miami (USA): **Randall Bailey** KO 1 Carlos Gonzalez (WBO)
08-21-1999 Miami (USA): **Konstantin "Kostya" Tszyu** TKO 10 Miguel Angel Gonzalez (WBC)
07-22-2000 Miami (USA): **Ener Julio** W 12 Randall Bailey (WBO)
02-03-2001 Las Vegas (USA): **Konstantin "Kostya" Tszyu** TKO 7 Sharmba Mitchell (WBC/WBA)
06-30-2001 Las Vegas (USA): **DeMarcus Corley** TKO 1 Felix Flores (WBO)
11-03-2001 Las Vegas (USA): **Konstantin "Kostya" Tszyu** TKO 2 Zab Judah (WBC/WBA/IBF)
01-04-2003 Washington (USA): **DeMarcus "Chop Chop" Corley** W 12 Randall Bailey (WBO)
01-18-2003 Melbourne (AUS): **Konstantin "Kostya" Tszyu** ret 7 Jesse James Leija (WBA/WBC/IBF)

LIGHTWEIGHT

06-01-1896 London (GBR): **George "Kid" Lavigne** KO 17 Dick Burge
07-03-1899 Buffalo (USA): **Frank Erne** W 20 Kid Lavigne
05-12-1902 Fort Erie (CAN): **Joe Gans** KO 1 Frank Erne
07-04-1908 San Francisco (USA): **Battling Nelson** KO 17 Joe Gans
02-22-1910 Port Richmond (USA): **Ad Wolgast** TKO 40 Battling Nelson
11-28-1912 Daly City (USA): **Willie Ritchie** disq 16 Ad Wolgast
07-07-1914 London (GBR): **Freddie Welsh** W 20 Willie Ritchie
05-28-1917 New York (USA): **Benny Leonard** TKO 9 Freddie Welsh
Jan. 1925 *Leonard relinquishes his title.*
07-13-1925 Long Island (USA): **Jimmy Goodrich** TKO 2 Stanislaus Loayza
12-07-1925 Buffalo (USA): **Rocky Kansas** W 15 Jimmy Goodrich
07-03-1926 Chicago (USA): **Sammy Mandell** W 10 Rocky Kansas
07-17-1930 New York (USA): **Al Singer** KO 1 Sammy Mandell
11-14-1930 New York (USA): **Tony Canzoneri** KO 1 Al Singer
06-23-1933 Chicago (USA): **Barney Ross** W 10 Tony Canzoneri
April 1935 *Ross relinquishes his title.*
05-10-1935 New York (USA): **Tony Canzoneri** W 15 Lou Ambers
09-03-1936 New York (USA): **Lou Ambers** W 15 Tony Canzoneri
08-17-1938 New York (USA): **Henry Armstrong** W 15 Lou Ambers
08-22-1939 New York (USA): **Lou Ambers** W 15 Henry Armstrong (NBA)
The NBA withdraws recognition of Ambers because he does not defend his title.
05-03-1940 Louisville (USA): **Sammy Angott** W 15 Davey Day (NBA)
05-10-1940 New York (USA): **Lew Jenkins** TKO 3 Lou Ambers
12-19-1941 New York (USA): **Sammy Angott** W 15 Lew Jenkins (unifies titles)
Nov. 1942 *Angott retires temporarily from professional sport.*
12-18-1942 New York (USA): **Beau Jack** KO 3 Tippy Larkin (NY)
05-21-1943 New York (USA): **Bob Montgomery** W 15 Beau Jack (NY)
10-27-1943 Los Angeles (USA): **Sammy Angott** W 15 Slugger White (NBA)
11-19-1943 New York (USA): **Beau Jack** W 15 Bob Montgomery (NY)
03-03-1944 New York (USA): **Bob Montgomery** W 15 Beau Jack (NY)
03-08-1944 Hollywood (USA): **Juan Zurita** W 15 Sammy Angott (NBA)
04-18-1945 Mexico City (MEX): **Ike Williams** KO 2 Juan Zurita (NBA)
08-04-1947 Philadelphia (USA): **Ike Williams** KO 6 Bob Montgomery (NY/NBA)
05-25-1951 New York (USA): **Jimmy Carter** TKO 14 Ike Williams
05-14-1952 Los Angeles (USA): **Lauro Salas** W 15 Jimmy Carter
10-15-1952 Chicago (USA): **Jimmy Carter** W 15 Lauro Salas
03-05-1954 New York (USA): **Paddy DeMarco** W 15 Jimmy Carter
11-17-1954 San Francisco (USA): **Jimmy Carter** TKO 15 Paddy DeMarco
06-29-1955 Boston (USA): **Wallace "Bud" Smith** W 15 Jimmy Carter
08-24-1956 New Orleans (USA): **Joe Brown** W 15 Wallace "Bud" Smith
04-21-1962 Las Vegas (USA): **Carlos Ortiz** W 15 Joe Brown
04-10-1965 Panama City (PAN): **Ismael Laguna** W 15 Carlos Ortiz
11-13-1965 San Juan (PUR): **Carlos Ortiz** W 15 Ismael Laguna
06-29-1968 Santo Domingo (DOM): **Carlos Teo Cruz** W 15 Carlos Ortiz
02-18-1969 Los Angeles (USA): **Mando Ramos** TKO 11 Carlos Teo Cruz
03-03-1970 Los Angeles (USA): **Ismael Laguna** ret 9 Mando Ramos
09-26-1970 San Juan (PUR): **Ken Buchanan** W 15 Ismael Laguna
06-26-1972 New York (USA): **Roberto Duran** KO 13 Ken Buchanan (WBA)
06-28-1972 Madrid (ESP): **Mando Ramos** W 15 Pedro Carrasco (WBC)
09-15-1972 Los Angeles (USA): **Chango Carmona** TKO 8 Mando Ramos (WBC)
11-10-1972 Los Angeles (USA): **Rodolfo Gonzalez** W 12 Chango Carmona (WBC)
04-11-1974 Tokyo (JPN): **Suzuki "Guts" Ishimatsu** KO 8 Rodolfo Gonzales (WBC)

05-08-1976 San Juan (PUR): **Esteban De Jesus** W 15 Suzuki "Guts" Ishimatsu (WBC)
01-21-1978 Las Vegas (USA): **Roberto Duran** KO 12 Esteban De Jesus (WBC/WBA)
Jan. 1979 *Duran relinquishes his titles because he fails to make weight.*
04-17-1979 Glasgow (GBR): **Jim Watt** TKO 12 Alfredo Pitalua (WBC)
06-16-1979 San Juan (PUR): **Ernesto Espana** KO 13 Claude Noel (WBA)
03-02-1980 Detroit (USA): **Hilmer Kenty** TKO 9 Ernesto Espana (WBA)
04-12-1981 Atlantic City (USA): **Sean O'Grady** W 15 Hilmer Kenty (WBA)
06-20-1981 London (GBR): **Alexis Arguello** W 15 Jim Watt (WBC)
Aug. 1981 *The WBA vacates O'Grady's title due to an argument over his contract.*
09-12-1981 Atlantic City (USA): **Claude Noel** W 15 Rodolfo Gonzales (WBA)
12-05-1981 Las Vegas (USA): **Arturo Frias** KO 8 Claude Noel (WBA)
05-08-1982 Las Vegas (USA): **Ray Mancini** TKO 1 Arturo Frias (WBA)
Feb. 1983 *Arguello relinquishes his title.*
05-01-1983 Hato Rey (PUR): **Edwin Rosario** W 12 José Luis Ramirez (WBC)
01-30-1984 Atlantic City (USA): **Charlie "Choo Choo" Brown** W 15 Melvin Paul (IBF)
04-15-1984 Atlantic City (USA): **Harry Arroyo** TKO 14 Charlie "Choo Choo" Brown (IBF)
06-01-1984 Buffalo (USA): **Livingstone Bramble** TKO 14 Ray Mancini (WBA)
11-03-1984 San Juan (PUR): **José Luis Ramirez** TKO 4 Edwin Rosario (WBC)
04-06-1985 Atlantic City (USA): **Jimmy Paul** W 15 Harry Arroyo (IBF)
08-10-1985 New York (USA): **Hector Camacho Jr.** W 12 José Luis Ramirez (WBC)
09-26-1986 Miami Beach (USA): **Edwin Rosario** KO 2 Livingstone Bramble (WBA)
12-05-1986 Las Vegas (USA): **Greg Haugen** W 15 Jimmy Paul (IBF)
May 1987 *Camacho Jr. relinquishes the WBC title because he fails to make weight.*
06-07-1987 Providence (USA): **Vinny Pazienza** W 15 Greg Haugen (IBF)
07-19-1987 St. Tropez (FRA): **José Luis Ramirez** W 12 Terrence Alli (WBC)
11-21-1987 Las Vegas (USA): **Julio Cesar Chavez** TKO 11 Edwin Rosario (WBA)
02-06-1988 Atlantic City (USA): **Greg Haugen** W 15 Vinny Pazienza (IBF)
10-29-1988 Las Vegas (USA): **Julio Cesar Chavez** Tech Dec 11 José Luis Ramirez (WBC/WBA)
02-18-1989 Hampton (USA): **Pernell Whitaker** W 12 Greg Haugen (IBF)
05-08-1989 Santa Ana (USA): **Mauricio Aceves** W 12 Amancio Castro (WBO)
May 1989 *Chavez relinquishes his WBA and WBC titles.*
07-09-1989 Atlantic City (USA): **Edwin Rosario** TKO 6 Anthony Jones (WBA)
08-20-1989 Norfolk (USA): **Pernell Whitaker** W 12 José Luis Ramirez (WBC/IBF)
04-04-1990 New York (USA): **Juan Nazario** TKO 8 Edwin Rosario (WBA)
08-11-1990 Stateline (USA): **Pernell Whitaker** KO 1 Juan Nazario (WBA/WBC/IBF)
09-22-1990 Brownsville (USA): **Dingaan Thobela** W 12 Mauricio Aceves (WBO)
Feb. 1992 *Whitaker relinquishes all titles to fight at junior welterweight.*
06-12-1992 Portland (USA): **Joey Gamache** ret 8 Chil-Sung Chun (WBA)
08-24-1992 Mexico City (MEX): **Miguel Angel Gonzalez** W 9 Wilfredo Rocha (WBC)
01-10-1993 Atlantic City (USA): **Fred Pendleton** W 12 Tracy Spann (IBF)
July 1992 *Thobela relinquishes the WBO title to fight for the WBA title.*
09-25-1992 Voghera (ITA): **Giovanni Parisi** TKO 10 Javier Altamirano (WBO)
10-24-1992 Portland (USA): **Tony Lopez** TKO 11 Joey Gamache (WBA)
06-26-1993 Sun City (RSA): **Dingaan Thobela** W 12 Tony Lopez (WBA)
10-30-1993 Johannesburg (RSA): **Orzoubek Nazarov** W 12 Dingaan Thobela (WBA)
02-19-1994 Inglewood (USA): **Rafael Ruelas** W 12 Fred Pendleton (IBF)
07-29-1994 Las Vegas (USA): **Oscar De La Hoya** KO 2 Jorge Paez (WBO)
05-06-1995 Las Vegas (USA): **Oscar De La Hoya** TKO 2 Rafael Ruelas (IBF)
July 1995 *De La Hoya relinquishes his IBF title.*
08-19-1995 Sun City (RSA): **Phillip Holiday** ret 11 Miguel Julio (IBF)
Feb. 1996 *Miguel Angel Gonzalez relinquishes the WBC title to fight at junior welterweight.*
04-20-1996 Paris (FRA): **Jean-Baptiste Mendy** W 12 Lamar Murphy (WBC)
09-24-1996 Berlin (GER): **Artur Grigorian** KO 2 Gene Reed (WBO)
03-01-1997 Paris (FRA): **Steve Johnston** W 12 Jean-Baptiste Mendy (WBA)
08-02-1997 Uncasville (USA): **Shane Mosley** W 12 Phillip Holiday (IBF)
05-16-1998 Paris (FRA): **Jean-Baptiste Mendy** W 12 Orzoubek Nazarov (WBA)
06-13-1998 El Paso (USA): **Cesar Bazan** W 12 Steve Johnston (WBC)
02-27-1999 Miami (USA): **Steve Johnston** W 12 Cesar Bazan (WBC)
04-10-1999 Paris (FRA): **Julien Lorcy** TKO 6 Jean-Baptiste Mendy (WBA)
08-07-1999 Chester (USA): **Paul Spadafora** W 12 Israel Cardona (IBF)
11-13-1999 Las Vegas (USA): **Gustavo Serrano** TKO 10 Stefano Zoff (WBA)
06-17-2000 Bell Gardens (USA): **Jose Luis Castillo** W 12 Steve Johnston (WBC)
07-01-2001 Tokyo (JPN): **Julien Lorcy** W 12 Takanori Hatakeyama (WBA)
10-08-2001 Paris (FRA): **Raul Horacio Balbi** W 12 Julien Lorcy (WBA)
01-05-2002 San Antonio (USA): **Leonard Dorin** W 12 Raul Horacio Balbi (WBA)
04-20-2002 Las Vegas (USA): **Floyd Mayweather Jr.** W 12 Jose Luis Castillo (WBC)
01-18-2003 Essen (GER): **Artur Grigorian** W 12 Maciej Matt Zegan (WBO)
04-19-2003 Fresno (USA): **Floyd Mayweather Jr.** W 12 Victoriano Sosa (WBC)
05-17-2003 Pittsburgh (USA): **Paul Spadafora** D 12 Leonard Dorin (IBF/WBA)

SUPER FEATHERWEIGHT (ALSO CALLED JUNIOR LIGHTWEIGHT)
11-18-1921 New York (USA): **Johnny Dundee** disq 5 George "KO" Chaney
05-30-1923 New York (USA): **Jack Bernstein** W 15 Johnny Dundee
12-17-1923 New York (USA): **Johnny Dundee** W 15 Jack Bernstein
06-20-1924 Brooklyn (USA): **Steve "Kid" Sullivan** W 10 Johnny Dundee
04-01-1925 Philadelphia (USA): **Mike Ballerino** W 10 Steve "Kid" Sullivan

12-02-1925 Los Angeles (USA): **Tod Morgan** ret 10 Mike Ballerino
12-19-1929 New York (USA): **Benny Bass** KO 2 Tod Morgan
Jan. 1930 *New York withdraws recognition of Bass.*
07-15-1931 Philadelphia (USA): **Kid Chocolate** TKO 7 Benny Bass (NBA)
Sept. 1932 *The NBA also withdraws recognition of this weight division.*
12-26-1933 Philadelphia (USA): **Frankie Klick** TKO 7 Kid Chocolate
Klick fails to defend the title.
12-06-1949 Cleveland (USA): **Sandy Saddler** W 10 Orlando Zulueta
07-20-1959 Providence (USA): **Harold Gomes** W 15 Paul Jorgensen
03-16-1960 Quezon City (PHI): **Gabriel "Flash" Elorde** KO 7 Harold Gomes
06-15-1967 Tokyo (JPN): **Yoshiaki Numata** W 15 Gabriel "Flash" Elorde
12-14-1967 Tokyo (JPN): **Hiroshi Kobayashi** KO 12 Yoshiaki Numata
Oct. 1968 *The WBC strips Kobayashi of the title for failing to defend. Kobayashi remains WBA champion.*
02-15-1969 Manila (PHI): **Rene Barrientos** W 15 Ruben Navarro (WBC)
04-05-1970 Tokyo (JPN): **Yoshiaki Numata** W 15 Rene Barrientos (WBC)
07-29-1971 Aomori (JPN): **Alfredo Marcano** KO 10 Hiroshi Kobayashi (WBA)
10-10-1971 Sendai (JPN): **Ricardo Arredondo** KO 10 Yoshiaki Numata (WBC)
04-25-1972 Honolulu (USA): **Ben Villaflor** W 15 Alfredo Marcano (WBA)
03-12-1973 Honolulu (USA): **Kuniaki Shibata** W 15 Ben Villaflor (WBA)
10-17-1973 Honolulu (USA): **Ben Villaflor** KO 1 Kuniaki Shibata (WBA)
02-28-1974 Tokyo (JPN): **Kuniaki Shibata** W 15 Ricardo Arredondo (WBC)
07-05-1975 Mito (JPN): **Alfredo Escalera** KO 2 Kuniaki Shibata (WBC)
10-16-1976 San Juan (PUR): **Sam Serrano** W 15 Ben Villaflor (WBA)
06-28-1978 Bayamon (PUR): **Alexis Arguello** TKO 13 Alfredo Escalera (WBC)
08-02-1980 Detroit (USA): **Yasutsune Uehara** KO 6 Sam Serrano (WBA)
Oct. 1980 *Arguello relinquishes the WBC title to fight at lightweight.*
12-11-1980 Los Angeles (USA): **Rafael Limon** KO 15 Ildefonso Bethelmy (WBC)
03-08-1981 Stockton (USA): **Cornelius Boza-Edwards** W 15 Rafael Limon (WBC)
04-09-1981 Wakayama (JPN): **Sam Serrano** W 15 Yasutsune Uehara (WBA)
08-29-1981 Viareggio (ITA): **Rolando Navarrete** KO 5 Cornelius Boza-Edwards (WBC)
05-29-1982 Las Vegas (USA): **Rafael Limon** KO 12 Rolando Navarrete (WBC)
12-11-1982 Sacramento (USA): **Bobby Chacon** W 15 Rafael Limon (WBC)
01-19-1983 San Juan (PUR): **Roger Mayweather** KO 8 Sam Serrano (WBA)
June 1983 *The WBC strips Chacon of his title due to arguments over his contract.*
08-07-1983 San Juan (PUR): **Hector Camacho Jr.** TKO 5 Rafael Limon (WBC)
02-26-1984 Beaumont (USA): **Rocky Lockridge** KO 1 Roger Mayweather (WBA)
04-22-1984 Seoul (KOR): **Hwan-Kil Yuh** W 15 Rod Sequenan (IBF)
June 1984 *Camacho relinquishes the WBC title to fight at lightweight.*
09-13-1984 Los Angeles (USA): **Julio Cesar Chavez** KO 8 Mario Martinez (WBC)
02-15-1985 Melbourne (AUS): **Lester Ellis** W 15 Hwan-Kil Yuh (IBF)
05-19-1985 San Juan (PUR): **Wilfredo Gomez** W 15 Rocky Lockridge (WBA)
07-12-1985 Melbourne (AUS): **Barry Michael** W 15 Lester Ellis (IBF)
05-24-1986 Hato Rey (PUR): **Alfredo Layne** TKO 9 Wilfredo Gomez (WBA)
09-27-1986 Sun City (RSA): **Brian Mitchell** TKO 10 Alfredo Layne (WBA)
08-09-1987 Windsor (GBR): **Rocky Lockridge** ret 8 Barry Michael (IBF)
Nov. 1987 *Chavez relinquishes the WBC title to fight at lightweight.*
02-29-1988 Los Angeles (USA): **Azumah Nelson** W 12 Mario Martinez (WBC)
07-23-1988 Sacramento (USA): **Tony Lopez** W 12 Rocky Lockridge (IBF)
04-29-1989 San Juan (PUR): **John-John Molina** W 12 Juan LaPorte (WBO)
Sept. 1989 *Molina relinquishes the WBO title to fight for the IBF title.*
10-07-1989 Sacramento (USA): **John-John Molina** TKO 10 Tony Lopez (IBF)
12-09-1989 Terano (ITA): **Kamel Bou-Ali** KO 8 Antonio Rivera (WBO)
05-20-1990 Reno (USA): **Tony Lopez** W 12 John-John Molina (IBF)
April 1991 *Mitchell relinquishes the WBA title to fight for the IBF title.*
06-28-1991 Lewiston (USA): **Joey Gamache** TKO 10 Jerry N'Gobeni (WBA)
09-13-1991 Sacramento (USA): **Brian Mitchell** W 12 Tony Lopez (IBF)
Oct. 1991 *Gamache relinquishes the WBA title because he fails to make weight.*
11-22-1991 Epernay (FRA): **Genaro Hernandez** ret 9 Daniel Londas (WBA)
Jan. 1992 *IBF champion Brian Mitchell retires from professional sport.*
02-22-1992 Sun City (RSA): **John-John Molina** KO 4 Jackie Gunguluza (IBF)
03-21-1992 San Rufo (ITA): **Daniel Londas** W 12 Kamel Bou-Ali (WBO)
09-04-1992 Copenhagen (DEN): **Jimmi Bredahl** W 12 Daniel Londas (WBO)
03-05-1994 Los Angeles (USA): **Oscar De La Hoya** ret 10 Jimmi Bredahl (WBO)
05-07-1994 Las Vegas (USA): **Jesse James Leija** W 12 Azumah Nelson (WBC)
June 1994 *De La Hoya relinquishes the WBO title to fight at lightweight.*
09-17-1994 Las Vegas (USA): **Gabriel Ruelas** W 12 Jesse James Leija (WBC)
09-24-1994 Rotterdam (NED): **Regilio Tuur** W 12 Eugene Speed (WBO)
Jan. 1995 *Molina relinquishes the IBF title to fight at lightweight.*
04-22-1995 Atlantic City (USA): **Ed Hopson** KO 7 Moises Pedroza (IBF)
07-09-1995 Reno (USA): **Tracy Patterson** TKO 2 Ed Hopson (IBF)
Aug. 1995 *WBA champion Hernandez relinquishes the WBA title.*
10-21-1995 Salta (ARG): **Yong Soo Choi** TKO 10 Victor Hugo Paz (WBA)
12-01-1995 Indio (USA): **Azumah Nelson** TKO 5 Gabriel Ruelas (WBC)
12-15-1995 New York (USA): **Arturo Gatti** W 12 Tracy Patterson (IBF)
Jan. 1997 *WBO champion Tuur retires from professional sport.*
03-22-1997 Corpus Christi (USA): **Genaro Hernandez** W 12 Azumah Nelson (WBC)
12-19-1997 London (GBR): **Barry Jones** W 12 Wilson Palacios (WBO)
Feb. 1998 *IBF champion Gatti relinquishes the title.*
03-13-1998 Miami (USA): **Roberto Garcia** W 12 Harold Warren (IBF)

April 1998 *The WBO strips Jones of the title.*
05-16-1998 Paris (FRA): **Anatoli Alexandrov** TKO 8 Arnulfo Castillo (WBO)
09-05-1998 Tokyo (JPN): **Takanori Hatakeyama** W 12 Yong Soo Choi (WBA)
10-03-1998 Las Vegas (USA): **Floyd Mayweather Jr.** ret 8 Genaro Hernandez (WBC)
06-27-1999 Tokyo (JPN): **Lakva Sim** TKO 5 Takanori Hatakeyama (WBA)
08-07-1999 Le Cannet (FRA): **Acelino Freitas** KO 1 Anatoly Alexandrov (WBO)
10-23-1999 Las Vegas (USA): **Diego Corrales** TKO 7 Roberto Garcia (IBF)
10-31-1999 Pusan (KOR): **Baek Jong-Kwon** W 12 Lakva Sim (WBA)
05-21-2000 Kansas City (USA): **Joel Casamayor** TKO 5 Baek Jong-Kwon (WBA)
12-03-2000 Miami (USA): **Steve Forbes** TKO 8 John Brown (IBF)
01-12-2001 Las Vegas (USA): **Acelino Freitas** W 12 Joel Casamayor (WBA/WBO)
08-24-2002 Tokyo (JPN): **Sirimongkol Singmanasak** KO 2 Kengo Nagashima (WBC)
2002 *Floyd Mayweather Jr. relinquishes the WBC title.*
01-13-2003 Tokyo (JPN): **Sirimongkol Singwancha** W 12 Yongsoo Choi (WBC)
02-01-2003 Las Vegas (USA): **Carlos Hernandez** W td 8 Daniel Santos (IBF)
03-15-2003 Chicago (USA): **Acelino Freitas** TKO 4 Juan-Carlos Ramirez (WBA/WBO)

FEATHERWEIGHT

01-13-1890 San Francisco (USA): **Billy Murphy** KO 14 Ike Weir
09-02-1890 Sydney (AUS): **Young Griffo** TKO 15 Billy Murphy
Griffo does not compete any more at featherweight.
06-27-1892 Coney Island (USA): **George Dixon** KO 14 Fred Johnson
11-27-1896 New York (USA): **Frank Erne** W 20 George Dixon
03-24-1897 New York (USA): **George Sullivan** W 25 Frank Erne
10-04-1897 San Francisco (USA): **Solly Smith** W 20 George Dixon
07-01-1898 New York (USA): **Ben Jordan** W 25 George Dixon (British World Title)
09-26-1898 Coney Island (USA): **Dave Sullivan** W 5 Solly Smith
11-11-1898 New York (USA): **George Sullivan** W 10 Dave Sullivan
10-10-1899 New York (USA): **Eddie Santry** KO 15 Ben Jordan (British World Title)
01-09-1900 New York (USA): **Terry McGovern** KO 8 George Dixon
11-28-1901 Hartford (USA): **Young Corbett II** KO 2 Terry McGovern
Corbett II does not compete any more at featherweight.
09-03-1903 St. Louis (USA): **Abe Atell** W 25 Johnny Reagan
02-22-1912 Vernon (USA): **Johnny Kilbane** W 20 Abe Atell
Kilbane is stripped of his title for not defending.
06-06-1912 London (GBR): **Jim Driscoll** KO 12 Jean Poesy (British + European World Title)
1913 *Driscoll temporarily resigns from professional sport.*
08-15-1922 Brooklyn (USA): **Johnny Dundee** KO 9 Danny Frush
06-02-1923 New York (USA): **Eugene Criqui** KO 6 Johnny Kilbane
07-26-1923 New York (USA): **Johnny Dundee** KO 6 Eugene Criqui
Dundee relinquishes his title because he fails to make weight.
01-02-1925 New York (USA): **Louis "Kid" Kaplan** ret 9 Danny Kramer
09-19-1927 Philadelphia (USA): **Benny Bass** W 10 Red Chapman (NBA)
10-24-1927 New York (USA): **Tony Canzoneri** W 15 Johnny Dundee (NY)
09-28-1928 New York (USA): **Andre Routis** W 15 Tony Canzoneri
09-23-1929 Hartford (USA): **Battling Battalino** W 15 Andre Routis
05-26-1932 Detroit (USA): **Tommy Paul** W 15 Johnny Pena (NBA)
June 1932 *Battalino relinquishes the title because he fails to make weight.*
10-13-1932 New York (USA): **Kid Chocolate** TKO 12 Lew Feldman (NY)
01-13-1933 Chicago (USA): **Freddie Miller** W 10 Tommy Paul (NBA)
May 1934 *Kid Chocolate is stripped of the NY title for not defending.*
05-11-1936 Washington (USA): **Peter Sarron** W 15 Freddie Miller (NBA)
09-03-1936 New York (USA): **Mike Belloise** KO 9 Dave Crowley (NY)
10-27-1936 Los Angeles (USA): **Henry Armstrong** W 10 Mike Belloise (NY)
10-05-1937 Algier (ALG): **Maurice Holtzer** W 15 Phil Dolhem (IBU)
10-29-1937 New York (USA): **Henry Armstrong** KO 6 Peter Sarron (NBA/NY)
May 1938 *The IBU withdraws recognition of Holtzer.*
Aug. 1938 *Armstrong relinquishes his titles.*
10-17-1938 New York (USA): **Joey Archibald** W 15 Mike Belloise (NY)
12-29-1938 Chicago (USA): **Leo Rodak** W 10 Leone Efrati (NBA)
04-18-1939 Providence (USA): **Joey Archibald** W 15 Leo Rodak (NBA/NY)
05-20-1940 Baltimore (USA): **Harry Jeffra** W 15 Joey Archibald (NY)
May 1940 *Archibald is stripped of the NBA title for not defending.*
07-10-1940 Hartford (USA): **Petey Scalzo** W 15 Bobby "Poison" Ivy (NBA)
05-12-1941 Washington (USA): **Joey Archibald** W 15 Harry Jeffra (NY)
07-01-1941 Los Angeles (USA): **Richie Lemos** KO 5 Petey Scalzo (NBA)
09-11-1941 Washington (USA): **Chalky Wright** KO 11 Joey Archibald (NY)
11-18-1941 Los Angeles (USA): **Jackie Wilson** W 12 Richie Lemos (NBA)
11-20-1942 New York (USA): **Willie Pep** W 15 Chalky Whright (NY)
01-18-1943 Providence (USA): **Jackie Callura** W 15 Jackie Wilson (NBA)
08-16-1943 New Orleans (USA): **Phil Terranova** KO 8 Jackie Callura (NBA)
03-10-1944 Boston (USA): **Sal Bartolo** W 15 Phil Terranova (NBA)
06-07-1946 New York (USA): **Willie Pep** KO 12 Sal Bartolo (NBA/NY)
10-29-1948 New York (USA): **Sandy Saddler** KO 4 Willie Pep
02-11-1949 New York (USA): **Willie Pep** W 15 Sandy Saddler
09-08-1950 New York (USA): **Sandy Saddler** ret 7 Willie Pep
Jan. 1957 *Saddler retires from professional sport.*
07-24-1957 Paris (FRA): **Hogan Bassey** W 10 Cherif Hamia
03-18-1959 Los Angeles (USA): **Davey Moore** ret 13 Hogan Bassey

03-21-1963 Los Angeles (USA): **Sugar Ramos** ret 10 Davey Moore
09-26-1964 Mexico City (MEX): **Vicente Saldivar** ret 11 Sugar Ramos
Oct. 1967 *Saldivar retires from professional sport.*
01-23-1968 London (GBR): **Howard Winstone** TKO 9 Mitsunori Seki (WBC)
03-28-1968 Los Angeles (USA): **Raul Rojas** W 15 Enrique Higgins (WBA)
07-24-1968 Porthcawl (GBR): **José Legra** TKO 5 Howard Winstone (WBC)
09-28-1968 Los Angeles (USA): **Shozo Saijo** W 15 Raul Rojas (WBA)
01-21-1969 London (GBR): **Johnny Famechon** W 15 José Legra (WBC)
05-09-1970 Rome (ITA): **Vicente Saldivar** W 15 Johnny Famechon (WBC)
12-11-1970 Tijuana (MEX): **Kuniaki Shibata** TKO 14 Vicente Saldivar (WBC)
09-02-1971 Tokyo (JPN): **Antonio Gomez** TKO 5 Shozo Saijo (WBA)
05-19-1972 Tokyo (JPN): **Clemente Sanchez** KO 3 Kuniaki Shibata (WBC)
08-19-1972 Maracay (VEN): **Ernesto Marcel** W 15 Antonio Gomez (WBA)
12-16-1972 Monterrey (MEX): **José Legra** KO 10 Clemente Sanchez (WBC)
05-05-1973 Brasilia (BRA): **Eder Jofre** W 15 José Legra (WBC)
May 1974 *Marcel retires from professional sport.*
June 1974 *Jofre is stripped of the WBC title for not defending.*
07-09-1974 Inglewood (USA): **Ruben Olivares** KO 7 Zensuke Utagawa (WBA)
09-07-1974 Los Angeles (USA): **Bobby Chacon** TKO 9 Alfredo Marcano (WBC)
11-23-1974 Inglewood (USA): **Alexis Arguello** KO 13 Ruben Olivares (WBA)
06-20-1975 Inglewood (USA): **Ruben Olivares** TKO 2 Bobby Chacon (WBC)
09-20-1975 Inglewood (USA): **David "Poison" Kotey** W 15 Ruben Olivares (WBC)
June 1976 *Arguello relinquishes the WBA title because he fails to make weight.*
11-13-1976 Accra (GHA): **Danny Lopez** TKO 15 David "Poison" Kotey (WBC)
01-15-1977 Panama City (PAN): **Rafael Ortega** W 15 Francisco Coronado (WBA)
12-17-1977 Torrelavega (ESP): **Cecilio Lastra** W 15 Rafael Ortega (WBA)
04-15-1978 Panama City (PAN): **Eusebio Pedroza** KO 13 Cecilio Lastra (WBA)
02-02-1980 Phoenix (USA): **Salvador Sanchez** TKO 13 Danny Lopez (WBC)
02-15-1982 New York (USA): **Juan LaPorte** ret 10 Mario Miranda (WBC)
03-04-1984 Seoul (KOR): **Min Keun-Oh** KO 2 Joko Arter (IBF)
03-31-1984 Hato Rey (PUR): **Wilfredo Gomez** W 12 Juan LaPorte (WBC)
12-08-1984 San Juan (PUR): **Azumah Nelson** TKO 11 Wilfredo Gomez (WBC)
06-08-1985 London (GBR): **Barry McGuigan** W 15 Eusebio Pedroza (WBA)
11-29-1985 Chonju (KOR): **Ki-Yung Chung** TKO 15 Min Keun-Oh (IBF)
06-23-1986 Las Vegas (USA): **Steve Cruz** W 15 Barry McGuigan (WBA)
08-30-1986 Osan (KOR): **Antonio Rivera** ret 10 Ki-Yung Chung (IBF)
03-06-1987 Fort Worth (USA): **Antonio Esparragoza** TKO 12 Steve Cruz (WBA)
01-23-1988 Gamaches (FRA): **Calvin Grove** TKO 4 Antonio Rivera (IBF)
Jan. 1988 *Nelson relinquishes his WBC title to fight at super featherweight.*
03-07-1988 Sydney (AUS): **Jeff Fenech** TKO 10 Victor Callejas (WBC)
08-04-1988 Mexicali (MEX): **Jorge Paez** W 15 Calvin Grove (IBF)
01-28-1989 Milan (ITA): **Maurizio Stecca** TKO 6 Pedro Nolasco (WBO)
11-11-1989 Rimini (ITA): **Louie Espinoza** TKO 7 Maurizio Stecca (WBO)
04-07-1990 Las Vegas (USA): **Jorge Paez** W 12 Louie Espinoza (WBO/IBF)
06-02-1990 Manchester (GBR): **Marcos Villasana** TKO 8 Paul Hodkinson (WBC)
Jan. 1991 *Paez relinquishes both titles to fight at lightweight.*
01-26-1991 Sassari (ITA): **Maurizio Stecca** W 12 Armando Reyes (WBO)
03-30-1991 Kwangju (KOR): **Kyung-Yung Park** W 12 Antonio Esparragoza (WBA)
06-03-1991 Las Vegas (USA): **Troy Dorsey** KO 1 Alfred Rangel (IBF)
08-12-1991 Los Angeles (USA): **Manuel Medina** W 12 Troy Dorsey (IBF)
11-13-1991 Belfast (GBR): **Paul Hodkinson** W 12 Marcos Villasana (WBC)
05-16-1992 London (GBR): **Colin McMillan** W 12 Maurizio Stecca (WBO)
09-26-1992 London (GBR): **Ruben Palacios** W 8 Colin McMillan (WBO)
02-26-1993 Melun (FRA): **Tom Johnson** W 12 Manuel Medina (IBF)
April 1993 *Palacios relinquishes the title after testing HIV-positive.*
04-17-1993 Washington (USA): **Steve Robinson** W 12 John Davison (WBO)
04-28-1993 Dublin (IRL): **Gregorio Vargas** ret 7 Paul Hodkinson (WBC)
12-04-1993 Reno (USA): **Kevin Kelley** W 12 Gregorio Vargas (WBC)
12-04-1993 Kwangmong (KOR): **Eloy Rojas** W 12 Kyun-Yung Park (WBA)
01-07-1995 San Antonio (USA): **Alejandro Gonzalez** ret 11 Kevin Kelley (WBC)
09-23-1995 Sacramento (USA): **Manuel Medina** W 12 Alejandro Gonzalez (WBC)
09-30-1995 Cardiff (GBR): **Naseem Hamed** TKO 8 Steve Robinson (WBO)
12-11-1995 Tokyo (JPN): **Luisito Espinosa** W 12 Manuel Medina (WBC)
05-18-1996 Las Vegas (USA): **Wilfredo Vasquez** TKO 11 Eloy Rojas (WBA)
02-08-1997 Millwall (GBR): **Naseem Hamed** TKO 8 Tom Johnson (IBF/WBO)
Sept. 1997 *Hamed is stripped of the IBF title after the unification of the IBF and WBO championships.*
12-13-1997 Pompano Beach (USA): **Hector Lizarraga** TKO 11 Welcome Ncita (IBF)
March 1998 *Vasquez is stripped of his title for not defending.*
04-03-1998 Bayamon (PUR): **Freddie Norwood** W 12 Antonio Cermeno (WBA/IBF)
Sept. 1998 *Norwood is stripped of the WBA title because he fails to make weight.*
10-03-1998 Caracas (VEN): **Antonio Cermeno** KO 4 Genaro Rios (WBA)
05-29-1999 San Juan (PUR): **Freddie Norwood** W 12 Antonio Cermeno (WBA)
05-15-1999 El Paso (USA): **Cesar Soto** W 12 Luisito Espinosa (WBC)
05-29-1999 San Juan (PUR): **Freddy Norwood** W 12 Antonio Cermeno (WBA)
10-22-1999 Detroit (USA): **Naseem Hamed** W 12 Cesar Soto (WBC/WBO)
Hamed relinquishes the title and remains WBO champion.
11-13-1999 Hull (GBR): **Paul Ingle** W 12 Manuel Medina (IBF)
04-14-2000 Merida (MEX): **Gustavo Espadas** Tech Dec 11 Luisito Espinosa (WBC)
09-09-2000 New Orleans (USA): **Derrick Gainer** TKO 11 Freddy Norwood (WBA)
12-16-2000 Sheffield (GBR): **Mbulelo Botile** TKO 12 Paul Ingle (IBF)

01-27-2001 Munich (GER): **Istvan Kovacs** TKO 12 Antonio Diaz (WBO)
04-06-2001 Las Vegas (USA): **Frank Toledo** W 12 Mbulelo Botile (IBF)
06-16-2001 Budapest (HUN): **Julio Pablo Chacon** TKO 6 Istvan Kovacs (WBO)
11-16-2001 Las Vegas (USA): **Manuel Medina** TKO 6 Frank Toledo (IBF)
04-24-2002 New York (USA): **Johnny Tapia** W 12 Manuel Medina (IBF)
10-19-2002 Glasgow (GBR): **Scott Harrison** W 12 Julio Pablo Chacon (WBO)
  Jan. 2003 *Johnny Tapia is stripped of the IBF title for failing a drugs test.*
02-01-2003 Las Vegas (USA): **Juan-Miguel Marquez** TKO 7 Manuel Medina (IBF)
02-22-2003 Mexico City (MEX): **Erik Morales** TKO 3 Eddie Croft (WBC)
March 2003 *Naseem Hamed relinquishes the IBO featherweight title.*
03-22-2003 Glasgow (GBR): **Scott Harrison** W 12 Wayne McCullough (WBO)
04-12-2003 Las Vegas (USA): **Derrick "Smoke" Gainer** splt 12 Oscar Leon (WBA)
05-03-2003 Las Vegas (USA): **Erik Morales** TKO 5 Fernando Velardez (WBC)

SUPER BANTAMWEIGHT (ALSO CALLED JUNIOR FEATHERWEIGHT)
04-03-1976 Panama City (PAN): **Rigoberto Riasco** ret 8 Waruinge Nakayama (WBC)
10-10-1976 Tokyo (JPN): **Royal Kobayashi** TKO 8 Rigoberto Riasco (WBC)
11-24-1976 Seoul (KOR): **Dong-Kyun Yum** W 15 Royal Kobayashi (WBC)
05-21-1977 Hato Rey (PUR): **Wilfredo Gomez** KO 12 Dong-Kyun Yum (WBC)
11-26-1977 Panama City (PAN): **Soo Hwang Hong** KO 3 Hector Carasquilla (WBA)
05-06-1978 Seoul (KOR): **Ricardo Cardona** TKO 12 Soo Hwang Hong (WBA)
05-04-1980 Seattle (USA): **Leo Randolph** TKO 15 Ricardo Cardona (WBA)
08-09-1980 Spokane (USA): **Sergio Palma** KO 5 Leo Randolph (WBA)
06-12-1982 Miami Beach (USA): **Leonardo Cruz** W 15 Sergio Palma (WBA)
  April 1983 *Gomez relinquishes the WBC title because he fails to make weight.*
06-15-1983 Los Angeles (USA): **Jaime Garza** TKO 2 Bobby Berna (WBC)
12-14-1983 Seoul (KOR): **Bobby Berna** ret 11 Seung-In Suh (IBF)
02-22-1984 Milan (ITA): **Loris Stecca** TKO 12 Leonardo Cruz (WBA)
04-15-1984 Seoul (KOR): **Seung-In Suh** KO 10 Bobby Berna (IBF)
05-26-1984 Guaynabo (PUR): **Victor Callejas** TKO 8 Loris Stecca (WBA)
11-03-1984 Kingston (USA): **Juan Meza** KO 1 Jaime Garza (WBC)
01-03-1985 Seoul (KOR): **Ji-Won Kim** KO 10 Seung-In Suh (IBF)
08-18-1985 Mexico City (MEX): **Lupe Pintor** W 12 Juan Meza (WBC)
01-18-1986 Bangkok (THA): **Samart Payakarun** KO 5 Lupe Pintor (WBC)
  Dec. 1986 *The WBA strips Callejas of the title for failing to defend.*
01-16-1987 Phoenix (USA): **Louie Espinoza** TKO 4 Tommy Valoy (WBA)
01-18-1987 Pohang (KOR): **Seung Hon Lee** KO 9 Prayoonsak Muangsurin (IBF)
05-08-1987 Sydney (AUS): **Jeff Fenech** TKO 4 Samart Payakarun (WBC)
11-28-1987 San Juan (PUR): **Julio Gervacio** W 12 Louie Espinoza (WBA)
  Jan. 1988 *Fenech relinquishes the WBC title to fight at featherweight.*
02-27-1988 San Juan (PUR): **Bernardo Pinango** W 12 Julio Gervacio (WBA)
02-29-1988 Los Angeles (USA): **Daniel Zaragoza** TKO 10 Carlos Zarate (WBC)
March 1988 *Lee relinquishes the IBF title to fight for the WBC title.*
05-21-1988 Bucaramanga (COL): **Jose Sanabria** KO 6 Moises Fuentes (IBF)
05-28-1988 Tijuana (MEX): **Juan Jose Estrada** W 12 Bernardo Pinango (WBA)
03-10-1989 Limoges (FRA): **Fabrice Benichou** W 12 Jose Sanabria (IBF)
04-29-1989 San Juan (PUR): **Kenny Mitchell** W 12 Julio Gervacio (WBO)
12-09-1989 Teramo (ITA): **Valerio Nati** disq 4 Kenny Mitchell (WBO)
12-11-1989 Inglewood (USA): **Jesus Salud** disq 9 Juan Jose Estrada (WBA)
03-10-1990 Tel Aviv (ISR): **Welcome Ncita** W 12 Fabrice Benichou (IBF)
  April 1990 *WBA strips Salud of the title for not defending.*
04-23-1990 Inglewood (USA): **Paul Banke** TKO 9 Daniel Zaragoza (WBC)
05-12-1990 Sassari (ITA): **Orlando Fernandez** KO 10 Valerio Nati (WBO)
09-11-1990 Miami (USA): **Luis Mendoza** TKO 3 Ruben Palacios (WBA)
11-05-1990 Inglewood (USA): **Pedro Decima** TKO 4 Paul Banke (WBC)
02-03-1991 Nagoya (JPN): **Kiyoshi Hatanaka** TKO 8 Pedro Decima (WBC)
05-24-1991 Corpus Christi (USA): **Jesse Benavides** W 12 Orlando Fernandez (WBO)
10-07-1991 Inglewood (USA): **Raul Perez** W 12 Luis Mendoza (WBA)
03-20-1992 Calais (FRA): **Thierry Jacob** W 12 Daniel Zaragoza (WBC)
03-27-1992 Mexico City (MEX): **Wilfredo Vasquez** TKO 3 Raul Perez (WBA)
06-23-1992 Albany (USA): **Tracy Patterson** TKO 2 Thierry Jacob (WBC)
10-15-1992 London (GBR): **Duke McKenzie** W 12 Jesse Benavides (WBO)
12-02-1992 Tortoli (ITA): **Kennedy McKinney** KO 11 Welcome Ncita (IBF)
06-09-1993 London (GBR): **Daniel Jimenez** W 12 Duke McKenzie (WBO)
08-20-1994 Hammanskraal (RSA): **Vuyani Bungu** W 12 Kennedy McKinney (IBF)
08-26-1994 Atlantic City (USA): **Hector Acero-Sanchez** W 12 Tracy Patterson (WBC)
03-31-1995 Anaheim (USA): **Marco Antonio Barrera** W 12 Daniel Jimenez (WBO)
05-13-1995 Bayamon (PUR): **Antonio Cermeno** W 12 Wilfredo Vasquez (WBA)
11-06-1995 Inglewood (USA): **Daniel Zaragoza** W 12 Hector Acero Sanchez (WBC)
11-22-1996 Tampa (USA): **Junior Jones** disq 5 Marco Antonio Barrera (WBO)
09-06-1997 El Paso (USA): **Erik Morales** TKO 11 Daniel Zaragoza (WBC)
  Sept. 1997 *Cermeno relinquishes the WBA title to fight at featherweight.*
12-19-1997 New York (USA): **Kennedy McKinney** TKO 4 Junior Jones (WBO)
02-08-1998 Lake Charles (USA): **Enrique Sanchez** W 12 Rafael Del Valle (WBA)
  May 1998 *McKinney relinquishes the WBO title.*
10-31-1998 Atlantic City (USA): **Marco Antonio Barrera** ret 3 Richie Wenton (WBO)
12-12-1998 Indio (USA): **Nestor Garza** W 12 Enrique Sanchez (WBA)
March 1999 *Bungu relinquishes the IBF title to fight at featherweight.*
05-29-1999 Hammanskraal (RSA): **Lehlohonolo Ledwaba** W 12 John Michael Johnson (IBF)

02-19-2000 Las Vegas (USA): **Erik Morales** W 12 Marco Antonio Barrera (WBC/WBO)
03-04-2000 Las Vegas (USA): **Clarence Adams** W 12 Nestor Garza (WBA)
09-08-2000 Manchester (GBR): **Willie Jorrin** W 12 Michael Brodie (WBO)
06-23-2001 Las Vegas (USA): **Manny Pacquiao** TKO 6 Lehlohonolo Ledwaba (IBF)
06-23-2001 Las Vegas (USA): **Agapito Sanchez** TKO 7 Jorge Pabon Monsalvo (WBO)
02-21-2002 Dankhuntod (THA): **Yoddamrong Sithyodthong** PS 12 Yober Ortega (WBA)
05-18-2002 Saitama (JPN): **Osamu Sato** TKO 8 Yoddamrong Sithyodthong (WBA)
  2002 *Agapito Sanchez relinquishes the WBO title.*
08-17-2002 Cardiff (GBR): **Joan Guzman** KO 3 Fabio Oliva (WBO)
10-09-2002 Tokyo (JPN): **Salim Medjkoune** W 12 Osamu Sato (WBA)
11-01-2002 Sacramento (USA): **Oscar Larios** TKO 1 Willie Jorrin (WBC)

BANTAMWEIGHT
06-05-1889 New York (USA): **Chappie Moran** W 10 Tommy Kelly
01-31-1890 New York (USA): **Tommy Kelly** KO 10 Chappie Moran
05-09-1892 New York (USA): **Billy Plimmer** W 10 Tommy Kelly
11-25-1895 London (GBR): **Pedlar Palmer** disq 14 Billy Plimmer
09-12-1899 Tuckahoe (USA): **Terry McGovern** KO 1 Pedlar Palmer
  Dec. 1899 *McGovern is stripped of his title because he fails to make weight.*
03-18-1901 London (GBR): **Harry Harris** W 20 Pedlar Palmer
          Harris relinquishes the title to fight at featherweight.
04-02-1901 Memphis (USA): **Harry Forbes** W 15 Casper Leon
08-13-1903 San Francisco (USA): **Frankie Neil** KO 2 Harry Forbes
10-17-1904 London (GBR): **Joe Bowker** W 20 Frankie Neil
          Bowker relinquishes the title.
10-20-1905 Chelsea (USA): **Jimmy Walsh** W 15 Digger Stanley
  1905 *Walsh relinquishes his title because he fails to make weight.*
01-20-1906 Newcastle (GBR): **Digger Stanley** W 20 Ike Bradley (British World Title/IBU)
04-03-1907 London (GBR): **Owen Moran** W 20 Al Delmont (World Title)
06-26-1908 San Francisco (USA): **Jimmy Walsh** KO 11 Jimmy Carroll (USA Title)
  1909 *Walsh changes back to featherweight.*
06-19-1909 San Francisco (USA): **Monte Attell** TKO 18 Frankie Neil (USA Title)
02-22-1910 Vernon (USA): **Frankie Conley** ret 42 Monte Attell (USA Title)
03-06-1910 New Orleans (USA): **Johnny Coulon** KO 19 Jim Kendrick (USA Title)
06-23-1912 Dieppe (FRA): **Charles Ledoux** KO 7 Digger Stanley (British World Title)
06-24-1913 Vernon (USA): **Eddie Campi** W 20 Charles Ledoux (British World Title)
01-31-1914 Los Angeles (USA): **Kid Williams** KO 12 Eddie Campi (British World Title/European World Title)
06-09-1914 Los Angeles (USA): **Kid Williams** KO 3 Johnny Coulon (World Title)
01-09-1917 New Orleans (USA): **Pete Herman** W 20 Kid Williams
12-22-1920 New York (USA): **Joe Lynch** W 15 Pete Herman
07-25-1921 New York (USA): **Pete Herman** W 15 Joe Lynch
09-23-1921 New York (USA): **Johnny Buff** W 15 Pete Herman
07-10-1922 New York (USA): **Joe Lynch** ret 14 Johnny Buff
03-21-1924 New York (USA): **Abe Goldstein** W 15 Joe Lynch
12-19-1924 New York (USA): **Eddie "Cannonball" Martin** W 15 Abe Goldstein
03-20-1925 New York (USA): **Charlie Phil Rosenberg** W 15 Eddie "Cannonball" Martin
          The New York State Boxing Commission suspends Rosenberg because they suspect him of a secret agreement.
05-05-1927 London (GBR): **Teddy Baldock** W15 Archie Bell (British World Title)
06-24-1927 Chicago (USA): **Bud Taylor** W10 Tony Canzoneri (NBA)
10-06-1927 London (GBR): **Willie Smith** W 15 Teddy Baldock (British World Title)
          Smith changes to featherweight.
  Aug. 1928 *Taylor relinquishes his NBA title to fight at featherweight.*
06-18-1929 New York (USA): **Al Brown** W 15 Vidal Gregorio
  May 1934 *Brown is stripped of his title for not defending.*
06-26-1934 Montreal (CAN): **Sixto Escobar** KO 9 Baby Casanova (NBA)
11-01-1934 Tunis (TUN): **Al Brown** KO 10 Young Perez (NY/IBU)
06-01-1935 Valencia (ESP): **Baltazar Sangchili** W 15 Al Brown (NY/IBU)
08-26-1935 New York (USA): **Lou Salica** W 15 Sixto Escobar (NBA/NY)
11-15-1935 New York (USA): **Sixto Escobar** W 15 Lou Salica (NBA/NY)
06-29-1936 New York (USA): **Tony Marino** KO 14 Baltazar Sangchili (IBU)
08-31-1936 New York (USA): **Sixto Escobar** TKO 13 Tony Marino (World Title)
09-23-1937 New York (USA): **Harry Jeffra** W 15 Sixto Escobar
02-20-1938 San Juan (PUR): **Sixto Escobar** W 15 Harry Jeffra (NBA/IBU)
          The IBU strips Escobar of the title.
03-04-1938 Paris (FRA): **Al Brown** W 15 Baltazar Sangchili (IBU)
          The IBU withdraws recognition of Brown to unify the titles.
04-02-1939 San Juan (PUR): **Sixto Escobar** W 15 Kayo Morgan (NBA/IBU)
  Oct. 1939 *Escobar is stripped of the title because he fails to make weight.*
09-24-1940 New York (USA): **Lou Salica** W 15 Georgie Pace (NBA)
04-25-1941 Baltimore (USA): **Lou Salica** W 15 Lou Transparenti (World Title)
08-07-1942 Hollywood (USA): **Manuel Ortiz** W 12 Lou Salica
01-06-1947 San Francisco (USA): **Harold Dade** W 15 Manuel Ortiz
03-11-1947 Los Angeles (USA): **Manuel Ortiz** W 15 Harold Dade

05-31-1950 Johannesburg (RSA): **Vic Toweel** W 15 Manuel Ortiz
11-15-1952 Johannesburg (RSA): **Jimmy Carruthers** KO 1 Vic Toweel (NBA/IBU)
  May 1954 *Carruthers retires from professional sport.*
09-19-1954 Bangkok (THA): **Robert Cohen** W 15 Chamrern Songkitrat (NBA/IBU)
03-09-1955 San Francisco (USA): **Raul Macias** KO 11 Chamrern Songkitrat (NBA)
  May 1955 *The NBA strips Cohen of the title for not defending.*
06-29-1956 Rome (ITA): **Mario D'Agata** W 6 Robert Cohen (EBU/NY)
04-01-1957 Paris (FRA): **Alphonse Halimi** W 15 Mario D'Agata (EBU)
11-06-1957 Los Angeles (USA): **Alphonse Halimi** W 15 Raul Macias (World Title)
07-08-1959 Los Angeles (USA): **José Becerra** KO 8 Alphonse Halimi (NBA/EBU)
  Aug. 1960 *Becerra retires from professional sport.*
10-25-1960 London (GBR): **Alphonse Halimi** W 15 Freddie Gilroy (European World Title)
11-18-1960 Los Angeles (USA): **Eder Jofre** KO 6 Eloy Sanchez (NBA)
01-18-1962 São Paulo (BRA): **Eder Jofre** ret 10 John Caldwell (World Title)
05-18-1965 Nagoya (JPN): **Masahiko "Fighting" Harada** W 15 Eder Jofre
02-26-1968 Tokyo (JPN): **Lionel Rose** W 15 Masahiko "Fighting" Harada
08-22-1969 Inglewood (USA): **Ruben Olivares** KO 5 Lionel Rose
10-16-1970 Mexico City (MEX): **Jesus "Chuchu" Castillo** KO 14 Ruben Olivares
04-03-1971 Inglewood (USA): **Ruben Olivares** W 15 Jesus "Chuchu" Castillo
03-19-1972 Mexico City (MEX): **Rafael Herrera** KO 8 Ruben Olivares
07-30-1972 Panama City (PAN): **Enrique Pinder** W15 Rafael Herrera
  Dec. 1972 *WBC strips Pinder of the title.*
01-20-1973 Panama City (PAN): **Romeo Anaya** KO 3 Enrique Pinder (WBA)
04-15-1973 Monterrey (MEX): **Rafael Herrera** TKO 12 Rodolfo Martinez (WBC)
11-03-1973 Johannesburg (RSA): **Arnold Taylor** KO 14 Romeo Anaya (WBA)
07-03-1974 Durban (RSA): **Soo Hwan-Hong** W 15 Arnold Taylor (WBA)
12-07-1974 Merida (MEX): **Rodolfo Martinez** TKO 4 Rafael Herrera (WBC)
03-14-1975 Inglewood (USA): **Alfonso Zamora** KO 4 Soo Hwan-Hong (WBA)
05-08-1976 Inglewood (USA): **Carlos Zarate** KO 9 Rodolfo Martinez (WBC)
11-19-1977 Los Angeles (USA): **Jorge Lujan** KO 10 Alfonso Zamora (WBA)
06-03-1979 Las Vegas (USA): **Lupe Pintor** W15 Carlos Zarate (WBC)
08-29-1980 Miami (USA): **Julian Solis** W 15 Jorge Lujan (WBA)
11-14-1980 Miami Beach (USA): **Jeff Chandler** TKO 14 Julian Solis (WBA)
  July 1983 *Pintor relinquishes the title due to injuries after a motorcycle accident.*
09-01-1983 Los Angeles (USA): **Albert Davila** KO 12 Francisco "Kiko" Bejines (WBC)
04-07-1984 Atlantic City (USA): **Richard Sandoval** TKO 15 Jeff Chandler (WBA)
04-16-1984 Kashiwara (JPN): **Satoshi Shingaki** TKO 8 Elmer Magallano (IBF)
  Feb. 1985 *The WBC strips Davila of the title due to inactivity.*
04-26-1985 Sydney (AUS): **Jeff Fenech** TKO 9 Satoshi Shingaki (IBF)
05-04-1985 Aruba (ANT): **Daniel Zarazoga** disq 7 Freddie Jackson (WBC)
08-09-1985 Miami (USA): **Miguel Lora** W 12 Daniel Zarazoga (WBC)
03-10-1986 Las Vegas (USA): **Gaby Canizales** TKO 7 Richard Sandoval (WBA)
06-04-1986 East Rutherford (USA): **Bernardo Pinango** W 15 Gaby Canizales (WBA)
  Feb. 1987 *Pinango relinquishes the WBA title because he fails to make weight.*
  Feb. 1987 *Fenech relinquishes the IBF title to fight at super bantamweight.*
03-29-1987 Moriguchi (JPN): **Takuya Muguruma** KO 5 Azael Moran (WBA)
05-15-1987 Cartagena (COL): **Kelvin Seabrooks** KO 5 Miguel Maturana (IBF)
05-24-1987 Moriguchi (JPN): **Chang-Yong Park** TKO 11 Takuya Muguruma (WBA)
10-04-1987 Seoul (KOR): **Wilfredo Vasquez** TKO 10 Chang-Yong Park (WBA)
05-09-1988 Bangkok (THA): **Kaokor Galaxy** W 12 Wilfredo Vasquez (WBA)
07-09-1988 Atlantic City (USA): **Orlando Canizales** TKO 15 Kelvin Seabrooks (IBF)
08-14-1988 Seoul (KOR): **Sung-Il Moon** Tech Dec 6 Kaokor Galaxy (WBA)
10-29-1988 Las Vegas (USA): **Raul Perez** W 12 Miguel Lora (WBC)
02-03-1989 Caracas (VEN): **Israel Contreras** KO 1 Maurizio Lupino (WBO)
07-08-1989 Bangkok (THA): **Kaokor Galaxy** W 12 Sung-Il Moon (WBA)
10-18-1989 Bangkok (THA): **Luisito Espinosa** TKO 1 Kaokor Galaxy (WBA)
  Jan. 1991 *Contrerras relinquishes the WBO title to fight for the WBA title.*
02-25-1991 Los Angeles (USA): **Greg Richardson** W 12 Raul Perez (WBC)
03-12-1991 Detroit (USA): **Gaby Canizales** KO 2 Miguel Lora (WBO)
06-30-1991 London (GBR): **Duke McKenzie** W 12 Gaby Canizales (WBO)
09-19-1991 Tokyo (JPN): **Joichiro Tatsuyoshi** ret 10 Greg Richardson (WBC)
10-19-1991 Manila (PHI): **Israel Contreras** KO 5 Luisito Espinosa (WBA)
March 1992 *Tatsuyoshi relinquishes the WBC title due to an injury.*
03-15-1992 Las Vegas (USA): **Eddie Cook** KO 5 Israel Contreras (WBA)
03-30-1992 Los Angeles (USA): **Victor Rabanales** Tech Dec 9 Yong-Hoon Lee (WBC)
05-13-1992 London (GBR): **Rafael Del Valle** KO 1 Duke McKenzie (WBO)
10-09-1992 Cartagena (COL): **Jorge Eliecer Julio** W12 Eddie Cook (WBA)
03-28-1993 Kyungju (KOR): **Jung-Il Byun** W 12 Victor Rabanales (WBC)
10-23-1993 Atlantic City (USA): **Junior Jones** W 12 Jorge Eliecer Julio (WBA)
12-23-1993 Nagoya (JPN): **Yasuei Yakushiji** W 12 Jung-Il Byun (WBC)
04-22-1994 Las Vegas (USA): **John Michael Johnson** TKO 11 Junior Jones (WBA)
07-16-1994 Bangkok (THA): **Daorung MP Petroleum** TKO 1 John Michael Johnson (WBA)
07-30-1994 London (GBR): **Alfred Kotey** W 12 Rafael Del Valle (WBO)

Dec. 1994 *Canizales relinquishes the IBF title.*
01-21-1995 Cartagena (COL): **Harold Mestre** TKO 8 Juvenal Berrio (IBF)
04-29-1995 Johannesburg (RSA): **Mbulelo Botile** KO 2 Harold Mestre (IBF)
07-30-1995 Nagoya (JPN): **Wayne McCullough** W 12 Yasuei Yakushiji (WBC)
09-17-1995 Nongtha Buri (THA): **Veeraphol Sahaprom** W 12 Daorung MP Petroleum (WBA)
10-21-1995 London (GBR): **Daniel Jimenez** W 12 Alfred Kotey (WBO)
01-27-1996 Kanchunburi (THA): **Nana Yaw Konadu** TKO 2 Veeraphol Sahaprom (WBA)
04-26-1996 Cardiff (GBR): **Robbie Regan** W 12 Daniel Jimenez (WBO)
10-27-1996 Uttaradit (THA): **Daorung MP Petroleum** Tech Dec 10 Nana Yaw Konadu (WBA)
  Jan. 1997 *Regan retires from professional sport due to health problems.*
  Feb. 1997 *McCullough relinquishes the WBC title to change to a higher weight division.*
06-21-1997 Tampa (USA): **Nana Yaw Konadu** TKO 7 Daorung MP Petroleum (WBA)
07-19-1997 Nashville (USA): **Tim Austin** TKO 8 Mbulelo Botile (IBF)
07-28-1997 Los Angeles (USA): **Jorge Julio** W 12 Oscar Maldonado (WBO)
11-22-1997 Osaka (JPN): **Joichiro Tatsuyoshi** TKO 7 Sirimongkol Singmanassak (WBC)
12-05-1998 Atlantic City (USA): **Johnny Tapia** W 12 Nana Yaw Konadu (WBA)
12-29-1998 Osaka (JPN): **Veeraphol Sahaprom** KO 6 Joichiro Tatsuyoshi (WBC)
06-26-1999 Las Vegas (USA): **Paulie Ayala** W 12 Johnny Tapia (WBA)
01-08-2000 Albuquerque (USA): **Johnny Tapia** W 12 Jorge Eliecer Julio (WBO)
  Tapia relinquishes his title.
09-08-2000 Manchester (GBR): **Mauricio Martinez** TKO 5 Lester Fuentes (WBO)
03-15-2002 Boca del Rio (MEX): **Cruz Carbajal** TKO 9 Mauricio Martinez (WBO)
02-15-2003 Las Vegas (USA): **Rafael Marquez** TKO 8 Tim Austin (IBF)

SUPER FLYWEIGHT (ALSO CALLED JUNIOR BANTAMWEIGHT)

02-01-1980 Caracas (VEN): **Rafael Orono** W 15 Seung-Hoon Lee (WBC)
01-24-1981 San Cristobal (VEN): **Chul-Ho Kim** KO 9 Rafael Orono (WBC)
09-12-1981 Buenos Aires (ARG): **Gustavo Ballas** TKO 8 Sok-Chul Baek (WBA)
12-05-1981 Panama City (PAN): **Rafael Pedroza** W 15 Gustavo Ballas (WBA)
04-08-1982 Osaka (JPN): **Jiro Watanabe** W 15 Rafael Pedroza (WBA)
11-28-1982 Seoul (KOR): **Rafael Orono** KO 6 Chul-Ho Kim (WBC)
11-27-1983 Pattaya (THA): **Payao Poontarat** W 12 Rafael Orono (WBC)
12-10-1983 Osaka (JPN): **Joo-Do Chun** KO 5 Ken Kasugai (IBF)
07-05-1984 Osaka (JPN): **Jiro Watanabe** W 12 Payao Poontarat (WBC)
  July 1984 *The WBA strips Watanabe of his title after he has become WBC champion.*
11-21-1984 Bangkok (THA): **Khaosai Galaxy** KO 6 Eusebio Espinal (WBA)
05-03-1985 Jakarta (INA): **Elly Pical** TKO 8 Joo-Do Chun (IBF)
02-15-1986 Jakarta (INA): **Carlos Cesar Polanco** W 15 Elly Pical (IBF)
03-30-1986 Itami City (JPN): **Gilberto Roman** W 12 Jiro Watanabe (WBC)
07-05-1986 Jakarta (INA): **Elly Pical** KO 3 Carlos Cesar Polanco (IBF)
March 1987 *Pical relinquishes the IBF title to fight for the WBA title.*
05-16-1987 Reims (FRA): **Santos Laciar** TKO 11 Gilberto Roman (WBC)
05-17-1987 Pusan (KOR): **Tae-Il Chang** W 15 Soon-Chun Kwan (IBF)
08-08-1987 Miami (USA): **Sugar Baby Rojas** W 12 Santos Laciar (WBC)
10-17-1987 Jakarta (INA): **Elly Pical** W 15 Tae-Il Chang (IBF)
04-08-1988 Miami Beach (USA): **Gilberto Roman** W 12 Sugar Baby Rojas (WBC)
09-09-1989 San Juan (PUR): **Jose Ruiz** TKO 1 Juan Carazo (WBO)
10-14-1989 Roanoke (USA): **Juan Polo Perez** W 12 Elly Pical (IBF)
11-07-1989 Mexico City (MEX): **Nana Yaw Konadu** W 12 Gilberto Roman (WBC)
01-20-1990 Seoul (KOR): **Sung-Il Moon** Tech Dec 9 Nana Yaw Konadu (WBC)
04-21-1990 Sunderland (GBR): **Robert Quiroga** W 12 Juan Polo Perez (IBF)
  Jan. 1992 *WBA champion Galaxy retires from professional sport.*
02-22-1992 Las Vegas (USA): **Jose Quirino** W 12 Jose Ruiz (WBO)
04-10-1992 Tokyo (JPN): **Katsuya Onizuka** W 12 Thalerngsak Sithbaobey (WBA)
09-04-1992 Copenhagen (DEN): **Johnny Bredahl** W 12 Jose Quirino (WBO)
01-16-1993 San Antonio (USA): **Julio Cesar Borboa** TKO 12 Robert Quiroga (IBF)
11-13-1993 Pohang (KOR): **Jose Luis Bueno** W 12 Sung-Il Moon (WBC)
05-04-1994 Yokohama (JPN): **Hiroshi Kawashima** W 12 Jose Luis Bueno (WBC)
  Aug. 1994 *Bredahl relinquishes the WBO title.*
08-29-1994 Inglewood (USA): **Harold Grey** W 12 Julio Cesar Borboa
09-18-1994 Tokyo (JPN): **Hyung-Chul Lee** TKO 9 Katsuya Onizuka (WBA)
10-12-1994 Albuquerque (USA): **Johnny Tapia** TKO 11 Henry Martinez (WBO)
07-22-1995 Seoul (KOR): **Alimi Goitia** KO 4 Hyung-Chul Lee (WBA)
10-07-1995 Mar del Plata (ARG): **Carlos Salazar** W 12 Harold Grey (IBF)
04-27-1996 Cartagena (COL): **Harold Grey** W 12 Carlos Salazar (IBF)
08-24-1996 Kamphaeng Phetch (THA): **Yokhtai Sithoar** TKO 8 Alimi Goitia (WBA)
08-24-1996 Albuquerque (USA): **Danny Romero** KO 2 Harold Grey (IBF)
02-20-1997 Tokyo (JPN): **Gerry Penalosa** W 12 Hiroshi Kawashima (WBC)
07-18-1997 Las Vegas (USA): **Johnny Tapia** W 12 Danny Romero (IBF/WBO)
12-23-1997 Nagoya (JPN): **Satoshi Iida** W 12 Yokthai Sit-Oar (WBA)
  Feb. 1998 *Tapia relinquishes the IBF and WBO titles to fight at bantamweight.*
08-29-1998 Seoul (KOR): **In-Joo Choo** W 12 Gerry Penalosa (WBC)
12-23-1998 Nagoya (JPN): **Jesus Rojas** W 12 Satoshi Iida (WBA)

04-24-1999 Washington (USA): **Mark Johnson** W 12 Ratanachai Sorvoraphin (IBF)
06-07-1999 Tijuana (MEX): **Diego Morales** ret 11 Victor Godoi (WBO)
07-31-1999 Nagoya (JPN): **Hideki Todaka** W 12 Jesus Rojas (WBA)
11-20-1999 Las Vegas (USA): **Antonio Adonis Rivas** W 12 Diego Morales (WBO)
07-22-2000 Miami (USA): **Felix Machado** W 12 Julio Gamboa (IBF)
08-27-2000 Osaka (JPN): **Masamori Tokuyama** W 12 In-Joo Choo (WBC)
10-09-2000 Nagoya (JPN): **Leo Gamez** KO 7 Hideki Todaka (WBA)
03-11-2001 Yokohama (JPN): **Celes Kobayashi** TKO 10 Leo Gamez (WBA)
06-16-2001 Panama City (PAN): **Pedro Alcazar** W 12 Antonio Adonis Rivas (WBO)
02-09-2002 Tokyo (JPN): **Alexander Munoz** TKO 8 Celes Kobayashi (WBA)
06-22-2002 Las Vegas (USA): **Fernando Montiel** TKO 6 Pedro Alcazar (WBO)
01-04-2003 Washington (USA): **Luis Perez** W 12 Felix Machado (IBF)
01-18-2003 Los Mochis (MEX): **Fernando Montiel** TKO 3 Roy Doliguez (WBO)

FLYWEIGHT

04-11-1913 Paris (FRA): **Sid Smith** W20 Eugene Criqui
06-02-1913 London (GBR): **Bill Ladbury** TKO 11 Sid Smith
01-26-1914 London (GBR): **Percy Jones** W 29 Bill Ladbury
05-15-1914 Plymouth (GBR): **Joe Symonds** KO 18 Percy Jones
11-16-1914 London (GBR): **Jimmy Wilde** W 15 Joe Symonds
01-25-1915 London (GBR): **Tancy Lee** TKO 17 Jimmy Wilde
10-18-1915 London (GBR): **Joe Symonds** TKO 16 Tancy Lee
02-14-1916 London (GBR): **Jimmy Wilde** TKO 12 Joe Symonds
06-18-1923 New York (USA): **Pancho Villa** KO 7 Jimmy Wilde
July 1925 *Death of Villa.*
08-22-1925 Los Angeles (USA): **Fidel LaBarba** W 10 Frankie Genaro
Aug. 1927 *LaBarba retires from professional sport.*
10-22-1927 Bridgeport (USA): **Pinky Silverburg** disq 7 Ruby Bradley (NBA)
Nov. 1927 *Silverburg is stripped of the title for not defending.*
12-16-1927 New York (USA): **Cpl Izzy Schwartz** W 15 Newsboy Brown (NY)
12-19-1927 Toronto (CAN): **Albert "Frenchy" Belanger** W 12 Ernie Jarvis (NBA/IBU)
02-06-1928 Toronto (CAN): **Frankie Genaro** W 10 Albert "Frenchy" Belanger (NBA)
08-29-1928 London (GBR): **Johnny Hill** W 15 Newsboy Brown (British World Title)
03-02-1929 Paris (FRA): **Emile Pladner** KO 1 Frankie Genaro (NBA)
04-18-1929 Paris (FRA): **Frankie Genaro** disq 5 Emile Pladner (NBA/IBU)
08-22-1929 Newark (USA): **Willie La Morte** W 15 Cpl Izzy Schwartz (NY)
New York does not recognize La Morte as champion and declares the title vacant.
03-21-1930 New York (USA): **Midget Wolgast** W 15 Black Bill (NY)
10-27-1931 Paris (FRA): **Victor "Young" Perez** KO 2 Frankie Genaro (NBA/IBU)
10-31-1932 Manchester (GBR): **Jackie Brown** TKO 13 Victor "Young" Perez (NBA/IBU)
09-09-1935 Manchester (GBR): **Benny Lynch** ret 2 Jackie Brown (NBA)
09-16-1935 Oakland (USA): **Small Montana** W 10 Midget Wolgast (NY)
01-19-1937 London (GBR): **Benny Lynch** W 15 Small Montana (NY)
June 1938 *Lynch is stripped of the title because he fails to make weight.*
09-22-1938 Liverpool (GBR): **Peter Kane** W 15 Jackie Jurich (NBA/IBU)
May 1939 *Kane relinquishes the title and changes to bantamweight.*
02-21-1941 Honolulu (USA): **Little Dado** W 19 Jackie Jurich (NBA)
1942 *Dado loses the title to Peter Kane because he fails to make weight.*
06-19-1943 Glasgow (GBR): **Jackie Paterson** KO 1 Peter Kane (NBA)
July 1947 *Paterson is stripped of the title because he fails to make weight.*
10-20-1947 London (GBR): **Rinty Monaghan** W 15 Dado Marino (NBA)
03-23-1948 Belfast (GBR): **Rinty Monaghan** KO 7 Jackie Paterson (World Title)
March 1950 *Monaghan retires undefeated from professional sport.*
04-25-1950 London (GBR): **Terry Allen** W 15 Honore Pratesi
08-01-1950 Honolulu (USA): **Dado Marino** W 15 Terry Allen
05-19-1952 Tokyo (JPN): **Yoshio Shirai** W 15 Dado Marino
11-26-1954 Tokyo (JPN): **Pascual Perez** W 15 Yoshio Shirai
04-16-1960 Bangkok (THA): **Pone Kingpetch** W 15 Pascual Perez
10-10-1962 Tokyo (JPN): **Masahiko "Fighting" Harada** KO 11 Pone Kingpetch
01-12-1963 Bangkok (THA): **Pone Kingpetch** W 15 Masahiko "Fighting" Harada
09-18-1963 Tokyo (JPN): **Hiroyuki Ebihara** KO 1 Pone Kingpetch
01-23-1964 Bangkok (THA): **Pone Kingpetch** W 15 Hiroyuki Ebihara
04-23-1965 Rome (ITA): **Salvatore Burruni** W 15 Pone Kingpetch
Nov. 1965 *The WBC withdraws recognition of Burruni because he does not defend his title.*
12-02-1965 Sydney (AUS): **Salvatore Burruni** KO 13 Rocky Gattellari (WBC)
03-01-1966 Tokyo (JPN): **Horacio Accavallo** W 15 Katsutoshi Takayama (WBA)
06-14-1966 London (GBR): **Walter McGowan** W 15 Salvatore Burruni (WBC)
12-30-1966 Bangkok (THA): **Chartchai Chionoi** W 15 Walter McGowan (WBC)
Oct. 1968 *Accavallo retires from professional sport due to an eye injury.*
02-23-1969 Mexico City (MEX): **Efren Torres** TKO 8 Chartchai Chionoi (WBC)
03-30-1969 Sapporo (JPN): **Hiroyuki Ebihara** W 15 Jose Severino (WBA)
10-19-1969 Osaka (JPN): **Bernabe Villacampo** W 15 Hiroyuki Ebihara (WBA)
03-20-1970 Bangkok (THA): **Chartchai Chionoi** W 15 Efren Torres (WBC)

04-06-1970 Bangkok (THA): **Berkrerk Chartvanchai** W 15 Bernabe Villacampo (WBA)
10-21-1970 Tokyo (JPN): **Masao Ohba** TKO 13 Berkrerk Chartvanchai (WBA)
12-07-1970 Bangkok (THA): **Erbito Salavarria** TKO 2 Chartchai Chionoi (WBC)
Nov. 1971 *After his win over Betulio Gonzalez Salavarria is found guilty of doping. The title goes to Gonzalez.*
09-29-1972 Bangkok (THA): **Venice Borkorsor** KO 10 Betulio Gonzalez (WBC)
Jan. 1973 *WBA champion Ohba is killed in a car accident.*
05-17-1973 Bangkok (THA): **Chartchai Chionoi** ret 5 Fritz Chervet (WBA)
July 1973 *Borkorsor relinquishes the WBC title to fight at bantamweight.*
08-04-1973 Maracaibo (VEN): **Betulio Gonzalez** W 15 Miguel Canto (WBC)
10-01-1974 Tokyo (JPN): **Shoji Oguma** W 15 Betulio Gonzalez (WBC)
10-18-1974 Yokohama (JPN): **Susumu Hanagata** TKO 6 Chartchai Chionoi (WBA)
01-08-1975 Sendai (JPN): **Miguel Canto** W 15 Shoji Oguma (WBC)
04-01-1975 Yokohama (JPN): **Erbito Salavarria** W 15 Susumu Hanagata (WBA)
02-27-1976 Manila (PHI): **Alfonso Lopez** TKO 15 Erbito Salavarria (WBA)
10-02-1976 Los Angeles (USA): **Gustavo "Guty" Espadas** TKO 13 Alfonso Lopez (WBA)
08-13-1978 Maracay (VEN): **Betulio Gonzalez** W 15 Guty Espadas (WBA)
03-18-1979 Pusan (KOR): **Chan-Hee Park** W 15 Miguel Canto (WBC)
11-16-1979 Maracay (VEN): **Luis Ibarra** W 15 Betulio Gonzalez (WBA)
02-16-1980 Seoul (KOR): **Taeshik Kim** KO 2 Luis Ibarra (WBA)
05-18-1980 Seoul (KOR): **Shoji Oguma** KO 9 Chan-Hee Park (WBC)
12-13-1980 Los Angeles (USA): **Peter Mathebula** W 15 Taeshik Kim (WBA)
03-28-1981 Soweto (RSA): **Santos Laciar** KO 7 Peter Mathebula (WBA)
05-12-1981 Mito (JPN): **Antonio Avelar** KO 7 Shoji Oguma (WBC)
06-06-1981 Buenos Aires (ARG): **Luis Ibarra** W 15 Santos Laciar (WBA)
09-26-1981 Merida (MEX): **Juan Herrera** KO 11 Luis Ibarra (WBA)
03-20-1982 Tampico (MEX): **Prudencio Cardona** KO 1 Antonio Avelar (WBC)
05-01-1982 Merida (MEX): **Santos Laciar** TKO 13 Juan Herrera (WBA)
07-24-1982 Merida (MEX): **Freddie Castillo** W 15 Prudencio Cardona (WBC)
11-06-1982 Los Angeles (USA): **Eleoncio Mercedes** W 15 Freddie Castillo (WBC)
03-15-1983 London (GBR): **Charlie Magri** TKO 7 Eleoncio Mercedes (WBC)
09-27-1983 London (GBR): **Frank Cedeno** TKO 6 Charlie Magri (WBC)
12-24-1983 Seoul (KOR): **Soon-Chun Kwon** KO 5 Rene Busayong (IBF)
01-18-1984 Tokyo (JPN): **Koji Kobajashi** TKO 2 Frank Cedeno (WBC)
04-09-1984 Tokyo (JPN): **Gabriel Bernal** KO 2 Koji Kobajashi (WBC)
10-08-1984 Bangkok (THA): **Sot Chitalada** W 12 Gabriel Bernal (WBC)
July 1985 *Laciar relinquishes the WBA title to fight at super flyweight.*
10-05-1985 Panama City (PAN): **Hilario Zapata** W 15 Alonzo Gonzalez (WBA)
12-20-1985 Taegu (KOR): **Chong-Kwang Chung** TKO 4 Soon-Chun Kwon (IBF)
04-27-1986 Pusan (KOR): **Bi-Won Chung** W 15 Chong-Kwang Chung (IBF)
08-02-1986 Inchon (KOR): **Hi-Sup Shin** TKO 15 Bi-Won Chung (IBF)
02-13-1987 Baranquilla (COL): **Fidel Bassa** W 15 Hilario Zapata (WBA)
02-22-1987 Inchon (KOR): **Dodie Penalosa** KO 5 Hi-Sup Shin (IBF)
09-05-1987 Manila (PHI): **Chang-Ho Choi** KO 11 Dodie Penalosa (IBF)
01-16-1988 Manila (PHI): **Rolando Bohol** W 15 Chang-Ho Choi (IBF)
07-24-1988 Pohang (KOR): **Yong-Kang Kim** W 12 Sot Chitalada (WBC)
10-05-1988 London (GBR): **Duke McKenzie** KO 11 Rolando Bohol (IBF)
03-03-1989 Medellin (COL): **Elvis Alvarez** W 12 Miguel Mercedes (WBO)
06-03-1989 Trang (THA): **Sot Chitalada** W 12 Yong-Kang Kim (WBC)
06-07-1989 London (GBR): **Dave McAuley** W 12 Duke McKenzie (IBF)
09-30-1989 Barranquilla (COL): **Jesus Rojas** W 12 Fidel Bassa (WBA)
Oct. 1989 *Alvarez relinquishes the WBO title.*
03-10-1990 Taejon (KOR): **Yul-Woo Lee** W 12 Jesus Rojas (WBA)
07-28-1990 Mito (JPN): **Yukihito Tamakuma** TKO 10 Yul-Woo Lee (WBA)
08-18-1990 Ponce (PUR): **Isidro Perez** TKO 12 Angel Rosario (WBO)
02-15-1991 Ayuthaya (THA): **Muangchai Kittikasem** TKO 6 Sot Chitalada (WBC)
03-14-1991 Tokyo (JPN): **Elvis Alvarez** W 12 Yukihito Tamakuma (WBA)
06-01-1991 Seoul (KOR): **Yong-Kang Kim** W 12 Elvis Alvarez (WBA)
03-18-1992 Glasgow (GBR): **Pat Clinton** W 12 Isidro Perez (WBO)
06-11-1992 Bilbao (ESP): **Rodolfo Blanco** W 12 Dave McAuley (IBF)
06-23-1992 Tokyo (JPN): **Yuri Arbachakov** KO 8 Muangchai Kittikasem (WBC)
09-26-1992 Pohang (KOR): **Aquilez Guzman** W 12 Yong-Kang Kim (WBA)
11-29-1992 Bangkok (THA): **Pichit Sitbangprachan** KO 3 Rodolfo Blanco (IBF)
12-15-1992 Caracas (VEN): **David Griman** W 12 Aquilez Guzman (WBA)
05-15-1993 Glasgow (GBR): **Jake Matlala** TKO 8 Pat Clinton (WBO)
02-13-1994 Bangkok (THA): **Saensor Ploenchit** W 12 David Griman (WBA)
Nov. 1994 *Sitbangprachan is stripped of the IBF title for not defending.*
02-11-1995 Hammanskraal (RSA): **Alberto Jimenez** TKO 8 Jake Matlala (WBO)
02-18-1995 Cartagena (COL): **Francisco Tejedor** TKO 7 Jose Luis Zepeda (IBF)
04-22-1995 Las Vegas (USA): **Danny Romero** W 12 Francisco Tejedor (IBF)
Jan. 1996 *Romero relinquishes the IBF title to fight at super flyweight*
05-04-1996 Anaheim (USA): **Mark Johnson** KO 1 Francisco Tejedor (IBF)
11-24-1996 Ubon Ratchatani (THA): **Jose Bonilla** W 12 Saensor Ploenchit (WBA)
12-13-1996 Buenos Aires (ARG): **Carlos Salazar** TKO 10 Alberto Jimenez (WBO)
11-12-1997 Sapporo (JPN): **Chatchai Sasakul** W 12 Yuri Arbachakov (WBC)
05-29-1998 Los Angeles (USA): **Hugo Soto** W 12 Jose Bonilla (WBA)

08-14-1998 Mexicali (MEX): **Ruben Sanchez** Tech Dec 8 Carlos Salazar (WBO)

Oct. 1998 *Johnson relinquishes the IBF title to fight at super flyweight.*

12-03-1998 Phuttamonthon (THA): **Manny Pacquaio** TKO 8 Chatchai Sasakul (WBC)

03-13-1999 New York (USA): **Leo Gamez** KO 3 Hugo Soto (WBA)

04-10-1999 Barranquilla (COL): **Irene Pacheco** TKO 9 Luis Cox (IBF)

04-23-1999 Saragossa (ESP): **Jose Antonio Lopez** KO 3 Ruben Sanchez (WBO)

09-03-1999 Mukdahan (THA): **Sornpichai Pisnurachan** KO 8 Leo Gamez (WBA)

09-17-1999 Nakhon Si Thammarat (THA): **Medgoen Singsurat** KO 3 Manny Paquiao (WBC)

12-18-1999 Indio (USA): **Isidro Garcia** W 12 Jose Lopez (WBO)

05-19-2000 Udon Thani (THA): **Malcolm Tunacao** TKO 7 Medgoen Singsurat (WBC)

08-05-2000 Madsion (USA): **Eric Morel** W 12 Sornpichai Pisnurachan (WBA)

12-15-2000 Ciudad Obregon (MEX): **Fernando Montiel** TKO 7 Isidro Garcia (WBO)

2001 *Kobayashi relinquishes the WBC title.*

03-02-2001 Pichit (THA): **Pongsaklek Wonjongkam** TKO 1 Malcolm Tunacao (WBC)

2002 *Fernando Montiel relinquishes the WBO title.*

05-04-2002 Managua (NCA): **Antonio Adonis Rivas** W 12 Jair Jimenez (WBO)

07-13-2002 Buenos Aires (ARG): **Omar Andres Narvaez** W 12 Antonio Adonis Rivas (WBO)

LIGHT FLYWEIGHT (ALSO CALLED JUNIOR FLYWEIGHT)

04-04-1975 Milan (ITA): **Franco Udella** disq 12 Valentin Martinez (WBC)

Aug. 1975 *The WBC strips Udella of the title for not defending.*

08-23-1975 Panama City (PAN): **Jaime Rios** W 15 Rigoberto Marcano (WBA)

09-13-1975 Caracas (VEN): **Luis Estaba** KO 4 Rafael Lovera (WBC)

07-01-1976 Santo Domingo (DOM): **Juan Guzman** W 15 Jaime Rios (WBA)

10-10-1976 Kofu (JPN): **Yoko Gushiken** KO 7 Juan Guzman (WBA)

02-19-1978 Caracas (VEN): **Freddy Castillo** KO 14 Luis Estaba (WBC)

05-06-1978 Bangkok (THA): **Netrnoi Vorasingh** W 15 Freddy Castillo (WBC)

09-30-1978 Seoul (KOR): **Sung-Jun Kim** KO 3 Netrnoi Vorasingh (WBC)

01-03-1980 Tokyo (JPN): **Shigeo Nakajima** W 15 Sung-Jun Kim (WBC)

03-24-1980 Tokyo (JPN): **Hilario Zapata** W 15 Shigeo Nakajima (WBC)

03-08-1981 Okinawa (JPN): **Pedro Flores** ret 12 Yoko Gushiken (WBA)

07-19-1981 Taegu (KOR): **Hwan-Jin Kim** TKO 13 Pedro Flores (WBA)

12-16-1981 Sendai (JPN): **Katsuo Tokashiki** W 15 Hwan-Jin Kim (WBA)

02-06-1982 Panama City (PAN): **Amado Ursua** KO 2 Hilario Zapata (WBC)

04-13-1982 Tokyo (JPN): **Tadashi Tomori** W 15 Amado Ursua (WBC)

07-20-1982 Kanazawa (JPN): **Hilario Zapata** W 15 Tadashi Tomori (WBC)

03-26-1983 Daejon (KOR): **Jung Koo Chang** KO 3 Hilario Zapata (WBC)

07-10-1983 Tokyo (JPN): **Lupe Madera** Tech Dec 4 Katsuo Tokashiki (WBA)

12-10-1983 Osaka (JPN): **Dodie Penalosa** TKO 11 Satoshi Shingaki (IBF)

05-19-1984 Maracaibo (VEN): **Francisco Quiroz** KO 9 Lupe Madera (WBA)

03-29-1985 Miami Beach (USA): **Joey Olivo** W 15 Francisco Quiroz (WBA)

12-08-1985 Taegu (KOR): **Myung-Woo Yuh** W 15 Joey Olivo (WBA)

July 1986 *Penalosa is stripped of the IBF title when he fights for the WBA flyweight title.*

12-07-1986 Pusan (KOR): **Jum-Hwan Choi** W 15 Cho-Woon Park (IBF)

Oct. 1988 *WBC champion Chang retires from professional sport.*

11-05-1988 Manila (PHI): **Tacy Macalos** W 12 Jum-Hwan Choi (IBF)

12-11-1988 Kimhae (KOR): **German Torres** W 12 Soon-Jung Kang (WBC)

03-19-1989 Taejon (KOR): **Yul-Woo Lee** KO 9 German Torres (WBC)

05-02-1989 Bangkok (THA): **Muangchai Kittikasem** W 12 Tacy Macalos (IBF)

05-19-1989 San Juan (PUR): **Jose de Jesus** TKO 9 Fernando Martinez (WBO)

06-25-1989 Chongju (KOR): **Humberto Gonzalez** W 12 Yul-Woo Lee (WBC)

07-29-1990 Phoenix (USA): **Michael Carbajal** TKO 7 Muangchai Kittikasem (IBF)

12-19-1990 Inglewood (USA): **Rolando Pascua** KO 6 Humberto Gonzalez (WBC)

03-25-1991 Inglewood (USA): **Melchor Cob Castro** TKO 10 Rolando Pascua (WBC)

06-03-1991 Las Vegas (USA): **Humberto Gonzalez** W 12 Melchor Cob Castro (WBC)

12-17-1991 Osaka (JPN): **Hiroki Ioka** W 12 Myung-Woo Yuh (WBA)

May 1992 *The WBO strips de Jesus of the title due to inactivity.*

07-31-1992 San Juan (PUR): **Josue Camacho** KO 6 Eduardo Vallejo (WBO)

11-18-1992 Osaka (JPN): **Myung-Woo Yuh** W 12 Hiroki Ioka (WBA)

03-13-1993 Las Vegas (USA): **Michael Carbajal** KO 7 Humberto Gonzalez (WBC/IBF)

Sept. 1993 *WBA champion Yuh retires from professional sport.*

10-21-1993 Tokyo (JPN): **Leo Gamez** TKO 9 Shiro Yahiro (WBA)

02-19-1994 Inglewood (USA): **Humberto Gonzalez** W 12 Michael Carbajal (WBC/IBF)

07-15-1994 Phoenix (USA): **Michael Carbajal** W 12 Josue Camacho (WBO)

Oct. 1994 *Carbajal relinquishes the WBO title to challenge WBC and IBF champion Gonzalez.*

11-23-1994 Irvine (GBR): **Paul Weir** W 12 Paul Oulden (WBO)

02-04-1995 Ulsan (KOR): **Hi Yong Choi** W 12 Leo Gamez (WBA)

07-15-1995 Inglewood (USA): **Saman Sorjaturong** TKO 7 Humberto Gonzalez (WBC/IBF)

07-15-1995 Glasgow (GBR): **Jake Matlala** Tech Dec 5 Paul Weir (WBO)

Jan. 1996 *Sorjaturong relinquishes the IBF title and remains WBC champion.*

01-13-1996 Miami (USA): **Carlos Murillo** W 12 Hi Yong Choi (WBA)

03-16-1996 Las Vegas (USA): **Michael Carbajal** W 12 Melchor Cob Castro (IBF)

05-21-1996 Osaka (JPN): **Keiji Yamaguchi** W 12 Carlos Murillo (WBA)

12-03-1996 Osaka (JPN): **Pichitnoi Sithbangprachan** TKO 2 Keiji Yamaguchi (WBA)

01-18-1997 Las Vegas (USA): **Mauricio Pastrana** W 12 Michael Carbajal (IBF)

May 1997 *Pastrana is stripped of the IBF title because he fails to make weight.*

May 1997 *Matlala relinquishes the WBO title.*

05-31-1997 Las Vegas (USA): **Jesus Chong** TKO 2 Eric Griffin (WBO)

08-25-1997 Los Angeles (USA): **Melchor Cob Castro** W 12 Jesus Chong (WBO)

12-13-1997 Pompano Beach (USA): **Mauricio Pastrana** KO 3 Manuel Herrera (IBF)

01-17-1998 Santiago del Estero (ARG): **Juan Cordoba** W 12 Melchor Cob Castro (WBO)

Aug. 1998 *Pastrana is stripped of the IBF title because he fails to make weight.*

12-05-1998 Tijuana (MEX): **Jorge Arce** W 12 Juan Cordoba (WBO)

12-16-1998 Fort Lauderdale (USA): **Will Grigsby** W 12 Ratanapol Sorvoraphin (IBF)

07-31-1999 Tijuana (MEX): **Michael Carbajal** TKO 11 Jorge Arce (WBO) *Carbajal relinquishes the title.*

10-02-1999 Las Vegas (USA): **Ricardo Lopez** W 12 Will Grigsby (IBF)

10-17-1999 Seoul (KOR): **Choi Yo-Sam** W 12 Saman Sorjaturong (WBC)

02-19-2000 Brakpan (RSA): **Masibulele Makepula** W 12 Jake Matlala (WBO)

07-22-2000 Miami (USA): **Will Grigsby** W 12 Nelson Dieppa (WBO)

08-12-2000 Las Vegas (USA): **Bebis Mendoza** disq 7 Rosendo Alvarez (WBA)

03-03-2001 Las Vegas (USA): **Rosendo Alvarez** W 12 Bebis Mendoza (WBA)

04-14-2001 New York (USA): **Nelson Dieppa** KO 11 Andy Tabanas (WBO)

07-06-2002 Seoul (KOR): **Jorge Arce** TKO 6 Yo-Sam Choi (WBC)

Jan. 2003 *IBF champion Ricardo Lopez retires.*

02-15-2003 Las Vegas (USA): **Jose Victor Burgos** TKO 12 Alex Sanchez (IBF)

03-31-2003 Little Rock (USA): **Rosendo Alvarez** W 12 Beilbis Mendoza (WBA)

STRAW WEIGHT (ALSO CALLED MINI-FLYWEIGHT)

01-14-1987 Bujok (KOR): **Kyung-Yun Lee** KO 2 Masaharu Kawakami (IBF)

10-18-1987 Osaka (JPN): **Hiroki Ioka** W 12 Mai Thornburifarm (WBC)

Dec. 1987 *Lee relinquishes the IBF title to fight for the WBC title.*

01-10-1988 Pusan (KOR): **Leo Gamez** W 12 Bong-Jun Kim (WBA)

03-24-1988 Bangkok (THA): **Samuth Sithnaruepol** TKO 11 Domingo Lucas (IBF)

11-13-1988 Osaka (JPN): **Napa Kiatwanchai** W 12 Hiroki Ioka (WBC)

Feb. 1989 *Gamez relinquishes the WBA title to fight at junior flyweight.*

04-16-1989 Pohang (KOR): **Bong-Jun Kim** TKO 7 Augustin Garcia (WBA)

06-17-1989 Jakarta (INA): **Nico Thomas** W 12 Samuth Sithnaruepol (IBF)

08-31-1989 Santo Domingo (DOM): **Rafael Torres** W 12 Yamil Caraballo (WBO)

09-21-1989 Jakarta (INA): **Eric Chavez** KO 5 Nico Thomas (IBF)

11-12-1989 Seoul (KOR): **Jum-Hwan Choi** TKO 12 Napa Kiatwanchai (WBC)

02-07-1990 Tokyo (JPN): **Hideyuki Ohashi** KO 9 Jum-Hwan Choi (WBC)

02-22-1990 Bangkok (THA): **Phalan Lukmingkwan** TKO 7 Eric Chavez (IBF)

10-25-1990 Tokyo (JPN): **Ricardo Lopez** TKO 5 Hideyuki Ohashi (WBC)

02-02-1991 Pusan (KOR): **Hi-Yon Choi** W 12 Bong-Jun Kim (WBA)

May 1992 *The WBO strips Torres of the title due to inactivity.*

09-06-1992 Bangkok (THA): **Manny Melchor** W 12 Phalan Lukmingkwan (IBF)

10-14-1992 Tokyo (JPN): **Hideyuki Ohashi** W 12 Hi-Yon Choi (WBA)

12-10-1992 Bangkok (THA): **Ratanapol Sorvoraphin** W 12 Manny Melchor (IBF)

02-10-1993 Tokyo (JPN): **Chana Porpaoin** W 12 Hideyuki Ohashi (WBA)

05-15-1993 Glasgow (GBR): **Paul Weir** TKO 7 Fernando Martinez (WBO)

Dec. 1993 *Weir relinquishes the WBO title to fight at junior flyweight.*

12-22-1993 San Juan (PUR): **Alex Sanchez** TKO 1 Orlando Malone (WBO)

12-02-1995 Bangkok (THA): **Rosendo Alvarez** W 12 Chana Porpaoin (WBA)

08-23-1997 New York (USA): **Ricardo Lopez** TKO 4 Alex Sanchez (WBC/WBO)

12-27-1997 Songkhia (THA): **Zolani Petelo** TKO 4 Ratanapol Sorvoraphin (IBF)

March 1998 *The WBO strips Lopez of the title. Lopez remains WBC champion.*

05-30-1998 Las Vegas (USA): **Kermin Guardia** ret 5 Eric Jamili (WBO)

Nov. 1998 *The WBA strips Alvarez of his title before a world championship title bout with WBC champion Lopez.*

01-31-1999 Pattaya (THA): **Songkram Porpaoin** Tech Dec 9 Ronnie Magramo (WBA)

10-09-1999 Caracas (VEN): **Noel Arambulet** W 12 Joma Gamboa (WBA)

02-11-2000 Samut Sakorn (THA): **Jose Antonio Aguirre** W 12 Wandee Chor Chareon (WBC)

08-20-2000 Tokyo (JPN): **Joma Gamboa** W 12 Noel Arambulet (WBA)

12-06-2000 Yokohama (JPN): **Keitaro Hoshino** W 12 Joma Gamboa (WBA)

04-16-2001 Yokohama (JPN): **Chana Porpaoin** W 12 Keitaro Hoshino (WBA)

04-29-2001 New York (USA): **Roberto Leyva** W 12 Daniel Reyes (IBF)

08-25-2001 Yokohama (JPN): **Yutaka Niida** W 12 Chana Porpaoin (WBA)

2001 *Niida relinquishes the WBA title.*

01-29-2002 Yokohama (JPN): **Keitaro Hoshino** W 12 Joma Gamboa (WBA)

2002 *Kermin Guardia relinquishes the WBO title.*

06-29-2002 Palma de Mallorca (ESP): **Jorge Mata** KO 9 Reynaldo Frutos (WBO)

07-29-2002 Yokohama (JPN): **Noel Arambulet** W 12 Keitaro Hoshino (WBA)

08-09-2002 Las Vegas (USA): **Miguel Barrera** W 12 Roberto Leyva (IBF)

02-22-2003 Mexico City (MEX): **Jose Antonio Aguirre** ret 7 Juan Alfonso Keb (WBC)

03-22-2003 Las Vegas (USA): **Miguel Barrera** KO 3 Roberto Leyva (IBF)

03-28-2003 Madrid (ESP): **Eduardo "Ray" Marquez** TKO 11 Jorge Mata (WBO)

GLOSSARY

Aficionado
(Span. *afición* "affection, fancy"), ardent and knowledgeable devotee of boxing, a fan.

All-time great
a boxer who is unanimously considered to belong to the best in the history of his sport (e.g., Jack Dempsey, Sugar Ray Robinson, Muhammad Ali).

Athletic Commission
the supervising administrative body in the USA or the parent organization of the respective federal states.

Bag gloves
training gloves for exercising at the punching bag.

Ballyhoo
a promotional build-up before a boxing match.

Banger
a type of boxer who attempts to achieve an early victory by throwing powerful single punches.

Bareknuckle
a boxing bout fought with bare fists, a historic precursor to modern boxing with padded gloves. As an illegal form of entertainment people can bet on, it occasionally still occurs in Anglo-American culture.

Bleeder
a boxer who is predisposed to heavily bleeding lacerations due to his sensitive skin.

Bobbin' and Weavin'
a strategy of boxers with a smaller reach to evade hostile punches by constant turning and twisting movements of the head and shoulders and, if possible, to hit the opponent from half-distance (e.g., Joe Frazier, Mike Tyson).

Body shot
each blow, be it a hook or a straight punch, that connects with the body.

Boil & Bite
a mouthpiece which, in contrast to an individually fitted product, gains the best fit by warming it up inside the mouth and chewing on it.

Booking agent
an independent agent who, assigned by a matchmaker, finds suitable opponents for a match.

Boxe Française
(also Savate), early form of modern boxing in France, which allowed foot techniques similar to Karate.

Boxing booth
a movable boxing stall at historic fairs where experienced athletes competed with laymen to the general amusement of the audience. Has survived as an event at fairs until today.

Braggadocio
(Engl. "to brag"), Italo-American for the pretentious self-advertisement of boxers and their entourage before fights. Is often accompanied by denigrating and insulting the opponent.

Brawler
a type of boxer who tries to wear out his opponent through a permanent exchange of punches at close range.

Bum
an inferior opponent who is usually defeated by the favorite without any problems. Also called "bum of the month" after a series of questionable world championship defenses by Joe Louis (1941).

Buy rate
sales rate at pay TV.

Canvas
the cloth that covers the ring. The expression *to hit the canvas,* therefore, refers to a boxer going down after a punch.

CAT scan
a computerized axial tomography of the cranium to discover potential lesions (e.g., *hematoma*) early on. More and more countries have made an annual CAT scan a precondition for prolonging the professional license.

Caestus
a leather strip fitted with metal studs that was wrapped around the hands and forearms in fist fights in ancient Rome.

Championship
the world championship title. Also the period of time during which a boxer holds and defends a title.

Clinch
a move of holding on to one's opponent, often performed by the groggy or less-fit contender.

Closed-circuit
the live transmission of a fight in a series of venues (cinemas, theaters etc.), particularly popular in the 1950s and in the beginning of the 1960s.

Color bar
an expression for the phase of segregation in professional boxing during which duels between white and non-white opponents were considered undesirable—white title-holders drew the "color bar."

Combination
a series of punches.

Conoscendi
(Ital. *conoscere* "to get to know"), the experts, also the insiders at the ringside.

Contender
a challenger. Originally, this expression referred to a boxer who was listed among the best ten fighters of his weight division and, therefore, entitled to challenge the champion.

Cornermen
the boxer's assistants in the corner of the ring—usually chief second or trainer, second and cut-man.

Counter-boxer
a boxer who specializes in counterattacks as a fighting tactic.

Cross
a counter punch delivered across the opponent's straight punch (see Boxing Basics, pp. 186–191).

Cross-town fight
a classic local derby between opponents from the same city.

Cut
a laceration caused by a regular hit or a deliberate or accidental foul.

Cut-man
the expert in the corner responsible for closing a boxer's lacerations and bringing down facial swellings during the break.

Diehard
generally an athlete with great stamina. In the ring, a boxer who continues fighting even when inferior or hampered by severe injuries.

Double jumping
a difficult variant of rope skipping in which the rope is swung twice around on each jump.

Double hits
a series of punches executed by the same hand, e.g., left hook to the body, left hook to the head (see Boxing Basics, pp. 186–191).

Down, but not out
a colloquial expression for the groggy boxer who has been knocked down but is not yet defeated.

Eight count
The referee counts out the standing boxer to a count of eight to determine if the boxer is well enough to continue—not mandatory at all world federations. If a boxer takes three standing eights in a round or four in a bout, the contest is stopped and the opponent declared the winner.

Electronic scoring
in amateur boxing the scoring of hits by a computerized scoring system (see The Scoring Machine, p. 57).

Entourage
the not quite official circle of seconds assisting a boxer (besides chief second, second etc.) which can include masseurs and press officials and also renowned ring announcers and hired applauders.

Feint
the most common deceptive maneuver in the ring—a punch is faked but not thrown in its entirety, to induce the opponent to open up into a vulnerable position.

Fight card
the program of a boxing event or a list of matches. Can be synonymous with the match itself: "to hold a fight card."

Finisher
a boxer who continues to bring his opponent into trouble until he finally wins by knockout. Boxers who excel at this are praised as "good finishers."

Floor-to-ceiling ball
a training ball which is strung up between the floor and ceiling (see Punchbag & Co., pp. 182–183).

Footwork
the way a boxer moves his legs to unify balance and flexibility.

Game
the rating of a boxer with great fighting spirit.

Glass jaw
allegory for a boxer who is prone to be knocked out.

Golden Gloves
the most renowned series of amateur tournaments in the USA, named after its sole prize, a pair of golden gloves (see Golden Gloves, pp. 56–57).

Gym rat
the insider fan who regularly watches boxers work out at their gyms. Can also be a former contender or trainer.

Gym war
a sparring duel in which local rivalries, personal enmities, etc. cause an exaggerated display of aggressiveness.

Heavy bag
also punching bag, mandatory training tool for punches and combinations (see Punchbag & Co., pp. 182–183).

Home crowd
the local fans of a boxer who support him at matches either at home or out of town.

House fighter
the favorite contender of a promoter and his regular audience who can be sure to be cheered and supported.

Hype
(Greek *hypo* "over, above, concerning"), loud and colorful campaign to attract the public's attention to a boxing match, similar to *braggadocio* in its exaggerated tone.

Infight
the close-range fight between opponents.

Intergender bout
an exhibition fight between a man and a woman. Entertainment generally reserved for boxing booths at fairs.

Jab
a straight punch thrown with the lead hand (left straight punch, right straight punch; see Boxing Basics, pp. 186–191).

Journeyman
an expression for a moderately strong occasional boxer who signs up for bouts in various towns, often on very short notice.

Judges
the officials of the boxing associations who score the bout (see The Judges, p. 278).

Knockdown
Counting is started when a boxer is in contact with the canvas with any part of his body other than his feet.

Knockout
a premature end to the bout that is caused when the boxer is still down by the time the referee has managed to count to ten. Acronym "KO."

Live gate
the sum of the proceeds from the ticket sales.

Local hero
a high-ranking boxer that usually resides close to where he performs. The local favorite.

Low blow
a punch thrown below the belt, which goes against the regulations.

Lucky punch
an accidental, rather than deliberate, knockout punch thrown by the until-then inferior boxer, enabling him to win the match.

Maize ball
training equipment which hangs freely from the ceiling and is used to improve a boxer's skill of hitting the mark. It is seldom used in today's professional training (see Punchbag & Co., pp. 182–183).

Matchmaker
the sporting director of a boxing event who organizes the fights on behalf of the promoter (see Matchmakers and Booking Agents, p. 376).

Megafight
an exceptional fight which attracts a high amount of public attention before taking place (e.g., Evander Holyfield vs. Mike Tyson, Shane Mosley vs. Oscar De La Hoya).

Million-dollar-gate
a boxing event where the proceeds from ticket sales exceed one million dollars (this occurred for the first time on July 2, 1921 in New Jersey: Dempsey vs. Carpentier).

Mouthpiece
a mouthguard to protect a boxer's teeth (see Brief Product History, pp. 146–147).

Muffler
the first form of padded training gloves (in use in Great Britain since the 18th century).

Noble art
an old English expression for the art of self-defense.

No contest
the official result of bouts which were not scored due to irregular conditions or passivity of the opponents.

No-decision bouts
Fights which were not finished by a knockout were considered undecided in the no-decision era. Later the expression often also included pure show and demonstration bouts.

No-decision era
the historic period at the beginning of the 20th century when in New York and elsewhere decisions on points were officially prohibited concordant with the Frawley Law (1911–20) to prevent the fixing of fights.

Olympic-style boxing
a synonym for amateur boxing.

Opponent
originally a neutral expression for any adversary. However, it has by now turned derogatory to refer to an unknown tune-up boxer without the slightest chance of winning the bout.

Pancratium
a brutal form of athletic contest in ancient Greece which allowed both boxing and wrestling techniques.

Pound-for-pound ratings
a rating list which ranks the official champions of all weight divisions according to their athletic capabilities, regardless of their weight limit. The pound-for-pound champion is therefore a prestigious title.

Promoter
the person who organizes, advertises, and produces a professional boxing match.

Protective cup
the padded support worn by contenders to protect themselves against blows beneath the belt (see Brief Product History, pp. 128–129).

Psyching out
strategy to intimidate the opponent by demonstrations of self-assuredness or threatening gestures (visual contact etc.).

Punchbag
a stuffed leather bag which can be used for training in boxing, also called heavy bag.

Punchdrunk
(Lat. *dementia pugilistica*), a condition which includes mental confusion resulting from numerous effective punches to the head during a boxer's career.

Puncher
a boxer who relies on his great punching power and a stoppage victory.

Record
the fighting record, also the overall rating of a boxer's athletic capabilities (e.g., 30–2; 30 wins, 2 losses).

Rematch
a return match between opponents where a fight for any reason is considered unfair or unjust.

Ringsider
slang for the insiders and regular observers at the ringside.

Roadwork
the rigorous physical training (running, sprints, etc.) required to enhance a boxer's fighting condition.

Rope dancing
a tactical variant to use the elasticity of the ropes to outbalance the punches of an opponent. Also known as *rope-a-dope* due to Muhammad Ali.

Round card girls
the young women holding up the cards in between rounds indicating the number of the current round.

Rubber match
the decisive match (mostly the third) between two boxers to determine the overall winner.

Rules meeting
a discussion of regulations and preliminaries (e.g., choice of gloves) between managers, seconds, etc., and the officials. Usually occurs on the evening before the boxing event.

Rumble in the jungle
the unofficial title of the heavyweight world championship bout between winner Muhammad Ali and George Foreman on October 30, 1974 in Kinshasa, Zaire.

Sanctioning fee
the fee for the supervising organization which sanctions a boxing match (usually several percent).

Saved by the bell
a situation in which a groggy fighter about to be knocked out just as the bell sounds can use the break period to rest and recover. The leading federations generally allow this only in the final round as a means to score each individual round.

Scorecards
slips of paper or printed forms to record the judges' scores (see The Judges, p. 276).

Shell style
a defensive style with arms thrust out and crossed to block the opponent's blows.

Side step
a step to the side to evade an opponent's punches (see Boxing Basics, pp. 186–191).

Slugger
a boxer who wants to decide the bout early with single, wide-reaching punches.

Southpaw
the right straight punch which holds the right hand thrust forward in the basic position.

Sparring
the duel in the ring during contact training.

Speedball
a punching technique that trains the coordination and strengthens the muscles of the lower arms (see Punchbag & Co., pp. 182–183).

Split decision
a decision by the judges which is not unanimous (e.g., there are two votes for boxer A, and only one vote or no decision for boxer B).

Staredown
an occurrence where contenders exchange menacing looks during the referee's instructions shortly before the bout begins; often influencing the outcome of the match.

Stinker
slang for a boxer who evades any exchange of punches (usually a counter-boxer).

Suspension list
the international file with all currently suspended professional fighters (because they lost due to a KO or positive doping results, etc.).

Swabsticks
a cotton wool tip for the treatment of bleeding lacerations used by the cut-man. Also named swabs for short.

Sweet science
American author A.J. Liebling is credited with coining this expression to refer to the high art of boxing.

Tale of the tape
the information about the boxer's physical measurements from weight and height to reach and size of fist.

Technical decision
an early decision which is consulted after a break-off of the bout due to an unintentional injury.

Technical draw
an early neutral decision reached after a bout has been broken off within the first few rounds if the fight does not allow a definite score.

They never come back
a melodramatic expression for the observation—valid until Floyd Patterson's comeback in 1960—that heavyweight world champions cannot win their title back once they have lost it.

Thumbing
an act where the thrust-out thumb is more or less intentionally poked into the opponent's eye. The models of thumb-attached gloves generally in use today make this tactic virtually impossible.

Timekeeper
the person at the ringside who signals the beginning, end, or interruption of a round.

TKO
a judge's decision in which a groggy fighter is removed from the bout after one or more knockdowns, or due to the simple inability to defend himself. The referee declares a technical knockout without counting the inferior contender out.

Tomato can
a greatly inferior fighter whose body is beaten bloody due to the inability to defend himself properly.

Touch gloves
a ritualized greeting of one's opponent as a sign of athletic fairness. The fighters slap their gloves after the referee's instructions. Can also be a gesture of apology after a foul.

Trial horse
a resilient, experienced professional tune-up opponent who is not easily defeated. Often a former-ranking boxer.

Umpire
old English for the referee as neutral third man in the ring. In the 18th and 19th centuries, there were originally two of them in Great Britain.

Underdog
the athletic (generally, also the social) outsider.

Unification bout
a boxing match between two champions of rival federations in which the winner unifies the titles.

Uppercut
an upward punch that comes underneath the opponent's guard, useful when boxing at close range. (see Boxing Basics, pp. 186–191).

Vegetable
slang for a former boxer whose mental and intellectual abilities are severely impaired resulting in chronic clouding of consciousness due to *dementia pugilistica* among other things.

Walk-in
The boxer's walk into the ring is accentuated by show-elements and often by a piece of music especially chosen or composed for this occasion (walk-in theme).

Weigh-in
the date (and event) of weighing the boxers, usually on the evening before the fight (see The Weigh-In, pp. 198–199).

White hope
an expression in the early days of boxing for the racist wish of some white Americans for a white champion during the White Hope Era when Jack Johnson, the first African-American, won the title.

INDEX

PICTURE CREDITS

The publishers would like to thank the museums, archives and photographers for their permission to reproduce their works.
The publishers have made every effort to contact all the copyright holders of images prior to the completion of the final production. Private and institutional image copyright holders who may not have been contacted are hereby requested to write to the publisher.

© AKG, Berlin
Erich Lessing 223t, 224
AP 309t
© Frank Bodenmüller, Berlin 6/7, 66, 67 (10 ill.), 278m r, 280b, 380bl
© Bongarts Sportfotografie, Hamburg 57, 69b
Martin Rose 184
H. Schneider 185lt, 185ml
Mark Sandten 185mt, 185mm, 185bl, 185bm
S. Schupfner 185tr
M. Kienzler 185mr
D. Gohlke 185br
A. Hassenstein 215b, 285r
© CNRI/Okapia, Frankfurt 64l, 65r
© Bettmann/CORBIS, Hamburg 96, 109, 133, 134, 141, 142, 143, 219, 237, 261 2fl, 276 2fr, 300, 304 (2 ill.), 306 (2 ill.), 307, 311, 372 (2 ill.), 373t, 374 (2 ill.), 376, 394/395
© dpa/ZB, Frankfurt 303, 346/347, 347r
© Das Fotoarchiv, Essen
Sebastian Bolesch 60/61
Frankie Berger 119
Lisa Quinones 60, 166, 167
Sonia Katchlan 246, 247b, 286m, 309b
SVT 111tl, 163l, 276r, 284r, 294, 362, 364b, 365 (2 ill.)
© George Eastman House/Hulton|Archive 233t
© Getty Images, London 22/23, 43 (3 ill.), 124, 170mr, 253 (small ill.), 275mr, 281t, 283l, 310
Scott Barbour 201br, 254/255
Al Bello 12/13 (background), 13 (small ill.), 14/15, 16, 17tl tm tr, 18/19, 26, 27, 44, 45l, 47bl, 50/51, 52/53, 73, 74bl, 75, 111tr, 112/113, 123l, 150, 158/159, 160/161, 164, 177, 178/179, 180, 181, 182 (2 ill.), 183b, 198tm b, 199 (4 ill.), 201tm, 202, 206, 207t, 214b, 231, 256r, 257, 258/259, 259b, 261l, 262 (2 ill.),

263 (2 ill.), 270, 275bl, 277 2fl, 283br, 286b, 287tr mr, 326/327, 338, 339, 341, 344 (4 ill.), 345 (4 ill.), 354m, 361, 363, 368, 380 bm, 402
Markus Boesch 120/121
Philippe Bordas 318, 319 (2 ill.)
Frederick M. Brown 74br
Clive Brunskill 265r
Simon Bruty 21, 129r
Chris Cole 201m
Glenn Cratty 360
Stephen Dunn 261r, 315 (4 ill.), 353, 382/383
Stuart Franklin 47tr
John Gichigi 17bm, 30/31, 69m, 130/131, 162b mr t, 170b, 171t, 197b, 213br, 249, 261 2fr, 269r, 275t (2 ill.), 277 2fr, 284l, 302t, 322, 323, 336, 336/337, 337, 340r, 356/357, 358/359, 378 (small ill.), 380br, 381r, 385b, 392, 393 (2 ill.)
Jeff Gross 183t, 276 2fl, 287br
Elsa Hasch 248b
Hulton|Archive 10/11, 24, 28, 29, 32, 33, 36/37, 38 (2 ill.), 39 (2 ill.), 49, 55t, 58/59, 68b, 69t, 76/77 (background), 77, 79 (background), 80, 81, 82 (3 ill.), 83, 84, 85 (2 ill.), 86, 87, 88 (2 ill.), 89, 90 (2 ill.), 91, 93l, 97, 98 (2 ill.), 99, 101, 104, 105, 106 (2 ill.), 107, 108, 116/117 (background), 118, 125, 126, 127, 132, 135, 136/137 (background), 137, 144, 144/145 (background), 152, 153, 154, 155 (2 ill.), 156tr t2fr, 157 (4 ill.), 163bl m br tr, 170t, 170ml, 170/171m, 171b, 183m, 186, 208/209, 214t, 215t, 220/221, 226 (2 ill.), 227 (2 ill.), 228, 229 (4 ill.), 232, 233bl bm br, 234, 235 (3 ill.), 236, 238, 239 (3 ill.), 240, 241 (2 ill.), 244 (2 ill.), 245, 247tl tr, 260l, 260 2fl, 264, 266/267, 280t, 282/283, 283tr, 285l, 290 (3 ill.), 291 (2 ill.), 292, 293 (2 ill.), 296 (2 ill.), 297 (2 ill.), 298, 301, 308, 333r, 334/335, 340l, 348/349, 350, 350/351, 352 (2 ill.), 355 (2 ill.), 364t, 367, 370b, 373b, 375, 385t, 387 (8 ill.), 388, 390, 391 (2 ill.), 396/397, 398 (2 ill.), 400
Jed Jacobsohn 45r, 47tl br, 138/139, 148/149, 201tr, 203, 212, 213tr bl, 272/273, 275ml, 287tl, 302b, 328/329 (3 ill.), 330tl tr ml mr br, 331tl tr ml b
David Leeds 115, 147tr, 201tl, 271b, 371b
Ken Levine 17ml, 168/169, 314 (4 ill.), 325, 378/379 (background)
Andy Lyons 46l, 369
Bob Martin 196, 277l, 312
Jamie McDonald 194/195
Zoran Milich 165

Stephen Munday 265l
Mark Morrison 17bl, 78, 192/193, 204/205 (6 ill.), 386l
Gray Mortimore 62/63
Doug Pensinger 54, 55b, 74bm, 256l
Mike Powell 117, 122 (background), 162ml, 172/173, 174, 250, 251 (2 ill.), 260r
Gary M. Prior 287ml
Ben Radford 386r
Todd Rosenberg 42r
Eliot J. Schechter 242
Ezra Shaw 70/71, 248t, 380t
Rick Solomon 288/289, 379 (small ill.)
Jamie Squire 102/103, 197t, 218, 320/321
Brian Spurlock 42l
Holly Stein 8/9, 17 mr, 68t, 72, 94/95, 114, 123r, 147tl, 175, 176, 198tr, 200, 207b, 213tl, 230, 258b, 275br, 277r, 281b, 286t, 287bl, 313 (3 ill.), 316, 317 (2 ill.), 324b, 354l r, 370t, 371t, 381l
Matthew Stockman 46r
Rick Stuart 210/211
Mark Thompson 17 br, 25, 147b, 201bl
Ian Walton 268 (2 ill.), 269l, 271t
Todd Warshaw 330bl, 331mr
Patty Wood 79tr
© Golden Gloves, Denver, USA 56 (2 ill.)
© Gordian Heindrichs, Rémelfing, France 216/217 (8 ill.)
© Carlos Irusta, Buenos Aires, Argentina 252, 253l r
© Marianne Müller, Düsseldorf 34 (6 ill.), 35 (6 ill.), 198tl
© L. Mulvehill/PR ScienceSc./Okapia, Frankfurt 64/65m
© New York Times Co./Ernest Sisto/Archive Photos 299
© Pat Orr, The International Boxing Hall of Fame 389 (2 ill.)
© The Ring, Fort Washington, USA 140, 151, 156tl t2fl, 260 2fr, 295, 305, 332/333, 377, 399 (3 ill.)
© Rolli Arts, Essen (Grafiken) 20, 181, 187-191, 273, 278l, 324t
© Mario Rivera Martino, San Juan, Puerto Rico 243 (2 ill.)
© Scala Group S.p.A., Firenze, Italy 222 (3 ill.), 223b, 225
© Werner Stapelfeldt, Düsseldorf 4/5, 92, 93r, 110/111, 128, 129l, 146 (2 ill.)
© Duif du Toit/Touchline Photo 276l
© Underwood & Underwood/CORBIS 100

CAPTIONS FOR THE INTRODUCTORY PAGES OF EACH CHAPTER

Pages 8/9 The Boxers:
Pernell Whitaker vs. Oscar De La Hoya, Las Vegas 1997.

Pages 10/11 The True Spirit:
Carl "Bobo" Olson (right) around 1955.

Pages 22/23 Winners and Losers:
No information available.

Pages 50/51 The Amateurs:
John Dovi vs. Michael Simms, Houston 1999.

Pages 62/63 The Professionals:
Joe Frazier, George Foreman and Muhammad Ali (from left to right)

Pages 158/159 The Training:
Prince Naseem Hamed at a demonstration training for advertisement shots in New York.

Pages 160/161 Gyms and Camps:
Evander Holyfield at the Church Street Gym, New York 1999.

Pages 172/173 Training methods:
Oscar De La Hoya during a workout, 1999.

Pages 192/193 The Fights:
George Foreman vs. Tommy Morrison, Las Vegas 1987.

Pages 194/195 The Whole Drama:
Mpush Makambi vs. Adrian Dodson, London, 1998.

Pages 254/255 The Cornermen:
Audley Harrison with coach Ian Irwin after the Olympic quarterfinals, Sydney 2000.

Pages 266/267 The Officials:
Bill Bodell vs. Jack Drover under supervision of the referee Harry Gibbs, London 1971.

Pages 286/287 Great Duels:
From top left to bottom right:
James Toney vs. Roy Jones Jr., Las Vegas 1994;
Felix Trinidad vs. Oscar De La Hoya, Las Vegas 1999;
Arturo Gatti vs. Tracy Patterson, Atlantic City 1997;
Muhammad Ali vs. George Foreman, Kinshasa 1974;
Joe Calzaghe vs. Ritchie Woodhall, Sheffield 2000;
Evander Holyfield vs. Lennox Lewis, Las Vegas 1999;
Riddick Bowe vs. Andrew Golota, New York, 1996;
Mike Tyson vs. Donovan "Razor" Ruddock, Las Vegas 1991;
Floyd Mayweather Jr. vs. Diego Corrales, Las Vegas 2001.

Pages 320/321 Sensations:
Great Chaos after the duel between Evander Holyfield vs. Mike Tyson, Las Vegas 1997.

Pages 334/335 Fateful Fights:
Rival fans put up a fight after the break-off of the bout between Dick Richardon vs. Brian London in Welsh Porthcawl, 1960.

Pages 348/349 Only in Boxing:
Muhammad Ali vs. Anthony Inoki, Tokyo 1976.

Pages 356/357 The Business:
Casino table at the Mandalay Bay Hotel before the heavyweight world championship bout between Lewis vs. Tua, 2000.

Pages 358/359 The Impresarios:
Promoter Don King with rival world champions Evander Holyfield and Lennox Lewis, Las Vegas 1990.

Pages 382/383 The Public:
Sky-TV commentator Ian Darke and Glen McCrory report from the duel between Joe Calzaghe vs. Rick Thornberry in Cardiff, Wales 1999.

Page 401 Appendix:
The ex-boxer Jake Bellows sweeps the ring at the Blue Horizon, Philadelphia 1997.

COUNTRY CODES IN ALPHABETICAL ORDER

ALG	Algeria	GER	Germany	PAN	Panama
ANT	Antigua and Barbuda	GHA	Ghana	PHI	Philippines
ARG	Argentina	HUN	Hungary	PUR	Puerto Rico
AUS	Australia	INA	Indonesia	RSA	Republic of
AUT	Austria	IRL	Ireland		South Africa
BRA	Brazil	ISR	Israel	SEN	Senegal
CAN	Canada	ITA	Italy	SWE	Sweden
COL	Colombia	JAM	Jamaica	THA	Thailand
CUB	Cuba	JPN	Japan	TRI	Trinidad and Tobago
DEN	Denmark	KOR	South Korea	TUN	Tunisia
DOM	Dominican Republic	MAR	Morocco	UGA	Uganda
ESP	Spain	MON	Monaco	USA	United States
FRA	France	MEX	Mexico	VEN	Venezuela
	and Guadeloupe	NCA	Nicaragua	ZAI	Zaire (now:
GBR	Great Britain and	NED	Netherlands		Democratic Republic
	Northern Ireland	NGR	Nigeria		of the Congo)

Getty Images is the leading provider of imagery for a wide range of professional clients, including advertising and design agencies, magazines and newspapers, television organizations and production companies, and, last but not least, new media publishing companies. With a prize-winning collection of more than 70 million images and 30,000 hours of film, Getty Images supplies unique still and moving imagery to creative professionals, journalists and the advertising industry.

Two of Getty Images' collections provided this book with precious and invaluable imagery: the unique resources of Hulton|Archive go back to the early days of photography and have images at their disposal of a wide range of subjects, Allsport Concepts comprehensively covers the field of current high-quality sports photography.

We would especially like to thank the photographers Al Bello in the United States and John Gichigi in the United Kingdom. They know most of the heavyweight contenders on both sides of the Atlantic Ocean personally and, in addition, have often worked together as a team. John and Al have captured some of the most impressive imagery at the ringside and have won many new fans for this sport.

www.gettyimages.com

101 Bayham Street
London NW1 0AG
United Kingdom
Contact: Liz Ihre
liz.ihre@getty-images.com